I0885015

Societal Approaches to AI, Psychology, and Digital Culture

Zuhal Akmeşe
Dicle University, Turkey

Serhat Erdem
Atatürk University, Turkey

IGI Global
Scientific Publishing
Publishing Tomorrow's Research Today

Vice President of Editorial	Melissa Wagner
Director of Acquisitions	Mikaela Felty
Director of Book Development	Jocelynn Hessler
Production Manager	Mike Brehm
Cover Design	Jose Rosado

Published in the United States of America by
IGI Global Scientific Publishing
701 East Chocolate Avenue
Hershey, PA, 17033, USA
Tel: 717-533-8845 | Fax: 717-533-7115
Website: https://www.igi-global.com E-mail: cust@igi-global.com

Copyright © 2026 by IGI Global Scientific Publishing. All rights reserved. No part of this publication may be reproduced, stored or distributed in any form or by any means, electronic or mechanical, including photocopying, without written permission from the publisher. Use of this publication to train generative artificial intelligence (AI) technologies is expressly prohibited. The publisher reserves all rights to license its use for generative AI training and machine learning model development.

Product or company names used in this set are for identification purposes only. Inclusion of the names of the products or companies does not indicate a claim of ownership by IGI Global Scientific Publishing of the trademark or registered trademark.

Library of Congress Cataloging-in-Publication Data

LCCN: 2025040368 (CIP Data Pending)
ISBN13: 9798337369709
Isbn13Softcover: 9798337369716
EISBN13: 9798337369723

British Cataloguing in Publication Data
A Cataloguing in Publication record for this book is available from the British Library.

All work contributed to this book is new, previously-unpublished material.
The views expressed in this book are those of the authors, but not necessarily of the publisher.
This book contains information sourced from authentic and highly regarded references, with reasonable efforts made to ensure the reliability of the data and information presented. The authors, editors, and publisher believe the information in this book to be accurate and true as of the date of publication. Every effort has been made to trace and credit the copyright holders of all materials included. However, the authors, editors, and publisher cannot assume responsibility for the validity of all materials or the consequences of their use. Should any copyright material be found unacknowledged, please inform the publisher so that corrections may be made in future reprints.

Editorial Advisory Board

M. Nur Erdem, *Ondokuz Mayıs University, Turkey*
Suat Gezgin, *Yeditepe University, Turkey*
Selçuk Hünerli, *İstanbul University, Turkey*
Ceyhan Kandemir, *İstanbul University, Turkey*
Neşe Kars, *Fenerbahçe University, Turkey*
Şükrü Sim, *İstanbul University, Turkey*
M. Nurdan Taşkıran, *Medipol University, Turkey*
Recep Yılmaz, *Ondokuz Mayıs University, Turkey*
Ergün Yolcu, *İstanbul University, Turkey*

Table of Contents

Detailed Table of Contents

The integration of digitalization and artificial intelligence into visual communication design offers new opportunities for educators and students. The ethical and conscious use of these technologies can help shape more skilled and innovative designers. Evaluating how digital tools and AI are included in curricula is key to assessing educational quality. This study analyzes how digitalization and AI are reflected in the curricula of Visual Communication Design departments within Communication Faculties at public and foundation universities in Turkey. Using content analysis, it reviews eight-semester course plans for the 2024–2025 academic year to assess the presence of digitalization and AI themes in theoretical and practical courses. Findings show progress in integration; however, practical courses and AI-based content remain limited. This may negatively impact students' industry readiness. Updating curricula to include digital literacy, data analysis, and AI-supported production, along with creative and critical thinking approaches, is essential for enhancing student competencies.

This study investigates the evolution of wayfinding and signage systems in Kuala Lumpur from 1960 to the present, focusing on their critical role in facilitating urban navigation amidst the city's rapid demographic and technological transformations. As Malaysia's capital transitions from traditional to digital signage, this research aims to assess the impact of these systems on urban mobility and propose adaptive strategies for future challenges. Utilising a sequential explanatory mixed method, the study combines quantitative surveys and qualitative interviews to gather comprehensive data. The survey, involving respondents across various demographics, evaluates public perceptions of current wayfinding effectiveness, particularly at high-traffic hubs like Kuala Lumpur International Airport (KLIA). This is supplemented by interviews with experts, including a long-term resident and teaching academic, to delve deeper into the practical applications and historical context of wayfinding systems. Findings reveal that efficient wayfinding significantly enhances urban mobility.

This study examines the impact of artificial intelligence technologies on the production processes of creative industries such as cinema, public relations, and advertising through a thematic content analysis approach. The introduction outlines the increasing role of AI in creative sectors and presents the research problem and objective. The development section classifies and analyzes AI-based tools used in screenwriting, pre-production, production, post-production, and distribution-marketing stages. Additionally, AI-supported practices in content creation and advertising strategies within public relations are addressed. The conclusion emphasizes that AI not only enhances operational efficiency but also transforms creative decision-making processes, giving rise to new ethical, aesthetic, and professional debates. The study underlines the growing need for sustainable production models based on human–AI collaboration in order to ensure balanced integration of technology and creativity.

This chapter explores the impact of deepfake technology on cinema and visual storytelling, focusing on its aesthetic, ethical, and theoretical dimensions. Once linked to digital deception, deepfakes now serve as creative tools in art, education, and media. Yet, they also raise concerns about visual trust, authenticity, and identity manipulation. By redefining concepts like performance, originality, and spectatorship, deepfakes enable the digital resurrection of actors, scene recreation, and simulated narratives. Through notions like digital twins and algorithmic acting, cinema becomes a site of epistemological production. The chapter draws on theories from Benjamin, Baudrillard, Deleuze, and Rancière to argue that deepfake aesthetics signal a paradigm shift—cinema is no longer just about telling stories but about engineering new realities.

Maria João Frade, Faculty of Economics, Universidade do Algarve, Portugal
Célia M. Q. Ramos, CinTurs, ESGHT, Univeristy of Algarve, Portugal

Combining Data Storytelling concepts and Artificial Intelligence algorithms presents a powerful alliance for the analysis and communication of complex data, in a more intuitive environment and with higher levels of engagement. The main goal was to understand and present the potential of combining these two areas, where sentiment analysis was the method considered to represent Artificial Intelligence. The considered methodology consists, in a first phase of literary review, followed by sentiment analysis. The findings of this research culminate in the development of the definition of Data Storytelling, its potential, and its relationship with Artificial Intelligence systems, presenting a Dashboard Data Storytelling incorporated with AI.

Hülya Semiz Türkoğlu, Faculty of Communication, Istanbul University, Turkey
Süleyman Türkoğlu, Faculty of Communication, Istanbul University, Turkey

Digital transformation is causing radical changes in the media and journalism field; while traditional media organizations are struggling to keep up with this rapid transformation, AI-based news platforms offer a new paradigm. AI technologies play an active role in algorithms at many stages from the writing of the news to its distribution. AI systems, which assume the role of reporters and editors in traditional journalism, select and process content within the framework of predefined rules and present it to digital platforms. In this context, the foundations of AI-based journalism are shaped by algorithmic content management. In this study, emotional expressions in news content were examined with both qualitative and quantitative analysis methods through the example of Dipnot.tv. The findings obtained reveal that AI journalism has not only technical but also emotional and human dimensions. As a result, AI-based news platforms are taking a central position in the future of journalism; they blur the boundaries between digital and traditional media.

The aim of the study is to reveal the relationship between higher education students' digital burnout levels and fear of missing out (FoMO). It can be interpreted that as fear of missing out (FoMO) increases, digital burnout increases with a significant and moderate relationship.In order to reveal whether fear of missing out (FoMO) has a predictive effect on digital burnout, simple linear regression analysis was conducted and it was concluded that fear of missing out positively predicts digital burnout. According to this result, it can be said that as individuals' fear of missing out increases, their digital burnout also increases.

This study examines the mediating roles of social comparison and FoMO in the effect of exposure to influencers on conspicuous consumption. The findings reveal a strong, positive, and significant relationship between the level of exposure to social media influencers and FoMO, and a moderate, positive, and significant relationship with conspicuous consumption. Additionally, the relationship between FoMO and conspicuous consumption is found to be strong, positive, and significant. However, no statistically significant relationships were identified between social comparison and the other variables. Moreover, FoMO was found to mediate the relationship between exposure to influencers and conspicuous consumption. The results suggest that, in the context of influencer exposure, FoMO functions as a significant external motivational factor influencing conspicuous consumption behavior.

The present research aims to investigate the relationship between attitudes toward selfie-taking, social appearance anxiety, and online self-presentation. According to

Foreword

The intersection of artificial intelligence, psychology, and digital culture represents one of the most defining issues of our time. AI has moved far beyond the laboratory and is now deeply embedded in the ways we think, feel, create, and connect. This book, *Societal Approaches to AI, Psychology, and Digital Culture*, provides an essential contribution to understanding these transformations from a holistic, interdisciplinary perspective.

What makes this volume significant is its ability to move past narrow technological narratives. The contributors reveal how AI not only transforms cognitive and emotional processes but also reshapes cultural production, communication, and social interaction. Equally, they emphasize the ethical and political stakes of living in an age where algorithms influence creativity, identity, and collective decision-making.

This book speaks to scholars, students, and practitioners across multiple fields, offering both critical reflection and constructive guidance. By situating AI as a socio-cultural phenomenon as well as a technological one, it encourages us to imagine a digital future that is not only innovative but also ethical, inclusive, and human-centered.

I commend this volume to its readers with confidence that it will inspire deeper understanding, dialogue, and action in shaping the society of tomorrow.

Selçuk Hünerli
İstanbul University-Cerrahpaşa, Turkey

Preface

INTRODUCTION

In an era defined by the convergence of artificial intelligence, psychology, and digital culture, societies are undergoing rapid transformations that reshape human experience at its core. This book, *Societal Approaches to AI, Psychology, and Digital Culture*, emerges from the need to critically explore these intersections within a global and interdisciplinary framework. Bringing together diverse scholars and perspectives, the volume examines how algorithmic systems affect cognition, emotional well-being, identity formation, and cultural production across different social contexts.

The goal of this collection is not only to analyze the technological dimensions of AI but also to emphasize its societal implications. From the psychological impact of digital environments to the ethical dilemmas of algorithmic governance, and from cultural narratives shaped by AI-driven platforms to new models of communication and creativity, the chapters demonstrate the complex interplay of human and machine. By situating AI as both a technological innovation and a socio-cultural actor, the book underscores the necessity of interdisciplinary approaches that move beyond single-discipline boundaries.

In doing so, this volume contributes to a deeper understanding of how AI influences daily life, governance, education, and cultural practices. It invites readers to critically engage with the challenges and opportunities of living in an algorithmically mediated world, and to reflect on the ethical, inclusive, and human-centered pathways necessary for the future.

CHAPTER OVERVIEW

Chapter 1 by *Saadet Zeynep Varlı Gürer, Nihan Dönmez & Zeynep Ebrar Doğan* assess the integration of AI and digital literacy into visual communication curricula in Turkish universities.

Chapter 2 by *Stephen Poon* traces the development of wayfinding systems in Kuala Lumpur, assessing how digital signage affects urban navigation.

Chapter 3 by *Deniz Oğuzcan & Anıl Uğur Oğuzcan* investigate AI-supported processes in cinema, PR, and advertising, and their effects on creative decision-making.

Chapter 4 by *Alper Erçetingöz & Taner* Kızılhan explore the theoretical and aesthetic dimensions of deepfake technologies in cinema and digital storytelling.

Chapter 5 by *Maria João Frade & Célia M.Q. Ramos* combine data storytelling and AI to enhance engagement and comprehension in complex data narratives.

Chapter 6 by *Hülya Semiz Türkoğlu & Süleyman Türkoğlu* explore AI-based journalism practices through a case study of Dipnot.tv, highlighting both technological and emotional dimensions.

Chapter 7 by *Mehmet Ulaş & Abuzer Yeşil* investigate the correlation between digital burnout and FOMO among higher education students.

Chapter 8 by *Nurcan Yılmaz & Seril Çakmak Ekinci* analyze the mediating role of FOMO in the relationship between influencer exposure and conspicuous consumption.

Chapter 9 by *Özgür Kılınç, Ali Arıcı & Sadık Çalışkan* examine the link between selfie-taking, social appearance anxiety, and online self-presentation.

Chapter 10 by *Andrej Kapcar* explores how video games function as spiritual and symbolic spaces in modern digital occultism.

Chapter 11 by *Tatiana Ferreira, Tatiana Batista, Pedro Malheiro, Tiago Lopes, João Vitorino & João Paulo Sousa* have attempted to provide a comprehensive mapping of the scientific literature on video game monetization methods.

Chapter 12 by *Ronit Kumar* addresses smartphone and social media addiction and its implications for interpersonal relationships.

CONCLUSION

This book has sought to highlight the multifaceted intersections of artificial intelligence, psychology, and digital culture from a societal perspective. Across its chapters, contributors have revealed how AI permeates not only technical infrastructures but also shapes cognition, emotions, cultural narratives, and social relations. The volume has emphasized that AI is more than a tool of efficiency; it is a cultural and psychological force that redefines identity, creativity, and community in the digital age.

As societies move deeper into algorithmic environments, the debates surrounding ethics, inclusivity, and human agency become increasingly urgent. The contributions in this volume collectively argue for a human-centered and culturally sensitive integration of AI—one that recognizes both opportunities and risks. By addressing issues such as surveillance, bias, creativity, digital well-being, and social belonging, this book offers a critical roadmap for scholars, practitioners, and policy-makers alike.

Ultimately, *Societal Approaches to AI, Psychology, and Digital Culture* stands as both an academic contribution and a reflective guide. It encourages readers to imagine futures where technology supports psychological health, strengthens cultural diversity, and sustains ethical responsibility. In this spirit, the book affirms that the dialogue between humanity and intelligent systems must remain guided by values of dignity, inclusivity, and critical awareness.

Zuhal Akmeşe
Dicle University, Turkey

Serhat Erdem
Atatürk University, Turkey

Chapter 1
Reflections of the Digital Age in Visual Communication Design Education

Saadet Zeynep Varlı Gurer
https://orcid.org/0000-0003-2362-9277
Communication Faculty, Kocaeli University, Turkey

Nihan Dönmez
https://orcid.org/0000-0003-2500-8431
Communication Faculty, Kocaeli University, Turkey

Zeynep Ebrar Doğan
https://orcid.org/0000-0002-6990-9605
Communication Faculty, Kocaeli University, Turkey

ABSTRACT

The integration of digitalization and artificial intelligence into visual communication design offers new opportunities for educators and students. The ethical and conscious use of these technologies can help shape more skilled and innovative designers. Evaluating how digital tools and AI are included in curricula is key to assessing educational quality. This study analyzes how digitalization and AI are reflected in the curricula of Visual Communication Design departments within Communication Faculties at public and foundation universities in Turkey. Using content analysis, it reviews eight-semester course plans for the 2024–2025 academic year to assess the presence of digitalization and AI themes in theoretical and practical courses. Findings show progress in integration; however, practical courses and AI-based

DOI: 10.4018/979-8-3373-6970-9.ch001

© 2026, IGI Global Scientific Publishing. Copying or distributing in print or electronic forms without written permission of IGI Global Scientific Publishing is prohibited. Use of this chapter to ...erative artificial intelligence (AI) technologies is expressly prohibited. The publisher reserves all rights to license its use for generative AI training and machine learning model development.

content remain limited. This may negatively impact students' industry readiness. Updating curricula to include digital literacy, data analysis, and AI-supported production, along with creative and critical thinking approaches, is essential for enhancing student competencies.

INTRODUCTION

Visual Communication Design is a multidimensional field situated at the intersection of art, communication, and technology, and it is directly influenced by ongoing digital transformations. The creative production processes accelerated by digitalization not only offer students new tools and methods but also enable the redefinition of design in more participatory, accessible, and experiential ways. AI-based design applications expand students' creative capacities and accelerate production through automation, allowing them to explore alternative forms of design. However, these technologies also raise certain ethical and legal concerns. New communication environments shaped by social media are transforming visual culture production, making the updating of educational content a necessity.

This study aims to analyze the four-year curricula of Visual Communication Design departments within the Faculties of Communication at both public and foundation universities in Turkey using a content analysis method. The primary goal of the research is to examine the extent to which the themes of "digitalization" and "artificial intelligence" are integrated into the 2024–2025 academic year programs, and how these themes are represented across theoretical, practical, and elective courses. In this context, different university programs are compared to evaluate their levels of adaptation to technological transformation in education. The study aims to provide a constructive framework for understanding the current state of visual communication design education and to offer insights for future curriculum development.

THE IMPACTS OF DIGITALISATION AND ARTIFICIAL INTELLIGENCE ON DESIGN

According to Naisbitt (2004), one of the primary reasons for humanity's reliance on technology is *"to make life easier, to alleviate suffering, reduce mundane tasks, maintain existence, and attain a comfortable life through affordable, labor-saving tools.* This motivation has led technology to become not only an essential part of our lives but also a force that governs them. Technological advancements have brought about significant changes in human and societal life, encapsulated by the concept of digitalisation. The technological breakthroughs initiated by the Industrial Revolution have laid the foundation for what is now called the "digital age."

Digitalisation is defined as the process of replacing analog operations with digital technologies, transforming business and educational models, creating new value, and offering added-value opportunities (Gartner, 2021; WalkMe, 2024). Artificial intelligence, on the other hand, is a scientific and engineering discipline that enables computer systems to mimic complex human intelligence functions such as learning, reasoning, problem-solving, decision-making, and creative production (IBM, 2024). Visual communication design, through the use of color, form, typography, and interactive elements, aims to convey information and messages effectively, and with the support of digital tools and AI-based systems, provides more dynamic, personalized, and interactive experiences (Falmouth University, 2023).

The "First Industrial Revolution," which took place in Britain during the 18th and 19th centuries, refers to a period marked by rapid social, economic, and demographic changes (Marshall, 1999, p. 632). Transition to urban life, industrialisation, and the introduction of steam-powered mass production were major developments of that era. In the "Second Industrial Revolution," electricity was integrated into production, leading to widespread industrial automation. The era that lasted until the late 20th century is referred to as the "Third Industrial Revolution," also known as the "digital revolution" (Schwab, 2016, p.11). The ongoing digitalisation we experience today is largely a continuation of the infrastructure established during this revolution. The "Fourth Industrial Revolution" is characterized by the term Industry 4.0 and signifies a phase where technologies such as artificial intelligence, the Internet of Things, and big data bring profound changes across all sectors—from production to everyday life (Akıncı & Kahraman, 2024, p.78).

This historical continuity also reveals that artificial intelligence has evolved through its own milestones. One of the most critical moments in AI research occurred in the 1950s with Alan Turing's publication of the article *Computing Machinery and Intelligence*, in which he proposed the "Imitation Game" (Turing Test). According to Turing, a machine can be considered intelligent if it can converse with a human without the person realizing they are interacting with a machine (Ilıcak & Çinko, 2021). This test is regarded as one of the first concrete indications of how theoretical foundations and real-world applications of AI can merge effectively.

Charles Babbage's *Difference Engine*, developed in the 19th century, is considered the first mechanical device to simulate basic operations of the human mind. Following the introduction of the term "artificial intelligence" at the 1956 Dartmouth Conference, early applications such as ELIZA and expert systems evolved with the development of neural networks. Today, AI applications based on big data and deep learning provide automated visual production and personalization solutions in fields such as healthcare, finance, agriculture, and graphic design (Aliefendioğlu, 2024).

When evaluating the contributions of digitalisation and AI to visual communication design, it becomes evident that these developments have profoundly transformed education, as in every other aspect of life. AI-supported tools have initiated deep transformation in the educational ecosystem—from course content to student-instructor interaction. Artificial intelligence, as a discipline, aims to replicate the learning, reasoning, and problem-solving capacities of human intelligence in computers (Öztemel, 2020, p. 101). Rapid technological progress in the internet, mobile communication, and big data fields has ushered humanity into a new era marked by intense digitalisation (Gawer, 2022, pp. 110–124). Online course platforms, AI-powered personalized learning management systems, and adaptive assessment tools now deliver dynamic content tailored to student needs, while learning analytics provide instructors with real-time feedback. Digital technologies have transformed the ways individuals access information, resulting in fundamental changes across communication, daily life, and social structures. MOOCs (Massive Open Online Courses), for instance, support equitable access to information through global participation (Friedman & Friedman, 2013). Virtual laboratories and augmented reality applications enhance abstract learning through tangible experiences. Digital platforms such as social media, blogs, and video portals enable individuals to both easily access and share knowledge, making information available anytime, anywhere.

The evolutionary transformation of knowledge in the digital age has repositioned educators from mere transmitters of content to guides in the learning process, profoundly redefining pedagogical approaches. This transformation has also necessitated the integration of new-generation competencies—such as digital literacy, data security, and ethical technology use—into educational practices. While the conceptual framework discussed here offers tangible contributions to both teaching and application in visual communication design, unmet educational needs continue to drive educators to develop safe, effective, and scalable technology-based solutions. Educators who actively use AI-supported tools in their daily lives are increasingly questioning how these technologies can enhance teaching. At the same time, they remain aware of associated risks, including data privacy, security, algorithmic bias, and ethical concerns. Integrating AI into educational technologies is a collective endeavor involving both opportunities and responsibilities (USDOE, 2023, p. 1). This technology- and AI-driven transformation has influenced curricula and instructional methods in university-level visual communication design programs, necessitating syllabus revisions and the introduction of new course content. Visual design elements are crucial communication tools and form an extensive system of thought that helps individuals and institutions express themselves and make sense of their environments.

From both educational and industry perspectives, digitalisation and artificial intelligence have significant impacts on design. Digital technologies, led by artificial intelligence, play a key role in reshaping education systems. Their contributions manifest in enhanced access to knowledge, accelerated learning processes (optimization of time and outcomes), rapid access to information (through research tools and bibliometric analyses), and the personalization of learning experiences and models (Folcu , Manta & Militaru, 2024, p. 1). AI systems successfully perform a wide range of tasks including learning, prediction, problem-solving, decision-making, natural language processing, speech and image recognition, automation, robotics, and game design. These systems are typically implemented through the integration of advanced techniques such as deep learning, machine learning, and natural language processing (Doğan & Türkoğlu, 2019, p. 71).

AI systems are generally classified into three categories: "narrow AI," which performs specific tasks; "strong AI," capable of human-like cognitive functions such as learning and problem-solving; and "super AI," which surpasses human intelligence and possesses autonomous decision-making capacity (Kaynar, 2024). While narrow AI has long been used in applications like computer-aided design, advancements in deep learning and machine learning have enabled strong AI to generate outputs that closely resemble human creativity (Bozüyük, Yağcı & Gökçe, 2005). Generative approaches such as Generative Adversarial Networks (GANs), diffusion models, and transformer-based networks have brought the concept of "computational creativity" to the forefront by producing a wide range of content—from motion graphics and design to creative texts and music (Elgammal et al., 2017). Today, many stages of visual communication design—from idea generation and creative storytelling to prototyping and the creation of animated or 3D visuals—can be conducted with AI support. Generative AI puts these theoretical foundations into practice by creating entirely new works from text, images, sound, and other data types. It provides designers with high computational power and vast memory resources, accelerating production and enriching the creative process with diverse sources of knowledge and inspiration compared to traditional methods.

Generative AI tools produce visual content both automatically and semi-automatically (Goodfellow et al., 2014; Elgammal et al., 2017). Notable examples include Midjourney, known for its creative capabilities (Midjourney, 2024); DALL·E 2, which generates high-detail visuals from textual descriptions and supports API integration (OpenAI, 2023); RunwayML, which enables real-time video style transfer (RunwayML, 2024); and Adobe Firefly, which is embedded in Photoshop and Illustrator and offers commercially licensed outputs (Adobe, 2024). Other platforms include Stable Diffusion, Canva AI (Magic Design, Magic Edit), DreamStudio, Figma AI (Figma Autoflow, Designer Bots), Designs.ai, and Let's Enhance / Gigapixel AI. These tools enhance the design process by enabling quick sketching at the ideation stage, alternative compositions during prototyping, and student-focused output production with low technical thresholds for accessibility. However, issues such as copyright uncertainties, model biases, and cloud-based infrastructure costs must be carefully considered in educational settings (Elgammal et al., 2017; Goodfellow et al., 2014; U.S. Department of Education, 2023). These AI platforms are categorized in the following table.

Table 1. Artificial Intelligence Platforms in Visual Communication Design

Tool	Use in Education	Use in Professional Studios	Free Access	Key Features
Midjourney	In advanced training	Highly preferred	Paid	Creative concept design
DALL·E 2 / 3 (OpenAI)	Widespread use	Concept and illustration generation	Limited free credits	Photorealistic or abstract visuals, style transfer, variation generation
Stable Diffusion	May require technical knowledge	Customization and project design	Open source	Open-source, customizable output, text-to-image generation
RunwayML	In multimedia projects	Video and visual editing	Some basic features are free	Video editing, scene alteration, AI-powered media production
Adobe Firefly	In licensed schools	Integrated use with Adobe Creative Suite	Adobe subscription may be required	Background replacement, text effects, artistic generation
Canva AI (Magic Design, Magic Edit)	Widely used in schools	Used for simple tasks	Basic version is free	Quick design suggestions, drag-and-drop editing, AI-assisted content
DreamStudio (Stable Diffusion tabanlı)	For advanced users	Artistic production and experimental designs	Limited free credits	Detailed style and content control, text-to-image generation
Figma AI (Autoflow, Designer Botlar)	Widely used in UI/UX education	Used in professional interface design	Basic version is free	Auto-alignment, flowchart drawing, prototype design

(OpenAI ChatGPT, 2025)

Brief Descriptions of AI Platforms:

Midjourney: Launched in 2022, Midjourney is an open-access software developed to convert textual descriptions into visuals. It synthesizes new images aligned with user prompts by referencing billions of visuals available online. Users can generate visuals using phrases such as "sadness" or "man with a red hat" (Vincent, 2022).

Stable Diffusion: Stable Diffusion is an open-source, customizable generative AI model that produces image content from text. Users can generate visuals in different aesthetic styles and perform edits on existing images.

DALL·E 2: The name DALL·E is derived from a combination of Salvador Dalí's artistic creativity and Pixar's character WALL-E. Developed by OpenAI, this model was trained on a dataset comprising text and image data using approximately 12 billion parameters (OpenAI, 2021). DALL·E can anthropomorphize animals and objects, transform written texts into visuals, and reinterpret scenes in various artistic styles. "Text-to-image synthesis dates back to 1983 and marked a significant evolution" (Koh et al., 2020). Thanks to generative approaches such as GANs, photorealistic image generation has become possible.

RunwayML: Developed for artists and designers, RunwayML offers a variety of AI-supported features including visual generation, background removal, video editing, text-to-image synthesis, and real-time media transformation (Runway, n.d.).

Adobe Firefly: Adobe Firefly is a generative AI-based platform that allows users to create images, videos, audio, and vector graphics. It supports functions such as ideation, concept development, and multilingual natural voice synthesis, while offering an intuitive 3D workspace (Adobe, n.d.).

Canva AI (Magic Design, Magic Edit): Canva enables anyone to easily create visual content through a user-friendly drag-and-drop interface. It supports professional-quality design production through templates, stock images, and advanced collaboration tools (Canva, n.d.).

DreamStudio: Developed by Stability AI, DreamStudio is based on the Stable Diffusion model. In addition to text-to-image generation, it offers features such as image-to-image transformation, inpainting, and resizing (Lopez, 2023).

Figma AI (Autoflow, Designer Bots): Figma AI helps designers quickly create initial drafts, convert static designs into interactive prototypes, and automatically name layers. It optimizes design processes with features such as visual search and content translation (Figma, n.d.).

The AI platforms listed in the table are notable not only for their technical capabilities but also for their impact on visual communication design processes. These tools accelerate the ideation phase, analyze large datasets to generate alternative prototype variations, and shorten design cycles. In particular, Figma AI supports the creation of personalized interface and interaction designs by analyzing user data. Generative models activate the concept of "computational creativity," showcasing the ability of computer systems to produce original and valuable outputs. The ability to generate content in areas such as motion graphics, graphic design, text, and music introduces flexibility and creativity into the design cycle.

Platforms like Stable Diffusion and Midjourney contribute to the democratization of design by enabling users without technical expertise to produce high-quality visual content. However, uncertainties regarding copyright, data licensing, and ethical usage persist in AI-supported design practices (Litmus Branding Pvt. Ltd., n.d.; OpenAI, 2023). Additionally, biases present in the datasets on which algorithms are trained create imbalances in cultural representation, thereby limiting the diversity of creative output and posing a risk of standardizing "creativity" (European Commission, 2019).

This process is transforming design practice on both theoretical and practical levels. Generative AI enhances flexibility and speed in the design process by enabling rapid prototyping and alternative composition through prompts, while enriching individual creative contributions through algorithmic feedback. From a pedagogical transformation perspective, the integration of generative AI tools into educational environments is reshaping the nature of design education. Students are not only learning traditional design methods but also the principles of computational creativity and the use of generative AI; in doing so, they develop critical thinking, ethical judgment, and creative problem-solving skills. As a result, visual communication design education is becoming more inclusive, dynamic, and responsive to the needs of the contemporary age.

In conclusion, AI-supported tools increase efficiency in visual communication design, diversify modes of creative expression, and expand sources of inspiration. In the educational context, generative AI applications enhance both students' technical skills and creative thinking capacities, leading to the adoption of faster, more flexible, and user-centered approaches in the design process. However, the ethical, legal, and cultural dimensions of these technologies must be carefully addressed to ensure that future design practices evolve on a fairer, more inclusive, and original foundation. Therefore, visual communication design education is being redefined in the age of AI-assisted creativity.

THE LANGUAGE OF DESIGN: THE EVOLUTION AND EDUCATION OF VISUAL COMMUNICATION

Visual communication design is the process of effectively delivering messages to a receiver through visual elements. As a discipline that integrates with numerous fields, it plays a significant role in cinema, graphic design, advertising, digital media, and animation. In recent years, with the rapid advancement of digital technologies and the increasing prominence of visual media in social life, the importance of visual communication design has grown steadily. Consequently, the demand for visual communication design education to train competent professionals in this field is rapidly increasing.

Interest in visual communication design education is rising proportionally with the development pace of communication technologies, both globally and in Turkey. The current visual age encompasses factors such as the visualization of messages, adapting them to the characteristics of different media, and capturing the audience's attention and interest. Ensuring uninterrupted and effective communication requires integrating technological advancements into the field. In this context, it is beneficial to first define the development of visual communication design and then project its educational trajectory.

The Development of Visual Communication Design in the World and in Turkey

People understand and interpret the world visually. As many sources indicate, before the development of linguistic skills, humanity expressed its perception of the world through cave drawings. These are considered the earliest examples of visual communication dating back to 15,000 BCE (Uçar, 2004; Ketenci and Bilgili, 2006; Günay, 2021). Prior to writing, visual imagery was the most effective tool for conveying emotion, thought, and information. These early visuals also represent some of the oldest examples of belief in the power of imagery (Uçar, 2004). According to Parsa (2004), "images helped humans to communicate before they translated messages into written language." Language, the foundation of communication, varies widely across regions, which can act as a barrier to communication. In contrast, visual communication is more inclusive and unifying due to its universality. Unlike auditory communication, visual messages tend to have greater longevity and impact. Humans learn to see before they learn to speak (Günay, 2021, p.110); thus, visuality has always been central to human life. In a world with many different languages, visual communication is one of the fastest and easiest ways for people to connect. People grasp information about their surroundings visually. According to Ketenci and Bilgili (2006, p.274), referencing English philosopher John Locke, humans learn 1% through tasting, 2% through reading, 4% through smelling, 10% through hearing, and 83% through observing their environment. This 83% statistic underscores the importance of using visual materials, signs, and symbols accurately and effectively in visual communication. Hence, visual communication has become the most dominant communication method in daily life.

Visual communication design involves the creation of visuals and text according to specific design principles with the goal of message transmission. The core objective is to establish visual-based communication between sender and receiver. According to Meggs, visual communication design is "the process of creating meaningful visuals, often using various visual technologies, to convey ideas and messages to a specific audience or the general public," regardless of whether the intent is to persuade, entertain, inform, or enlighten (as cited in Yeo, 2014, p.52). Karaahmet Balcı (2017) defines visual communication design as follows:

> *"Visual communication design encompasses a creative process aimed at delivering planned marketing goals and strategies related to a product, service, idea, or institution. It involves organizing text and image elements on two- or*

three-dimensional surfaces and across all digital platforms to communicate information to a predetermined target audience using various media tools."

From birth certificates to gravestones, newspapers to children's books, traffic signs to product packaging, street posters to daily television programs, notes on doors to printed publications, and film credits to street signs—all are elements of graphic arts (Kavuran and Çetinkaya, 2012, p.612). Surrounded by a visual world, humans have developed interpretation and meaning-making skills accordingly.

In visual communication, the eye is the primary sensory organ, followed by the brain, which interprets what is seen. Thus, the human effort to communicate visually has increased proportionally with the development of mass communication technologies. In today's image-dominated era, we live in an image-centric world. With the invention of the camera, followed by motion picture and television technologies, the world rapidly began transforming under the rules of a unique audiovisual language (Parsa, 2004). McCoy defined the emergence of visual communication design as "a spontaneous response to the communication needs of capitalist, market-based economies during the industrial revolution" (as cited in Yeo, 2014, p.52). Visual communication design products have been significantly influenced by technological advancements, the spread of communication tools, and the rapid progression of consumer society. With the rise of consumerism, the interpretation and use of art have also undergone major transformations (Günay, 2021, p.109). Technology has transformed the methods and practices of visual communication design, covering areas from typography and illustration to motion graphics and web design (Yeo, 2014, p.52). The transition from traditional print to digital platforms has also led to the formation of a multilayered structure encompassing various disciplines. Designs must now be interactive and user-centered in addition to being artistic and aesthetically driven. As such, visual communication design defines a dynamic field that is continuously evolving and transforming.

As a visual language, graphic design became a core element of communication in the late 19th and early 20th centuries, coinciding with the rise of mass communication. Influenced by the modern art movements that shaped European art and design in the early 20th century, the conceptual framework and function of graphic design began to shift. Art movements of the time also impacted design processes. The paradigm shifts in graphic design that began in the 1930s continued into the 1980s, influenced by visual, communicational, sociological, economic, technological, cultural, ecological, and educational factors. As a result of these transformations, the term "visual communication design" became more commonly used than "graphic design" (Karaahmet Balcı, 2017, p.153). The term gained popularity during the World Design Conference held in Tokyo, Japan, in 1960. It refers not only to the design of print materials such as newspapers, magazines, and posters, but also to media such as film, television, and electronic billboards. Visual communication design is defined as an art form encompassing expressive and impactful designs that convey content through the eye and serve modern commerce (Jun, 2023, p.88). The transition from graphic design to visual communication design reflects the growing importance of communication and storytelling in the design industry. While traditional graphic design focuses on visual elements such as logos, typography, and illustrations, visual communication design represents a more holistic approach that considers the entire user experience (Creativani, 2023, p.283).

The field of visual communication design has rapidly advanced due to digitalisation, the rise of new media technologies, and the transformation of social needs. Once transmitted on stone tablets and later on paper, information now circulates within complex digital networks. Technology has increasingly appealed to visual and auditory senses, making the acquisition and transmission of knowledge faster and easier (Doğan, 2015, p.17). With globalization, the expansion of international communication platforms, and increased access to information, traditional and static design methods have transformed in response to diverse human needs (Jun, 2023, p.88). These developments have supported the evolution of the field through the visualization of knowledge and the improved comprehension of visualized information. Interactivity, personalized design, and technological advancements offered by new media have reinforced human-centered thinking in visual communication design. The dynamic processes of visual communication design facilitate more accurate and direct content delivery, enhancing the effectiveness of communication and aligning with the rapid development of contemporary society (Guo, 2022).

In Turkey, as elsewhere, graphic design gained significant momentum with the expansion of mass media and the development of advertising. The growth of graphic arts has been shaped by Turkey's modernization efforts in relation to the West, the spread of printing, the emergence of advertising, and the transformation of visual culture. Historically, it is appropriate to describe this as a multilayered development process. The advancement of graphic arts and design has paralleled the evolution of communication technologies, increasing the power of visual communication. This progression, particularly influenced by digital technologies, has enabled design to serve not only as an aesthetic practice but also as an effective communication tool.

Specialization in graphic arts in Turkey began after the declaration of the Republic. In the 1920s, figures like Münif Fehim, İhap Hulusi, and Kenan Temizan produced original and high-quality works in areas such as book covers, press advertisements, and poster design, establishing themselves as pioneers of Turkish graphic design (Kavuran and Çetinkaya, 2012, p.613). Graphic design education in Turkey began in 1933 with Mithat Özer's initiative in the poster studio of the Academy of Fine Arts. For many years, this institution focused on traditional arts such as painting, sculpture, and architecture. As an alternative, the State School of Applied Fine Arts was established in Istanbul in 1957 to train specialists in industrial arts and design

(Ketenci and Bilgili, 2006, p.286). These developments contributed to defining graphic art as an academic discipline. Many German academics were involved in the founding of the school, and education began in five fields: graphic design, interior architecture, textiles, ceramics, and decorative painting. In 1978, Turkish graphic designers organized under the "Graphic Designers Professional Association" to institutionalize professional solidarity. This organization made significant contributions in areas such as protecting designers' rights, establishing wage standards, and organizing exhibitions (Kavuran and Çetinkaya, 2012, p.613). Following the 1980s, with the influence of globalization, Turkey's media, advertising, and publishing sectors began to grow rapidly, and the integration of computers into the design process led to significant changes in graphic design. The Higher Education Law enacted in 1982 brought the Academy of Fine Arts and the State School of Applied Fine Arts into university status (Ketenci and Bilgili, 2006, p.286). After this milestone, the establishment of departments such as "Graphic Design" and "Visual Communication Design" within different university faculties contributed to the accumulation of both knowledge and experience in the field, enabling the training of specialized professionals.

Visual Communication Design Educatication

Contemporary society has entered a visual culture era in which the centrality of language and print culture has diminished, and the public's way of perceiving the world has significantly changed. In this era, which places visuality and imagery-based expression at its core, visual communication design education has become increasingly important (Sun & Zhu, 2022). Visual communication design is an interdisciplinary field that brings together art, communication, technology, and creativity in today's rapidly changing digital world. The field addresses the limitations of traditional media, particularly in marketing practices, by utilizing both art and technology. This emerging area requires a practice-based education in higher education institutions, equipping students with effective communication-design-technology skills while also training qualified professionals for the industry (Doğan, 2015, p.20). Therefore, visual communication design education must offer a comprehensive curriculum aligned with this interdisciplinary structure. In recent years, accreditation processes and restructuring efforts within institutions have led to the revision and renewal of educational programs and teaching methods in accordance with technological developments, industry demands, and student expectations.

Visual communication design is a new discipline rooted in graphic design, aiming to address the needs of social development. It effectively integrates graphic design principles with multimedia technology and artistic design (Zhou & Ghazali, 2023). Moreover, interdisciplinary approaches such as psychology, media studies, and technology integration contribute to the formation of new paradigms in visual communication design education (Creativani, 2023).

As an essential component of the design field, visual communication is not merely an area focused on teaching design techniques, but a complex and systematic process aimed at developing knowledge, intuition, and thought. Enhancing design quality requires more than technical skills. A designer must be proficient not only in design techniques but also in the historical evolution and future trends of design, possess the ability to evaluate design aesthetically, interpret and comprehend design holistically, and explore personal visual thinking in depth (Jun, 2023). Furthermore, Karaahmet Balcı (2017) notes: "If marketing is considered an active part of the cultural process, then advertising—which serves marketing—and consequently visual communication design will evolve under the influence of cultural paradigms. In such a case, it becomes even more essential for visual communication design students to acquire cultural competence" (p.163). Yeo (2014) asserts that "one potential way to enhance design practice is to equip design students with research literacy and frame it as a valuable contribution" (p.52). Brown (2012) also emphasizes that designers must learn scientific methods because such approaches enable them to "ask the right questions, formulate better hypotheses, design effective experiments, and most importantly, share what they learn with others" (p.20). In today's context, designers must not only produce visual messages but also value research and possess the ability to decode and analyze cultural codes. Thus, visual communication design education must adopt a multidisciplinary framework that fosters students' development in critical thinking, cultural analysis, and visual literacy.

The insights presented in Zhou & Ghazali's (2023) study are particularly valuable in revealing the limitations of traditionally structured design education. According to the authors, traditional visual communication design curricula mostly emphasize tools and techniques while neglecting the theoretical and conceptual dimensions of the field. Moreover, conventional teaching methods such as in-class lectures and textbook-based learning are still widely used, resulting in a lack of practical engagement and real-world connection. In the digital age, instructional methods should not be confined to the classroom alone—they should also include online learning, social media engagement, and design competitions. However, due to limited familiarity with these new methods, visual communication design education in universities often remains strongly tied to traditional teaching paradigms. One of the findings in Günay's (2021) study also confirms the crucial role of technical programs in the postmodern phase of visual communication design. While digital technologies provide many technical conveniences, they may also cause visual errors and clutter in practice. Therefore, it is emphasized that individuals using these tools must be sensitive, knowledgeable, intuitive, and competent designers (p.121).

The digital revolution has fundamentally transformed visual communication design in areas such as editing, typography, layout, and illustration. The speed, multi-dimensionality, and storage capabilities of digital technologies have also influenced educational processes. Staying current is essential in visual communication design education. Thanks to the tools of the digital age, students can easily access information from all over the world through databases and the internet (Sun & Zhu, 2022). However, Zhou & Ghazali (2023) argue that despite the field's continuous evolution, traditional textbooks and course content often fail to meet student needs. For example, traditional graphic design courses no longer align with industry expectations; students must now acquire digital design skills such as web design and UI/UX design. As such, programs that maintain traditional methods fail to meet contemporary requirements and produce graduates who are unprepared for industry needs.

Faculty members play a central role in shaping visual communication design curricula. It is essential to revise course content and instructional approaches in response to the demands of the age and student needs. It is also worth highlighting the importance of communication between universities, faculty, and students in enhancing educational quality (Lim, 2023). Not only should course content reflect current trends, but educators must also update their knowledge and skills regularly. Following industry developments and advancements in information and communication technologies is critical in this regard. Additionally, visual communication design serves as a powerful tool in education—applicable from course materials to student projects. Educators should create environments where students can freely express their creativity, provide the necessary technical infrastructure, and guide their development. While this field was initially taught based on professional experience, it has since become enriched through academic research, resulting in a more comprehensive structure. The effective use of visual elements in the classroom deepens learning, enhances creativity, and transforms traditional educational models (Creativani, 2023, p.287).

In light of these considerations, visual communication design education must evolve from a field focused solely on technical skill development into a multidimensional discipline encompassing cultural, theoretical, and creative thinking. In the age of visual culture, educational programs in this field must be supported by comprehensive, current, and practice-based curricula that address both industry expectations and student needs. To cultivate designers who are research-oriented, capable of cultural analysis, and skilled in following and utilizing technological advancements, educators must not only revise their course content but also continuously update their own expertise. In this context, visual communication design education should offer a dynamic, layered, and interdisciplinary learning environment that integrates critical thinking, creativity, and digital competence.

Importance and Purpose of the Study

The rapid development of digitalisation and artificial intelligence systems is transforming and reshaping the structure of contemporary society. This transformation affects not only the economy through its technological dimensions, but also everyday life experiences in fields such as health, art, and communication. The proliferation of visual culture has increased with digitalisation, reshaping the ways individuals communicate through images. Consequently, visual communication design has emerged as one of the most significant fields of the new era. In order for this discipline to meet contemporary needs, it must incorporate an educational curriculum aligned with new communication technologies. In this context, the purpose of the present study is to determine the prevalence of digital and artificial intelligence-themed courses based on the four-year undergraduate curricula of Visual Communication Design departments located within the Faculties of Communication at public and foundation universities in Turkey for the 2024–2025 academic year.

One of the pioneering studies in this field is Eda Doğan's 2015 article titled *A General Status Analysis of Visual Communication Design Departments in Turkey*, which offered a comparative analysis of theoretical and practical courses within the curricula of all Communication and Fine Arts faculties in Turkey offering Visual Communication Design programs based on 2015 data. Similarly, in her 2017 article *Reflections of Changing Paradigms on Undergraduate and Graduate Programs in Visual Communication Design*, Selma Karaahmet Balcı addressed the terminological issues between the concepts of graphic and visual communication design and their educational implications. Her study examined various universities in Turkey and abroad, comparing faculties, departments, and course structures in graphic/visual communication design education to identify key differences. The present study differs from these earlier works in terms of its currency and its focused aim of identifying how "digitalisation" and "artificial intelligence" are reflected in the curricula of Visual Communication Design departments located specifically within Faculties of Communication. This makes the study particularly important in terms of assessing whether the curricula reflect a contemporary and future-ready educational approach.

METHOD

This study adopts a content analysis method. By identifying themes related to digitalisation and the use of artificial intelligence, content analysis allows for an assessment of the extent to which curricula are aligned with current technologies and tools. Within this scope, the compulsory and elective courses most commonly included in the four-year plans of both public and foundation universities were identified, along with whether these courses were theoretical or practical. These were quantitatively assessed.

Courses in Visual Communication Design departments were systematically examined through a theme-based classification and coding system. In the final stage of the analysis, the courses were grouped under three main themes: "Artificial Intelligence" (T1), "Digitalisation" (T2), and "Artificial Intelligence and Digitalisation" (T3). Each theme included more specific subcategories (K1–K16), under which the courses were further analysed.

Limitations

The universe of this research comprises all Visual Communication Design departments in Turkey. The sample consists of those departments that are affiliated with Faculties of Communication. In order to ensure up-to-date data, only courses listed in the four-year undergraduate curricula for the 2024–2025 academic year were included. Course plans publicly available on the official websites of the respective Faculties of Communication were reviewed. Within this context, it was identified that among the 53 Visual Communication Design departments in Turkey, 21 are housed within Communication Faculties. Among these, 5 are public and 16 are foundation universities. Of these, 20 programs were included in the study based on the accessibility of their course plans. The program at Avrasya University was excluded due to the inaccessibility of its curriculum. Although the course list for Fırat University was available, the classification of courses as compulsory or elective was not provided, which also limited its inclusion in the dataset.

FINDINGS

Table 2. Number of Courses in Visual Communication Design Departments within Communication Faculties of Universities

	University Name	Type of University	Number of Courses in the 4-Year Curriculum
1	Bahçeşehir University	Foundation	73
2	Kadir Has University	Foundation	106
3	Aydın Adnan Menderes University	State	75
4	Kocaeli University	State	73
5	Bolu İzzet Baysal University	State	76
6	İstinye University	Foundation	56

continued on following page

Table 2. Continued

	University Name	Type of University	Number of Courses in the 4-Year Curriculum
7	Yeditepe University	Foundation	124
8	İstanbul Topkapı University	Foundation	85
9	İstanbul Aydın University	Foundation	129
10	İstanbul Ticaret University	Foundation	67
11	Fırat University	State	73
12	Hasan Kalyoncu University	Foundation	74
13	Maltepe University	Foundation	157
14	İstanbul Beykent University	Foundation	81
15	İstanbul Arel University	Foundation	196
16	İstanbul Yeni Yüzyıl University	Foundation	77
17	Yaşar University	Foundation	96
18	Üsküdar University	Foundation	69
19	İstanbul Bilgi University	Foundation	44
20	Süleyman Demirel University	State	88
	Total		**1819**

As shown in Table 2, the total number of courses is 1,819. Of these, 1,434 are offered by foundation universities, while 385 are offered by public universities. Foundation universities account for 78.83% of the total courses, whereas public universities account for 21.17%. The primary reason for this disparity lies in the relatively lower number of public universities in quantitative terms. It has been observed that foundation universities generally offer a higher number of courses. Furthermore, it was identified that Visual Communication Design departments established within Communication Faculties of public universities remain more limited in comparison to those at foundation universities.

Table 3. Number of Courses Themed on Digitalisation and Artificial Intelligence in Visual Communication Design Departments

University Name	F	S	Digitalisation	Artificial Intelligence	Digitalisation and Artificial Intelligence
Bahçeşehir University		X	13	2	-
Kadir Has University		X	22	-	-
Aydın Adnan Menderes University	X		12	1	1
Kocaeli University	X		9	1	-
Bolu İzzet Baysal University	X		12	-	-
İstinye University		X	9	1	-

continued on following page

Table 3. Continued

University Name	F	S	Digitalisation	Artificial Intelligence	Digitalisation and Artificial Intelligence
Yeditepe University		X	13	-	-
İstanbul Topkapı University		X	12	-	1
İstanbul Aydın University		X	18	1	1
İstanbul Ticaret University		X	12	4	-
Fırat University	X		11	-	-
Hasan Kalyoncu University		X	15	-	1
Maltepe University		X	9	-	-
İstanbul Beykent University		X	11	2	1
İstanbul Arel University		X	13	1	3
İstanbul Yeni Yüzyıl University		X	9	-	-
Yaşar University		X	12	2	-
Üsküdar University		X	7	-	-
İstanbul Bilgi University		X	9	-	-
Süleyman Demirel University	X		10	-	-
Total			**238**	**15**	**8**

Within the scope of this study, the courses offered in the Visual Communication Design departments of the examined universities were categorized based on their focus on digitalisation, artificial intelligence, and content addressing both themes simultaneously. Table 3 presents the number of such courses, distinguishing between public and foundation universities. This distribution reveals that the study predominantly focuses on the curricula of foundation universities. All universities examined include courses related to digitalisation in their curricula. The number of digitalisation-themed courses ranges from 7 to 22. Kadir Has University offers the highest number of such courses (22), while Üsküdar University offers the lowest (7). These findings indicate that digitalisation has become a fundamental component of visual communication design education. However, the wide range in course counts demonstrates variations in the emphasis and integration of this theme across different universities. Courses on artificial intelligence are relatively limited in many universities. Istanbul Ticaret University offers the highest number of AI-themed courses (4). In contrast, some universities (e.g., Bolu İzzet Baysal University, Fırat University, Üsküdar University) do not offer any courses focused on artificial intelligence. This finding suggests that AI has not yet been fully integrated into the visual communication design curriculum and remains underrepresented. Courses that combine the themes of digitalisation and artificial intelligence are offered by only a few universities. Istanbul Arel University stands out for offering the highest number of such integrated courses (3). This indicates that thematic integration is still an emerging area and that the majority of universities tend to address these two domains separately within their curricula. Foundation universities offer a greater number of courses in both digitalisation and artificial intelligence compared to public universities. In particular, the number of AI-related courses in public universities is quite limited. Foundation universities appear to adapt more swiftly to innovative curriculum development. This trend may be associated with factors such as financial resources, curricular flexibility, and the capacity to respond quickly to industry dynamics.

Table 4. Teaching Methods of Courses Themed on Digitalisation and Artificial Intelligence in Visual Communication Design Departments

			Tematik Dersler		
University Name	F	S	Theoretical	Practical	Theoretical + Practical
Bahçeşehir University		X	2	-	13
Kadir Has University		X	-	-	22
Aydın Adnan Menderes University	X		6	-	8
Kocaeli University	X		7	-	3
Bolu İzzet Baysal University	X		2	-	10
İstinye University		X	6	-	4
Yeditepe University		X	-	-	13
İstanbul Topkapı University		X	2	-	11
İstanbul Aydın Üniversitesi		X	15	-	5
İstanbul Ticaret University		X	5	-	11
Fırat University	X		6	-	5
Hasan Kalyoncu University		X	6	-	10
Maltepe University		X	-	-	9
İstanbul Beykent University		X	4	-	10
İstanbul Arel University		X	16	-	1
İstanbul Yeni Yüzyıl University		X	-	-	9
Yaşar University		X	3	-	11
Üsküdar University		X	1	-	7
İstanbul Bilgi University		X	9	-	-
Süleyman Demirel University	X		9	-	1
Total			**99**	**0**	**163**

An examination of the theoretical and practical structures of digitalisation- and artificial intelligence-themed courses in Visual Communication Design programs across universities reveals that the vast majority of these courses are theory-oriented. According to the data presented in the table, nearly all courses are either delivered entirely in a theoretical format or structured as hybrid courses combining both theoretical and practical components. It is particularly noteworthy that foundation universities such as Kadir Has University and Yeditepe University tend to offer curricula heavily based on theoretical instruction, whereas public universities such as Aydın Adnan Menderes University and Kocaeli University include a limited number of practice-based elements alongside theoretical education. However, it appears that practice-oriented courses do not exist as a distinct and independent category but are generally integrated into theoretical content. This situation indicates that the development of practical skills in visual communication design education is positioned as a secondary priority, while theoretical foundation remains the main backbone of the curriculum. In conclusion, the course structures of the universities analyzed prioritize the accumulation of conceptual knowledge, but also point to the need for further curricular revisions to enhance practice-based competencies.

Table 5. Distribution of Compulsory and Elective Courses Themed on Digitalisation and Artificial Intelligence in Visual Communication Design Departments

			Thematic Courses	
University Name	F	S	Compulsory	Elective
Bahçeşehir University		X	8	7
Kadir Has University		X	20	2
Aydın Adnan Menderes University	X		9	5
Kocaeli University	X		8	2
Bolu İzzet Baysal University	X		2	10
İstinye University		X	6	4
Yeditepe University		X	5	8
İstanbul Topkapı University		X	8	5
İstanbul Aydın University		X	5	15
İstanbul Ticaret University		X	7	9
Fırat University	X		-	-
Hasan Kalyoncu University		X	7	9
Maltepe University		X	4	5
İstanbul Beykent University		X	12	2
İstanbul Arel University		X	14	3
İstanbul Yeniyüzyıl University		X	2	7
Yaşar Üniversitesi		X	10	4
Üsküdar University		X	5	2
İstanbul Bilgi Üniversitesi		X	8	1
Süleyman Demirel University	X		4	6
Total			**144**	**106**

An analysis of the distribution of thematic courses in Visual Communication Design programs according to their status as compulsory or elective reveals that most of the courses are offered as compulsory. Among the 20 universities analyzed, some institutions place greater emphasis on compulsory courses, while others diversify elective course offerings to support students in pursuing their individual interests.

For instance, Kadir Has University offers 20 compulsory and only 2 elective courses, indicating a highly structured curriculum with limited student autonomy. In contrast, Istanbul Aydın University provides 5 compulsory and 15 elective courses, reflecting a more flexible learning environment. It appears that foundation universities generally offer a greater number of elective courses, whereas public universities tend to follow a curriculum dominated by compulsory courses. Nevertheless, certain public universities such as Bolu İzzet Baysal University stand out as notable exceptions, where the number of elective courses exceeds that of compulsory ones. The absence of data on compulsory and elective course distinctions at Fırat University constitutes one of the limitations of the study, possibly due to gaps in curriculum planning or publicly available information.

Overall, the balance between compulsory and elective courses reflects the pedagogical orientation of universities and the degree to which they embrace a student-centered educational philosophy.

Table 6. Classification of Courses within Visual Communication Design Departments in the Context of Digitalisation and Artificial Intelligence Themes

Theme	Theme Name	Kod	Kod Adı	Ders Sayısı
T1	Artificial Intelligence	K1	Design	7
T1	Artificial Intelligence	K2	Ethics	3
T1	Artificial Intelligence	K3	Data Visualization	3
T1	Artificial Intelligence	K4	*Machine Learning*	1
T2	Digitalisation	K5	Graphic Design	40
T2	Digitalisation	K6	Media Design	23
T2	Digitalisation	K7	Interaction and Interface Design	28
T2	Digitalisation	K8	Programming	48
T2	Digitalisation	K9	*Digital Culture*	33
T2	Digitalisation	K10	Gaming and Virtualisation	19
T2	Digitalisation	K11	Content Production	14
T2	Digitalisation	K12	Digital Marketing	15
T2	Digitalisation	K13	Theoretical Approaches	18
T3	Artificial Intelligence and Digitalisation	K14	Digital Ecosystems	4
T3	Artificial Intelligence and Digitalisation	K15	Data-Based Technologies	3
T3	Artificial Intelligence and Digitalisation	K16	Technology Management	1

An analysis of the distribution of courses based on thematic coding in Visual Communication Design programs clearly reveals that curricula are predominantly structured around digitalisation. According to the data presented in the table, courses coded under the theme of "Digitalisation" (T2) exhibit a significantly higher concentration compared to other themes. In particular, areas such as Programming (K8, 48 courses), Graphic Design (K5, 40 courses), and Interaction and Interface Design (K7, 28 courses) demonstrate that production processes based on digital technologies occupy a central position in the curricula. By contrast, courses under the "Artificial Intelligence" theme (T1) are relatively limited in scope. A total of 14 courses were identified under subcategories such as Design and Artificial Intelligence (K1, 7 courses), Ethics (K2, 3 courses), Data Visualization (K3, 3 courses), and Machine Learning (K4, 1 course), indicating that AI-focused content remains an emerging area within visual communication design education. Under the "Artificial Intelligence and Digitalisation" theme, the focus shifts to more managerial and system-oriented topics such as Digital Ecosystems (K14, 4 courses), Data-Based Technologies (K15, 3 courses), and Technology Management (K16, 1 course). In conclusion, the thematic distribution suggests that education in Visual Communication Design departments is heavily concentrated in areas such as digital production, graphical communication, and interface design, while domains related to AI-driven innovation and data analytics still exhibit potential for development. In the future, increasing the number of interdisciplinary courses that integrate both artificial intelligence and digitalisation will support these departments in adapting more effectively to ongoing transformations in the industry.

CONCLUSION AND RECOMMENDATIONS

The accelerating process of digitalisation in recent years, the widespread use of social media, and the growing capacity of artificial intelligence technologies to offer practical solutions across various domains have made it imperative for educational content to adapt to these transformations. In today's image-dominated era, Visual Communication Design departments—with their eclectic structure encompassing art, technology, and communication—are among the fields that must adapt most rapidly to digital transformation. Within this context, the present study analyzed the level of adaptation to technological transformation in education by comparing various university programs. The analyses conducted aimed to reveal the extent to which digitalisation and artificial intelligence themes are incorporated into the curricula of Visual Communication Design departments in Turkey. The examination of course plans for the 2024–2025 academic year at both public and foundation universities revealed that courses focused on digitalisation are significantly more prevalent than those related to artificial intelligence. The prioritization of areas such as digital literacy, programming, and digital media production in the majority of programs reflects the industry's demand for technology-proficient designers. However, it also points to the limited access students have to hands-on, experiential learning processes. Although artificial intelligence remains an emerging area, its direct integration into curricula is still limited and generally addressed through more specific topics such as machine learning, data visualization, and ethics.

Another striking finding of the study is that the thematic structures of courses are primarily theory-oriented. The lack of fully practice-based courses suggests that opportunities for applied learning remain limited. Furthermore, it was observed that foundation universities offer a wider range of elective courses compared to public universities, providing students with greater flexibility to adapt to technological changes. However, the limited number of interdisciplinary and AI-focused courses, as well as the restricted emphasis on practice-based instruction, indicates that students may not be sufficiently supported in terms of their post-graduation competitiveness and capacity for innovative thinking. This points to a shortfall in current educational programs in meeting the multifaceted requirements of the digital and AI-driven design industries.

In the process of restructuring educational programs, it is essential that students be equipped not only with traditional design skills but also with contemporary competencies in digital literacy, data analysis, and AI-supported production processes. The integration of such content into curricula will not only strengthen students' technical knowledge but also enhance their ability to think strategically, develop interdisciplinary approaches, and compete effectively in the professional sector. Particularly in fast-evolving domains like digitalisation and AI, incorporating more flexible and elective course structures into curricula will enable students to better adapt to industry dynamics and even shape the ongoing transformation.

Within this framework, the study concludes that it is necessary to increase the number of courses themed on "digitalisation" and "artificial intelligence" in Visual Communication Design departments housed within Communication Faculties, and to place greater emphasis on practice-oriented content in curriculum planning. In light of the findings, it is clear that Visual Communication Design programs must be restructured around a holistic approach that centers on digitalisation and AI literacy. In this context, merely expanding course content will not suffice; pedagogical strategies aimed at fostering skills such as creative problem-solving, critical thinking, ethical awareness, and technological competence must also be updated. This will enable universities to not only meet the current demands of the industry but also to take a leading role in training designers who can actively shape the digital transformation.

It should also be noted that this study is limited to the 2024–2025 curricula of Visual Communication Design departments located within Communication Faculties in Turkey. Consequently, it does not include a comparative analysis with other faculties or programs offering similar education at national or international levels. Future studies should incorporate comparative evaluations of educational models in different countries to assess how Turkish curricula align with international standards and to draw insights from best practices. In conclusion, promoting interdisciplinary, multidimensional, and data-driven research in the field of visual communication design will enable the development of more innovative, inclusive, and technology-oriented educational models through a visionary approach.

REFERENCES

Adobe. (n.d.). Adobe Firefly. Retrieved May 4, 2025, from https://firefly.adobe.com/

Akıncı, H., & Kahraman, Ü. G. (2024). Endüstri 4.0: Yönetim bilişim sistemleri bakış açısıyla değerlendirme. *MAKÜ Uygulamalı Bilimler Dergisi*, *8*(1), 76–99. DOI: 10.31200/makuubd.1442339

Aliefendioğlu, B. (2024). Artırılmış çağda yapay zekâ teknolojilerinin grafik tasarımı alanına etkisi. *International Journal of Media. Culture and Literature*, *10*(1), 69–96.

Bozüyük, T., Yağcı, C., & Gökçe, İ. (2005). Yapay zekâ teknolojilerinin endüstrideki uygulamaları. *Dicle Üniversitesi Mühendislik Fakültesi Mühendislik Dergisi*, *2*(2), 95–105.

Brown, T. (2012). From blueprint to genetic code: the merits of an evolutionary approach to design. *Rotman Magazine, Spring.*

Canva. (n.d.). Canva: Tasarım herkes için. Retrieved May 4, 2025, from https://www.canva.com/tr_tr/

Creativani, K. (2023). Exploring the potential of visual communication design education: Transforming education paradigm. *Visual Heritage: Jurnal Kreasi Seni dan Budaya*, 5(2), 281–289. https://doi.org/DOI: 10.30998/vh.v5i2.8242

Doğan, E. (2015). Türkiye'deki görsel iletişim tasarımı bölümleri üzerine genel bir durum analizi. *İletişim Çalışmaları Dergisi*, 1(1), 15–33.

Doğan, F., & Türkoğlu, İ. (2019). Derin öğrenme modelleri ve uygulama alanlarına ilişkin bir derleme. *Dicle Üniversitesi Mühendislik Fakültesi Mühendislik Dergisi*, *10*(2), 409–445. DOI: 10.24012/DUMF.411130

Elgammal, A., Liu, B., Elhoseiny, M., & Mazzone, M. (2017). CAN: Creative adversarial networks—Generating "art" by learning about styles and deviating from style norms. In Goel, A., Jordanous, A., & Pease, A. (Eds.), *Proceedings of the 8th International Conference on Computational Creativity* (pp. 96–103). Georgia Institute of Technology. https://arxiv.org/abs/1706.07068

European Commission. (2019). *Ethics guidelines for trustworthy AI.* Publications Office of the European Union., DOI: 10.2759/346720

Falmouth University. (2023). What is visual communication? Retrieved May 4, 2025, from https://www.falmouth.ac.uk/news/what-is-visual-communication

Figma. (n.d.). Your creativity, unblocked with Figma AI. Retrieved May 4, 2025, from https://www.figma.com/ai/

Folcu , O., Manta, O., & Militaru, I. (2024, January 15). Education, artificial intelligence, and the digital age. *Qeios.*

Friedman, L. W., & Friedman, H. H. (2013). Using social media technologies to enhance online learning. *The Journal of Educators Online*, *10*(1). Advance online publication. DOI: 10.9743/JEO.2013.1.5

Gartner. (2021). Definition of digitalization. Retrieved May 4, 2025, from https://www.gartner.com/en/information-technology/glossary/digitalization

Gawer, A. (2022). Digital platforms and ecosystems: Remarks on the dominant organizational forms of the digital age. *Innovation (North Sydney, N.S.W.)*, *24*(1), 110–124. DOI: 10.1080/14479338.2021.1965888

Goodfellow, I., Pouget-Abadie, J., Mirza, M., Xu, B., Warde-Farley, D., Ozair, S., Courville, A., & Bengio, Y. (2014). Generative adversarial nets. *In Advances in Neural Information Processing Systems* (Vol. 27, pp. 2672–2680). https://www.researchgate.net/publication/263012109_Generative_Adversarial_Networks

Günay, M. (2021). Design in visual communication. *Art and Design Review*, *9*, 109–122. DOI: 10.4236/adr.2021.92010

Guo, H. (2022). Innovation and development of visual communication design in the new media era. *Frontiers in Business, Economics and Management*, *3*(3), 49–51.

IBM. (2024). What is artificial intelligence (AI)? Retrieved May 4, 2025, from https://www.ibm.com/think/topics/artificial-intelligence

Ilıcak, N. G., & Çinko, K. (2021). Yapay zekânın yarattığı masal: Prenses ile tilki. *Uluslararası Türkçe Edebiyat Kültür Eğitim Dergisi*, *10*(2), 703–719.

Jun, X. Y. (2023). The construction of designers' visual design thinking in the visual communication design perspective. *World Journal of Educational Research (Los Angeles, Calif.)*, *10*(5), 88–93.

Karaahmet Balcı, S. (2017). Değişen paradigmaların görsel iletişim tasarımı lisans ve lisansüstü eğitim programlarına yansımaları. *Turkish Studies International Periodical for the Languages. Literature and History of Turkish or Turkic*, *12*(23), 151–172.

Kavuran, T., & Çetinkaya, A. (2012). Görsel iletişim açısından film afişlerinin grafik çözümlemeleri (2000–2010 yılları arasında Antalya Altın Portakal Film Festivali'nde ödül alan sinema film afişlerinin değerlendirilmesi). *International Communication Symposium:* Kyrgyzstan Turkey Manas University Publications.

Kaynar, M. (2024). Yapay zekâ, yapay zekâ etiği ve insan doğasının geleceği (Yüksek lisans tezi, İstanbul Sabahattin Zaim Üniversitesi, Lisansüstü Eğitim Enstitüsü, Felsefe ve Din Bilimleri Anabilim Dalı, Felsefe ve Din Bilimleri Bilim Dalı). İstanbul, Türkiye.

Ketenci, F., & Bilgili, C. (2006). *Görsel İletişim ve Grafik Tasarım: Yoncaların 10.000 Yıllık Gizemli Dansı*. Beta Yayınevi.

Koh, Y. J., Baldridge, J., Lee, H., & Yang, Y. (2020). Text-to-image generation grounded by fine-grained user attention. Google Research. https://arxiv.org/abs/2011.03775

Lim, S. (2023). A qualitative study of the curriculum of visual communication design majors at University A: Based on NASAD, a design certification system in the U.S. *Archives of Design Research, 36*(2), 323–337.

Litmus Branding Pvt. Ltd. (n.d.). Ethical issues in AI-based design. Retrieved May 4, 2025, from https://www.litmusbranding.com/

Lopez, J. (2023, May 17). Stability AI releases StableStudio, the open source future of DreamStudio. Stability AI. https://stability.ai/news/stablestudio-open-source-community-driven-future-dreamstudio-release

Marshall, G. (1999). *Sosyoloji sözlüğü* (O. Akınhay & D. Kömürcü, Çev.). Bilim ve Sanat Yayınları.

Open, A. I. (2021). Organizational update. Retrieved January 14, 2021, from https://openai.com/blog/organizational-update/

Open, A. I. (2023). DALL·E 2 [Computer software]. https://openai.com/dall-e-2

Open, A. I. ChatGPT. (2025, May 4). Görsel iletişim tasarımında kullanılan yapay zeka botları: Eğitim, profesyonel kullanım ve ücretsiz erişim özellikleri tablosu. OpenAI ChatGPT. https://chat.openai.com/

Öztemel, E. (2020). Yapay zekâ ve insanlığın geleceği. In Şeker, M., Bulduklu, Y., Korkut, C., & Doğrul, M. (Eds.), *Bilişim Teknolojileri ve İletişim: Birey ve Toplum Güvenliği* (pp. 95–112). Türkiye Bilimler Akademisi Yayınları.

Parsa, A. F. (2004). İmgenin gücü görsel kültürün yükselişi. In Işık, M. (Ed.), *Medyada Yeni Yaklaşımlar* (pp. 215–237). Eğitim Kitapevi Yayınları.

Runway. (n.d.). Studios. Retrieved May 4, 2025, from https://runwayml.com/studios

Schwab, K. (2016). The fourth industrial revolution. World Economic Forum.

Sun, Q., & Zhu, Y. (2022). Teaching analysis for visual communication design with the perspective of digital technology. *Hindawi Computational and Mathematical Methods in Medicine, 2022*, 1–10. DOI: 10.1155/2022/2411811 PMID: 35903440

Uçar, T. F. (2004). *Görsel İletişim ve Grafik Tasarım.* İnkılap Kitapevi.

U.S. Department of Education. (2023, May). Artificial intelligence and the future of teaching and learning: Insights and recommendations (M. A. Cardona, R. J. Rodríguez, & K. Ishmael, Eds.). Office of Educational Technology. https://eric.ed.gov/?q=source%3A%22Office+of+Educational+Technology%2C+US+Department+of+Education%22&id=ED631097

WalkMe. (n.d.). What is digitalization? Retrieved May 4, 2025, from https://www.walkme.com/glossary/digitalization/

Yeo, H.-J. P. (2014). An overview of research methods in visual communication design education. *International Journal of Design Creativity and Innovation, 2*(1), 51–62.

Zhou, Q., & Ghazali, M. (2023). Research on the curriculum of visual communication design. *Journal of Humanities, Arts and Social Science.* https://doi.org/DOI: 10.26855/jhass.2023.07.031

ADDITIONAL READING

Becer, E. (2002). *İletişim ve grafik tasarım.* Dost Kitabevi Yayınları.

Bedir Erişti, S. D. (2025). *Yeni medya ve görsel iletişim tasarımı.* Pegem Akademi.

Berger, J. (2005). *Görme biçimleri (Y. Salman, Çev.).* Metis Yayınları.

Gürdal, G. (2024). *Eylül 27). Eğitim ve araştırmada yapay zeka* [Çalıştay sunumu]. İYTE Eğitim Çalıştayı, İzmir Yüksek Teknoloji Enstitüsü.

İnceağaç, M., & İnceağaç, S. (2019). Eğitimde küreselleşme ve görsel sanatlar eğitimi. In Sağer, T., Arapgirlioğlu, H., Akgül, K. P., & Sürmeli, K. (Eds.), *Uluslararası SANAD bildiri kitabı* (pp. 173–181). Gece Akademi.

Karamustafa, S. (2003). 21. yüzyıl Türkiyesi'nde görsel iletişim tasarımı eğitimi: Gelişmiş iletişim teknolojileri çağında, Türkiye'deki grafik tasarımı eğitiminin geleceğine ilişkin bir model önerisi [Sanatta yeterlik tezi, Mimar Sinan Üniversitesi Sosyal Bilimler Enstitüsü]. YÖK Ulusal Tez Merkezi. https://acikerisim.msgsu.edu.tr/xmlui/handle/20.500.14124/4636

Kavut, S. (2024). *Yapay zeka ve iletişim.* Çizgi Kitabevi.

Liu, X., & Yao, R. (2023). Design of visual communication teaching system based on artificial intelligence and CAD technology. *Computer-Aided Design and Applications, 20*(S10), 90–101. https://app.scinito.ai/article/W4362659706

Üsküdar Üniversitesi İletişim Fakültesi. (2020). *7. Uluslararası iletişim günleri: Dijital çağda iletişim eğitimi sempozyumu bildiri kitabı* [Proceedings book]. Üsküdar Üniversitesi.

Zhao, K., Peng, C., & Wu, Y. (2024). Exploring the teaching path of visual communication in the digital era. *International Journal of Web-Based Learning and Teaching Technologies, 19*(1), 1–17. DOI: 10.4018/IJWLTT.340937

KEY TERMS AND DEFINITIONS

AI-Supported Design Platforms: These platforms contribute to design processes by performing tasks similar to those of humans. They offer advantages such as creativity, originality, speed, convenience, innovation, efficiency and personalization. By employing machine learning and deep learning models, they can analyze visual and textual data, thereby enabling data-driven insights and automating aspects of the design process.

Artificial Intelligence: Artificial intelligence is software that can imitate the human brain, generate thought and action, establish relationships between concepts, make interpretations, adapt to new situations, and operate for purposes such as prediction, classification, and recommendation, utilizing various modes of learning.

Digitalisation: Digitalisation refers to the transformation of information, objects, and processes into digital formats, encompassing tools and platforms such as artificial intelligence, mobile applications, software, online resources, videos, articles, advertisements, music, podcasts, audiobooks, virtual reality, digital art, and e-commerce. It constitutes a holistic technological ecosystem that facilitates, accelerates, and supports individuals' tasks and workflows.

Graphic Design: Graphic design refers to the creation of visual and textual content using design principles within an artistic and aesthetic framework. Unlike visual communication design, it prioritizes artistic expression. Its focus lies in producing visually engaging outcomes through elements like typography, color theory, photography, and illustration.

Visual Communication Design Education: Visual communication design education is an interdisciplinary field combining technology and design to communicate messages effectively and creatively. It includes applied courses and theoretical subjects to prepare adaptable graduates for the demands of a rapidly evolving industry.

Visual Communication Design: Visual communication design involves creating visual and textual content based on specific design principles to effectively convey messages. It entails adapting a message from source to receiver using visual elements suited to the medium and target audience. Distinguished from graphic design by its multilayered structure, the field integrates insights from the humanities, aesthetics, communication theories, research methods, emerging media technologies, and multimodal tools such as photography, video, and animation.

Visual Culture: Visual culture refers to a cultural structure in which visual images, media messages, and technology play a central role in how people perceive and interpret the world. Within this culture, photographs, videos, advertisements, digital content, and two-dimensional and three-dimensional visual elements hold significant functions. In contemporary society, visuals are not only used for transmitting information but also for conveying emotions, thoughts, and ideologies, and they play a crucial role in the expression of individual identity.

Chapter 2
Navigating Complexity: Tracing the Development of Wayfinding Design in Busy Urban Environments

Stephen T. F. Poon
https://orcid.org/0000-0003-0780-1903
MILA University, Malaysia

ABSTRACT

This study investigates the evolution of wayfinding and signage systems in Kuala Lumpur from 1960 to the present, focusing on their critical role in facilitating urban navigation amidst the city's rapid demographic and technological transformations. As Malaysia's capital transitions from traditional to digital signage, this research aims to assess the impact of these systems on urban mobility and propose adaptive strategies for future challenges. Utilising a sequential explanatory mixed method, the study combines quantitative surveys and qualitative interviews to gather comprehensive data. The survey, involving respondents across various demographics, evaluates public perceptions of current wayfinding effectiveness, particularly at high-traffic hubs like Kuala Lumpur International Airport (KLIA). This is supplemented by interviews with experts, including a long-term resident and teaching academic, to delve deeper into the practical applications and historical context of wayfinding systems. Findings reveal that efficient wayfinding significantly enhances urban mobility.

DOI: 10.4018/979-8-3373-6970-9.ch002

© 2026, IGI Global Scientific Publishing. Copying or distributing in print or electronic forms without written permission of IGI Global Scientific Publishing is prohibited. Use of this chapter to ...erative artificial intelligence (AI) technologies is expressly prohibited. The publisher reserves all rights to license its use for generative AI training and machine learning model development.

INTRODUCTION

Malaysia, now home to over 34.6 million residents as of April 2024 according to *WorldOMeter* (2024), continues to thrive as a major tourist destination. The tourism sector, significantly impacted by global events such as the COVID-19 pandemic, is projected to rebound strongly. According to recent statements by Deputy Tourism, Arts and Culture Minister Khairul Firdaus Akbar Khan, the country expects to generate RM375.3 billion in tourism revenue over the next three years (Carvalho et. al., 2024). This optimism is fuelled by anticipated tourist arrivals increasing yearly, culminating in an estimated 35.6 million tourists by the *Visit Malaysia Year 2026*. This research examines the evolution of wayfinding and signage design in Kuala Lumpur from 1960 to today, highlighting its pivotal role in enhancing urban navigation. The study tracks the progression from basic early signs to today's advanced digital systems, reflecting significant technological and societal shifts, including the adoption of multilingual signs and universal design principles. This transition not only facilitates the smooth flow of city life but is also essential for maintaining the economic vitality of a city renowned for its high population density and rapid pace. Through a mix of qualitative and quantitative methods, the study captures public perceptions and evaluates the effectiveness of these evolving wayfinding systems.

Aims

The objective of this research is twofold: firstly, to underscore the significance of efficient wayfinding systems in busy urban environments where time is a precious commodity, and secondly, to chart the developmental trajectory of these systems over several decades. By understanding the evolution of wayfinding in Kuala Lumpur, this study seeks to demonstrate its impact on urban mobility and to propose ways in which these systems can continue to evolve in response to future urban challenges. The hypothesis posits that superior wayfinding systems have significantly contributed to the positive navigation experiences of both locals and tourists, reflecting a broader trend of continuous improvement in urban infrastructure. Through this comprehensive analysis, the research aims to provide actionable insights that can guide future urban planning and design initiatives in Kuala Lumpur and similar urban settings worldwide.

LITERATURE REVIEW

Signage and wayfinding systems are intricately designed with human behaviour in mind, recognising that people generally seek the most straightforward and least cognitively demanding paths to their destinations. According to Neville (2021), effective wayfinding systems implant the memory of a location's geography in the minds of its users through strategic placement of landmarks, orientation cues, and navigational aids, both consciously and unconsciously guiding them to their desired destinations.

Understanding the Essentials of Signage and Wayfinding

Research plays a pivotal role in this design process, as it provides designers with a deep understanding of the environmental context, user behaviours, and critical areas where sign legibility can be optimised. There are four fundamental types of signs integral to an effective wayfinding system: *informational signs, directional signs, identification signs,* and *warning signs*. To coordinate these elements effectively, the use of a design grid is recommended, helping to organise signs in a visually coherent manner across various sizes and scales. This approach prevents information overload, which can occur if too much data is condensed into a single sign. Instead, distributing information across multiple signs can enhance clarity and comprehension. Design consistency in typography, icons, material choices, and colour schemes is also crucial to maintain an intuitive navigation experience.

The Confusion between 'Wayfinding' and 'Signage'

The terms *wayfinding* and *signage* are often used interchangeably, though they refer to distinct concepts within the design field (Jalees, 2020). Iftikhar and Luximon (2022) define wayfinding as an information system that guides individuals through a physical environment, facilitating navigation in complex spaces like campuses and public transportation systems. This system relies on a combination of maps, symbols, and directional cues to aid users in forming a mental map of their surroundings, simplifying their navigation to the greatest extent possible. In modern settings, advancements such as digital displays and wireless technologies are increasingly integrated to enhance these systems. Signage, on the other hand, is the visual component of the wayfinding system, comprising graphic displays that convey location-specific information to guide individuals toward their destinations (Kocaturk et al., 2024). Effective signage not only provides clear directions but also contributes to the learning and environmental engagement of its users, helping to establish and reinforce the character of a place. The strategic placement of signs is the key, with locations chosen to maximise functionality and visibility, often turning transitional spaces into mini destinations within larger environments. Overall, while wayfinding encompasses the broader communication system within which signage operates, signage itself focuses on the conveyance of navigational and informational content. Both elements are indispensable, without signage, the wayfinding system lacks a medium to communicate, and without wayfinding principles, signage would be devoid of strategic context and purpose. Together, they create a cohesive navigational aid that addresses the complexities of human movement and orientation within built and natural environments.

Evolving Dynamics of Modern Wayfinding Systems

The evolution of wayfinding systems, particularly in urban environments, underscores a complex interplay of design, technology, and user interaction. The *WalkNYC* programme serves as a quintessential example of modern wayfinding initiatives that have transformed the navigation landscape in New York City (*NYC DOT*, 2024). This development process encompasses extensive research, collaboration with field specialists, and the application of precedent studies to inform design decisions. A critical step in this process involves selecting prominent landmarks and integrating them into the navigation aids to enhance spatial recognition and orientation. An essential component of contemporary wayfinding is the adherence to design standards, such as those established by the *American Institute of Graphic Arts* (AIGA). These standards ensure that signage not only communicates effectively but also maintains a visual harmony that reduces cognitive load on users. For instance, the AIGA symbol design adopted in the *WalkNYC* programme exemplifies how standardised symbols can streamline navigation in complex urban spaces while minimising visual dissonance (Pepple, 2014).

Figure 1. The adaptation of AIGA signage design by Michael Bierut

Source: Assets.dwell.com. (2016). [online]. http://assets.dwell.com/sites/default/files/2013/08/28/walk-nyc-logos.jpg

In today's digital age, technology plays a pivotal role in shaping wayfinding systems. The integration of smartphones and digital technology has profoundly influenced projects like *WalkNYC*, enhancing how information is conveyed and accessed. Modern mapping systems offer advancements well beyond traditional, static maps; they provide dynamic orientation with real-time updates. Despite these technological enhancements, the challenge remains to balance digital interaction with the intuitive need to engage directly with the environment. For many, the physical act of navigating, looking around and interpreting signs directly within the streetscape, remains preferable to mediated experiences through a device. Moreover, the effectiveness of a wayfinding system is often judged by its ability to resonate with the identity of its location. For New Yorkers and visitors alike, the design of the *WalkNYC* system aims to evoke a sense of place, making it unmistakably representative of the city's unique character. This aspect of design, ensuring that users not only find their way but also connect with the environment, is crucial for a wayfinding system's success (Figure 1). Thus, the development of wayfinding systems, as exemplified by New York City's approach, involves a careful consideration of various elements, from research and standardisation to the integration of technology and local identity. Each component is vital to creating an effective and user-friendly navigation system that meets the demands of contemporary urban life.

Navigational Strategies at Kuala Lumpur International Airport (KLIA)

The KLIA serves as a critical hub for both local and international travellers, making its wayfinding system an essential component of airport operations (Batouei et al., 2020). The design of KLIA's wayfinding system is meticulously planned to accommodate a myriad of functionalities such as accessibility and connectivity, ensuring that all passengers navigate the airport efficiently.

Figure 2. Wayfinding system in KLIA2

The wayfinding system at KLIA is specifically engineered to manage three main types of traffic: *aviation, pedestrian,* and *vehicle*. Each category is addressed through tailored signage to guide the respective users effectively. The pedestrian traffic, in particular, receives significant attention due to the high volume of footfall within the airport premises. Signage for pedestrian traffic is strategically deployed to streamline the flow of passengers across different areas, including arrivals, departures, and transfer pathways. This is depicted in Figures 2 and 3, which illustrate the comprehensive signage framework within KLIA2, a terminal of KLIA.

Figure 3. Wayfinding system in KLIA2

The signage system is categorised into three types, each serving a unique purpose. *Informational signs* cater to individual needs by directing passengers to specific facilities like prayer rooms, lounges, or restaurants. *Identification signs* serve to mark significant locations without providing directional guidance; for example, restrooms are typically indicated with such signs. *Directional signs* are crucial as they guide passengers towards specific areas, utilising visual commands and arrows to lead the way.

Figure 4. Wayfinding system in KLIA2

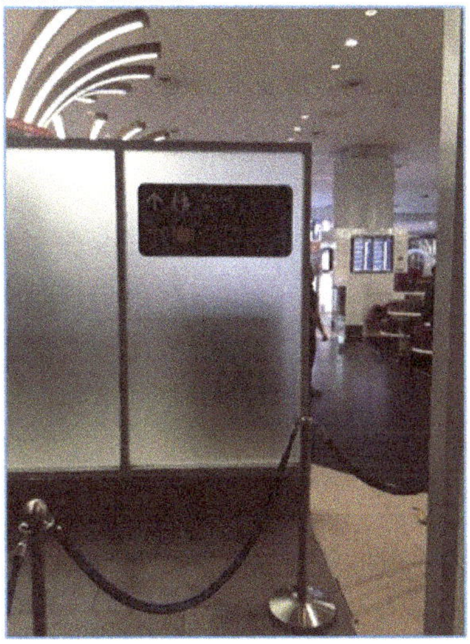

In the design of signage systems, particularly those in complex environments like KLIA, several key attributes must be carefully considered to ensure functionality and user-friendliness. These attributes include the shape, ergonomics, size, symbols, colour, and layout of the signage. Each element plays a critical role in the effectiveness of the signage in guiding vast numbers of passengers, both locals and tourists, through the airport's expansive and intricate spaces. At KLIA, the signage system is designed to facilitate navigation between major areas, such as the transition from the main building to the satellite building. However, challenges arise due to the architectural features and spatial configurations of these areas. Notably, the circular design of the satellite building has been a point of contention and confusion for many passengers. The wayfinding signs, while visible, often fall short in terms of *readability* and *understandability*, critical factors that directly impact the overall effectiveness of the system.

Figure 5. Wayfinding system in KLIA2

Figures 4, 5, and 6 in the study illustrate various aspects of the wayfinding system within KLIA2. These images depict the signage deployed across different junctures within the airport, highlighting both the strengths and weaknesses of the current designs. For instance, while Figure 4 may show signage that is prominently displayed, its effectiveness is diminished if the information presented is not immediately comprehensible to a diverse, international audience. Similarly, Figures 5 and 6 provide further examples of how signage is utilised within the airport to manage passenger flow through key transit points. These images capture the physical placement and visual design of the signs, which should ideally guide passengers smoothly from one section of the airport to another.

Figure 6. Wayfinding system in KLIA2

Despite the strategic placement and visibility of these signs, the feedback from users indicates that improvements are necessary to enhance the readability and understandability of the information provided. The signage must not only direct effectively but also be easily interpretable at a glance, which is crucial in a high-traffic environment where time and clarity are of the essence. Therefore, while KLIA's signage system includes several well-thought-out design elements, the overall integration of these elements needs refining to better serve the needs of all airport users, ensuring a seamless and stress-free navigation experience.

Overcoming Language Barriers through Effective Wayfinding Design

Airports serve as international hubs that welcome millions of tourists from various nationalities to Malaysia each year. The diversity of languages spoken by these visitors presents a significant challenge in terms of navigation within the airport. Effective wayfinding systems are crucial not only for efficient human traffic flow but also for bridging the language divides among multicultural passengers (Alkharoubi, 2020). To address the language barriers effectively, the design of airport wayfinding and signage systems can be approached through several strategies: a combination of symbols and text, text-only, or symbols-only. Among these, the use of universally understood symbols, such as the directional arrow, is particularly effective. According to Green (2023), the directional arrow is a prime example of symbol standardisation at its most effective, prominently featured in navigation systems worldwide due to its clarity and universal recognition.

Effective communication within wayfinding systems relies on five key principles: *consistency, repetition, simplicity, rehearsal,* and *continuity*. Emphasising the standardisation of signage designs across different languages and cultures can significantly enhance navigational ease, reducing the need for visitors to decode multiple cultural references. This approach is not only practical but also time-efficient, bypassing the complexities involved in accommodating a wide array of cultural specifics. Looking forward, there is a growing consideration among specialists for the incorporation of advanced technological solutions, such as talking and video signs. These innovations promise to further enhance the wayfinding experience by providing dynamic, interactive guidance that can adapt to the needs of a diverse passenger base, potentially revolutionising how information is conveyed in high-traffic environments like airports.

Gaps in the Literature

While existing literature acknowledges the importance of wayfinding systems in urban environments, there is a noticeable lack of comprehensive studies focusing on the evolution of these systems over extended periods, particularly in rapidly developing cities like Kuala Lumpur. Most current research, such as that by Batouei et al. (2020), primarily examines wayfinding effectiveness in isolated contexts, often neglecting the broader historical and cultural shifts that influence these systems. This gap in longitudinal analysis leaves a critical void in understanding how wayfinding has adapted to the growing complexities of urban life, including the integration of digital technologies. Addressing this gap is essential, as it will provide insights into how historical trends and technological advancements have shaped the current state of wayfinding systems, offering a more nuanced perspective that can guide future developments.

Another significant gap in the literature relates to the specific challenges faced by multicultural and multilingual urban populations in navigating increasingly digital wayfinding systems. Although research by Iftikhar and Luximon (2022) explores the synthesis of static and mobile wayfinding information, it does not fully address the unique needs of diverse populations who may face language barriers when interacting with digital signage. This oversight is critical, as cities like Kuala Lumpur, which attract a wide range of international visitors, require wayfinding solutions that are both universally accessible and culturally inclusive. By investigating these challenges, this study aims to fill the gap by providing actionable recommendations for designing wayfinding systems that bridge linguistic and cultural divides.

Furthermore, while the role of wayfinding systems in enhancing urban mobility is generally well-recognised (Steg & De Groot, 2019), there is limited exploration of why emphasising this significance remains necessary, particularly in the context of time-sensitive environments like busy urban centres. The current literature often assumes the importance of wayfinding without fully investigating the specific factors that make efficient wayfinding critical in modern urban life. This study aims to clarify this necessity by examining how wayfinding systems directly impact the efficiency of urban mobility, with a focus on the unique pressures of densely populated areas where time is a precious commodity. Through this approach, the research seeks to contribute a deeper understanding of the strategic importance of wayfinding in contemporary urban design.

Theoretical Framework

This study on the evolution of wayfinding and signage design in Kuala Lumpur from 1960 to the present is grounded in environmental psychology and semiotics.

This framework helps to understand how individuals interact with their surroundings and how symbols and signs facilitate this interaction. Environmental psychology posits that the design of an environment influences human behaviour (Steg & De Groot, 2019). This concept is particularly relevant to wayfinding systems as they are integral to how people perceive and navigate public spaces. The wayfinding systems are designed not only to direct but also to enhance the user's understanding of the space, which can significantly affect their movement and psychological comfort within that environment. Semiotics, the study of signs and symbols and their use or interpretation, further supports the framework by examining how wayfinding elements act as communicative tools (Chmielewska, 2001; De Jesus, 1994). This approach is crucial in understanding the effectiveness of different signs and symbols used in public spaces like airports, where clarity and universality are essential to accommodate a diverse, international populace. By applying semiotic theory, the study assesses how effectively these symbols bridge language barriers and cultural differences, aiding in seamless navigation. Together, these theoretical perspectives provide a comprehensive foundation for analysing the changes in wayfinding design over the decades, exploring how technological advancements and shifts in urban demographics have influenced design choices. The framework facilitates an understanding of why certain designs succeed or fail in enhancing navigational efficacy and user experience in complex environments such as Kuala Lumpur, reflecting broader trends in urban design and technology integration. This approach also considers the potential future directions of wayfinding systems, including the integration of digital technologies and interactive elements that could redefine navigational practices in urban settings.

RESEARCH METHODOLOGY

This study employs a sequential explanatory approach, which integrates quantitative data collection followed by qualitative data analysis to provide depth and context. Initially, the quantitative phase involves conducting a survey targeting a diverse population without restrictions on gender or age, encompassing 150 respondents. This broad-based data collection aims to gather a wide array of perceptions and experiences related to wayfinding and signage efficiency within Kuala Lumpur. Following the analysis of the survey results, the qualitative phase is introduced to enhance the findings and address any nuances the quantitative data alone might not fully capture. This stage of the methodology involves in-depth interviews with key informants who have substantial experience with the local context. Specifically, an interview is conducted with an *IELTS* (International English Language Testing System) lecturer who has resided in Kuala Lumpur for the past 20 years, providing insights into the evolution and effectiveness of wayfinding systems over two decades. A critical question explored during the interviews is: *"Are the symbols in signage/wayfinding nowadays could be a language barrier between people?"* This enquiry is essential for understanding the communicative effectiveness of the signage in a multicultural and multilingual urban setting like Kuala Lumpur. By addressing this question, the research seeks to uncover the impact of wayfinding designs on navigational ease and to gather comprehensive information about the positive transformations induced by effective signage systems in contemporary urban environments.

RESULTS AND DISCUSSION

Quantitative Research Findings

The primary research methodology employed in this study is quantitative, conducted through a structured survey. This survey is divided into three sections, which explore respondents' basic understanding of wayfinding and signage design, their observations of wayfinding systems in society, and the advancements in wayfinding technologies. The quantitative approach is complemented by a qualitative method, which serves as a secondary means of data collection.

Section 1: Basic knowledge of Wayfinding and Signage Design

Wayfinding and signage design are crucial elements in the architecture of public spaces, playing a vital role in facilitating efficient navigation and improving the overall user experience. Effective wayfinding systems significantly ease the process of locating important public amenities and destinations, particularly in high-traffic environments like airports, where clarity and ease of navigation are paramount. In this section, the researcher analysed responses from a structured survey that explored public perceptions and the effectiveness of wayfinding systems, with a particular focus on environments like KLIA.

The survey responses indicate that public transportation is a fundamental part of daily life for many respondents. A considerable portion of the respondents reported using public transportation either daily or at least once a week. This regular interaction with public transport highlights the critical importance of efficient wayfinding systems, as they are instrumental in ensuring smooth and hassle-free navigation for a large segment of the population. When asked about the effectiveness of signage and wayfinding systems, a significant majority of respondents affirmed their usefulness in navigating to their destinations and identifying public transportation infrastructure.

Specifically, 64 respondents (42.7%) emphasised the value of signage in orienting them toward their destinations, while 70 respondents (46.7%) recognised the role of wayfinding systems in identifying public transportation hubs and facilities. This overwhelming consensus underscores the critical role that signage and wayfinding play in supporting daily mobility and access to essential services.

Regarding the effectiveness of specific wayfinding systems, respondents showed a marked preference for the system implemented at KLIA. Nearly half of the survey respondents identified KLIA's wayfinding system as the most exemplary in the city, attributing their preference to the system's visibility, understandability, and readability. These factors, which were highlighted as needing improvement in other systems, contribute significantly to the effectiveness of KLIA's wayfinding design. The survey results suggest that the familiarity and frequency of use among daily users of the airport also play a role in their positive assessment of the system. The survey findings further reveal that visibility of content is a primary factor influencing the positive evaluation of KLIA's wayfinding system. Many respondents indicated that clear and easily visible signage was crucial to their navigation experience. However, it is important to note that the other half of the respondents, who favoured different locations, may not necessarily believe that those systems surpass KLIA's in efficacy. Rather, their preferences likely reflect habitual use and familiarity with those particular environments, illustrating a general tendency among individuals to favour systems with which they are most acquainted.

In summary, the survey responses analysed in this section strongly support the importance of effective signage and wayfinding systems in public spaces. The data demonstrate general satisfaction with these systems at places like KLIA, while also indicating specific areas for improvement, particularly in enhancing the understandability and readability of signage. These insights are invaluable for urban planners and designers who aim to optimise navigational aids in public spaces, ensuring that they meet the diverse needs of user groups and contribute to a more accessible and user-friendly environment. By addressing these aspects, wayfinding systems can significantly improve the user experience, particularly in complex and busy settings like airports.

Section 2: The Evolution and Current Trends in Wayfinding within Society

The evolution of wayfinding and signage systems is closely tied to broader societal shifts, particularly in response to technological advancements and the dynamic nature of urban environments. This section explores how society has integrated these systems and the preferences that have emerged, drawing on data collected through structured survey questions. The focus is on understanding how public perceptions of wayfinding have shifted from traditional methods to modern digital solutions, and how these changes influence daily navigation within urban spaces.

The survey responses indicate a widespread perception among participants that wayfinding systems have undergone significant transformation over the years. Many respondents recognised that advancements in technology and changes in urban dynamics have led to notable shifts in the design and implementation of wayfinding systems. However, when asked to specify the nature of these changes, nearly 116 respondents (77.3%) expressed uncertainty, unable to clearly differentiate whether these transformations represented a true development or simply an evolution of existing practices. This confusion among respondents highlights a broader uncertainty regarding the impact of technological advancements on traditional wayfinding practices. It suggests that while the public is aware of the changes occurring in wayfinding systems, there is a lack of clarity on how these changes fundamentally alter the way people navigate urban environments. The blending of traditional and digital methods may contribute to this uncertainty, as it can be challenging for users to distinguish between enhancements that offer new functionalities and those that are merely modernised versions of long-standing practices. The findings emphasise the need for clearer communication and education regarding the benefits and implications of modern wayfinding systems. As cities continue to integrate digital solutions into their infrastructure, it becomes increasingly important for urban planners and designers to ensure that these innovations are not only user-friendly but also clearly understood by the public. By addressing the uncertainties surrounding the evolution of wayfinding systems, stakeholders can better align these systems with the needs and expectations of urban residents, ultimately improving the efficiency and accessibility of navigation in modern cities.

The subsequent second question aimed to clarify respondents' preferences between traditional paper-based guides and modern digital wayfinding solutions. The responses were varied and highlighted a division in preference as shown in Table 1. These responses illuminate the on-going debate between the reliability of traditional methods and the convenience of digital technology in wayfinding systems. The transition from paper to digital reflects a broader trend towards digitisation in all aspects of life. However, this shift is not without its detractors, who raise valid concerns about the reliability of digital systems in the face of technological failures.

Table 1. Survey Response Section 2 Question

Respondent No.	Answer to the Question
37	*Digital wayfinding/signage would be preferable since nowadays people live in high-tech based communities, so it's a good thing to have it in a digital form. Besides that, it may be helpful in conserving the usage of paper which means saving a lot of trees.*
101	*Digital wayfinding solutions can link with a consumer's mobile phone and put turn-by-turn directions and other important directional information directly on to a handset.*
117	*Paper based. Its more hands on and graphical.*
122	*Digital. It's a common thing to digitalise everything since we are leaving in the modern era.*
124	*Paper based, no internet or 3G needed, not reliable to network, more convenient.*
150	*Paper, unpredictable problem won't occur.*

The responses gathered reveal a split in preference, with some respondents favouring digital wayfinding solutions while others prefer traditional paper-based guides. Respondent No.37, for instance, highlights the modern trend towards digitisation, emphasising the benefits of digital solutions in terms of convenience and environmental conservation. They argue that digital signage is more aligned with today's high-tech communities and can contribute to reducing paper usage, thereby saving trees. In contrast, Respondent No.117 expresses a preference for paper-based guides, valuing their hands-on and graphical nature. This respondent's preference suggests a tactile and visual comfort with traditional methods, which digital solutions might not fully replicate. Similarly, Respondent No.124 points out the reliability issues associated with digital systems, such as dependence on internet connectivity. They find paper guides more convenient in situations where network reliability is a concern. Respondent No.150 echoes this sentiment, emphasising the unpredictability of problems that can arise with digital systems. They express a clear preference for paper-based solutions, viewing them as more reliable in avoiding potential technical issues. These varied responses illustrate the on-going debate between the reliability and traditional familiarity of paper-based guides versus the convenience and modern appeal of digital solutions. This division reflects broader societal trends, where the shift towards digitalisation is met with both enthusiasm and resistance, depending on individual concerns about reliability and environmental impact.

The societal impact of changes in wayfinding systems is further examined through the survey, revealing significant insights into how cultural shifts influence the development of these systems. More than half of the respondents, totalling 126 respondents (84%), agreed that a *"busy culture"* significantly drives the evolution of wayfinding systems. This observation reflects a broader cultural shift toward faster, more efficient lifestyles, which in turn demands wayfinding solutions that can match the increasing tempo of daily activities. As urban environments become more fast-paced, the need for clear, intuitive, and quickly accessible wayfinding systems becomes paramount. The respondents' agreement on this point suggests that the pressures of modern life, characterised by tight schedules, rapid movement, and the need for instant information, are key factors shaping the design and implementation of contemporary wayfinding systems. This cultural shift requires that wayfinding solutions not only provide accurate directions but also do so in a manner that minimises delays and enhances the overall efficiency of navigation in urban spaces. These findings underscore the importance of developing wayfinding systems that are responsive to the demands of a busy, modern society. Urban planners and designers must consider the pace of life in contemporary cities and ensure that wayfinding systems are equipped to handle the complexities and speed of urban movement. By doing so, they can create navigational aids that support the efficiency and productivity of urban residents, contributing to a more seamless and stress-free experience in public spaces.

The importance of efficient navigation is echoed in the responses to the fourth survey question as depicted in Table 2, where a significant majority underscored the critical role of effective signage in avoiding disorientation and enhancing the efficiency of their movements through busy urban spaces. Respondent No.4 emphasises the potential chaos that could ensue in the absence of signage, highlighting its fundamental role in helping individuals locate their intended destinations. This response underscores the notion that signage acts as a crucial guide in unfamiliar environments, preventing confusion and disorder. Similarly, Respondent No.58 points out the practical implications of inadequate signage, particularly in time-sensitive situations. The importance of signage is linked to avoiding the frustration and potential consequences of getting lost, especially when one is in a hurry to catch a ride or meet a deadline. This practical perspective resonates with many users who rely on clear and accessible guidance to navigate efficiently.

Table 2. Survey Response Section 2 Question

Respondent No.	Answer to the Question
4	*Very important. Without signage it will be a chaotic situation because it will be very hard for us to find out where actually we want to go.*
58	*Very important since getting lost, especially when being in a hurry for example to catch a ride, is certainly something we would like to avoid.*
65	*Very important, to get to the destination faster.*
69	*Very important because today's lifestyle need to be efficient and easy.*
72	*Important, to get to the destination we want faster.*
75	*Very important, we wouldn't get lost easily with signage. Faster finding our transportation as well as our destination.*

Respondents No.65 and No.69 both focus on the efficiency that signage brings to modern lifestyles. They note that in today's fast-paced world, where time is often at a premium, the ability to reach one's destination quickly and easily is highly valued. Signage is seen as a facilitator of this efficiency, enabling users to navigate with minimal delays. Respondent No.72, while agreeing with the others on the importance of signage, uses slightly less emphatic language, categorising it as *"important"* rather than *"very important"*. However, their reasoning aligns with the others in emphasising the need to reach destinations quickly. Finally, Respondent No.75 echoes the earlier sentiments, adding that signage not only prevents one from getting lost but also aids in quickly locating transportation options. This response highlights the dual function of signage in both navigating to a destination and efficiently finding transportation to get there. Overall, the responses collectively underscore the critical role of signage in wayfinding. The emphasis on speed, efficiency, and the prevention of disorientation reflects the respondents' strong preference for clear and accessible guidance in their navigation experiences. This insight is crucial for understanding the expectations and needs of users in environments where wayfinding is essential.

In summary, as Malaysia and similar contexts continue to develop and urbanise at a rapid pace, the importance of sophisticated and user-friendly wayfinding systems cannot be overstated. Such systems not only support the dynamic nature of modern urban life but also enhance safety, reduce stress, and improve the overall efficiency of public and private transportation networks. The strong public consensus on the necessity of effective wayfinding reflects a clear mandate for urban planners and designers to prioritise the development and continuous improvement of these systems, ensuring they meet the evolving needs of a busy populace.

Section 3: Advancements in Digital Wayfinding and Signage Systems

The progression toward digital wayfinding systems marks a significant advancement in the field of navigation aids, reflecting a shift towards more interactive, user-friendly, and technologically sophisticated signage. This section examines the effectiveness of digital wayfinding systems, focusing on their ability to provide clear, concise, and consistent signs with strong contrast and visibility, as well as their role in overcoming language barriers in multicultural environments like Kuala Lumpur. The first question of this section explored whether digital wayfinding and signage designs are perceived as providing clear, concise, and consistent information. Responses varied, highlighting both the strengths and areas for improvement in current implementations. These responses indicate that while many users find digital wayfinding systems effective, there is a notable portion of feedback suggesting that the design and functionality of these systems can be inconsistent. For instance, at high-traffic locations like KLIA, users have identified gaps in the signage system, suggesting that while advancements have been made, implementation remains uneven across different settings.

Most respondents express a positive view of digital wayfinding, citing various benefits that enhance the user experience, as depicted in Table 3. Respondent No.5 highlights the practicality of digital systems in providing not just directions but also additional information such as the distance remaining and estimated travel time. This functionality is particularly valuable for users who need precise and timely information to navigate effectively. Respondent No.25 emphasises the interactive nature of digital wayfinding systems, noting that this interactivity can make the information easier to understand. The ability to interact with the system, whether through touch screens or other interfaces, allows users to customise their experience and access the specific information they need more intuitively. Similarly, Respondent No.37 appreciates the design elements of digital wayfinding, such as effective design, attractive visuals, and clear text. These elements combine to create a user-friendly experience that enhances comprehension and makes the signage more appealing to a broader audience. This response underscores the importance of not just the functionality but also the aesthetic and communicative aspects of digital wayfinding. Respondent No.100 takes this a step further by highlighting the advanced capabilities of digital systems, such as the use of 3D models, individual route planning, and an immersive experience of the environment. These features provide users with a more detailed and engaging way to navigate, which can be particularly useful in complex or large spaces.

Table 3. Survey Response Section 3 Question

Respondent No.	**Answer to the Question**
5	*Yes. It shows direction and distance left from one place to another. It even calculates estimated time taken.*
25	*Yes, digitals would be more interactive which would be easier to understand.*
37	*Yes, it is. The effective design along with the attractive picture and background added with simple text that explains the sign will provide a great understanding for those people who read the digital wayfinding/signage design.*
100	*Yes, can offer 3D models of an environment, individual route planning, and an 'immersive' impression of the area that enhances directions.*
115	*No, some just simply made and not really helpful to people.*
124	*No, some of digital wayfinding is moving, when u move too example in the car, it is pretty hard to read and concentrate at the road at the same time.*

On the other hand, there are some dissenting views. Respondent No.115 points out that not all digital wayfinding systems are effective, noting that some are simply made and do not provide the necessary guidance to users. This critique suggests that the quality and design of digital systems can vary significantly, potentially leading to frustration if the system does not meet user expectations. Respondent No.124 also expresses a negative view, particularly in the context of using digital wayfinding while driving. They note that moving digital displays can be difficult to read and may distract drivers, highlighting a significant safety concern. This response underscores the need for careful consideration of context and user needs when designing and implementing digital wayfinding systems. Overall, the responses reveal a general appreciation for the capabilities of digital wayfinding systems, particularly in terms of interactivity, design, and advanced features. However, they also highlight the importance of ensuring these systems are well-designed and context-appropriate to avoid potential drawbacks, such as user confusion or safety issues.

The second question addressed the potential of signage to serve as a bridge over language barriers, an important consideration in a multicultural hub like Kuala Lumpur. The survey responses here, as depicted in Table 4, were overwhelmingly positive, emphasising the universal language of symbols. The overwhelming consensus among the respondents is that language does not constitute a major barrier when it comes to understanding signage, particularly when symbols are used. Respondent No.11 provides a straightforward example, noting that universally recognised symbols, such as those indicating male and female restrooms, are immediately understood by people regardless of language. This response highlights the power of symbols to transcend language barriers, making signage universally accessible. Similarly, Respondent No.19 reinforces this point by emphasising the international use of symbols. They express confidence that most people will interpret common symbols in the same way, thereby eliminating language as a potential barrier. This perspective aligns with the global trend towards standardising symbols for common facilities and directions, ensuring that they are easily understood across different cultures and languages. Respondent No.24 also dismisses the notion of a language barrier, arguing that signage should operate as a *"universal language"* that all types of people can understand. They assert that if users fail to comprehend the signage, it represents a failure of the design, rather than an issue of language. This response suggests that the success of signage lies in its ability to communicate effectively through universally recognised symbols and clear design, rather than relying on written language.

Table 4. Survey Response Section 3 Question

Respondent No.	Answer to the Question
11	*No, for example, sign of man and woman, people will know is toilet.*
19	*No, symbols are internationally used nowadays, and I believe most people will have the same interpretation towards some common symbol used in the signage, so it shouldn't be a language barrier.*
24	*I don't think so. Personally, I think when it comes to signage/wayfinding it should be a universal language where all types of people can understand. If users can't really get it, then it's definitely a failure.*
36	*No, with symbol it is more understandable even though to people who do not understand the language.*
37	*Not really that much as long as the used symbols have to be as clear and precise as possible so that people will not get a misunderstanding from their interpretation of the symbols.*
62	*No, when people see the signage, they will know what it is about, such as toilet signage, the symbols of women and men are very clear.*

Respondent No.36 echoes these sentiments, pointing out that symbols are often more understandable than text, even to individuals who do not understand the language. This underscores the importance of using clear and universally recognised symbols in signage to ensure that it can be understood by a diverse audience. Respondent No.37 provides a nuanced view, acknowledging that while language may not be a significant barrier, the symbols used must be clear and precise to avoid any potential misunderstanding. This response highlights the importance of careful symbol selection and design to ensure that signage communicates its intended message without ambiguity. Lastly, Respondent No.62 reiterates the idea that symbols, particularly those used in common signage such as restrooms, are very clear and widely recognised. They argue that people will generally understand the meaning of such symbols *immediately* reinforcing the idea that language is not a significant barrier in effective signage. Overall, the responses suggest a strong belief in the effectiveness of symbols in overcoming language barriers in signage and wayfinding systems. The consensus is that as long as symbols are clear, precise, and universally recognised, they can effectively communicate the necessary information to a diverse audience, regardless of language differences. This insight is crucial for the design of wayfinding systems that aim to be inclusive and accessible to all users.

In conclusion, the transition towards digital wayfinding systems has introduced significant improvements in navigational aids, providing users with interactive, engaging, and informative signage. While these advancements have enhanced the user experience in many aspects, the feedback indicates that there is room for further refinement, particularly in ensuring consistency and readability under various conditions. Additionally, the effective use of universal symbols in signage plays a crucial role in bridging language gaps, crucial for a country like Malaysia, with its diverse visitor demographics. These insights are pivotal for urban planners and designers as they continue to innovate and enhance wayfinding systems to meet the evolving needs of a global populace.

Qualitative Research Findings

In the qualitative segment of the study, the exploration of wayfinding and signage systems merges personal insights with broader societal trends, providing a nuanced understanding of the preferences and impacts of both traditional and digital wayfinding solutions. The interview responses illuminate the diverse perspectives on these systems, reflecting on both their evolution and current relevance in the context of a rapidly changing society. The first interview question delves into the preference between paper-based and digital wayfinding systems, highlighting a tendency towards traditional methods. One participant expressed a preference for paper-based designs, citing their simplicity, ease of understanding, and cost-effectiveness. This perspective suggests that while digital advancements are prevalent, there remains a significant appreciation for the straightforwardness and directness of traditional wayfinding methods.

The second interview question addressed the impact of societal changes, such as increased population and tourism, on the development of wayfinding and signage systems. The response indicated that the escalating pace of social life and the consequent development in infrastructure necessitate more effective wayfinding solutions. This reflects a broader understanding that as societies become busier and more complex, the demands on wayfinding systems to provide clear and efficient guidance also increase. In response to the third interview question about the clarity, consistency, and visibility of digital signage, the interviewee acknowledged the effectiveness of traditional designs in achieving these qualities. The preference for traditional over digital options was again noted for their cost-effectiveness and simplicity, suggesting that while digital solutions are advancing, there is still considerable value seen in traditional approaches.

The fourth interview question explored the potential language barriers imposed by modern signage symbols. The response was clear: *modern symbols are universally understood and do not constitute a significant language barrier.* This indicates a successful standardisation of symbols within wayfinding systems, which are recognised across different cultural and linguistic backgrounds, facilitating easier navigation for both locals and tourists. Finally, the fifth interview question emphasised the critical importance of effective wayfinding systems, particularly in high-traffic areas like MRT interchange stations. The participant highlighted the role of good signage in avoiding delays and ensuring smooth transitions between routes, underscoring the value of clear and efficient wayfinding in managing the flow of large numbers of people efficiently.

Collectively, these qualitative insights underscore the on-going relevance of both traditional and digital wayfinding systems. They reflect a society in transition, where the integration of modern technology and traditional methods could potentially offer a balanced approach to navigation in urban spaces. The preference for traditional methods does not diminish the potential benefits of digital advancements but rather highlights a spectrum of user needs and preferences that designers and urban planners must consider. The emphasis on efficiency, clarity, and universal design in signage reflects a universal theme across the responses: *the critical role of wayfinding systems in facilitating smooth, efficient, and accessible navigation for all users in increasingly complex urban environments.*

Enhancing Brand Image through Effective Wayfinding at Airports

The role of wayfinding systems at airports extends beyond mere functionality; they are pivotal in shaping the brand image and overall experience of a country, city, or the airport itself. Effective wayfinding contributes significantly to place branding, a concept that emphasises the identity and reputation of a location as perceived by its visitors. Airports often serve as the first point of contact between a destination and its visitors, making the initial experience critical in setting the tone for their stay. A well-designed wayfinding system can communicate efficiency, hospitality, and modernity, thereby enhancing the brand image of the location. For instance, the seamless integration of culturally relevant symbols and multilingual signs at KLIA not only aids in navigation but also reinforces Malaysia's image as a welcoming and diverse nation. The ease with which visitors can navigate the airport, coupled with the aesthetic and cultural elements embedded in the signage, contributes to a positive first impression, aligning with the broader branding objectives of the country.

Furthermore, the effectiveness of airport wayfinding systems directly impacts the overall brand experience, influencing how travellers perceive the city and country. A positive experience at the airport, characterised by clear, intuitive, and aesthetically pleasing signage, can enhance the visitor's perception of the destination as a whole. Conversely, a confusing or poorly executed wayfinding system can lead to frustration and dissatisfaction, negatively affecting the visitor's experience and, by extension, the brand image of the city or country. In the context of place branding, the consistency and quality of wayfinding systems are crucial in creating a cohesive brand narrative that extends from the airport to the city itself. By investing in advanced, user-friendly, and culturally resonant wayfinding systems, airports like KLIA can significantly contribute to strengthening the brand identity of Kuala Lumpur and Malaysia, making it a preferred destination for international travellers.

CONCLUSIONS AND RECOMMENDATIONS

This research has systematically explored the evolution and significance of wayfinding and signage systems in Kuala Lumpur, revealing their vital role in enhancing urban mobility and the overall user experience. The findings affirm that efficient wayfinding systems are essential in managing the dynamic flow of both residents and tourists in densely populated urban areas. As cities like Kuala Lumpur continue to grow and diversify, the need for adaptable and user-friendly navigation aids becomes increasingly critical. It is recommended that future urban planning and design initiatives prioritise the integration of both digital and traditional wayfinding elements to address the varied needs of a multicultural populace. Emphasis should also be placed on standardising signage to overcome language barriers effectively, ensuring that signs are clear, intuitive, and accessible to all users. By continuing to innovate and refine wayfinding systems, urban planners can significantly enhance the functionality of public spaces, making cities more navigable and welcoming for everyone.

Practical Implications

The findings of this study have substantial practical implications for urban development and public space management in rapidly urbanising cities. By highlighting the crucial role of effective wayfinding systems, the research underscores the need for strategic integration of these systems into the urban infrastructure to support growing populations and increasing tourist activity. For urban planners and policymakers, the study advocates for investment in both digital innovations and the preservation of traditional wayfinding methods, ensuring inclusivity and accessibility. This approach is particularly vital in multicultural urban centres like Kuala Lumpur, where navigation systems must cater to diverse populations, including varying language capabilities and technological access. Additionally, the standardisation of signage, which has been shown to effectively bridge language barriers, should be implemented universally to improve clarity and reduce navigation errors in public spaces. Ultimately, these strategies aim to enhance the quality of urban life, facilitating smoother transitions in busy environments and contributing to the overall safety and satisfaction of both residents and visitors.

REFERENCES

Alkharoubi, A. M. (2020) *Wayfinding for pedestrians in the crowded areas of Al-Hajj: How can wayfinding system designs increase the efficiency of wayfinding and navigation performances for pedestrian pilgrims during the Islamic pilgrimage (Al-Hajj)* [Doctoral dissertation, University of Minnesota]. https://search.proquest.com/openview/22bbf5a8b9a21dfcb66c8605586f8104/1?pq-origsite=gscholar&cbl=18750&diss=y

Batouei, A., Iranmanesh, M., Mustafa, H., Nikbin, D., & Ping, T. A. (2020). Components of airport experience and their roles in eliciting passengers' satisfaction and behavioural intentions. *Research in Transportation Business & Management, 37*, 100585. https://www.sciencedirect.com/science/article/abs/pii/S221053952030122X?via%3Dihub

Carvalho, M., Yunus, A., & Lee, B. (2024) Tourism sector to bring in RM375bil over three years, Dewan Rakyat told. https://www.thestar.com.my/news/nation/2024/03/11/tourism-sector-to-bring-in-rm375bil-over-three-years-dewan-rakyat-told

Chmielewska, E. (2001) *Implaced communication: wayfinding and informational environments.* https://escholarship.mcgill.ca/concern/theses/zk51vj42x

De Jesus, S. C. (1994). *Environmental communication: design planning for wayfinding. Design Issues, 10(3).* MIT Press., DOI: 10.2307/1511691

Green, L. N. (2023) *The Variability of Typographic Wayfinding Systems.* Kent State University. https://search.proquest.com/openview/dbf12a2bbf207e3781714e2f39e9ff60/1?pq-origsite=gscholar&cbl=18750&diss=y

Iftikhar, H., & Luximon, Y. (2022). The syntheses of static and mobile wayfinding information: An empirical study of wayfinding preferences and behaviour in complex environments. *Facilities*, *40*(7/8), 452–474. DOI: 10.1108/F-06-2021-0052

Jalees, D. (2020). Design thinking in the library space: Problem-solving signage like a graphic designer. *Art Libraries Journal*, *45*(3), 114–121. DOI: 10.1017/alj.2020.17

Kocaturk, T., Greuter, S., Hoang, T., & Wang, R. (2024) Enhancing human-building interaction and spatial experience in cultural spaces. *International Journal of Architectural Computing.* https://journals.sagepub.com/doi/epub/10.1177/14780771231225702

Neville, S. (2021) *Immersive Participation: Futuring, Training Simulation, Dance and Virtual Reality.* [Doctoral dissertation, Coventry University]. https://pureportal.coventry.ac.uk/files/80837135/Neville2022PhD.pdf

NYC DOT. (2024). WalkNYC. https://www.nyc.gov/html/dot/html/pedestrians/walknyc.shtml

Pepple, S. (2014). Evaluating and Presenting Points of Interest in Wayfinding and Navigation Systems. *ResearchGate*. https://dl.acm.org/doi/pdf/10.1145/2541831.2541849?casa_token=41-kX6q9b00AAAAA:V10GPPClKSdp4lw_sB4EoNmA_smMS-VeOvVM3HcaiqF7CJv5peoXtlP1l4kOGJxg3jltWaStBeP0

Steg, L., & De Groot, J. I. (2019) *Environmental psychology: An introduction*. 2nd Ed. BPS Textbooks in Psychology. New Jersey: Wiley-Blackwell. https://www.hse.ru/data/2019/03/04/1196348199/%5BLinda_Steg_Judith_I._M._de_Groot%5D_Environmental_P(b-ok.cc).pdf

WorldOMeter. (2024) Malaysia Population (LIVE).https://www.worldometers.info/world-population/malaysia-population/#:~:text=The%20current%20population%20of%20Malaysia,latest%20United%20Nations%20data%201

Chapter 3

A Thematic Content Analysis on the Use of Artificial Intelligence in the Production Process of Cinema, Advertising, and Public Relations Films

Deniz Oğuzcan
https://orcid.org/0000-0002-1999-8400
Faculty of Communication, Altınbaş University, Turkey

Anıl Uğur Oğuzcan
https://orcid.org/0000-0002-0376-7632
Tirebolu Faculty of Communication, Giresun University, Turkey

ABSTRACT

This study examines the impact of artificial intelligence technologies on the production processes of creative industries such as cinema, public relations, and advertising through a thematic content analysis approach. The introduction outlines the increasing role of AI in creative sectors and presents the research problem and objective. The development section classifies and analyzes AI-based tools used in screenwriting, pre-production, production, post-production, and distribution-marketing stages. Additionally, AI-supported practices in content creation and advertising strategies within public relations are addressed. The conclusion emphasizes that AI not only enhances operational efficiency but also transforms creative decision-making pro-

DOI: 10.4018/979-8-3373-6970-9.ch003

© 2026, IGI Global Scientific Publishing. Copying or distributing in print or electronic forms without written permission of IGI Global Scientific Publishing is prohibited. Use of this chapter to ıerative artificial intelligence (AI) technologies is expressly prohibited. The publisher reserves all rights to license its use for generative AI training and machine learning model development.

cesses, giving rise to new ethical, aesthetic, and professional debates. The study underlines the growing need for sustainable production models based on human–AI collaboration in order to ensure balanced integration of technology and creativity.

INTRODUCTION

It is possible to assert that artificial intelligence (AI), one of the most significant developments of the 21st century, has created a comprehensive transformation in communication technologies. Research reveals that AI has substantially altered communication professions. Machine learning and big data analytics offer new possibilities in various fields. AI diversifies suggestion and solution alternatives in areas such as strategy development, content production, video creation, and analysis of information sources. AI tools not only enhance data collection and processing capacities but also offer new opportunities in core areas such as meaning-making, content creation, discourse analysis, and strategic communication management.

These technologies, which find applications across a wide spectrum ranging from social media analysis to big data mining, from automated news writing to text, visual, and video production, are transforming both the quantitative and qualitative dimensions of communication processes. Particularly with the advancement of natural language processing (NLP) techniques, discourse analyses have become more systematic, scalable, and multilayered, thus enabling communication theories to be interpreted with data support. Moreover, the micro-level analysis of target audiences and the development of personalized communication strategies have strengthened the role of AI in the field of strategic communication.

However, these developments bring not only technical advancements but also ethical, cultural, and critical concerns to the forefront of communication studies. Risks such as algorithmic bias, lack of transparency, and the contribution of artificial content to disinformation necessitate new research agendas. Communication education is also being updated in response to this transformation, aiming for students to gain competencies in AI-assisted media analysis, content production, and digital strategy development. In this context, it is essential to evaluate the impact of AI tools on communication studies not only from a technical instrumentalization perspective but also through critical, ethical, and epistemological dimensions.

These advancements have also led to a transformation in the roles of communication professionals. The effective use of AI technologies has become one of the fundamental elements of a successful communication strategy. AI provides significant advantages in content production for professionals working in cinema, public relations, advertising, and journalism. Thanks to NLP and machine learning methods, AI systems can generate content tailored to the interests and needs of target audiences, viewers, or readers. This accelerates the content production process and contributes to more effectively reaching individuals (Kozan, 2025, p. 318).

The influence of AI technologies on communication studies has been increasingly addressed with growing academic interest in recent years. Especially in digital communication environments, AI-based applications such as big data analysis, natural language processing, and automated content generation indicate a structural transformation in communication processes (Van Dijck, 2013). The algorithmic shaping of social media platforms has led to profound changes in the structure of the public sphere and the circulation of information (Couldry & Mejias, 2019). In this context, it is argued that AI functions not only as a technical tool but also as a new regulator of communication.

Particularly in the fields of big data and social media analytics, studies show that the capacity of AI tools to monitor and predict audience behavior has radically influenced the design of communication strategies (Tüfekçi, 2014). In parallel, automated content generation systems (e.g., robot journalism applications used in news agencies) have reopened debates on journalistic ethics, accuracy, and responsibility (Carlson, 2015).

Strategic communication studies reveal that AI-supported micro-targeting techniques are employed across a wide range, from political campaigns to marketing communications. Examples such as the Cambridge Analytica scandal have exposed the impacts of AI and data mining on individual privacy and democratic processes (Zuboff, 2019).

NLP technologies have particularly enabled the development of new methodological approaches in discourse analyses. Going beyond traditional content analysis, these tools can more quickly and broadly uncover latent patterns, themes, and ideological tendencies across texts (Boyd & Crawford, 2012). Thanks to NLP, significant progress has been made in text analysis, language generation, and sentiment analysis, leading to more intelligent and user-friendly applications such as chatbots and virtual assistants. Machine learning-based recommendation systems and targeting mechanisms are widely used in content production processes within mass media. Automated content generation enables the rapid and effective creation of visual content, video content, news articles, blog posts, and marketing materials. Voice and image recognition technologies, through AI-powered voice assistants and automatic subtitling systems, have also facilitated and accelerated the production of audiovisual media. However, these automation processes do not replace the researcher's critical interpretive skills and, due to algorithmic biases and issues of data representation, also give rise to new ethical responsibilities (Noble, 2018).

When it comes to visual content, the film production process stands out as one of the first areas undergoing transformation through AI technologies. The relationship between film production and technology has been a continuously evolving and deepening bond since the emergence of cinema. Today, AI—being the latest stage of technology—has brought revolutionary changes to the film production process, introducing numerous innovations in the pre-production, production, and post-production phases. AI-supported tools are particularly transforming creative processes during pre-production, in stages such as scriptwriting, location selection, and production design. For instance, AI algorithms can analyze viewer preferences by working on large datasets and assist in constructing story structures or character profiles based on this data (McCosker & Wilken, 2020). As a result, traditional creative processes are being supported by data-driven predictive models, enabling more targeted narratives.

The influence of AI is also striking in the post-production phase. Editing, color correction, and visual effects can be carried out more rapidly and efficiently with machine learning-based software. For example, AI engines such as Adobe Sensei automate processes like scene recognition, object tracking, and image enhancement, thereby facilitating the editing workflow (Adobe, 2025).

All these developments are redefining not only the technical aspects but also the creative processes of filmmaking. However, issues such as artistic freedom of expression, ethical boundaries, and impacts on the workforce in AI-based production processes continue to constitute significant areas of debate within communication and media studies (Manovich, 2019). Therefore, when evaluating the use of AI in film production, it is crucial to consider not only the technical capabilities but also the cultural, ethical, and societal dimensions.

In this study, the impact of artificial intelligence applications on film production processes in communication-oriented sectors such as cinema, public relations, and advertising has been examined; by analyzing the ways in which AI-supported technologies are utilized in these fields and their contribution to sectoral transformation, the current position of artificial intelligence in film production has been identified.

ARTIFICIAL INTELLIGENCE TECHNOLOGIES IN FILM PRODUCTION PROCESSES

From its inception, cinema has always maintained a close relationship with technology, functioning as a technological apparatus and undergoing significant ruptures in line with developments in this field. Revolutionary technological advancements in film production have extended into areas such as distribution and exhibition, ultimately reaching a point where they shape the audience itself.

Lev Manovich (2002, p. 244) raises the following questions regarding the virtualization of film material: "How does computerization affect our concept of moving images? Does it offer new possibilities for film language? Has it enabled the development of entirely new film forms?" To explore these questions, he categorizes the influence of computerization on cinema into two main areas:

1. The use of computer techniques in traditional film production:
    - Three-dimensional computer animation / digital compositing.
      Example: Titanic (James Cameron, 1997)
    - Digital coloring.
      Example: Forrest Gump (Robert Zemeckis, 1994)
    - Virtual actors / motion capture.
      Example: Titanic (James Cameron, 1997)
2. New computer-based cinematic forms:
    - Typographic cinema: Films composed of a blend of graphic design and typographic animation.
    - Net.cinema: Films produced exclusively for internet distribution.
    - Games and interactive films composed of film-like sequences. These sequences may be created using traditional cinematic techniques (e.g., the *Johnny Mnemonic* game) or computer animation (e.g., the *Blade Runner* game)

As can be seen, computer technologies have created new possibilities and platforms within the film industry. Virtual reality, augmented reality, and entirely computer-generated three-dimensional animations have triggered major technological revolutions in the traditional film industry.

In recent years, the rapid development of artificial intelligence (AI) technologies has had profound effects on creative industries, particularly catalyzing a major transformation in film production processes. The cinema industry is undergoing significant changes in production, distribution, and exhibition through the adoption of these new technologies. The growing influence of AI in the production phase has sparked important debates within the industry. The dynamics of traditional filmmaking are being reshaped by AI-powered software, algorithms, and automation tools. Thanks to AI-based applications and design systems, audiovisual content that once required extensive time and resources can now be created much more efficiently and made available to audiences with ease.

From script development and project planning in pre-production, to image generation and scene management during production, and editing, visual effects, and sound design in post-production, AI solutions are being actively utilized across all phases of filmmaking. AI not only accelerates technical operations but is also being integrated into creative decision-making processes, transforming various elements of cinematic language—from storytelling to visual aesthetics.

As crucial as the creation of a film itself is in the realm of mass communication, understanding audience preferences and tendencies is equally vital. Today's advanced AI systems can even conduct highly precise analyses of viewer reactions, tracking facial expressions, consumption behaviors, and body movements in response to a film.

In this context, alongside the opportunities offered by AI in filmmaking, issues such as artistic originality, ethical responsibility, and creative autonomy have also come to the forefront of both academic and professional debates. To fully comprehend the role of AI technologies in film production, it is essential to examine how these tools function within creative practices and how they contribute to broader dynamics of industry transformation from a multidimensional perspective.

Screenwriting with Artificial Intelligence

Artificial intelligence (AI) technologies have increasingly become instrumental tools in the domain of screenwriting. Various applications and methods are being developed in this field, providing support to screenwriters in overcoming creative blocks and generating new ideas. AI-based writing tools offer assistance by analyzing elements such as narrative consistency, character development, and pacing—thereby contributing to the enhancement of screenplays. Moreover, these tools can guide writers in adhering to screenplay formatting and industry standards, streamlining the writing process.

The incorporation of AI into creative writing processes has sparked significant interest in the film industry in recent years. With advances in natural language processing (NLP) and machine learning, AI systems have begun to play an active role in scriptwriting. AI-driven screenwriting relies on the creation of narrative structures, character profiles, and dialogue patterns based on specific data sets. These systems analyze extensive screenplay databases to learn narrative conventions and apply them to generate new texts (Kember & Zylinska, 2012). For example, models such as OpenAI's GPT or Google's T5 (Text-to-Text Transfer Transformer) possess the capacity to produce coherent and structurally meaningful texts.

AI-assisted screenwriting offers several advantages. Above all, its ability to increase speed and efficiency aligns with the film industry's demand for rapid production cycles (Lubart, 2005). AI systems can suggest ways to overcome creative stagnation, inspire alternative plotlines or character developments, and assist in generating novel story concepts (McCormack et al., 2019).

It is fair to argue that AI has introduced transformative changes in script development. Among the primary areas where AI is utilized in screenwriting are plot construction, storyline generation, dialogue creation, and character development. By analyzing large datasets, AI screenwriting applications support writers in their creative processes and offer narrative pathways that may not have been previously considered (Dayo, Memon & Dharejo, 2023, pp. 27–28).

According to research conducted by Yuying Tang and colleagues, screenwriters primarily employ AI in various creative stages such as structuring narratives, generating plotlines, drafting scripts, and crafting dialogue. However, attitudes toward the integration of AI in creative processes vary. While some screenwriters perceive AI as a creative collaborator, others express concerns about its potential to undermine originality and creative control. Tang et al. classify screenwriters' expectations of AI into four categories: the "performer" (offering creative ideas), the "audience" (providing feedback), the "expert" (offering insights and suggestions), and the "executor" (handling technical tasks). This classification provides valuable insight into how AI could evolve into a more effective and collaborative tool for screenwriting (Tang et al., 2025).

Several experimental initiatives have emerged in the film industry that explore AI-assisted screenwriting. For instance, the 2016 short film *Sunspring*, created by Oscar Sharp and Ross Goodwin, was based entirely on a script generated by an AI system, marking one of the earliest experimental cases in this field (Sharp & Goodwin, 2016). The AI used in *Sunspring* was a Long Short-Term Memory (LSTM) neural network trained on science fiction scripts, which produced unpredictable and often absurd dialogues that defied traditional narrative conventions. Another example is *Zone Out* (2020), a project that also employed AI-driven writing processes, contributing to narrative experimentation in a novel way.

Today, major film studios have also shown interest in AI-assisted storytelling tools. In 2020, Warner Bros. invested in Cinelytic—a company that develops AI-powered software for film analysis and distribution—to explore how AI could be used in decision-making processes (Spangler, 2020). Although such tools are currently employed more for project selection and risk assessment than for direct script generation, it is anticipated that creative processes will increasingly intersect with automation in the near future.

Nevertheless, the role of AI in screenwriting has become a subject of intense debate in recent years. These discussions encompass a broad range of issues, including the potential of AI in creative processes, intellectual property rights, creative responsibility, transparency, and fair use.

Additionally, concerns have been raised about the limitations of AI systems, particularly their lack of genuine creative intuition and cultural contextual awareness. These limitations may result in texts that are superficial, formulaic, or devoid of emotional depth (Boden, 2016). Furthermore, algorithmic biases can reproduce existing discriminations within datasets, increasing the risk of generating content that is sexist, racist, or culturally problematic (Noble, 2018).

The growing use of AI in screenwriting processes has brought with it important ethical and legal considerations in the creative industries. AI's contribution to story development, character design, and dialogue construction necessitates a rethinking of the boundaries of creative labor and authorship. One pressing issue is whether AI-generated scripts fall within the scope of copyright protection. Current practices of the U.S. Copyright Office stipulate that only works created by human authors are eligible for copyright protection (Quinn Emanuel Urquhart & Sullivan, LLP, 2023). Therefore, fully autonomous AI-generated content is excluded from such protection, although hybrid works involving human creative input may be partially safeguarded.

The nature of the datasets used to train AI is another key ethical concern. Large-scale datasets often include copyrighted materials, raising issues around the unauthorized use of creative works and the potential loss of income for original creators (Georgetown University Library, 2023). In this context, obtaining creators' consent and ensuring transparent data usage must be prioritized within ethical design principles.

Moreover, concealing AI's contribution or leaving its role ambiguous may mislead audiences and readers. In professions grounded in strong individual authorship, failure to acknowledge AI's input can pose ethical and representational challenges. Transparency is therefore essential not only during the production phase but also in the reception and evaluation of creative works (Radanliev, 2025).

There exist significant national differences regarding legal regulations. In the United Kingdom, a proposal has been put forward to introduce a "collective licensing" system that would enable payments to copyright holders for works used to train artificial intelligence. This proposal is regarded as a positive step toward protecting creative labor (The Guardian, 2025a). In contrast, gaps in the European Union's AI legislation have been criticized for potentially enabling indirect copyright infringements (The Guardian, 2025b).

The 2023 Writers Guild of America (WGA) strike in Hollywood is considered a major resistance against the use of AI technologies in screenwriting. This strike brought ethical and legal debates about AI's role in creative processes to the forefront and became a symbol of the struggle to protect the rights of creative workers. During the 148-day strike, WGA members expressed concerns that AI's use in scriptwriting would devalue writers' labor and threaten job security. Particularly, studios' attempts to employ AI for script production pose serious risks regarding authors' copyright and creative control. Following the strike, the WGA reached an agreement imposing significant restrictions on AI usage: AI cannot be recognized as a writer, nor can it be used for scriptwriting or rewriting. Studios are required to explicitly disclose when materials have been generated by AI, and AI-generated content will not affect writers' copyright or creative rights (Watercutter, 2023).

This strike and its outcomes serve as a critical precedent not only for writers in Hollywood but for all workers in creative industries. The struggle over the role and limits of AI in creative processes provides guidance for protecting labor rights against future technological advancements (Kinder, 2024).

The widespread adoption of AI in screenwriting calls for profound ethical and legal reassessments regarding the nature of creative labor. Copyright protection, transparency, definitions of creative responsibility, and ethical principles in data usage constitute the core areas of debate in this new era. Ensuring fair and sustainable human-AI collaboration in scriptwriting requires not only technological adjustments but also cultural and legal transformations.

Significant advances in AI-supported screenwriting are expected in the coming years, particularly in the realm of "co-creation" models. In this paradigm, AI systems would serve as collaborative assistants rather than fully autonomous content producers, working alongside human writers to aid story development (McCormack et al., 2019). Such collaboration could enable AI use that supports human creativity, inspires new ideas, and proposes alternative narrative solutions. Additionally, AI-assisted screenwriting integrated with emerging narrative platforms such as virtual reality (VR) and augmented reality (AR) can transform storytelling into an interactive, multi-layered, and personalized experience (Kember & Zylinska, 2012).

In conclusion, the field of AI-driven screenwriting opens new possibilities within the creative industries, while simultaneously raising fundamental issues around originality, ethics, diversity, and aesthetic values. Therefore, alongside technological progress, it is crucial to develop a critical, culturally informed, and human-centered approach to safeguard both the art of cinema and the future of creative industries.

THE USE OF ARTIFICIAL INTELLIGENCE IN THE PRE-PRODUCTION PHASE

The use of artificial intelligence (AI) in the pre-production phase enhances the efficiency, speed, and data-driven nature of film production planning and organization. This phase is one of the most critical stages in film production, as the majority of creative decisions are made here and all preparations for the shooting process are carried out. AI is actively employed in various tasks during pre-production.

Script Analysis Process

One of the key applications of AI in pre-production is script analysis and scene structuring. AI-based script analysis tools can automatically parse a script to identify scenes, characters, locations, and plotlines. This enables faster visual planning of the script.

The ScriptBook application, used for script analysis, evaluates the commercial success potential, character distribution, emotional intensity, and target audience compatibility of scripts. Film producers can thus make more informed investment decisions based on these analyses (Zengin, 2020, p. 161). Additionally, it automatically applies criteria such as the Bechdel Test to analyze scripts in terms of gender equality.

AI can group scenes in a script and organize them according to the shooting schedule, thereby facilitating the creation of shooting calendars. Another AI tool, Scry, analyzes the emotional impact of scripts by assessing characters' emotional journeys and the story's potential effect on viewers, guiding producers to enhance the emotional depth of the screenplay.

Vault AI is an application that analyzes scripts to predict box office success and return on investment. By analyzing over 300,000 data points, it assesses the commercial potential of scripts, providing producers and studios with valuable insights to inform investment decisions (Vaultai, 2025). For example, Warner Bros. uses the AI tool Cinelytic to forecast the potential box office performance of film projects. 20th Century Fox employs Merlin, a system leveraging AI and machine learning to match films with specific genres and audiences, as well as to provide comprehensive demographic data for any given film. Sony Pictures has utilized ScriptBook to analyze 62 of its films (Andriasyan, 2025).

Furthermore, AI can group scenes to optimize shooting schedules and analyze scene descriptions to suggest appropriate filming locations or optimize shooting calendars. For instance, the science fiction film *Annihilation* (2018) used AI-assisted tools to optimize script analysis and scene planning, allowing complex visual effects and set designs to be implemented more effectively (Vakhtin, 2023). Netflix adopts innovative approaches to script analysis and scene structuring through AI technologies, thereby increasing the efficiency of its content production processes (Levy, 2025).

AI-supported script analysis and scene structuring tools enhance efficiency in film production and enable more informed creative decisions. These technologies offer valuable contributions to producers and screenwriters during script development and production planning stages.

Use of Artificial Intelligence in the Casting Process

Artificial intelligence is transforming casting processes in the film industry by enabling producers and casting directors to make more informed and data-driven decisions. AI tools assist in identifying the most suitable actors for a project by analyzing their past performance data. Additionally, automated analysis and recommendations help speed up and economize casting procedures, saving both time and costs. Moreover, AI supports more fair and objective casting decisions by minimizing human biases. Tools like Casting Droid analyze candidate profiles to suggest the best matches, thereby accelerating the casting process (Cmsproductions, 2025).

For example, Warner Bros. uses the AI tool Cinelytic to evaluate the commercial success potential of actors in casting decisions. This system analyzes actors' past performances, box office success, and influence in international markets to predict which actor might generate the highest commercial return for a given project (Frawley, 2023). Another AI tool, Largo.ai, analyzes scripts to create character profiles and recommends the most suitable actors based on these profiles. It assesses actors' previous roles, physical attributes, and performances, comparing them with the script's character profiles to provide "compatibility percentage" suggestions. By offering the best actor matches, it supports producers' and directors' decision-making processes (Largo.ai, 2025).

AI tools also accelerate audition processes, saving time and resources in casting. For instance, they automatically schedule audition times, facilitate communication with talent agencies, and speed up feedback cycles.

AI applications used for automatic pre-screening of actor submissions analyze videos, resumes, and demo reels sent by actors, highlighting those who best meet the role criteria (Massive.io, 2025). Some AI applications even analyze actors' facial expressions, vocal tones, and body language to assess their suitability for specific roles (2immersive4u.com, 2025).

Art Direction, Location Selection, and Costume Planning

Artificial intelligence enhances creativity and production efficiency in processes such as location selection, art direction, and costume planning. Location selection is one of the most time-consuming and costly aspects of film production. AI-powered tools are used to accelerate and optimize this process.

Art direction draws the film's atmosphere, period, and setting, immersing the audience into the story. This process visually supports the characters' emotional states and the film's themes. In other words, it expresses the characters' experiences and the meaning of the story through visual design elements (Wille, 2015). Consistent art direction strengthens the audience's suspension of disbelief, transporting them to different times or worlds (Deguzman, 2023).

The integration of AI with art direction, a fundamental element shaping a film's visual narrative, supports creative workflows and increases production efficiency. For example, AI-based tools like Midjourney and DALL·E enable art directors to create location designs in various styles and lighting, facilitating faster creative decisions in early production phases (DiTommaso, 2025). The 2019 film *The Lion King* was produced entirely using virtual production technologies and AI-supported visual processing methods, creating the effect of real locations (Söğütlüler, 2024). Such applications make it possible to digitally stage scenes instead of relying on physical locations, saving time and budget during art direction (Mast & Kawin, 2011).

In the film *The Brutalist*, AI-assisted architectural and location design tools were used to develop original structures that fit the film's atmosphere. AI gives art directors the freedom to create more imaginative worlds beyond traditional physical locations (Tatlerasia, 2025).

Locations are not just physical spaces but dramatic devices that carry the story and concretize relationships between characters. Especially in period films, accurate historical design of locations directly impacts the film's credibility (Cave & Dihal, 2020). With advances in AI technology, location design in film production is increasingly transformed by digital tools. Trained AI models can generate digital location sketches with desired aesthetic qualities and atmospheres.

One such AI tool, superscout.ai, allows users to create and manage their own location databases. Locations can be added by uploading addresses or photos, organized into collections, and searched quickly (Superscout.ai, 2025). Lumalabs ai creates photorealistic 3D models from simple videos, enabling virtual exploration of locations (Lumalabs.ai, 2025). The AI tool Massif Network optimizes location selection by providing detailed data such as sunlight predictions, environmental analyses, and logistics information. Cinelytic, used by major studios like Warner Bros., analyzes thousands of hours of footage with AI algorithms to identify suitable filming locations (Sahota, 2024).

AI is also used in shooting planning through spatial data analysis. AI-based location analysis systems combine geographic information system (GIS) data to recommend the most suitable locations for scenes, considering physical conditions and aesthetic parameters. This optimizes time and budget planning, especially for outdoor shoots (Shaw, 2024). The virtual production technology StageCraft, used in *The Mandalorian* series, allowed real-time creation of digital locations using AI-assisted visualization tools (Tatlerasia, 2025).

Another crucial area in art direction is costume design. Costume design in cinema is not limited to the clothes characters wear but is a key visual narrative device reflecting the story, period, the character's inner world, social status, and cultural identity. Thus, costume design is a fundamental component of film aesthetics and storytelling.

Costumes reflect a character's personality and transformation. For instance, in *Black Swan* (2010), the costumes of Natalie Portman's character symbolically represent her oscillation between innocence and darkness. Costumes can define the historical period, geographic, and cultural context of a film. Period films like

Marie Antoinette (2006) use costumes to establish a character's social status and the atmosphere of the era. According to Laura Mulvey (2006), costumes support metaphors within the film. In *The Matrix* (1999), black leather outfits represent the characters' hacker identity fighting against the system and the boundaries between digital and physical realities.

In recent years, the integration of AI technologies into visual design has brought a paradigm shift in costume design practices at both aesthetic and production levels. AI is no longer just a technical tool but has assumed the role of a "co-creator" participating in creative decision-making processes (McCormack et al., 2019). The use of AI in costume design occurs at three main levels: reference generation through data analytics, visual prototyping and simulation, and creative production.

In the future, AI may become not only a supportive tool but an autonomous creative agent capable of making design decisions. AI-equipped visual stylists could provide instant costume suggestions tailored to different film genres and target audiences and even analyze audience reactions (e.g., feedback gathered from social media) to guide costume design (Manovich, 2018). However, these developments raise ethical questions. To what extent can the emotional and cultural dimensions of design be represented by algorithmic suggestions? How will the designer's identity as an "artist" be redefined in collaboration with AI?

It is noted that AI-designed costumes may sometimes fall short in terms of originality, contextuality, and cultural representation. Particularly, systems trained on Western-centric datasets risk overlooking diverse cultural representations or ethnic details within global cinema, which is a subject of criticism (Broussard, 2018). In this context, conscious, ethical, and multicultural human-AI collaboration is of great importance.

In conclusion, the use of AI has faced criticism for potentially weakening elements such as creative originality and the human touch (Whittaker et al., 2018). While AI tools in art direction increase production efficiency, the ultimate artistic vision is still seen as requiring guidance from human art directors (Cave & Dihal, 2020).

Use of Artificial Intelligence in the Production Phase of Filmmaking

The integration of artificial intelligence (AI) into the film industry in recent years has led to profound transformations during the production phase of filmmaking. Traditionally, the production process required intensive coordination among the director, cinematographer, art director, and various technical teams, often proving to be time-consuming and labor-intensive. However, the incorporation of AI-supported systems into this phase has brought significant improvements in terms of efficiency, cost control, and creativity (Chen et al., 2024).

Scene Planning, Camera Angles, and Camera Movements

In conventional filmmaking, scene planning and camera angles were manually determined based on storyboards and the director's expertise, a process often lengthy and expensive. Today, AI plays a critical role in automating and optimizing these tasks.

For instance, the CinePreGen system enables users to dynamically control camera movements and storyboards. Utilizing game engine-supported diffusion models, CinePreGen integrates cinematic camera movements into AI-based video previsualization, offering solutions to the limited control issues present in existing models. With its parametrized camera field, CineSpace, and storyboard-based interface, the system provides detailed visual narrative adjustments. By incorporating scene-specific "ground truth" data such as depth, motion, and mask information, production becomes both visually consistent and creatively flexible (Chen et al., 2024).

Another notable AI application, ChatCam, allows users to direct camera movements through natural language commands. Leveraging CineGPT—a GPT-based autoregressive model—and the Anchor Determinator module for object-centric positioning, ChatCam can generate high-quality video scenes based on radiance field representations such as NeRF and 3DGS. This system transforms user inputs into multi-step plans, effectively shaping camera trajectories. The GPT-4-powered agent analyzes input commands and guides CineGPT and Anchor Determinator accordingly, automating the production of complex camera movements (Liu et al., 2024).

Traditionally performed manually by skilled cinematographers, camera movements are increasingly automated by AI tools. For example, CineMPC automates drone camera movements, focusing, and scene composition in real time. Integrated with drone technology, this system optimizes camera positioning, movement, and focus according to specific scenarios, preserving the director's aesthetic vision while enabling faster and more efficient shoots. Furthermore, CineMPC's automation minimizes human errors and prevents cinematographic mistakes (Pueyo et al., 2024).

EditIQ, another AI-driven system, automatically edits static wide-angle videos into cinematic sequences. It analyzes footage, suggesting enhancements to visual aesthetics by optimizing camera movements and lighting, and managing color tones and contrast. Additionally, EditIQ can modulate scene pacing based on content analysis, offering filmmakers significant time and cost savings by reducing manual intervention (Girmaji et al., 2025).

Examples of AI use in cinematography include the short film *Zone Out* (2020), directed by Oscar Sharp in collaboration with AI researcher Ross Goodwin. This film gained attention not only for its AI-generated screenplay but also for employing

AI-supported systems in camera planning and shooting phases. Camera movements and scene arrangements were proposed and applied by algorithms aligned with cinematic aesthetics, synchronizing close-ups and panning to highlight characters' emotional transitions (Goodwin & Sharp, 2020). This case demonstrates AI's potential to influence both narrative and visual composition in cinema.

Looking ahead, AI is anticipated not only as a supportive tool but as a directive force in cinematography. Beyond optimizing visual aesthetics, AI can contribute data-driven insights to creative processes, reducing human labor while enhancing production quality. Simultaneously, it offers filmmakers greater creative freedom, accelerates production workflows, and decreases costs. The impact of AI on cinematography marks a significant step in redefining the role of technology within the art of cinema.

Virtual Production Technologies

The increasing prominence of digital technologies in the film industry is progressively transforming traditional production methodologies. One of the pioneering concepts in this transformation is virtual production, which, when combined with recent advances in artificial intelligence (AI) technologies, offers enhanced creative and technical possibilities.

Virtual production is a hybrid filmmaking technique that merges physical and digital elements. Replacing traditional methods such as green screens, it utilizes LED volume stages surrounded by LED panels and game engines like Unreal Engine to enable shooting within digital environments (Whissel, 2014). This technology allows directors and cinematographers to view scenes in real time, seamlessly integrating physical sets with digital backgrounds. The virtual production process generally includes the following components:

- LED Screens and Real-Time Rendering: Large LED panels display digital backgrounds in real time, providing natural lighting for actors and cameras.
- Game Engines: Engines such as Unreal Engine are employed to create and manage digital environments, offering real-time rendering and physics simulations.
- Camera Tracking Systems: Cameras' movements are tracked via sensors and synchronized with digital environments, ensuring perspective alignment and naturalistic motion.
- AI-Assisted Environment Generation: AI algorithms analyze large datasets to automatically generate 3D environments and characters, facilitating rapid creation of expansive and detailed scenes.

One of the most critical stages in virtual production is 3D world design, where virtual sets constructed digitally are prepared for filming through real-time rendering engines such as Unreal Engine and Unity. This technology has gained widespread popularity with productions like *The Mandalorian* (2019), providing a compelling alternative to traditional set construction (Desowitz, 2020). Virtual set design not only reduces production costs but also offers directors and cinematographers unprecedented creative freedom.

The virtual world creation process comprises three main elements: environment modeling, lighting, and material/texture design. Environment modeling involves procedural techniques using software like Houdini to generate landscapes automatically, photogrammetry for 3D scans of real-world locations, and the use of asset libraries such as Quixel Megascans (Kerlow, 2009). Lighting systems employ solutions like Unreal Engine 5's Lumen global illumination technology and HDRI skyboxes to simulate realistic lighting conditions. Material and texture design leverage Physically Based Rendering (PBR) techniques and high-polygon optimization systems such as Nanite. Unreal Engine stands out as one of the most widely used engines in virtual production, offering tools like Landscape Tool for natural environments, Foliage System for automatic vegetation placement, Niagara FX for particle effects, and Sequencer for cinematic camera movement planning. For LED volume integration, tools such as nDisplay and Live Link enable real-time background changes, as exemplified in *The Mandalorian*. Similarly, *The Lion King* (2019) showcases photorealistic animal animations created using Unreal Engine (Silva Jasaui et al., 2024).

Unity is another popular alternative, especially favored in indie productions and AR/VR projects. Unity provides a performance-oriented architecture via its Entity Component System (ECS), cinematic-quality lighting and shadow effects through High Definition Render Pipeline (HDRP), and intelligent virtual camera systems via Cinemachine (Unity, 2025). The short film *The Heretic* (2022) serves as a successful example of Unity's real-time rendering capabilities applied to cinema.

Despite its advantages, virtual set design faces criticism. While offering limitless creative freedom to filmmakers, the technology is sometimes criticized for causing practical skill erosion due to over-digitization (Zettl, 2016). Nonetheless, the inclusion of Unreal Engine-based courses in film school curricula worldwide highlights the growing importance of technical training in this domain (Kerlow, 2009).

Several productions demonstrate this integration. The "StageCraft" system developed by ILM for *The Mandalorian* enables real-time shooting in Unreal Engine-powered virtual environments, where scene content is automatically updated by AI algorithms in response to lighting conditions (Desowitz, 2020). In *Avatar: The Way of Water*, James Cameron's team utilized AI-assisted analysis techniques for underwater performance capture.

AI-enhanced virtual production offers numerous advantages. It provides real-time feedback, allowing directors and cinematographers to visualize the final scene during shooting. It reduces constraints related to location and time, thereby shortening production schedules. Additionally, it facilitates the creation of complex scenes independent of physical limitations. However, high costs, the need for technical expertise, and concerns about AI's impact on creativity remain points of contention. Consequently, the integration of virtual production and AI represents not only a technical innovation but a comprehensive transformation influencing filmmaking's aesthetic and economic dimensions.

THE USE OF ARTIFICIAL INTELLIGENCE IN POST-PRODUCTION

In recent years, artificial intelligence (AI) and machine learning have brought profound changes to various sectors of the film and advertising industries. Particularly in post-production processes, AI applications have enhanced both time and cost efficiency while simultaneously transforming creative workflows. Post-production encompasses all editing, visual effects, sound processing, and color grading tasks carried out after the principal photography or production phase of a film project. These processes traditionally require extensive time and a collaborative team effort; however, with the advancement of AI, many of these steps have become automated, yielding more precise outcomes (Selby-Lara & Howard, 2025).

Numerous films have incorporated AI technologies during post-production. One notable example is Ang Lee's *Gemini Man* (2019), where AI-powered facial modeling and animation techniques were employed to create a younger digital version of Will Smith, enabling the portrayal of a 23-year-old iteration of the then 50-year-old actor. Similarly, *Blade Runner 2049* (2017) utilized AI to recreate the character Rachel, originally portrayed by Sean Young in the 1982 film, through AI-supported facial modeling and voice synthesis. In *Avengers: Endgame* (2019), Marvel Studios applied AI in scene composition, motion capture, and facial animation, notably for characters such as Hulk and Thanos, whose movements were generated using AI-enhanced animation methods.

In the realm of advertising and public relations films, a significant number of productions are fully generated using AI technologies. Many brands have released commercials produced with AI tools. For instance, Coca-Cola launched a New Year advertisement in 2024 created entirely by AI. Toys "R" Us utilized OpenAI's Sora technology to produce a brand film narrating the story of its founder, Charles Lazarus, entirely via AI. Under Armour accelerated its production process and reduced costs by integrating AI technologies in an advertising campaign featuring Anthony

Joshua. In 2021, the late Turkish actor Kemal Sunal was digitally resurrected in a commercial using deep learning and AI-driven audiovisual reconstruction, marking a significant example of creative AI application in Turkey. Given the creative and operational advantages AI offers in the post-production of advertising and promotional films, it is anticipated that the industry's adoption of AI will continue to grow.

Editing Phase

In the editing phase of post-production, AI-powered automated video editing tools analyze raw footage to select the most suitable scenes and arrange them sequentially according to a predefined structure. For instance, Adobe Premiere Pro's Auto Reframe feature automatically reformats videos to fit different social media platform requirements (Selby-Lara & Howard, 2025). Furthermore, AI algorithms are capable of analyzing the emotional intensity and dramatic structure of scenes to inform editorial decisions (Aliyev, 2025).

AI-supported editing systems fundamentally operate through techniques such as scene recognition, sentiment analysis, facial and object detection. These systems analyze visual and auditory materials to identify key segments, create timelines, and design edits aligned with the intended emotional or thematic narrative. For example, in documentary filmmaking, AI can highlight impactful sentences and dramatic moments from interviews to generate an automatic structure. Throughout this process, the system evaluates scene content, vocal tones, dialogues, and visual density to autonomously construct the framework of the edit (Ghosh, 2023; Coursera, 2024).

The use of AI in film and advertising editing has become increasingly prevalent. *The Editor* short film stands out as one of the first projects entirely edited by artificial intelligence. In this film, AI analyzed scenes to maintain narrative coherence and optimize dramatic flow (Ghosh, 2023). Another example is Lexus's *Driven by Intuition* advertising campaign, where an AI engine developed by IBM Watson analyzed driver behavior and emotional response data to determine scene sequencing and construct the advertisement's edit. Similarly, Canva's AI-supported video editing tool is widely used for producing educational and social media content, offering content creators a fast and efficient video montage capability (Canva, 2025).

AI-based editing systems offer significant advantages such as time and cost savings, automatic transcript generation, audio/video synchronization, and customizable editing templates. These systems reduce workload by preparing rough cuts, especially in content-heavy projects, thereby assisting human editors. However, the limitations of AI-driven editing should not be overlooked. Particularly in the nuanced structure of dramatic storytelling, AI may fail to fully interpret emotional context. AI-generated edits might lack the creative and artistic intuition essential to filmmaking. Therefore, AI should be positioned as a supportive tool, with final creative decisions and refinements performed by human editors.

Visual Effects and Color Grading

Visual effects (VFX) and color grading are two essential post-production processes that play a critical role in the aesthetic success of a film. These stages are employed to enhance the emotional impact on the audience, make the narrative world believable, and ensure cinematographic coherence. Traditionally, these tasks have required high technical skill and time-consuming manual workflows; however, recent advances in artificial intelligence have accelerated these processes while rendering them more predictable and consistent.

It is possible to state that visual effects applications have become faster through AI integration. In VFX workflows, AI tools eliminate the need for manual masking by enabling efficient object tracking and motion capture. AI assumes responsibilities such as object and face recognition, motion tracking, and image synthesis within the visual effects production pipeline. Particularly in action, science fiction, and fantasy genres—where intensive VFX use is prevalent—AI-supported systems provide significant time and cost savings.

Color grading involves balancing the colors of footage after shooting, while color classification refers to applying an artistic or thematic color palette to the image. These processes are crucial in determining the film's mood and atmosphere. AI-based software substantially reduces manual intervention at this stage and increases consistency and efficiency, especially in multi-scene projects. Certain AI-driven tools offer automatic adjustment of scenes to optimal color tones. To maintain color coherence across different scenes, the color profile of a reference scene can be automatically applied to others. Moreover, AI can suggest color palettes based on scene content (e.g., sunset, nighttime, indoor settings). Simultaneously, by analyzing the emotional tone of the scene—such as sadness, joy, or tension—AI can perform appropriate color adjustments (Canva, 2025).

One notable example of AI usage in visual effects is Martin Scorsese's *The Irishman*. The film utilized AI-powered algorithms for facial de-aging VFX. The younger versions of actors like Robert De Niro and Al Pacino were dynamically integrated into scenes with natural light, shadows, and facial muscle movements. The VFX system employed real-time facial analysis models powered by AI. Another example is *Avengers: Endgame*, where CGI characters such as Thanos and Hulk had their emotional reactions modeled through AI-supported facial muscle and micro-movement analysis. This approach prevented the plastic appearance often seen in visual effects and delivered a more believable character experience (Coursera, 2024).

Sound Design

In film and video production, sound design is as crucial as visual elements for enabling the audience to experience the atmosphere effectively. Within this scope, artificial intelligence (AI) is increasingly utilized in sound processing (e.g., noise reduction, mixing), audio content analysis (speech-to-text, emotion detection), music composition, and dubbing. Traditionally manual and time-consuming, these processes have become faster, more accessible, and more efficient through AI-based systems (Coursera, 2024). In the film and advertising industries, AI has evolved beyond mere analytical tools to creative applications such as sound generation and voice cloning.

One of the primary applications is sound processing, especially for cleaning audio recorded in outdoor environments. Tools like Adobe Audition, RX iZotope, and Krisp leverage AI to analyze sound frequencies and automatically eliminate background noise, reverberation, and distortions. These systems can filter not only static-frequency noise but also environmental sounds mixed with human speech (Adobe, 2025).

Moreover, these tools employ AI-powered learning models to isolate dialogues from background noise, perform leveling, and optimize sound frequencies. This allows sound engineers to work with automatic recommendations rather than manual equalizer adjustments, thereby saving time and cost (Coursera, 2024).

AI also offers solutions in voice cloning and synthetic voice production. Platforms such as ElevenLabs, Descript, Resemble.AI, and Meta Voicebox can generate a person's voice profile from just a few minutes of audio and then use that profile to synthesize speech for different texts.

In particular, in fictional and documentary film dubbing, these systems can synchronize with actors' facial expressions, supported by "lip-sync AI" models that match lip movements with speech timing. Netflix provides an example of this technology: for some of its multilingual productions, English original dialogues have been automatically dubbed into German, Spanish, and Japanese using AI (Mohamed, 2025). Meta's Voicebox system not only performs voice cloning but also supports automatic translation and multilingual dubbing with the same voice tone. This presents a scalable, cost-effective, and rapid localization solution for global streaming platforms (Meta, 2023).

Automatic Speech Recognition (ASR) technologies are particularly important for video editing and content accessibility. Platforms like YouTube, Vimeo, and Adobe Premiere Pro utilize AI-based audio analysis to automatically generate subtitles. AI can analyze speech tempo, accent, and context to create synchronized subtitle text in terms of both content and timing (Coursera, 2024). Systems such as Google's Speech-to-Text API and OpenAI's Whisper model support multiple languages and can rapidly transcribe long texts. These technologies are applied in various domains, from podcast editing to film post-production (OpenAI, 2022).

Additionally, music composition represents another significant area of AI application. AI-driven composing platforms such as Amper Music, AIVA, Soundraw, and Ecrett Music generate music pieces suited to the emotional tone and tempo of film scenes. Users can simply provide keywords such as "action," "melancholy," or "suspense" to receive custom compositions. These tools are commonly preferred in Hollywood short documentaries and promotional videos. For instance, some commercial tracks produced via Soundraw are designed for multi-platform release without copyright issues (Soundraw, 2025). In *The Mandalorian*, machine learning-based modeling was used to create sound effects and atmospheric sound layers. Background sounds were digitally resynthesized based on diverse microphone recordings learned by AI (Adobe, 2025). The documentary *Welcome to Chechnya* (2020) used AI-based voice alteration and cloning techniques to preserve the authenticity of interviewees while anonymizing their identities.

AI's role in sound processing and audio content analysis is not only as a technical enhancement but also as a creative and accessible narrative tool. Providing fast and scalable solutions for both low-budget independent productions and large studio projects, it is expected that AI will increasingly be integrated into sound design workflows in cinema, advertising, and public relations films.

The Use of Artificial Intelligence in Film Distribution and Marketing

Artificial intelligence (AI) is revolutionizing the distribution and marketing processes of the film industry, rapidly transforming traditional methods. Particularly through big data analytics and machine learning algorithms, comprehensive insights can be obtained regarding target audiences' viewing habits, social media interactions, and content preferences. These insights are employed in various domains, including the personalization of film trailers, optimization of advertising strategies, and even scheduling of cinema screenings.

Digital platforms such as Netflix and Amazon Prime enhance user experience and improve content distribution efficiency through AI-powered recommendation systems. Furthermore, natural language processing techniques analyze film scripts to predict which scenes will be more effective from a marketing perspective (Zhang et al., 2020). These technologies not only help to expand the viewer base but also enable filmmakers to allocate marketing budgets more strategically.

Netflix is renowned for its advanced recommendation algorithms that analyze users' viewing histories. By utilizing artificial neural networks and deep learning, Netflix personalizes content suggestions and increases audience engagement (Amatriain & Basilico, 2012). Additionally, interactive productions such as *Bandersnatch* employed AI systems that analyze user choices in real time.

20th Century Fox employed IBM's AI tool, Merlin Video, to predict the performance of film trailers. This system analyzes visual elements in trailers to forecast which scenes attract greater viewer interest. Warner Bros collaborated with the AI platform Cinelytic to optimize marketing decisions. Cinelytic analyzes film scripts to predict the commercial viability of projects, allowing studios to manage high-risk investments more judiciously (Vincent, 2020).

PURPOSE AND SIGNIFICANCE OF THE STUDY

Artificial intelligence (AI) tools are rapidly increasing in number, and their areas of application are expanding accordingly. While initially developed for simple tasks, AI tools now play a significant role in a wide range of creative and productive functions, offering substantial convenience to professionals across sectors. These developments are transforming the operational dynamics of the industry, making it critical to investigate how AI tools are used and to define frameworks for their effective integration.

Cinema, advertising, and public relations are inherently creative and production-oriented fields. However, there is a notable lack of systematic and comparative research examining the impact of AI on content creation processes within these domains. This study aims to fill this gap by constructing a thematic intersection among these three sectors. Accordingly, the research focuses on identifying the contributions, application areas, and functions of AI tools within the film production processes specific to cinema, advertising, and public relations. In doing so, the study not only aims to contribute to academic knowledge, but also to offer practical guidance for production studios, advertising agencies, public relations professionals, educational institutions, and media policymakers.

The film industry is a technology-driven sector that evolves rapidly. Therefore, the integration of AI tools into the film production process has the potential to mark the beginning of a new era, enabling more efficient, creative, and commercially successful productions. AI-driven practices can help reduce production costs, increase labor productivity, and generate more compelling visual effects. From this perspective, the present study is expected to make a significant contribution to both academic discourse and professional practice concerning technology use in the film industry.

The primary objectives of this research include categorizing the use of AI in film production, analyzing its functionality, impact on creativity, and ethical implications, and identifying thematic models of human–AI collaboration. Additionally, the study aims to explore how AI tools can be utilized within the film industry, how they contribute to different stages of the production process, what types of innovations they introduce, how these innovations may be reflected in the industry, and how the use of AI tools may transform existing production practices.

Research Methodology

This study aims to examine the impact of artificial intelligence technologies on the production processes within visual-auditory communication fields such as cinema, advertising, and public relations through a thematic perspective. To this end, the research is designed within a qualitative research framework and conducted using the descriptive content analysis method. Descriptive content analysis enables the systematic examination of documents related to a specific topic in order to generate conceptual categories and thematic patterns (Krippendorff, 2004).

In this research, a document-based qualitative content analysis was performed, and a thematic coding strategy was employed throughout the analysis process. Through the identification of recurring themes, the study explores how AI technologies are integrated into production processes, the stages at which they are utilized, and the purposes they serve. The analysis focuses on the most widely used AI tools and is limited to the tools selected within the scope of the study.

The relevant themes, their descriptions, content types, and usage examples are presented in the table 1 below:

Table 1. Relevant themes, their descriptions, content types, and usage examples

Theme	Description	Content Type	Example of Use
AI–Screenwriting	Use of AI in scriptwriting, character development, and narrative structure design	All	Story development with ChatGPT
AI–Pre-production	Scene and shot planning, automatic storyboard generation, casting and location selection	Cinema, Advertising	Scene design using Midjourney
AI–Production	On-set use of digital effects, facial synthesis, and deepfake applications	Cinema	Real-time digital face creation
AI–Post-production	Editing, voice synthesis, automated dubbing, visual effects creation, scene sequencing, trailer editing	Cinema, Advertising	Voice generation with Replica Studios
AI–Distribution and Marketing	Audience analytics, social media content suggestions, automatic trailer cutting	Advertising, Public Relations	Netflix's AI-driven recommendation systems

Artificial Intelligence Tools Used in Screenwriting

The use of artificial intelligence (AI) tools in screenwriting is increasingly preferred to support, accelerate, and enrich the creative process. These tools are utilized at various stages by both amateur writers and professional screenwriters. The use of AI in screenwriting helps save time, provide inspiration, overcome creative blocks, and speed up trial-and-error processes. The main areas where AI is applied in screenwriting include:

- Idea development and brainstorming
- Character creation
- Plot structuring and development
- Dialogue writing
- Revisions and editing
- Genre transformation and adaptation
- Database scanning

AI tools used in screenwriting can be categorized as follows table 2:

Table 2. AI tools used in screenwriting

Theme	AI Tool	Purpose of Use	Description
AI-Screenwriting	ChatGPT (OpenAI)	Idea development, dialogue writing, structure	Used for writing dialogues, editing scripts, generating creative ideas, and suggesting scenes.
AI-Screenwriting	DeepStory	Automated story writing	Generates scripts automatically by creating characters and plots based on user input.
AI-Screenwriting	Runway ML (Gen-2)	Visual-based story generation	Produces descriptive texts and scene ideas based on video or visual inputs.
AI-Screenwriting	Plot Generator	Story templates and character suggestions	Creates short stories, characters, and events based on simple data inputs.
AI-Screenwriting	NovelAI	Creative writing using large language models	Generates stories and scripts based on user-defined characters, settings, or plots.
AI-Screenwriting	Rytr	Story ideas and script drafts	Creates original content based on keywords and topics defined by the user.
AI-Screenwriting	Cinelytic	Market-oriented script analysis	Analyzes scripts for financial and audience potential; serves as a pre-production decision support tool.
AI-Screenwriting	Sudowrite	Creative writing and paragraph completion	Suggests continuations in the writer's tone to enhance originality and flow.

continued on following page

Table 2. Continued

Theme	AI Tool	Purpose of Use	Description
AI-Screenwriting	CapCut	Web-based scriptwriting	Used to create short or feature-length scripts in various genres like comedy, mystery, and thriller.
AI-Screenwriting	Jasper AI	Advertising and marketing copy	Produces creative texts for social media, emails, and marketing campaigns.
AI-Screenwriting	Scalenut	SEO-friendly content and script generation	Optimizes scripts for online video ads according to SEO criteria.
AI-Screenwriting	ShortlyAI	Long-form text generation	Develops detailed scenes from brief inputs during the writing process.
AI-Screenwriting	Cohesive	Content for marketing, sales, and personal use	Assists users in writing tailored scripts and blog posts based on needs.
AI-Screenwriting	Copy.ai	Ad copy and creative content	Preferred for rapid production of creative texts such as product descriptions and ad spots.
AI-Screenwriting	WriteSonic	Promotional scripts and video content	Offers creative content for YouTube descriptions, ads, and short films.
AI-Screenwriting	Storyboard That	Visual storytelling and storyboarding	Designs visual panels and scenes before or after scriptwriting.
AI-Screenwriting	Notion AI	Writing planning and creative support	Used for taking notes, developing ideas, and planning script structure.
AI-Screenwriting	AI Dungeon	Interactive story generation	Creates immersive content for ads or interactive scripts.
AI-Screenwriting	Dramatron (DeepMind)	Script structure and dramatic theory support	Optimizes relationships between characters, scenes, and events based on narrative theory.
AI-Screenwriting	HyperWrite	Automatic writing and expansion	Develops script sections by adding more detail and enriching the content.
AI-Screenwriting	INK Editor	Creative writing and optimization	Edits scripts to improve style, originality, and readability.
AI-Screenwriting	Quillbot	Text paraphrasing	Suggests sentence rewordings to make the script sound more natural.
AI-Screenwriting	Papercup AI	Multilingual dialogue translation	Automatically translates and localizes scripts into various languages with voiceover.
AI-Screenwriting	Narrative Device	Randomized story structure suggestions	Provides unique scene connections for experimental or creative storytelling.
AI-Screenwriting	OpenAI Whisper	Audio-to-text transcription	Converts interviews or improvised voice recordings into written text.
AI-Screenwriting	Kafkai	SEO and ad-focused script generation	Generates short scripts automatically to meet ad agencies' content demands.

AI Tools Examined Under the Theme of AI-Screenwriting

ChatGPT is an artificial intelligence system developed by OpenAI, based on large-scale language modeling (LLM). This tool, which can be used in various areas such as human-like text generation, dialogue simulation, story construction, and creative writing, provides creative support particularly in processes like script drafting, character development, and thematic diversification within the film and media industries. Thanks to its natural language processing capabilities, ChatGPT generates contextually meaningful and coherent responses to user inputs and functions as a digital writing partner by offering suggestions both in terms of content and form during the creative writing process.

DeepStory is a platform developed to structure the AI-assisted creative writing process in screenplay format. This system creates scenes and dialogues in the format of a film script based on the characters, plotlines, and themes defined by the user, offering support particularly in terms of dramatic structure and narrative continuity. By analyzing textual inputs, DeepStory generates the tone of the writing, emotional progression, and character dynamics in accordance with specific cinematic theories, thereby presenting an AI-based alternative to traditional screenwriting tools.

Runway ML (Gen-2) is a groundbreaking artificial intelligence model with text-to-video generation capabilities, playing a transformative role in the field of creative visual production. This system converts textual descriptions provided by the user into high-resolution, scene-based videos and is used in the film pre-production process to create concept scenes, storyboard-like visual previews, and visual representations. Incorporating components such as image synthesis, motion simulation, and visual stylization, Runway ML has become an essential tool that democratizes and accelerates creative visualization processes.

Plot Generator is a text-based artificial intelligence tool that automatically generates story drafts and plotlines based on user inputs (such as character names, setting, genre, etc.). Modeling traditional narrative structures (e.g., three-act structure, the hero's journey), this system can be used to create short stories, novel openings, or basic structures for film scripts. Thanks to its generation mechanism based on trained language patterns, it serves as a guiding source for individuals new to the creative writing process, particularly in terms of idea generation, genre variation, and character development.

NovelAI is an AI-powered writing platform developed to personalize the creative writing process and produce literary texts tailored to the user. Offering in-depth narrative creation in genres such as interactive novels, role-playing stories, and fantasy fiction, this system stands out with its ability to mimic stylistic features of language. Thanks to a structure shaped by continuous feedback and user intervention, stories can dynamically evolve with internal consistency and character development.

NovelAI is one of the pioneering platforms demonstrating how artificial intelligence can be effectively used in literary production for stylistic coherence, narrative voice, and atmosphere building.

Rytr is an AI-supported text generation platform focused on short-form content creation. This system, which can rapidly produce marketing texts such as blog posts, social media content, and product descriptions, analyzes user inputs to generate personalized texts in terms of tone, language structure, and topic relevance. It is particularly preferred for saving time in digital marketing and content production processes.

Cinelytic is an artificial intelligence analysis platform designed for the film industry and is particularly used to assess the commercial potential of film projects. It models components such as cast, genre, budget, and distribution plans to forecast box office success and provides data-driven decision support to producers and distributors. In this regard, it is one of the pioneering systems that combine content evaluation with algorithmic prediction.

Sudowrite is an AI tool developed specifically to support the creative process in literary writing and fiction production. It provides contextually relevant alternative expressions, metaphors, descriptions, and plot suggestions based on the user's text. It is used to overcome productivity blocks commonly known as "writer's block" in creative writing.

CapCut is an AI-powered video editing tool developed for TikTok and other short video platforms. With features like automatic subtitle generation, face tracking, filter applications, and timing-based scene cuts, it makes visual content production accessible and fast. It is widely used in visual storytelling and social media marketing.

Jasper AI is an advanced AI writing platform that supports multilingual and multimodal content generation. Capable of producing content in various formats, from advertising copy to long-form blog posts, the system is optimized for marketing, sales, and content strategies. It stands out with its brand voice alignment, tone customization, and SEO-targeted output capabilities.

Scalenut offers AI solutions for SEO-friendly content planning and creation. With features such as keyword research, content brief generation, and automated writing, it provides an end-to-end content production pipeline, especially for digital marketers. It adopts a data-driven approach to AI-supported content strategy development.

ShortlyAI is a platform aimed at supporting creative writing for long-form content, particularly novels, stories, and essays. It continues the user's text contextually, offers suggestions, or rewrites specific sections. Its minimalist design offers a writer-focused experience.

Cohesive is a writing and collaboration platform that synchronizes with AI. It focuses on maintaining coherence, style, and structural balance in content production. It is especially used for internal document sharing and maintaining structural consistency in creative projects.

Copy.ai is an AI platform developed for marketing-focused content production. It generates content in formats such as ad copy, email campaigns, and landing page texts. It stands out for its ability to quickly produce product-focused content in multiple languages.

WriteSonic is a versatile AI writing tool used to automate marketing, e-commerce, and blog content. It is particularly effective in generating SEO-optimized titles, meta descriptions, and product summaries. It is positioned as a digital strategy tool combining AI with content automation.

Storyboard That is a digital storyboard tool used to visualize storytelling. With its drag-and-drop interface, it allows users to organize scenes, characters, and dialogue boxes. It is widely used in education, advertising, and film pre-production.

Notion AI is the AI extension of the multifunctional productivity application Notion. It provides generative AI support in functions such as note-taking, content drafting, summarization, task planning, and text editing. It accelerates information management in collaborative digital workspaces.

AI Dungeon is an interactive storytelling-based role-playing (RPG) game that uses GPT models to generate narratives in real time based on user input. It offers a gamified story creation experience and produces open-ended stories directly shaped by user commands.

Dramatron, developed by DeepMind, is an AI writing tool that automatically creates scripts, plays, and story structures while offering suggestions to the user. It provides creative collaboration in components such as character development, plot creation, and dialogue generation. It is a notable example of "AI-assisted screen-writing."

HyperWrite is a generative AI platform developed to accelerate the writing process by offering real-time suggestions to the writer. It assists users with sentence completion, text editing, and style alignment. It can also be used for business writing formats like emails, reports, and articles.

INK Editor is an AI-supported writing platform that combines SEO optimization with writing quality. It performs NLP-based analysis to improve content ranking and provides suggestions during writing based on metrics such as readability, keyword density, and originality.

Quillbot is a natural language processing tool used for paraphrasing, summarizing, grammar correction, and adapting texts to academic writing style. It is widely used by students, academics, and content creators for simplifying and improving texts.

Papercup AI is a voice technology platform that performs automatic dubbing by translating videos into different languages. With AI-powered voice synthesis, it preserves the original speaker's emotional tone while translating into the target language. It facilitates the localization process in international video distribution.

Narrative Device is an AI tool aimed at creative writers that builds stories based on theoretical narrative structures. By modeling classic structures such as Joseph Campbell's "Hero's Journey," it provides guidance in plot, theme, and character motivation. It uniquely combines theoretical structure with generative AI in fictional storytelling.

Whisper, developed by OpenAI, is a multilingual automatic speech recognition (ASR) system. It transcribes audio content with high accuracy and is used for subtitle generation, video transcription, and audio archiving. It plays an important role in film post-production, news media, and accessibility services.

Artificial Intelligence Tools Used in the Pre-Production Stage

The pre-production phase of the filmmaking process is the planning and preparation stage of a film. The use of artificial intelligence (AI) tools during this phase offers significant advantages in terms of both time and cost. AI tools used in pre-production shorten production timelines, help detect errors early, accelerate the visualization process, increase efficiency in budgeting and logistics, and enable creative experimentation.

The main areas where AI is used during the pre-production stage are as follows:

- Script development and analysis
- Character and casting planning
- Location and production design
- Storyboarding and visual planning
- Music and sound planning
- Shooting schedule and logistics optimization
- Budgeting and risk management
- Testing and feedback simulations

AI tools used in the pre-production stage are categorized as follows table 3:

Table 3. AI tools used in the pre-production stage

Theme	AI Tool	Purpose of Use	Description
AI - Pre-Production	ScriptBook	Script analysis	Analyzes structural elements of a screenplay; provides feedback on pacing, characters, and plot development.
AI - Pre-Production	Dramatron (DeepMind)	Dramatic structure support	Optimizes dramatic elements such as plot and character development.
AI - Pre-Production	Casting Networks AI	Casting matching	Matches suitable actors from the database based on role descriptions.
AI - Pre-Production	Quriosity AI	Talent analysis	Evaluates actors' suitability for roles based on past performances and demo reels.
AI - Pre-Production	Runway ML	Visual reference generation	Generates visual references for art direction, set, and costume design.
AI - Pre-Production	Midjourney	Concept design	Provides aesthetically rich concept designs for characters, locations, and costumes.
AI - Pre-Production	StyleGAN	Costume & character design	Produces variations of faces and costumes for design experimentation.
AI - Pre-Production	Kaedim	2D to 3D conversion	Quickly creates 3D scene models from concept sketches.
AI - Pre-Production	Promethean AI	Set layout	Automatically arranges props and scenes in virtual environments.
AI - Pre-Production	Archit AI	Location visualization	Designs and selects locations based on architectural images.
AI - Pre-Production	Descript	Voice scene analysis	Transcribes audio recordings and assists in evaluating actor performances.
AI - Pre-Production	OpenAI Whisper	Speech transcription	Transcribes audio from casting sessions and aids in performance analysis.
AI - Pre-Production	Fotor AI	Costume fitting preview	Digitally outfits characters in various costumes for visual previews.
AI - Pre-Production	Artbreeder	Character design	Creates visual character concepts by blending features like face, hair, and clothing.
AI - Pre-Production	Wonder Dynamics	Digital casting test	Inserts AI-generated characters into real scenes to test alternative casting options.
AI - Pre-Production	Kive.ai	Moodboard creation	Generates visual moodboards to define the overall aesthetic style of a production.
AI - Pre-Production	Plask	Motion analysis	Evaluates physical performances of actors for action or dance scenes.
AI - Pre-Production	EbSynth	Costume test scene creation	Produces scenes by overlaying digital costumes onto footage of real actors.

AI Tools Examined Under the Theme of Pre-Production

ScriptBook is an AI-based analysis tool developed to digitize and objectify the script evaluation processes in the film industry. Utilizing natural language processing (NLP) and machine learning techniques, this system evaluates the structural, thematic, and emotional components of a screenplay; analyzing elements such as character distribution, emotional flow, narrative structure, and diversity through quantitative data. The primary goal of ScriptBook is to predict the commercial potential of a script, its suitability for the target audience, and its cinematic success. It has been used by producers, distributors, and investors to conduct risk analysis at early stages and to guide content selection through data-driven insights. Although the platform ceased its commercial operations after 2019, ScriptBook's methodology is still recognized as a pioneering example of how AI can be utilized in content evaluation processes.

Dramatron, developed by DeepMind, is an AI tool designed to support screenwriters during the creative writing process. Powered by large language models (LLMs), the system generates essential screenplay components such as character lists, plot outlines, scene drafts, and dialogue suggestions based on user input. Dramatron aims to accelerate the creative workflow particularly in areas like constructing dramatic arcs, developing thematic variations, and generating multiple narrative alternatives. Based on the concept of "AI as co-author," the tool is designed to be used in collaboration with producers, screenwriters, and playwrights. In this context, it has also laid the groundwork for research into how generative AI can be ethically, aesthetically, and practically integrated into creative industries. Since its outputs require human editorial intervention, Dramatron positions AI as a complementary creative partner rather than a replacement.

Casting Networks AI is an AI-supported platform that aims to digitize casting processes to allow for faster, data-driven, and unbiased decision-making. Operating through machine learning algorithms applied to actor databases, the system automatically matches and ranks suitable candidates for specific roles. It evaluates a wide range of parameters such as physical characteristics, previous experience, performance history, and special talents. Additionally, it can analyze self-tape submissions by examining gestures, tone of voice, and emotional expression. Casting Networks AI provides producers and casting directors with time and cost savings while enabling a more inclusive and objective casting process.

Quriosity AI is an artificial intelligence platform designed for content curation and data-driven creative insight generation. It enhances the creative process by providing content suggestions, headline variations, and idea chains tailored to specific topics or areas of interest. It is particularly effective in digital media strategy, creative brainstorming, and topic exploration workflows.

Runway ML is a versatile AI platform capable of performing tasks such as text-to-video generation, automatic video editing, object tracking, and image segmentation. Especially with its Gen-2 model, it has gained the capability to produce realistic video scenes from user-provided text prompts. It has been widely adopted in fields such as filmmaking, advertising, and virtual production due to its capacity to accelerate the creation of visual content.

Midjourney is an advanced AI tool used for generating high-quality visuals from text descriptions. Known for producing aesthetically compelling results, Midjourney is employed in illustration, fashion design, game development, and film previsualization to generate original and visually rich concept designs.

StyleGAN (Style-based Generative Adversarial Network), developed by NVIDIA, is a generative neural network that revolutionized the production of highly realistic human faces and styles. Capable of generating photorealistic variations based on input style vectors, it is used in fields such as game design, character modeling, and digital portrait creation. StyleGAN has also been the subject of ethical debates, particularly concerning its potential for misuse.

Kaedim is an AI tool that rapidly transforms 2D sketches into 3D models. It is particularly favored in the game and animation industries for swiftly converting concept designs into prototypes. By saving time for 3D artists, the system accelerates the integration of visual ideas into production pipelines.

Promethean AI is an AI-supported content creation platform used for virtual world design. Developers and designers can create 3D game environments or digital scenes using only natural language commands. It is one of the most prominent examples of human + AI collaborative creativity in the architecture and gaming sectors.

Archit AI is an AI system that automatically generates architectural concept designs based on text input. It creates plans, renderings, and volumetric suggestions according to the user's structural, functional, and aesthetic requirements. It is used to accelerate the architectural pre-design process and promote creative diversity.

Descript is an AI-based media editing platform that enables users to edit audio and video via text. Its "Overdub" feature can synthesize speech from text using the user's own voice, allowing the generation of new sentences. It plays a revolutionary role in podcast production, video editing, and audio content creation.

Whisper is a multilingual, highly accurate automatic speech recognition (ASR) system. It transcribes video and audio recordings into text, widely used for subtitle creation, speech analysis, and content accessibility. It saves time in film, media, and news archiving processes and offers the advantage of multilingual support.

Fotor AI is an AI-powered image editing and style transfer tool. In addition to basic functions like photo retouching, face enhancement, and background removal, it can apply artistic effects. It provides practical solutions in visual marketing, social media content, and digital art production.

Artbreeder is a collaborative generative AI platform that allows users to blend various visuals to create new ones. It is especially used in character design, fantasy creature generation, and environment visualization. By combining user inputs with genetic algorithms, it enables creative diversity.

Wonder Dynamics is an AI system that automatically removes real actors from a scene and replaces them with digital characters. It adapts to camera movements, lighting, and actor actions to provide cinematic-level character integration. It is an innovative tool that automates CGI integration in film and game production.

Kive.ai is a platform that uses AI to optimize visual content organization, curation, and analysis for creative teams. It enables the creation of vision boards using moodboards, reference images, and project-specific folders. It enhances team alignment in visual memory and creative productivity processes.

Plask is an AI tool that performs motion capture from video using a markerless method. It is used to model natural character movements in animation, gaming, and virtual reality production. It offers a budget-friendly alternative to expensive motion capture systems.

EbSynth is an AI tool that creates animations based on style transfer by applying a visual style or artistic texture from a single video frame to the rest of the frames. The effect painted by the artist on one frame is reflected throughout the scene, providing aesthetic continuity in animation and music videos.

These tools are concrete examples of the transformative capabilities AI offers in fields such as visual production, architectural design, audio processing, and creative storytelling. Each contributes to time savings, creative support, and technical optimization at various stages of production, creating value for both individual artists and professional studios.

AI Tools Used During the Production Stage

In the production (filming) phase of filmmaking, artificial intelligence (AI) is actively used in many areas, including scene shooting, image analysis, camera control, and sound tracking. These technologies not only optimize the physical production process but also offer significant savings in time, labor, and costs. The use of AI during this stage enhances shooting quality, reduces human error, prevents time loss, accelerates decision-making through real-time feedback, and improves safety by solving risky scenes in virtual environments.

The main areas where AI tools are used during the production phase include:

- Smart camera systems and automatic framing
- Real-time image processing and feedback
- Sound tracking and noise reduction

- Digital doubles and virtual characters
- Live performance capture (motion capture)
- Virtual production environments
- Production process management
- Real-time VFX and previsualization

The AI tools used during the production phase are categorized as follows table 4:

Table 4. AI tools used during production phase

Theme	AI Tool	Purpose	Description
AI-Production	Magic Camera (Runway)	Real-time scene tracking	Enables the camera to recognize scene elements and analyze composition.
AI-Production	Wonder Dynamics	Real-time character placement	Integrates AI characters into live scenes.
AI-Production	TimeBolt	Automatic silence removal	Automatically removes repetitions and silent parts.
AI-Production	Cuebric	Virtual production scene creation	Creates virtual scenes as an alternative to green screens.
AI-Production	Kinetix	Real-time motion capture	Applies actors' movements to live scenes using AI.
AI-Production	LucidPix AI	3D camera effects	Generates 3D visual layers on mobile devices.
AI-Production	Aiva AI	Original music during filming	Suggests music based on emotional tone of scenes.
AI-Production	ShotDeck AI	Visual references	Offers aesthetic and framing suggestions from similar scenes.
AI-Production	Topaz Video Enhance AI	Image quality enhancement	Upscales resolution in post-production.
AI-Production	ShotPro AI	Script and scene analysis	Automatically analyzes scenes and provides optimization suggestions.
AI-Production	Celtx AI	Script and shooting schedule generation	Supports scriptwriting and shoot planning with AI.
AI-Production	Arraiy (AI Camera Tracking)	Automatic camera movements	Provides smart camera systems that follow actors or objects.
AI-Production	NVIDIA Broadcast	Smart camera settings and filters	Offers auto-focus, tracking, and background effects using AI.
AI-Production	Move.ai	Motion capture and camera choreography	Optimizes camera angles with real-time motion analysis.
AI-Production	Unreal Engine MetaHuman	Realistic digital characters	Creates hyper-realistic human models with AI.
AI-Production	DeepMotion	Real-time motion capture	Generates animations from camera and sensor data.

continued on following page

Table 4. Continued

Theme	AI Tool	Purpose	Description
AI-Production	NVIDIA Omniverse	Virtual set design and simulation	Enables collaborative real-time virtual production environments.
AI-Production	AI-powered Green Screen (Adobe)	Smart green screen and background switch	Performs real-time background replacement and composition using AI.
AI-Production	Disguise (AI-Powered VP)	Dynamic virtual production	Provides real-time VFX and virtual set integration.

AI Tools Examined Under the Theme of AI-Driven Production

Magic Camera is a real-time image processing feature powered by Runway ML's AI technology. It enables users to remove backgrounds, correct lighting, and apply instant effects using webcam or video input without the need for a green screen. This system offers professional-level visual control and aesthetics, particularly for live broadcasts, interviews, and social media content, accelerating content creation by reducing post-production requirements.

Wonder Dynamics is an AI-powered visual effects platform that automatically integrates 3D digital characters in place of real actors. By analyzing camera movement, lighting, and performance data, digital characters are inserted into live-action scenes without user intervention. It makes CGI integration more accessible, especially for independent productions and low-budget projects.

TimeBolt is an AI tool that automatically removes silent sections, gaps, and repetitive content from video footage. It enables faster editing, particularly for YouTube videos, educational content, and podcasts, significantly reducing manual labor in the editing of long raw recordings and optimizing the production process.

Cuebric is a tool that integrates scene planning and virtual background creation in film and video production with AI. AI-generated scene visuals can be automatically placed according to composition analysis. It is particularly suited for integration with LED volume-based virtual production techniques and stands as a strong example of the "AI-assisted previsualization" approach.

Kinetix is an AI platform that generates animated 3D avatars and animations from text or video inputs. Designed to democratize character animation for gaming, metaverse, and virtual reality applications, it allows users without technical expertise to produce professional-quality content through its markerless motion capture capabilities.

LucidPix AI is an AI tool that transforms 2D images into 3D visuals with parallax effects. By predicting depth maps, it creates dynamic perspectives within scenes, making it ideal for eye-catching content in social media and mobile applications. This technology adds layered visual storytelling and aesthetic depth to creative design.

AIVA is an AI-based composer developed to produce original music for film, advertising, games, and television. Working with algorithms grounded in classical music theory, the system creates unique musical compositions based on genre and emotional tone. AIVA serves as an inspiring creative partner for human composers and offers advantages in both time and copyright costs.

ShotDeck AI is a platform that facilitates visual reference discovery in film and video production, offering visual search and scene data analysis. With AI-powered tagging and image recognition, users can search through thousands of scenes based on themes, color palettes, camera angles, or compositions. It is a powerful tool used for visual planning and cinematographic referencing.

Topaz Video Enhance AI is an AI-powered video super-resolution tool that upgrades low-resolution videos to high resolution. Utilizing deep learning models, it reconstructs image details and reduces motion blur. It serves as an effective solution for archival restoration, film enhancement, and boosting professional video quality.

ShotPro AI is a platform that simulates visual elements such as scene planning, camera angles, actor movement, and lighting placement in a 3D environment for film and television productions. It accelerates storyboard creation and scene design with AI support, helping creative decisions materialize during the pre-production phase.

Celtx AI is the AI-supported version of an integrated platform that combines screenwriting and production planning. It provides automated suggestions while building story structure and contributes to content consistency through character and plotline analysis. With modules for scheduling, budgeting, and scene planning, it enables end-to-end production management.

Arraiy is a platform that develops AI-based real-time camera and object tracking systems used in film and advertising production. Compared to traditional motion tracking methods, Arraiy reduces labor and time costs by analyzing scenes on set in terms of depth, position, and movement data. It enables background replacement and synchronization with virtual environments without requiring green screens. As one of the early pioneers of virtual production, Arraiy has been especially utilized in VP and VFX integration processes.

NVIDIA Broadcast is a real-time audio and video processing platform developed for streamers and content creators. Its AI-powered features include background noise removal, face-tracking auto-focus, background removal (without a green screen), and advanced echo reduction. Running on a GPU-based system, it combines hardware acceleration with AI optimization to deliver professional-grade broadcast quality. It is widely used in both game streaming and remote work environments.

Move.ai is a markerless motion capture system that uses AI to perform skeletal motion analysis from video data. By analyzing multi-camera video inputs, it produces highly accurate 3D motion data. It stands out for its ability to function independently of clothing, body type, or lighting variations—making it especially useful in animation, game development, and virtual character management.

MetaHuman Creator, developed by Epic Games and integrated with Unreal Engine, is a platform for creating highly realistic digital humans. It delivers high-fidelity outputs in areas such as facial anatomy, skin texture, hair, expressions, and voice synchronization. Users can create photorealistic characters for use in games, films, or virtual universe projects in just a few minutes. It has had a significant impact on virtual production, cinema, and the metaverse.

DeepMotion is an AI system that generates automatic character animation based on video input. It maps human movement captured from ordinary videos onto 3D character skeletons. This approach is more accessible than traditional motion capture systems and is compatible with game engines like Unreal and Unity. It can capture a wide range of movements, including facial expressions and gestures, for use in virtual character animation.

NVIDIA Omniverse is a real-time, AI-assisted 3D collaboration platform that connects multiple software tools, engines, and users. It allows synchronized work between developers, artists, and engineers and is used for physically accurate lighting modeling, animation simulation, and scene management. With capabilities like AI-powered character animation, environment synchronization, and data integrity, it is groundbreaking for filmmaking, virtual reality, and digital twin creation.

Adobe's AI-based green screen technology enables real-time background removal during video editing without the need for a physical screen. Using AI segmentation and deep learning, it accurately isolates the edges of people or objects, resulting in faster and more mobile production workflows. It is integrated into tools like Adobe Premiere Pro and After Effects.

Disguise is a comprehensive platform offering AI-powered solutions for virtual production and real-time scene visualization. Commonly used on LED volume stages, the system provides real-time background rendering, lighting simulation, and camera tracking synchronization based on camera positions. AI enhances the virtual production environment by analyzing scene transitions, lighting adaptations, and script variations, making VP setups smarter and more adaptive.

These tools represent the transformative power of artificial intelligence in areas such as filmmaking, video editing, scene design, music composition, real-time production, motion capture, audio/video processing, digital character creation, and animation. Especially in film and game production, they reduce production costs, enhance visual quality, and overcome physical limitations—placing AI tools at the very heart of modern cinema and digital content creation.

AI Tools Used in the Post-Production Phase

The post-production phase of filmmaking is the most critical stage where the film is finalized both aesthetically and technically. In this phase, artificial intelligence (AI) tools offer significant advantages by automating traditionally time- and cost-intensive tasks such as editing, color correction, sound mixing, and visual effects. These advantages include automating workflows to save time, improving technical quality, reducing human error, enabling experimentation with multiple versions, and allowing small teams to accomplish large-scale work.

The main application areas of AI tools in the post-production phase include:

- Automated video editing
- Color correction
- Visual effects (VFX) and background replacement
- Audio cleaning, dubbing, and sound effects
- Subtitling and dialogue transcription
- Scene stabilization and image enhancement
- Content analysis and summarization
- Test screening and audience analysis

AI tools used in the post-production phase are categorized as follows table 5:

Table 5. AI tools used in the post-production phase

Theme	AI Tool	Use Case	Description
AI – Post-Production	Adobe Sensei	Automated editing and color correction	Automates video editing processes.
AI – Post-Production	Runway ML	Rotoscoping and VFX	Enables background removal, object tracking, and effect generation.
AI – Post-Production	Boris FX	VFX and Face Synthesis	Provides tools for rotoscoping, face synthesis, and other VFX tasks.
AI – Post-Production	DaVinci Resolve AI	Color and sound analysis	Performs automatic color matching and audio balancing.
AI – Post-Production	Topaz Video AI	Image enhancement	Converts low-resolution video to high quality.
AI – Post-Production	Deep Compositing and GAN	Natural integration of VFX into scenes	Balances lighting and perspective automatically to prevent unrealistic VFX.

continued on following page

Table 5. Continued

Theme	AI Tool	Use Case	Description
AI – Post-Production	Cleanvoice AI	Audio cleanup	Removes breathing sounds, filler words, and noise.
AI – Post-Production	iZotope Neutron	Audio mixing	Optimizes audio editing and mixing processes.
AI – Post-Production	Respeecher	Voice cloning	Used to adapt actors' voices into different languages.
AI – Post-Production	Flawless AI	Dubbing and lip sync	Synchronizes lip movements with dubbed languages.
AI – Post-Production	Boomy	AI music composition	Creates original music for film scenes.
AI – Post-Production	Descript Overdub	Automated voice dubbing	Edits audio via text and generates dialogue.
AI – Post-Production	Papercup AI	Translation and voiceover	Dubs videos into different languages.
AI – Post-Production	Reface AI	Face swapping	Provides deepfake-style face replacement.
AI – Post-Production	ElevenLabs	Natural voice generation	Enables dubbing with realistic synthetic voices.
AI – Post-Production	Suno AI	Original music generation	Composes music based on genre and emotion.
AI – Post-Production	Pictory	Video summarization	Extracts short summary clips from long videos.
AI – Post-Production	Magisto	Smart editing	Automatic video montage.
AI – Post-Production	Synthesia.io	Avatar-based narration, auto voiceover and editing	Used for corporate presentations and training videos.
AI – Post-Production	Canva Magic Design	Creates videos based on user prompts, adds automatic transitions and subtitles	Used in educational and promotional content.
AI – Post-Production	Steve.AI	Text-to-video conversion, smart editing suggestions	For animated and narrative videos.
AI – Post-Production	Soundraw	AI music composition	Creates scene-specific music.
AI – Post-Production	AutoSub	Automatic subtitles	Produces synchronized multilingual subtitles.
AI – Post-Production	DeepDub	AI dubbing	Generates multilingual voices similar to the actor's.
AI – Post-Production	Rev.ai	Automatic transcription	Provides text-based video analysis for editing.
AI – Post-Production	Kaiber	Visual effect generation	Creates aesthetic effects suitable for scenes.

continued on following page

Table 5. Continued

Theme	AI Tool	Use Case	Description
AI – Post-Production	Synthesia	Use of AI actors	Produces AI characters for digital presentations.
AI – Post-Production	Colourlab AI	Color correction	Offers automatic color correction and stylization.
AI – Post-Production	Filmbox	Color grading	AI-assisted color grading.
AI – Post-Production	Color.io	Color analysis	Provides smart color suggestions.
AI – Post-Production	Palette.fm	Color editing	Changes photo colors using AI.
AI – Post-Production	Neural Love	Restoration of old footage	Enhances low-quality visuals.
AI – Post-Production	D-ID	Photo animation	Animates old photos.
AI – Post-Production	MyHeritage	Face animation	Brings historical figures to life.

AI Tools Used in the Post-Production Phase

Adobe Sensei is an AI and machine learning platform integrated into all Adobe Creative Cloud and Document Cloud applications. It algorithmically optimizes processes such as image editing, object recognition, auto-framing, color correction, and content-aware fill. Adobe Sensei accelerates creative workflows while enhancing intuitive editing capabilities, offering a hybrid model that integrates AI with aesthetic decisions.

Runway ML is a comprehensive generative AI platform that supports various creative tasks, including text-to-video generation, object removal, background replacement, automatic rotoscoping, and style transfer. Especially with its Gen-2 model, it enables the generation of realistic video sequences from textual input, creating new possibilities in cinema, advertising, and digital art production. Runway is one of the tools democratizing real-time content creation.

Boris FX develops advanced software for VFX, color correction, and image stabilization used in film and video post-production. With AI-supported planar tracking systems such as Mocha Pro, it enables high-precision masking and rotoscoping in moving images. Frequently used by Hollywood studios, Boris FX tools minimize manual labor in complex visual effects processes.

DaVinci Resolve AI is the AI engine within the DaVinci Resolve editing software developed by Blackmagic Design. It is used for tasks such as auto color correction, face recognition, object tracking, scene detection, and smart audio separation. Integrated with AI, this system supports creative decisions in editing and color workflows through technical automation, offering both speed and quality advantages.

Topaz Video AI is a video super-resolution tool that uses deep learning techniques to enhance the quality of low-resolution videos. It enables upscaling by reconstructing details in images using AI-powered algorithms, also offering functions like deblurring, frame interpolation, and noise reduction. It is widely used in film restoration and digitizing archival footage.

Deep compositing, an AI-based VFX method, combines image layers shot at different depth levels. When combined with GANs (Generative Adversarial Networks), it can generate missing scene information or depth of field. This technology enables seamless integration of virtual backgrounds with physical footage and plays a groundbreaking role in virtual production and CGI.

Cleanvoice AI is an AI tool focused on speech editing that removes filler words ("uh," "um"), background noise, and echo from audio recordings. It automates manual editing processes for podcast producers, audiobook editors, and educational content creators, elevating audio quality to a professional level. It maintains the timing of speech sections to ensure flow is preserved.

iZotope Neutron is an AI-powered audio mixing tool with advanced analysis and suggestion systems used in music production, film sound design, and broadcasting. Its Mix Assistant detects frequency clashes and helps create a balanced sound stage. With channel-based dynamic processors, it allows users without technical audio expertise to produce professional-quality mixes.

Respeecher is an advanced voice cloning technology that synthesizes one person's voice with another's, used in dubbing, voice-over documentaries, and film synchronization. It produces synthetic voices based on real recordings while preserving emotion, tone, and emphasis. It is used ethically in processes such as recreating voices of deceased actors or multilingual localization.

Flawless AI is a visual AI platform working on dubbing alignment (AI lip sync) and digital actor placement. Translated dialogues are reconstructed to synchronize with actors' lip movements. This narrows the gap between dubbing quality and scene realism, enhancing cross-cultural accessibility in international film distribution.

Boomy is an AI composer that allows users to create original music tracks in just a few clicks. Customized music can be generated based on inputs such as style, tempo, and mood, and tracks can be published directly on digital platforms. It democratizes music production for amateurs while serving as a unique sound design tool for content creators.

Overdub, a feature within the Descript platform, enables AI-based text-to-speech production in the user's own voice. Sentences forgotten or needing correction during recording can be re-generated simply by editing the text. By preserving individual vocal styles, it makes voice editing as easy as text editing.

Papercup AI is an AI-based automatic video dubbing and multilingual voice translation tool. It mimics the speaker's tone and pace while translating into different languages, making content sound more natural and audience-appropriate. It is preferred by international media distributors, news agencies, and educational platforms for accessibility.

Reface AI combines face swap technology with AI to develop realistic face replacement applications in videos. Besides being used for entertainment and short content production, it is also applied in virtual character animation and digital identity simulation. With GAN-based algorithms, it provides highly compatible face transitions.

ElevenLabs is an AI platform delivering advanced performance in natural voice synthesis, capable of producing multilingual and emotion-sensitive speech. Used especially in audiobooks, podcasts, and dubbing, it offers personalized synthetic voice experiences by creating unique voice profiles. It excels in replicating nuances such as intonation, speed, and emphasis.

Suno AI is a generative AI platform that creates fully vocal songs from text prompts. Based on user-specified style, tempo, and theme, it synthesizes music, vocal melodies, and lyrics in an integrated way. Rather than replacing human creativity, this system acts as a collaborative AI partner in music production, reducing copyright concerns by providing original soundtracks for digital content creators.

Pictory is an AI-powered video editing platform that automatically creates summary video clips from text or long-form videos. With features such as transcription-based editing, automatic subtitle generation, and social media-optimized content creation, it is particularly preferred for transforming marketing, educational, and news content into video formats.

Magisto is an AI video editor that analyzes user-uploaded images and video clips to automatically perform editing, transition effects, music integration, and title application. Based on emotional analysis of visual content, the system selects style and tempo, making it easy for small businesses and individual content creators to produce professional-looking videos.

Synthesia is an AI video generation platform that produces talking-head videos using realistic digital avatars from text-based input. Users can select from various face models and languages to create training, marketing, or informational videos within minutes. This technology reduces the need for human actors, making video production scalable on a global level.

Magic Design, part of Canva, is an AI-assisted automated design suggestion system. Based on uploaded content (text, image, logo, etc.), it offers templates, color palettes, and layout variations. Combining visual storytelling with algorithmic design aesthetics, this system saves time and ensures consistency in visual communication.

Steve.AI is an AI platform that generates videos and animations automatically from text input. Blog content or text documents are directly transformed into visual scenes, combined with character animations, subtitles, and music. It is ideal for accelerating the production of explanatory videos in education, advertising, and presentations.

Soundraw is an AI music composition platform that generates original, royalty-free music tracks based on user-defined inputs such as theme, tempo, and mood. With an interface that allows user intervention, music composition can be semi-automated. It reduces copyright burdens in sectors like film, gaming, and content marketing.

AutoSub is an open-source automatic speech recognition (ASR) tool that transcribes speech in audio and video files into subtitle files (SRT, TXT). Thanks to language model training, it provides high-accuracy, time-coded transcription and is especially used in film post-production, academic video archiving, and accessibility projects.

DeepDub is an AI-powered automatic dubbing and localization platform. It translates video content into different languages while generating synchronized dubbing using synthetic voices that match the original actor's tone and speaking style. This technology offers cost-effective and culturally adaptive solutions for global media distribution.

Rev.ai, offered by Rev, is an AI-based speech recognition and transcription API. Capable of real-time and multilingual transcription, this system can be integrated into subtitles, speech analysis, and voice search systems. With AI-powered speech analytics, it enhances efficiency in the media industry.

Kaiber is a generative AI platform that transforms static images or text descriptions into dynamic video content. By converting visual storytelling into moving scenes, this system is used in music videos, artistic narratives, and digital storytelling projects. It enables creative applications in visual abstraction and stylization.

Synthesia, frequently used in corporate video production, is an AI avatar-based video synthesis system. Eliminating the need for human presenters, it provides time and cost advantages for presentations, training modules, and multilingual informational videos. It stands out with advanced facial expressions, dubbing synchronization, and multilingual support.

Colourlab AI is a professional film color tool that optimizes the video color grading process using AI. With functions such as visual composition analysis, LUT suggestions, and automatic color matching, it brings visual coherence to cinematic storytelling. It is especially used in the film industry due to integration with tools like DaVinci Resolve.

Filmbox is a cinematic analysis platform focused on optimizing visual components such as lighting, camera angles, and scene layout for film production. By analyzing scenes using AI, it strengthens cinematographic consistency and provides a technical foundation for creative decisions in pre-production planning.

Color.io is a browser-based, AI-supported digital color management platform offering color space transformation, LUT design, and visual analysis features. Centered on color science in film, photography, and video content, this tool combines technical accuracy with aesthetic control in creative projects.

Palette.fm is a platform that automatically colorizes black-and-white photos using AI. By classifying elements like object types, faces, and clothing in the image, it offers realistic color suggestions. It is used in digital history, family archives, and creative restoration.

Neural Love is a visual restoration platform that enhances, colorizes, and animates low-resolution or old images using AI. It yields particularly successful results with portraits and historical materials. Using GAN-based algorithms, it reconstructs missing details.

D-ID is a system that transforms static facial images into talking, moving video avatars using AI. It is used to create virtual hosts or characters in areas such as education, guidance, and customer experience. It is highly popular for personal or commercial video avatar production.

MyHeritage Deep Nostalgia is an AI service that creates "living portraits" by adding moving expressions and eye movements to historical photos. Through deep learning-based facial animation technology, it brings emotional depth to static images and is effective in digitizing memories and reviving nostalgic experiences.

Masterpiece Studio is a digital content creation platform offering AI-supported tools to produce virtual characters and 3D assets. Managing modeling, rigging, and animation processes integratively, it enables users to create professional-grade 3D characters and objects. It plays an important role in game and VR/AR content production.

These tools combine creativity with automation and algorithmic aesthetics across areas such as video synthesis, sound generation, facial animation, color management, and dubbing—making digital content production more accessible, scalable, and multilingual. In filmmaking and media production, they provide advanced solutions that enhance automation, quality, and productivity in fields such as post-production, sound engineering, VFX, dubbing, and synthetic content creation. In disciplines like cinema, advertising, and public relations, AI has become not just a supportive element but a generative actor.

Artificial Intelligence Tools Used in Distribution and Marketing

In the film industry, the distribution and marketing phase is a critical process that directly impacts the commercial success of a production. In this phase, artificial intelligence (AI) tools are used in various areas such as target audience analysis, advertising strategies, poster design, trailer production, and audience behavior prediction—enabling data-driven, personalized, and highly effective campaigns. The use of AI in this process offers advantages such as more accurate targeting, cost-effective yet high-performing campaigns, rapid production of multi-channel content versions, data-based decision-making, and optimized release timing.

The main areas where AI tools are used in the distribution and marketing phase include:

- Target audience analysis and segmentation
- Personalized promotional strategies
- Trailer and promotional video production
- Poster and digital design creation
- Audience response and sentiment analysis
- Marketing campaign performance prediction
- Distribution strategy planning
- Chatbot usage and interactive marketing

The AI tools used during the distribution and marketing phase are categorized as follows table 6:

Table 6. AI tools used during the distribution and marketing phase

Theme	AI Tool	Purpose of Use	Description
AI – Distribution & Marketing	Vault AI	Audience reaction	Analyzes trailers through emotion mapping.
AI – Distribution & Marketing	Cinelytic	Film investment and marketing decisions	Analyzes film scripts to predict commercial success and assists production companies in investment decisions.
AI – Distribution & Marketing	Largo AI	Film success prediction	Provides marketing strategy recommendations based on film analytics.
AI – Distribution & Marketing	Merlin Video (IBM)	Trailer analysis	Uses image recognition technology to analyze scenes in film trailers and predict viewer interest.

continued on following page

Table 6. Continued

Theme	AI Tool	Purpose of Use	Description
AI – Distribution & Marketing	Netflix Recommendation System	Content distribution and personalized marketing	A deep learning-based system that analyzes users' viewing history to suggest content, increasing engagement and user loyalty.
AI – Distribution & Marketing	Google Cloud Video Intelligence	Visual content labeling and analysis	Tags and analyzes objects, faces, and speech in films and trailers to provide insights for marketing analytics.
AI – Distribution & Marketing	ChatGPT / GPT-4 (OpenAI)	Marketing content creation, customer communication	Used for generating film promotion texts, social media content, and interactive chatbot communication with audiences.
AI – Distribution & Marketing	Adobe Sensei	Content analysis and creative process support	Accelerates creative processes in areas such as visual editing and automated marketing campaign creation.
AI – Distribution & Marketing	Persado	Marketing language optimization	Uses AI-based language analysis to test and optimize the most effective email and ad copy variations.
AI – Distribution & Marketing	Movio	Target audience analysis and campaign optimization	Analyzes cinema audience behavior data to deliver personalized marketing campaigns.
AI – Distribution & Marketing	Clarifai	Image recognition and content classification	Classifies objects in trailers and promotional visuals to support marketing segmentation.
AI – Distribution & Marketing	KAIROS	Audience reaction measurement via facial recognition	Analyzes facial expressions of test viewers watching trailers to identify which scenes are most impactful.

AI Tools Examined Under the Theme of Distribution and Marketing

Vault AI is an artificial intelligence platform that uses natural language processing (NLP) and machine learning models to predict the commercial potential of content, spanning processes from script analysis to marketing strategies. Particularly in the film and television industry, it evaluates scripts using metrics such as success probability, audience interest, and market fit, offering data-driven insights for producers' decision-making processes. Vault AI is one of the pioneering systems that combines the "creative intelligence" approach with automated content evaluation.

Cinelytic is an AI-powered decision support system that predicts a film project's box office success by analyzing variables such as cast, genre, budget, script, and distribution strategies. Operating with big data analytics and AI prediction models, the platform helps studios optimize their investment decisions. It provides strategic foresight in the film industry through functions like pre-production risk analysis and portfolio management.

Largo AI is a multi-layered AI system that determines a film's target audience, box office success, marketing strategy, and casting recommendations based on the script. It has been used by various European production companies since the 2019 Cannes Film Festival. By evaluating elements such as visual analysis, dialogue density, pacing, and emotional distribution, it provides a numerical foundation for creative decision-making.

Merlin Video, developed by IBM Research, is a visual understanding and tagging system that analyzes video content scene by scene. With functions like image recognition, object classification, facial analysis, and emotion detection, it makes videos more searchable, indexable, and recommendable. This technology forms the backbone of content recommendation algorithms in OTT platforms.

Netflix's recommendation system is based on deep learning and content-based filtering algorithms that analyze user behavior, watch duration, rating history, and content attributes. Aiming to increase user retention through personalized content recommendations, this system processes millions of content-decision relationships with high accuracy and optimizes watch times. It is considered one of the most effective applications of modern recommendation systems.

Google Cloud Video Intelligence is a video content analysis API that automatically detects scene transitions, objects, speech, and text in video files. Also used in YouTube infrastructure, this system is utilized for media archiving, content security, and automatic subtitle generation. With the integration of computer vision and speech recognition, it enables fast semantic analysis of large-scale video content.

ChatGPT, based on OpenAI's GPT-4, is a generative language model used in content creation, dialogue writing, summarization, sentiment analysis, and idea generation. In the film and media industry, it supports various content types, from script writing to marketing texts, acting as an AI writer. Its ability to interact with users in natural language also makes it a modular component for recommendation systems.

Adobe Sensei is an AI engine integrated into Adobe products that optimizes processes such as visual editing, content creation, and data analytics. It supports creative processes with functions like object recognition in visuals, automatic color correction, and suggestion systems. By analyzing user habits, it offers personalized suggestions and automatic optimizations — an example of AI's contribution to creative productivity within Creative Cloud tools.

Persado is a language generation platform that performs emotion-based optimization of marketing texts using AI and linguistic science techniques. It tests different emotional tones to determine the message variant that will generate the most positive response from users. It is used in film promotions, trailer scripts, and advertising campaigns to boost conversion rates.

Movio is an AI platform that develops personalized film promotions and targeted marketing strategies by analyzing cinema audience data. It uses demographic and behavioral data such as age, gender, viewing frequency, and genre preferences to optimize trailers, posters, and recommendation systems on a viewer-by-viewer basis. In this way, it stands out as a data-driven micro-targeting tool in film distribution.

Clarifai is an AI visual analysis platform focused on object, face, text, and emotion recognition in visual content. It is used in tasks such as video security, archiving, automatic tagging, and content classification. In the media industry, it enables rapid indexing and management of large-scale image or video datasets.

Kairos is an AI platform focused on human facial recognition and demographic analysis. Used in advertising and film marketing to analyze viewer reactions, the system analyzes metrics such as age, gender, race, and emotion to aid in audience profiling and content optimization. Developed within an ethical framework, Kairos is also utilized in content sensitivity research.

These tools provide strategic decision support to producers, distributors, and platforms in critical areas such as content strategy, audience analytics, content discovery, and marketing within the film and media industry. In the era of data-driven creative economy, such tools are not only technological but also cultural transformation agents.

CONCLUSION

As we enter the second quarter of the 21st century, the impact of artificial intelligence (AI) technologies on creative industries should be interpreted not merely as a transformation but as a paradigm shift. This study has examined how AI technologies are used in communication-based production domains such as cinema, advertising, and public relations; and how these technologies are redefining creative processes, labor structures, ethical norms, and sectoral competition conditions. The findings point not only to the automation of production processes but also to the digitalization of creative decision-making mechanisms. Thus, the transformation observed is not merely practical but also epistemological and normative in nature.

The extensive use of AI in the cinema industry—from pre-production to post-production—opens up a renewed discussion about the nature of creative labor. Particularly in areas such as screenwriting, scene planning, location selection, visual effects creation, and sound design, AI plays both a supportive and directive role. While these technologies do not entirely replace traditional creative processes, they lead to the widespread adoption of “co-creative partnership” models. GPT-based scriptwriting systems have become valuable partners for filmmakers in generating ideas, building characters, and constructing narrative structures. Simultaneously, virtual production technologies have largely eliminated the material and temporal constraints associated with physical set construction. However, the impact of these technological capabilities on core values such as artistic freedom, aesthetic integrity, and cultural authenticity still requires in-depth and critical examination.

In the fields of advertising and public relations, AI offers major advantages particularly in areas like audience targeting, content personalization, emotional intensity prediction, and automated video production. Data-driven campaign planning and micro-targeting have increased the impact of messaging, while fast production cycles offer savings in time and cost. Nevertheless, these sectors also bring forth critical ethical questions: How does an AI-generated brand narrative affect perceptions of authenticity and sincerity among consumers? Does increased automation lead to the devaluation of creative labor? These questions demand not only a technological discussion but also a reevaluation of the ethical and political dimensions of the communication discipline.

The analysis presented in this study demonstrates that the relationship between the opportunities offered by AI and sectoral expectations is transforming not only production practices but also the epistemological foundations of the industries themselves. As creative decision-making increasingly relies on data analytics, "intuitive creativity" tends to be replaced by "computable creativity." This trend manifests differently across sectors: in cinema, creative intuition and cultural context still play a decisive role, whereas in advertising, AI-supported content production is rapidly becoming centralized and often constitutes the core of the final product.

Looking ahead, it is foreseeable that AI technologies will influence creative industries in three major directions:

1. Autonomous content production,
2. AI models sensitive to cultural context,
3. Creative production systems based on human–AI collaboration.

These three trends will require new strategic approaches in both technical and normative contexts. In the film industry, AI-assisted scriptwriting and visual storytelling systems are likely to be integrated not only into production but also into audience feedback mechanisms. In advertising and public relations, the real-time and emotionally responsive nature of content generation will make algorithmic ethics an unavoidable area of debate.

In this context, communication faculties within universities and sectoral institutions must develop more systematic and interdisciplinary approaches to the effects of AI technologies on education, professional ethics, and cultural production. Otherwise, the instrumentalization of creative labor through automation may undermine fundamental values such as originality, diversity, and freedom of expression. The digital future of creative industries can only be sustained through a human-centered, critical, and ethically grounded AI literacy.

REFERENCES

Adobe. (2025). Audio Enhancement Powered by Adobe Sensei. https://www.adobe.com/sensei.html

Aliyev, R. A. (2025). Artificial Intelligence as a Key Driver of Energy Security Transformation. *Post-Soviet Issues*, *12*(1), 30–48.

Amatriain, X., & Basilico, J. (2012). Netflix Recommendations: Beyond the 5 stars. Netflix Tech Blog. https://netflixtechblog.com/netflix-recommendations-beyond-the-5-stars-part-1-55838468f429

Andriasyan, S. (2025). How Artificial Intelligence Is Used in the Film Industry. https://smartclick.ai/articles/how-artificial-intelligence-is-used-in-the-film-industry

Boden, M. A. (2016). *AI: Its nature and future*. Oxford University Press.

Boyd, D., & Crawford, K. (2012). Critical Questions for Big Data: Provocations for A Cultural, Technological, and Scholarly Phenomenon. *Information Communication and Society*, *15*(5), 662–679.

Broussard, M. (2018). *Artificial Unintelligence: How Computers Misunderstand the World*. MIT Press.

Canva. (2025). AI Video Editor – Create & Edit Videos with AI. https://www.canva.com/video-editor/ai/

Carlson, M. (2015). The Robotic Reporter: Automated Journalism and The Redefinition of Labor, Compositional Forms, and Journalistic Authority. *Digital Journalism (Abingdon, England)*, *3*(3), 416–431.

Cave, S., & Dihal, K. (2020). *Imagining AI: How the World Sees Intelligent Machines*. Oxford University Press.

Chen, Y., Rao, A., Jiang, X., Xiao, S., Ma, R., Wang, Z., Xiong, H., & Dai, B. (2024). CinePreGen: Camera Controllable Video Previsualization via Engine-powered Diffusion. arXiv preprint arXiv:2408.17424.

Cmsproductions (2025). https://www.cmsproductions.com/blog/ai-tools-for-film-producers

Couldry, N., & Mejias, U. A. (2019). *The Costs of Connection: How Data Is Colonizing Human Life and Appropriating It for Capitalism*. Stanford University Press.

Coursera. (2024). What Is AI Video Editing? https://www.coursera.org/articles/ai-video-editing

Dayo, F., Memon, A. A., & Dharejo, N. (2023). Scriptwriting in the Age of AI: Revolutionizing Storytelling withArtificial Intelligence. *Journal of Media & Communication*, *4*(1), 24–38.

Deguzman, K. (2023). What is Production Design in Film- How to Tell Stories Visually. https://www.studiobinder.com/blog/what-is-production-design-in-film

Desowitz, B. (2020). The Mandalorian: How ILM's Innovative StageCraft Tech Created a Star Wars Virtual Universe. https://www.indiewire.com/features/general/the-mandalorian-ilm-stagecraft-1202212389/

DiTommaso, L. (2025). Conversations about Artificial Intelligence in Filmmaking. https://www.productiondesignerscollective.org/single-post/conversations-about-artificial-intelligence-in-filmmaking

Frawley, C. (2023). What Generative AI Could Look Like for Actors. https://www.backstage.com/magazine/article/ai-actors-explained-76361

Georgetown University Library. (2023). Copyright and AI. https://guides.library.georgetown.edu/ai/copyright

Ghosh, A. (2023). Artificial Intelligence as an Innovation in the Film Industry. *Research Inspiration*, *3*(3), 12–16.

Girmaji, R., Beri, B., Subramanian, R., & Gandhi, V. (2025). EditIQ: Automated Cinematic Editing of Static Wide-Angle Videos via Dialogue Interpretation and Saliency Cues. In *Proceedings of the 30th International Conference on Intelligent User Interfaces* (pp. 609-623).

Goodwin, R., & Sharp, O. (2020). *Zone Out* [Short film]. NYU AI Film Lab.

2. immersive4u. (2025). https://2immersive4u.com/

Kember, S., & Zylinska, J. (2012). *Life after new media: Mediation as a vital process*. MIT Press.

Kerlow, I. (2009). *The Art of 3D Computer Animation and Effects*. Wiley Publishing.

Kinder, M. (2024). Hollywood writers went on strike to protect their livelihoods from generative AI. Their remarkable victory matters for all workers. https://www.brookings.edu/articles/hollywood-writers-went-on-strike-to-protect-their-livelihoods-from-generative-ai-their-remarkable-victory-matters-for-all-workers/

Kozan, E. (2025). Emerging Opportunities and Threats for Filmmaking In The Age of Artificial Intelligence In Communications. 15th International Congresses on Social, Humanities, Administrative, and Educational Sciences in a Changing World Congress Proceedings Book, pp. 317-323. https://doi.org/DOI: 10.30546/19023.978-9952-8545-8-9.2025.601

Krippendorff, K. (2004). *Content analysis: An introduction to its methodology* (2nd ed.). Sage Publications.

Largo.ai. (2025). https://home.largo.ai/

Levy, C. (2025). 'Not Just 50% Cheaper.' Netflix's Ted Sarandos Has His Own Take After James Cameron Revised His Thoughts On AI In Hollywood. https://www.cinemablend.com/movies/ted-sarandos-take-james-cameron-revised-thoughts-ai-in-hollywood

Liu, X., Tai, Y.-W., & Tang, C.-K. (2024). ChatCam: Empowering Camera Control through Conversational AI. arXiv preprint arXiv:2409.17331.

Lubart, T. I. (2005). How can computers be partners in the creative process: Classification and commentary on the special issue. *International Journal of Human-Computer Studies*, *63*(4–5), 365–369.

Lumalabs.ai. (2025). https://lumalabs.ai/

Manovich, L. (2002). *The Language of New Media. Londra.* The MIT Press.

Manovich, L. (2019). *AI Aesthetics*. Strelka Press.

Massive.ai. (2025). https://massive.io/

Mast, G., & Kawin, B. (2011). *A Short History of the Movies. 11Th Edition.* Pearson.

McCormack, J., Gifford, T., & Hutchings, P. (2019). Autonomy, Authenticity, Authorship and Intention in Computer Generated Art. In *International Conference on Computational Intelligence in Music, Sound, Art and Design*, 35-50. Cham: Springer International Publishing.

McCosker, A., & Wilken, R. (2020). *Automating vision: The social impact of the new camera consciousness.* Routledge.

Meta, A. I. (2023). Voicebox: A Multilingual, Context-Aware Text-to-Speech System. https://ai.facebook.com/blog/voicebox-meta-generative-ai-model-speech

Mohamed, E. (2025). Netflix's 'Deepfake Dubbing' Sparks Outrage. https://www.meer.com/en/92522-netflixs-deepfake-dubbing-sparks-outrage

Mulvey, L. (2006). *Death 24x a Second Stillness and the Moving Image*. Reaktion Books.

Noble, S. U. (2018). *Algorithms of Oppression: How Search Engines Reinforce Racism*. NYU Press.

Open, A. I. (2022). Whisper Speech Recognition System. https://openai.com/research/whisper

Pueyo, P., Dendarieta, J., Montijano, E., Murillo, A. C., & Schwager, M. (2024). Cinempc: A fully autonomous drone cinematography system incorporating zoom, focus, pose, and scene composition. *IEEE Transactions on Robotics*, *40*, 1740–1757.

Quinn Emanuel Urquhart & Sullivan, LLP. (2023). Client Alert: Copyright Protection for Works Made With AI Tools. https://www.quinnemanuel.com/the-firm/publications/client-alert-copyright-protection-for-works-made-with-ai-tools

Radanliev, P. (2025). AI Ethics: Integrating Transparency, Fairness, and Privacy in AI Development. *Applied Artificial Intelligence*, *39*(1). Advance online publication. DOI: 10.1080/08839514.2025.2463722

Sahota, N. (2024). The AI Takeover In Cinema: How Movie Studios Use Artificial Intelligence. https://www.forbes.com/sites/neilsahota/2024/03/08/the-ai-takeover-in-cinema-how-movie-studios-use-artificial-intelligence

Selby-Lara, A., & Howard, C. (2025). Robotic Rhythm: A Contemporary Look At AI-Driven Editing Tools. LMU Digital Commons. https://digitalcommons.lmu.edu/honors-thesis/572

Sharp, O., & Goodwin, R. (2016). *Sunspring* [Short film]. End Cue.

Shaw, L. (2024). Four Experts Explain How AI Will Change Hollywood. https://www.bloomberg.com/news/newsletters/2024-08-18/four-experts-explain-how-ai-will-change-hollywood

Silva Jasaui, D., Martí-Testón, A., Muñoz, A., Moriniello, F., Solanes, J. E., & Gracia, L. (2024). Virtual Production: Real-Time Rendering Pipelines for Indie Studios and the Potential in Different Scenarios. *Applied Sciences (Basel, Switzerland)*, *14*(6), 2530. DOI: 10.3390/app14062530

Söğütlüler, T. (2024). The Future of the Moving Image: Virtual Production Technology. *Türkiye Film Araştırmaları Dergisi*, *4*(2), 214–234. DOI: 10.59280/film.1530664

Soundraw. (2025). AI Music Generator for Creators. https://soundraw.io

Spangler, T. (2020). Warner Bros. Taps AI for Film Marketing Decision-Making. https://variety.com/2020/digital/news/warner-bros-cinelytic-ai-1203452420/

Superscout.ai. (2025). https://superscout.ai/

Tang, Y., Li, H., Lan, M., Ma, X., & Qu, H. (2025). Understanding Screenwriters' Practices, Attitudes, and Future Expectations in Human-AI Co-Creation. In *CHI Conference on Human Factors in Computing Systems*. Yokohama, Japan. https://doi.org/DOI: 10.1145/3706598.3714120

Tatlerasia (2025). https://www.tatlerasia.com/lifestyle/entertainment/ai-in-movies

The Guardian. (2025a). Collective licence to ensure UK authors get paid for works used to train AI, says trade body. https://www.theguardian.com/books/2025/apr/23/collective-licence-to-ensure-uk-authors-get-paid-for-works-used-to-train-ai

The Guardian. (2025b). EU accused of leaving devastating copyright loophole in AI act. https://www.theguardian.com/technology/2025/feb/19/eu-accused-of-leaving-devastating-copyright-loophole-in-ai-act

Tüfekçi, Z. (2014). Big Questions for Social Media Big Data: Representativeness, Validity and Other Methodological Pitfalls. *Proceedings of The Eighth International AAAI Conference On Weblogs And Social Media*, 505–514.

Unity. (2025). https://learn.unity.com/

Vakhtin, D. (2023). AI for filmmaking: Script breakdowns in seconds. https://filmustage.com/blog/ai-for-filmmaking-script-breakdowns-in-seconds

Van Dijck, J. (2013). *The Culture Of Connectivity: A Critical History of Social Media*. Oxford University Press.

Vault.ai. (2025). https://vault-ai.com/research-and-insights/

Vincent, J. (2020). Warner Bros. Signs AI Startup That Claims to Predict Film Success. https://www.theverge.com/2020/1/9/21058094/ai-film-decision-making-warner-bros-signs-cinelytic

Watercutter, A. (2023). The Hollywood Strikes Stopped AI From Taking Your Job. But for How Long? https://www.wired.com/story/hollywood-saved-your-job-from-ai-2023-will-it-last

Whissel, K. (2014). *Spectacular Digital Effects: CGI and Contemporary Cinema*. Duke University Press.

Whittaker, M., ... (2018). AI Now Report 2018. AI Now Institute. https://ainowinstitute.org/wp-content/uploads/2023/04/AI_Now_2018_Report.pdf

Wille, C. I. (2015). Shaping Dreams: Design Ideas and Design Fiction in Movie and Television Production Design. Artifact, Volume 3, Issue 4, 9.1-9.10. https://doi.org/DOI: 10.14434/artifact.v3i4.12812

Zengin, F. (2020). Akıllı Makine Çağı Sinemasına Giriş: Sinema Sanatında Yapay Zekâ Teknolojilerinin Kullanımı. İletişim Çalışmaları Dergisi, 6(2), 151-177.

Zettl, H. (2016). *Sight, Sound, Motion: Applied Media Aesthetics* (8th ed.). Cengage Learning.

Zhang, Q., Lu, J., & Jin, Y. (2020).. . *Artificial Intelligence in Recommender Systems*, *7*(6), 1–19.

Zuboff, S. (2019). *The Age Of Surveillance Capitalism: The Fight for A Human Future at The New Frontier of Power*. Public Affairs.

ADDITIONAL READING

Anadolu, B. (2019). Dijital Hikâye Anlatıcılığı Bağlamında Yapay Zekânın Sinemaya Etkisi: Sunspring ve It's No Game Filmlerinin Analizi. *Erciyes İletişim Dergisi*, (1), 39–56.

Boztepe Taşkıran, H., & Önay Doğan, B. (2024). Halkla ilişkiler ve Reklamcılık Perspektifinden Yapay Zeka Çalışmaları: Ulusal Alan Yazının Bibliyometrik Analizi. *Uluslararası Halkla İlişkiler ve Reklam Çalışmaları Dergisi*, *7*(2), 9–35. DOI: 10.61766/hire.1472693

Çeber, B. (2023). *Yapay Zeka ve Halkla İlişkiler: Kullanım Alanları, Etki, Sınır ve Zorluklar*. Nobl Yayıncılık.

Çeber, B. (2024). *Yapay Zekâ Etiği ve İletişim: Sorunlar, Sınırlar ve Zorluklar*. Nobel Yayıncılık.

Coşkuner, A. (2023). Sinemanın Denetimsiz Teknolojiyle Sınavı: Yapay Zeka'nın Film Endüstrisine Etkisi. *Türkiye Film Araştırmaları Dergisi*, *3*(1), 32–47.

Frías, C. L. (2024). The Paradox of Artificial Intelligence in Cinema. *Cultura Digital*, *2*, 5–25.

Oğuzcan, D. (2025). *Metamodern Sinema: Dijitalleşme, Sanal Gerçeklik, Metaverse ve Yapay Zeka Ekseninde Dönüşen Sinema*. Eğitim Yayınevi.

Pradeep, A., Satmuratov, A., Yeshbayev, I., Khasan, O., Iqboljon, M., & Daniyor, A. (2023, August). The Significance of Artificial Intelligence in Contemporary Cinema. *Second International Conference on Trends in Electrical, Electronics, and Computer Engineering*, 111-116.

Türten, B. (2024). Yapay Zekâ ve Sinema: Film Yapımında Olanaklar ve Fırsatlar. *Anadolu ve Balkan Araştırmaları Dergisi*, *7*(14), 399–425.

KEY TERMS AND DEFINITIONS

Artificial Intelligence: Artificial intelligence (AI) refers to computer systems that mimic human-like thinking and learning abilities. It automates processes such as data analysis, pattern recognition, and decision-making. It encompasses subfields such as machine learning and deep learning. Today, it is used in numerous sectors including healthcare, finance, art, media, and defense.

Content Creation in Public Relations: Content creation in public relations is the strategic process of producing messages to ensure effective and continuous communication between an organization and its target audience. These contents can take various formats such as press releases, blog posts, social media updates, videos, or event texts. The goal is to strengthen the organization's image, build trust, and inform the public. The content should be planned to capture the target audience's attention, be up-to-date, and reflect the unique identity of the organization. Successful content production directly enhances the effectiveness of public relations campaigns.

Creativity in Advertising: Creativity in advertising is the process of developing original and striking ideas to influence the target audience. It allows messages to be delivered in unconventional ways and establishes an emotional connection between the brand and the consumer. It is also one of the most powerful tools for standing out in a competitive environment.

Deep Learning: Deep learning is an advanced form of machine learning, which is a subfield of artificial intelligence. It operates through artificial neural networks that mimic the human brain's neural structures. It excels in learning and analyzing complex patterns, especially with large datasets. It achieves high success in areas such as image recognition, voice commands, and natural language processing. It is utilized in a wide range of technologies, from autonomous vehicles to medical diagnostic systems.

Digital Cinema: Digital cinema refers to a form of filmmaking in which movies are produced, distributed, and exhibited using digital technologies instead of analog film stock. All stages—from shooting and editing to sound design and screening—use digital tools. Instead of film reels, digital files are used via hard drives, memory cards, or the internet. It offers advantages such as high resolution, lower costs, and easier distribution. Visual effects, color grading, and post-production processes can be handled more flexibly in digital environments. This enables opportunities for independent filmmakers and creates new possibilities for cinematic language and aesthetics.

Production: Virtual production is a filmmaking method that combines physical and digital elements using real-time computer graphics and green screen technologies. Using LED walls and game engines, realistic environments can be simulated. Virtual backgrounds synchronized with camera movements allow directors and actors to visualize the scene on set. It provides more flexible, faster, and cost-effective solutions compared to traditional production. It is widely used in science fiction, fantasy, and commercial films. It has gained even more importance with the rise of remote filming and hybrid sets following the pandemic.

Visual Effects: Visual effects (VFX) refer to the digital creation of scenes in film or video that are difficult or impossible to capture in live-action. These effects, generated in a computer environment, are integrated with real footage to create a seamless scene. Elements like explosions, creatures, natural phenomena, or fantastical settings are brought to life this way. Techniques such as 3D modeling, animation, compositing, and motion tracking are used. VFX is widely applied in cinema, television, advertising, and the gaming industries.

Chapter 4

Deepfake in Visual Storytelling and Cinema: New Horizons in Digital Aesthetics

Alper Erçetingöz
https://orcid.org/0000-0002-9168-5740
Aydın Adnan Menderes University, Turkey

Taner Kızılhan
https://orcid.org/0000-0002-3501-415X
Aydın Adnan Menderes University, Turkey

ABSTRACT

This chapter explores the impact of deepfake technology on cinema and visual storytelling, focusing on its aesthetic, ethical, and theoretical dimensions. Once linked to digital deception, deepfakes now serve as creative tools in art, education, and media. Yet, they also raise concerns about visual trust, authenticity, and identity manipulation. By redefining concepts like performance, originality, and spectatorship, deepfakes enable the digital resurrection of actors, scene recreation, and simulated narratives. Through notions like digital twins and algorithmic acting, cinema becomes a site of epistemological production. The chapter draws on theories from Benjamin, Baudrillard, Deleuze, and Rancière to argue that deepfake aesthetics signal a paradigm shift—cinema is no longer just about telling stories but about engineering new realities.

INTRODUCTION

This chapter offers a critical theoretical examination of the transformative impact of deepfake technologies on visual storytelling, with a particular emphasis

DOI: 10.4018/979-8-3373-6970-9.ch004

© 2026, IGI Global Scientific Publishing. Copying or distributing in print or electronic forms without written permission of IGI Global Scientific Publishing is prohibited. Use of this chapter to generative artificial intelligence (AI) technologies is expressly prohibited. The publisher reserves all rights to license its use for generative AI training and machine learning model development.

on the aesthetic, ethical, and epistemological shifts introduced by algorithmically generated imagery. Through the analysis of representative examples, it demonstrates that these technologies expand creative possibilities while also presenting structural risks. When considered within the context of the post-truth era, deepfake technologies have given rise to intense debates in contemporary digital culture concerning authenticity, the boundaries of representation, and the legitimacy of visual media. Their growing influence across cinema and other visual narrative forms is reshaping production processes and altering how narratives are constructed, perceived, and experienced by audiences.

Defined simply, a deepfake is a video, image, or audio recording that appears real but has been artificially manipulated using machine learning techniques. Applications such as AI-powered face replacement, motion capture, and virtual character creation are transforming visual storytelling and film production. With the rise of generative AI models, the use of deepfake technologies has become increasingly widespread. As many observers have noted, these technologies have introduced a new aesthetic paradigm and production logic, altering the very foundations of cinematic design.

Artificial intelligence and deepfake technologies are not merely visual effects tools; they are reshaping the role of visual design in cinema, leading to a new aesthetic sensibility. These developments are changing not only the production process but also the audience's perception and cinema's narrative power. Artificially generated characters now make it possible to reconstruct the past and create alternative historical narratives, further blurring the line between reality and fiction. To ensure that the industry is not adversely affected by the risks associated with these transformations, it is crucial to establish new aesthetic codes, expressive forms, and ethical standards in the field of cinematic design.

The new horizons opened by deepfake technologies, along with the risks they introduce, reflect a complex transformation process that continues to be debated from both artistic and ethical perspectives.

From this perspective, the present study aims to critically examine the transformative impact of deepfake technologies on cinema and visual storytelling by exploring their aesthetic, ethical and epistemological implications. Rather than focusing on a single case, the analysis is grounded in theoretical frameworks drawn from media theory, digital aesthetics, and posthuman philosophy, supported by a comprehensive review and critical evaluation of the relevant literature. By engaging with concepts such as Baudrillard's simulation, Deleuze's time-image, and Benjamin's aura, the study situates deepfake technologies within broader debates on authenticity, representation, and the algorithmic reconstruction of reality. In this paradigm, deepfake cinema is regarded not merely as a technological innovation, but as a cultural and ontological rupture that redefines the relationship between the image, truth, and the spectator. In doing so, it seeks to provide the reader with a comprehensive theoretical perspective on both the opportunities and the threats posed by deepfake technologies in the context of contemporary visual culture.

DEEPFAKE: DEFINITION SCOPE AND CONCEPTUAL FOUNDATIONS

Definition and Scope

It seems important to first touch upon the definition of the deepfake concept, its etymological roots and scope, to render the subject more intelligible. In the contemporary era, characterized by the expeditious generation, duplication and dissemination of media content, the way reality is perceived has undergone a profound metamorphosis in the wake of artificial intelligence. This paradigm shift has engendered a plethora of novel difficulties and challenges for the general populace, including the capacity to discern between reality and its simulacrum. The advent of deepfake technologies and culture has had a profound impact on the pervasive emergence of these difficulties. This technology has significantly augmented the ease with which synthetic visual and audio content can be produced, encompassing not only human subjects but also animals, machines, and inanimate objects (eSafety, 2022, p.1). The advent of artificial intelligence that can be defined as the ability to think like humans, to perceive data, to make rational decisions based on that data, and to act accordingly (Ermeydan & Etlioğlu Erçetingöz, 2024, s. 1420) has rendered it impossible to distinguish between images and sounds that are produced by the naked eye, thus challenging the conventional boundaries between reality and fiction. In this context, the concept of "deepfake" can be defined as "the artificial manipulation of faces or voices in photos or videos to generate new, synthetic outputs" (Belada, 2024, p.323).

Etymologically, the term "Deep", which forms the concept, is derived from the term "Deep Learning" and emphasizes the use of deep neural networks and the learning process of artificial intelligence. As Holdsworth and Scappichio (2024) explain, 'deep learning is a subset of machine learning that uses multilayered neural networks, called deep neural networks, to simulate the complex decision-making power of the human brain'. The success of this approach is dependent upon the availability of large quantities of data. The following logic underpins the operation of deepfakes: "In order to generate convincing content, the majority of contemporary deepfake technologies necessitate substantial quantities of authentic data (e.g. images, footage or sound recordings). However, it should be noted that technical capability is advancing at a rapid pace, with the result that in the near future only a small number of original files will be required to create a deepfake" (eSafety, 2022, p.1). It is therefore evident that the word "deep" is of significant importance in this context. The term 'fake', as employed in this context, underscores the contrived character of the content produced by means of this technology.

The term "Deep" is of a semantic nature and is of central importance in the conceptualisation of the phenomenon. In this sense, "Deepfake" technology has become one of the most powerful tools of the post-truth era. The term "post-truth" is defined as "relating to situations in which people respond with emotions and beliefs rather than facts" (Oxford Learner's Dictionaries, 2025). The advent of deepfake content has been a significant catalyst in this trend, fundamentally eroding trust in information by presenting fabricated information as authentic. As the distinction between reality and fiction becomes increasingly indistinct, the term "Deepfakes" is employed not solely to denote visual manipulation, but also to signify a crisis of reality. As Karnouskos (2020, p. 1) asserts, "The application of sophisticated capabilities of deep learning allows for the creation or alteration of images, text and voices in a highly realistic manner." In essence, the capacity of deepfake technology is such that it can substitute or imitate a person's face, voice or movements with data belonging to another individual. Consequently, even content that is deemed unreal can be presented to an audience as if it were authentic. The situation is accompanied by a multitude of threats, risks and negatives, as will be discussed in the following section.

The term 'Deep Learning' is employed to emphasize the utilization of deep neural networks and the learning process of artificial intelligence. As Holdsworth and Scappichio (2024) explain, 'deep learning is a subset of machine learning that uses multilayered neural networks, called deep neural networks, to simulate the complex decision-making power of the human brain'. The success of this approach is dependent upon the availability of large quantities of data. The following logic underpins the operation of deepfakes: "In order to generate convincing content, the majority of contemporary deepfake technologies necessitate substantial quantities of authentic data (e.g. images, footage or sound recordings). However, it should be noted that technical capability is advancing at a rapid pace, with the result that in the near future only a small number of original files will be required to create a deepfake" (eSafety, 2022, p.1). It is therefore evident that the word "deep" is a fundamental component of the concept under discussion. The employment of the term 'fake' in the concept is intended to underscore the contrived nature of the concept itself.

Digital Reality Crisis: Risks and Threats of Deepfake Technology

The application of deepfake technologies invariably gives rise to a multitude of risks, threats and problems. As previously discussed, the notion that reality can be readily modified and replicated through digital technologies has precipitated a crisis within society.

It is evident that a significant proportion of content created with the assistance of deepfake technology is of a detrimental and malicious nature. For instance, research undertaken by DeeptraceLabs in 2022 revealed that a significant proportion of content created with the use of deepfake technologies is of a pornographic nature. Indeed, the same study found that "96% of the videos contain fake pornographic content with celebrities, attracting more than 134 million views (Misirlis & Munawar, 2023, p. 26). These videos and audio recordings, which appear to be authentic but are in fact fabricated, are frequently accepted and disseminated by users. Nevertheless, there is a possibility that the reputation of the targeted individuals may be compromised. It is important to note that such attacks can be directed not only at public figures, such as celebrities and politicians, but also at ordinary individuals. The threats posed by deepfake technologies are not limited to this type of content. Furthermore, the damage caused by content produced with this technology can often reach irreversible levels. For instance, as stated by Chen and Magramo (2024), "in February 2024, an employee of a multinational financial company in China was defrauded after a video conference meeting with the company's chief financial officer and other employees, after making a $25 million transaction". It was not evident to him that each of the individuals with whom he was convening in order to attend the aforementioned meeting had in fact been replicated as a result of the use of deepfake technology, with the result that they were exact replicas of the company's employees.

It is evident that the repercussions of technologies produced with deepfake extend to various domains, including the infringement of privacy and the potential for political manipulation. Firstly, within the context of political manipulation, it has been demonstrated that disinformation, in the form of videos, images or audio recordings, is capable of influencing public opinion by creating the impression that leaders have made statements which they in fact did not make, or have committed actions which they did not in fact perform. For instance, during the Russia-Ukraine war, a deepfake video was released in which Ukrainian President Volodymyr Zelenskiy was shown instructing his army to surrender. As Holroyd and Olorunselu (2022) state, one iteration of this "deepfake" was viewed more than 120,000 times on the social media platform Twitter. The dissemination of such content has the potential to erode public confidence in leaders, to influence public opinion, and to impact the integrity of electoral processes. As evidenced by the case of Zelensky, they have the capacity to initiate or conclude a war. While social media manipulation is not a new phenomenon, the emergence of deepfakes has substantially intensified the scale and impact of this threat. "Earlier forms of false content, such as 'cheapfakes,' were more reputable due to their low quality, limiting their adverse effects on democratic processes" (Kilavuz, 2024, p. 8). Such political deepfakes can undermine trust in democratic institutions and deepen polarization within society.

Despite the potential for deepfake technologies to engender a multitude of negatives and risks, there is an absence of comprehensive legal regulations that can effectively address these concerns, and these regulations have yet to be widely adopted across many countries. This absence of legislation engenders uncertainty regarding the categorization of crimes perpetrated through deepfakes, thereby complicating the delineation of the elements constituting these criminal acts. In many cases, victims are compelled to pursue recourse through the established legal framework, encompassing provisions such as defamation, fraud, and violations of privacy, among others. Conversely, the utilization of digital media content as evidence within judicial proceedings has also become increasingly intricate. It is challenging to ascertain the authenticity of video and audio recordings presented in court, which consequently impedes the ability to reach a just decision during the judicial process.

Consequently, the credibility of online content is significantly compromised. As the veracity of visual and audio content becomes increasingly uncertain, individuals are compelled to interrogate the authenticity of the videos or audio recordings to which they are exposed, thereby engendering an overarching atmosphere of distrust on media platforms. This distrust is not only directed towards the content itself, but also towards the individuals and institutions that disseminate it, and even the media as an institution. Consequently, the social circulation of information and digital interaction processes are disrupted, and the healthy functioning of the digital public is seriously threatened.

The question therefore arises as to whether the use of deepfake technologies is invariably detrimental and poses a significant risk. It is imperative to comprehend the fundamental question in order to gain a comprehensive understanding of the technology in question. Furthermore, addressing the ensuing discourse from a more expansive standpoint is contingent upon this fundamental grasp of the technology.

Beyond the Illusion: Exploring the Creative Potential of Deepfake Technology

Despite the tendency to associate deepfake content with disinformation, privacy violations, and trust crises, it can also facilitate the development of creative and innovative applications in areas such as cinema, art, education, and digital communication. Consequently, this technology is not merely a threat, but has the potential to function as a tool that can engender social benefit when employed responsibly and transparently. The utilization of deepfakes in entertainment, education, medicine and other domains is conducive to numerous positive applications, particularly in the fields of modelling and predicting behavior (eSafety, 2022, p.1).

This technology offers unique opportunities in areas such as overcoming language barriers. The employment of artificial intelligence (AI)-driven lip-syncing and voice transformation techniques has enabled the realistic depiction of individuals speaking in languages other than their own. For instance, in a 2019 awareness campaign, David Beckham was digitally recreated with his original voice and face to deliver messages in nine different languages (Oakes, 2019). The objective is to facilitate the seamless adaptation of content to multilingual audiences residing in diverse cultural contexts and utilizing a variety of languages, thereby aiming to dismantle language barriers. In the context of news media, the employment of virtual news anchors, created with artificial intelligence, in digital news presentations is a noteworthy development. For instance, in China, in 2018, Xinhua, the state news agency, unveiled Qiu Hao, a digital news presenter, who promised to bring viewers the news "24 hours a day, 365 days a year" (Milmo & Hawkins, 2024). These applications have been demonstrated to facilitate global communication, thereby enabling media content to reach a much wider audience.

Another area in which deepfake technologies are being used is in the sphere of education and associated cultural activities, such as those taking place in museums. In these areas, the potential of deepfake technology to play a pioneering role in the presentation of historical and cultural content is significant. The advent of digital reconstructions of historical figures has engendered a novel opportunity for students and museum visitors to engage with significant figures from the past in a manner that is akin to being in physical proximity to them. This development has the potential to profoundly impact the realm of digital storytelling and the experience it offers. In this context, a notable example is the Salvador Dalí Museum in the United States. In the relevant museum, visitors are greeted by a life-size avatar of the renowned artist Salvador Dalí, animated by artificial intelligence, which recounts the artist's life story (The Dali, 2025). The incorporation of audiovisual animations in museum exhibitions has been demonstrated to enhance interactivity and engender a memorable experience for visitors. When evaluated within the context of educational environments, the integration of audiovisual educational materials augmented with deepfakes has been demonstrated to enhance the quality of education by providing a concrete representation of abstract concepts. Indeed, during the pandemic period, an academician who taught online courses by projecting themselves as an anime-style digital character significantly increased students' attention and participation (Shen, 2020).

In the domain of art and creative narrative forms, the advent of deepfake technologies has engendered a paradigm shift, paving the way for novel forms of expression by facilitating the emergence of experimental art practices. A significant number of innovative art projects are employing this technology to obfuscate the line between reality and fiction, thereby offering the audience extraordinary experiences. To illustrate this point, consider the work of German-Iraqi artist Nora Al-Badri, who employed deepfake techniques to reinterpret historical artefacts exhibited in museums in the digital age. In her project entitled Babylonian Vision, she produced 200 imaginary objects inspired by ancient Mesopotamian artefacts using GAN-based machine learning methods with the aim of reviving cultural heritage in a digital environment (Al-Badri, 2023). In the context of digital performances, stage artists have the opportunity to adopt multiple characters in a single show by using deepfake-supported avatars. Using avatar representations, artists are able to create a virtual body of themselves or a fictional character, subsequently using this as the focal point of a narrative. It is evident that, in this manner, characters that are not physically present are rendered animate in a manner that approximates reality, thereby affording creative narratives novel manifestations.

Deepfake technology is evolving into a potent medium for creative expression, transcending its initial application as a mere instrument of imitation or deception within the artistic domain. Consequently, the subsequent sections of this study will address the application of deepfake technology within the domain of cinema, which is recognized as one of the most significant forms of visual narrative and storytelling. These sections will also explore the impact of deepfake technologies on these areas.

SIMULATED REALITIES

The Transformative Power of Deepfake Technology in Visual Storytelling

In the digital age, storytelling takes place not only through traditional text or video, but also through new forms of media powered by artificial intelligence. Deepfake technology adds a new dimension to digital visual storytelling, enabling the creation of scenes and characters that were previously impossible. For example, deepfake has made it possible to add modern actors to a classic film scene, or to create an alternate history by bringing together people who have never met. An example of the this is the resurrection of the late actress Carry Fisher as Princess Lea in *Star Wars: Rogue One* after her death, thanks to deepfake technology (Black & Fullerton, 2020). As another example, in web series such as Sassy Justice, created by the creators of *South Park*, sketches featuring a satirical news anchor conducting "interviews" with various world leaders (e.g. Facebook CEO Mark Zuckerberg) are entirely composed of deepfake characters. Such examples show that deepfake technologies can be a creative tool in entertainment and artistic storytelling. Indeed, more and more examples are appearing every day, and as can be seen from these examples, deepfake technologies can push the boundaries of visual storytelling and offer viewers unique and immersive experiences.

However, the use of deepfakes in digital visual narratives should also be evaluated with a critical eye. The fact that “anything is possible” thanks to technology can blur the line between reality and fiction, thus damaging the viewer's sense of truth. The historical reputation of visual media was built on the notion that “pictures don't lie”. A photograph or video was assumed to be direct evidence of an event that had actually taken place. However, with the advent of deepfake technology, the adage “seeing is believing” is beginning to lose its validity. This situation lies at the heart of the authenticity crisis. The proliferation of artificially produced images blurs the concept of reality conveyed by the media. Baudrillard's theory of simulation provides an important theoretical framework for understanding this phenomenon. Baudrillard (1994) argues that in modern society images have replaced reality, creating a hyperreality, and simulations have overtaken truth. According to him, truth itself has now disappeared, replaced by a continuous flow of simulations that conceal the fact that there is no truth at all. Deepfakes have precisely the simulacrum quality that Baudrillard describes: copies that imitate reality but have no original (Baudrillard, 1994). In conclusion, even a completely fictional deepfake video can be mistaken by viewers for the real thing, or conversely, real footage can be suspected of being manipulated. This calls into question the reliability and documentary value of visual narratives.

In this context, it would be appropriate to mention how deepfake technology can be used in documentary and digital archive projects, which are other types of visual narrative. One of the most notable uses of deepfake technology is the visual recreation of historical events and people. Documentary filmmakers and digital archive projects have begun to use deepfakes to recreate scenes that were not recorded in the past, or to 'resurrect' historical figures and make them speak. In this context, examples of what might be called historical simulations have emerged. The *In Event of Moon Disaster* project carried out by MIT in 2020 is an important example in this respect. In this project, the speech that US President Richard Nixon would have made if the moon landing had failed in 1969 was recorded by using artificial intelligence to animate Nixon's face and voice, and an “alternative history” scenario was visually presented (MIT Open Learning, 2020). The resulting seven-minute video is highly convincing and provides a striking example of how powerful deepfake technology can be. This type of simulation pushes the boundaries of digital storytelling while reintroducing the concepts of truth and ethics into documentary filmmaking. The aim of the *In Event of Moon Disaster* project is precisely to stimulate this debate: to approach images with skepticism and to increase media literacy in the age of deepfakes.

The use of deepfakes in documentary is not only used to recreate 'unlived' scenarios, but also to recreate moments that occurred but were not recorded, or to give voice to historical figures. For example, "the 2020 documentary *Welcome To Chechnya*, which depicts the human rights crisis of the LGBTQ+ community in Russia, used technology to protect the identities of the oppressed individuals in the film, according to Dazed" (Recker, 2022). In this way, real people were protected while their stories were conveyed to the audience. This creative method has been praised in documentary film as both an ethical solution (protecting privacy) and a narrative tool (allowing the viewer to empathize with a natural facial expression rather than distracting mosaic censorship).

On the other hand, the re-voicing of historical figures using deepfake techniques is also a controversial topic on the agenda. In the documentary *Roadrunner* (2021), which recounts the life of Anthony Bourdain, excerpts from the late celebrity chef's own emails were read by Bourdain's voice, created using artificial intelligence. "Although Neville described his use of AI technology as a "modern storytelling technique", critics on social media expressed concern about the unannounced use of a "deepfake" voice to speak sentences that Bourdain never spoke" (Yang, 2021). Despite the emotional impact of a historical figure speaking with a deepfake, Bourdain's example has sparked debates about consent and authenticity. These interventions also carry the risk of overstepping the boundaries of historical reality and producing a kind of "historical fiction". A critical assessment suggests that while the use of deepfakes in documentary and archival studies offers great narrative potential, this potential should be carefully managed within a framework of ethical and truthful principles.

Another area where the creative impact of deepfake technologies is being felt strongly is in social media and the digital identities created through social media. With deepfakes, any user's face can be adapted to another body or scene, and their voice can be imitated, making online identity virtually plastic. In fact, virtual influencers created entirely with artificial intelligence can now reach millions of followers. For example, "fictional characters like Miquela Sousa, who has 2.5 million followers on Instagram, or Lu do Magalu, a Brazilian synthetic influencer who has a staggering 7.1 million Instagram followers and promotes products from mobile phones to makeup, have had a say in fashion and pop culture narratives despite not being real" (Pandey, 2024). These AI influencers demonstrate that young audiences may be less likely to seek out a human face in content, and the distinction between the real and the artificial may become less important. While the proliferation of this technology in social media concretizes the concept of fluid identity, it also magnifies the problem of content verification and trust. As a result, deepfake applications both expand and complicate the concept of identity and representation in social media narratives, making it critical for users and platforms to establish ethical principles and develop media literacy among their audiences.

Another phenomenon related to these fluid representations of identity in social media are avatar representations and personal narratives realized through these avatar representations. It has become common practice for individuals to tell their own life stories or fictional stories on digital platforms. Deepfake technology offers a new way to enrich these personal digital narratives: digital avatars. An avatar is a virtual character that represents the user (D-ID, 2024). Thanks to deepfakes, avatars can now be given a real face and voice, bringing the narrator closer to the audience. People can also give their own faces to AI, create a talking avatar and tell their stories through that avatar. In this way, anonymity can be maintained and the effect of face-to-face storytelling can be captured. "Today, various online tools and applications allow individuals to create special artificial avatars with a few photos or short video recordings and make them talk" (Miller, 2024). As this technology matures, people will be able to create content on their blogs or vlogs by featuring virtual twins of themselves rather than their real selves.

The use of deepfake avatars in personal digital narratives such as these increases the creative control and expressiveness of the narrator, while providing a more immersive experience for the viewer. Of course, ethical and privacy issues should not be ignored: Impersonating a person as an avatar without their permission, or creating avatars of deceased relatives, can cause emotional damage. Therefore, the use of deepfake avatars, even in personal stories, should be done within a framework of consent and respect, and manipulation beyond the purpose of the narrative should not be resorted to.

In conclusion, as algorithms evolve and computing power increases, almost any user can create convincing media content with the help of a computer that is difficult to distinguish from reality. In this sense, deepfake technology is emerging as a two-way tool with great potential and transformative impact on visual storytelling in the digital age. In the context of visual art and visual storytelling, the creative potential of deepfake technology in terms of narrative potential is quite high. For all the dangers it poses, deepfake technology is creating a new narrative language for the first time in history, producing scenes that are disconnected from reality but as striking as the real thing; viewers can see a dead artist speak again and witness events that never happened. The place of deepfake technology in visual storytelling will depend on the intentions of those using it and on social norms. If the creative industries, educational institutions and media professionals combine this tool with responsible innovation, it will be possible to tell more immersive and powerful stories with deepfakes.

Among all these narrative forms, cinema stands out as the visual narrative form that has the potential to be most affected by this situation due to its technical and creative nature.

A New Cinema or a New Reality: Cinema's New Reality Crisis

The digital transformation of the 21st century has fundamentally changed the production and consumption practices of cinema. One of the most striking examples of this transformation is AI-powered deepfake technology. Thanks to this technology, "artificial actors," once found only in science fiction texts, have become part of the film industry and our perception of visual reality. Deepfake is a reproduction tool that can combine a human face, voice, and facial expressions with another face using algorithms to present a performance that never actually existed with a convincing level of realism. The use of this technology in cinema has reignited discussions about fundamental cinematic concepts such as traditional acting, representation, identity, and truth.

For example, in Martin Scorsese's *The Irishman* (2019), Robert De Niro's digitally rejuvenated face created an "uncanny valley"[1] effect in viewers; the actor's familiar yet unsettling artificial expressions raised the question, "Is the person in front of us really the actor himself, or just an image made up of data?"[2] (Okeke et al., 2024, pp. 46-49). Similarly, examples such as the digital resurrection of a deceased actor in the *Star Wars* series or the AI-driven de-aging of Harrison Ford in *Indiana Jones and the Dial of Destiny* (2023) demonstrate that this technology has become widespread across the industry and has deepened ethical and artistic debates, going beyond being merely an aesthetic choice (The Guardian, 2023; Yamazaki, 2024).

The emergence of deepfake technology in cinema can be interpreted as a development that blurs the boundaries between fiction and reality, necessitating a reexamination of fundamental issues in film theory. In this context, the aim of this study is to evaluate the aforementioned technological transformation not merely as a technical advancement, but as a disruptive force that poses both a threat and an opportunity for the fundamental elements of the art of cinema. The study will address questions such as how deepfake technology is transforming cinema aesthetics; how the concept of artificial acting is redefining the art of acting; how the introduction of artificial characters is determining the ethical boundaries of representation; and to what extent viewers now believe what they see. These questions are as meaningful for cinema as they are for digital culture, as the images we watch are increasingly becoming algorithmically generated simulated realities. Indeed, in 2023, Hollywood actors went on strike against the unauthorized use of their digital copies and artificial performances, highlighting the urgency of the practical and ethical consequences of this transformation (Yamazaki, 2024). Therefore, this study aims to go beyond contributing to the aesthetic history of cinema and offer a critical perspective on the future of cinema.

Digital Aesthetics in Cinema and "Machine Vision"

Digital transformation has reshaped production practices in cinema, as well as the modes of perception and the meaning of the represented. New AI-powered cinema tools are producing a new type of vision called "machine vision,"[3] which transcends traditional aesthetic norms. Machine vision refers to the ability of computers or algorithms to visually "read," analyze, and make decisions about the world through cameras, sensors, and artificial intelligence systems. These processes include applications such as facial recognition, object classification, and motion tracking. According to Chávez Heras, this concept is as much an aesthetic and epistemological issue as it is a technological one (2024, p. 5). The concept of machine vision questions how machines 'see' the world, and even how they present the world to us humans. In this sense, it creates a new form of visual experience in cinema beyond narrative. In particular, the integration of surveillance, simulation, artificial intelligence, and data-driven imaging techniques into cinema redefines the relationship between the viewer and the image. In this context, machine vision signifies a shift from the traditional human-centered gaze to a computational and algorithmic gaze. As Chávez Heras points out, this new perspective has the potential to go beyond representing human experience and take the place of humans themselves (2024, pp. 1-22). Cinema is no longer solely an art form created by humans; it is becoming an epistemic plane where algorithmic processes simultaneously occupy the roles of both producer and spectator. The films we watch consist not of images in the traditional sense, but of data. Scenes and frames are composed of computable meta-data. This data-driven structure is fundamentally transforming cinematic aesthetic values. Today, the value of an image is determined as much by how it is processed as by its content. Indeed, in today's films, many images are filtered, colored, encoded, and restructured by algorithms before reaching the audience. What emerges is not an image in the classical sense, but a visual proposition created by a machine. This proposition often appeals to the viewer's cognitive responses rather than traditional aesthetic tastes. Deepfake technology is one of the extreme examples of this data-aesthetic regime. For while it mimics the human image, it also reveals the simulacral reality of machine vision. Thus, the viewer is not merely watching a scene but is also exposed to how a machine "sees." The scene is no longer constructed from the perspective of a subject but as the product of a sequence of code.

At this point, a fundamental question arises: If a scene appears to be real, does it matter that it is not? The rupture created by deepfake cinema becomes clear here. While traditional cinema relies on the viewer's desire for "willing suspension of disbelief," deepfake technology is designed to be so believable that it renders this desire unnecessary. The image produced is created with the explicit aim of being convincing from the very beginning. Deepfake technology undermines fictional productions and also shakes the truth claim of documentary cinema. For instance, making a historical figure say things they never actually said through deepfake technology destabilizes the existential foundation of the documentary film and undermines its ethics of representation (Lees, 2024). Indeed, David France's documentary *Welcome to Chechnya* (2020) used deepfake face-swapping technology to conceal the identities of real people under threat. This allowed the faces of LGBT activists to be digitally replaced with those of other people for their protection. However, this creative solution adds a fictional layer to the documentary narrative, opening up a debate about the documentary's relationship with reality (Rothkopf, 2020). This example demonstrates that even when used to protect the truth, deepfake technology can challenge the "image=reality" equation of documentary cinema and give rise to new ethical dilemmas in the representation of reality.

Artificial Acting and the Limits of Representation

In traditional cinema, acting is an art form based on physical performance, bodily memory, inner motivations, and emotional fluctuations. However, with AI-supported production methods, this definition has begun to change radically. Today, it is no longer necessary for a character to be physically present on set in order to exist within a scene. Applications such as digital twins created through deepfake technologies, which are used to resurrect deceased actors or to animate individuals who never actually existed, are indicators of an aesthetic, ethical, and ontological transformation that challenges the very nature of representation.

Although it may initially appear as a technical convenience, the concept of artificial acting, which raises the question "do we still need actors?", also brings with it deeper inquiries into the very essence of art. The emergence of a "manufactured" acting performance blurs the lines between genuine acting and the imitation of reality, thereby necessitating a reevaluation of the relationship between performance and truth. If we update Gilles Deleuze's concept of "time-image" in his film theory, we now have an "algorithm-image."[4] Cinema is based on fluid data rather than fluid time. In this context, Ari Folman's film *The Congress* (2013) is significant in that it foreshadows a possible dystopian future. In the film, Robin Wright sells all rights to her digital self to a studio, becoming her own "digital twin." As a result, the actor is no longer defined by their physical presence but exists as a licensed digital object open to infinite reproduction. This marks the surrender of the "story of the face"—one of the cornerstones of cinematic history—to an algorithmic artificiality.

In cinema, the phenomenon of representation is a matter of the image, but at the same time, it is also an ethical relation. Artificially recreating a character or historical figure raises the question of "who has the right to tell whose story?" As Dominic Lees emphasizes in his analysis of documentary cinema, the claim of deepfake technology to represent reality carries the risk of ethical manipulation (2024, pp. 109-110). For example, digitally bringing a person who lived in the past onto the screen in a documentary or having them speak with an artificial voice can undermine the viewer's sense of trust and the dignity of the person being represented. Especially in the narration of a historical trauma, such an intervention can completely erase the ethical distance between reality and fiction.

On the other hand, the concept of artificial acting has also been transformed into concrete initiatives in the film industry. In 2019, a production company announced that it would feature the late actor James Dean in a new film using digital effects and existing footage (the *Finding Jack* project), sparking a heated debate in the industry (Saad, 2019). Many actors and directors have criticized this initiative, arguing that using an actor's digital likeness on the big screen without their consent constitutes an excessive intervention. Some even argued that such artificial acting applications would harm the creative essence of cinema and violate ethical values (Saad, 2019; Pavis, 2021). Today, even active actors in Hollywood are seeking to protect their rights out of concern that their digital twins could be used without permission. Indeed, Tom Hanks publicly revealed that his face had been placed in an advertisement using deepfake technology without his consent, issuing a warning against such violations (The Guardian, 2023). The real-world reflections of the phenomenon of artificial acting clearly demonstrate how deepfake technology can challenge the creative and ethical paradigms of cinema.

Identity, Memory, and Digital Twins in Cinema

One of the most striking questions raised by AI-assisted cinematic practices is this: Who does the self in the image belong to? The fact that the entity we refer to as "I" in cinema is now treated as a digital construct derived solely from datasets necessitates a rethinking of the question of identity. As Rosi Braidotti (2013) describes in her concept of the "posthuman subjectivity," such selves are no longer conscious entities experiencing the world but rather ontological codes reduced to data. The theme of identity has been at the center of many powerful narratives in cinema history, ranging from immigration to gender, class, and ethnicity. The theory of performative identity argues that identity is constructed through social practices and forms of representation (Butler, 1990). However, in the digital age, identity is increasingly shifting from performance to algorithm-based profiling. As Liz W. Faber emphasizes in her work *Robot Suicide*, the suicidal behavior of artificial intelligence-generated characters demonstrates that they are designed as carriers of ethical and psychological identity (2023, p. 71). In this context, cinema is now more about data-driven profiling than personality[5]. As conceptualized by Shoshana Zuboff (2019), the "extraction of behavioral surplus" means that the existence of a character no longer depends on an actor but on sufficient data. Lev Manovich (2001)'s concepts of "database cinema" and "algorithmic media" explain the technical dimension of this transformation: The character is no longer a dramatic entity but a sequence of images composed of combinations of data sets. This means that identity ceases to be an experienced subject and becomes an object that is analyzed and controlled.

Indeed, in many major film productions today, digital scans of lead actors are made to create a "digital twin" archive. Film studios record actors' facial and body data and store them digitally, enabling the actor's digital likeness to be used in stunt scenes, aging or de-aging effects, or future productions (Şeylan, 2023, p. 1456). This application normalizes the data-based reproduction of an actor's image, thereby separating film characters from physical reality.

Characters and scenes created using digital technologies transform the concept of memory by presenting experiences that never happened in the past as if they did. For example, the use of Mark Hamill's digital twin as the young Luke Skywalker from the 1980s in the *Star Wars* universe's *The Mandalorian* (2021) series is a striking example of presenting an unlived past as real, evoking a nostalgic effect in the viewer. This allows viewers to perceive scenes they have never experienced in their own lives as if they were part of their memories. The created emotional familiarity produces a false collective memory, thereby transforming cinema into an algorithmic tool that directs and shapes cultural memory. This example demonstrates that digital twin technologies can even construct concepts such as nostalgia and memory in popular culture through data. Ultimately, identity and memory have ceased to be characteristics of biological existence in cinema, becoming instead codable and manipulable data sets.

Ethical Dilemma: Representation, Copyright, and Authencity

Artificial intelligence and deepfake-supported new cinema create profound ethical dilemmas regarding the accuracy of representation (authenticity), artists' rights, and intellectual property. In cinema, an authentic performance has traditionally relied on the physical presence of an actor's body and voice in the moment. The slightest hesitation of an actor, or even the way they breathe, points to the authenticity of the performance. Today, however, it is possible to teach a facial expression or gesture to an AI through machine learning and reproduce the same emotion repeatedly. In this way, the distinction between lived experience and algorithmic imitation becomes increasingly blurred. For example, the character Samantha (voiced by

Scarlett Johansson) in Spike Jonze's *Her* (2013) is presented as an emotional subject. However, the audience is not actually connected to a human voice, but to a programmed simulation. At this point, the audience cannot tell whether the voice they hear represents real emotions or predetermined responses. As Liz W. Faber points out, today even sound itself can be treated as a pile of data and reproduced; therefore, sound is no longer an acoustic phenomenon but rather an artificial sign that contains social codes (2020, pp. 159-181).

With the rise of deepfake technology, there is a need to restructure intellectual property (copyright) rights in cinema. An actor's face, voice, facial expressions, and even posture must now become their property. In the digital age, an actor's digital image is just as valuable as their physical presence. However, the current legal system focuses on tangible products such as written texts or audio recordings, leaving it unclear whether a face or a glance falls under copyright protection. The issue of digitally replicating an actor's likeness gained concrete visibility in the film *Rogue One: A Star Wars Story* (2016), when the late actor Peter Cushing was brought back to life as a "digital twin" with the permission of his family. It is likely that in the near future, actors will need contracts specifying whether they consent to being digitally represented after their death. Indeed, in 2023, the Hollywood actors' union SAG-AFTRA[6], went on strike demanding that the use of digital twins and artificial performances not occur without permission and that fair compensation be provided to the rights holders. As a result of this strike, new contract provisions were accepted and implemented, including clauses requiring explicit consent for the use of actors' digital likenesses and additional compensation (Yamazaki, 2024). This marks a significant step forward for the industry in recognizing and controlling the rights to artificial performances.

The main issue here is not whether a person can be represented digitally after their death, but under what conditions, for what purpose, and within what moral framework they can be represented. Some recent studies highlighting the current legal vacuum emphasize that existing regulations are inadequate in the face of artificial performances and suggest that expanding the concept of "performer's rights" in this area could be effective in protecting actors' digital likenesses (Pavis, 2021). The fact that actors are now considered a licensable visual data set rather than an entity in digital production processes emphasizes that commercial logic takes precedence over the artistic creativity of the subject in cinema. Indeed, an increasing number of films are being written by artificial intelligence, actors are being digitally produced, and scenes are being designed using simulation technologies. This development signals a transformation in the artistic production process, shifting from human to code. Code not only replaces the artist but also eliminates their creative uncertainty. However, uncertainty is the source of creativity in art, while code is based on specific formulas. Nevertheless, as the productive capabilities of artificial intelligence increase, the role of the artist is also changing. Artists are no longer content creators, but rather content selectors, editors, and directors. This can be considered a paradigm shift in the history of cinema.

The Transformation of Narrative: Post-Truth Cinema

While the tension between reality and fiction was emphasized in postmodern narratives of the 20th century, this tension has been transferred to a completely different level in the post-truth environment of the 21st century. What is at stake now is not the representation of reality, but its direct production and replacement with fiction. Deepfake-supported cinema has become one of the sharpest narrative forms of the post-truth era. Post-truth, as defined by the Oxford Learner's Dictionaries (2025), refers to an era in which emotions and personal beliefs are more influential than objective facts. This definition directly influences the narrative dynamics of deepfake cinema. For this type of cinema does not seek to convince the audience of reality but rather to falsely reproduce a reality that the audience has already chosen to believe in. In this sense, making a historical figure speak digitally with words they never actually said can be seen as an aesthetic experiment and at the same time a political intervention. Such scenes blur the line between "what actually happened" and "what we want to happen." Thus, cinema ceases to be a medium of storytelling and turns into a machine that ideologically reconstructs reality. Today, many productions supported by digital platforms use technology to reshape the perception of truth. This situation weakens the ability of young viewers in particular to distinguish between reality and fiction. Deepfake cinema is also transforming the classical narrative structure. The narrative is moving away from its linear, chronological, and causality-based structure, taking on a pattern where repetitive motifs and artificial emotion triggers come to the fore. In this new aesthetic, images exist not so much to produce meaning as to produce impact (emotion). In this structure, where the meaning-content connection is weakened, pre-calculated montages and scene compositions are designed to trigger certain emotions in the viewer. Chávez Heras defines such structures as "micro affective resonances" (2024, p. 30). The resulting understanding of cinema validates Walter Benjamin's concept of the loss of "aura" in a completely different context. For the scene no longer carries the traces of a lived performance, but rather the emotional arithmetic of predefined data points. Indeed, an advanced artificial intelligence model introduced in 2024 was able to generate short video clips solely based on a written text. This suggests that cinematic narratives may be produced in the future without the need for human creativity, directly through algorithmic imagination (Yamazaki, 2024).

The impact of deepfake technology on documentary cinema is also noteworthy in this context. Documentary cinema has always claimed to represent reality. However, deepfake is fundamentally transforming this type of production. While documentaries once relied on reenactments or archival footage to support the truth, they can now present scenes that never actually occurred as if they were part of reality. When viewers cannot be certain that the person on screen is real, the documentary's evidence-based narrative loses its value. This goes beyond an aesthetic preference and becomes a democratic issue. For in an environment where truth cannot be represented, social decision-making processes also become susceptible to manipulation.

Audience and Artificial Aesthetic Sensitivity

In cinema, the act of "willing suspension of disbelief" has evolved into a new dimension in the age of deepfakes. Deepfake cinema does not require the audience to make a traditional effort to believe; rather, it claims to convince them that what they see is real. Instead of questioning the authenticity of the scenes they see, viewers are exposed to their impact. This weakens the ability to distinguish between reality and fiction. The viewing experience is reduced to reflexive emotional responses rather than conscious analysis. Especially scenes designed to target the audience's emotions, which are artificially produced and tailored to evoke specific feelings, immerse the viewer in an unprecedented automatic reaction process. The emotions triggered in these scenes do not stem from an original experience but from premodeled cognitive response templates. As Gillian Murphy and colleagues (2023) point out, today's audience responds not to visual reality, but to aesthetic possibility. For the audience, it is not so much whether a scene is real or not, but whether it feels real. However, the same study also revealed that a significant portion of the audience approaches the use of deepfake actors with caution. Participants emphasized that the use of artificially produced actors in cinema carries the potential to spread misinformation and the risk of creating false memories in people's minds. Therefore, while the audience may respond to scenes that feel real, they have clear concerns about the artificiality behind them.

At the same time, artificial intelligence functions as a system that analyzes the viewer's preferences and habits. On today's digital platforms, what content is presented to viewers is largely determined by past viewing data. This situation is shaking up classic cinema aesthetics. This is because it is no longer the viewer's subjective perception that determines the structure and flow of a film, but rather the objective data collected about them. While AI-supported cinema promises a personalized aesthetic experience, it can also create an "echo chamber" effect, trapping viewers in a cycle that reinforces their own worldview. As Belarusian technology critic Evgeny Morozov (2013) pointed out in his critique of "technological solutionism,"[7] algorithmic recommendation systems shape the viewing experience and, along with it, the architecture of perception. As a result, the viewer is directed toward a predetermined flow, independent of their choices.

In deepfake cinema, the audience is no longer a subject captivated by the narrative, but has become a consumer of images bombarded with stimuli. Images produced or manipulated by artificial intelligence appear one after another at a speed and intensity that disrupts the rhythm of classic cinema. The rapid succession of visually stunning scenes creates a viewing experience focused on instant gratification, overshadowing the nuances of traditional cinema. The importance of framing, lighting, or actor direction in a film is now overshadowed by the impact of the scene itself. The viewer is conditioned to react rather than establish a meaningful connection with the scene[8]. Thus, the process of perceiving cinema as an art form gives way to a regime of consumption as content.

CONCLUSION

Deepfake technology marks one of the most radical transformations in the history of cinema. This transformation can be seen as a technical evolution, but it can also be interpreted as an ontological, ethical, and aesthetic rupture. Cinema today is an art form that involves storytelling as well as the construction of reality. Reality itself is becoming a construct, a possibility, a pile of data presented to the audience. As seen in this study, deepfake technology is transforming many fundamental elements of cinema. Acting is now based on data sets rather than the physical presence of the body and voice. Representation is being redefined through synthetic production and copyright rather than originality. Narrative is no longer linear but woven with emotional algorithms. Viewing is evolving from a conscious act of participation into a guided form of exposure. All these transformations are shifting cinema away from the classical notion of representing reality, turning it into an aesthetic space where reality can be reconstructed, replicated, and simulated. This shift is felt across numerous dimensions, from artistic understanding to perceptions of truth, ethical norms, and social consciousness.

Will artists or data architects produce cinema in the future? Will what make a scene real be considered the actual presence of those involved, or merely their appearance? Will we continue to watch authentic representations or merely simulations that we are prepared to believe in? These questions will continue to preoccupy our minds in the posthuman, post-truth, and postbody eras of cinema, which has long since transcended its role as a medium of artistic expression. Deepfake technology, meanwhile, appears poised to continue replicating, fragmenting, and reinventing this new visual language. Ultimately, we will have to accept that what stands before us is no longer merely a new form of cinema, but a new form of reality.

Discussion: Four Conceptual Approaches beyond Current Theories toward a Post-Deepfake Cinema

Throughout the history of cinema, the image has been regarded not only as an aesthetic element but also as a window into truth. In this context, the connection between cinema and reality has been grounded in the actor's physical presence, the inscription of light onto time, and the camera's capacity to bear witness. However, with the advent of deepfake technology, the ability to produce images without any reference to reality is fundamentally shaking the ontological foundations of cinema. Similar to Immanuel Kant's distinction between phenomenon and noumenon, the image is no longer a representation of a "thing" but has become a simulacrum that grounds its own existence.[9] Jean Baudrillard's theory of simulation provides an important reference point here, but today's digital production techniques have reached the level of "hyper-simulacrum"[10] where simulation can be simulated. The image is no longer a trace of the past or a vision of the future; it is merely the output of algorithmic production. This situation transforms cinema from an ontological art form into an epistemological design field. Cinema is no longer a machine that represents reality but one capable of producing the non-existent. In an ontological context, this creates a rupture that invalidates representation. Because what is represented no longer has any reality; it only has visibility. The existence of the image conceals the absence of reality.

At the same time, the growing prevalence of deepfake technologies in popular culture is reshaping individual viewing experiences and contributing to a broader transformation of collective memory structures. Scenes produced using these technologies, particularly in nostalgia-focused productions, create emotional effects that feel as though they happened in the past, even though they never did. This leads individuals to remember the past through fiction and brings the concept of "synthetic memory"[11] to the forefront. Here, cinema goes beyond the technical reproduction defined by Walter Benjamin and reproduces memory itself. Viewers can now internalize events that have never intersected with their personal history as part of their memories. This implies that cinema is becoming a kind of collective memory engineer. The collective remembrance of something unreal as if it were real artificializes individual identities, cultural affiliations, and historical memories. At this point, cinema is more of a tool for constructing the desired past than recording the truth. Therefore, in the future, social memory of historical events may rely directly on cinematic artificial productions. This situation means that Hannah Arendt's (2006) idea of "public truth" is replaced by "emotionally accepted artificial images."[12] Thus, even social truth becomes determined by cinema's emotional design capabilities.

On the other hand, the increasing use of digitally created characters produced by artificial intelligence is radically transforming the concept of acting in cinema. The assumption that an actor is not merely an interpreter but an artistic creator with both physical and emotional presence is being replaced by algorithmic modeling. This transformation is also eliminating the notion of "embodied presence", one of the fundamental aesthetic values of cinema, along with the profession of acting. Digital characters created with artificial intelligence can mimic the effect of authenticity, but since they do not have a real body, no intercorporeal relation (Sobchack, 1992, p. 58) can be established between the viewer's bodily presence and the actor's bodily presence in the film. For example, an actor shedding tears, the movement of facial muscles through micro-expressions, or the trembling of the body is not merely a visual effect, but a cinematic transmission of embodied experience. Digital characters, on the other hand, present this experience as a data-driven and superficial simulation.

Today, in cinema, a face is no longer just an aesthetic element; it has become an interface optimized by deep learning systems. This represents a post-human transformation of Deleuze and Guattari's concept of the "faciality": The face is no longer a surface that produces meaning, but a masking device that replaces meaning.[13] This situation gives rise to a cinema practice that produces representation without the need for the actor's physical and spiritual presence, known as "post-acting aesthetics." In the aesthetics that emerges from this digitized form of acting, the emotional connection established with the viewer is not to a human body but to a data-based facial image that reveals its artificiality through its perfection. The cinematic face is no longer an extension of embodied existence but of algorithmic simulation. In this context, a Deleuzian "regime of defacialization" is emerging in cinema. Since actors' faces can be altered, replicated, or erased as data objects, the face has ceased to be an authentic representation and has become a mutable surface. Faces now produce a form of representation that belongs to everyone and no one at the same time. This may fundamentally alter the viewer's capacity for empathy, as empathy requires not only recognizability but also encounter and resistance. In contrast, nothing in a digital face resists; it merely appears.

Finally, emotional response design in AI-powered content production is becoming one of the new frontiers of cinema. Especially with the ability of artificial intelligence to analyze viewer data such as eye movement, attention span, and preference history, it becomes possible to optimize the emotional impact of scenes. This development signifies a shift from storytelling to emotion engineering. Narrative is no longer just a sequential arrangement of events. Scenes are constructed based on predetermined emotional thresholds. Here, cinema becomes a system that directly intervenes in the viewer's emotional state. At this point, the concept of "algorithmic affect design" can be proposed: Elements such as scene structure, music selection, pacing, and color tone are calculated by artificial intelligence to produce a specific emotional response in the viewer. This means that in cinema, fictionality is being replaced by calculability. The viewer is no longer part of a narrative but is positioned as an object to be affected. Jacques Rancière's (2009) idea of the "emancipation of the spectator" is reversed here. The audience is no longer a free interpreter but an emotional machine shaped by a series of reactions. This transformation has aesthetic as well as ethical and political consequences. For the pre-designation of emotions can also eliminate the spectator's capacity for subjectivation. Thus, cinema becomes not merely a visual but a biopolitical tool.

REFERENCES

Al-Badri, N. (2023). *Works.* https://www.nora-al-badri.de/works-index

Arendt, H. (2006). *Between past and future: Eight exercises in political thought.* Penguin Books.

Baudrillard, J. (1994). *Simulacra and simulation* (Glaser, S. F., Trans.). University of Michigan Press.

Belada, N. E. S. (2024). Deepfake disinformation. *Journal of Information Technology Law*, *6*(1), 321–358. DOI: 10.55009/bilisimhukukudergisi.1387306

Black, J., & Fullerton, C. (2020). Digital deceit: Fake news, artificial intelligence, and censorship in educational research. *Open Journal of Social Sciences*, *8*, 71–88. DOI: 10.4236/jss.2020.87007

Braidotti, R. (2013). *The posthuman.* Polity Press.

Bukatman, S. (1997). *Blade Runner.* BFI Publishing.

Butler, J. (1990). *Gender trouble: Feminism and the subversion of identity.* Routledge.

Chávez Heras, D. (2024). *Cinema and machine vision: Artificial intelligence, aesthetics and spectatorship*. Edinburgh University Press.

Chen, H., & Magromo, K. (2024, May 4). Finance worker pays out $25 million after video call with deepfake 'chief financial officer'. *CNN.* https://edition.cnn.com/2024/02/04/asia/deepfake-cfo-scam-hong-kong-intl-hnk

D-ID. (2024). *Digital avatar.* https://www.d-id.com/resources/glossary/digital-avatar/

Deleuze, G. (1989). *Cinema 2: The time-image* (Tomlinson, H., & Galeta, R., Trans.). University of Minnesota Press.

Deleuze, G., & Guattari, F. (1987). *A thousand plateaus: Capitalism and schizophrenia* (Massumi, B., Trans.). University of Minnesota Press.

Ermeydan, D., & Etlioğlu Erçetingöz, S. (2024). Avrupa Birliği Yapay Zekâ Tüzüğü uyarınca kişilik kapsamında yapay zekâ. *Bahçeşehir Üniversitesi Hukuk Fakültesi Dergisi*, *19*(223), 1417–1454.

eSafety. (2022). *Deepfake trends and challenges - Position statement.* https://www.esafety.gov.au/sites/default/files/2022-01/Deepfake-position-statement%20_v2.pdf

Faber, L. W. (2020). *The computer's voice: From Star Trek to Siri*. University of Minnesota Press.

Faber, L. W. (2023). *Robot suicide: Death, identity, and AI in science fiction.* Lexington Books.

Holdsworth, J., & Scappichio, M. (2024). *What is deep learning?* IBM. https://www.ibm.com/think/topics/deep-learning

Holroyd, M., & Olorunselu, F. (2022, March 16). Deepfake video shows Zelenskyy's false call for Ukraine to surrender. *Euronews.* https://www.euronews.com/my-europe/2022/03/16/deepfake-zelenskyy-surrender-video-is-the-first-intentionally-used-in-ukraine-war

Kant, I. (1998). *Critique of pure reason* (Guyer, P., & Wood, A. W., Trans.). Cambridge University Press.

Karnouskos, S. (2020). Artificial intelligence in digital media: The era of deepfakes. *IEEE Transactions on Technology and Society, 1*(3), 138–147. DOI: 10.1109/TTS.2020.3001312

Kellner, D. (1995). *Media culture: Cultural studies, identity and politics between the modern and the postmodern.* Routledge.

Kilavuz, İ. F. (2024). *Deepfaked democracy': The next-generation menace to global politics.* TRT World Research Centre. https://researchcentre.trtworld.com/wp-content/uploads/2024/09/Deepfaked-Democracy-to-publish-1.pdf

Lees, D. (2024). Deepfakes in documentary film production: Images of deception in the representation of the real. *Studies in Documentary Film, 18*(2), 108–129. DOI: 10.1080/17503280.2023.2284680

Manovich, L. (2001). *The language of new media.* The MIT Press.

Merrin, W. (2005). *Baudrillard and the media: A critical introduction.* Polity Press.

Miller, E. (2024). Easy steps to make a talking avatar with AI from any photos. *Wondershare Virbo.* https://virbo.wondershare.com/talking-photo/make-ai-talking-avatar.html

Milmo, D., & Hawkins, A. (2024, May 18). How China is using AI news anchors to deliver its propaganda. *The Guardian.* https://www.theguardian.com/technology/article/2024/may/18/how-china-is-using-ai-news-anchors-to-deliver-its-propaganda

Misirlis, N., & Munawar, H. B. (2023). From deepfake to deep useful: Risks and opportunities through a systematic literature review (No. arXiv:2311.15809). *arXiv.* https://doi.org//arXiv.2311.15809DOI: 10.48550

MIT Open Learning. (2020). *Tackling the misinformation epidemic with "In Event of Moon Disaster"*. MIT News. Massachusetts Institute of Technology. https://news.mit.edu/2020/mit-tackles-misinformation-in-event-of-moon-disaster-0720

Morozov, E. (2013). *To save everything, click here: The folly of technological solutionism*. PublicAffairs.

Murphy, G., Ching, D., Twomey, J., & Linehan, C. (2023). Face/off: Changing the face of movies with deepfakes. *PLoS One*, *18*(7), e0287503. DOI: 10.1371/journal.pone.0287503 PMID: 37410765

Oakes, O. (2019). "Deepfake" voice tech used for good in David Beckham malaria campaign. *Campaign*. https://www.campaignlive.co.uk/article/deepfake-voice-tech-used-good-david-beckham-malaria-campaign/1581378?utm_source=website&utm_medium=social

Okeke, A. O., Nwosu, C. J., Asogwa, J., & Dada, O. (2024). Utilization of deepfake technology in the film industry: Analysing Al-generated performances in the Hollywood film *The Irishman* and its impact on Artistic Integrity. *Scholarly Journal of Social Sciences Research*, *3*(6), 35–51. DOI: 10.5281/zenodo.13989607

Oxford Learner's Dictionaries. (2025). Post-truth [adjective]. *Oxford Advanced Learner's Dictionary*. https://www.oxfordlearnersdictionaries.com/definition/english/post-truth?q=post+truth

Pandey, E. (2024). The rise of fake influencers. *Axios*. https://www.axios.com/2024/09/07/fake-ai-influencers-lil-miquela

Pavis, M. (2021). Rebalancing our regulatory response to deepfakes with performers' rights. *Convergence (London)*, *27*(4), 974–998. DOI: 10.1177/13548565211033418

Rancière, J. (2009). *The emancipated spectator* (Elliott, G., Trans.). Verso Books.

Recker, J. (2022). This deepfake exhibition shows how convincing the new technology can be. *Smithsonian Magazine*. https://www.smithsonianmag.com/smart-news/this-deepfake-exhibition-shows-how-convincing-the-new-technology-can-be-180979619/

Rothkopf, J. (2020, July 1). Deepfake technology enters the documentary world. *The New York Times*. https://www.nytimes.com/2020/07/01/movies/deepfakes-documentary-welcome-to-chechnya.html

Saad, N. (2019, November 8). Director says James Dean CGI film is still on despite backlash. *Los Angeles Times*. https://www.latimes.com/entertainment-arts/movies/story/2019-11-08/cgi-james-dean-director-backlash

Şeylan, S. (2023). Dijital ikiz teknolojilerinin sinemaya yansımaları ve etik sorunlar. *Motif Akademi Halkbilimi Dergisi*, *16*(43), 1450–1468.

Shen, X. (2020, March 12). Professor's online students prefer when he teaches classes as anime girl. *South China Morning Post*. https://www.scmp.com/abacus/news-bites/article/3074961/professors-online-students-prefer-when-he-teaches-classes-anime

Sobchack, V. (1992). *The address of the eye: A phenomenology of film experience*. Princeton University Press.

The Dali. (2025). *Dalí lives (via artificial intelligence)*. https://thedali.org/exhibit/dali-lives/

The Guardian. (2023, October 2). Tom Hanks says AI version of him used in dental plan ad without his consent. *The Guardian*. https://www.theguardian.com/film/2023/oct/02/tom-hanks-dental-ad-ai-version-fake

van Dijck, J. (2007). *Mediated memories in the digital age*. Stanford University Press.

Virilio, P. (1994). *The vision machine*. Indiana University Press.

Yamazaki, A. (2024). Digital replicas and democracy: Issues raised by the Hollywood actors' strike. *Humanities & Social Sciences Communications*, *11*, 1661. Advance online publication. DOI: 10.1057/s41599-024-04204-w

Yang, M. (2021, July 16). Anthony Bourdain documentary sparks backlash for using AI to fake voice. *The Guardian*. https://www.theguardian.com/food/2021/jul/16/anthony-bourdain-documentary-ai-voiceover-roadrunner

Zuboff, S. (2019). *The age of surveillance capitalism: The fight for a human future at the new frontier of power*. PublicAffairs.

ADDITIONAL READING

Allen, G. (2025). *Representing the new AI in film and television*. Bloomsbury Academic.

Butterfield, J. (2024). *AI for visual artists: Transforming creativity through technology*. Independent, Amazon.

Filimovicz, M. (2022). *Deepfakes: algorithms and society*. Routledge.

Foster, T. (2005). *The souls of cyberfolk: Posthumanism as vernacular theory*. University of Minnesota Press.

Lundberg, E., & Mozelius, P. (2024). The potential effects of deepfakes on news media and entertainment. *AI & Society*. Advance online publication. DOI: 10.1007/s00146-024-02072-1

Lyon, B., & Tora, M. (2023). *Exploring deepfakes: Deploy powerful AI techniques for face replacement and more with this comprehensive guide*. Packt Publishing.

McLean, S. T. (2008). *Digital storytelling: The narrative power of visual effects in film*. MIT Press.

Sawant, O. D. (2024). *Visual storytelling with generative AI: A practical handbook for modern filmmakers and content creators*. Independent, Amazon.

Street, J. (2023). *Silicon valley cinema*. Edinburgh University Press.

Xu, Y. (2025). Balancing creativity and automation: The influence of AI on modern film production and dissemination. *arXiv preprint*. https://arxiv.org/abs/2504.19275

KEY TERMS AND DEFINITIONS

Ai-Mediated Perception: AI-mediated perception describes how artificial intelligence is shaping what and how we see. From generating deepfakes to curating visual feeds, AI is changing the lens through which we experience media. The term draws attention to the machine-driven reconstruction of visual reality.

Algorithmic Storytelling: Algorithmic storytelling involves the use of data-driven systems and AI algorithms to influence or generate narratives. These systems may suggest plot structures, simulate performances or edit visual content. In deepfake-based narratives, algorithms often act as co-creators. This method redefines authorship and creativity in media production.

Aura Loss: Aura loss is a concept introduced by Walter Benjamin, referring to the diminishing uniqueness and originality of a work of art due to mechanical reproduction. In the age of deepfakes, this loss is intensified as faces and voices can be endlessly replicated. It challenges the notion of authenticity and presence in digital media.

Deepfake Technology: Deepfake technology refers to synthetic media created using artificial intelligence, especially by manipulating or generating realistic images, videos or voices. This technology blurs the line between reality and fiction. It can replicate human likenesses with striking accuracy. While it offers creative opportunities in media and design, it also raises ethical concerns about deception and authenticity.

Post-Truth Aesthetics: Post-truth aesthetics refer to visual narratives formed in an era where emotional appeal and manipulated realities often override factual accuracy. Deepfakes contribute to this aesthetic by creating believable yet fictional content. This visual style questions the reliability of what is seen. It emphasises perception over verifiable reality in storytelling and communication.

Synthetic Media: Synthetic media is media content generated or manipulated by algorithms, especially AI-based systems. It includes images, videos and voices that mimic reality without being captured from real-world events. Synthetic media offers limitless creative possibilities for storytelling. But it also challenges traditional notions of originality and truth in media.

Visual Authenticity: Visual authenticity refers to the perceived authenticity or trustworthiness of an image or video. Deepfakes disrupt this notion by making it difficult to distinguish between real and fake visuals. As a result, audiences become more sceptical of visual media. The concept is crucial to journalism, cinema and digital storytelling.

ENDNOTES

1 The term "uncanny valley" was coined in 1970 by Japanese robotics engineer Masahiro Mori. As the similarity to humans increases, so does the emotional closeness felt toward an object. However, when this similarity reaches a point where it is almost entirely human but still not "fully human," the viewer experiences a sense of discomfort, unease, or alienation. Deepfake technology's ability to present human faces in a way that is very close to reality but not 100% flawless can evoke a disturbing feeling in viewers. This effect becomes more pronounced when artificial elements are noticeable in details such as eye movements, facial expressions, and lip synchronization.

2 The same questions apply to digital twins, synthetic voices, and even characters created entirely by artificial intelligence.

3 Paul Virilio's concept of the "vision machine" refers to the separation of visual perception from the human body and its realization through automatic systems. Virilio (1994) regards this transformation as both a technical evolution and an epistemological and ethical crisis; for seeing is no longer a cognitive experience of the human subject, but is becoming an autonomous activity of the machine. Daniel Chávez Heras' concept of "machine vision" is a contemporary continuation of this line of thought. Heras defines the concept of machine vision, as discussed in the context of cinema, as a regime that restructures human perception on an aesthetic and cultural level. Thus, Heras reinterprets

Virilio's critique of the “vision machine” within the context of contemporary digital cinema and artificial intelligence aesthetics (Chávez Heras, 2024).

4 The concept of “algorithm-image” is a reinterpretation of Gilles Deleuze's “time-image” theory in the digital age, and was introduced to understand the effects of artificial intelligence, machine learning, and algorithmic processes on cinema and visual culture. Deleuze's classification of images in his film theory and his ideas about the cinematic representation of time form the foundation of this concept. Deleuze's (1989) concept of “time-image” refers to the direct representation of time and non-linear narratives in cinema, while the term “algorithm-image” emphasizes the impact of digital technologies and algorithmic processes on visual narratives. In this context, Lev Manovich's analysis of the structural characteristics of digital media and the role of algorithms in visual culture in his work *The Language of New Media* (2001) provides the theoretical foundation for the concept of “algorithm-image.” Manovich argues that algorithms are decisive in the production and editing of digital images. Additionally, Daniel Chávez Heras's *Cinema and Machine Vision* (2024) examines the impact of machine vision on aesthetic and narrative structures in cinema, discussing the role of algorithmic processes in the formation of cinematic images. Heras notes that machine vision creates a new visual regime in cinema, transforming traditional cinematic understanding. Among the concrete examples of the “algorithm-image” concept, Guy Maddin's *Seances* (2016) project stands out. In this project, algorithms are used to offer each viewer a different film experience, thus shaping cinematic narrative through algorithmic processes. Similarly, Eve Sussman's *whiteonwhite:algorithmicnoir* (2012) presents unique film experiences created by combining 3,000 video clips, 80 voiceovers, and 150 music tracks through algorithms.

5 The concept of profiling refers to the replacement of subjective identity in the digital age with data-based representations. In this process, individuals cease to be subjects shaped by their own experiences and narratives; instead, they are represented by behavioral patterns derived from their digital traces by algorithms. As defined by Shoshana Zuboff, this situation means that individuals are included in a surveillance capitalism system based on the “extraction of behavioral surplus” (Zuboff, 2019). In the context of cinema, profiling is used in algorithmic recommendation systems aimed at the viewer, and it also plays a key role in AI-based character creation. Rather than relying on character psychology or dramatic acting, digital replicas are generated from a large set of data samples. This reduces the representation of identity from a unique subject to an analyzable object (Manovich, 2001; Braidotti, 2013).

6 Screen Actors Guild-American Federation of Television and Radio Artists

7 Morozov criticizes technological solutionism that is the belief that complex social and political problems can be solved solely through technology. According to him, this approach offers superficial solutions by ignoring the root causes of problems and undermines democratic processes. With this criticism, Morozov emphasizes the need to be cautious about Silicon Valley's technology-focused solutions. The concept is also discussed today in fields such as education, healthcare, and public policy.

8 Mise-en-scène, a French term meaning "putting on stage" refers in the context of cinema to the deliberate arrangement of every element within a scene — including the positioning of actors, their movements, gaze direction, body language, posture, and spatial placement. Actor's mise-en-scène specifically encompasses the actor's position within the frame, physical movements, gestures and facial expressions, as well as their spatial and emotional relationships with other actors. These elements are orchestrated by the director and the cinematographer in accordance with the narrative rhythm and emotional tone of the scene. Representing the nuanced staging and acting aesthetics of traditional cinema, this concept is increasingly giving way in the digital age to spectacle-driven staging — such as explosions, dynamic camera movements, and visual effects.

9 The distinction between phenomenon and noumenon in Immanuel Kant's theory of knowledge deserves to be reconsidered in terms of the representation of images produced by artificial intelligence and deepfake technologies in contemporary cinema. According to Kant, the phenomenon refers to the world of appearances that we experience through the mind's perceptions and concepts, while the noumenon is the "thing-in-itself" that exists outside the mind and beyond experience, yet can never be directly known (Kant, 1998, pp. 360-361). Deepfake videos and scenes created with artificial intelligence present images that appear real to the viewer; these images are phenomena. However, access to the truth behind these phenomena—that is, the noumenon in Kantian terms—is either blocked or completely obscured. Especially in the post-truth era, the relationship between the image and truth weakens, and at times it becomes unclear whether there is any reality behind the image at all. While reality, for Kant, is an inaccessible yet enduring fact, in today's digital representations, reality often transforms into speculative fiction. This situation demonstrates that cinema is no longer merely a visual aesthetic but has become an epistemological and ethical problem.

10 The concept of "hyper-simulacrum" is based directly on Jean Baudrillard's theory of simulation, although the term does not appear explicitly in his texts. The concept has been developed by post-Baudrillard media theorists, particularly as an extension of the concept of hyperreality. According to Baudrillard, the simulacrum is a level of representation that no longer refers to any reality but circulates independently. The extreme point of simulation is hyperreality: "the simulation of reality that replaces reality" (Baudrillard, 1994, pp. 1-6). Hyper-simulacrum, on the other hand, transcends this level, canceling out both the references to reality and representation, and is defined as a visual system that repeats and multiplies itself (see Kellner, 1995; Merrin, 2005). Deepfake images or digital twins, which appear in AI-supported cinema practices, are hyper-simulacra that have no ontological basis but produce an effect of reality. In this context, hyper-simulacra expresses a postmodern visual epistemology that operates in an amorphous plane between fiction and direct representation.

11 The concept of "synthetic memory" refers to the way in which individual memory has been reshaped in the digital age through its intertwining with technology. This concept describes false but seemingly real memory constructs based not on direct experiences but on visual representations, narratives, and digital manipulations. According to José van Dijck, in the digital environment, memory is no longer recalled but is reconstructed through algorithms and images; therefore, individuals often remember a "constructed" past as if it were their own experience (2007, p. 12). One of the most striking representations of this concept in cinema is seen in the character Rachel in the film *Blade Runner* (Ridley Scott, 1982). Her memories of the past are not biological but synthetic, having been uploaded into her memory (Bukatman, 1997). Similarly, scenes created through today's deepfake technologies can evoke genuine feelings about a non-existent past by presenting images of events that never happened in a nostalgic context. In this context, the synthetic memory represents a critical conceptual threshold that signals the transformation of both cinematic aesthetics and collective memory. Because technological representations can replace individual memory over time and artificially reconstruct "the truth of the past."

12 According to Hannah Arendt, public truth relies not only on personal opinions but also on a shared ground of reality accessible to all; without this ground, public debate, ethical judgment, and political action become impossible. Arendt, particularly in her essay *Truth and Politics* (1967), argues that the distortion of public truth draws individuals into a false reality, which is one of the most powerful tools of totalitarian regimes (2006, pp. 231-233). Today, cinema plays an important role in the construction of this false universe. In particular,

AI-supported production forms and deepfake technologies produce emotional versions of the desired past rather than representing the truth. These productions create aesthetically convincing but epistemologically problematic “realities” while reconstructing historical events. Arendt's concept of “public truth” should be reconsidered in this context to question how artificially produced cinematic narratives transform the collective perception of truth. Cinema does not merely aestheticize the past; it also produces narrative frameworks that will shape social memory in the future. This situation points to the emergence of a “post-truth cinema regime” in which truth is no longer nourished by its provability but by its emotional acceptability.

13 Gilles Deleuze and Félix Guattari’s concept of “faciality” suggests that the face, as a biological entity, is a socially coded surface that produces meaning. According to them, the face is a “coding space” regulated by modern forms of power; the individual is recognized, controlled, and classified through this surface (Deleuze & Guattari, 1987, pp. 115-122). However, in the digital age, especially with AI-supported visual production techniques, this system of meaning-making is undergoing a radical transformation. The face is no longer a natural extension of the body, but a data-constructed, optimized, and staged interface. This digital image of the face does not belong to the individual or to a social memory; rather, it produces a false intimacy created by algorithmic processes. The face simulates emotion rather than expressing it. Thus, the “faciality” ceases to be a representational space and evolves into a visual masking regime that replaces truth. This transformation also alters the nature of the aesthetic relationship between the viewer and the character: The face no longer belongs to a subject bearing identity, but to a digital object reprogrammed in each scene. This reconfiguration of the face in cinema leads to the erasure of embodied presence and results in the disappearance of the ethical dimension of representation.

Chapter 5
Synergizing Data Storytelling and AI:
Enhancing Engagement in Complex Data Communication

Maria João Frade
Faculty of Economics, Universidade do Algarve, Portugal

Célia M. Q. Ramos
https://orcid.org/0000-0002-3413-4897
CinTurs, ESGHT, Univeristy of Algarve, Portugal

ABSTRACT

Combining Data Storytelling concepts and Artificial Intelligence algorithms presents a powerful alliance for the analysis and communication of complex data, in a more intuitive environment and with higher levels of engagement. The main goal was to understand and present the potential of combining these two areas, where sentiment analysis was the method considered to represent Artificial Intelligence. The considered methodology consists, in a first phase of literary review, followed by sentiment analysis. The findings of this research culminate in the development of the definition of Data Storytelling, its potential, and its relationship with Artificial Intelligence systems, presenting a Dashboard Data Storytelling incorporated with AI.

INTRODUCTION

Throughout society, in general but especially in the business sector, it's easy to notice the shift in paradigm felt with galloping advances regarding data collection and processing and technology with access to AI, with its ability to influence, and

DOI: 10.4018/979-8-3373-6970-9.ch005

© 2026, IGI Global Scientific Publishing. Copying or distributing in print or electronic forms without written permission of IGI Global Scientific Publishing is prohibited. Use of this chapter to ıerative artificial intelligence (AI) technologies is expressly prohibited. The publisher reserves all rights to license its use for generative AI training and machine learning model development.

even make, important decisions. The development of capturing means and reading different types of data has generated such voluminous datasets (Big Data) that their treatment, extraction of insights and communication from them has become an almost impractical task without the intervention of Artificial Intelligence and advanced analysis and visualisation software. Consequently, resources such as Data Storytelling, among others, become fundamental to understanding this new reality, as well as providing a basis for its practice, according to the study Big Data and AI-driven Product Design: A Survey (Quan *et al.*, 2023):

> *"In recent years, big data and AI-driven product design have become a significant research hotspot. However, to the best of our knowledge, before this work, there has been almost no comprehensive summary of the applications of big data in product design. Therefore, a thorough literature review is necessary to provide theoretical foundations that can be utilised to develop scientific insights in this area." (Quan et al., 2023, p. 33).*

The main challenge of appropriately analysing and transmitting the massive amount of data that has been intensifying is what Data Storytelling aims to solve. In addition to the problem of absorbing useful information, there is the added difficulty of communicating it. Feigenbaum and Alamalhodaei (2020) warn that:

> *"But while datasets and digital archives grow bigger and more open, information remains difficult to collect, complex to analyse, and challenging to communicate. As we've seen over the past two decades of this proliferation, more data does not necessarily lead to better data stories" (Feigenbaum & Alamalhodaei, 2020, p. 4).*

This argument highlights the relevance of systems optimisation, and Storytelling associated with Data visualisation can be the solution to these demands. Data is one of the most precious business assets today, and companies that can convert their data into insights and those insights into knowledge will stand out, become smarter and outperform their competition. In a data-driven world, telling stories is a crucial aspect that will contribute to the success of organisations (Dykes, 2020).

Given and in addition to what was presented above, this study also aims to understand the impact these tools have on decision-making. The inclusion of Business Intelligence is fundamental. In this context, the main goals are:

- Familiarisation with the fundamental principles of Artificial Intelligence (AI) applied to data analysis, combined with Data Storytelling concepts.
- Present a case study related to the potential of combining these two areas and the creation of stories based on the insights obtained.

This study is divided into five sections, each one focusing on different aspects. Introduction establishes the context of the study, presenting the goals and the importance of the topic in focus, namely, the use of Data Storytelling and Artificial

Intelligence. Section two will focus on Artificial Intelligence, addressing its definitions, methods and the interconnection with Data Storytelling, and is fundamental to continuing the exploration of Artificial Intelligence. How can it improve data analysis and visualisation? The third section presents the methodology used to develop the study, followed in the text section by a detailed description of projects related to this topic. Finally, the last section presents the final considerations, the limitations of the study and presents future research paths.

DATA STORYTELLING AND ARTIFICIAL INTELLIGENCE

With the increase of Artificial Intelligence (AI) in data analysis, its approach in this study, and its intersection with Data Storytelling, are thus essential. AI has lately proven its potential and benefits to such an extent that AI-Powered Analytics products have been developed capable of analysing large amounts of data and extracting relevant insights in real time and interactively. The centre issue ends up being its communication, the way in which this information is transmitted and perceived. This communication must be streamlined through Data Storytelling, and AI must be able to use this technique to facilitate the transmission of the desired message.

Artificial Intelligence

Artificial Intelligence is a scientific area with quite some history that gained significant prominence in recent decades, and its rise is due to important milestones resulting from the work of several researchers. In the 1950s. British mathematician and computer scientist Alan Turing published an article (Computing Machinery and Intelligence) where he introduced the famous "Turing Test" as a way to determine the intelligence of a machine (Ergen, 2019: 6). During this period, the perceptron, a more primitive form of Artificial Neural Network (ANN), also emerged. "*The put forward perceptron by Professor Rosenblatt in 1956, before the basis of today's artificial intelligence*" (Ergen, 2019, p.5). Hence, the consolidation of the term "Artificial Intelligence" - AI - as an area of study. In 1956, the term Artificial Intelligence was first coined by John McCarthy. Artificial Intelligence would be the science and engineering of making intelligent machines, especially intelligent computer programs (Morais *et al.*, 2020). Shortly thereafter, Samuel trademarked the term Machine Learning (ML) to describe systems capable of learning through the insertion and manipulation of data. "*One year later, after introducing the per-*

ceptron, American computer scientist Arthur Samuel coined the term 'machine learning." (Ergen, 2019, p. 6).

In the 1960s, the concept of learning was expanded by stacking multiple perceptrons to create Deep Neural Networks (DNN) - [...] *resembling today's deep-learning architectures inspired from Neural Networks (NN) of the human brain.*" (Ergen, 2019, p. 6). However, interest in AI waned from the 1970s onwards, with few notable advances until the end of the decade.

In 1980, there was a resurgence of AI with Geoffrey Hinton, who developed the backpropagation algorithm, a fundamental technique for ANN training. At this time, other important techniques were also introduced, such as Convolutional Neural Networks (CNNs) for recognising presented images (Ergen, 2019).

The 90s brought some advances, such as Support Vector Machines (SVMs) for sentiment classification and Natural Language Processing (NLP). Recurrent Neural Networks (RNNs) and Long-Short Term Memory (LSTM) have also been introduced for advanced speech-to-text translation (Ergen, 2019).

In the early 2000s, Deep Learning (DL) was developed, an approach within AI's field that uses artificial neural networks (ANNs) with multiple layers that learn from data (Ergen, 2019: 6). Geoffrey Hinton was one of the pioneers introducing the concept of DL to the world, as well as demonstrating its abilities on several pattern recognition problems. To overcome some of its disadvantages and reduce training time, Transfer Learning (TL) was promoted, which consists of refusing knowledge from one problem to another related but different problem, using a pre-trained model (Ergen, 2019). "*In ML, you need to choose for yourself which features to include in the model. In order to overcome the drawback of insufficient data and reduce the training time, Transfer Learning (TL) is gaining popularity.*" (Ergen, 2019, p. 7).

Nowadays, AI is increasingly present in our daily lives and plays a crucial role in many areas. Although there are concerns about its impact on jobs, politics, the economy, and the structure of society in general, it can bring many significant benefits if used responsibly and ethically. (Ergen, 2019).

> *"Expectations in AI will create more jobs than it will destroy. The AI hype will die eventually when AI becomes another thread as on the Internet, electricity, and transportation. Today, AI is promising, or in some cases threatens, changes in business and society at large. The industrial era let machines do the physical work; the information era enabled machines to do the computation and storage, now the AI era will let machines make the decisions" (Ergen, 2019, p. 7).*

In more recent years, AI has spread and evolved due to its social and economic impact, especially due to the advances seen in DL. However, the complexity and opaque nature of DNNs make it difficult to understand the decision-making of these models, which limits their safe use. To solve this problem, eXplainable Artificial Intelligence (XAI) methods have been developed, but these have also been challenged.

This has driven Concept-based eXplainable Artificial Intelligence (C-XAI) methods, which are based on concepts and offer more understandable explanations, similar to human reasoning, making models more robust and effective (Poeta *et al.*, 2023).

In order to better comprehend the model, explanations based on C-XAI concepts offer an interesting alternative, as they provide a more holistic view of the inner workings of the model and the network. Poeta *et al.* (2023) state that: "*By explaining the model's predictions in terms of human-understandable attributes or abstractions, concept-based explanations better resemble the way humans reason and explain.*" (Poeta *et al.*, 2023, p. 2). They also allow users to gain depth regarding the insights and their underlying reasoning, helping detect deviations from the model and improve their classification (Poeta *et al.*, 2023).

AI is often confused with automatization or digitalization, and is now everywhere, including most areas of science, but it is still far from having an appropriate universal definition, because on the one hand it belongs to the scientific field, on the other it has roots in biology, mathematics, psychology, philosophy and metaphysics, which makes its conceptualization a complex task. The definition of it as a concept has sparked discussion in the scientific community in recent years and has generated disagreements. "*A further inspection of the history shows that many have attempted to define AI. Every definition has been criticized and has failed to obtain consensus within each of these disciplines, let alone universal consensus.*" (Abbass, 2021, p. 95).

There is a need to ensure that the definition of AI can retain its true meaning and scope. The literature does not allow redundant definitions such as "AI is intelligence that is artificial". "*We need to ensure that a definition is a "good" definition. The literature tells us that we should avoid self-referential statements; we should not offer a circular definition such as that "AI is intelligence that is artificial.*" (Abbass, 2021, p. 94). It isn't unreasonable that a definition of a term such as AI's begins with exactly the two words that compose it: "intelligence" and "artificial". One possible starting point can be beginning by defining these two words. For instance, intelligence as: cognition, learning, processing or gathering information; and artificial as: man-made, non-biological, imitating nature, unfaithful to nature, unfaithful to reality or manufactured (Abbass, 2021).

Thus, it is possible that AI is the automation of cognition, and the word "cognition" comes from the Latin word "cogito" (meaning "to know"), and that is not exclusive to humans. "*It could be the cognition of an animal or even the cognition of a different AI agent.*" (Abbass, 2021, p. 95). AI must be seen beyond its status as a technological product and more as a sociocognitive phenomenon. Although no theoretical definition of AI is yet error-free, sufficiently universal or concisely ambiguous, Abbass (2021), in his article *What is Artificial Intelligence?* presents the following definition:

"Artificial Intelligence is a social and cognitive phenomena that enable a machine to socially integrate with a society to perform competitive tasks requiring cognitive processes and communicate with other entities in society by exchanging messages with high information content and shorter representations." (Abbass, 2021, p. 95)

Given the vast scope and capabilities of AI, the finding of a concise, clear and comprehensive concept that defines it is a difficult task. However, Morais *et al.* (2020) state the following:

"Uma Inteligência Artificial é uma estrutura composta e articulada por softwares e eventualmente, hardwares, cuja finalidade é auxiliar os seres humanos na tomada de decisão com base na associação de dados históricos e no reconhecimento de padrões". (Morais et al., 2020, p. 98).

Artificial Intelligence and Data Analysis

AI combined with Data Analysis is known as AI-powered Analytics. It is a proven but fairly recent technological advancement. Many companies have invested heavily in DL, a subcategory of ML (Machine Learning), which is in turn a subcategory of AI. DL and artificial neural networks enable image recognition, audio, NLP (Natural Language Processing), and other tools have been developed. Today, most modern Analytics solutions have recently started developing NLP that allows end users to use everyday language to ask questions about data. But it is undeniable that AI-powered Analytics will help organisations create and develop their most important strategies, and thus focus their business on the most important activities, instead of wasting valuable time with vast reports. "*AI and Machine Learning assist, augment, and amplify work. And when done right, these insights can empower everyone in the company, not just a few specialists.*" (Jyoti, 2021, p. 22).

It is necessary to act concretely, that is, to collect and process all the data generated by consumers and use it so effectively that it exceeds everyone's expectations. Analysis and insights are means to an end, not the end in themselves, and AI and ML allow, in addition to identifying the best action to take, also to automate some processes, which could translate into a benefit for everyone, companies and consumers (Jyoti, 2021).

Sometimes, developing and evaluating hypotheses and separating correlations from casualties to explain an unexpected anomaly or an upward trend can be a job that takes many hours and even days. AI-powered Analytics and ML techniques are able to classify billions of rows in seconds and show the indicators and main causes implicit in the data, guiding and increasing work efficiency, and giving greater consistency, accuracy and reliability to the results. These techniques are capable of presenting analyses and predictions with depth and detail unattainable by human hand alone. They can, for instance, assume a hypothesis and abandon it if the data does not corroborate it, continuing in another more favourable direction until the best possible result is reached. These systems learn and become more intelligent as they receive more data and thus improve their ability to detect and correct anomalies over time (Jyoti, 2021).

AI-powered Analytics can help automate lifecycle tasks, augment human intelligence, or support human-to-human collaboration (Jyoti, 2021) as shown in Figure 1.

Figure 1. AI-powered Analytics performance in the enterprise scope

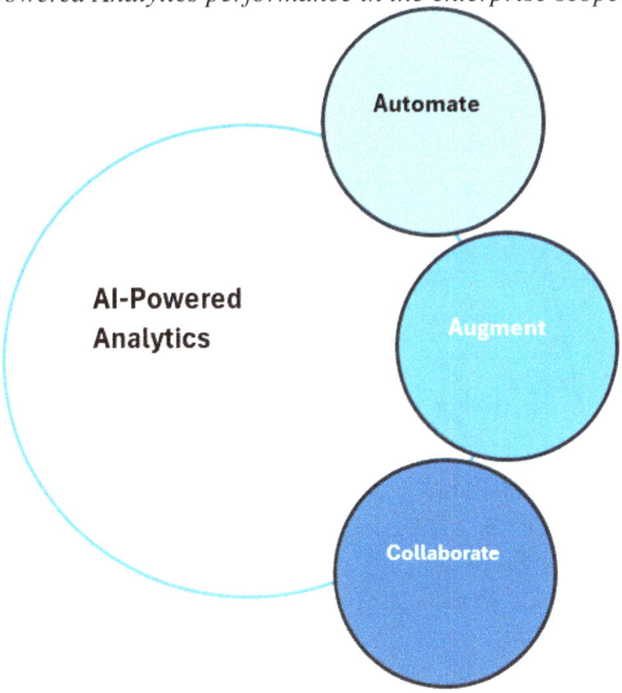

Source: Adapted from Jyoti (2021, p. 26).

Data analysis and AI algorithms allow us to discern what previously happened, project insights into the present, and make predictions about the future; that is, there are three types of analysis that can be performed (Liu, 2021):

Descriptive Analysis - The simplest type and usually the first step in the data analysis process, as it manages to consolidate data in a form that allows the generation of appropriate analyses and reports.

Predictive Analysis - Uses statistical models and ML to make predictions about future outcomes based on patterns found in existing data.

Prescriptive Analysis - Uses the results of previous analyses to create prescriptions or recommendations on the best actions to be taken to achieve the objective.

The essence of data analysis remains the same; what changes is the vast amount of data inside and outside organisations, as well as the enormous increase and development of computing power that can be used for its processing.

Data Science starts with data generation, which nowadays happens on a massive scale; everything is recorded, evaluated and stored. Data analysis and modelling are just some parts of the extensive data science cycle, as illustrated in Figure 2.

Figure 2. Data Science's life cycle

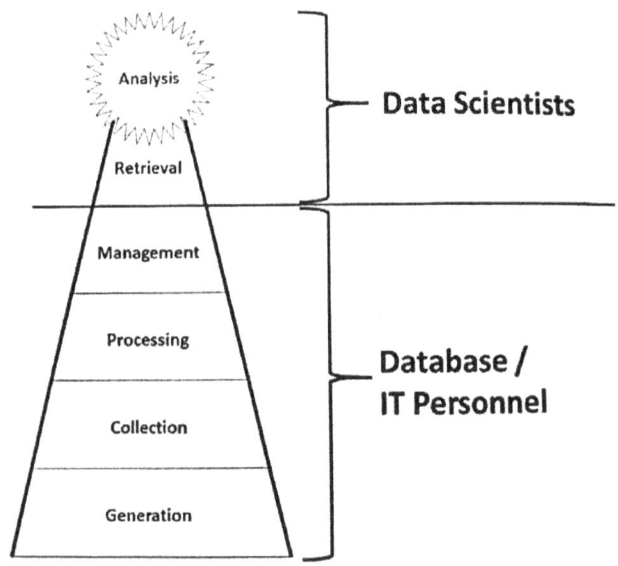

Source: Nelson (2021, p. 10).

The comprehensive diversity of data types and their processing can bring as many benefits as challenges. Elements such as video, images or sounds must be indexed with keywords so that they can be processed, and a large amount of information will remain uncategorized. This can represent a major problem as long as organisations and companies do not realise the value of unstructured data (Nelson, 2021).

After obtaining and cleaning the data, the step that follows is to decide which data to use, understand what is needed for analysis and what may be missing, meaning, how one can find the data that reveals what one needs to know. This process known as Data Wrangling can be effectively assisted by AI, which can process all types of data types through the data lake (repository for storing Big Data, and structured and unstructured data). Nelson (2021) states:

"Data must be processed. Data Scientists must be able to trust the data provenance. [...] "Data wrangling" is the new data science buzzword. [...] However,

unstructured is proving difficult to manage. [...] AI can assist with this type of data by performing some of the wrangling by processing data through a "data lake". (Nelson, 2021, p. 11).

AI has the remarkable ability to examine and transform structured and unstructured data environments into relevant data, to identify important elements, categorise and purify these elements, and store them for later retrieval (Nelson, 2021, p. 7).

For these reasons, AI is essential to the future of data science and thus enters the field of Data Science Artificial Intelligence (DSAI) (Nelson, 2021). Therefore, the data science life cycle includes a very important aspect: understanding the business (Nelson, 2021).

Nelson (2021) argues that through the Analytics Life Cycle (ALC) all elements of analysis can be treated from start to finish in a business context, and divides ALC into 11 direct steps, shown in Figure 3, intuitive and useful that can be applied when you want to change something, especially if you want a change with some impact, and which are (Nelson, 2021, p. 8):

1- Comprehend the business environment.
2- Understand the business.
3- Understand the business's goal.
4- Comprehend the business's strategy.
5- Recognise and understand the business's struggles.
6- Develop questions.
7- Use data science life cycles.
8- Understand the analytic model through its visualisation.
9- Evaluate the analytic model.
10- Apply the model back to the questions (send unanswered questions by the model through the process).
11- Apply the answered question(s) to the business' problem(s).

Figure 3. Analytics Life Cycle

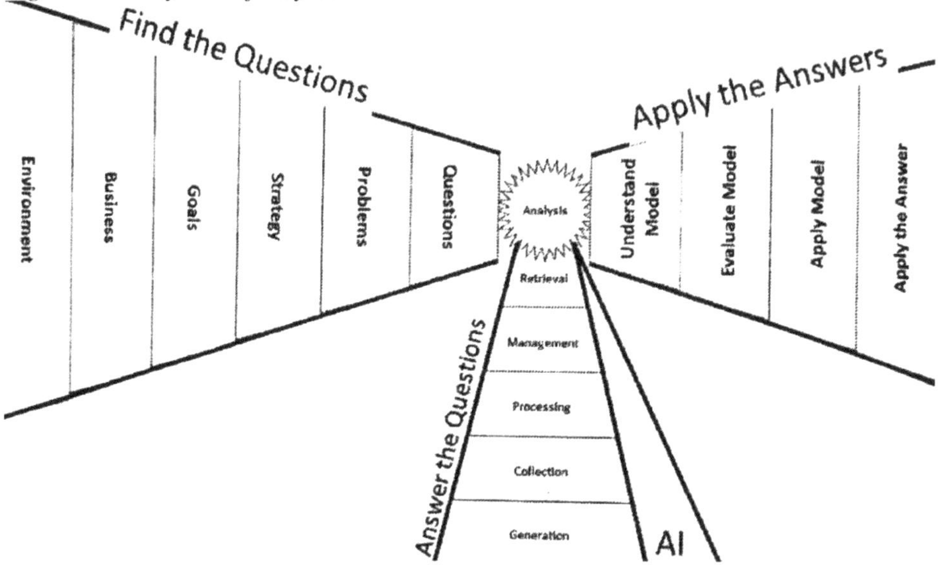

Source: Nelson (2021, p. 14).

These are some of the most popular approaches, in which analytics is seen as a "maturity journey" that progresses from the descriptive stage to the predictive stage, culminating in the perspective state. The synergies between AI and data analysis (AIA - Artificial Intelligence Analytics) are still a young science, but with a lot of potential, and professionals lack a lot of support. To address this shortcoming, Anderson and Zettlemeyer (2021) developed their framework, which they considered more suited to the real and current business world, shown in Figure 4.

Anderson and Zettlemeyer's (2021) framework focus on three specific types of analysis:

- **Exploratory Analysis**: Describes the data, explains how it was generated, and supports understanding the variability among the data.
- **Predictive Analysis**: Uses AIA models to anticipate future results.
- **Causal Analysis**: Uses AIA models to influence future outcomes.

The distinction between Predictive and Causal analysis is tenuous, but relevant. Firstly, because the business questions that can be addressed with Predictive analysis are different from those that can be addressed with Causal analysis. Secondly, the sources required to support a Predictive versus Causal analysis job can be quite different. Analysis is not the end goal; in order to determine the best action, it is necessary to link the analysis with the business's goals (Anderson & Zettelmeyer, 2021).

Figure 4. Artificial Intelligence Framework for decision making

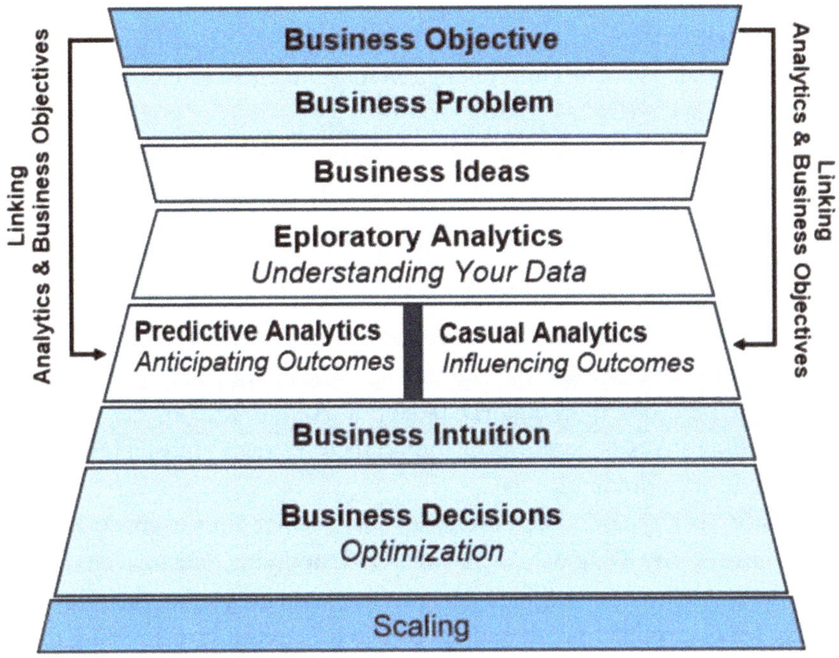

Source: Anderson and Zettelmeyer (2021, p. 27).

Artificial Intelligence and Data Storytelling

To relate AI and Storytelling, it is relevant to understand the importance and impact that communication has on humanity (Harari, 2011):

> *"That was the key success of sapiens. [...] In a conflict of hundreds, Neanderthals didn't stand a chance. They could share information about the location of lions, but they probably couldn't tell - and reframe - stories about tribal spirits. Without the ability to compose fiction, Neanderthals were unable to cooperate effectively in large numbers, just as they were unable to adapt their social behaviour to rapidly changing challenges. [...] The immense diversity of imagined realities that sapiens invented, as well as the resulting diversity of behaviour patterns, are the main components of what we call "cultures". Once cultures emerge, they never stop changing and developing, and it is these unstoppable changes that we call "history". (Harari, 2011, pp. 50-53).*

As we continue today with the same eagerness, depending on, creating, searching for, and especially consuming stories. Imagining and communicating stories is inherent to the human condition. This reality is emphasised with the arrival of AI, which can learn and produce logical reasoning more effectively and quickly than the human brain, but cannot imagine and communicate stories with creativity, empathy and feeling, meaning, it is precisely the imaginary side of the human brain that distinguishes it as such. This conception must be taken into consideration and used to our advantage (Dykes, 2020).

Data visualisation and Data Storytelling focus on the perception and cognition of data, respectively. Therefore, data storytelling is expected to be applied in scenarios where analysis results need to capture their interest and trust. Compared to raw data, data stories are more easily memorable and cognitively more engaging. Additionally, they can align with naturally human characteristics and offer a higher level of experiential engagement. Throughout the narrative exploration of a story, there is continuous communication and interaction with the audience, feedback and revision of the plot, based on data (Daradkeh & Atalla, 2023). Thus, research on Data Storytelling takes on significant importance for data representation and the development of data products.

A data story is a type of data product or service that aims to meet the specific needs of a business by using data as raw material, applying data analysis and modelling methods to extract valuable insights from it, and presenting them in the form of a story to a determined target audience. The process of transforming data into a data story is called Data Storytelling. A data story is the end product of a Data Storytelling process, combining the objectivity of data and the subjectivity of the story. A data story starts from the needs of a targeted business, always relies on data as evidence, and involves sequential stages of analysis.

Currently, applying Data Storytelling can be organised into two main categories (Daradkeh & Atalla, 2023):

- **Direct data stories Generation**: this genre develops and delivers data products in story form to the audience, such as data journalism, dashboards, and academic presentations.

- **Data Storytelling Software Product Development**: This type provides and implements methods and techniques to support platforms or tools used to generate data stories. Currently, Data Storytelling platforms or tools can be subclassified into two categories: those that incorporate Data Storytelling capabilities into Data Visualisation or Business Intelligence, such as Tableau, TIBCO Spotfire, Flexdashboard, Qlik Sense, ShortHand and Microsoft Power BI; and those that are specifically developed for Data Storytelling, such as Banjo. Generally, Data visualisation software that supports Data Storytelling products, and the number of specialised tools designed specifically for Data Storytelling is relatively limited.

This last genre of Data Storytelling is where the core of this work lies. In this type of Data Storytelling - Development of Data Storytelling Software Products - is where the intersection with AI occurs, where one can observe the performance of the algorithm in the creation of narratives, and more specifically, in visual narratives. In other words, it falls in the first subcategory: Development of Data Storytelling Software Products that incorporate Data Storytelling capabilities into Data Visualisation or Business Intelligence tools. According to Daradkeh and Atalla (2023):

> *"Currently, data storytelling platforms or tools can be classified into two categories: those that incorporate data storytelling features into existing data visualization tools or business intelligence software, such as Tableau, D3.js, TIBCO Spotfire, Flexdashboard, Qlik Sense, ShortHand, and Microsoft Power BI; and those that are specifically developed for data storytelling, such as Banjo and Narratives for Tableau. Generally, visualisation software that supports data storytelling is the mainstream approach in the development of data storytelling software products, while the number of specialised tools specifically designed for data storytelling generation is relatively limited" (Daradkeh and Atalla, 2023, p. 551).*

From a perspective of automatic generation and engineering refinement, the data story creation process can be decomposed into six main activities: understanding the data and the business, analysing data and insights, modelling the narrative, formalising the storytelling description, narration and interaction, and audience interaction and reflexive behaviour. According to Dradkeh and Attalla (2023), such as illustrated in Figure 5.

Figure 5. Main activity of Data Narratives

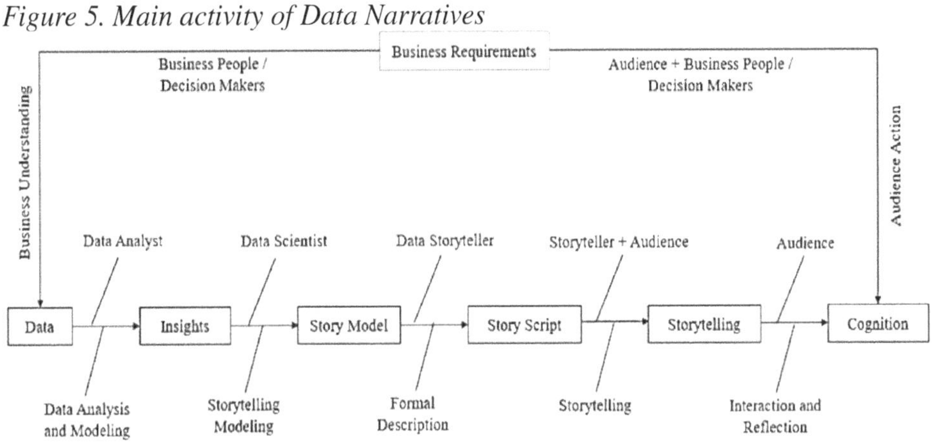

Source: Daradkeh and Atalla (2023, p. 552).

Crafting visually appealing data stories requires creativity, logic, sensitivity and other diverse skills, data analysis being one of them, allied to a keen awareness of the audience and context (Li *et al.*, 2024), however there remains a gap in literature on Data Storytelling tools, especially from a human-AI collaboration perspective (Li *et al.*, 2024).

On human-AI collaboration in existing Data Storytelling tools, Li *et al.* (2024) cite the importance of the different detailed stages: data analysis, data story planning, data story implementation, and its communication (Li *et al.*, 2024). And at each stage, collaboration patterns are examined through creators, reviewers, optimisers and assistants (Li *et al.*, 2024: 2)- Separating roles makes it easier to understand how humans and AI contribute to each stage of Data Storytelling. When combining these aspects, it is possible to comprehensively understand the design of human-AI collaboration. Figure 6 illustrates the framework of human-AI collaboration in Data Storytelling tools. It characterises collaborative data storytelling tools between humans and AI, based on the phases they encompass and the role they partake in these collaborations per phase.

Figure 6. Human-AI Collaborative Data Storytelling Tools

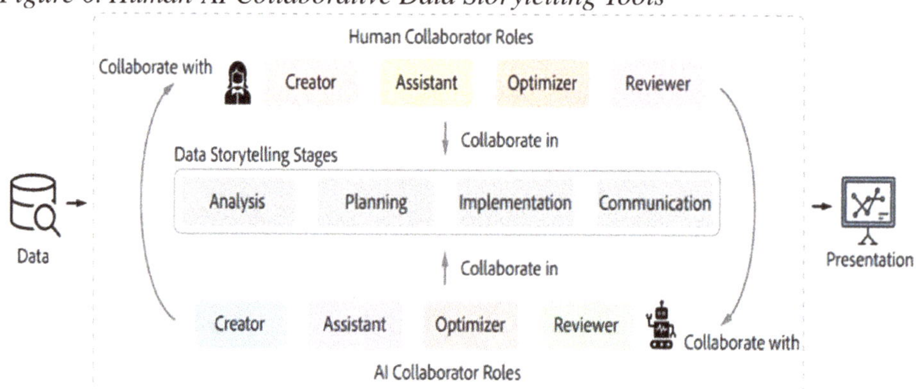

Source: Li et al., (2024, p. 1).

The distinctive roles - creator, assistant, optimizer and reviewer - for a worthy understanding of this process, translates into the following matrix that defines the four types of human-AI collaborations (Li *et al.*, 2024), where the coding of the collaboration patterns between humans and AI in Data Storytelling is done by the author himself and which are represented in Figure 7.

Figure 7. Four types of Human-AI Collaborations

Role	Definition
Human-creator, AI-creator	The collaborator who finishes most of the work from scratch
Human-assistant, AI-assistant	The collaborator who works with creators together to reduce the workload or compensate for inability
Human-optimizer, AI-optimizer	The collaborator who automatically improves the entire or part of the data stories
Human-reviewer, AI-reviewer	The collaborator who assesses the content in data stories and provides assessment results or suggestions

Source: Li et al., (2024, p. 5).

Researchers have extensively investigated collaborative ways between humans and AI to automate Data Storytelling whilst considering human control. This aligns with the creative nature of Data Storytelling, where designing stories should be taken as a creative task and it is difficult to define a clear goal to be achieved automatically by AI (Li *et al.*, 2024), since the creation of data stories still rely on the experience and judgement of humans, it is crucial to have human control throughout the Data Storytelling process, and simultaneously optimize the automation process.

In conclusion, there is interest and many advances regarding applying Data Storytelling in AI systems; however, this process still depends on the human touch to give it the genuineness that distinguishes it and makes it effective. Li *et al.* (2024) also propose two directions: exploring more design options in collaborative human-AI data storytelling tools and considering storytelling tools in conjunction with general visualisation creation and creativity support tools.

Data Storytelling and Artificial Intelligence for Data Analysis

The conjunction of the disciplines of Data Visualisation and Data Storytelling gives rise to the terminology of Visual Storytelling, as previously noted in this work. According to concepts stipulated in the study by Daradkeh and Atalla (2023, p. 552), and discussed previously in this study, Visual Storytelling is: "*A primarily visual storytelling approach that emphasises the importance of visualisation techniques in data storytelling*."

Popular sayings such as "a picture is worth a thousand words" or "judging a book by its cover" are based on the common and widespread observation of human behaviour in society. If the story is the key element to captivate an audience, visualisation is no less important. And sometimes, more important than the plot of the story is the way it is presented. If the challenge in data analysis is - how to express an insight through numbers; in data visualisation - how to present data visually; in Data Storytelling - how to tell a story with data that expresses the desired insights; in Data Visualisation, the challenge will be - how to tell that data story visually.

In the wide range of communications, there are different types and elements, and specifically, visual communication encompasses verbal communication (text) and non-verbal communication (images). Although visual communication of data always requires some textual communication, it should be strictly the minimum and necessary; graphics and images should prevail, highlighting their immediate and intuitive nature, which allows for faster, easier and clearer interpretation (Knaflic, 2015). Within the images, there are also animated images and videos that, like other visual elements, must be carefully inserted.

Generative AI, although recent, can be found in the task of automatically completing emails, for example, and therefore it is mostly used in co-writing and education. Lo Duca's (2023) study then focuses on how to assign a narrative to a data product in terms of annotations and introduces Generative AI to enrich data visualisation. "*Applying data storytelling to data visualisation means adding a narrative that better explains the visual and engages the audience. Generative AI can help transform data visuals into data stories*" (Lo Duca, 2023, p. 512).

Generative AI has opened new possibilities for the enhancement of data visualisation with narrative elements. Generative AI is a subfield of AI that uses Large Language Models (LLM) to generate new text based on a given prompt. It can be useful for different purposes, including text, audio and image generation (Lo Duca, 2023). There has been an effort made to identify the most common approaches to constructing stories in the media and news, and seven genres of visual narrative for journalistic stories have been recorded: magazine style, annotated graphic, partitioned poster, flowchart, comic book style, slideshow, and video (Lo Duca, 2023). And the semantics of the content of textual descriptions of the graphics is organised into two levels: enumerating the visualisation construction priorities, reporting statistical concepts and relationships, identifying perceptual and cognitive phenomena, and explaining domain-specific insights (Lo Duca, 2023).

AI Data Storytelling (AI-DaST) is a framework that allows for improving data visualisation and graphics through Generative AI. Figure 8 shows the AI-DaST architecture, which comprises three main elements: the Main Editor, the Textual Annotator Editor, and the Graphical Annotator.

Figure 8. AI Data Storytelling Architecture

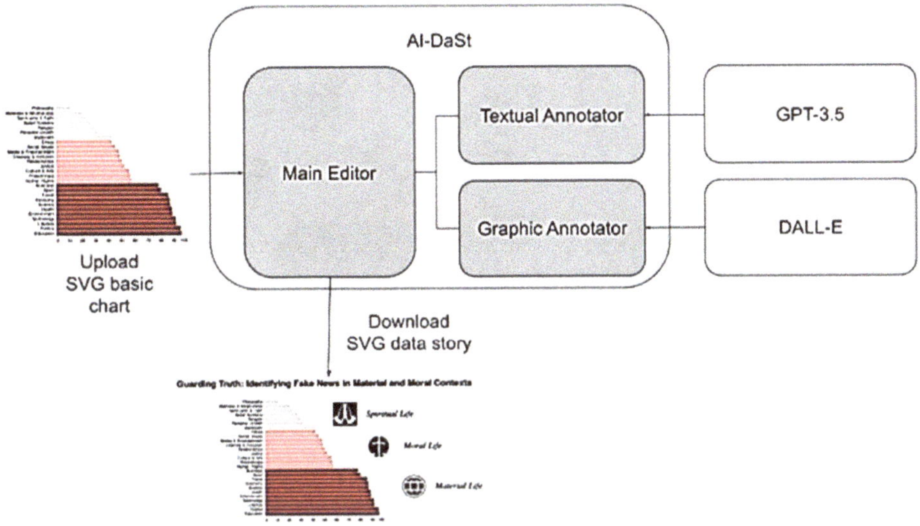

Source: Lo Duca (2023, p. 514).

The AI-DaST architecture considers four types of annotations (Lo Duca, 2023):

- Title - a concise sentence that summarises the main purpose of the chart, and the way it is written influences its interpretation.
- Comment - a brief comment providing additional information or context to the chart.
- Note - a brief written observation that gives additional information about a specific point in the chart.
- Image - a visual representation of the main subject of the graphic, an image that helps to engage the audience from an emotional point of view (Lo Duca, 2023: 514).

For a better understanding of these concepts, Figure 9 reveals the differences between graphs with and without AI-DaST. That is, the left side presents an initial graphical representation, and the right side presents the graph after using the Graphic Annotator.

Figure 9. Applying Data Storytelling in Graphics (Before and After)

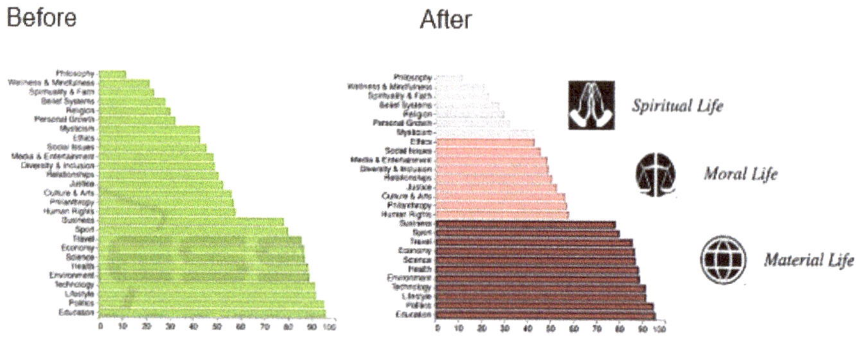

Source: Adapted from Do Luca (2023, pp. 516 - 517).

In this example by Do Luca (2023), the automatic change in the way the graph is read after applying Data Storytelling is noticeable, as shown in Figure 9. Compared to the original graph (on the left), the graph that represents Data Storytelling techniques is much more appealing, enlightening and quickly understandable (on the right). The main differences reside in the added elements, but also in the way they are integrated and add perceptual features. Applying short, highlighted text that serves as a caption (Textual Annotator), of colours to create structured divisions and of icons as signage (Graphic Annotator), instinctively guides the eye towards faster, more informed and useful reading.

The improvement of Data Storytelling in AI systems is the concluding point of this section, which takes as an example and establishes a connection with another developed by Do Luca, who states that in the future, it may involve the additional refinement of the AI-DaST framework, addressing scalability challenges and exploring additional forms of applying AI in data storytelling.

METHODOLOGIES

The methodology used for this study has a first stage, where the research and consultation of relevant bibliographic references for the acquisition of knowledge about Data Storytelling and the interconnection with Artificial Intelligence will take place.

For this study, the following stages, mainly qualitative methods, will be used. In particular, the participant observation technique will be used as a reference to implement Data Storytelling and Visual strategies.

Finally, a methodology will be presented to combine Artificial Intelligence, through the consideration of Sentiment Analysis, with concepts of Data Storytelling.

Data Storytelling

The first stage consisted of defining Data Storytelling, based on the literature review. For this purpose, and after a set literature review, the following definition was considered: Data Storytelling is the process of transforming raw data into understandable and engaging narratives by combining data analysis with narrative and visual elements. Its purpose is to facilitate the understanding and retention of complex information, helping the decision-making process and engaging the public. For doing so, it uses graphics, charts and visual design to present insights in a clear and persuasive form, making it an essential tool in business, journalism, education and public health.

Sentiment Analysis

In the second stage, the goal is to develop a project where an artificial intelligence algorithm will be applied to Sentiment Analysis on satisfaction comments about an event, as a demonstrative example of the potential of combining AI with Data Storytelling, an approach with ML that is a subcategory of AI, as a "proof of concept".

Sentiment Analysis (SA) (also known as Opinion Mining, Opinion Extraction and Subjectivity Analysis) focuses on the extraction of people's opinions, emotions, feelings and attitudes toward entities such as organisations, brands, personalities, services, products, issues, events or topics (Liu, 2021). With the growth of social media databases on the Internet, the amount of opinion data in digital form is as large and accessible as ever. Therefore, since the 2000s, SA has become one of the most interesting research topics in the field of Natural Language Processing (NLP). Due to its important contribution to decision-making, applying it has been spread to areas such as Marketing, Finance, Politics and Health, and many companies are currently dedicated to providing SA services. Several applied studies have demonstrated its useful contribution in predicting sales performance, election results and market trends (Liu, 2021).

Sentiment Analysis can be considered and applied at three levels (Liu, 2021):

- **Document Level**: involves classifying an entire document as expressing a positive or negative sentiment. This approach is limited to documents that evaluate a single entity and is not suitable for texts that compare multiple entities.

- **Sentence Level**: Focuses on analysis at the level of each sentence, identifying whether it expresses positive, negative or neutral opinion, it is associated with the subjectivity classification that distinguishes factual sentences from subjective sentences. However, they still don't capture all the nuances.
- **Entity and Aspect Level**: Performs a more refined analysis by specifically identifying which aspects of an entity were appreciated and the ones that were criticised. Rather than analysing documents or sentences as a whole, this level looks directly at the sentiment associated with entities and their individual attributes. This level transforms unstructured text into structured data, facilitating detailed qualitative and quantitative analyses.

SA has several steps to be completed for its conclusion; these steps constitute the methodology for applying SA to comments. The author El-Masri *et al.* (2017) present a schematic methodology for the SA process, as shown below in Figure 10.

Figure 10. Sentiment Analysis Methodological Process

Source: El-Masri et al., (2017, p. 3).

The different steps that are part of the SA methodology are as follows (El-Masri *et al.*, 2017):

- **Data Gathering**: Opinions can be collected from a variety of sources, the most common currently being social networks such as Facebook and Twitter, which are multi-domain and contain opinions on different topics. It is also possible to collect data from specialised sites, such as TripAdvisor for tourism reviews, IMDB for movie reviews and Amazon for product reviews.
- **Data Processing**: Processing means the process of cleaning data in order to remove unwanted elements, thereby increasing the accuracy of results and reducing the chance of errors. However, excessive use of these techniques can lead to the loss of important information. Processing techniques include:
  - Tokenise text: Split and categorise a text, words, sentences or characters.
  - Remove stopwords: Words that are irrelevant to sentiment analysis are eliminated, which improves effectiveness.

- Remove or identify punctuation: Punctuation marks are generally removed, but some, such as the exclamation point, can indicate emotional polarity.
- Convert text to lower or upper case: Capital letters can suggest strong emotion.
- Stemming the word: Reducing words to their basic form, a more complex process in certain languages such as Arabic and Chinese.
- Check the Spelling: Correct common typos, especially in social media data.
- Letter replacement: substitutions can be made to improve the accuracy of the data analysis. For instance, Twitter data requires additional techniques, such as removing hashtags, ERULs, and user mentions, as well as dealing with emojis and specific characters. Dialect manipulation is also important. In some cases, "unique" tokens are added for rare words in short tweets. And all these techniques help transform unstructured text into structured data, facilitating qualitative and quantitative analysis. Some of the text enrichment techniques in NPL are part-of-speech tagging (identifying grammatical functions of tokens), and syntactic analysis (building the syntactic structure of sentences) (Liu, 2021).

- **Feature Extraction**: Feature extraction allows for more accurate sentiment analysis and detailed summarisation of results. The most common features in SA are n-grams and POS (Part of Speech) tagging. Due to the complexity of the Arabic language, some studies have explored other specific linguistic features. The extracted characteristics can be of various types: stylistic, syntactic, semantic, lexical, and other specific needs.
- **Analysis Application**: There are three main methods of SA: Machine Learning, Lexicon-based, and hybrid or combined methods. In SA, the concepts of polarity (which can be positive, negative or neutral), subjectivity (which refers to feelings and opinions) and objectivity (referring to information, concrete data and facts) stand out (Costa, 2018).
- **Results Evaluation**: The evaluation of the results must be done taking into account the objective/problem initially defined, and possible limitations such as: the correct recognition of dialects, expressions and figures of speech (metaphor, sarcasm, irony, etc.); translation or interpretations eros; inability to compare opinions with each other; the lack of literary enrichment and colloquial language; and the appropriate classification of feelings and subjectivities. (El- Masri *et al.*, 2017).

The extractions of information for effective SA depend on the information gathered for it, since in this study, it was not possible to use company data; only the methodology to be considered for future studies is presented.

Based on the notions of SA, this point aims to highlight the importance and explore the methodology of applying Data Storytelling in the presentations of results, which integrate results from sentiment analysis. And to these ends, the proposed framework is as follows:

1. Collect data from social networks which represent consumer opinions, corresponding to the Data Gathering Phase.
2. Clean and process the collected data so that it can be analysed, corresponding to the Data Processing phase. This stage includes the following steps (Liu, 2021):
   a) Tokenisation: Break text into meaningful tokens.
   b) Stop words removal: Eliminate words that do not add value.
   c) Normalisation: Standardise tokens and convert uppercase to lowercase.
   d) Stemming and lemmatisation: Reducing words to their primary form.
   e) Spell correction: Correct typing errors.
3. Organise/Identify what to analyse in terms of characteristics or aspects to be investigated, corresponding to the Feature Extraction phase.
4. Applying the Sentiment Analysis Algorithm.
5. Assessment of SA results.
6. Present the SA results on dashboards, according to Data Storytelling concepts presented above.
7. Integration of other data in the company, such as financial data and development of dashboards that allow the analysis and comparison of SA results with financial results, detecting possible patterns in them.

SA is thus defined as something complex, something where it is of importance to structure the problem to objectively identify and understand effects and causes. This structured definition makes it easier to solve the challenges associated with unstructured natural language text and to analyse a wide range of opinions, reducing their subjectivity and combining them with emotions.

APPLYING AI WITH DATA STORYTELLING

Opinions are crucial for the decision-making process and influence our behaviours and choices, and SA studies how feelings, evaluations, attitudes and emotions shape our perceptions. The task of finding and analysing these opinions continues to be challenging due to the large volume and diversity of the available data, and therefore, investment and research in automated SA systems become increasingly essential (Liu, 2012).

Towards this end, we proceeded to apply a satisfaction survey to a considered event, where the concepts of Data Storytelling were applied, combined with AI methods. This process took into consideration the Sentiment Analysis methodology proposed by El-Masri *et al.* (2017) described above, which includes the following steps:

1. Collect

Data was collected through a satisfaction survey carried out with event participants. As they contain responses with text and are subject to SA, the following questions were considered for the purpose of this Sentiment Analysis:

> Question 2: What were the main reasons for your rating above?
> Question 3: Were there any specific sections or topics you found particularly valuable? Please mention them.
> Question 4: Were there any specific sections or topics you found lacking in quality or relevance. Please mention them.

2. Clean

This particular task began with cleaning up the text. Special characters, emojis, irrelevant words, and extra blanks were removed, as well as some spelling corrections that were made, thus preparing the text for the next stage.

3. Process

When processing this data, normalisation was carried out to convert all words to lowercase. It was also necessary to remove stopwords.

4. Organise

Since the only goal is to present a "proof of concept", only a small set of responses (16 in total) were considered, where the aspects analysed were not identified, leading to only the application of Sentiment Analysis at the global comment to be considered.

5. Applying the Algorithm

The algorithm was applied, tested and trained to create an analysis model. In this context, the chosen algorithm was VADER, given that it is considered the most suitable for analysing comments made on social networks. – "*Interestingly, the VAD-*

ER lexicon performs exceptionally well in the social media domain. [...] *it is more sensitive to sentiment expressions in social media contexts while also generalizing more favourably to other domains.*" (Hutto & Gilbert, 2014).

6. Results Analysis

In the analysis of the results of this SA, the examination is carried out question by question (2,3,4), highlighting the best and worst results, and the average. Word clouds were also generated based on the obtained responses, allowing the visualisation of the most used words and a clearer perception of the expressed sentiment.

RESULTS

Data collection was carried out through a digital satisfaction survey aimed at event participants. In total, 16 surveys were answered. Based on the responses obtained, analyses were carried out that correspond to the questions in the survey, to understand public satisfaction and identify aspects that can be improved in the organisation of a future event of a similar nature.

Question 2 - What were the main reasons for your ranking above?

In this question, the answer with the highest sentiment was "*Very enjoyable conference with opportunities to make it even better!*", with a value of 4.5. The response with the lowest sentiment was "*Nice programme, but announcements not very clear. Also missing a coffee/tea break in the afternoon and I think there should have been a bar/drinks place open at the venue, even if we would have to pay*.", with a value of 0.7. The average sentiment recorded was 2.9, and Figure 11 represents the word cloud generated from the collected responses, showing "*Good*", "*Conference*", "*Organization*" and "*Speaker*" as the main influencers of the overall evaluation of the event.

Figure 11. Word cloud generated through the responses to question 2

Source: Own elaboration on Orange Data Mining.

Question 3 - Were there any specific sections or topics you found particularly valuable? Please mention them.

Amongst the answers given to this question, the one that registered the highest values was "*Inspirational topics were very good. I also enjoyed the startups competition.*", with a value of 4.6. And the one that presented the lowest sentiment was "*The Future of Search and AI.*", presenting a value of 2.5. The average sentiment value is also 2.9, and Figure 12 shows the word cloud revealing "*AI*", "*Future*", "*Search*" and "*Startups*" as the most captivating topics.

Figure 12. Word cloud generated through the responses to question 3

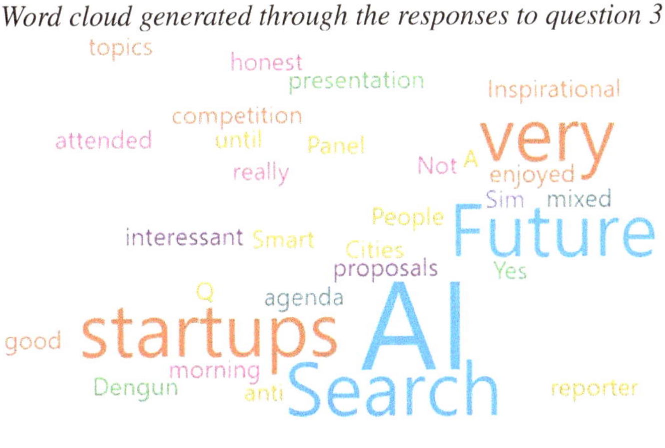

Source: Own elaboration on Orange Data Mining.

Question 4 - Were there any specific sections or topics you found lacking in quality or relevance. Please mention them.

Please note that in the following answers, there are concrete names, such as speaker names, which have been replaced by "###" to protect their identity and comply with current data protection policies.

The answer with the highest sentiment for this question was "*### - is it for normal people like me? It seems really high-end and the speaker kep saying that we could contribute and this project is for us - honestly couldn't see that. In what way can one participate and how can we benefit from it.*", with a score of 4.5, the one with the lowest sentiment was "*Yes, ### and ### presentations were bad.*" Figure 13 shows the word cloud based on the text resulting from the provided answers, which reveals "Presentations", "No", "All" and "Speaker" as the most representative terms.

Figure 13. Word cloud generated through responses to question 4

Source: Own elaboration on Orange Data Mining.

In this analysis, the Orange software and the VADER algorithm were used, as already mentioned. This algorithm performs SA based on rules and a lexical dictionary: "[…] *then combine these lexical features with consideration for five general rules that embody grammatical and syntactical conventions for expressing and emphasising sentiment intensity. Interestingly, using our parsimonious rule-based model to assess the sentiment.*" (Hutto & Gilbert, 2014). VADER only works with text in English since all the answers were given in English; in this case, there is no need for translation. To start this process, it is necessary to load the corpus file so that it can be linked to the SA, and by calculating the negative, neutral and positive scores, the column with the value resulting from the combination of all these scores (sentiment) is generated.

Sentiment is expressed from -1 to 1, where a value of -1 expresses the most negative sentiment and +1 expresses the most positive sentiment. To facilitate reading and analysis of the data, as well as comparison with other scales, the sentiment value was converted to a scale from 0 to 5 (where a value less than 2.5 represents negative sentiment and a value greater than 2.5 represents a positive sentiment). The conversion was performed using the following equation (Chen, 2020).

Based on the analysis of the results presented, it can be concluded that the overall balance is favourable. The majority of responses were indicative of people being pleased with the experience and its attributes. In general, the graphs represent positive values, revealing negative responses on a smaller scale. The level of "Very Satisfied" is reached in almost every graph, and although evident and not residual, it allows us to affirm a satisfactory evaluation of the event by the participants surveyed.

Dashboard Results

To present these results in a more readable and attractive way, a graphical representation was used, and the software chosen was Microsoft Power BI.

The goal here is to create a dashboard with the SA results, based on the responses given to the satisfaction survey. The aim is to apply the acquired knowledge coherently, develop the skills of crossing the studied tools, and highlight their usefulness and importance.

Dashboards are essential for the synthesis of large volumes of data into understandable visualisations, facilitating analysis and strategic decision-making, and for this reason, they play a fundamental role in competitive management. Through Data Storytelling, dashboards transform large amounts of complex data into clear and accessible visualisations, promoting faster, deeper and more enlightening assimilation of data sets. In turn, AI enhances not only the ability of dashboards to provide advanced information, such as predictive analysis and automated insights, which allow companies to respond quickly and conveniently to the challenges they face.

Figure 14 presents the dashboard built to communicate the results of the SA carried out on the responses from the event participants who took part in the satisfaction surveys, displaying Visual Storytelling techniques that apply in several aspects. Regarding text, titles were added and adapted for quick understanding of the graphs, with colour and font suited to the easy reading and general aesthetics of the panel, which were stylised for more intuitive communication. Colours were chosen according to their ability to facilitate highlighting and suggestion of automatic associations of the issues being analysed in the final graph that interconnects them, also highlighted. Dashboard data is linked in a way that allows cross-highlighting between its elements, making evident the selected results in all graphs simultaneously, and allowing perception of the related components.

One of the Data Storytelling focuses of this dashboard lies in the positioning of the visual elements. In line with the common reading orientation, from left to rights, it begins with the graph corresponding to the question about the intention to repeat the experience of the event again, with the other graphs on the right that analyse different isolated categories, and ending with the graph that interconnects them and shows their relationship, highlighted in colour in the lower left corner.

Figure 14. Final Dashboard of Sentiment Analysis and Participant Satisfaction

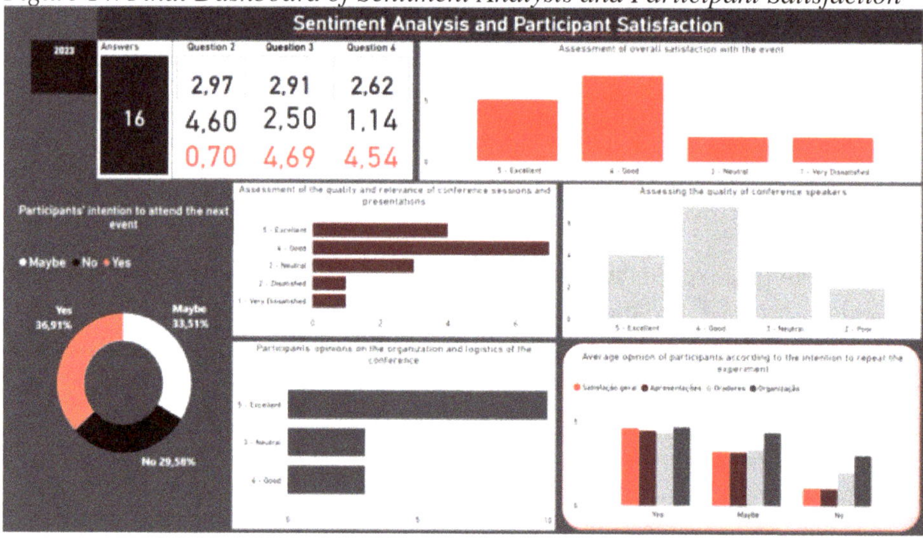

Source: Own elaboration on Microsoft Power BI.

This dashboard, based on the previously discussed Data Storytelling practices, allowed for adequate graphical visualisation of the results, as well as the relevance of applying AI tools to data processing. The combination of Data Storytelling with AI has proven to be an operational collusion for presenting complex insights in a concrete way, allowing for objective communication of results.

CONCLUSIONS

This work begins with a literary review on Data Storytelling, its definition and the combination of its application with AI tools. Starting by understanding what AI and Data Analysis are, what they are for, and how they work.

Data Storytelling refers to transforming data into engaging narratives, combining analysis and graphical visualisation to facilitate decision-making and understanding complex information. AI, in turn, is introduced to assist and improve the analysis and presentation of data, being applied, for instance, in Sentiment Analysis and in the creation of dashboards that allow for more flexible interpretation of Big Data.

AI can also be integrated into data analytics processes, creating accurate predictions about customer behaviour, providing businesses with a competitive advantage. In short, combining these tools can not only improve a company's analytical capabilities but also provide a more effective and accessible understanding and communication of the insights generated.

Nonetheless, the most striking limitation of this study was the lack of data to obtain more interesting results. The lack of access to some of the company's key data did not allow other types of information to be included in this study.

One of the topics worthy of deeper investigation would be the distinction, and respective systematisation, between "creation" and "extraction" of Data Stories. Data-driven stories can be drawn from a dataset, but they can also be adapted or fictionalised and still be based on factual data. Comprehending these differences and their methodology would also be important to decide when to use software with Data Storytelling resources (e.g. Microsoft Power BI), or one that is specific to carry out Data Storytelling (e.g. Banjo). Another aspect to be included would be the concepts associated with color and their effect on users' emotions.

Since these tools are advancing and seen as indispensable in the near future, it would be very important to develop a study aimed at Generation Z to examine their relationship with data visualisation.

A more detailed study on the influence, the application and the good practices of data visualisations with AI to transform complex information could also result in a valuable contribution, understanding what can enhance engagement, attention and empathy of the general public. As such, it is important to investigate phenomena like this, whether from an academic, artistic or social point of view.

The study's reliance on a small sample size (16 survey responses) significantly limits the generalizability of its findings. While the sentiment analysis provided preliminary insights, the narrow dataset risks overlooking nuanced patterns or biases inherent in larger, more diverse populations. A critical examination reveals that such constraints may skew results, particularly in sentiment analysis, where cultural, linguistic, and contextual variability play pivotal roles. Future research should prioritise larger, stratified samples to enhance reliability and capture broader sentiment trends, ensuring findings are robust and actionable for real-world applications.

The methodology, though well-structured, could benefit from deeper exploration of human-AI collaboration, particularly in how biases in AI algorithms (e.g., VADER's English-language limitations) interact with human interpretation. Ethical considerations—such as data privacy, transparency in AI decision-making, and the risk of automating subjective judgments—warrant further discussion. For instance, while AI streamlines sentiment analysis, human oversight remains crucial to validating results, address ambiguities (e.g., sarcasm), and ensure ethical data usage. Integrating frameworks like Explainable AI (XAI) could bridge this gap, fostering trust and accountability in AI-aided storytelling processes.

To advance this field, future studies could explore the integration of multimodal sentiment analysis, combining text with visual and audio data to capture richer emotional cues, while also addressing ethical challenges such as algorithmic bias and data privacy. Additionally, investigating adaptive human-AI collaboration frameworks—where AI handles data processing and humans refine narratives—could optimise the balance between automation and creativity in data storytelling. Another promising avenue is examining the impact of cultural and linguistic diversity on sentiment analysis accuracy, alongside developing more inclusive AI tools to mitigate biases and improve cross-cultural applicability. Longitudinal studies assessing the real-world effectiveness of AI-enhanced dashboards in organisational decision-making would further validate their practical utility.

ACKNOWLEDGEMENT

This paper is financed by National Funds provided by FCT- Foundation for Science and Technology through project UID/04020: Research Centre for Tourism, Sustainability and Well-*being.*

REFERENCES

Abbass, H. (2021). Editorial: What is Artificial Intelligence? *IEEE Transactions on Artificial Intelligence*, *2*(2), 94–95.

Anderson, E., & Zettelmeyer, F. (Eds.). (2021). *Leading with AI and Analytics: Build your data IQ to drive business value*. McGraw Hill.

Chen, W., Xu, Z., Zheng, X., Yu, Q., & Luo, Y. (2020). Research on sentiment classification of online travel review text. *Applied Sciences (Basel, Switzerland)*, *10*(15), 52–75.

Costa, B. M. (2018). Mas afinal, para que serve a Análise de Sentimento? *YouTube*. https//www.youtube.com/watch?v=JMQaFBYNLno

Daradkeh, M., & Atalla, S. (2023). From Data to Narrative: Automating and Engineering the Art of Data Storytelling. In *International Conference on Information Technology* (Vol. 23, pp. 550-555).

Dykes, B. (2020). *Effective Data Storytelling: How to Drive Change with Data, Narrative and Visuals*. John Wiley & Sons.

El-Masri, M., Altrabsheh, N., & Mansour, H. (2017). *Successes and challenges of Arabic sentiment analysis research: a literature review*. Qatar University.

Ergen, M. (2019). What is Artificial Intelligence? Technical Considerations and Future Perception. *The Anatolian Journal of Cardiology*, *22*, 5–7.

Feigenbaum, A., & Alamalhodaei, A. (2020). *The Data Storytelling Workbook*. Routledge.

Harari, Y. N. (2011). Sapiens: História Breve da Humanidade - De Animais a Deuses. (7ª ed.). Elsinore.

Hutto, C. J., & Gilbert, E. (2014). VADER: A Parsimonious Rule-based Model for Sentiment Analysis of Social Media Text. In *Proceedings of the Eighth International AAAI Conference on Weblogs and Social Media*. Association for the Advancement of Artificial Intelligence, 216-225.

Jyoti, R. (2021). Unlock The True Power of Data Analytics with Artificial Intelligence. In Liebowitz, J. (Ed.), *Data Analytics and AI* (pp. 21–30). CRC Press.

Knaflic, C. N. (2015). *Storytelling with data: A data visualization guide for business professionals*. John Wiley & Sons.

Li, H., Wang, Y., & Qu, H. (2024). *Where Are We So Far? – Understanding Data Storytelling Tools from the Perspective of Human-AI Collaboration*. The Hong Kong University of Science and Technology.

Liu, Y. (2021). Natural Language Processing in Data Analytics. In Liebowitz, J. (Ed.), *Data Analytics and AI* (pp. 117–131). CRC Press.

Lo Duca, A. (2023). Towards a Framework for AI-Assisted Data Storytelling. In *Proceedings of the 19th International Conference on Web Information Systems and Technologies* (pp. 512-519).

Morais, D. M., Oliveira, V., Junger, A. P., & Facó, J. F. (2020). O Conceito de Inteligência Artificial Usado no Mercado de Softwares, na Educação Tecnológica e na Literatura Científica. *Revista Educação Profissional e Tecnológica*, *4*(2), 98–109.

Nelson, J. H. (2021). Data Science Life Cycle. In Liebowitz, J. (Ed.), *Data Analytics and AI* (pp. 1–7). CRC Press.

Poeta, E., Ciravegna, G., Pastor, E., Cerquitelli, T., & Baralis, E. (2023). Concept-based Explainable Artificial Intelligence: A Survey. *Politecnico di Torino*.

Quan, H., Li, S., Zeng, C., Wei, H., & Hu, J. (2023). Big Data and AI-Driven Product Design: A Survey. *Applied Sciences (Basel, Switzerland)*.

KEY TERMS AND DEFINITIONS

Artificial Intelligence (AI): A scientific field focused on creating machines or systems capable of performing tasks that typically require human intelligence, such as learning, reasoning, and decision-making. AI is applied in areas like data analysis, automation, and problem-solving, transforming industries through advanced algorithms and computational power.

AI-Powered Analytics: The use of AI algorithms to analyse large datasets in real time, extract actionable insights, and automate decision-making processes. It combines machine learning and natural language processing to enhance data interpretation, enabling businesses to uncover trends and optimise strategies efficiently.

Data Storytelling: The process of transforming raw data into compelling narratives by combining analysis, visuals, and storytelling techniques. It simplifies complex information, engages audiences, and supports data-driven decision-making in fields like business, journalism, and public policy.

Data-Driven Decisions: Decisions based on evidence derived from data analysis rather than intuition. By leveraging analytics tools, organisations identify patterns, predict outcomes, and implement strategies with greater accuracy, improving efficiency and competitive advantage. **Marketing:** Strategies and techniques used to promote products, services, or brands by addressing consumer needs. Modern marketing relies on data and AI to personalise campaigns, optimise engagement, and measure effectiveness across digital and traditional channels.

Sentiment Analysis: A natural language processing technique that detects emotions, opinions, and attitudes in text (e.g., social media comments). It classifies sentiment as positive, negative, or neutral, helping businesses gauge public perception and improve customer experiences.

Visual Storytelling: An approach that uses visual elements (charts, infographics, videos) to communicate data-driven stories. It enhances comprehension and retention by blending aesthetics with narrative, making complex information accessible and engaging for diverse audiences.

Chapter 6
The Digital Transformation of Journalism:
The Example of dipnot.tv, a New Generation News Platform Based on Artificial Intelligence

Hülya Semiz Türkoğlu
https://orcid.org/0000-0002-7177-1959
Faculty of Communication, Istanbul University, Turkey

Süleyman Türkoğlu
https://orcid.org/0000-0003-2102-678X
Faculty of Communication, Istanbul University, Turkey

ABSTRACT

Digital transformation is causing radical changes in the media and journalism field; while traditional media organizations are struggling to keep up with this rapid transformation, AI-based news platforms offer a new paradigm. AI technologies play an active role in algorithms at many stages from the writing of the news to its distribution. AI systems, which assume the role of reporters and editors in traditional journalism, select and process content within the framework of predefined rules and present it to digital platforms. In this context, the foundations of AI-based journalism are shaped by algorithmic content management. In this study, emotional expressions in news content were examined with both qualitative and quantitative analysis methods through the example of Dipnot.tv. The findings obtained reveal

DOI: 10.4018/979-8-3373-6970-9.ch006

© 2026, IGI Global Scientific Publishing. Copying or distributing in print or electronic forms without written permission of IGI Global Scientific Publishing is prohibited. Use of this chapter to ‑nerative artificial intelligence (AI) technologies is expressly prohibited. The publisher reserves all rights to license its use for generative AI training and machine learning model development.

that AI journalism has not only technical but also emotional and human dimensions. As a result, AI-based news platforms are taking a central position in the future of journalism; they blur the boundaries between digital and traditional media.

INTRODUCTION

When we look at the history of humanity, every technological leap that has occurred in the means of communication has transformed not only the forms of information transfer but also social structures and interpersonal relationships. While cables laid under the ocean and nefs transmission processes that lasted for weeks were once seen as a great revolution, today's network-based digital communication systems that reach millions of people in seconds reveal the point this historical development has reached. This radical digital transformation has fundamentally affected not only the forms of communication but also the processes of news production and distribution, and therefore the understanding of journalism. The letters, telegrams and written newspapers of the analog age have given way to a digital media system where internet-based, instant and personalized content is rapidly produced.

In the new media environment, not only professional journalists but also ordinary individuals can actively participate in the news production process. This new dynamic developing through social media platforms has brought the concept of "citizen journalism" to the agenda and caused the centralization in journalism to break down. However, in today's digital media environment, not only people but also artificial intelligence-supported software and robot systems have become active actors in news production. This development has brought about ethical and philosophical discussions not only in terms of the content of the news but also in terms of the identity, responsibility and professional competence of the producer.

Artificial intelligence technologies are defined as "the ability of a computer or a computer-controlled system to perform tasks associated with intelligent living beings". Artificial intelligence systems, which are used in many areas from daily life practices to the business world, from education to production processes, now also undertake functions such as collecting, editing, analyzing and distributing content in news production. The concept of "robot journalism" that emerged in line with this development points to a media production practice in which news texts are written by algorithms instead of humans. However, the fact that these systems produce content devoid of emotional context and based solely on data creates a controversial area, especially in matters where news should be evaluated in an ethical, cultural and social context.

AI-supported journalism applications are transforming not only technological advances but also the definition, role, and application practices of the journalism profession. Pavlik (2023) states that generative AI technologies—especially large language models such as ChatGPT—are creating a new paradigm in content production. This paradigm shift repositions journalists not only as content providers but also as "hybrid professionals" who work in collaboration with technological systems, managing and interpreting data. Similarly, Diakopoulos (2019) argues that the future of journalism will be shaped by a hybrid model in which humans and AI work together. It is stated that this hybrid structure should provide a balance between technological efficiency and ethical reasoning.

Indeed, many media organizations in the West have integrated AI-supported systems into their newsrooms in the last decade (Putranto et al., 2021). Algorithms have become decisive at many points, from editorial decision-making processes to content distribution. AI-based systems analyze large data sets and provide news content customized to users' interests; this enables media organizations to achieve significant gains in terms of speed, efficiency, and accessibility. However, the ethical, social, and professional risks that these developments bring are also noteworthy. Hermida and Young (2019) emphasize that the ethical problems that AI systems may cause in journalism should be addressed, especially within the scope of journalism education.

In order to evaluate this process in Turkey, Dipnot.tv, a pioneering example among AI-based news platforms, is the focus of the study. Founded by Cüneyt Özdemir, this platform adopts a user-centered approach and integrates AI technologies into content production, analysis, and distribution processes. In this context, Dipnot.tv is evaluated as a model that embodies the impact of digital transformation on journalism practices, beyond being just a news platform. The functions of emotional expressions and algorithmic structures in the news published on this platform were examined with both descriptive and content analysis methods. Additionally, positive and negative criticisms towards artificial intelligence journalism were re-evaluated in the example of Dipnot.tv.

This study aims to examine how journalism has evolved during the digital transformation process, the role of artificial intelligence-supported systems in journalism, and the social, ethical, and professional dimensions of this transformation in a multi-layered manner. Revealing both the potential advantages and the risks that artificial intelligence-based content production processes may create will contribute to a holistic assessment of contemporary journalism practices. Thus, it is aimed to understand the place of artificial intelligence and robot journalism in the media ecosystem and to develop strategic predictions for the future.

Innovations Brought by Digitalization to Journalism

Digitalization has led to radical changes in the field of journalism and transformed the traditional media approach. With the widespread use of the internet, news production and distribution processes have accelerated, and instant information flow has been provided. Social media platforms allow individuals to play an active role in news production, while also enabling journalists to reach wider audiences. In addition, the use of data journalism and multimedia content enables news to be presented more effectively. Digital tools increase audience interaction and encourage readers' participation in news. However, the information pollution and reliability problems brought by digitalization bring new ethical discussions to the agenda in the practice of journalism. As a result, while digitalization makes journalism more dynamic and interactive, it also brings new challenges. (Türkoğlu & Doğan, 2018)

The rapid development of the Internet as a dominant tool in the field of information has brought with it many innovations arising from the nature of digital networked media. Communication has gained a new dimension with digitalization. The Internet, which connects millions of computers around the world and is called the "network of networks", has provided its users with the opportunity to choose the content they follow. In addition, one-way communication has given way to interaction. The Internet, which enables an individual to send a message to more than one person or multiple people to a single person in real time or within a certain time period, is an interactive tool that enables media content to be sent to a small target audience or large audiences between two networks (Castells, 2009, p. 55). This communication tool has also been used in journalism for many years. The internet, which has been used in journalism since the early 1990s, has quickly become an important complement to journalism. Access to archives, maps, sound and image recordings or materials that will support the news has become significantly easier with the internet (Tokgöz, 2010, p. 90).

In the early 2000s, as a result of the use of the internet in news, it became easier for people to be informed about developments in other parts of the world than to learn about events in their immediate surroundings. During this period, internet journalism was carried out differently than today. In general, online news sites where traditional publishing organizations were active were used to introduce content produced for traditional media or to publish content that was normally offline online (Salwen, 2005, p. 47). This situation has also changed with the development of technology and the spread of the internet.

With digitalization, the areas of use of artificial intelligence have increased, causing serious changes and transformations in traditional media. With artificial intelligence, it has now become possible to report data in a short time and serve it to online readers at low cost. Internet journalism has paved the way for the formation of a new universe of automatic news content developed by artificial intelligence algorithms to meet the reader's demand for news. Every stage of the news is designed with automation from its emergence to its delivery and can be delivered to the reader within seconds.

Artificial intelligence algorithms, which are expected to have an important place in today's journalism, are changing people's lives and perspectives on events. These algorithms, which facilitate internet journalism, transfer the ability to analyze and make decisions that are unique to humans to artificial intelligence software. Artificial intelligence is known as the modeling of human learning by machines that emerged with the imitation of human intelligence. Media organizations that want to be permanent and successful may now have to switch to artificial intelligence journalism. Artificial intelligence algorithms will help news organizations process their data quickly and automate the process of news. Artificial intelligence used in journalism refers to algorithms and spreadsheets rather than a physical robot. Artificial intelligence in newsrooms is not a physical entity or an autonomous robot, but rather software that can automatically create news content, process and analyze data, and personalize content (Peretti, 2022). However, researchers state that today's artificial intelligence is only advanced enough to replace humans in a specific and narrow task, and does not have general human intelligence.

When the studies on the subject are evaluated, it is seen that algorithmic journalism is addressed from different perspectives, both critically and from mainstream perspectives. For example, Anderson et al. (2015, p. 33) emphasize that this type of journalism has a commercial dimension, especially in the context of American journalism, and state that journalistic practices are becoming increasingly negative. Researchers argue that good journalism practice is possible by examining what kinds of tasks machines and journalists successfully perform. It is stated that computers are superior, especially in organizational functions, but humans are ahead of machines in areas such as "competence, originality, creativity and charisma". These studies, which emphasize the importance of the original and creative perspective of human origin, draw attention to the need for transformation in the working styles of journalists.

On the other hand, the analyses conducted by Ay (2023) on the content produced or monitored on the AI-supported news platforms 'Knowherenews.com' and 'The Bipartisanpress.com' reveal that AI journalism is not as impartial as expected. Ay explains the news production process in detail and discusses the various ethical and practical dimensions of this process.

Figure 1. News Production Process in Artificial Intelligence Journalism

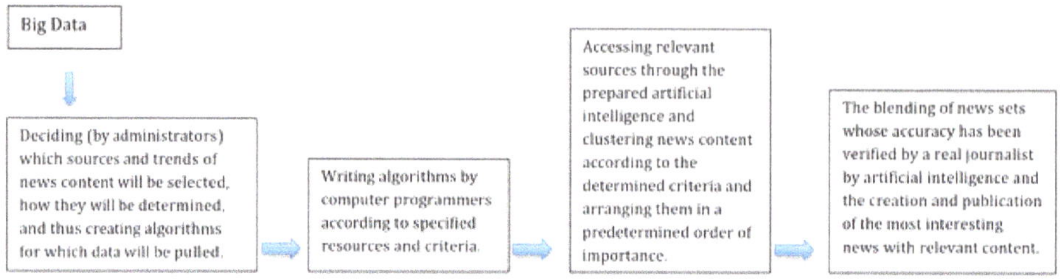

(Ay, 2023: 430)

The administrators of news sites are the decision makers in the design of algorithms and prioritization of sources. Content verified by real journalists is mapped by artificial intelligence and the most interesting ones are published. This process makes the impartiality claim of artificial intelligence journalism significantly questionable.

Readers in traditional media can become active people with the transfer of news to the internet. This transformation can therefore affect the concept of gatekeeping. The production processes from selecting, collecting and monitoring the subject of the news are provided by gatekeepers. Therefore, gatekeeping refers to the selection, display, presentation, timing, storage and monitoring of various data in the interpretation of the message or message content. Manipulating a news by drowning in details or not reflecting certain news clearly upon request can show how important the concept of gatekeeping is. However, comments from readers can also be monitored by gatekeepers as in traditional journalism. Gatekeepers can transfer their own ideas to internet platforms without being censored thanks to artificial intelligence. Thus, ideas and opinions circulating on the internet are published without being bound to any value (Carter, 1998: 392). An interactive news understanding can be developed by taking user comments into account through platforms.

DIGITALIZATION, ARTIFICIAL INTELLIGENCE AND THE EVOLUTION OF ROBOT JOURNALISM IN THE NEW MEDIA ECOSYSTEM

Artificial intelligence, one of the most important building blocks of the digital transformation process, has become the pioneer of radical changes in the field of media and journalism, as in many sectors today. Artificial intelligence is a scientific and engineering-based discipline that aims to perform cognitive processes such as learning, reasoning and problem solving, which traditionally require human intelligence, through machines. Artificial intelligence systems, which are widely used in application areas such as natural language processing, visual recognition, pattern perception and decision support systems; have the capacity to produce solutions to many complex problems, especially from supply chains to healthcare services.

Machine learning, an important subfield of artificial intelligence, offers an approach based on analyzing the relationships between data and extracting meaning from these relationships, unlike traditional algorithms. The development of these technologies has not only been limited to the increase in technical competencies, but has also made it possible to develop solutions for much more complex problems with deep learning techniques. Especially thanks to unlimited data circulation and increasing processing power, artificial learning models can make predictions with increasing accuracy, making them indispensable tools in a wide variety of fields. (Nilson, 2018).

With the development of Web 4.0 technologies, artificial intelligence-supported systems have been integrated into many sectors, from social networks to public services. In this process, algorithms stand out as one of the basic building blocks of digitalization; They are at the center of the processes of creating meaning in the digital environment by undertaking functions such as collecting, classifying and analyzing data. Especially today, an extraordinary amount of data is produced, and making this data meaningful is not only a technical but also a social necessity (Harari, 2016). Algorithms are not only mechanisms that process data; They are also considered as cognitive structures that play an active role in digital decision-making processes. These algorithms, which feed the learning cycle of artificial intelligence systems, reshape the information processing practices of the digital age by enabling machines to learn from experience.

In the field of journalism, one of the most striking applications of artificial intelligence and algorithm-based systems is robot journalism (automated journalism). Robot journalism refers to algorithmic systems that can automatically produce news texts from predefined data sets. These systems are widely used in news types based on regular and structured data sources, especially finance, sports and weather. While robot journalism provides speed and efficiency in news production, it also transforms the information consumption habits of digital media users thanks to the opportunity to offer personalized content.

The most well-known example of robot journalism is given by the Los Angeles Times newspaper. The QuakeBot system includes the algorithms necessary to write earthquake news. This system was used by the Los Angeles Times to write about the 4.4 magnitude earthquake that occurred in southern California in 2013 (Graefe, 2016: 24). Accordingly, regardless of the time of the earthquake, the news text is automatically created and presented to the reader without the need for any reporter. The area of use of robot journalism is not only in earthquake news; News is produced on many topics such as sports, weather, technology, and the news produced can even be presented by robot announcers.

With the widespread use of Internet of Things (IoT) technologies, data obtained from daily life is being accumulated in large data silos through environmental sensors and mobile devices. Artificial intelligence engineers are developing advanced algorithms to make sense of these data sets and identify social trends. In this context, the approach that Alex Pentland calls "social physics" focuses on understanding social behavior patterns by analyzing billions of digital traces left by individuals in digital environments (Latar, 2018: 3). Robot journalism systems can also produce more targeted and context-sensitive news content at individual and social levels thanks to algorithms that have the capacity to analyze these digital traces.

However, AI-supported news production also carries risks that should be carefully considered, especially in terms of ethical and social impacts. Although robot journalism systems appear to be based on seemingly impartial data analysis, the possibility that they can be directed in a way that serves certain commercial, ideological or political interests in the background can create serious problems in terms of the accuracy and objectivity of the news. (Carro, 2018) At this point, the transparency and accountability of algorithmic systems have become one of the most fundamental areas of discussion in digital journalism.

In this context, what is expected from journalists and media organizations is not only to increase their technological competence; but also to develop sensitivity to the ethical, legal and social problems that artificial intelligence and algorithm-based systems may create. If automated content production becomes independent of journalism practice, basic democratic principles such as the right to receive news and access to public information may be at risk. Therefore, artificial intelligence and robot journalism applications are not only technologies; they are also communication tools that should be directed with a sense of social responsibility (Salaverría & de-Lima-Santos, 2020).

Artificial Intelligence and Algorithm-Based Journalism in the Digitalization Process: A New Phase of Media Transformation

Today, the acceleration of digitalization has created radical transformations in the media sector, as in many other areas. Artificial intelligence technologies, which are at the center of this transformation, have fundamentally affected the traditional understanding of journalism and have led to the emergence of innovative applications in processes ranging from news production to distribution. Data can now be processed and reported in very short periods of time and delivered to online readers at low cost. This process has created serious changes not only in the production and distribution stages, but also in the forms of interaction established with the reader.

Internet journalism has become a dynamic, fast and interactive platform, exceeding the limited possibilities of traditional media. Artificial intelligence algorithms developed in order to respond to the reader's demand for news have made it possible to produce automatic content. Thus, a new era has begun in journalism; a structure in which human intervention is reduced and automation is at the forefront has been adopted. All stages such as the collection, organization, presentation and distribution of news can be completed by algorithms in seconds (Dalen, 2012: 648–649).

As a result of these developments, journalism practice is becoming based on statistical information and stereotyped language patterns; the content of the news is shaped more by software-based systems (Clearwall, 2014). Computer software has now assumed a role that is not only supportive but also content-producing; it has become a determining factor in processes such as access to, sharing and publishing news. This situation directly affects not only the technical infrastructure of the media but also journalistic ethics, the accuracy of the news and the perception of the reader.

The new media environment has transformed the relationship between the reader and the journalist into a more interactive and dynamic structure. Readers, who were passive in traditional media, have ceased to be individuals who only received information with digitalization and have become active actors contributing to content production. Thanks to digital tools such as social media platforms, blogs and online comment areas, users are directly involved in news processes; they take on active roles in processes such as expressing opinions, sharing news and even creating news. These developments form the basis of the interactive journalism approach, enabling journalists to communicate with readers simultaneously and build a more participatory news environment.

One of the main sectors transformed by digital transformation is journalism. In this context, artificial intelligence technologies have increasingly begun to play a role in news production. Many media institutions, especially leading international news organizations such as The New York Times, Los Angeles Times and The Washington Post, actively use artificial intelligence as part of the editorial process (Çavuş, 2020, p. 252). Many media organizations, large and small, are diversifying, accelerating and automating content production through artificial intelligence robots and algorithms developed with digital technologies.

However, these developments also lead to some concerns among media professionals. In particular, discussions that artificial intelligence-based news systems can replace traditional journalists create serious uncertainty and anxiety within the sector. How artificial intelligence-supported systems will affect the journalism profession opens up new areas of discussion in the context of the ethical principles and professional responsibilities of journalism.

Artificial intelligence algorithms, which have an important place in today's media, deeply affect not only news production processes but also the ways individuals relate to daily life and social events. Artificial intelligence-supported news systems play an active role in stages such as news collection, analysis, classification and presentation, thus accelerating the news production process and increasing the level of automation. However, this technological transformation should not be evaluated only as a technical advancement; it should also be addressed with its ethical, sociological and ideological dimensions.

Different discussions on the effects of artificial intelligence are also on the agenda in the field of communication transformed by computer and communication technologies. These discussions are shaped around two basic approaches: techno-optimists and those with a critical perspective. Techno-optimists believe that artificial intelligence technologies will have constructive and positive effects on the journalism profession. According to them, artificial intelligence will increase news accuracy, improve data journalism and lighten the workload of journalists, allowing them to focus more on creativity (Marconi, 2020).

However, the fact that the algorithms are created by human hands also raises doubts that artificial intelligence systems will always be impartial and objective. This situation is called "algorithmic bias" in the literature. The prejudices of the people who program artificial intelligence systems can also be reflected in the decision-making mechanisms of these technologies. Especially in a field that is extremely sensitive in terms of politics and ideology, such prejudices can infiltrate media content and lead to serious problems such as misleading the public. For this reason, it is of great importance that artificial intelligence is used in media applications in accordance with principles such as transparency, auditability and ethical responsibility. (Manning, 2020)

Artificial intelligence technologies are defined as systems that model human intelligence. These systems undertake decision-making processes that humans can do by imitating cognitive processes such as learning, problem solving, reasoning and language understanding. For media organizations aiming for permanent and sustainable success, the transition to artificial intelligence-supported journalism has become inevitable. These technologies, used in many areas from big data analysis to natural language processing, from machine learning to user behavior tracking, make it possible to present news quickly, efficiently and in a personalized way.

Artificial intelligence applications have led to the emergence of a new type of news in the journalism profession, referred to as "algorithmic journalism" (Clearwall, 2014: 520). This type of news redefines the role of the journalist in news production; It refers to a structure in which algorithms are decisive in stages such as the collection, classification, processing and publication of news. The development of artificial intelligence first came to the agenda in the 1950s with the concept of "thinking machines", and after the 1990s, it began to be used effectively in many areas of life. These technologies, which emerged from the synthesis of computer science and human intelligence, have led to a significant transformation in the field of media over time (Akyazı, 2018: 21).

The role of artificial intelligence in journalism has ceased to be a mere technical tool and has become one of the main actors shaping content production. Data is converted into numerical expressions through algorithms, and meaningful results are extracted from this data and converted into information. Solving particularly difficult problems with artificial intelligence algorithms provides great convenience in the journalism profession. However, the most important point to be considered here is to protect ethical principles and not to ignore the human factor. (Tableau, 2024)

With digitalization, the reader profile has also changed. Readers who are passive in traditional media can turn into active content producers on digital platforms, and this transformation directly affects the concept of "gatekeeping" in news production. Gatekeepers play a decisive role in processes such as selection, collection, control and preparation of news for publication. According to Donohue's definition, gatekeeping is a process that includes various decisions in stages such as presentation, timing, storage and control of the message or content (Donohue, 1972: 53).

However, the gatekeeping function has transformed in internet journalism. Readers' comments and contributions are communicated through platforms, but these comments are again filtered by AI-supported systems or editors. While artificial intelligence offers gatekeepers the opportunity to share their ideas directly, without being subject to censorship, it can also cause content that is open to manipulation to spread uncontrollably (Carter, 1998: 392). This situation causes ethical problems to become more visible in digital journalism.

The transformation experienced in the media environment with digitalization has made the reader-journalist relationship more interactive, and the spread of artificial intelligence technologies has radically redefined the practice of journalism. However, this transformation process should not be evaluated solely on the basis of technological possibilities; it should also be analyzed multidimensionally with its social, ethical and ideological consequences. While evaluating the possibilities of artificial intelligence technologies, the journalism of the future should not ignore a human-centered, transparent and responsible approach to journalism.

Artificial Intelligence Based New Generation News Platform: Analysis on the Example of Dipnot.tv

Rapid developments in artificial intelligence technologies have radically changed the direction of the relationship between journalism and artificial intelligence; this has also brought about the transformation of news production practices. Research shows that investigative journalists have been using computer technologies in data analysis and news writing processes for over fifty years (Thurman et al., 2019;

Zamith, 2019, p.1). Especially since the mid-2010s, automatic or semi-automatic systems have become increasingly common in newsrooms for news gathering, filtering and sharing processes. In line with these developments, traditional news production norms, formats and routines have transformed; established acceptances and professional practices related to journalism have once again become a subject of debate.

It is known that algorithms are used on social media platforms to filter content, select newsworthy content and inform journalists. In this context, the artificial intelligence-supported content production applications that have emerged are defined in the literature as "automatic journalism" or "robot journalism"; This new approach is reshaping the nature and ethical boundaries of the journalism profession.

Surjatmodjo et al. (2024) emphasize that this problem has not only technological but also ethical and professional dimensions by revealing the increasingly complex structure of disinformation in the digital age. In this context, the proposed analytical framework lays the foundations of a multi-layered verification system by integrating disinformation combat strategies into daily journalism practices. This system aims to provide a more effective approach in the detection and analysis of false information by combining human judgment and artificial intelligence algorithms.

The inclusion of artificial intelligence in editorial decision-making processes necessitates a reinterpretation of the concept of objectivity, one of the fundamental principles of journalism. In this context, transparency is not limited to information sources alone, but also requires that algorithmic functioning and news production processes be clear and understandable. The proposed analytical framework provides both a theoretical basis and a practical model for the integration of AI technologies into the sector while preserving journalistic ethics. It also makes significant contributions to updating journalism education, encouraging ethical innovation and preserving the quality of public discourse.

An Innovative Model in Artificial Intelligence-Supported Digital Journalism: The Dipnot.tv Example

The digital transformation of journalism is undergoing a significant evolution with the rise of AI-based platforms. The example of Dipnot.tv shows how this transformation takes place and how it transforms the user experience. The interaction between traditional journalism and new generation platforms is reshaping the understanding of journalism and changing the way users access information. Artificial intelligence is becoming one of the elements that will determine the future of journalism by offering innovative solutions in many areas from content production to user interaction. In this context, the opportunities and challenges brought by digitalization will continue to affect the dynamics of the journalism sector.

As an AI-based news platform, Dipnot.tv offers content customized according to users' interests. The platform analyzes user feedback to optimize the news flow and provides a more interactive experience.

As one of the innovative media platforms leading the evolution of digital journalism in Turkey, Dipnot.tv stepped into the digital media world in 2011 with the visionary approach of journalist Cüneyt Özdemir. Adapting to the dynamics of digital media with its interactive publishing approach, the platform has attracted attention especially in user-centered content production and has quickly become one of the leading actors of digital journalism.

Today, Dipnot.tv has undergone a radical transformation with the integration of artificial intelligence technologies and has become the first completely artificial intelligence-based news platform in Türkiye. This transformation is important not only as a technological innovation, but also in terms of redefining journalism practices and restructuring media production in the digital age. The platform aims to deliver content to users in a faster, more accurate and more customized way thanks to artificial intelligence algorithms that enable the automation of news production processes.

Dipnot.tv's artificial intelligence-based infrastructure was developed by Roide Technology, and content production processes were supported by Matnon. This technical infrastructure allows content to be created with data-based analyses, news to be personalized according to user interests and accuracy rates to be increased. Thus, the platform has gone beyond being a medium that only provides information and has gained a structure that focuses on user interaction and experience.

In addition, Dipnot.tv aims to raise the sectoral standards of digital journalism by developing collaborations with experts in areas such as digital marketing, business development and special content production. This multi-disciplinary approach offers a sustainable media production model in both technological and content terms; and reveals the application potential of AI-supported journalism in Turkey.

PURPOSE AND METHOD OF THE RESEARCH

The main purpose of this study is to examine the concept of "mechanized journalism", which is increasingly prominent in today's digital media environment, through the example of Dipnot.TV, an artificial intelligence-based digital news platform. In this context, the structure, functioning and emotional aspects of artificial intelligence-supported journalism were evaluated by analyzing the current news content published on the platform.

A two-stage methodological framework was adopted within the scope of the research. In the first stage, the news published on Dipnot.TV was examined using the quantitative content analysis method, based on the topicality criterion. In this analysis, the news was divided into 11 categories: Dipnot Special, Agenda, Business and Economy, Politics, Sports, Science and Technology, Art and Culture, Life, Health, Education and Environment. In the sample selection, a purposeful random sampling method that combines systematic and random qualities was used. According to Marshall and Rossman (2014), this sampling method ensures that the sample cases selected in accordance with the purpose of the study increase the validity and reliability of the research results.

In the second stage, the qualitative dimension of the study was addressed, and the emotional expressions in the selected news were evaluated in detail using the descriptive content analysis method. In this stage, a total of 10 news items belonging to the "Agenda" and "Footnote Special" sections, which were determined using the purposeful sampling method and were among the news categories that received the most attention in the public, were analyzed in depth. The news items in question were found suitable for evaluation in terms of the density of their content and the diversity in the use of artificial intelligence-supported language.

Thanks to this methodological approach, both the thematic distribution of artificial intelligence-based content and the emotional dimension of the language used in these contents were revealed. Thus, a multidimensional analysis was carried out not only in terms of the technical and structural aspects of the mechanized journalism process, but also in terms of the human and emotional elements in content production.

FINDINGS

This section is structured under three main headings in order to systematically present the data obtained in the study: "General View of Dipnot.TV" and "Basic Findings Regarding the Examined News".

The subheading "General View of Dipnot.TV" addresses the structural features of the platform, news presentation format, artificial intelligence integration and content policies. In this context, a general framework is drawn regarding the platform's position within the digital journalism approach.

Dipnot.TV is an online news platform operating in the field of digital journalism and drawing attention with its artificial intelligence-based content production. The site offers various content categories that appeal to different areas of interest of users. The main headings on the platform are as follows: "Dipnot Special", "Agenda",

"Business and Economy", "Politics", "Sports", "Science and Technology", "Art and Culture", "Life", "Health", "Education" and "Environment".

This categorical structure aims to classify news content thematically and provide easy access to areas of interest to users. In addition, it is seen that the platform has a rich range in terms of news diversity and content strategy. In this context, Dipnot. TV's content organization aims to both improve user experience and systematize content production with artificial intelligence algorithms.

Figure 2. Visual Interface Design of the Upper Section of Dipnot.TV Home Page

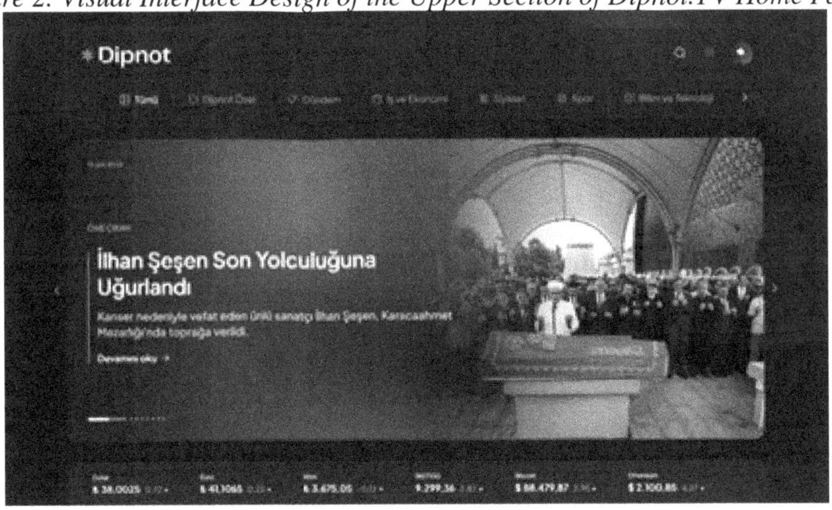

There is a section titled "Hot Agenda" just below the main categories. This section usually presents headline-worthy and prominent current news content published in the last 1-2 days. The "Hot Agenda" section stands out as an area where the platform's most current news flows dynamically and thematic diversity can be observed. Exchange rate information is located just below this section, enabling instant tracking of economic developments. Below the exchange rates, there are square-shaped visuals that summarize the news in the "Hot Agenda" section. These visuals are supported by short headlines prepared by artificial intelligence using algorithmic summarization techniques for news content. These sections, which provide the user with a brief idea of the content, provide clickable links for readers who want to read the full news to detailed pages.

Figure 3. Weather, Current Headlines and Featured News in the Sub-Section of Dipnot.TV Home Page

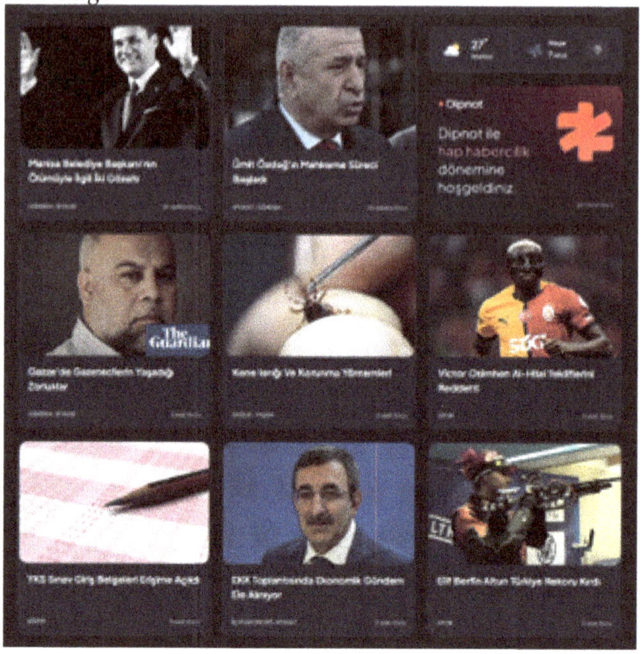

As you move towards the bottom of the page, the number of news content presented to the user increases and thematic diversity expands. When the cursor is placed on the news cards, the category to which the relevant news belongs, a short summary text, information about the publication time (for example, how many hours ago it was published) and the phrase "Read in Detail" become visible. This structure allows users to preview the content and to more easily select the news that interests them and go to the detail pages.

Figure 4. News on Dipnot.TV Home Page

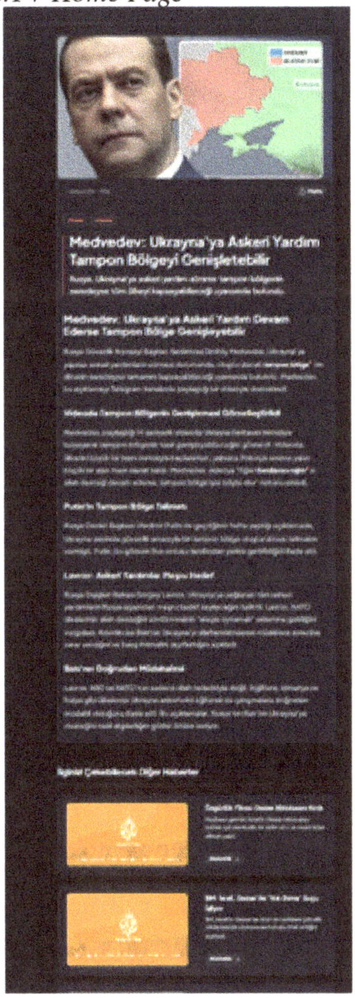

On the Dipnot TV news site, reader comments are not included under the news content, which eliminates the opportunity for users to directly react to the content, express their opinions or participate in discussions. This situation shows that the two-way communication opportunities commonly seen on digital news platforms are limited and user participation remains at a passive level.

AI-Based Footnote TV Content Classification on News Sites

In understanding the content structure and algorithmic tendencies of AI-based news sites, news headlines and the categories they belong to play a critical role.

Therefore, these elements are discussed in detail in the study. The headlines, categories and publication dates of the first ten news analyzed within the scope of qualitative analysis are systematically presented in Table 1.

Table 1. News Headlines and Categories

News No	Headlines	Categories	Date
1	Overseas Sacrifice Campaign from Turkish Red Crescent	Life Footnote Special	May 28, 2025
2	New Developments in Mehmet Çetin's Disappearance	Agenda Footnote Special	May 20, 2025
3	Unknown Video Footage of Ataturk Found	Art and Culture Footnote Special	May 19, 2025
4	The Epic Fight of the 57th Regiment in Çanakkale	Agenda Footnote Special	April 24, 2025
5	New Development in 11-Year-Old Child Murder Investigation in Şanlıurfa	Agenda Footnote Special	April 10, 2025
6	UK Imposes Sanctions on Israeli Ministers	Agenda Politics	June 10, 2025
7	Russia-Ukraine War: Developments of Day 1,198	Agenda Politics	June 10, 2025
8	Security Issues of Women and Children in the Metaverse	Agenda Science and Technology	June 10, 2025
9	Prof. Dr. Gazi Yaşargil Passed Away	Health Science and Technology	June 11, 2025
10	Türkiye is Third in Europe in Information Technology and Artificial Intelligence Education	Education Science and Technology	June 8, 2025

When the news text regarding the Turkish Red Crescent International Sacrifice Campaign numbered 1 is examined, it is determined that expressions that emphasize human emotions such as “empathy”, “helpfulness”, “brotherhood” and “hope” are included. It is seen that expressions such as “those in need”, “solidarity”, “bridge of goodness” and “millions of people in need of help” are used throughout the text, aiming to arouse compassion and social sensitivity in the reader. In addition, it is determined that the expression “the names of the proxy holders are read one by one” is used, thus emphasizing the spiritual dimension of aid activities.

In addition, expressions such as “peace of sharing”, “abundance” and “tranquility” show that the news presents the act of aid as a social and spiritual value. The news does not only aim to inform, but also to create an emotional impact.

When the news text regarding the disappearance of Mehmet Çetin numbered 2 is examined, it is determined that expressions reflecting strong human emotions such as loss, uncertainty, pain, hope and the search for justice are frequently included in the text. It has been determined that the expressions "hopeful in the search for justice", "mysterious loss", "unsolved" and "years of search" are used; it has been determined that both the emotional burden experienced by the family and the anxiety at the social level are reflected through these expressions. In addition, it has been determined that structures such as "the family… claimed" and "contradictory expressions" are used in the text; it has been determined that these expressions reflect emotions such as doubt, faith and determination.

The news text aims to evoke empathy and sensitivity in the reader by appealing not only to information but also to human emotions.

When the news text numbered 3 titled "Unknown Video Footage of Atatürk Found" is examined, it has been determined that the language used and the expressions chosen carry an emotional and meaningful structure that can be encountered in human-written news texts, despite the fact that the text is produced by artificial intelligence. It has been determined that expressions such as "unknown video footage" and "emerged" are used in the text; it has been determined that the sense of curiosity and discovery is tried to be triggered in the reader through these expressions. In addition, it was determined that structures such as "very rarely known" and "could have been in the hands of collectors for years" were used; it was concluded that these expressions served to increase emotional interest by emphasizing the special and valuable nature of the event. When the news text was examined, it was determined that expressions such as "documenting how young our Ataturk looked", "drawing attention to his youth" and "giving him as a gift" were used. It was seen that these expressions reflected the feelings of nostalgia, loyalty and attribution of historical value. In addition, it was determined that the use of the word "Atamız" undertook an important function in the transmission of collective feelings such as national belonging, love and respect. In addition, the use of words such as "important" and "needs to be documented" in context can be evaluated as presenting a value-laden narrative that can be associated with historical responsibility and attribution of meaning. In this respect, the news text contains discourse structures that aim to establish an emotional bond, appeal to the reader's historical memory and perception of national identity; thus, despite the artificial production, it exhibits a human-centered narrative style.

When news text number 4 was examined, it was determined that although it was produced by artificial intelligence, human emotions that can be encountered in human-written texts were frequently included. It was determined that expressions such as "epic struggle", "heroic story" and "symbolizes courage and resistance" were used in the text; feelings such as pride, courage, determination and love of country were highlighted through these expressions. In addition, it was determined that "Atatürk's words 'I order you to die'" were used as a strong expression of devotion and sacrifice, and concepts such as "strategic importance", "gaining superiority" and "victory" reflected the feelings of respect and collective pride for historical success. As a result, it was observed that the news text went beyond providing information and presented a narrative that aimed to create an emotional impact, and in this respect, it gave the impression of human narration despite the artificial production.

When the language and narrative style in the news text number 5 was examined, it was determined that although the text was produced by artificial intelligence, it contained human emotion elements that are frequently encountered in human-written texts. It was determined that expressions such as "child", "playing" and "lost" were used in the text; innocence, need for protection and feelings of loss were highlighted through these expressions. In addition, words such as "murder", "corpse" and "suspects" were used; it was seen that these words reflected pain, fear, anger and the search for justice. In addition, expressions such as "an important step", "new evidence was reached" and "justice was provided" were used; it was determined that these structures triggered feelings of hope, expectation and optimism in the reader. It was determined that structures such as "years of work" and "continuing their work" presented a narrative that expressed patience and determination. It was determined that all these expressions allowed the reader to establish an emotional bond with the event and that the text went beyond conveying information and offered content that touched human emotions.

When the news text numbered 6 was examined, it was determined that although it had a structure that was mainly political and diplomatic, it also included some linguistic elements related to human emotions, despite being produced by artificial intelligence. It was determined that expressions such as "infuriating", "unacceptable" and "reaction" were used in the text; these expressions expressed emotions such as anger, resentment and opposition, especially in a framework reflecting the international public opinion's criticism of Israel. It was also determined that the concept of "pressure" was used to define international demands for aid to Gaza and that it evoked feelings of tension and responsibility in this context. In addition, it was determined that the expression "awaited with curiosity" was used to convey the expectation and interest in developments in the public. As a result, it was determined that although the news text was mainly shaped on a political level, it indirectly touched on human emotions such as anger, curiosity and pressure through certain words and expressions and in this respect, it presented a human-centered narrative despite being an artificial production.

As a result of the analysis of the news text numbered 7, it was determined that, despite being created by artificial intelligence, the text contained expressions that triggered human emotion and empathy. It was determined that expressions such as "humanitarian aid", "call for a ceasefire", "civilian population" and "having difficulty meeting their basic needs" were used in the text; it was observed that an emotional connection was established in the reader by emphasizing the suffering experienced by people, their need for protection and their demands for basic rights through these expressions. In addition, it was determined that concepts such as "problems in accessing health services" and "displaced persons" were used; it was evaluated that these expressions concretized the dimensions of the humanitarian crisis and triggered emotions such as charity and solidarity. As a result, it was determined that the news text not only conveyed information, but also adopted a humane language that enabled the reader to empathize and presented a narrative structure that prioritized human sensitivity despite being an artificial production.

The emotional expressions used in the news text number 8 provide a narrative framework that reflects individual and social security concerns. It was determined that expressions such as "security issues" and "source of concern" were used in the text; it was determined that these expressions aroused a perception of threat and feelings of anxiety in the reader. In addition, it was determined that expressions such as "sexual harassment", "abuse" and "threats of violence" were used; it was determined that these expressions drew attention to the trauma experienced by the victims and the need for social sensitivity. In addition, it was determined that concepts such as "responsibility" and "effective policies" were used; it was evaluated that these concepts aimed to create an emotional and social consciousness towards the search for a solution. As a result, it was determined that the news text presented a narrative structure aimed at creating a strong impact on both emotional and cognitive levels.

It was determined that the expressions in the news text number 9 aimed to reflect strong human feelings such as respect and admiration, as well as a deep sense of sadness and loss. It was determined that expressions such as "lost his life" and "passed away" were used in the text; It was evaluated that these expressions expressed the weight of the loss experienced at individual and social levels. In addition, it was determined that statements containing religious and cultural elements such as "may his place be heaven, may his rank be high" were used; it was seen that these expressions contributed to the meaning of the loss within the framework of spiritual consolation and respect. In addition, it was determined that expressions such as "his life dedicated to science", "his unique studies" and "left a permanent mark" were used. It was evaluated that these expressions emphasized the contributions made by the deceased throughout his life and drew attention to his scientific and social legacy. In the respect and admiration dimension, it was determined that praise expressions such as "the best brain surgeon of the century", "Turkish scientist" and "awarded with a medal of honor" were included; it was concluded that these expressions served to give the news text a positive and monumental tone as a reflection of the social appreciation and gratitude. As a result, it was determined that the news text presented a narrative structure with a strong human aspect, balancing the themes of loss and sadness with feelings of respect and admiration, creating both empathy and inspiration in the reader.

It has been determined that expressions reflecting feelings of success, progress and social appreciation are used intensively in the news text created by artificial intelligence number 10. It has been determined that expressions such as "achieved success", "significant success" and "demonstrated a successful performance" are used in the text. These expressions highlight the achievements achieved at the individual or institutional level and evoke feelings of pride, motivation and belonging in the reader. Thus, it has been observed that the language is not limited to conveying information only, but also adds a human dimension to the news through positive emotions. In addition, it has been determined that expressions such as "pioneer country" and "successful in gender equality in education" are used. Such expressions reflect the collective achievements of societies and their efforts towards progress, reinforcing feelings of social appreciation, hope and confidence in the future. This situation contributes to the strengthening of the positive identity perception and social responsibility awareness in individuals who read the news. As a result, it has been determined that discourses focused on success and appreciation support the objective content of the news text with emotional depth and provide a narrative structure that strengthens feelings of motivation, inspiration and confidence at the individual and social level.

CONCLUSION

In today's world where digitalization is accelerating and media production is largely transferred to technology-based tools, AI-supported journalism applications are becoming increasingly widespread and are replacing traditional journalism practices. While this transformation offers advantages such as speed, cost-effectiveness and access to multiple data sources in journalism, it also brings with it important discussions on issues such as the nature of content production, ethical responsibilities and emotional transfer. Considering the function of news not only to provide information but also to direct social emotions, establish empathy and create public opinion, the extent to which content produced by AI can carry these aspects emerges as a critical problem in terms of media research.

In this study, the effect of AI-supported news production on human emotional expression was examined; ten news texts published on the Dipnot.tv platform, one of the pioneers in this field in Turkey, were selected as a sample. In the study, the qualitative content analysis method was used to analyze which emotions were conveyed in the news produced by AI and how, at the level of language and discourse. The selected news items; It consists of different thematic categories such as social events, cultural content, environmental disasters and science-technology developments.

As a result of the analysis, although emotional language elements are clearly used in most of the news, it has been determined that this language is generally used in a stereotyped, superficial and contextually insufficient manner. For example, while dramatic but repetitive patterns such as "urgent measures must be taken" and "nature is taking revenge" are encountered in news about environmental disasters, it has been observed that expressions emphasizing nostalgia, national pride or traditional values are prominent in cultural news. However, it has been observed that these forms of narration offer limited creative variety compared to the style of human journalists and their potential to interact with the reader remains weak. The lack of contextual richness and emotional resonance of the news makes it difficult to comprehend the content in depth and to affect the reader emotionally.

These findings reveal that while the integration of artificial intelligence into news production processes transforms journalistic practices, it is still open to development in terms of ethics, narrative quality and human-centeredness. Especially in news that requires emotional expression, the limited context-building capacity of artificial intelligence-supported systems and their inability to fully internalize social sensitivity reduce the impact of the content and make it difficult for the news to fulfill its social function.

Recommendations

In this context, the following recommendations are presented for AI-supported journalism to gain a more humane, ethical and effective dimension:

Editorial Human Control: News texts produced with AI should be ethically, content-wise and linguistically controlled by human editors before publication; especially in emotional news, the guidance of human journalists should be taken as a basis.

Algorithmic Transparency and Ethical Principles: Transparency should be provided regarding how AI systems that produce news work, and these systems should be structured with ethical codes within the framework of universal journalism principles.

Cultural and Emotional Data Sets: In order for AI systems to produce more qualified content, they should be trained with large data sets that include cultural sensitivity and emotional diversity. Thus, their capacity to establish context and create empathy can be increased.

Education and Awareness Programs: Journalism professional organizations should organize training programs that explain the opportunities and limitations offered by AI technologies to journalists; digital media literacy should be increased.

Hybrid News Models: Hybrid news models should be developed that are not based entirely on artificial intelligence, but rather where human-journalist and artificial intelligence collaborate. In this way, both speed and efficiency can be achieved and human sensitivity can be preserved.

In conclusion, while AI-supported journalism is an inevitable part of the digital age, human touch, control and guidance are needed for this technology to be used in the media field in a sustainable, reliable and ethical way. In this context, establishing a balance between the possibilities of technology and the ethical foundations of the journalism profession is essential for acting with a sense of social responsibility in new media environments.

REFERENCES

Akyazı, A. (2018). *Gazetecilikte Dijitalleşe ve Haber Üretimine Yansıması: Robot Gazeteciler, Dijital Medya ve Gazetecilik*. Eğitim Yayınevi.

Anderson, C. W., Bell, E., & Shirky, C. (2015), Post-Industrial Journalism: Adapting to the Present. Geopolitics, History, and International Relations, 7(2), 32–123. https://www.jstor.org/

Ay, A. (2023). Gazetecilik 4.0: Yapay Zekâ Haberciliğinin Güncel Örneklerine Yönelik Bir İnceleme. *Süleyman Demirel Üniversitesi Vizyoner Dergisi*, *14*(38), 412–435. 10.21076/ vizyoner.1141093

Carro, B. (2018). Pros and Cons of Robot Journalism, https://www.mediego.com/en/blog/pros-and-cons-of-robot-journalism/. Erişim Tarihi:12.04.2025

Carter T. B. (1998), "Electronic Gatekeepers: Locking Out The Marketplace Of Ideas". Communication Law and Policy. 3:3., 389-408.

Castells, M. (2009). *Communication Power*. Oxford University Press.

Çavuş, S. (2020). Gazetecilik ve Yapay Zekâ. H. Bakırtaş, & S. Çavuş içinde, Yapay Zekâ Disiplinleri Dönüştürüyor Değişime Hazır mıyız? (s. 242-255 S:250). Konya: Ekin

Diakopoulos, N. (2019). *Automating the News*. Harvard University Press.

Dipnot.tv. https://dipnot.tv/tr-TR/ilhan-sesen-son-yolculuguna-ugurlandi, Access Date: May 29, 2025 https://dipnot.tv/tr-TR, Access Date: May 29, 2025

Donohue, G. A., Tichenor, P. J., & Olien, C. N. (1972). Gatekeeping: mass media systems and information control. In Kline, F. G., & Tichenor, P. J. (Eds.), *Current Perspectives in Mass Communication Research* (pp. 41–70). Sage.

Graefe, A. (2016). Guide to Automated Journalism. Tow Center for Digital Journalism Report. Erişim Tarihi (25.04.2025) http://towcenter.org/research/guide-to-automated-journalism/

Harari, N. Y. (2016). *Homo Deus Yarının Kısa Bir Tarihi. P. N. Taneli (Çev.).* Kolektif Kitap.

Hermida, A., & Young, M. L. (2019). *Data Journalism and the Regeneration of News*. Routledge.

Latar, N. L. (2018). *Robot Journalism: Can Human Journalism Survive?* World Scientific.

Manning, C. (2020). Artificial Intelligence Definitions. hai.stanford: https://hai.stanford.edu/sites/default/files/2020-09/AI-Definitions-HAI.pdf

Marconi, F. (2020). *Newsmakers: Artificial Intelligence and the Future of Journalism.* Columbia University Press.

Marshall, C. & Rossman, G. B. (2014). Designing Qualitative Research. NewYork: Sage.

Nilson, N. J. (2018). *Yapay Zekâ Geçmişi ve Geleceği.* Boğaziçi Üniversitesi Yayınevi.

Pavlik, J. V. (2023). Collaborating with ChatGPT: Considering the implications of generative artificial intelligence for journalism and media education. *Journal. Mass Commun. Educ.*, *78*, 84–93. DOI: 10.1177/10776958221149577

Peretti, M. (2022). 10 Things You Should Know About AI in Journalism. gijn.org: https://gijn.org/stories/10-things-you-should-know-aboutai-in-journalism/

Putranto, A., Utoyo, W. A., & Delliana, S. (2021). Robotic Journalısm Practıce, Journalis Twilight. The 3rd Open Society Conference (OSC 2021) (s. 218-228). Jakarta, Endonezya: Faculty of Law, Social and Political Sciences Universitas Terbuka.

Salwen, M. B. (2005). Online News Trends. M. B. Salwen, B. Garrison, & P. D. Driscoll içinde, Online News and the Public, Lawrence Erlbaum Associates. stable/26805941

Surjatmodjo, D., Unde, A. A., Cangara, H., & Sonni, A. F. (2024). Information pandemic: A critical review of disinformation spread on social media and its implications for state resilience. *Soc. Sci.*, *13*, 418. DOI: 10.3390/socsci13080418

Tableau. (2024). Artificial intelligence (AI) algorithms: a complete overview. Tableau: https://www.tableau.com/datainsights/ai/algorithms#:~:text=So%2C%20at%20the%20essential%20level,and%20their%20ability%20to%20learn

Thurman, N., & Lewis, S. C., ve Kunert, J. (2019). Algorithms, Automation, and News. *Digital Journalism (Abingdon, England)*, *7*(8), 980–992. DOI: 10.1080/21670811.2019.1685395

Tokgöz, O. (2010). *Temel Gazetecilik.* İmge Kitabevi.

Türkoğlu, H. S., & Doğan, B. Ö. (2018). Sosyal Medya Üzerinden Okurun Değişimi ve Bilgi Güvenirliği. *Erciyes İletişim Dergisi*, *5*(4), 371–385.

Van Dalen, A. (2012). The algorithms behind the headlines: How machine-written news redefines the core skills of human journalists. *Journalism Practice*, *6*(5-6), 648–658.

ADDITIONAL READING

Bulut, S. (2020). Dijital Çağda Medya: Makine Öğrenmesi, Algoritmik Habercilik Ve Gazetecilikte İşlevsiz İnsan Sorunsalı. *Selçuk İletişim*, *13*(1), 294–313.

Florıdı, L., & Chırıattı, M. (2020). Gpt-3.5: Its Nature, Scope, Limits, And Consequences. *Minds and Machines*, *30*, 681–694.

Graefe, A. (2016). *Guide to Automated Journalism.* Tow Center for Digital Journalism, Columbia Journalism School.

Moschovakis, Y. N. (2001). What is an Algorithm?B. Engquist ve W. Schmid (Ed.), İçinde Mathematics Unlimited-2001 and Beyond (ss. 919-936). Springer.

Russell, S. J., Norvig, P., & Davis, E. (2010). *Artificial intelligence: A modern approach* (3rd ed.). Prentice Hall.

SEN. J. (2022). Machine Learning Algorithms, Models and Applications. London: IntechOpen.

Tiwari, S. (2024). The Role Of Artificial Intelligence In Automated Journalism: Transforming News Production. 12(5).

Whittaker, J. (2019). *Tech Giants, Artificial Intelligence, and the Future of Journalism*. Routledge.

KEY TERMS AND DEFINITIONS

Algorithmic Content: Algorithmic content is a type of digital content automatically selected, ranked, or generated by algorithms based on user data, interaction behavior, and specific parameters. The visibility and accessibility of content in digital environments such as social media platforms, news sites, and search engines are largely determined by these algorithmic systems. This raises significant ethical and epistemological debates regarding the objectivity of news, its agenda-setting power, and access to public information.

Artificial Intelligence Journalism: Artificial intelligence journalism is a new journalistic practice shaped by the use of artificial intelligence technologies in news production and distribution processes. By leveraging AI in areas such as text generation, data analysis, automated content generation, and news presentation based on the analysis of user interactions, the goal is to both accelerate production processes and reach a wider audience. This process means that news is edited and even written using algorithms rather than human hands. This situation raises new debates regarding both ethics and accuracy.

Digital Transformation: Digital transformation is the process of integrating digital technologies into social, cultural, economic, and institutional structures, radically altering the way these structures operate, their relationships, and their production processes. Specifically, in the media sector, digital transformation refers to the transition from traditional publishing to online platforms, the production of content across multiple media, and a user-focused, data-driven approach to journalism. This transformation encompasses not only a technical adaptation but also a structural and cultural shift.

Dipnot.tv: Dipnot.tv, distinguished by its innovative and interaction-based publishing approach, has become one of the leading platforms in digital journalism in Turkey. Today, leveraging artificial intelligence technologies, it operates as Turkey's first fully AI-based news platform. It offers alternative reporting, video content, and original analysis within the framework of its digital journalism approach. Dipnot.tv, which pursues a more independent, innovative, and online-focused publishing policy compared to traditional media, is considered one of the prominent new media initiatives in the digital transformation process. The platform particularly appeals to young and digitally literate audiences.

Media Innovation: Media innovation refers to the process of developing and implementing new technologies, production processes, distribution channels, and content formats emerging in the media sector. In the media landscape transformed by digitalization, this concept encompasses innovative solutions in many areas, from content production and audience interaction to data analytics and revenue models. Media innovation is considered a multidimensional transformation process that considers not only technological advancements but also their social, cultural, and economic impacts. In this context, it is of strategic importance for media institutions to increase their competitiveness, establish more interactive relationships with audiences, and ensure sustainability.

Personalized News: Personalized news is news content selected by algorithms based on individuals' online behavior, interests, and past consumption data and presented specifically to the user. This model prioritizes content that is likely to appeal to each individual based on user profiling, aiming to enhance the user experience. However, this also raises questions about concepts like filter bubbles and confirmation bias, leading to criticisms that it narrows public debate and weakens the democratic flow of information.

Robot Journalism: Robot journalism (or automated journalism) refers to the automatic production of news content without human intervention, leveraging artificial intelligence and natural language processing technologies. This practice is typically used in data-driven fields such as finance, sports, and weather. While robot journalism offers advantages such as speed, consistency, and scalability, it has also sparked discussions surrounding ethical responsibilities, editorial oversight, and news accuracy. From an academic perspective, the impact of this technology on journalism practices is evaluated within the framework of concepts such as journalistic ethics, the transformation of professional roles, and digital labor.

Chapter 7
The Relationship Between Digital Burnout Levels and FoMo Among Higher Education Students

Mehmet Ulaş
https://orcid.org/0000-0002-6131-7509
İnönü University, Turkey

Abuzer Yeşil
https://orcid.org/0000-0001-6163-3432
Malatya Turgut Özal Üniversitesi, Turkey

ABSTRACT

The aim of the study is to reveal the relationship between higher education students' digital burnout levels and fear of missing out (FoMO). It can be interpreted that as fear of missing out (FoMO) increases, digital burnout increases with a significant and moderate relationship.In order to reveal whether fear of missing out (FoMO) has a predictive effect on digital burnout, simple linear regression analysis was conducted and it was concluded that fear of missing out positively predicts digital burnout. According to this result, it can be said that as individuals' fear of missing out increases, their digital burnout also increases.

INTRODUCTION

The process of digitalization, which has particularly intensified in the 21st century, has produced a profound transformative effect on all aspects of life, spanning from

DOI: 10.4018/979-8-3373-6970-9.ch007

© 2026, IGI Global Scientific Publishing. Copying or distributing in print or electronic forms without written permission of IGI Global Scientific Publishing is prohibited. Use of this chapter to ıerative artificial intelligence (AI) technologies is expressly prohibited. The publisher reserves all rights to license its use for generative AI training and machine learning model development.

the economy and politics to society, culture, education, health, sports, and urbanization. While it has introduced immense conveniences into people's lives, it has also generated novel problems that did not previously exist. This duality has made it crucial and necessary to conduct studies on the overall impact of digitalization on humanity within each of the aforementioned domains. In this context, digital burnout and Fear of Missing Out (FoMO) stand out as two significant phenomena on the negative side of this process that warrant scholarly attention.

In their study on the digital experiences of faculty members and university students, Gower et al. (2023) concluded that both groups exhibited above-average levels of digital burnout. The rates of digital burnout were identified as 67.4% for students and 54.3% for faculty members. The researchers attributed this difference to the fact that older individuals spend less cumulative time using digital technology. In his 2022 study, Göldağ examined the relationship between the digital burnout levels of university students and their perceived stress, concluding that students' digital burnout levels were above average, while their perceived stress levels were moderate. Karataşlıoğlu and Özkanal (2023) investigated the impact of remote education on digital burnout among middle school teachers during the COVID-19 pandemic, finding that individuals were affected by it in multiple ways. In their 2024 field study, Saboor et al., 2024 found that high levels of digital transformation intensity and work pressure were positively correlated with feelings of digital burnout. In their 2021 study, Şirin et al. examined the digital burnout levels of physical education teachers and observed a slight increase following the COVID-19 pandemic. Erten (2020) developed a scale to measure digital burnout levels. The scale comprises three sub-factors: digital attrition, digital deprivation, and emotional exhaustion. Similarly, Tutar and Mutlu (2024) developed a scale to measure the digital fatigue of employees working in environments with intensive digital technology use. Choi and Kim (2024) conducted a study aimed at investigating the factor structure and validating the reliability and validity of the Korean version of the Digital Burnout Scale (DBS) among Generation Z university students.

A review of the literature concerning Fear of Missing Out (FoMO) reveals studies that approach its relationship with social media, health, social life, marketing, and consumption from diverse perspectives. In their study examining the relationship between FoMO and individuals' social media use practices, Casale et al. (2018) concluded that a direct relationship exists between the two. A study by Blackwell et al. (2017), which addressed the impact of FoMO on individuals' health status, revealed that it causes them to experience feelings of loneliness and leads to significant health problems such as distraction, anxiety, and depression. In their work on the relationship between FoMO and social life practices, Shabahang et al. (2021) found that individuals with high levels of FoMO feel a need to access the latest or most current sources of information within their social spheres, concluding that this need, in turn, further increases their FoMO levels over time. Another finding of the study was that this fear of missing out on current developments leads to increased anxiety and negatively impacts individuals' character traits. Studies examining the relationship between FoMO and individual-level psychological issues have gradually given way to those investigating the link between FoMO and marketing and consumption (Gürdin, 2019, p. 1260). A study on the relationship between FoMO and hedonic consumption concluded that individuals' fear of missing out increases their social media use practices, which in turn affects their hedonic consumption (Çopuroğlu, 2021, pp. 4317-4318). Similarly, in a study examining the connection between FoMO and news consumption, it was found that individuals experience a fear of social exclusion from their communities and therefore feel compelled to follow current events. The study concluded that this sense of obligation heightens the importance, for these individuals, of being able to access developments regardless of time and place (Yeniceler Kortak, 2024, pp. 170-172).

A review of the literature indicates that while the phenomena of digital burnout and Fear of Missing Out (FoMO) have been subjects of research in various contexts, studies focusing on the relationship between the two have not been encountered. This gap highlights the significance of the present study. Accordingly, the purpose of this research is to determine the relationship between the digital burnout levels of higher education students and their Fear of Missing Out (FoMO). In line with this objective, the study was designed based on a correlational research model. Data were collected using the survey method, a quantitative research technique, and the collected data were subsequently analyzed using the SPSS 26.0 software. As data collection instruments, the study utilized a personal information form, the Digital Burnout Scale developed by Erten (2020), and the Fear of Missing Out (FoMO) Scale, which was originally developed by Przybylski et al. (2013) and adapted into Turkish by Gökler et al. (2016). The study's population comprised 35,366 students at İnönü University, while the sample consisted of 381 randomly selected students, calculated with a 95% confidence interval and an alpha level of α=0.05.

DIGITAL BURNOUT

According to the joint report by We Are Social and Meltwater (2024), there are 5.61 billion unique mobile phone users worldwide. When non-unique connections are accounted for, this figure rises to 8.65 billion, representing a penetration rate of 107%. Furthermore, 5.35 billion people use the internet, equivalent to over 66% of the global population, and there are more than 5 billion social media users, accounting for 62.3%. When examining the data for Turkey from the same report, it is observed that although the country's mobile connection rate of 93.8% is below the global average, it surpasses the world average with an 86.5% internet user rate and a 66.8% social media user rate. These data demonstrate that digital technologies have become a central phenomenon in human life.

The fact that digital technology has become an inevitable part of human life inherently entails an impact on the ecosystem of their existence. As Postman (2004) stated, any new technological development is not a mere addition to human life; instead, it changes one's entire life. In this sense, while the ease of use and speed of digital technology can enhance quality of life, the digitalization of daily life also has various adverse effects due to the excessive time spent on digital devices, such as mental and behavioral health problems, academic performance issues, sleep disturbances, and musculoskeletal health problems (Daraj et al., 2023, pp. 1-14). Digital burnout is one of the negative phenomena resulting from the use of digital technology. As a new phenomenon defined internationally and initially identified among employees, digital burnout has attracted the attention of psychologists due to its psychological dimension. However, owing to its impact on employee well-being manifesting as low productivity, stress, an inability to cope with routine, and disengagement it has also become a topic of interest in numerous fields outside of psychology. For instance, in a study by Yener (2018) examining the relationship between technology-based stress (technostress) and job performance among computer-using office workers, the concept of burnout was central. The study's findings revealed that burnout functions as a mediating factor in the connection between technostress and performance. In other words, individuals experiencing burnout due to technological stress exhibit a decline in their job performance.

In recent years, work environments and conditions have undergone significant transformations. With the advancement of technology, desktop computers have been replaced by laptops, tablets, and smartphones, a shift that has accelerated the transition to flexible working hours both inside and outside the office. The rapid development of digital devices has enabled remote work by offering employees the freedom to work from anywhere as long as they remain online. Particularly during the COVID-19 pandemic, the use of complementary and accessible technologies brought the concept of digital burnout to the forefront (Çelik Durmuş et al, 2022, pp. 1-7). Lockdown restrictions and efforts to avoid crowded places led people to isolate themselves in environments such as their homes and workplaces, causing them to spend excessive time with digital devices. This, in turn, paved the way for the emergence of digital burnout. The intense demand for digital technologies during the pandemic played a crucial role in the manifestation of the digital burnout phenomenon (Sharma et al., 2020, pp. 171-172).

Digital burnout, also known as digital fatigue, emerges as a consequence of being unable to cope with the information overload from the internet, social media, and digital tools. It represents a stress-induced problem rather than a medical condition.

This state can lead to negative outcomes such as a diminished enjoyment of life, a constant feeling of tiredness, exhaustion, and a decline in productivity (Sharma et al., 2020, pp. 171-172). Following trends on social media, sharing content, engaging with others, and watching various types of content are all indicators of spending an intensive amount of time with technology. Furthermore, the heavy use of computers, the internet, and technological tools for work and other responsibilities triggers feelings of fatigue, exhaustion, and being overwhelmed in individuals. Excessive internet use, often described by terms like internet addiction, pathological internet use, or internet use disorder, has been linked to emotional exhaustion. It has been determined that heavy internet users are susceptible to negative consequences such as emotional exhaustion and depression (Peterka-Bonetta et al., 2019, p. 195). Among students, problematic internet use can lead to the emergence of academic burnout. As the duration of this problematic behavior increases, the level of burnout experienced also rises; and as burnout levels increase, individuals turn to the internet more frequently to escape their current state of mind. This situation leads to an increase in the time spent online. Consequently, problematic internet use can be considered both a cause and a consequence of academic burnout (Christy et al., 2020, p. 588). Spending extended periods in the digital world through social media applications also causes the manifestation of burnout symptoms. Being active on social media leads to a decrease in interest and attention in class; disrupts the balance of time and energy allocated to daily life and school responsibilities; and results in symptoms of fatigue and exhaustion as a consequence of prolonged exposure to technology (Hietajärvi et al., 2019, p. 19).

Digital burnout is a type of exhaustion that arises from the excessive and prolonged use of digital devices. No longer confined to the physical work environment, burnout is also linked to the impacts of technology on professional life and societal functioning. Breytenbach (2015) defines this condition according to the level of exhaustion experienced by individuals. People suffering from digital burnout may exhibit symptoms such as constant fatigue, difficulty concentrating, and trouble maintaining daily routines. This state can lead to diminished productivity as individuals struggle to focus on multiple tasks. Digital burnout manifests through both physical and psychological symptoms and is fundamentally a form of exhaustion resulting from the prolonged and intensive use of digital devices (McCarty, 2020, pp. 673-677). The hyper-connected and compulsive use of portable devices plays a significant role in the emergence of digital stress and burnout. The state of being constantly online can entail a perceived need to multitask and manage excessive communication from sources like digital media, news, and social media. This situation can strain users' coping mechanisms, increase environmental demands, and lead to digital stress. According to research by Reinecke et al. (2014), this stress is associated with negative psychological outcomes such as dissatisfaction, decreased productivity, persistent fatigue, loss of emotional control, and complete exhaustion or burnout. Information overload is another key contributor to this form of burnout. The intense flow of information from a wide variety of digital platforms causes individuals to become fatigued (Tutar & Mutlu, 2024, pp. 56-74). Digital burnout is a condition that arises from extended screen time and the excessive use of technology. Physically, its effects can be observed as eye strain, headaches, and neck pain; chronic fatigue; and sleep disturbances. Mentally, problems such as difficulty concentrating, forgetfulness, irritability, anxiety, and depression can occur (Abel et al., 2016, pp. 33-44). For example, the rising prevalence of digital burnout and mental health issues among educators can lead teachers to experience stress and distress, making it difficult for them to communicate effectively with students and provide quality education. This, in turn, can have negative consequences for the students (Abdulkareem et al., 2024, pp. 354-371).

FEAR OF MISSING OUT (FOMO)

As an inherent part of their ontological nature, individuals develop physical and emotional needs from the moment they engage in social life. A fundamental emotional dynamic for humans is the sense of curiosity. This drive to be curious constitutes one of the primary motivational factors enabling individual and societal progress, inventions, and the discovery of the unknown. The expression of this curiosity arguably takes on different forms depending on stages of personal development and large-scale societal shifts. By its very nature, the digital realm that has emerged with technological advancements provides a remarkably rapid response to the human drive for curiosity. It can be argued that social media platforms, which facilitate the spread of digital footprints across social spheres, are the primary catalyst in this process. While they significantly cater to an individual's curiosity, they also transform this innate sense into a high-level, perceived need. This dynamic shifts the gratification of curiosity from a mere desire into a necessity. Consequently, the potential for this need to go unfulfilled can be identified as the fundamental cause for the emergence of the Fear of Missing Out. This perceived fear, in turn, makes individuals more dependent on social media platforms while simultaneously establishing a pervasive foundation of anxiety.

The conceptualization of "Fear of Missing Out" was first used in 1996 by marketing strategist Dan Herman (2020). Herman viewed the Fear of Missing Out as a significant factor in the psychological background of individuals engaging in consumer practices. Consequently, he investigated the relationship between FoMO and consumer behaviors through the lenses of socio-cultural influences, motivational sources, and personal characteristics. In his research, Herman (2020, p. 330) defined FoMO as an attitude centered on the fear of not being able to seize current opportunities and the corresponding possibility of missing out on the anticipated joy this would bring. This conceptualization appears in English literature as "Fear of Missing Out," abbreviated as FoMO, and has been translated into Turkish as "gelişmeleri kaçırma korkusu." In the literature, the term is predominantly used to describe the fear that arises from the possibility of missing out on opportunities, new developments, and current topics of interest. Fear of Missing Out emerges as a consequence of technological advancements and individuals' quest to ground their existence in a meaningful way by belonging to a group (Aliçavuşoğlu & Boyraz, 2019, p. 684).

Among the technological advancements that significantly impact individuals' social life practices, developments related to the internet and social media platforms are paramount. The internet and social media platforms substantially cater to the human quest for information. Consequently, individuals increase their frequency of using these platforms to stay informed about current topics in their social spheres and to avoid the potential danger of falling behind. This increased frequency of use, in turn, can lead to dependency, which subsequently triggers a fear of missing out in the event of being disconnected or uninformed (Dossey, 2014, pp. 69-70). According to Saji Kumar et al. (2020), Fear of Missing Out reflects a significant state of social anxiety that arises from the motivational effect of regret, particularly when individuals miss out on interactions occurring on social media platforms. For individuals, this state of social anxiety can lead to considerable health problems.

According to Oberst et al. (2017), anxiety, feelings of loneliness, and social withdrawal are some of the health problems caused by the Fear of Missing Out (FoMO). However, it would be a reductionist approach to claim that the health issues stemming from FoMO are limited to this scope. Fear of Missing Out also leads to significant pathological health problems such as social anxiety and depression. Research conducted by Przybylski et al. (2013) concluded that the health issues caused by FoMO lead to significant changes in individuals' personality traits. Key findings from their study indicate that individuals with FoMO tend to have a mental disposition characterized by low motivation and experience lower levels of life satisfaction. Furthermore, the research found that individuals with FoMO frequently check their smartphones during social interactions and that a perceived lack of this control mechanism triggers significant anxiety.

In another study conducted by Modzelewski (2020), distinct findings were obtained regarding the behavioral practices exhibited by individuals with FoMO in their social lives. The research concluded that these individuals display a range of specific behaviors, such as: frequently checking their smartphones even when there are no notifications; photographing many things they see; unconditionally accepting invitations to events; frequently checking work emails via smartphone, even while on vacation; and attempting to imitate the consumption patterns of their social circle by stretching their financial limits. Ultimately, Fear of Missing Out represents a cognitive process related to the apprehension of falling behind on online developments—a process with numerous tangible consequences, ranging from shaping social behaviors to the emergence of psychological problems (Wegmann, Oberst, Stodt, & Brand, 2017, pp. 34-35).

In an experimental study conducted by Hunt et al. (2018), the use of social media platforms such as Instagram, Facebook, and Snapchat was limited to ten minutes per day over a three-week period. As a result of this limitation, it was concluded that there was a significant decrease in psychological issues such as depression, self-doubt, loneliness, and anxiety among the individuals in the experimental group. In short, FoMO represents a fear that arises from the prospect of being deprived of potential experiences or being unaware of others' activities, particularly on digital platforms like social media (Zhang, Jimenez, & Cicala, 2020, p. 1620). It can be argued that this fear causes significant changes and transformations in numerous areas, from the behavioral practices individuals exhibit in their social lives to their personality traits. Furthermore, advanced levels of FoMO can lead to both psychological and pathological health problems (Lemay, Doleck, & Bazelais, 2019, p. 485). In an article published in The New York Times, Wortham (2011) used the description "the emblem of the digital age" when defining the Fear of Missing Out.

In an era where digitalization and its associated technologies are actively used in many spheres of social life, the transformation of an individual's anxiety about being deprived of digital developments into an outright fear can be seen as a probable outcome of the digitalization process itself. For instance, the act of individuals sharing content or frequently checking digital platforms—even when physically present with their friends—is a significant indicator of digitalization's encroachment into daily life (Metz, 2019, pp. 464-467). This suggests that it is not the act of being disconnected from the digital world, but rather the mere thought of it, that induces a sense of potential deprivation in individuals. This feeling, in turn, gives rise to a fear, which ultimately manifests as the Fear of Missing Out. In short, Fear of Missing Out can be defined as a multifaceted desire to: be constantly and actively present on social media platforms, which are an output of digitalization; stay informed of developments through interaction on these platforms; replicate the various experiences of followed individuals; and emulate them in every aspect of life, from consumption patterns to daily practices. Simultaneously, the term characterizes the state of fear individuals experience as a result of the potential failure to realize these aspirations.

Fear of Missing Out (FoMO) is linked to the need for constant activity and engagement on social media platforms, a direct consequence of digitalization. This phenomenon is shaped by an individual's desire to stay informed of developments via social media, to observe the diverse experiences of those they follow, and to participate in these experiences. Moreover, individuals exhibit a tendency to emulate the lifestyles of others presented on social media. In this context, should these practices fail to materialize, individuals are prone to experiencing a state of fear over missing out on developments and the prospect of being excluded from social interactions. Consequently, it can be argued that social media use reinforces the human desire for social belonging and acceptance, while the deprivation of such interactions can generate anxiety and fear.

METHODOLOGY

Purpose and Significance of the Research

The 21st century can be described as a period in which technological advancements have had a profound impact on social life, making adaptation to these developments a necessity for both individuals and society. Social media platforms, in particular, as an output of the internet and new media technologies, constitute key channels of interaction that permeate many areas of daily life. The capacity of these platforms to meet a wide range of needs—from entertainment and news consumption to following current events and socializing—has arguably led to immense interest in this domain and its transformation into a phenomenon, especially in interdisciplinary studies. While meeting these numerous needs intensifies the use of social media, this pattern of use can also lead to a behavioral dependency, characterized by a sense of deprivation when engagement is unfulfilled. This dependency creates a state of anxiety when individuals perceive that others in their social circle are having fulfilling experiences on these platforms in their absence. This condition, termed Fear of Missing Out (FoMO), arguably drives individuals to increase the duration of their social media use to remain constantly active, up-to-date, and aware of developments within their social environment. This very increase in usage time, resulting from prolonged exposure to digital platforms, can then be identified as a cause of digital burnout. Based on this premise, the purpose of this study is to determine the relationship between the digital burnout levels and the Fear of Missing Out (FoMO) among higher education students. A review of the existing literature revealed no studies that have concurrently examined the relationship between digital burnout and FoMO. By investigating this relationship, the present study distinguishes itself from the current literature. This distinction, in turn, underscores the significance of the research.

In line with the purpose of the study, the following hypotheses were developed and tested:

- **H1.** Participants' levels of digital burnout and Fear of Missing Out (FoMO) differ based on demographic variables.
- **H2.** There is a relationship between participants' levels of digital burnout and Fear of Missing Out (FoMO).
- **H3.** There is a relationship between the dimensions of participants' digital burnout and their levels of Fear of Missing Out (FoMO).
- **H4.** There is a relationship between participants' levels of Fear of Missing Out (FoMO) and digital burnout.

Research Method

According to Patton (2005), quantitative research methods aim to objectively measure the behavioral practices of individuals within their social context through instruments such as tests, experiments, or observations. A key prerequisite for this approach is that the data obtained via these instruments must be expressible in a numerical format. Furthermore, statistically explaining the relationships between variables is a fundamental requirement of quantitative research. Accordingly, this study which aims to determine the relationship between the digital burnout levels of higher education students and their Fear of Missing Out (FoMO) employed a quantitative research method. The study was specifically structured using a correlational survey model, which is a type of survey research design. According to Fraenkel (2008), the correlational survey model is a design aimed at establishing the existence and strength of a presumed relationship between two or more quantitative variables through a correlation coefficient.

Population, Sample, and Limitations of the Research

According to Corbetta (2003), every scientific study has a unique population defined by specific characteristics. Researchers determine this population by considering these characteristics and the objectives of their study. A primary task for researchers is to correctly identify the population that will enable them to achieve their research goals. Similarly, Christensen et al. (2015) state that another crucial task for researchers is the selection of a sample group. This involves choosing a relatively smaller group of participants from the target population, based on specific rules and criteria, which is believed to be representative of that population and will aid in achieving the research objectives. According to Şimşek (2018), various sampling methods are used in quantitative research. One such method, which minimizes the probability of bias by basing the selection process on a random perspective, is probability sampling. A key technique within probability sampling is simple random sampling. Vogt et al. (2012) emphasize that simple random sampling is important because it offers every element in the population an equal chance of being selected. Accordingly, this study utilized the simple random sampling technique, a form of probability sampling. The study's population consisted of 35,366 students at İnönü University. The sample comprised 381 randomly selected students, calculated with a 95% confidence interval and an alpha level of $\alpha=0.05$. No limitations were imposed during the sample selection process, other than the requirement of being a student at İnönü University.

Data Collection and Analysis

Data for the study were collected using the survey technique, a quantitative research method, and subsequently analyzed using the SPSS 26.0 software. The data collection instruments for the study included a personal information form, the Digital Fatigue Scale developed by Erten (2020), and the Fear of Missing Out (FoMO) Scale, which was originally developed by Przybylski et al. (2013) and adapted into Turkish by Gökler et al. (2016). Participants were presented with questions regarding their demographic characteristics as well as items structured on a 5-point Likert scale. To save time and costs, the survey was created using Google Forms and distributed to potential participants via email and the WhatsApp application to solicit their participation. To initiate and conduct this process in accordance with the study's objectives, ethics approval was obtained from the İnönü University Scientific Research and Publication Ethics Committee (Decision No: 21/1, Date: 18.12.2024). A pilot study conducted with 30 participants revealed that two items in the questionnaire were not clearly understood. Based on this finding, the necessary revisions were made, and the final version of the questionnaire was established. The main data collection process was then initiated.

FINDINGS

Reliability and Validity Analysis

A Cronbach's Alpha reliability analysis was conducted to determine the reliability of the scales used in the research. According to the findings of the analysis, the Cronbach's Alpha value was found to be 0.937 for the Digital Burnout Scale and 0.862 for the Fear of Missing Out (FoMO) Scale. Given that both of these values are above the 0.5 threshold, the reliability of both scales is considered to be at an acceptable level (Altunışık et al., 2007, p. 124).

Descriptive Statistics and Normality Test

A normality test was conducted to assess whether the research data met the assumption of normality. The descriptive statistics and the results of the normality test for the scales are presented in the table below.

Table 1. Normality test

	Min.	Max.	Mean	Standart Error	Skewness	Kurtosis
Digital Burnout Scale	1,00	4,63	2,7532	,03541	,022	-,095
Fear of Missing Out (FoMO)	1,00	3,90	2,2911	,03288	,067	-,505

An examination of the descriptive statistics indicates that the mean and standard error (M ± SE) for the Digital Burnout Scale were 2.7532 ± 0.03541. For the Fear of Missing Out (FoMO) Scale, these values were 2.2911 ± 0.03288. According to Morgan et al. (2004, p. 49), when the skewness and kurtosis values of scales fall within the range of +1 to -1, it suggests that the data conform to the assumption of normality. The results presented in the normality test table show that the scales used in this research satisfy this assumption.

Findings on the Differences in Fear of Missing Out (FoMO) and Digital Burnout Based on Demographic Variables

Table 2. Demographic variables with FoMO

		Count	Column N %
Gender	Female	300	70,9
	Male	123	29,1
	Total	**423**	**100,0**
Age	17-22	309	73,0
	23-28	92	21,7
	29-34	2	,5
	35+	20	4,7
	Total	**423**	**100,0**

continued on following page

Table 2. Continued

		Count	Column N %
Income	2000 TL and under	114	27,0
	2001-4000 TL	159	37,6
	4001-6000 TL	64	15,1
	6001 TL and over	86	20,3
	Total	**423**	**100,0**
Time spent on digital media	1-3 hours	173	40,9
	4-7 hours	217	51,3
	8 hours and over	33	7,8
	Total	**423**	**100,0**
Most frequently used digital platform	Facebook	1	,2
	Instagram	238	56,3
	Linkedln	1	,2
	Tik Tok	39	9,2
	X (Twitter)	18	4,3
	YouTube	54	12,8
	WhatsApp	72	17,0
	Total	**423**	**100,0**
Purpose for using digital media	Shopping	18	4,3
	Social Validation	0	,0
	Information seeking	79	18,7
	Entertainment	167	39,5
	Social interaction	95	22,5
	Social escapism / Relaxation	64	15,1
	Total	**423**	**100,0**
Frequency of checking one's phone	Every 1-5 minutes	90	21,3
	Every 6-10 minutes	107	25,3
	Every 11-15 minutes	132	31,2
	Once an hour	72	17,0
	A few times a day	22	5,2
	Total	**423**	**100,0**

An examination of the table presenting the participants' demographic characteristics reveals that the sample was composed of 70.9% women and 29.1% men. In terms of age, 73% of participants were in the 17-22 age range, 21.7% in the 23-28 range, 0.5% in the 29-34 range, and 4.7% were aged 35 and over. Regarding income levels, 27% of participants reported an income of 2000 TL or less, 37.6% between 2001-4000 TL, 15.1% between 4001-6000 TL, and 20.3% had an income of 6001 TL or more. The distribution of daily time spent on digital media was as follows: 40.9% spent 1-3 hours, 51.3% spent 4-7 hours, and 7.8% spent 8 hours or more. The distribution of time spent across various digital platforms was: 56.3% on Instagram, 17% on WhatsApp, 12.8% on YouTube, 9.2% on TikTok, 4.3% on X (Twitter), 0.2% on Facebook, and 0.2% on LinkedIn. The primary purposes for using these platforms were identified as: entertainment (39.5%), social interaction (22.5%), information seeking (18.7%), social escape/relaxation (15.1%), and shopping (4.3%). Finally, the frequency of checking their phones during the day was reported as follows: every 11-15 minutes (31.2%), every 6-10 minutes (25.3%), every 1-5 minutes (21.3%), once an hour (17%), and a few times during the day (5.2%).

Table 3. User habits regarding FoMO

	Gender	n	$\bar{X}$	t-value	p-value
Fear of Missing Out (FoMO)	Female	300	2,31	-,065	,449
	Male	123	2,31		
Digital Burnout	Female	300	2,81	1,627	,509
	Male	123	2,68		

The table below presents the findings regarding whether Fear of Missing Out (FoMO) and digital burnout differ based on demographic variables. An independent samples t-test was conducted to determine whether there were significant differences in the levels of FoMO and digital burnout based on gender. The results of the analysis revealed no statistically significant difference between genders for either Fear of Missing Out (FoMO) (t = -0.065, p = .449) or digital burnout (t = 1.627, p = .509).

Table 4. Digital burnout and FoMO by dempographic

	Age	n	$\bar{X}$	f-value	p-value
Fear of Missing Out (FoMO)	17-22	309	2,33	1,923	,125
	23-28	92	2,28		
	29-34	2	1,25		
	35+	20	2,19		

continued on following page

Table 4. Continued

	Age	n	$\bar{X}$	f-value	p-value
Digital Burnout	17-22	309	2,81	1,525	,207
	23-28	92	2,70		
	29-34	2	2,02		
	35+	20	2,60		
	Income	**n**	$\bar{X}$	**f-value**	**p-value**
Fear of Missing Out (FoMO)	2000 TL and under	114	2,41	2,492	,060
	2001-4000 TL	159	2,35		
	4001-6000 TL	64	2,21		
	6001 TL and over	86	2,17		
Digital Burnout	2000 TL and under	114	2,80	,523	,667
	2001-4000 TL	159	2,78		
	4001-6000 TL	64	2,79		
	6001 TL and over	86	2,68		
	Time spent on digital media	**n**	$\bar{X}$	**f-value**	**p-value**
Fear of Missing Out (FoMO)	1-3 hours	173	2,17	6,722	,001
	4-7 hours	217	2,38		
	8 hours and over	33	2,57		
Digital Burnout	1-3 hours	173	2,51	21,512	,000
	4-7 hours	217	2,92		
	8 hours and over	33	3,15		
	Most frequently used digital platform	**n**	$\bar{X}$	**f-value**	**p-value**
Fear of Missing Out (FoMO)	Facebook	1	1,60	2,530	,020
	Instagram	238	2,40		
	Linkedln	1	1,60		
	Tik Tok	39	2,28		
	X (Twitter)	18	1,18		
	YouTube	54	2,26		
	WhatsApp	72	2,19		

continued on following page

Table 4. Continued

	Age	n	$\bar{X}$	f-value	p-value
Digital Burnout	Facebook	1	1,95	2,579	,018
	Instagram	238	2,87		
	Linkedln	1	2,33		
	Tik Tok	39	2,85		
	X (Twitter)	18	2,55		
	YouTube	54	2,70		
	WhatsApp	72	2,54		
	Purpose for using digital media	**n**	$\bar{X}$	**f-value**	**p-value**
Fear of Missing Out (FoMO)	Shopping	18	2,57	2,290	,059
	Social Validation	79	2,17		
	Information seeking	167	2,27		
	Entertainment	95	2,36		
	Social interaction	64	2,45		
Digital Burnout	Shopping	18	2,85	8,126	,000
	Social Validation	79	2,42		
	Information seeking	167	2,80		
	Entertainment	95	2,77		
	Social interaction	64	3,10		
	Frequency of checking one's phone	**n**	$\bar{X}$	**f-value**	**p-value**
Fear of Missing Out (FoMO)	Every 1-5 minutes	90	2,57	6,841	,000
	Every 6-10 minutes	107	2,40		
	Every 11-15 minutes	132	2,23		
	Once an hour	72	2,09		
	A few times a day	22	2,01		
Digital Burnout	Every 1-5 minutes	90	3,12	10,249	,000
	Every 6-10 minutes	107	2,78		
	Every 11-15 minutes	132	2,75		
	Once an hour	72	2,41		
	A few times a day	22	2,62		

In the study, a one-way analysis of variance (ANOVA) was used to determine whether there were significant differences in Fear of Missing Out (FoMO) and digital burnout across various demographic variables, including age, income, time spent on digital media, preferred digital application, purpose for using digital media, and frequency of checking one's phone. The results of the analysis indicated no statistically significant differences for the following variables:

- Between age and either Fear of Missing Out (FoMO) (F = 1.923, p = .125) or digital burnout (F = 1.525, p = .207).
- Between income level and either Fear of Missing Out (FoMO) (F = 2.492, p = .060) or digital burnout (F = .523, p = .667).

A statistically significant difference was found in Fear of Missing Out (FoMO) levels based on the variable of time spent on digital media (F = 6.722, *p* = .001). To identify which specific groups differed, a Tukey's HSD post-hoc test was conducted. The test results revealed significant differences in FoMO levels between:

- the "1-3 hours" group and the "4-7 hours" group (MD = -0.20584, *p* = .001).
- the "1-3 hours" group and the "8 hours or more" group (MD = -0.39469, *p* = .008).

Similarly, a statistically significant difference was also found in digital burnout levels based on the time spent on digital media (F = 21.512, *p* < .001). A Tukey's HSD post-hoc test was performed to determine the specific group differences. The test results showed significant differences in digital burnout levels between:

- the "1-3 hours" group and the "4-7 hours" group (MD = -0.41574, *p* < .001).
- the "1-3 hours" group and the "8 hours or more" group (MD = -0.64122, *p* < .001).

No other pairwise comparisons for either variable were found to be statistically significant.

Regarding the variable of preferred digital application, the analysis revealed a statistically significant difference in both Fear of Missing Out (FoMO) levels (F = 2.530, *p* = .020) and digital burnout levels (F = 2.579, *p* = .018).

For the variable purpose for using digital media, no statistically significant difference was found in FoMO levels (F = 2.290, *p* = .059). However, a statistically significant difference was observed for digital burnout (F = 8.126, *p* < .001). To identify the specific group differences for digital burnout, a Tukey's HSD post-hoc test was conducted. The results indicated significant differences between the following groups:

- "Information seeking" and "Entertainment" (MD = -0.37795, *p* = .001)
- "Information seeking" and "Social interaction" (MD = -0.34568, *p* = .015)

- “Information seeking” and “Social escape” (MD = -0.67943, $p < .001$)
- “Entertainment” and “Social escape” (MD = -0.30148, $p = .037$)
- “Social interaction” and “Social escape” (MD = -0.33375, $p = .035$)

No other pairwise comparisons for digital burnout based on purpose of use were found to be statistically significant.

The analysis revealed a statistically significant difference in Fear of Missing Out (FoMO) levels based on the frequency of checking one's phone ($F = 6.841$, $p < .001$). A Tukey's HSD post-hoc test was conducted to identify which specific groups differed. The results indicated significant differences in FoMO levels between the following groups:

- “Every 1-5 minutes” and “Every 11-15 minutes” (MD = -0.33136, $p = .004$)
- “Every 1-5 minutes” and “Once an hour” (MD = -0.47417, $p < .001$)
- “Every 1-5 minutes” and “A few times a day” (MD = -0.55182, $p = .007$)
- “Every 6-10 minutes” and “Once an hour” (MD = -0.30510, $p = .030$)

No other pairwise comparisons for FoMO were found to be statistically significant.

Similarly, a statistically significant difference was found in digital burnout levels based on the frequency of checking one's phone ($F = 10.249$, $p < .001$). A Tukey's HSD post-hoc test was performed, and the results showed significant differences in digital burnout levels between the following groups:

- “Every 1-5 minutes” and “Every 6-10 minutes” (MD = -0.33454, $p = .010$)
- “Every 1-5 minutes” and “Every 11-15 minutes” (MD = -0.36627, $p = .002$)
- “Every 1-5 minutes” and “Once an hour” (MD = -0.71007, $p < .001$)
- “Every 1-5 minutes” and “A few times a day” (MD = -0.49726, $p = .029$)
- “Every 6-10 minutes” and “Once an hour” (MD = -0.37552, $p = .006$)
- “Every 11-15 minutes” and “Once an hour” (MD = -0.34380, $p = .010$)

No other pairwise comparisons for digital burnout were found to be statistically significant.

Correlation Analysis

Table 5. Correlation between FoMO and digital burnout

Correlations			
		Fear of Missing Out (FoMO)	**Digital Burnout**
Fear of Missing Out (FoMO)	Pearson Correlation	1	,579**
	Sig. (2-tailed)		,000
	N	423	423
Digital Burnout	Pearson Correlation	,579**	1
	Sig. (2-tailed)	,000	
	N	423	423

**. Correlation is significant at the 0.01 level (2-tailed).

The table presents the results of the correlation analysis, which was used to determine the relationship between Fear of Missing Out (FoMO) and digital burnout. The findings revealed a moderate, positive, and statistically significant correlation between Fear of Missing Out (FoMO) and digital burnout ($r = .579, p < .05$). This finding can be interpreted to mean that as the level of Fear of Missing Out (FoMO) increases, the level of digital burnout also increases, with the relationship being moderate and statistically significant.

Regression Analysis

Table 6. Simple linear regression analysis

Correlations			
		Digital Burnout	**Fear of Missing Out (FoMO)**
Pearson Correlation	**Digital Burnout**	1,000	,579
	Fear of Missing Out (FoMO)	,579	1,000
Sig. (1-tailed)	**Digital Burnout**	.	,000
	Fear of Missing Out (FoMO)	,000	.
N	**Digital Burnout**	423	423
	Fear of Missing Out (FoMO)	423	423

The table presents the results of the simple linear regression analysis. According to the findings, a significant and positive relationship was found between individuals' levels of Fear of Missing Out (FoMO) and digital burnout. A review of the descriptive statistics shows that the mean score for FoMO was 2.31, while the mean for digital burnout was 2.77. This finding reveals that Fear of Missing Out (FoMO) is a significant predictor of digital burnout. This suggests that the degree of individuals' connectedness to the digital world can influence their levels of digital burnout.

CONCLUSION

Technological advancements in the field of communication have led to the emergence of new forms of life wherein digitalization holds a central position within social practices. In numerous domains, ranging from communication strategies to access to information sources, it is observed that digitalization has assumed a primary role, with its determinant influence steadily increasing. The digitalization of communication strategies and the quest for information sources by both individuals and social structures has rendered various requirements within the digital realm essential. Individuals' pursuit of information regarding the lives of others who constitute their social capital, particularly on digital platforms, also fosters an anxiety about missing out on potential developments in this sphere. While the intensive use of digital media—a primary strategy for individuals to alleviate this anxiety—may serve to eliminate the unease, it simultaneously leads to cognitive digital fatigue. Accordingly, the purpose of this study is to investigate the relationship between the digital burnout levels of higher education students and their Fear of Missing Out (FoMO).

To determine the reliability of the scales used in the research, a Cronbach's Alpha reliability analysis was conducted. According to the findings of the reliability analysis, the Cronbach's Alpha value for the Digital Burnout scale was found to be 0.937, and for the Fear of Missing Out (FoMO) scale, it was 0.862. Therefore, it can be concluded that the reliability levels of the scales employed in the study are within an acceptable range. Furthermore, the fact that the skewness and kurtosis values for the scales fell within the ± 1 range indicates that the assumption of normality was met.

When the research findings are analyzed based on demographic characteristics, it was determined that female participants took part in the study at a higher rate than male participants. Similar studies in the literature (Teke & Yılmaz, 2023, p. 7) have also reported a higher proportion of female participants. In this respect, the data obtained from the study are consistent with the literature. The age range of the participants was observed to be significantly concentrated between 17 and 22 years. It can be argued that the composition of the study's sample, which consists of university students, is a significant factor in this outcome. Regarding income levels, it was found that nearly half of the participants had an income in the 2001-4000 TL range. Furthermore, Instagram was identified as the digital platform where participants spend the most time. A similar finding was reported in the study conducted by Coşkun et al. (2021). This indicates that the result obtained in the current study aligns with the existing literature.

Additionally, it was found that digital platforms are used by participants primarily for entertainment purposes. This finding is consistent with several studies in the literature (e.g., Durak & Seferoğlu, 2016, p. 526). Although the frequency of daily phone checking among participants showed a relatively balanced distribution, the interval of checking every 11-15 minutes was the most prominent. Consequently, it can be suggested that participants frequently check their phones throughout the day, which may indicate a potential problem of dependency. Moreover, the participants' frequent phone checking can be interpreted as an indication of their fear of missing out on developments concerning themselves or their social circles. This behavior, in turn, can be said to support the presence of high levels of Fear of Missing Out (FoMO) among these individuals.

Based on the analyses conducted to determine whether Fear of Missing Out (FoMO) and digital burnout vary according to demographic variables, it was concluded that there was no statistically significant difference in participants' FoMO and digital burnout levels based on gender, age, or income. However, a significant difference was found between FoMO and digital burnout and the amount of time spent in digital environments. It was determined that participants who spent 4-7 hours and 8 or more hours online had higher levels of FoMO and digital burnout compared to those who spent 1-3 hours. No significant difference was found among the other groups. Furthermore, a significant difference was also found between FoMO and digital burnout and the type of digital application used. Consequently, it can be stated that individuals who spend extensive time on digital platforms also have a higher fear of missing out, and this exposure to the digital environment contributes to digital burnout.

The results showed no significant difference between Fear of Missing Out (FoMO) and the purpose of using digital media; however, a significant difference was found between digital burnout and this same variable. It can be suggested that participants who use digital platforms for information acquisition and entertainment have higher levels of FoMO and digital burnout compared to those who use them for other purposes. No significant difference was observed among the other groups. A significant difference was also found between the frequency of phone checking and both FoMO and digital burnout. It was determined that participants who check their phones every 1-5 minutes had higher levels of FoMO and digital burnout compared to other participants, with no significant differences found among the other groups. Based on these results, it can be argued that using digital platforms, particularly for entertainment, increases individuals' fear of missing out on developments within their social circles, which in turn leads to digital burnout. Furthermore, individuals' frequent checking of their phones at short intervals also indicates a fear of being left behind on potential developments.

A correlation analysis was conducted to determine the relationship between Fear of Missing Out (FoMO) and digital burnout. The results revealed a moderate, positive ($r = .579$), and significant ($p < .05$) relationship between the two variables. This finding can be interpreted to mean that as FoMO increases, digital burnout also increases in a significant and moderate manner. Subsequently, a simple linear regression analysis was performed to investigate the predictive effect of FoMO on digital burnout, and it was concluded that the fear of missing out positively predicts digital burnout. According to this result, it can be stated that as individuals' fear of missing out intensifies, so does their level of digital burnout.

In conclusion, it can be argued that the young generation, who constitute the "digital natives," exhibit high levels of attachment to digital media, which is a consequence of their fear of missing out on potential developments in their environment. This fear, in turn, brings about digital burnout. Excessive exposure leads to a loss of meaning on an individual scale, and individuals' frequent exposure to these environments causes the platforms themselves to lose significance. However, the persistent effort of individuals to maintain their presence on these platforms, which are undergoing a loss of meaning, represents a significant paradox. The fact that individuals' insistent monitoring of developments on these platforms causes burnout, yet this burnout and loss of meaning do not negatively impact usage rates, constitutes a critical problem that needs to be addressed. Nevertheless, it can be posited that individuals' relatively low levels of consciousness and awareness while using these platforms, coupled with the attribution of a reduced meaning to them—as merely tools for entertainment—precludes potential countermeasures and thus does not negatively affect the platforms' usage rates and practices.

REFERENCES

Abdulkareem, A. K., Ishola, A. A., Bello, M. L., & Adejumo, A. (2024). The dark side of digitalization: Examining the impact of digital overload on job autonomy and job satisfaction. *Journal of Information. Communication and Ethics in Society, 22*(3), 354–371.

Abel, J. P., Buff, C. L., & Burr, S. A. (2016). Social Media and the Fear of Missing Out: Scale Development and Assessment. *Journal of Business & Economics Research*, •••, 33–44.

Aliçavuşoğlu, Ç., & Boyraz, E. (2019). Kendimi Biliyorum, Kork(M)Uyorum! Yenilikleri Kaçırma Korkusu (Fomo) ve Sosyal Medya Dijital Üstbilişin Rolü. *International Journal of Social And Humanities Sciences Research (JSHSR)*, 682-697.

Blackwell, D., Leaman, C., Tramposch, R., Osborne, C., & Liss, M. (2017). Extraversion, Neuroticism, Attachment Style and Fear Of Missing Out As Predictors of Social Media Use and Addiction. *Personality and Individual Differences*, •••, 66–72.

Breytenbach, C. (2015, 02 10). *Tackling digital burnout in the workplace.* January 24, 2025 tarihinde http://www.destinyman.com/2015/02/10/tackling-digital-burnout-in-the-workplace/ adresinden alındı

Casale, S., Rugai, L., & Fioravanti, G. (2018). Exploring the Role of Positive Metacognitions in Explaining the Association Between the Fear of Missing Out and Social Media Addiction. *Addictive Behaviors*, •••, 83–87.

Çelik Durmuş, S., Gülnar, E., & Özveren, H. (2022). Determining digital burnout in nursing students: A descriptive research study. *Nurse Education Today*, (111), 1–7.

Choi, S.-Y., & Kim, J.-H. (2024). Validity and reliability of The Korean version of the Digital Burnout Scale. *Frontiers in Paublic Health*, 1-11.

Christensen, L., Johnson, B., & Turner, L. (2015). Araştırma Yöntemleri Desen ve Analiz. (A. Aypay, Çev.) Ankara: Anı Yayıncılık.

Christy, A., Sahrani, R., & Heng, P. H. (2020). Academic Burnout in Digital Era: Examining the Role of Problematic Smartphone Use, Core Self-Evaluations and Academic Achivement Burnout among Medical Students. *Advances in Social Science, Education and Humanities Research*, (439), 586–590.

Çopuroğlu, F. (2021). Tüketicilerin Sosyal Medya Kullanımı, FoMO ve Hedonik Tüketim Arasındaki İlişki. *OPUS Uluslararası Toplum Araştırmaları Dergisi*, 4298-4326.

Corbetta, P. (2003). *Social Research Theory, Methods and Techniques*. Sage Publications.

Daraj, L. R., AlGhareeb, M., Almutawa, Y. M., Trabelsi, K., & Jahrami, H. (2023). Systematic Review and Meta-Analysis of the Correlation Coefficients between Nomophobia and Anxiety, Smartphone Addiction, and Insomnia Symptoms. *Health Care*, *11*(14), 1–14.

Dossey, L. (2014). FOMO, Digital Dementia, and Our Dangerous Experiment. *Explore (New York, N.Y.)*, •••, 69–73.

Durak, H., & Seferoğlu, S. S. (2016). Türkiye'de Sosyal Medya Okuryazarlığı Ve Sosyal Ağ Kullanım Örüntülerinin İncelenmesi. *Uluslararası Sosyal Araştırmalar Dergisi The Journal Of International Social Research*, 526-535.

Erten, P. (2020). The Digital Burnout Scale Development Study. *İnönü University Journal of the Faculty of Education, 21*(2), 668-683.

Fraenkel, J., & Wallen, N. (2008). *How to Design and Evaluate Research in Education*. McGraw-Hill Education.

Göldağ, B. (2022). An Investigation of the Relationship between University Students' Digital Burnout Levels and Perceived Stress Levels. *Journal of Learning and Teaching in Digital Age*, *7*(1), 90–98.

Gower, D., Kachaturoff, M., & Caboral-Stevens, M. (2023). Digital Experience Among Faculty and Students in One Midwest University. *Education Journal*, *12*(3), 92–98.

Gürdin, B. (2019). Sosyal Medyanın Hedonik Tüketimi ve FoMO"nun Gücü. *Üçüncü Sektör Sosyal Ekonomi Dergisi*, 1259-1278.

Herman, D. (2020). Introducing Short-Term Brands: A New Branding Tool for a New Consumer Reality. *Journal of Brand Management*, •••, 330–340.

Hietajarvi, L., Salmela-Aro, K., Tuominen, H., Hakkarainen, K., & Lonka, K. (2019). Beyond screen time: Multidimensionality of socio-digital participation and relations to academic well-being in three educational phases. *Computers in Human Behavior*, (93), 13–24.

Hunt, M., Marx, R., Lipson, C., & Young, J. (2018). No more FOMO: Limiting social media decreases loneliness and depression. *Journal of Social and Clinical Psychology*, •••, 751–768.

Karataşlıoğlu, R. E., & Özkanal, B. (2023). Digital Burnout in Distance Education Process: Examination of Secondary School Teachers' Opinions. *Journal of Advanced Education Studies*, *5*(2), 319–341.

Lemay, D. J., Doleck, T., & Bazelais, P. (2019). Self-Determination, Loneliness, Fear of Missing Out, and Academic Performance. *Knowledge Management & ELearning*, 485-496.

McCarty, C. (2020). Resident assistant secondary trauma and burnout associated with student nonsuicidal self-injury. *Journal of American College Health*, *68*(7), 673–677.

Metz, J. (2019). Fomo and Regret for Non-Doings. *Social Theory and Practice*, •••, 451–470.

Modzelewski, P. (2020). FoMO (Fear of Missing Out) – An Educational and Behavioral Problem in Times of New Communication Forms. *Pedagogical Contexts*, 215-232.

Oberst, U., Wegmann, E., Stodt, B., Brand, M., & Chamarro, A. (2017). Negative consequences from heavy social networking in adolescents: The mediating role of fear of missing out. *Journal of Adolescence*, •••, 51–60.

Patton, M. Q. (2005). *Patton, M. Q. (2005). Qualitative Research*. John Wiley & Sons, Ltd.

Peterka-Bonetta, J., Sindermann, C., Sha, P., Zhou, M., & Montag, C. (2019). The relationship between Internet Use Disorder, depression and burnout among Chinese and German college students. *Addictive Behaviors*, (89), 188–199.

Postman, N. (2004). *Teknopoli. (M. E. Yılmaz, Çev.)*. Gelenek Yayıncılık.

Przybylski, A., Murayama, K., DeHaan, C., & Valerie, G. (2013). Motivational, Motional and Behavioral Correlates of Fear of Missing Out. *Computers in Human Behavior*, •••, 1841–1848.

Reinecke, L., Hartmann, T., & Eden, A. (2014). The Guilty Couch Potato: The Role of Ego Depletion in Reducing Recovery Through Media Use. *Journal of Communication*, (64), 569–589.

Saboor, A., Ali, K., Mugheri, A., & Fatima, M. (2024). The Impact of Digital Transformation on Educational Leadership: Assessing Digital Burnout and Mental Health in Virtual Teaching. *Review of Applied Management and Social Sciences*, *7*(4), 391–408.

Shabahang, R., Aruguete, M., & Shim, H. (2021). Online News Addiction: Future Anxiety, Fear of Missing Out on News, and Interpersonal Trust Contribute to Excessive Online News Consumption. *Online Journal of Communication and Media Technologies*, •••, 1–11.

Sharma, M. K., Anand, N., Ahuja, S., Thakur, P. C., Mondal, I., Singh, P., & Venkatesyan, S. (2020). Digital burnout: Covid-19 lockdown mediates excessive technology use stress. *World Social Psychiatry*, *2*(2), 171–172.

Şirin, T., Eratlı Şirin, Y., & Can, B. (2021). Beden Eğitimi Öğretmenlerinin Dijital Tükenmişlik Düzeylerinin İncelenmesi. *International Journal of Social. Humanities and Administrative Sciences*, *7*(42), 1236–1245.

Teke, D., & Yılmaz, T. (2023). Sosyal Ortamlardaki Gelişmeleri Kaçırma Korkusu (Fomo) Ve İlişkili Faktörlerin Değerlendirilmesi: Lisans Öğrencileri Üzerine Bir Alan Araştırması. *Yönetim Bilimleri Dergisi/Journal Of. Administrative Sciences*, •••, 1–24.

Tutar, H., & Mutlu, H. T. (2024). Dijital Yorgunluk Ölçeği (DİYÖ): Geçerlilik ve Güvenirlik Çalışması. *İletişim Kuram ve Araştırma Dergisi*(67), 56-74.

Vogt, P., Gardner, D., & Haeffele, L. (2012). *When To Use What Research Design*. Guilford Press.

Wegmann, E., Oberst, U., Stodt, B., & Brand, M. (2017). Online-Specific Fear of Missing Out and Internet-use Expectancies Contribute to Symptoms of Internet-Communication Disorder. *Addictive Behaviors Reports*, •••, 33–42.

Wortham, J. (2011, 4 9). *New York Times*. New York Times: https://www.nytimes.com/2011/04/10/business/10ping.html adresinden alındı

Yener, S. (2018). Teknostresin İş Performansı Üzerindeki Etkisi; Tükenmişliğin Aracı Rolü. *Afyon Kocatepe Üniversitesi Sosyal Bilimler Dergisi*, *20*(2), 85–101.

Yeniceler Kortak, İ. (2024). Gelişmeleri kaçırma korkusu ve haber tüketimi arasındaki ilişkinin incelenmesi. *Kastamonu İletişim Araştırmaları Dergisi (KİAD)*, 153-176.

Zhang, Z., Jimenez, F., & Cicala, J. (2020). Fear Of Missing Out Scale: A Self-Concept Perspective. *Psychology and Marketing*, •••, 1619–1634.

ADDITIONAL READING

Bozkurt, B. (2022). The relationship between teachers' emotional labor and digital burnout during the covid-19 pandemic process. *International Online Journal of Educational Sciences, 14*(4), 977–988.

Dogan, V. (2019). Why Do People Experience the Fear of Missing Out (FoMO)? Exposing the Link Between the Self and the FoMO Through Self-Construal. *Journal of Cross-Cultural Psychology, 50*(4), 524-538. https://doi.org/ (Original work published 2019)DOI: 10.1177/0022022119839145

Duan, H., & Zhao, W. (2024). The Effects of Educational Artificial Intelligence-Powered Applications on Teachers' Perceived Autonomy, Professional Development for Online Teaching, and Digital Burnout. *International Review of Research in Open and Distance Learning, 25*(3), 57–76. DOI: 10.19173/irrodl.v25i3.7659

Elhai, J. D., Yang, H., & Montag, C. (2021). Fear of missing out (FOMO): Overview, theoretical underpinnings, and literature review on relations with severity of negative affectivity and problematic technology use. *The British Journal of Psychiatry, 43*, 203–209. DOI: 10.1590/1516-4446-2020-0870

Hetz, P. R., Dawson, C. L., & Cullen, T. A. (2015). Social Media Use and the Fear of Missing Out (FoMO) While Studying Abroad. *Journal of Research on Technology in Education, 47*(4), 259–272. DOI: 10.1080/15391523.2015.1080585

Hodkinson, C. (2016). 'Fear of Missing Out' (FOMO) marketing appeals: A conceptual model. *Journal of Marketing Communications, 25*(1), 65–88. DOI: 10.1080/13527266.2016.1234504

Roberts, J. A., & David, M. E. (2019). The Social Media Party: Fear of Missing Out (FoMO), Social Media Intensity, Connection, and Well-Being. *International Journal of Human-Computer Interaction, 36*(4), 386–392. DOI: 10.1080/10447318.2019.1646517

Woods, C., & Davis, J. (2024). Exploring the Origins of Digital Burnout in the Music Industries and What to Do About It. In Arditi, D., & Nolan, R. (Eds.), *The Palgrave Handbook of Critical Music Industry Studies*. Palgrave Macmillan., DOI: 10.1007/978-3-031-64013-1_11

KEY TERMS AND DEFINITIONS

Analysis: It is a way of reaching a conclusion by breaking down a subject (material or intellectual) into its basic parts and then defining the parts and the relationships between them.

Digital Burnout: Feelings of anxiety, exhaustion and apathy caused by spending too much time on digital devices are a growing problem

Digital Media: Platforms that enable interaction and content generation.

Digital: All documents and papers that do not have a tangible existence and exist only in the virtual environment.

Fear of Missing Out (FoMO): It is the concern that a person does not know or misses the news, developments and information experienced in daily life.

SPSS: It is a widely used program for statistical analysis in social sciences.

Student: A person who studies at any educational institution such as primary, secondary, high school or university for the purpose of education.

Chapter 8

The Relationship Between Influencer Exposure and Conspicuous Consumption:

The Mediating Role of Social Comparison and FoMo

Nurcan Yılmaz
https://orcid.org/0000-0003-4707-857X
Inonu University, Turkey

Seril Çakmak Ekinci
https://orcid.org/0000-0002-2742-4642
İnonu University, Turkey

ABSTRACT

This study examines the mediating roles of social comparison and FoMO in the effect of exposure to influencers on conspicuous consumption. The findings reveal a strong, positive, and significant relationship between the level of exposure to social media influencers and FoMO, and a moderate, positive, and significant relationship with conspicuous consumption. Additionally, the relationship between FoMO and conspicuous consumption is found to be strong, positive, and significant. However, no statistically significant relationships were identified between social comparison and the other variables. Moreover, FoMO was found to mediate the relationship between exposure to influencers and conspicuous consumption. The results suggest that, in the context of influencer exposure, FoMO functions as a significant external motivational factor influencing conspicuous consumption behavior.

DOI: 10.4018/979-8-3373-6970-9.ch008

© 2026, IGI Global Scientific Publishing. Copying or distributing in print or electronic forms without written permission of IGI Global Scientific Publishing is prohibited. Use of this chapter to
ıerative artificial intelligence (AI) technologies is expressly prohibited. The publisher reserves all rights to license its use for generative AI training and machine learning model development.

INTRODUCTION

With the spread of digitalization and social media, brands have started to turn to influencer marketing to reach their target audiences. Influencers can have an impact on factors such as brand awareness, trust, purchase intention and conspicuous consumption by establishing strong relationships with their followers thanks to their characteristics such as expertise, sincerity and reliability. In this context, the role of influencers in marketing strategies is becoming increasingly important.

Social media influencers (SMIs) are online personalities who reach large followings on social networking sites and are positioned as an integral part of social media today (Rüther et al., 2023, p. 1). With the increasing popularity of SMIs, influencer marketing has become an important and indispensable element in the marketing strategies of brands (Vrontis et al., 2021, p. 617). Influencers are perceived by consumers as celebrities who have achieved their fame through social media and are called social media stars (Hudders et al., 2021, p. 333). According to Freberg et al. (2011, p. 90), influencers are independent third-party endorsers who shape the attitudes of audiences through social media. According to Delbaere et al. (2021, p. 111), influencers are micro-celebrities who have a large following on social media platforms. Influencers develop customer-brand relationships in different product categories by interacting with their followers. There is a previously established trust relationship between influencers and their followers. For this reason, followers refer to the content produced by influencers in order to access reliable information and advice. Influencers are labelled as nano, micro, macro and mega influencers according to their number of followers. Nano influencers have 1,000-10,000 followers, micro influencers have 10,000-100,000 followers, macro influencers have 100,000-1,000,000 followers, and mega influencers have 1,000,000 followers or more (Campbell & Farrell, 2020, p. 47). In addition, influencers have areas of expertise such as gaming, sports, photography, travel, beauty, fashion, parenting (Santora, 2021).

Influencers are social media users who gain online fame by reaching a significant number of followers through remarkable and engaging social media profiles. Influencers initially created a strong identity by sharing their interests on their personal blogs, and with the emergence of social networks such as Facebook, Instagram, YouTube and TikTok, they turned to social media. Influencers have a strong influence on the decision-making processes of their followers. For this reason, advertisers collaborate with influencers to promote products, brands, organisations or ideas through social media. This marketing strategy is called influencer marketing (Hudders et al., 2021, pp. 327-328). According to Lou and Yuan (2019, p. 59), influencer marketing is a marketing strategy that aims to direct consumers' brand awareness and purchasing decisions by using the influence of opinion leaders.

One of the most important features of influencers for marketers is the audience they reach. The follower base of influencers consists of consumers who voluntarily want to follow influencer content. Thanks to this target audience, marketers can provide organic access through influencer content, reach a niche target audience directly, and attract consumers' attention more effectively than traditional advertisements (Campbell & Farrell, 2020).

Characteristics such as expertise, authenticity and intimacy play a critical role in the success of influencers. These characteristics are important for influencers to increase their influence on the decision-making processes of their followers and to gain more followers. Influencers who are perceived as experts by their followers and share sincere and real information with their followers can reach a wider audience and be more effective in the decision-making processes of their followers (Hudders et al., 2021, p. 334). For example, in Trivedi and Sama's (2020) study, it was found that influencers' expertise and attractiveness characteristics indirectly affect consumers' purchase intentions through brand attitude and brand admiration. Reinikainen et al., (2020) found that consumers' parasocial interaction with influencers positively affects brand trust indirectly through influencer credibility. On the other hand, according to the research findings of Lee et al. (2016), parasocial interaction with influencers positively affects consumers' purchase intention indirectly through luxury brand perceptions.

It is an undeniable fact that social media platforms have a major impact on interpersonal and sociocultural interaction patterns. In particular, these platforms offer new possibilities for individuals to manage their personal networks and social activities. The interesting and complex interaction between technology and human behaviour is shaping an environment full of social comparisons (Qiu, 2024, p. 1).

Social comparison theory was first proposed by Festinger (1954) to explain how individuals perform self-evaluation processes through social interactions. Festinger suggested that individuals have an internal motivation to reduce uncertainties and evaluate themselves. In the absence of an objective evaluation criterion, individuals tend to make comparisons with others in order to evaluate their own abilities and performances (cited in Liu et al., 2016, p. 621). This theory suggests that individuals need to evaluate and make sense of themselves and therefore tend to reduce uncertainty by making comparisons with others in various aspects such as skills, opinions, appearance, and assets (Kim et al., 2023, p. 656; Liu et al., 2016, p. 619).

Social comparison is the practice of individuals making comparisons with others in order to evaluate themselves or to improve their selves (Suls et al., 2002, p. 159). In this process, individuals make social comparison by comparing their performance in a certain dimension with the people around them (Mundel et al., 2024, p. 836). Although individuals do not always make comparisons consciously, they can evaluate themselves in line with the information they obtain from their environment.

For example, even if a person does not directly prefer to make a comparison with someone who is different from him/her, this information may increase his/her self-confidence when he/she learns that he/she has the same opinion with that person (Suls et al., 2000, p. 221).

Social comparisons can be both upward (comparison with a superior person) and downward (comparison with someone who is in a worse situation). If the person being compared performs better in general or in terms of a specific characteristic (for example, intelligence, physical attractiveness, athletic ability, etc.), the individual feels worse in the encounter; when he/she perceives that other individuals are worse than him/her, he/she feels better (Liu et al., 2016, p. 621). In other words, an individual who compares himself/herself with someone who is in a better situation may experience negative emotions, whereas he/she may feel better when he/she compares himself/herself with someone who is in a worse position.

Once social media users interact with influencers, they are typically the primary source of social comparison (Dinh & Lee, 2024). In this context, exposure to influencer content on social media intensifies social comparison processes that affect both individuals' self-perceptions and purchasing behaviours (Mundel et al., 2024, p. 836). Therefore, social comparison in social media is not passively experienced by the users; individuals prefer to compare themselves with others according to the contents they watch (Qiu, 2024, p. 3). These comparison processes, combined with individuals' desire to stay updated on social media and stay up to date with their environment, can trigger fear of missing out on developments (FoMO).

Fear of missing out (FoMO) has become an increasingly important concept in the study of consumer behaviour, particularly in terms of social media marketing (Zhang et al., 2020, p. 1619). Social media plays an important role in the development of FoMO in individuals (Abel et al., 2016). Social media platforms provide information about individuals' social environments in a more diverse and comprehensive way every day. Thanks to social media, individuals can access information about activities and conversations in different social circles in real time. Therefore, the use of social media seems inevitable for individuals who are afraid of missing the developments. FoMO is defined as a state of constant anxiety that arises from the thought that rewarding experiences that the individual is not involved in are experienced by others, and this state is characterised by individuals' desire to constantly follow the actions of others (Przybylski, et al., 2013, p. 1841). According to Rozgonjuk et al. (2020, p. 1), FoMO is defined as the tendency to worry about missing rewarding experiences experienced by others.

Zhang et al., (2020, p. 1622), based on the self-concept theory, argue that FoMO is "an emotional response to perceived psychological threats to the individual's self-concept" and consider FoMO in two dimensions: personal and social FoMO. Personal FoMO refers to "the level of missing experiences related to one's own private life and social FoMO indicates the level of missing pleasant or rewarding experiences experienced by others".

Marketers target to influence consumers' purchasing preferences by using FoMO-oriented marketing strategies on social media. The use of FoMO messages through influencers has been found to significantly impact consumers' choice of travel destinations (Lee et al., 2023). According to the research findings of Setiawan et al. (2024), FoMO can indirectly affect touristic destination choices by influencing consumers' motivations, emotional reactions and behaviours. In addition, the study concluded that influencers play a decisive role in shaping consumers' perceptions of tourist destinations and guiding their travel preferences.

Influencers have a powerful influence on their followers as the first to introduce new products and trends in the market. Influencers affect the purchase intentions of their followers by conveying their opinions and experiences about products to their followers through the product promotion videos they post on social media. In this direction, the purchase behaviour that occurs with the influence of influencers is usually triggered by the fear of missing out on developments (Dinh & Lee, 2022, p. 351). For example, Laili et al., (2025) found that the beauty influencers have a significant effect on consumers' FoMO levels and brand image. In addition, FoMO was found to play an important mediating variable role in the relationship between beauty influencers and brand image and purchase intention.

The constant exposure of individuals to influencer content on social media leads individuals to compare themselves with influencers and think that influencers have more exclusive experiences or more valuable products. In addition, when individuals cannot follow current trends, they feel left behind and excluded from their social circles, which triggers the emergence of FoMO. On the other hand, the desire of individuals to maintain their commitment with influencers leads them to compare themselves with the lifestyles of influencers. This comparison process triggers the fear of missing out on the products and services used by influencers (Dinh & Lee, 2022, p. 351). Reer et al. (2019) found that individuals with a high tendency for social comparison are more likely to develop a sense of FoMO.

The theoretical concept of conspicuous consumption was first put forward by Thorstein Veblen in 1899. According to Veblen (1899), wealthy individuals consume remarkable and expensive goods and services in order to display their richness and thus achieve a higher social status (cited in Bagwell & Bernheim, 1996, p. 349). In this context, conspicuous consumption is defined as the consumer's purchase of expensive products by displaying his/her wealth in a wasteful manner to maintain his/her current status or to obtain a higher social status rather than meeting his/her utilitarian needs (cited in Eckhardt and et al., 2015, p. 807). Indeed, since Veblen and Simmel, the concept of 'luxury' has largely become synonymous with conspicuous consumption (Eckhardt et al., 2015, p. 807). These emotional and social processes pave the way for individuals to turn towards not only psychological but also symbolic forms of consumption.

Conspicuous consumption is a behaviour in which individuals display their material wealth by purchasing unnecessary and extravagant products to gain status and influence others (Griskevicius et al., 2007, p. 87; Nguyen et al., 2015, p. 17). This consumption style is regarded as a symbolic and visible form of self-presentation. Qattan and Khasawneh (2020, p. 1) define conspicuous consumption as a conscious behaviour based on the purchase, ownership and use of products and services with limited economic and cultural capital in order to convey a distinctive self-image.

The asynchronous nature of social media allows users to present more selective and idealised versions of themselves, enabling even ordinary consumer items to be presented in a pretentious manner. Through social media posts, individuals can display their consumption actions to a wide audience, thereby expressing their social status and participating in conspicuous consumption (Duan & Dholakia, 2017, p. 410).

Conspicuous consumption behaviour can differ at the individual level. The consumer's tendency to display wealth and show off in an attention-seeking manner when purchasing luxury goods is shaped by the personal value they attribute to conspicuous consumption (Pangarkar & Rathee, 2023, p. 1155). In this context, individual factors such as self-esteem also play an important role. Wai and Osman (2019, p. 336) propose that individuals with high and low self-esteem have different moderating effects on the relationship between social media use and conspicuous consumption.

While building a public identity for themselves in the digital environment, SMIs share their personal experiences, product evaluations and recommendations with their followers; in this process, they also display conspicuous consumption behaviours (Matheson & Sedgwick, 2021, p. 19). Studies have shown that SMIs have a positive effect on brand image, consumer attitudes, and purchase intention. However, it has been determined that brand image plays a mediating role in the relationships between SMIs, customer attitudes, and purchase intention (Rashid et al., 2023, p. 140).

As luxury products lose their importance as symbols of status, wealth or power to others; individuals have begun to seek alternative status symbols. In recent years, individuals have increasingly turned to social media to display their experiences and conspicuous consumption in order to gain approval and recognition. Therefore, social media not only offers new opportunities for the conspicuous consumption of experiential purchases but also provides various advantages for brands that offer such experiences (Siepmann et al., 2022, pp. 454, 456). In other words, social media serves both individuals' quest for social status and provides brands with benefits in terms of visibility and interaction. At this point, not only internal but also external motivations play a significant role in individuals' tendency towards conspicuous consumption on social media.

In addition to perception, personality, attitude, and learning, motivation also plays a key role in understanding behaviour (Akanbi, 2011, p. 4). Motivation is the driving force that explains why individuals behave and act in certain ways (Clanton Harpine, 2015, p. 87). Being motivated means having taken action to achieve something. Individuals who do not feel the desire or inspiration to take action are described as unmotivated, while those who act energetically and decisively towards a specific goal are considered motivated (Ryan & Deci, 2000, p. 54).

Contemporary approaches to behaviour suggest that an individual's actions can be driven by both internal and external motivation. External motivation is related to an individual's performance of an activity based on external factors such as rewards, approval or social expectations rather than its intrinsic value. In contrast, internal motivation arises simply because the activity is inherently interesting, engaging, or satisfying. These two types of motivation are considered the fundamental driving factors behind behaviour aimed at specific outcomes (Lee et al., 2005, p. 1097). This study focuses on social comparison and fear of missing out (FoMO) as mediating variables within the scope of external motivation. Both variables emerge based on individuals' responses to environmental stimuli and shape consumption behaviour in line with social expectations.

Studies in influencer marketing literature show that influencers positively affect brand attitude, brand trust, brand awareness, purchase intention, and word-of-mouth communication (Lee et al., 2016; De Veirman et al., 2017; Breves et al., 2019; De Jans et al., 2020; Trivedi and Sama, 2020; Reinikainen et al., 2020). However, there are only a limited number of studies examining influencers in terms of social comparison, FoMO, and conspicuous consumption (Lee et al., 2021; Dinh and Lee, 2022; Dinh and Lee, 2024). In this context, it is becoming increasingly important to examine the effects of influencer marketing not only on brand-based outcomes but also on individual psychological and social dynamics.

The purpose of this study is to examine how consumers' exposure to influencers is related to social comparison, FoMO, and conspicuous consumption tendencies. In addition, the study examines whether social comparison and FoMO play a mediating role in the relationship between exposure to influencers and conspicuous consumption. Within the scope of the stated purpose, the following research questions and hypotheses have been developed:

Q1: Is there a relationship between being exposed to social media influencers and social comparison?
H1: There is a significant relationship between being exposed to social media influencers and social comparison.
Q2: Is there a relationship between being exposed to social media influencers and FoMO?

H2: There is a significant relationship between being exposed to social media influencers and FoMO.
Q3: Is there a relationship between exposure to social media influencers and conspicuous consumption?
H3: There is a significant relationship between exposure to social media influencers and conspicuous consumption.
Q4: Is there a relationship between social comparison and FoMO?
H4: There is a significant relationship between social comparison and FoMO.
Q5: Is there a relationship between social comparison and conspicuous consumption?
Q5: There is a significant relationship between social comparison and conspicuous consumption.
Q6: Is there a relationship between FoMO and conspicuous consumption?
Q6: There is a significant relationship between FoMO and conspicuous consumption.
Q7: Does social comparison play a mediating role in the relationship between exposure to social media influencers and conspicuous consumption?
H7: Social comparison plays a mediating role in the relationship between exposure to social media influencers and conspicuous consumption.
Q8: Does FoMO play a mediating role in the relationship between exposure to social media influencers and conspicuous consumption?
H8: FoMO mediates the relationship between exposure to social media influencers and conspicuous consumption.
Q9: Does exposure to social media influencers differ according to demographic variables?
H9: Exposure to social media influencers differs significantly according to gender, age, income, and education level.
Q10: Does social comparison differ according to demographic variables?
H10: Social comparison shows significant differences according to gender, age, income, and education status.
Q11: Does FoMO differ according to demographic variables?
H11: FoMO shows significant differences according to gender, age, income, and education status.
Q12: Does conspicuous consumption differ according to demographic variables?
H12: Conspicuous consumption shows significant differences according to gender, age, income, and education status.

METHOD

A survey study was conducted to examine the relationship between consumers' exposure to influencers and their tendencies toward social comparison, FoMO, and conspicuous consumption, as well as the mediating role of social comparison and FoMO in the relationship between exposure to influencers and conspicuous consumption. The population of the study consisted of individuals aged 18 and older who live in Turkey and follow social media influencers. However, due to time and cost constraints, it was not possible to reach the entire population. Therefore, convenience sampling, one of the non-probability sampling methods, was used in this study. An online survey form was prepared to collect research data. Participants were asked questions regarding demographic information such as gender, age, educational status, and income level. Accordingly, the survey consists of a total of 23 items. The scales used were translated into Turkish by two researchers and then tested on 60 participants in a pilot study. Following the pilot study, the scale items were reviewed and necessary adjustments were made. Accordingly, data were obtained from 395 participants in the main data collection process; however, 11 invalid forms were identified and excluded from the analysis. As a result, data from 384 participants were analysed. According to Krejcie and Morgan (1970, p. 608), the appropriate sample size for a population of 1,000,000 is 384 individuals. Ethical approval for the conduct of the study was obtained from the Scientific Research and Publication Ethics Committee of İnönü University on 23 May 2025 (session no: 11 / decision no: 19).

In the online questionnaire, the measurement tools developed by Dinh and Lee (2024) by adapting the studies of various researchers, namely the 'Exposure to Social Media Influencers Scale,' 'Social Comparison Scale,' 'Fear of Missing Out Scale,' and 'Conspicuous Consumption Scale,' were used. 'The level of agreement with all statements was measured using a 5-point Likert scale, ranging from 1 = "Strongly Disagree" to 5 = "Strongly Agree." The findings of the reliability analyses for the scales are presented in Table 2.'

The data obtained in the study were analysed using the SPSS statistical programme and the Hayes PROCESS Macro add-on.

Descriptive Statistics and Normality Test

A normality test was conducted to test the suitability of the research data for the normality assumption. When examining the descriptive statistics in Table 1, the mean value of the social media exposure variable was determined as 2.35 and the standard deviation as 0.94911. The mean and standard deviation values for the social comparison variable are 3.77 and 1.07274, respectively. The mean value of the fear of missing out scale was found to be 1.98, and the standard deviation was 0.93727. The mean and standard deviation values for the conspicuous consumption variable were 1.98 and 1.08018, respectively.

Skewness and kurtosis values were examined to assess the normality of the data distribution. According to a generally accepted approach in the literature, skewness and kurtosis values between -2 and +2 indicate that the distribution is reasonably normal (Bachman, 2004, p. 74). As a result of this analysis, since the skewness and kurtosis values of the data remained within the relevant limits, it was concluded that the distribution is normal, and the data were deemed suitable for the application of parametric tests.

Table 1. Descriptive Statistics and Normality Test for the Scales

	Min.	Max.	Mean	Std. Deviation	Skewness	Kurtosis
Exposure to Social Media Influencers	1,00	5,00	2,35	,94911	,458	-,493
Social Comparison	1,00	5,00	3,77	1,07274	-,904	,186
FoMO	1,00	5,00	1,98	,93727	,916	-,017
Conspicuous Consumption	1,00	5,00	2,05	1,08018	,936	,082

Reliability Analysis

Table 2 presents the reliability analyses of the scales. Cronbach's Alpha value of 0.80 and above is considered high reliability, while 0.70 is considered acceptable reliability (Burns & Burns, 2008, p. 417). Therefore, it can be stated that the scales included in the study are reliable.

Table 2. Reliability Analysis of Scales

	Cronbach's Alpha
Exposure to Social Media Influencers	,788
Connecting with influencers through SNS platforms is part of my everyday activity.	
I dedicate a part of my daily schedule to connect with influencers through SNS platforms.	
I feel I am part of the influencers' community on SNS platforms.	

continued on following page

Table 2. Continued

	Cronbach's Alpha
Social Comparison	,921
Influencers can afford a better dwelling (apartment, house) than me.	
Influencers can afford better food and drink than me.	
Influencers can afford more expensive entertainment than me.	
Influencers can afford better and more clothes than me.	
Influencers can afford to pay school expenses more easily than me.	
FoMO	,919
I'm afraid I will feel sorry I didn't buy endorsed products later.	
I will worry that I'm missing out on endorsed products.	
I will worry that other people are having more rewarding experiences than me by using endorsed products.	
I feel concerned that other people are having more fun with endorsed products.	
I will feel left out of trends if I don't have endorsed products.	
I will feel sorry that I didn't experience endorsed products.	
I will feel anxious about not having endorsed products.	
I will feel bothered that I missed an opportunity to use endorsed products.	
Conspicuous Consumption	,882
I want to buy products to be noticed by others.	
I want to buy products because of the presence of others.	
I want to buy products to gain respect.	

RESULTS

Demographic Findings

Table 3. Demographic Characteristics

		N	%
Gender	Female	226	58,9
	Male	158	41,1
Age	18-29	325	84,6
	30-39	34	8,9
	40-49	20	5,2
	50 ve üzeri	5	1,3
Education level	Primary School	5	1,3
	High School	15	3,9
	Associate Degree	30	7,8
	Undergraduate Degree	312	81,3
	Postgraduate Degree	22	5,7
Income	20,000 or less	269	70,1
	20,001-30,000	40	10,4
	30,001-40,000	18	4,7
	40,001-50,000	15	3,9
	50,001 and above	42	10,9

N= 384

When Table 3 is examined, it is seen that 58.9% of the participants are women. When participants are evaluated in terms of age distribution, the 18-29 age group stands out with 84.6%. In terms of education distribution, the bachelor's degree level leads with 81.3%. In terms of income distribution, the income group earning 20,000 and below stands out with 70.1%.

Investigation of the Relationships Between Exposure to Social Media Influencers, Social Comparison, Fear of Missing Out (FOMO), and Conspicuous Consumption Through Pearson Correlation Analysis

The classification proposed by O'Rourke and colleagues (2005, p. 127) has been used to interpret the correlation coefficient. Accordingly, a value of 0.00 indicates no relationship between two variables; 0.01–0.20 indicates a weak relationship, 0.21–0.50 indicates a moderate relationship, 0.51–0.80 indicates a strong relationship, and 0.81–1.00 indicates a perfect relationship.

Table 4. Pearson Correlation Analysis of Exposure to Influencers, Social Comparison, FOMO, and Conspicuous Consumption

Correlations					
		Exposure to Social Media Influencers	**Social Comparison**	**FoMO**	**Conspicuous Consumption**
Exposure to Social Media Influencers	Pearson Correlation	1	,003	,590	,494
	Sig. (2-tailed)		,947	,000	,000
Social Comparison	Pearson Correlation		1	-,033	,059
	Sig. (2-tailed)			,522	,246
FoMO	Pearson Correlation			1	,723
	Sig. (2-tailed)				,000
Conspicuous Consumption	Pearson Correlation				1

The correlation is significant at the $p < 0.05$ level.

No significant relationship was found between exposure to social media phenomena and social comparison ($p<0.05$). A strong relationship ($r = .590$) was found between exposure to social media phenomena and fear of missing out, while a moderate positive relationship ($r = .494$) and a significant relationship were found between exposure to social media phenomena and conspicuous consumption ($p<0.05$). In other words, as participants' exposure to social media influencers increases, their fear of missing out and conspicuous consumption also increase significantly and strongly. On the other hand, no significant relationship was found between social comparison and fear of missing out or conspicuous consumption ($p<0.05$). In contrast, a strong, positive, and significant relationship was found between fear of missing out and conspicuous consumption ($r = 0.723$, $p < 0.05$). In other words, as participants' fear of missing out increased, their tendency toward conspicuous consumption also increased significantly. Therefore, H2, H3, and H6 were accepted; H1, H4, and H5 were rejected.

Findings Related to the Mediation Analysis

This study examined the mediating role of social comparison and FoMO in the effect of influencer exposure on conspicuous consumption. The results of the analyses revealed no statistically significant relationship between social comparison and other variables. Therefore, no mediation analysis was conducted for the social comparison variable. Additionally, H6 was rejected. In conclusion, it was determined that social comparison does not play a mediating or triggering role in this relationship.

Model 4 was preferred in Hayes Process Macro to determine the mediating role of FoMO in the relationship between exposure to influencers and conspicuous consumption. In Model 4, exposure to influencers (X) was defined as the independent variable, FoMO (M) as the mediating variable, and conspicuous consumption (Y) as the dependent variable (Hayes, 2022). The findings of the analysis results are presented in Tables 5, 6, 7, and 8. The criteria indicating that the research model is statistically significant include the confidence interval values (LLCI and ULCI) not including zero, the beta coefficient being significant, and the p-value being less than 0.05 (Preacher & Hayes, 2004; Abu-Bader & Jones, 2021).

Table 5. Model Results for Mediation Test

Model Summary							
R	**R²**	**MSE**	**F**	**df1**	**df2**	**p**	
,590	,348	,575	203,553	1,000	382,000	,000	
Variables		**Effects**					
		B	**SE**	**t**	**p**	**LLCI**	**ULCI**
Constant		,613	,104	5,918	,000	,410	,817
Exposure to Influencers FoMO		,582	,041	14,267	,000	,502	,662
Standardized Beta (β) Coefficient		, 590					

According to the findings in Table 5, exposure to influencers was found to have a positive and significant effect on FoMO (β= .582, 95% CI [.502; .662], t=14.267, p<0.05). Additionally, exposure to influencers explains 34.8% (R^2 = 0.348) of the variance in FoMO.

Table 6. Model Results for Mediation Test 2

Model Summary							
R	**R²**	**MSE**	**F**	**df1**	**df2**	**p**	
,494	,244	,885	123,215	1,000	382,000	,000	
Variables		**Effects**					
		B	**SE**	**t**	**p**	**LLCI**	**ULCI**
Constant		,734	,129	5,710	,000	,482	,987
Exposure to Influencers Conspicuous Consumption		,562	,051	11,100	,000	,462	,662
Standardized Beta (β) Coefficient		,494					

According to Table 6, before FoMO was included in the model, exposure to influencers positively and significantly affected conspicuous consumption (β= .562, 95% CI [.462; .662], t= 11.100, p<0.05). Additionally, exposure to influencers explains 24.4% of the variance in conspicuous consumption ($R^2 = 0.244$).

Table 7. Model Results for Mediation Test 3

Model Summary							
R	**R²**	**MSE**	**F**	**df1**	**df2**	**p**	
,727	,529	,552	214,148	2,000	381,000	,000	
Variables		**Effects**					
		B	**SE**	**t**	**p**	**LLCI**	**ULCI**
Constant		,267	,106	2,513	,012	,058	,476
Exposure to Influencers Conspicuous Consumption		,118	,050	2,388	,017	,021	,216
FoMO Conspicuous Consumption		,762	,050	15,196	,000	,664	,861
Standardized Beta (β) Coefficient							
Exposure to Influencers		,104					
Conspicuous Consumption		,661					

According to Table 7, when examining the combined effects of exposure to influencers and FoMO on conspicuous consumption, it is observed that the direct effect of exposure to influencers on conspicuous consumption (β= .118, 95% CI [.021; .216], t= 2.388, p<0.05) is significant. Additionally, FoMO (β = 0.762, 95% CI [0.664; 0.861], t = 15.196, p < 0.05) positively and significantly influences conspicuous consumption. Exposure to influencers and FoMO explain 52.9% of the variance in conspicuous consumption ($R^2 = 0.529$).

Table 8. Total, Direct and Indirect Effects

Total Effect **Exposure to Influencers Conspicuous Consumption**					
Effect	**SE**	**t**	**p**	**LLCI**	**ULCI**
,562	,051	11,100	,000	,462	,662
Direct Effect **Exposure to Influencers Conspicuous Consumption**					
Effect	**SE**	**t**	**p**	**LLCI**	**ULCI**
,118	,050	2,388	,017	,021	,216
Indirect Effect **Exposure to Influencers FoMO Conspicuous Consumption**					
Effect	**BootSE**	**BootLLCI**	**BootULCI**		
,444	**,044**	,359	**,533**		
Total Standardized Indirect Effect					
Effect	**BootSE**	**BootLLCI**	**BootULCI**		
,390	,035	,323	,459		

Table 8 presents the findings regarding the total, direct, and indirect effects of exposure to influencers on conspicuous consumption. The total effect of exposure to influencers on conspicuous consumption (β= 0.562, 95% CI [0.462; 0.662], t=11.100, p<0.05) and direct effect (β=, 118, 95% CI [,021;, 216], t= 2.388, p>0.05) on conspicuous consumption are positive and significant. The indirect effect is 44.4% (β=,444) and the confidence interval (95% CI [,359;, 533]) values do not include zero. In this regard, when FoMO is included in the model, the direct effect of exposure to influencers on conspicuous consumption does not lose its meaning, but the strength of the effect decreases. This finding shows that FoMO plays a partial mediating role.

It has been determined that FoMO plays a significant mediating role in the relationship between exposure to influencers and conspicuous consumption. This finding reveals that social media users' tendency to experience social exclusion anxiety when exposed to influencer content may influence their conspicuous consumption behaviour. Therefore, H8 were accepted.

Exposure to Influencer, Social Comparison, FoMO and Conspicuous Consumption: A Demographic Analysis

Table 9 presents findings on whether exposure to social media influencers, social comparison, FoMO, and conspicuous consumption vary according to demographic variables. In this context, an independent samples t-test analysis was conducted to determine whether the variables of exposure to social media influencers, social comparison, FoMO, and conspicuous consumption exhibit a significant difference based on gender. According to the analysis results, significant differences were found between gender and exposure to social media phenomena (t = -2.481; p = .014), FoMO (t = 3.418; p = .001), and conspicuous consumption (t = -5.116; p = .000). Based on this finding, it can be suggested that female individuals tend to follow social media influencers more frequently or are more exposed to such content. On the other hand, no difference was found between gender and the social comparison variable (t = -1.203; p = 0.045). This result indicates that individuals' tendencies toward social comparison are at a similar level regardless of gender.

Table 9. Demographic Variables and Exposure to Social Media Influencers, Social Comparison, Fear of Missing Developments, Conspicuous Consumption

	Gender	**N**	**Mean**	**t**	**Sig. (2-tailed)**
Exposure to Social Media Influencers	Female	226	2,25	-2,481	,014
	Male	158	2,50		
Social Comparison	Female	226	3,72	-1,203	,230
	Male	158	3,85		
FoMO	Female	226	1,84	-3,418	,001
	Male	158	2,18		
Conspicuous Consumption	Female	226	1,81	-5,116	,000
	Male	158	2,40		
	Education	**N**	**Mean**	**F**	**Sig.**
Exposure to Social Media Influencers	Primary School	5	3,0	4,123	,003
	High School	15	2,60		
	Associate Degree	30	2,87		
	Undergraduate Degree	312	2,30		
	Postgraduate Degree	22	2,01		
Social Comparison	Primary School	5	3,56	,225	,924
	High School	15	3,68		
	Associate Degree	30	3,64		
	Undergraduate Degree	312	3,79		
	Postgraduate Degree	22	3,81		

continued on following page

Table 9. Continued

	Gender	N	Mean	t	Sig. (2-tailed)
FoMO	Primary School	5	2,60	4,032	,003
	High School	15	2,35		
	Associate Degree	30	2,50		
	Undergraduate Degree	312	1,91		
	Postgraduate Degree	22	1,96		
Conspicuous Consumption	Primary School	5	2,66	4,087	,003
	High School	15	2,42		
	Associate Degree	30	2,67		
	Undergraduate Degree	312	1,96		
	Postgraduate Degree	22	2,18		
	Income	**N**	**Mean**	**F**	**Sig.**
Social Comparison	20,000 or less	269	3,89	2,840	,024
	20,001-30,000	40	3,49		
	30,001-40,000	18	3,45		
	40,001-50,000	15	3,66		
	50,001 and above	42	3,47		

One-way analysis of variance (One-Way ANOVA) was applied to determine whether demographic variables such as age, education, and monthly income showed a significant difference in terms of exposure to social media phenomena, social comparison, FoMO, and conspicuous consumption. H9, H10, H11, and H12 were partially supported.

The analysis revealed that there was no significant difference between the age variable and the variables of exposure to social media phenomena, social comparison, FoMO, and conspicuous consumption. Therefore, since no significant difference emerged, the findings were not included in the table (Table 9). This result indicates that individuals' attitudes toward these variables remain similar regardless of their age groups. In other words, it can be concluded that age does not influence these variables.

Significant differences were found between educational level and exposure to social media phenomena (F = 4.123; p = .003), FoMO (F = 4.032; p = .003) and conspicuous consumption (F = 4.087; p = .003). To determine which educational categories exhibited these differences, the 'Games-Hovell' post hoc test was applied. The analysis revealed significant differences between educational groups in terms of exposure to social media influencers. In particular, the difference between the associate degree and bachelor's degree groups (md = 0.56902; p = 0.022) and between the associate degree and postgraduate groups (md = 0.86263; p = 0.028) was found to be significant. Similarly, a significant difference was found between the associate degree and bachelor's degree groups (md = 0.59391; p = 0.034) in terms of FoMO. Additionally, a significant difference was found between the associate degree and bachelor's degree groups in terms of conspicuous consumption (MD = 0.71410; p = 0.027). On the other hand, no significant difference was found between educational level and social comparison (F = 0.225; p = 0.924). This indicates that individuals with higher educational levels are more active, interactive, and visibility-oriented on social media. Additionally, it can be considered that social comparison occurs at similar levels among individuals regardless of educational level.

A significant difference was found only between the monthly income variable and social comparison (F = 2.840; p = .024). No significant difference was found between the income variable and exposure to social media phenomena, FoMO, and conspicuous consumption. Therefore, these findings were not included in the table (Table 9). This finding indicates that individuals' levels of social comparison vary according to their income levels. Additionally, these results can be interpreted as suggesting that some attitudes and behaviours may emerge independently of demographic variables.

CONCLUSION

The fear of missing out (FoMO) can influence individuals' purchasing decisions. For example, individuals may prefer to purchase a more expensive or higher quality product in order to keep up with their friends and fit in with their social circle. Therefore, in such situations, individuals may change their consumption habits and purchasing decisions due to the social pressure and fear of rejection they feel (Abel et al., 2016). Social media platforms have increased the visibility of consumption preferences, potentially making almost all forms of consumption conspicuous (Anggarawati et al., 2023). In this context, marketing activities conducted through SMI are particularly effective on young consumers (Sun et al., 2021, p. 603) and contribute to the spread of conspicuous consumption in the digital age.

This study investigates how consumers' exposure to influencers is related to social comparison, FOMO, and conspicuous consumption tendencies. Additionally, it examines whether social comparison and FOMO play a mediating role in the relationship between exposure to influencers and conspicuous consumption.

According to the research results, the majority of participants are women. Participants are generally young, have a bachelor's degree, and belong to a low-income group. This indicates that the study focuses on young, educated individuals with limited income.

The findings of the correlation analysis conducted to determine the relationships between the research variables revealed strong, positive, and significant relationships between the level of exposure to social media phenomena and FoMO, and moderate, positive, and significant relationships between the level of exposure to social media phenomena and conspicuous consumption. This result shows that participants exposed to phenomenon content have significantly increased tendencies towards both FoMO and conspicuous consumption. Furthermore, the relationship between FoMO and conspicuous consumption is strong, positive, and significant. This finding reveals that individuals exposed to phenomenon content on social media feel a more intense anxiety about keeping up with current events and not missing any content. Therefore, it can be said that phenomenon content is a triggering factor for FoMO. This suggests that individuals who view phenomenon content may exhibit more conspicuous consumption behaviour in order to leave an impression on others. Additionally, individuals with high levels of FoMO may be more inclined to engage in conspicuous consumption in order to attract attention or stay up-to-date within their social circles. On the other hand, the absence of a significant relationship between social comparison and other variables indicates that individuals' social comparison tendencies are not directly related to exposure to phenomenon content, FoMO, or conspicuous consumption. This suggests that social comparison may have a limited effect in the sample of this study.

According to the research findings, no significant relationship was found between social comparison and other variables, leading to the conclusion that social comparison does not play a mediating or triggering role in this relationship. This finding can be interpreted as meaning that social comparison does not always trigger FoMO and does not have a direct effect on conspicuous consumption. On the other hand, this result differs from some studies in the literature. Social media users discover their social identities through the content of influencers they follow and tend to engage in social comparison (Kim et al., 2023, p. 657). Influencers are powerful actors who shape perceptions, values, and behaviours on social media. Their posts significantly influence users' social interactions and self-perceptions. They often present idealised lifestyles, setting difficult standards to achieve concepts such as beauty, success, and happiness. This encourages social comparison, especially among young users, and can lead to psychological outcomes such as feelings of inadequacy and disappointment (Qiu, 2024, pp. 3-4). As noted by Mundel et al. (2024, p. 836), exposure to influencer content increases social comparison processes that affect individuals' self-perceptions and purchasing behaviour. Similarly, Dinh & Lee (2024) state that social comparison is often primarily triggered by influencers when social media users interact with them. According to the researchers' findings, exposure to influencers triggers social comparison and FoMO, thereby increasing consumers' tendencies toward conspicuous consumption.

In today's world, conspicuous consumption is on the rise in both developed and developing countries. Social media platforms encourage social comparisons among individuals in areas such as wealth, status, and attractiveness, which in turn increases the motivation to acquire luxury products and triggers conspicuous consumption (Wai & Osman, 2019, p. 336). Research indicates that consumers' self-presentation behaviours on social media increase their tendency toward social comparison, and these tendencies support conspicuous consumption (Lu et al., 2024, p. 1206). It can be said that this form of consumption has become more visible and widespread through social media.

According to another research finding, exposure to influencers positively and significantly affects conspicuous consumption before being included in the FoMO model. With the addition of FoMO to the model, the effect of exposure to influencers on conspicuous consumption continues to decrease but remains statistically meaningful. This suggests that FoMO plays a partial mediating role in the relationship between influencer effect and conspicuous consumption. The findings reveal that FoMO plays a mediating or triggering role in the relationship between exposure to social media phenomena and conspicuous consumption. This result is similar to the findings of Dinh and Lee (2024), who also found that FoMO mediates the relationship between exposure to social media influencers (SMI) and conspicuous consumption. As stated by Dinh and Lee (2024), FoMO is an emotion that arises from the fear of missing out on trends after individuals evaluate themselves. Individuals are driven to consume products and services in order to obtain and maintain social status and avoid distress. Increased fear levels also enhance the tendency toward conspicuous consumption of approved products. This study determined that FOMO plays a mediating or triggering role in the relationship between exposure to social media phenomenon content and conspicuous consumption.

On the other hand, some studies in the literature that examine influencers and FoMO variables together have reached different results. Research findings reveal that imitating influencers has a significant effect on social comparison, materialism, and FoMO, and that these variables significantly influence the intention to purchase products endorsed by influencers (Dinh & Lee, 2021, p. 346). Additionally, it has been determined that FoMO plays a moderating role in the relationships between exposure to influencers and materialism and purchase intention (Dinh et al., 2023, p. 1). Barari's (2023, p. 1162) study shows that FoMO plays a mediating role in the relationship between social media influencers and consumer well-being. Furthermore, Lee and colleagues' (2021) research revealed that individuals with high levels of FoMO follow influencer accounts more frequently, which leads them to purchase products recommended by influencers more often and, consequently, increases their happiness levels. These findings demonstrate that influencer content can influence individuals' psychological tendencies and purchasing behaviour in a multidimensional manner.

The research findings reveal that FoMO is an external motivational factor that significantly influences conspicuous consumption behaviour in the context of exposure to influencers. In this regard, examining the effect of FoMO on conspicuous consumption within the framework of external motivation contributes to a better understanding of the decisive role of motivation types in consumer behaviour.

Indeed, in the study by Truong and McColl (2011, pp. 555-559), it is emphasised that external-oriented purchasing behaviour is based on the opinions of others as the primary source of motivation for consumers and is shaped by external goals such as social approval, desire for recognition and status.

The fact that participants were reached using a convenience sampling technique constitutes the main limitation of the study. In future studies, probability sampling techniques could be used to determine the sample, and research could be conducted by including different mediating variables. These findings provide important insights into the effects of social media phenomena on individuals' psychological processes and consumption behaviours; they also contribute to the existing literature on social media phenomena, social comparison, FoMO, and conspicuous consumption. Additionally, the results obtained are instructive for developing strategies for phenomena and marketing practitioners.

REFERENCES

Abel, J. P., Buff, C. L., & Burr, S. A. (2016). Social media and the fear of missing out: Scale development and assessment. *Journal of Business & Economics Research, 14*, 33–43.

Abu-Bader, S., & Jones, T. V. (2021). Statistical mediation analysis using the sobel test and hayes SPSS process macro. *International Journal of Quantitative and Qualitative Research Methods.*

Akanbi, P. A. (2011). Influence of extrinsic and intrinsic motivation on employees' performance. https://www.academia.edu/download/34792904/motivationworker.pdf

Anggarawati, S., Armelly, A., Salim, M., Odilawati, W., Saputra, F. E., & Atmaja, F. T. (2023). The mediating role of narcissistic behavior in the relationship between materialistic orientation and conspicuous online consumption behavior on social media. *Cogent Business & Management, 10*(3), 2285768. DOI: 10.1080/23311975.2023.2285768

Bachman, L. F. (2004). *Statistical analyses for language assessment book.* Cambridge University Press.

Bagwell, L. S., & Bernheim, B. D. (1996). Veblen effects in a theory of conspicuous consumption. *The American Economic Review, 86*(3), 349–373.

Barari, M. (2023). Unveiling the dark side of influencer marketing: How social media influencers (human vs virtual) diminish followers' well-being. *Marketing Intelligence & Planning, 41*(8), 1162–1177. DOI: 10.1108/MIP-05-2023-0191

Breves, P. L., Liebers, N., Abt, M., & Kunze, A. (2019). The perceived fit between Instagram influencers and the endorsed brand: How influencer–brand fit affects source credibility and persuasive effectiveness. *Journal of Advertising Research, 59*(4), 440–454.

Burns, R. P., & Burns, R. (2008). Business research methods and Sstatistics using SPSS. *Sage (Atlanta, Ga.).*

Campbell, C., & Farrell, J. R. (2020). More than meets the eye: The functional components underlying influencer marketing. *Business Horizons, 63*(4), 469–479.

Clanton Harpine, E. (2015). Is intrinsic motivation better than extrinsic motivation? Içinde E. Clanton Harpine (Ed.), *Group-Centered Prevention in Mental Health: Theory, Training, and Practice* (ss. 87-107). Springer International Publishing. https://doi.org/DOI: 10.1007/978-3-319-19102-7_6

De Jans, S., Van de Sompel, D., De Veirman, M., & Hudders, L. (2020). #Sponsored! How the recognition of sponsoring on Instagram posts affects adolescents' brand evaluations through source evaluations. *Computers in Human Behavior*, *109*, 106342.

De Veirman, M., Cauberghe, V., & Hudders, L. (2017). Marketing through Instagram influencers: The impact of number of followers and product divergence on brand attitude. *International Journal of Advertising*, *36*(5), 798–828.

Delbaere, M., Michael, B., & Phillips, B. J. (2021). Social media influencers: A route to brand engagement for their followers. *Psychology and Marketing*, *38*(1), 101–112.

Dinh, T. C. T., & Lee, Y. (2021). "I want to be as trendy as influencers" – how "fear of missing out" leads to buying intention for products endorsed by social media influencers. *Journal of Research in Interactive Marketing*, *16*(3), 346–364. DOI: 10.1108/JRIM-04-2021-0127

Dinh, T. C. T., & Lee, Y. (2022). "I want to be as trendy as influencers" – How fear of missing out leads to buying intention for products endorsed by social media influencers. *Journal of Research in Interactive Marketing*, *16*(3), 346–364. DOI: 10.1108/JRIM-04-2021-0127

Dinh, T. C. T., & Lee, Y. (2024). Social media influencers and followers' conspicuous consumption: The mediation of fear of missing out and materialism. *Heliyon*, *10*(16), e36387. DOI: 10.1016/j.heliyon.2024.e36387

Dinh, T. C. T., Wang, M., & Lee, Y. (2023). How Does the Fear of Missing Out Moderate the Effect of Social Media Influencers on Their Followers' Purchase Intention? *SAGE Open*, *13*(3), 21582440231197259. DOI: 10.1177/21582440231197259

Duan, J., & Dholakia, R. R. (2017). Posting purchases on social media increases happiness: The mediating roles of purchases' impact on self and interpersonal relationships. *Journal of Consumer Marketing*, *34*(5), 404–413. DOI: 10.1108/JCM-07-2016-1871

Eckhardt, G. M., Belk, Russell W., & and Wilson, J. A. J. (2015). The rise of inconspicuous consumption. *Journal of Marketing Management*, *31*(7-8), 807–826. DOI: 10.1080/0267257X.2014.989890

Freberg, K., Graham, K., McGaughey, K., & Freberg, L. A. (2011). Who are the social media influencers? *Public Relations Review*, *37*(1), 90–92. DOI: 10.1016/j.pubrev.2010.11.001

Griskevicius, V., Tybur, J. M., Sundie, J. M., Cialdini, R. B., Miller, G. F., & Kenrick, D. T. (2007). Blatant benevolence and conspicuous consumption: When romantic motives elicit strategic costly signals. *Journal of Personality and Social Psychology*, *93*(1), 85–102. DOI: 10.1037/0022-3514.93.1.85

Hayes, A. F. (2022). *Introduction to mediation, moderation, and conditional process analysis: A regression-based approach* (3rd ed.). The Guilford Press.

Hudders, L., De Jans, S., & De Veirman, M. (2021). The commercialization of social media stars: A literature review and conceptual framework on the strategic use of social media influencers. In De Jans, S., De Veirman, M., & Hudders, L. (Eds.), *Social media influencers in strategic communication* (pp. 24–67). Routledge.

Kim, D. Y., Park, M., & Kim, H.-Y. (2023). An influencer like me: Examining the impact of the social status of Influencers. *Journal of Marketing Communications*, *29*(7), 654–675. DOI: 10.1080/13527266.2022.2066153

Laili, E. F., Nadapdap, E., Respati, H., & Earlike, F. (2025). The influence of fear of missing out (FoMO) as a mediating variable between beauty influencers and brand image on purchase intention for Wardah products in Malang City. *East African Scholars Journal of Economics. Business and Management*, *8*(1), 30–36. DOI: 10.36349/easjebm.2025.v08i01.004

Lee, D., Wut, T. M., & Wan, C. (2023, July). The effect of fear-of-missing-out (FoMO) laden influencer marketing on travel destination promotion. In *Global Marketing Conference* (p. 118).

Lee, J. A., Bright, L. F., & Eastin, M. S. (2021). Fear of missing out and consumer happiness on Instagram: A serial mediation of social media influencer-related activities. *Cyberpsychology, Behavior, and Social Networking*, *24*(11), 762–766.

Lee, J. E., & Watkins, B. (2016). YouTube vloggers' influence on consumer luxury brand perceptions and intentions. *Journal of Business Research*, *69*(12), 5753–5760.

Lee, M. K. O., Cheung, C. M. K., & Chen, Z. (2005). Acceptance of Internet-based learning medium: The role of extrinsic and intrinsic motivation. *Information & Management*, *42*(8), 1095–1104. DOI: 10.1016/j.im.2003.10.007

Liu, J., Li, C., Carcioppolo, N., & North, M. (2016). Do our Facebook friends make us feel worse? A study of social comparison and emotion. *Human Communication Research*, *42*(4), 619–640. DOI: 10.1111/hcre.12090

Lou, C., & Yuan, S. (2019). Influencer marketing. *Journal of Interactive Advertising*, *19*(1), 58–73. DOI: 10.1080/15252019.2018.1533501

Lu, Y., Zhao, T., Song, S., & Song, W. (2024). Can self-presentation on social media increase individuals' conspicuous consumption tendency? A mixed-method empirical study on Wechat in China. *Journal of Theoretical and Applied Electronic Commerce Research, 19*(2), 2. Advance online publication. DOI: 10.3390/jtaer19020062

Matheson, E., & Sedgwick, D. (2021). Influencers and 21st Century Consumption. *Contexts, 20*(2), 18–23. DOI: 10.1177/15365042211012066

Mundel, J., Wan, Anan, & and Yang, J. (2024). Processes underlying social comparison with influencers and subsequent impulsive buying: The roles of social anxiety and social media addiction. *Journal of Marketing Communications, 30*(7), 834–851. DOI: 10.1080/13527266.2023.2183426

Nguyen, T., Ngamsiriudom, W., Pelton, L., & Dubinsky, A. J. (2015). Interrelationships among facets of self, motivation, and conspicuous and sustainable consumption behaviour. [IJBSAM]. *International Journal of Business Science and Applied Management, 10*(2), 16–31.

O'Rourke, N., Hatcher, L., & Stepanski, E. J. (2005). *A step-by-step approach to using SAS for univariate & multivariate statistics*. SAS Institute.

Pangarkar, A., & Rathee, S. (2023). The role of conspicuity: İmpact of social influencers on purchase decisions of luxury consumers. *International Journal of Advertising, 42*(7), 1150–1177. DOI: 10.1080/02650487.2022.2084265

Preacher, K. J., & Hayes, A. F. (2004). Spss and sas procedures for estimating indirect effects in simple mediation models. *Behavior Research Methods, Instruments, & Computers, 36*(4), 717–731.

Przybylski, A. K., Murayama, K., DeHaan, C. R., & Gladwell, V. (2013). Motivational, emotional, and behavioral correlates of fear of missing out. *Computers in Human Behavior, 29*(4), 1841–1848.

Qattan, J., & Khasawneh, M. A. (2020). The psychological motivations of online conspicuous consumption: A qualitative study. [IJEBR]. *International Journal of E-Business Research, 16*(2), 1–16. DOI: 10.4018/IJEBR.2020040101

Qiu, Y. (2024). Social Comparison on Social Media Platforms: A media and communication Perspective. *SHS Web of Conferences, 185*, 03008. https://doi.org/DOI: 10.1051/shsconf/202418503008

Rashid, S., Warraich, U., Peerjan, G., & Salman, F. (2023). Impact of social media opinion leaders influencers on individual consumption decisions of visually conspicuous products. *Market forces, 18*, 139-162. https://doi.org/DOI: 10.51153/mf.v18i2.637

Reer, F., Tang, W. Y., & Quandt, T. (2019). Psychosocial well-being and social media engagement: The mediating roles of social comparison orientation and fear of missing out. *New Media & Society*, *21*(7), 1486–1505.

Reinikainen, H., Munnukka, J., Maity, D., & Luoma-Aho, V. (2020). 'You really are a great big sister'–Parasocial relationships, credibility, and the moderating role of audience comments in influencer marketing. *Journal of Marketing Management*, *36*(3–4), 279–298.

Rozgonjuk, D., Sindermann, C., Elhai, J. D., & Montag, C. (2020). Fear of missing out (FoMO) and social media's impact on daily life and productivity at work: Do WhatsApp, Facebook, Instagram, and Snapchat use disorders mediate that association? *Addictive Behaviors*, *110*, 106487.

Rüther, L., Jahn, J., & Marksteiner, T. (2023). #influenced! The impact of social media influencing on self-esteem and the role of social comparison and resilience. *Frontiers in Psychology*, *14*, 1–8. DOI: 10.3389/fpsyg.2023.1216195

Ryan, R. M., & Deci, E. L. (2000). Intrinsic and extrinsic motivations: Classic definitions and new directions. *Contemporary Educational Psychology*, *25*(1), 54–67. DOI: 10.1006/ceps.1999.1020

Santora, J. (2021, June 29). 12 types of influencers you can use to improve your marketing. *Influencer Marketing Hub*. https://influencermarketinghub.com/types-of-influencers/

Setiawan, R., Garliani, G., & Rahmawati, D. (2024). Analysis of the influence of fear of missing out (FoMO) and the role of influencers on tourism destination selection. *Jurnal Wacana Ekonomi*, *23*(2), 65–72.

Siepmann, C., Holthoff, L. C., & Kowalczuk, P. (2022). Conspicuous consumption of luxury experiences: An experimental investigation of status perceptions on social media. *Journal of Product and Brand Management*, *31*(3), 454–468. DOI: 10.1108/JPBM-08-2020-3047

Suls, J., Martin, R., & Wheeler, L. (2000). Three kinds of opinion comparison: The Triadic Model. *Personality and Social Psychology Review*, *4*(3), 219–237. DOI: 10.1207/S15327957PSPR0403_2

Suls, J., Martin, R., & Wheeler, L. (2002). Social comparison: Why, with whom, and with what effect? *Current Directions in Psychological Science*, *11*(5), 159–163. DOI: 10.1111/1467-8721.00191

Sun, Y., Wang, R., Cao, D., & Lee, R. (2021). Who are social media influencers for luxury fashion consumption of the Chinese Gen Z? Categorisation and empirical examination. *Journal of Fashion Marketing and Management*, *26*(4), 603–621. DOI: 10.1108/JFMM-07-2020-0132

Trivedi, J., & Sama, R. (2020). The effect of influencer marketing on consumers' brand admiration and online purchase intentions: An emerging market perspective. *Journal of Internet Commerce*, *19*(1), 103–124.

Truong, Y., & McColl, R. (2011). Intrinsic motivations, self-esteem, and luxury goods consumption. *Journal of Retailing and Consumer Services*, *18*(6), 555–561. DOI: 10.1016/j.jretconser.2011.08.004

Vrontis, D., Makrides, A., Christofi, M., & Thrassou, A. (2021). Social media influencer marketing: A systematic review, integrative framework and future research agenda. *International Journal of Consumer Studies*, *45*(4), 617–644.

Wai, L. K., & Osman, S. (2019). The Influence of Self-esteem in the relationship of social media usage and conspicuous consumption. *International Journal of Academic Research in Business & Social Sciences*, *9*(2), 335–352. DOI: 10.6007/IJARBSS/v9-i2/5549

Zhang, Z., Jiménez, F. R., & Cicala, J. E. (2020). Fear of missing out scale: A self-concept perspective. *Psychology and Marketing*, *37*(11), 1619–1634. DOI: 10.1002/mar.21406

ADDITIONAL READING

Brown, D., & Hayes, N. (2008). *Influencer marketing: Who really influences your customers?* Routledge.

Featherstone, M. (2007). *Consumer culture and postmodernism* (2nd ed.). Sage Publications.

Frank, R. H. (2001). *Luxury fever: Why money fails to satisfy in an era of excess.* The Free Press.

Hennessy, B. (2018). *Influencer: Building your personal brand in the age of social media.* Citadel.

Katz, E., & Lazarsfeld, P. F. (1955). *Personal influence: The part played by people in the flow of mass communications.* Free Press.

McGinnis, P. J. (2020). *Fear of missing out: Practical decision-making in a world of overwhelming choice*. Sourcebooks.

Sammis, K., Lincoln, C., & Pomponi, S. (2015). *Influencer marketing for dummies*. Wiley.

Suls, J., & Wheeler, L. (Eds.). (2013). *Handbook of social comparison: Theory and research*. Springer.

Suls, J. M., & Miller, R. L. (Eds.). (1977). *Social comparison processes: Theoretical and empirical perspectives*. Hemisphere.

Veblen, T. (2017). *The theory of the leisure class*. Routledge.

KEY TERMS AND DEFINITIONS

Conspicuous Consumption: Conspicuous consumption refers to the act of purchasing expensive products not to fulfill utilitarian needs, but rather to display wealth in a wasteful manner with the aim of maintaining one's current status or achieving a higher social status.

FoMO: FoMO is the tendency to experience anxiety over the possibility of missing out on rewarding experiences that others are having.

Influencer Marketing: Influencer marketing is a marketing strategy that uses the influence of key individuals or opinion leaders to drive consumers' brand awareness and/or their purchasing decisions.

Influencers: Influencers are independent third-party endorsers who shape audience attitudes through social media.

Motivation: Motivation is the driving force that explains why individuals behave and act in certain ways.

Social Comparison: Social comparison refers to the process by which individuals evaluate themselves or enhance their self-concept by comparing themselves to others.

Social Media: Social media is a group of Internet-based applications that are built on the ideological and technological foundations of Web 2.0 and allow the creation and sharing of user-generated content.

Chapter 9

The Relationship Between Selfie-Taking, Social Appearance Anxiety, and Online Self-Presentation

Özgür Kılınç
https://orcid.org/0000-0002-8697-162X
Faculty of Communication, İnönü University, Turkey

Ali Arıcı
https://orcid.org/0000-0003-4027-8288
Bozüyük Vocational School, Bilecik Şeyh Edebali University, Turkey

Sadık Çalışkan
https://orcid.org/0000-0001-6899-0424
Faculty of Communication, İnönü University, Turkey

ABSTRACT

The present research aims to investigate the relationship between attitudes toward selfie-taking, social appearance anxiety, and online self-presentation. According to the research findings, a high level of consistency was found between participants' offline and online self-presentation, and the presentation of multiple online selves was found to be low. Moreover, it can be stated that participants reported low levels of social appearance anxiety and primarily took selfies for the purpose of creating memories. There is a moderate, positive, and significant relationship between selfie-taking and social appearance anxiety; likewise, a moderate, positive, and significant relationship was also found between selfie-taking and online self-presentation. On

DOI: 10.4018/979-8-3373-6970-9.ch009

© 2026, IGI Global Scientific Publishing. Copying or distributing in print or electronic forms without written permission of IGI Global Scientific Publishing is prohibited. Use of this chapter to generative artificial intelligence (AI) technologies is expressly prohibited. The publisher reserves all rights to license its use for generative AI training and machine learning model development.

the other hand, it has been revealed that there is a strong relationship between the dimensions of taking selfies - namely, "environmental enhancement," "attention seeking," "mood modification," and "self-confidence" - and online self-presentation.

INTRODUCTION

As a product of digitalisation, the selfie has become a popular concept with the proliferation of social media platforms. Selfies, which are taken based on various emotional or cognitive motivations, can be shared with other users on social media platforms. At this point, it would not be incorrect to position selfies as a form of content. These contents, which constitute the social media-mediated form of photography, are created for purposes such as remembering the moment, presenting the digital self, and fulfilling the need for social approval.

Although selfies, which are a digital self-portrait (Shah & Tewari, 2016, p. 864), have gained visibility with social media, especially the self-portraits of artists have become increasingly common since the 15th century, when quality mirrors were produced (Wade, 2014, p. 1142). Indeed, Saltz (2014) poses the question of whether the Italian painter Parmigianino's "Self-Portrait in a Convex Mirror" (1523-1524) could be considered the first selfie. Therefore, it can be said that selfies, which carry the characteristics of self-portraits, have a long-standing historical background. The selfie, which expresses, develops, expands, and intensifies the long history of self-portraiture (Mirzoeff, 2015, p. 31), has in recent years become a widespread practice due to technological advancements and socio-cultural contexts (Moreno, 2018, p. 54), emerging as a popular visual form of communication (Lobinger & Brantner, 2015, p. 1849).

The term "selfie" was chosen as the Word of the Year in 2013 by the Oxford English Dictionary (Senft & Baym, 2015, p. 1588), and it refers to a self-portrait photograph taken by a person, typically with a smartphone or camera (Qiu et al., 2015, p. 443). A selfie, which is called a kind of "life diary" (Liu et al., 2022, p. 1), expressing the visual announcement of ordinary life (Hand, 2012, p. 1), containing the motivations of "entertainment and memory storage" (de Vaate et al., 2018, p. 1392), is "a photo of the person taken by himself / herself, especially for publication on social networks" ([REMOVED HYPERLINK FIELD]Merriam-webster, n.d.). Motivations for taking selfies include attention seeking, communication, archiving, and entertainment (Sung et al., 2016, p. 260). However, selfies can also be taken to meet psychological needs such as identity formation, authenticity and independence (Lobo & Gowda, 2016, p. 147), and it is one of the ways in which individuals represent or express themselves (Lodha & De Sousa, 2019, p. 1).

As a cultural phenomenon (Choi & Behm-Morawitz, 2018, p. 345) and a networked representation of the self (Tiidenberg, 2018, p. 36), the selfie has been evaluated within the frameworks of narcissism (Halpern et al., 2016), body image (Mills et al., 2018), self-objectification (Salomon, 2021), self-worth (Shin et al., 2017), and addiction (El Khoueiry et al., 2021). Although taking selfies aims to create a positive impression, it can also be considered narcissistic (Krämer et al., 2017, p. 1), and narcissism has been found to be associated with sending selfies to social media platforms (Sorokowski et al., 2015). The selfie culture is argued to meet the "mirroring and idealization" needs of digital narcissism (Jin & Ryu, 2018, p. 570). Body image is suggested to influence selfie behaviors (Veldhuis et al., 2020), and self-objectification plays a significant role in taking selfies (Boursier et al., 2020a). It is stated that taking and editing selfies have negative effects on body image (Vandenbosch et al., 2022, p. 1), and the obsessive selfie-taking behavior known as selfitis (Balakrishnan & Griffiths, 2018) is strongly associated with narcissism (Puthiyakath et al., 2024, p. 1). Furthermore, selfie editing is negatively related to self-worth (Ozimek et al., 2023, p. 1). Fox et al. (2021, p. 193) claim that those who take selfies are more self-objectified, experience more negative moods, and have lower self-worth compared to those who photograph objects. Similarly, Wang et al. (2021, p. 57) suggest that selfie editing leads to an increase in self-objectification and appearance anxiety among adolescents over time. Moreover, it is stated that when adolescents receive positive feedback on their selfies, they tend to spend more time on social media to check likes and comments (Zeng et al., 2024, p. 451).

The behavior known as selfitis has been classified by the American Psychiatric Association (APA) as a mental disorder and is divided into the following three levels (Balakrishnan & Griffiths, 2018, pp. 722-723):

- Borderline (Taking photos of one's self at least three times a day but not posting them on social media)
- Acute (Taking photos of one's self at least three times a day and posting each of the photos on social media)
- Chronic (Uncontrollable urge to take photos of one's self round the clock and posting the photos on social media more than six times a day)

The above classification highlights various levels of selfitis behavior. In this context, it has been indicated that selfies may lead to a loss of self-confidence and self-esteem particularly among adolescents (Safna, 2017, p. 68); that individuals who take more selfies may possess lower self-esteem compared to those who do not (Imran et al., 2024, p. 26); that taking and editing selfies contributes to increased negative mood and heightened physical dissatisfaction (Tiggemann et al., 2020, p. 175); that there are associations between selfies and depression, anxiety, and eating disorders (Hashem, 2022, p. 1); and that selfie editing is related to heightened self-objectification (Xiao et al., 2023, p. 10656). On the other hand, various studies have emphasized aspects other than the negative effects of taking and sharing selfies. It has been stated that individuals who enjoy taking or sharing selfies tend to be in better psychological condition (Taskin et al., 2024, p. 77); that selfies serve as a creative means of expressing emotions (Diefenbach & Christoforakos, 2017, p. 2); that sharing selfies may enhance self-esteem and consequently reduce body image concerns (Kim, 2020, p. 10); that sharing selfies or receiving feedback on them has no significant effect on self-esteem or mood (Coulthard & Ogden, 2018, p. 7); and that self-esteem is generally not associated with selfie-sharing behavior (Sorokowska et al., 2016, p. 119). In this regard, it can be stated that the literature on the subject predominantly highlights the psychological negative effects of taking and sharing selfies.

Social appearance anxiety is a type of anxiety that arises from an individual's concern about being negatively evaluated by others due to their appearance (Hart et al., 2008, p. 48). As a specific form of social anxiety, social appearance anxiety has been reported to have a strong and positive association with symptoms of eating disorders (Levinson & Rodebaugh, 2011, p. 354; Levinson et al., 2013, p. 129), and is positively related to emotional and interpersonal difficulties (Claes et al., 2012, p. 406). Moreover, it has been indicated that low levels of self-esteem may lead to heightened social appearance anxiety (Antonietti et al., 2020, p. 1096), that the use of social media may increase appearance-related concerns (Papapanou et al., 2023, p. 1), and that there is a link between viewing idealized images on social media and dissatisfaction with one's own body (UOY, 2023). Similarly, Caner et al. (2022, p. 8424) suggest that social media addiction and being affected by social media phenomena increase social appearance anxiety in adolescents. Boursier et al. (2020b, p. 5) report strong correlations between selfie-related expectations, social appearance anxiety, and problematic social media use, particularly among adolescent males. On the other hand, Nesi et al. (2021, p. 488) state that adolescent girls share selfies more frequently than boys share and place greater importance on the feedback they receive about their selfies.

It has been argued that selfie editing behavior increases concerns about body image in the long term (Lau & Idang, 2022, p. 6), selfie editing is associated with self-objectification (Terán et al., 2020, p. 343), and there is a significant and positive correlation between selfie editing frequency and appearance anxiety (Ismail, 2024, p. 3487). Fastoso et al. (2021, p. 365) state that among youth with high body image discrepancy, selfie editing is positively associated with social media addiction and negatively associated with life satisfaction. In other words, as negative perceptions of body image increase, the tendency to engage in selfie editing behavior also rises. However, it has been suggested that increased appearance-based comparisons on social media are associated with a higher frequency of selfie-taking and sharing (Rousseau, 2021, p. 22), and that selfie-taking is positively related to social comparisons focused on physical appearance (Chae, 2017, p. 374).

The self is defined as an individual's perception of themselves (Shavelson et al., 1976, p. 411) and is a conscious reflection of his / her own existence or identity (Huitt, 2009) and the sum of his / her beliefs and attitudes about himself / herself (Valkenburg, 2017, p. 479). The self, which encompasses the totality of individuals' attitudes, beliefs, and evaluative judgments about themselves (Wehrle & Fasbender, 2019, p. 1), plays a significant role in one's psychological and social development. In particular, developing a clear and stable sense of self is important for psychological well-being and social development (Fullwood et al., 2016). Digital technologies offer new ways for individuals to expand their sense of self (Bartoli et al., 2023, p. 1136), while the internet has made it possible to present the self in multiple forms (Rui & Stefanone, 2013, p. 110; Fullwood et al., 2016). With the advancement of social media, the concept of the online self has begun to gain prominence. The concept of self plays an important role in online self-presentation (Strimbu & O'Connell, 2019, p. 804).

Online self-presentation refers to the ways in which individuals share certain aspects of themselves in order to project a specific image (Fullwood et al., 2020, p. 737). Online self-presentation is used as a means of conveying the "ideal self" (Chen et al., 2022, p. 369), and selfies, in particular, represent one of the key forms of online self-presentation content (de Vaate et al., 2020). 2020). In the digital age, photographs have become a medium for self-presentation (Chua & Chang, 2016, p. 191). The importance of "looking good" in social media photographs (Siibak, 2009, p. 4) embodies the effect of selfies on self-presentation. One of the purposes of sharing selfies on social media is to impress others and attract attention by presenting the photographic self (Hong et al., 2020, p. 2). Fullwood et al. (2020, p. 737) state that young adults and individuals with higher levels of social anxiety are more likely to present idealized versions of themselves online. In light of the aforementioned literature, it appears worthwhile to examine attitudes toward selfies within the framework of social appearance anxiety and online self-presentation. Accordingly, the aim of this study is to evaluate the relationship between selfie, social appearance anxiety and online self-presentation. In line with the stated objective, a survey study was conducted and the following research questions and hypotheses were developed:

Q1. What is the relationship between selfie-taking and social appearance anxiety?
H1. There is a significant relationship between selfie-taking and social appearance anxiety.
Q2. What is the relationship between selfie-taking and online self-presentation?

H2. There is a significant relationship between selfie-taking and online self-presentation.
Q3. What is the relationship between social appearance anxiety and online self-presentation?
H3. There is a significant relationship between social appearance anxiety and online self-presentation.
Q4. What is the relationship between the dimensions of selfie-taking and social appearance anxiety?
H4. There is a significant relationship between the dimensions of selfie-taking and social appearance anxiety.
Q5. What is the relationship between the dimensions of selfie-taking and online self-presentation?
H5. There is a significant relationship between the dimensions of selfie-taking and online self-presentation.

METHOD

A survey study was conducted to examine the relationship between selfies, social appearance anxiety, and online self-presentation. The population of the study consisted of individuals over the age of 18 residing in Türkiye. Since it was not possible to reach the entire population, the convenience sampling method was employed. Within this framework, the generalizability of the research findings is subject to certain limitations. The questionnaire developed for the study was distributed online by the researchers. Accordingly, the data obtained from a total of 481 participants were analyzed. For the conduct of the study, ethical approval was obtained from the Scientific Research and Publication Ethics Committee of İnönü University on 21.02.2025 (session no: 4 / decision no: 1).

The study utilized three scales. The first scale is the Presentation of Online Self Scale (POSS) (Fullwood et al., 2016), which consists of 21 items and 4 sub-dimensions: "ideal self," "multiple selves," "consistent self," and "online presentation preference." The items in the mentioned scale were adapted to social media contexts. The dimensions of the scale can be explained as follows (Fullwood et al., 2016):

- Ideal self that relates to the extent to which individuals present an idealised version of the self online
- Multiple selves describe the extent to which individuals present different versions of the self across online environments
- Consistent self relates to the extent to which an individual's offline and online self-presentation are analogous

- Online presentation preference describes the extent to which individuals prefer presenting themselves online

The second scale is the Social Appearance Anxiety Scale (SAAS), developed by Hart et al. (2008), consisting of 16 items and a single dimension. The third scale is the Selfitis Behavior Scale (SBS) (Balakrishnan and Griffiths, 2018) and consists of a total of 20 items and 6 sub-dimensions. These sub-dimensions are: "environmental enhancement," "social competition," "attention seeking," "mood modification," "self-confidence," and "subjective conformity." These dimensions can be defined as follows (Griffiths & Balakrishnan, 2018, p. 5):

- *Environmental enhancement (e.g., taking selfies in specific locations to feel good and show off to others)*
- *Social competition (e.g., taking selfies to get more 'likes' on social media), attention seeking (e.g., taking selfies to gain attention from others)*
- *Mood modification (e.g., taking selfies to feel better)*
- *Self-confidence (e.g., taking selfies to feel more positive about oneself)*
- *Subjective conformity (e.g., taking selfies to fit in with one's social group and peers)*

The scales were designed using a 5-point Likert format, ranging from 1 = Strongly disagree to 5 = Strongly agree. The items "I can't really be myself online" and "I find it difficult to be myself in the real world" from the POSS were reverse-coded based on the study by Strimbu et al. (2021, p. 5), as well as the item "I feel comfortable with the way I appear to others" from the SAAS (Hart et al., 2008, p. 53). However, the score ranges used for interpreting the scales were defined as follows: 1-1.80 = strongly disagree, 1.81-2.60 = disagree, 2.61-3.40 = neutral / uncertain, 3.41-4.20 = agree, and 4.21-5 = strongly agree (Nyutu et al., 2021, p. 89).

Based on the study of Strimbu et al. (2021, p. 2), a high score on the POSS scale represents a higher presentation of each factor, and the interpretation of the factors was grounded in the following inferences made by the aforementioned researchers:

> *A high ideal self score indicates that more ideal selves are presented online than offline self-representation, a high multiple selves score indicates that more than one self is presented online, a high consistent self score indicates higher consistency between the individual's offline and online self-representation, and a high online presentation preference score demonstrates a stronger preference for presenting the self online rather than offline.*

Similar to the POSS, higher scores on the SAAS indicate higher levels of social appearance anxiety (Lau & Idang, 2022, p. 3). Similarly, it was taken into consideration that the higher the score on the SBS, the greater the likelihood that the participant exhibits selfitis tendencies (Balakrishnan & Griffiths, 2018, p. 734).

Selfie editing behavior was assessed based on the items used in the study by Fox and Rooney (2015, p. 163), while the frequency of selfie posting was evaluated according to the expressions in Sung et al. (2016, p. 262). Selfie editing behavior was rated on a scale ranging from 1 = Never to 5 = Always. Participants were asked four demographic questions regarding age, gender, education level, and income status. Accordingly, the questionnaire consists of a total of 65 items. The scales were translated into Turkish by three researchers, and a pilot study was conducted with 50 participants. Following the pilot study, the items in the scales were revised. Table 1 presents the reliability analyses of the scales.

Table 1. Reliability Analysis of Scales

Scale	**Cronbach's Alpha**	**Item**
POSS	.774	21
SAAS	.940	16
SBS	.953	20

An examination of the reliability analyses reveals that the SAAS and SBS demonstrate excellent reliability, while the POSS shows a very high level of reliability (Taber, 2018, p. 1278).

3. RESULTS

3.1. Demographic Findings

Table 2. Demographic Characteristics

Gender	**Frequency**	**%**
Female	341	70.9
Male	140	29.1
Total	**481**	**100**
Age		
18-29	379	78.8
30-39	39	8.1

continued on following page

Table 2. Continued

Gender	**Frequency**	%
40-49	50	10.4
50-59	13	2.7
Total	**481**	**100**
Education level		
Primary School	7	1.5
High School	89	18.5
Associate Degree	121	25.2
Undergraduate Degree	220	45.7
Postgraduate Degree	44	9.1
Total	**481**	**100**
Income		
20000 TL or less	250	52
20001 - 30000 TL	85	17.7
30001 - 40000 TL	41	8.5
40001 - 50000 TL	33	6.8
50001 TL and above	72	15
Total	**481**	**100**

Table 2 shows the demographic characteristics of the participants. Of the participants in the study, 341 were female and 140 were male. A total of 379 participants were between the ages of 18 and 29, while 50 participants were between 40 and 49 years old. This age range is followed by the 30-39 and 50-59 age groups. In terms of education level, the majority of participants held a bachelor's degree, followed by those with an associate degree, high school education, postgraduate education, and primary education, respectively. While 250 participants have a monthly income of 20,000 TL or less, 72 participants have a monthly income of 50,001 TL or more.

3.2. Levels of Agreement with the Statements

Table 3. Mean Scores of POSS Items

Items	Mean	Standard Deviation
1. I find it difficult to be myself in the real world*.	3.89	1.05
2. I find it easier to communicate in face to face contexts.	3.79	1.05
3. I can't really be myself online*.	3.70	1.08
4. I am always my true self online.	3.69	1.10
5. I feel I am the same person in the cyber world that I am in the real world.	3.66	1.09
6. I feel more comfortable behaving how I want to online.	3.40	1.14
7. I can show my best qualities online.	3.23	1.05
8. Being online allows me to express myself.	3.04	1.10
9. I can talk to people who wouldn't usually talk to me in the real world.	2.93	1.30
10. I feel my personality online is the real me.	2.81	1.25
11. I prefer being online than offline.	2.71	1.10
12. I feel I can be my ideal self-online.	2.66	1.10
13. Communicating online allows me to say the things I can't say offline.	2.64	1.22
14. Being online allows me to create a new identity.	2.43	1.13
15. I can escape from myself online.	2.40	1.21
16. I like going online because it allows me to be a different person.	2.32	1.09
17. The way I present myself online differs significantly from real life.	2.18	1.10
18. I am a different person depending on which online space I'm in.	2.14	1.12
19. I very often act out different personas in certain online spaces.	1.97	.997
20. I enjoy acting out different identities online.	1.96	1.01
21. I regularly use different personas online.	1.90	1.01

Note: Items in this table are taken from Fullwood et al. (2016).
* Reverse coded
Ideal self: 6-7-8-9-12-13-15-16-17, Multiple selves: 14-18-19-20-21, Consistent self: 3-4-5-10, Online presentation preference: 1-2-11

An evaluation of the mean scores of the POSS items reveals that the five items with the highest averages are, respectively: "I find it difficult to be myself in the real world," "I find it easier to communicate in face-to-face contexts," "I can't really be myself online," "I am always my true self online," and "I feel I am the same person in the cyber world that I am in the real world." Since the mean scores of the five items are greater than 3.41, it can be concluded that participants agreed with these statements. The two items with the highest mean scores belong to the "online presentation preference" dimension. Therefore, the fact that these two items have the highest mean scores may be interpreted as an indication that participants exhibit a stronger inclination toward presenting themselves in online settings rather than in offline contexts, suggesting a preference for the curated and potentially more controllable nature of digital self-presentation. However, another notable finding is that the remaining three items with the highest mean scores belong to the "consistent self" dimension. Based on this finding, it is possible to infer that there is a high level of consistency between participants' offline and online self-presentations. In other words, there is no contradiction between the online and offline self-presentations of the participants.

The three items with the lowest mean scores are "I regularly use different personas online," "I enjoy acting out different identities online," and "I very often act out different personas in certain online spaces," all of which belong to the "multiple selves" dimension. This finding indicates that the presentation of multiple selves in online environments is low. In other words, the participants of the research do not present more than one self on online platforms. Therefore, it can be stated that the online and offline online self-presentations of the participants in the study exhibit a consistent appearance. Moreover, the fact that three of the top five items with the highest mean scores belong to the "consistent self" dimension supports this inference.

Table 4. The Mean Scores of the POSS Dimensions

Dimensions	Mean	Standard Deviation
Consistent self	3.46	-.798
Online presentation preference	3.46	.575
Ideal self	2.75	.710
Multiple selves	2.07	.877

Table 4 presents the mean scores of the POSS dimensions. The highest mean score, 3.46, was observed in both the "consistent self" and "online presentation preference" dimensions. As noted in the interpretation of Table 3, this finding can be evaluated as an indication that participants exhibit consistency between their online and offline self-presentations yet demonstrate a stronger preference for presenting themselves online rather than offline. The low score on the ideal self dimension indicates that participants do not tend to present a more idealized version of themselves online compared to offline. Similarly, the low score on the multiple selves dimension highlights that participants do not tend to present multiple versions of the self online.

Table 5. Means of SAAS Items

Items	Mean	Standard Deviation
I get tense when it is obvious people are looking at me.	3.11	1.27
I feel comfortable with the way I appear to others*.	2.92	1.09
I feel nervous when having my picture taken.	2.88	1.27
I am uncomfortable when I think others are noticing flaws in my appearance.	2.60	1.27
I worry that others talk about flaws in my appearance when I am not around.	2.59	1.20
I am concerned that people think I am not looking good.	2.48	1.27
I feel anxious when other people say something about my appearance.	2.46	1.22
I am concerned that I have missed out on opportunities because of my appearance.	2.40	1.24
I am concerned people would not like me because of the way I look.	2.38	1.22
I am afraid that people find me unattractive.	2.37	1.19
I worry that my appearance will make life more difficult for me.	2.33	1.19
I worry people will judge the way I look negatively.	2.32	1.19
I am concerned people will find me unappealing because of my appearance.	2.31	1.19
I worry that a romantic partner will/would leave me because of my appearance.	2.26	1.19
I am often afraid I would not meet others' standards of how I should look.	2.15	1.14
I get nervous when talking to people because of the way I look.	2.11	1.10

Note: Items in this table are taken from Hart et al. (2008).
* Reverse coded

The SAAS is a unidimensional scale, and the mean scores of its items are presented in Table 5. In this context, the fact that the item means range between 2.11 and 3.11 can be interpreted as an indication that participants either disagreed with the statements or remained neutral. Therefore, it can be stated that participants exhibit a low level of social appearance anxiety. However, the item with the highest mean score is "I get tense when it is obvious people are looking at me," although its average falls within the neutral range. In other words, participants are uncertain about whether they feel tense when they are being looked at by others. The item with the lowest average is "I get nervous when talking to people because of the way I look."

Table 6. Means of SBS Items

Items	Mean	Standard Deviation
1. I take selfies as trophies for future memories.	3.56	1,25
2. Taking selfies provides better memories about the occasion and the experience.	3,39	1,30
3. By posting selfies, I expect my friends to appraise me.	2.88	1,23
4. Taking selfies gives me a good feeling to better enjoy my environment.	2.65	1,16
5. I become more positive about myself when I take selfies.	2,57	1,18
6. I feel confident when I take a selfie.	2,52	1,22
7. Taking selfies immediately modifies my mood.	2,46	1,15
8. I take more selfies and look at them privately to increase my confidence.	2,46	1,15
9. Taking more selfies improves my mood and makes me feel happy.	2,44	1,18
10. I gain enormous attention by sharing my selfies on social media.	2.33	1,10
11. Taking different selfie poses helps increase my social status.	2.29	1,15
12. Sharing my selfies creates healthy competition with my friends and colleagues.	2,27	1,10
13. I became a strong member of my peer group through selfie postings.	2,26	1,13
14. I am able to reduce my stress level by taking selfies.	2.25	1,15
15. I use photo editing tools to enhance my selfie to look better than others.	2,23	1,19
16. I feel more popular when I post my selfies on social media.	2.22	1,13
17. I am able to express myself more in my environment through selfies.	2,17	1,09
18. I gain more acceptance among my peer group when I take a selfie and share it on social media.	2,09	1,05
19. I post frequent selfies to get more 'likes' and comments on social media.	2,03	1.08
20. When I don't take selfies, I feel detached from my peer group.	1.90	1,04

Note: Items in this table are taken from Balakrishnan and Griffiths (2018).
Environmental enhancement: 1-2-4-17, Social competition: 11-12-15-19, Attention seeking: 3-10-16, Mood modification: 7-9-14, Self-confidence: 5-6-8, Subjective conformity: 13-18-20

The SBS is a scale consisting of six dimensions, and Table 6 presents the means of the items in the scale. Among the items in the scale, the statement "I take selfies as trophies for future memories" recorded the highest mean score, indicating a stronger agreement among participants. In contrast, the statement "When I don't take selfies, I feel detached from my peer group" yielded the lowest mean score, reflecting comparatively lower levels of agreement. The item with the highest mean belongs to the "Environmental Enhancement" dimension, while the item with the lowest mean falls under the "Subjective Conformity" dimension. Based on the item with the highest mean, it can be inferred that participants are inclined to take selfies with the aim of creating positive memories (Balakrishnan & Griffiths, 2018, p. 730).

It is possible to conclude that the participants do not need to take selfies in order to adapt to any social group.

Table 7. Means of SBS Dimensions

Dimensions	Mean	Standard Deviation
Environmental enhancement	3.06	.655
Attention seeking	2.92	.825
Social competition	2.91	.525
Self - confidence	2.74	.673
Subjective conformity	2.65	.547
Mood modification	2.60	.658

An analysis of the mean scores across the dimensions of the SBS indicates that the "Environmental Enhancement" dimension received the highest average score, suggesting that participants predominantly associate selfie-taking with the intention of enhancing or enriching their surroundings. In contrast, the "Mood Modification" dimension yielded the lowest average score, implying that altering or regulating one's emotional state is a less prominent motivation among the participants. On the other hand, the mean score of 3.06 for the "Environmental Enhancement" dimension falls within the neutral / uncertain range, indicating that participants neither strongly agreed nor strongly disagreed with the items in this dimension.

Table 8. Average Scores of Photo Editing Technique Items

Items	Mean	Standard Deviation
Cropping	2.44	1.04
Use of Filters	2.31	1.07
Use of Photo Editing Applications	2.11	1.12

Note. The three items in this table are taken from Fox and Rooney (2015, p. 163).

The mean levels of agreement with the items related to photo editing techniques are relatively low. Since the mean scores for the three items -cropping, use of filters, and use of photo editing applications- are all below 2.60, it can be inferred that participants tended to express disagreement with these statements. Frequent selfie editing has been reported to be associated with social appearance anxiety (Lau & Idang, 2022, p. 1), with research also indicating that photo manipulation on social media is linked to body image concerns (McLean et al., 2015, p. 1132) and may be related to body dissatisfaction (Lonergan et al., 2019, p. 39). Therefore, this finding appears to be explainable by the relatively low levels of social appearance anxiety among the participants. In other words, the low levels of social appearance anxiety among participants do not appear to lead to selfie editing behavior.

Table 9. Frequency of Selfie Sharing on Social Media

	Frequency	%
Never	63	13.1
Very rarely	212	44.1
Once in a month	84	17.5
Every two weeks	49	10.2
Once a week	24	5
2-4 times a week	27	5.6
5-6 times a week	4	.8
Once a day	4	.8
Several times a day	14	2.9

Note. Items in this table are taken from Sung et al. (2016, p. 262).

Among the participants, 63 reported that they never share selfies on social media, 212 stated they do so very rarely, 84 indicated once a month, 49 every two weeks, 24 once a week, 27 two to four times a week, 4 five to six times a week, another 4 once a day, and 14 reported sharing selfies several times a day. However, it would be inaccurate to conclude that the participants are exhibiting selfitis behavior. It appears to be at least partially possible to infer that only 14 participants may be exhibiting signs of acute selfitis behavior. On the other hand, considering that acute selfitis behavior requires taking and sharing selfies at least three times a day (as cited in Balakrishnan & Griffiths, 2018, pp. 722-723), this inference also becomes controversial. These 14 participants represent only 2.9% of the total sample. As indicated in Table 6, the fact that the mean scores of all SBS items -except for "I take selfies as trophies for future memories"- fall below 3.41 can be interpreted as an indication that the participants do not exhibit selfitis behavior. The absence of selfitis behavior is also reflected in the relatively low frequency of selfie sharing on social media.

3.3. Findings Regarding the Relationship between Taking Selfies, Social Appearance Anxiety, and Online Self-Presentation

Table 10. Correlation Coefficient Analysis Regarding the Relationship between Taking Selfies, Social Appearance Anxiety, and Online Self-Presentation

		Social Appearance Anxiety
Selfie Taking	Pearson r	.443
	p	.001
		Online Self-Presentation
	Pearson r	.577
	p	.001

There is a moderate, positive, and significant relationship between taking selfies and social appearance anxiety, as well as a moderate, positive, and significant relationship between taking selfies and online self-presentation. In other words, since the r-value falls between 0.3 and 0.7, the relationship is considered to be of moderate strength (Ratner, 2009, p. 140). Therefore, H1 and H2 were accepted. This finding may be interpreted as an indication that a high frequency of selfie-taking could contribute to increased levels of social appearance anxiety. The existing literature also indicates a relationship between these two constructs. It is suggested that adolescent girls who regularly share selfies on social media internalize the thin ideal and exhibit greater body dissatisfaction compared to those who do not share selfies regularly (McLean et al., 2015, p. 1132). Additionally, excessive viewing of selfies is associated with high levels of dissatisfaction with one's facial appearance (Yang et al., 2020, p. 1). Selfie filtering may be linked to an increased interest in plastic surgery (Aldosari, 2020, p. 23), and taking and sharing selfies significantly heightens social anxiety and the desire for cosmetic surgery (Eldaly & Mashaly, 2022, p. 371).

3.4. Findings Regarding the Association between Social Appearance Anxiety and Online Self-Presentation

Table 11. Correlation Coefficient Analysis Regarding the Relationship between Social Appearance Anxiety and Online Self-Presentation

		Online Self-Presentation
Social Appearance Anxiety	Pearson r	.392
	p	.001

As shown in Table 11, there is a moderate, positive, and statistically significant correlation between social appearance anxiety and online self-presentation. In this context, H3 was accepted.

3.5. Findings Regarding the Relationship between the Dimensions of Taking Selfies and Social Appearance Anxiety

Table 12. Correlation Coefficient Analysis Regarding the Relationship between the Dimensions of Taking Selfies and Social Appearance Anxiety

		Social appearance anxiety
Environmental enhancement	**Pearson r**	**.269**
	p	**.001**
Social competition	Pearson r	.170
	p	.001
Attention seeking	Pearson r	.306
	p	.001
Mood modification	Pearson r	391
	p	.001
Self - confidence	Pearson r	.344
	p	.001
Subjective conformity	Pearson r	.202
	p	.001

There is a significant and positive relationship between all dimensions of selfie-taking and social appearance anxiety. On the other hand, the relationship is weak in the context of environmental enhancement, social competition, and subjective conformity, whereas it is of moderate strength in relation to attention seeking, mood modification, and self-confidence. Therefore, H4 was accepted.

3.6. Findings Regarding the Relationship between the Dimensions of Taking Selfies and Online Self-Presentation

Table 13. Correlation Coefficient Analysis Regarding the Relationship between the Dimensions of Taking Selfies and Online Self-Presentation

		Presentation of online self
Environmental enhancement	Pearson r	.794
	p	.001
Social competition	Pearson r	.661
	p	.001
Attention seeking	Pearson r	.739
	p	.001
Mood modification	Pearson r	.800
	p	.001
Self - confidence	Pearson r	.757
	p	.001
Subjective conformity	Pearson r	.660
	p	.001

There is a significant and positive relationship between all dimensions of selfie-taking and presentation of online self. On the other hand, this relationship is strong in the context of environmental enhancement, attention seeking, mood modification and self-confidence, and moderate in the context of social competition and subjective compliance. In this context, H5 was accepted.

As presented in Table 10, although there is a moderate relationship between taking selfies and online self-presentation, it is noteworthy that there is a strong relationship between taking selfies and the dimensions of environmental enhancement, attention seeking, mood modification, and self-confidence in relation to online self-presentation In other words, it can be stated that as an individual's level of environmental enhancement increases, the frequency of taking selfies also increases. The aforementioned finding underscores the motivation for taking selfies as a means of archiving (Sung et al., 2016, p. 260) and highlights that individuals take selfies to "capture memorable moments" (Choi & Behm-Morawitz, 2018, p. 345). In other words, individuals may be inclined to accumulate various visual memories, driven by the "everyday" nature of selfies.

It is observed that attention seeking is also associated with taking selfies. This finding appears to be explainable by the inference that attention seeking is among the motivations for sharing selfies (Chaudhari et al., 2019, p. 123). Therefore, it can be suggested that as an individual's expectation for attention seeking increases, the frequency of taking selfies also increases. Considering that, selfies are regarded as one of the tools for self-presentation and impression management (Sung et al., 2016, p. 263), the relationship between the need for attention seeking and selfies appears to be explainable within the framework of impression management. Individuals try to manage their impressions in their online self-presentations. Selfies constitute one of the aforementioned tools of impression management. It is suggested that "happiness" and "physical appearance" serve as motivating factors in conveying impressions through selfies (Pounders et al., 2016, p. 1880).

The significant and positive relationship between self-confidence and taking selfies appears to be explainable by the inference that taking selfies may enhance an individual's self-confidence (Moneva et al., 2020, p. 139). On the other hand, it would be appropriate to interpret this finding within the framework of self-worth. Because, as stated in the introduction of the study, taking selfies emphasizes a diminished level of self-worth (Fox et al., 2021, p. 193). Moreover, the fact that self-worth and self-confidence do not always coexist (Legere, 2020) may also explain the relationship between selfies and self-confidence. In other words, an individual may attempt to reinforce their self-confidence through taking selfies; however, this does not necessarily imply that the individual possesses self-worth.

CONCUSSION

The "selfie," as one of the methods of self-expression in the digital communication world, has gained popularity through social media sharing. This new-generation form of communication, which holds a place in contemporary self-concept discussions, appeals to the need for social approval. Although it has an analog history, the concept of the selfie, which has become ingrained in everyday language through digital technologies and social media, updates individuals' self-presentation practices. Selfies, which serve fundamental functions such as attention seeking, influencing others, archiving, identity formation, and entertainment, are used to engage with others on social media. Selfies, which function as "controlled media" for users, diversify the possibilities of digital representation and self-expansion.

Selfies, which stand out in terms of online self-presentation, help to create idealized selves. In this context, the concept of the selfie, as one of the cultural phenomena in the virtual world, brings with it discussions on digital narcissism, selfitis, body image, self-objectification, and appearance anxiety. It is discussed that obsessive selfie-taking (selfitis) may have psychological consequences such as depression, anxiety, social appearance anxiety, and eating disorders. Selfie communication, a topic worth researching due to its multifaceted psychological effects, is associated with social appearance anxiety and online self-presentation. In this context, attitudes towards selfie are evaluated within the framework of social appearance anxiety and online self-presentation.

In the study, five main hypotheses were tested, and the significance of taking selfies from the participants' perspective was examined. In this context, a survey conducted using the convenience sampling technique reached a total of 481 participants. The scales, structured in a 5-point Likert format ranging from "1 = Strongly Disagree" to "5 = Strongly Agree," were supplemented with demographic questions such as age, gender, education, and income level. Following the pilot study conducted with 50 participants, reliability analyses of the scales were performed, and the main study was initiated. The study, which predominantly included female participants, young adults (aged 18-29), and those with undergraduate and associate degrees, revealed the following prominent findings:

- It can be suggested that participants place more importance on real-world communication rather than the challenging presentation and perception management on social media. Furthermore, the majority of participants believe that their self-presentation in virtual environments is consistent with their self-presentation in the real world. This situation prompts a reconsideration of the relationship between self-presentation on social media and social appearance anxiety. In this context, participants may believe that they could receive uncontrollable reactions to their self-presentation in online environments. However, this does not change the fact that participants still prefer online self-presentation. This illustrates the impact of contemporary digital presentation practices on the younger generation. On the other hand, the fact that participants find themselves consistent about online and offline self-presentation is open to discussion as it is an internal evaluation.
- Displaying a different self and identity in the online environment compared to real life is among the items that participants disagreed with. Therefore, most of the participants state that they do not use social media to exhibit a different persona. This may indicate that participants see social media as an extension, repetition and / or mirror of real life. Of course, these results may include socio-cultural contexts within the scope of the limitations of the research. In other words, conducting the same research in another social structure can strongly affect the averages of the scales.

- Participants who strive to maintain a balanced preference between being online and offline do not perceive social media as an escape from reality in terms of self-presentation. The low averages of the "multiple selves" dimension in the POSS scale can describe this situation. This result seems to be compatible with the high averages of the "consistent self" and "online presentation preference" dimensions of the scale. In addition, participants are skeptical about whether the online environment helps to present them with ideal selves.
- When the findings in the context of the SAAS scale are examined, it is understood that the participants are generally undecided about social appearance anxiety. In general, participants who do not exhibit social appearance anxiety but feel tense when being observed may express this within the context of socio-cultural reasons. This is because the lowest averages on this scale correspond to the items that involve evaluations from others. In other words, participants mostly experience appearance anxiety not on a personal level, but within the framework of social contexts. The item with the highest average can be interpreted through cultural reality or social contexts. On the other hand, the item "I feel tense when my photo is taken," which has a high average, can be discussed in the context of ideal self-presentation.
- The majority of participants indicate that they use the selfie format functionally in accordance with the SBS scale. Participants who take selfies with motivations such as archiving, memory, and experiential value do not describe this communication format as a typical generational behavior. Participants who are inferred not to take selfies due to concerns such as social approval, conformity, or exclusion do not perceive this visual form as a tool for gaining popularity. Participants who report using photo editing tools at a low level behave consistently with the results of the SAAS scale. The fact that the participants who describe that they do not experience psychological problems such as social appearance anxiety, body anxiety, and body dissatisfaction rarely share selfies on social media may raise a question mark. In this context, it can be stated that except for 14 participants (2.9%), selfitis behavior was not observed, and the selfie format was not accepted at a high level. Within the framework of the aforementioned data, it can be stated that selfie content does not occupy a significant place in participants' social media usage practices.
- When examining the relationship between selfies, social appearance anxiety, and online self-presentation, it was found that the first three hypotheses were accepted: (1) there is a significant relationship between taking selfies and social appearance anxiety, (2) there is a significant relationship between taking selfies and online self-presentation, and (3) there is a significant relationship between social appearance anxiety and online self-presentation. There is a moderate, positive, and significant relationship (with an r-value between 0.3

and 0.7) between taking selfies, social appearance anxiety, and online self-presentation. In this context, it can be suggested that taking fewer selfies has a positive impact on reducing social appearance anxiety. Consistent with the relevant literature, the study indicates that when the frequency of taking selfies is low, the rate of experiencing social appearance anxiety is also low. Therefore, it can be argued that taking more selfies may pave the way for social appearance-related issues such as body dissatisfaction, social anxiety, and the desire for cosmetic surgery.

- Since there is a significant and positive relationship between selfie-taking and all dimensions of the SAAS scale, it is seen that the fourth hypothesis is also accepted. In other words, selfie can trigger social appearance anxiety as a form of communication and presentation. Similarly, when the correlation coefficient analysis for the relationship between the dimensions of selfie-taking and online self-presentation is examined, it is understood that the fifth hypothesis is also confirmed. In the context of the motivations for taking selfies mentioned above, this result is natural. Because the selfie form is accepted by the participants within the framework of "environmental enhancement."

REFERENCES

Aldosari, B. (2020). Do filters and pose in selfies have an effect on cosmetic procedures? *Saudi Journal of Otorhinolaryngology Head and Neck Surgery, 22*(1), 21–23. DOI: 10.4103/SJOH.SJOH_1_20

Antonietti, C., Camerini, A. L., & Marciano, L. (2020). The impact of self-esteem, family and peer cohesion on social appearance anxiety in adolescence: Examination of the mediating role of coping. *International Journal of Adolescence and Youth, 25*(1), 1089–1102. DOI: 10.1080/02673843.2020.1858888

Balakrishnan, J., & Griffiths, M. D. (2018). An exploratory study of "selfitis" and the development of the Selfitis Behavior Scale. *International Journal of Mental Health and Addiction, 16*(3), 722–736. DOI: 10.1007/s11469-017-9844-x

Bartoli, C., Nosi, C., Mattiacci, A., & Sfodera, F. (2023). Consumer self-concept in the cyberspace: How digitization has shaped the way we self-disclose to others. *Journal of Strategic Marketing, 31*(6), 1133–1154. DOI: 10.1080/0965254X.2022.2056501

Boursier, V., Gioia, F., & Griffiths, M. D. (2020a). Selfie-engagement on social media: Pathological narcissism, positive expectation, and body objectification–Which is more influential? *Addictive Behaviors Reports, 11*, 1–10. DOI: 10.1016/j.abrep.2020.100263

Boursier, V., Gioia, F., & Griffiths, M. D. (2020b). Do selfie-expectancies and social appearance anxiety predict adolescents' problematic social media use?. *Computers in Human Behavior, 110*, 1-8. 106395. https://doi.org/DOI: 10.1016/j.chb.2020.106395

Caner, N., Efe, Y. S., & Başdaş, Ö. (2022). The contribution of social media addiction to adolescent LIFE: Social appearance anxiety. *Current Psychology (New Brunswick, N.J.), 41*(12), 8424–8433. DOI: 10.1007/s12144-022-03280-y

Chae, J. (2017). Virtual makeover: Selfie-taking and social media use increase selfie-editing frequency through social comparison. *Computers in Human Behavior, 66*, 370–376. DOI: 10.1016/j.chb.2016.10.007

Chaudhari, B. L., Patil, J. K., Kadiani, A., Chaudhury, S., & Saldanha, D. (2019). Correlation of motivations for selfie-posting behavior with personality traits. *Industrial Psychiatry Journal, 28*(1), 123–129. DOI: 10.4103/ipj.ipj_30_19

Chen, S., van Tilburg, W. A., & Leman, P. J. (2022). Self-objectification in women predicts approval motivation in online self-presentation. *British Journal of Social Psychology, 61*(1), 366–388. DOI: 10.1111/bjso.12485

Choi, G. Y., & Behm-Morawitz, E. (2018). Teach me about yourself (ie): Exploring selfie-takers' technology usage and digital literacy skills. *Psychology of Popular Media Culture*, *7*(3), 345–360. DOI: 10.1037/ppm0000130

Chua, T. H. H., & Chang, L. (2016). Follow me and like my beautiful selfies: Singapore teenage girls' engagement in self-presentation and peer comparison on social media. *Computers in Human Behavior*, *55*, 190–197. DOI: 10.1016/j.chb.2015.09.011

Claes, L., Hart, T. A., Smits, D., Van den Eynde, F., Mueller, A., & Mitchell, J. E. (2012). Validation of the social appearance anxiety scale in female eating disorder patients. *European Eating Disorders Review*, *20*(5), 406–409. DOI: 10.1002/erv.1147

Coulthard, N., & Ogden, J. (2018). The impact of posting selfies and gaining feedback ('likes') on the psychological wellbeing of 16-25 year olds: An experimental study. *Cyberpsychology (Brno)*, *12*(2). Advance online publication. DOI: 10.5817/CP2018-2-4

de Vaate, A. J. N. B., Veldhuis, J., Alleva, J. M., Konijn, E. A., & van Hugten, C. H. (2018). Show your best self (ie): An exploratory study on selfie-related motivations and behavior in emerging adulthood. *Telematics and Informatics*, *35*(5), 1392–1407.

de Vaate, A. J. N. B., Veldhuis, J., & Konijn, E. A. (2020). How online self-presentation affects well-being and body image: A systematic review. *Telematics and Informatics*, *47*, 101316. DOI: 10.1016/j.tele.2019.101316

Diefenbach, S., & Christoforakos, L. (2017). The selfie paradox: Nobody seems to like them yet everyone has reasons to take them. An exploration of psychological functions of selfies in self-presentation. *Frontiers in Psychology*, *7*(8), •••. DOI: 10.3389/fpsyg.2017.00007

El Khoueiry, C., Sacre, H., Haddad, C., Akel, M., Saade, S., Hallit, S., & Obeid, S. (2021). Selfie addiction: The impact of personality traits? A cross-sectional study among the Lebanese population. *Perspectives in Psychiatric Care*, *57*(1), 167–178. DOI: 10.1111/ppc.12539

Eldaly, A. S., & Mashaly, S. M. (2022). The new dilemma of plastic surgery and social media: A systematic review. *European Journal of Plastic Surgery*, *45*, 371–382. DOI: 10.1007/s00238-021-01891-5

Fastoso, F., González-Jiménez, H., & Cometto, T. (2021). Mirror, mirror on my phone: Drivers and consequences of selfie editing. *Journal of Business Research*, *133*, 365–375. DOI: 10.1016/j.jbusres.2021.05.002

Fox, J., & Rooney, M. C. (2015). The Dark Triad and trait self-objectification as predictors of men's use and self-presentation behaviors on social networking sites. *Personality and Individual Differences*, *76*, 161–165. DOI: 10.1016/j.paid.2014.12.017

Fox, J., Vendemia, M. A., Smith, M. A., & Brehm, N. R. (2021). Effects of taking selfies on women's self-objectification, mood, self-esteem, and social aggression toward female peers. *Body Image*, *36*, 193–200. DOI: 10.1016/j.bodyim.2020.11.011

Fullwood, C., James, B. M., & Chen-Wilson, C. H. (2016). Self-concept clarity and online self-presentation in adolescents. *Cyberpsychology, Behavior, and Social Networking*, *19*(12), 716–720. DOI: 10.1089/cyber.2015.0623

Fullwood, C., Wesson, C., Chen-Wilson, J., Keep, M., Asbury, T., & Wilsdon, L. (2020). If the mask fits: Psychological correlates with online self-presentation experimentation in adults. *Cyberpsychology, Behavior, and Social Networking*, *23*(11), 737–742. DOI: 10.1089/cyber.2020.0154

Griffiths, M. D., & Balakrishnan, J. (2018). The psychosocial impact of excessive selfie-taking in youth: A brief overview. *Education for Health*, *36*(1), 3–6.

Halpern, D., Valenzuela, S., & Katz, J. E. (2016). "Selfie-ists" or "Narci-selfiers"?: A cross-lagged panel analysis of selfie taking and narcissism. *Personality and Individual Differences*, *97*, 98–101. DOI: 10.1016/j.paid.2016.03.019

Hand, M. (2012). *Ubiquitous photography*. Polity Press.

Hart, T. A., Flora, D. B., Palyo, S. A., Fresco, D. M., Holle, C., & Heimberg, R. G. (2008). Development and examination of the social appearance anxiety scale. *Assessment*, *15*(1), 48–59. DOI: 10.1177/1073191107306673

Hashem, R. E. S. M., Hassan, G. A. M., El-Sheikh, M. M., Hassan, H., & Azzam, L. A. B. I. (2022). Selfie phenomenon among a sample of Egyptian university students: Rate and psychiatric correlates. *Middle East Current Psychiatry*, *29*(103), 1–12. DOI: 10.1186/s43045-022-00254-5

Hong, S., Jahng, M. R., Lee, N., & Wise, K. R. (2020). Do you filter who you are?: Excessive self-presentation, social cues, and user evaluations of Instagram selfies. *Computers in Human Behavior*, *104*, 1–6. DOI: 10.1016/j.chb.2019.106159

Huitt, W. (2009). Self-concept and self-esteem. *Educational Psychology Interactive*. Valdosta, GA: Valdosta State University. (https://www.edpsycinteractive.org/topics/conation/self2.html). 25.02.2025.

Imran, H., Rehman, S., Khanum, S., & Shahzadi, M. (2024). Association of self-esteem, narcissistic tendencies, and selfie-posting behavior among young adults: Association between self-esteem, narcissism and selfies. *Pakistan Journal of Health Sciences*, *5*(1), 26–31. DOI: 10.54393/pjhs.v5i01.1266

Ismail, A. F. (2024). Excessive editing of selfies on social media: The illusion of sustainability in mental health among female adolescents. *Journal of Ecohumanism*, *3*(7), 3487–3494. DOI: 10.62754/joe.v3i7.4481

Jin, S. V., & Ryu, E. (2018). "The paradox of Narcissus and Echo in the instagram pond" in light of the selfie culture from Freudian evolutionary psychology: Self-loving and confident but lonely. *Journal of Broadcasting & Electronic Media*, *62*(4), 554–577. DOI: 10.1080/08838151.2018.1474881

Kim, M. (2020). Instagram selfie-posting and young women's body dissatisfaction: Investigating the role of self-esteem and need for popularity. *Cyberpsychology (Brno)*, *14*(4), 1–15. DOI: 10.5817/CP2020-4-4

Krämer, N. C., Feurstein, M., Kluck, J. P., Meier, Y., Rother, M., & Winter, S. (2017). Beware of selfies: The impact of photo type on impression formation based on social networking profiles. *Frontiers in Psychology*, *8*(188), 1–14. DOI: 10.3389/fpsyg.2017.00188

Lau, G. S. J., & Idang, J. (2022). The relationship between selfie-editing, self-esteem, and social appearance anxiety among university students. *International Journal of Advanced Research in Future Ready Learning and Education*, *26*(1), 1–8. DOI: 10.37934/frle.26.1.18

Legere, C. (2020). *What's the difference between self-esteem and self-confidence?* (https://www.torontopsychologists.com/whats-the-difference-between-self-esteem-and-self-confidence). 25.04.2025.

Levinson, C. A., & Rodebaugh, T. L. (2011). Validation of the Social Appearance Anxiety Scale: Factor, convergent, and divergent validity. *Assessment*, *18*(3), 350–356. DOI: 10.1177/1073191111404808

Levinson, C. A., Rodebaugh, T. L., White, E. K., Menatti, A. R., Weeks, J. W., Iacovino, J. M., & Warren, C. S. (2013). Social appearance anxiety, perfectionism, and fear of negative evaluation. Distinct or shared risk factors for social anxiety and eating disorders? *Appetite*, *67*, 125–133. DOI: 10.1016/j.appet.2013.04.002

Liu, Y., Zhu, J., & He, J. (2022). Can selfies trigger social anxiety? A study on the relationship between social media selfie behavior and social anxiety in Chinese youth group. *Frontiers in Psychology*, 13, 1-16. 1016538.

Lobinger, K., & Brantner, C. (2015). In the eye of the beholder: Subjective views on the authenticity of selfies. *International Journal of Communication*, *9*, 1848–1860.

Lobo, S. S., & Gowda, Y. (2016). The selfie phenomenon: Self-presentation and its implications. *International Journal of Computational Research and Development*, *1*(1), 147–153.

Lodha, P., & De Sousa, A. (2019). Selfie taking: Is there a socio-cultural risk? *Indian Journal of Mental Health*, *6*(4), 1–4.

Lonergan, A. R., Bussey, K., Mond, J., Brown, O., Griffiths, S., Murray, S. B., & Mitchison, D. (2019). Me, my selfie, and I: The relationship between editing and posting selfies and body dissatisfaction in men and women. *Body Image*, *28*, 39–43. DOI: 10.1016/j.bodyim.2018.12.001

McLean, S. A., Paxton, S. J., Wertheim, E. H., & Masters, J. (2015). Photoshopping the selfie: Self photo editing and photo investment are associated with body dissatisfaction in adolescent girls. *International Journal of Eating Disorders*, *48*(8), 1132–1140. DOI: 10.1002/eat.22449

Merriam-webster. (n.d.). *Selfie.* (https://www.merriam-webster.com/dictionary/selfie). 23.02.2025.

Mills, J. S., Musto, S., Williams, L., & Tiggemann, M. (2018). "Selfie" harm: Effects on mood and body image in young women. *Body Image*, *27*, 86–92. DOI: 10.1016/j.bodyim.2018.08.007

Mirzoeff, N. (2015). *How to see the world.* Pelican Books.

Moneva, J. C., Perolino, J. A., Jagobiao, M. C., & Ycong, S. T. (2020). Selfie and self-esteem. *International Journal of Social Science Research*, *8*(2), 131–142.

Moreno, S. (2018). Selfie-taking: A key semiotic practice within the 'show of the self'. *Punctum. International Journal of Semiotics*, *4*(2), 49–65. DOI: 10.18680/hss.2018.0019

Nesi, J., Choukas-Bradley, S., Maheux, A. J., Roberts, S. R., Sanzari, C. M., Widman, L., & Prinstein, M. J. (2021). Selfie appearance investment and peer feedback concern: Multimethod investigation of adolescent selfie practices and adjustment. *Psychology of Popular Media*, *10*(4), 488–499. DOI: 10.1037/ppm0000342

Nyutu, E. N., Cobern, W. W., & Pleasants, B. A.-S. (2021). Correlational study of student perceptions of their undergraduate laboratory environment with respect to gender and major. [IJEMST]. *International Journal of Education in Mathematics, Science, and Technology*, *9*(1), 83–102. DOI: 10.46328/ijemst.1182

Ozimek, P., Lainas, S., Bierhoff, H. W., & Rohmann, E. (2023). How photo editing in social media shapes self-perceived attractiveness and self-esteem via self-objectification and physical appearance comparisons. *BMC Psychology*, *11*(99), 1–14. DOI: 10.1186/s40359-023-01143-0

Papapanou, T. K., Darviri, C., Kanaka-Gantenbein, C., Tigani, X., Michou, M., Vlachakis, D., Chrousos, G. P., & Bacopoulou, F. (2023). Strong correlations between social appearance anxiety, use of social media, and feelings of loneliness in adolescents and young adults. *International Journal of Environmental Research and Public Health*, *20*(5), 4296. DOI: 10.3390/ijerph20054296

Pounders, K., Kowalczyk, C. M., & Stowers, K. (2016). Insight into the motivation of selfie postings: Impression management and self-esteem. *European Journal of Marketing*, *50*(9/10), 1879–1892. DOI: 10.1108/EJM-07-2015-0502

Puthiyakath, H. H., Anjali, R., Angel, S., & Goswami, M. P. (2024). Selfie syndrome: A study of selfitis and narcissism among young adults. *Journal of Creative Communications*, •••, 1–19. DOI: 10.1177/09732586231223603

Qiu, L., Lu, J., Yang, S., Qu, W., & Zhu, T. (2015). What does your selfie say about you? *Computers in Human Behavior*, *52*, 443–449. DOI: 10.1016/j.chb.2015.06.032

Ratner, B. (2009). The correlation coefficient: Its values range between+ 1/– 1, or do they? *Journal of Targeting. Measurement and Analysis for Marketing*, *17*, 139–142. DOI: 10.1057/jt.2009.5

Rousseau, A. (2021). Adolescents' selfie-activities and idealized online self-presentation: An application of the sociocultural model. *Body Image*, *36*, 16–26. DOI: 10.1016/j.bodyim.2020.10.005

Rui, J., & Stefanone, M. A. (2013). Strategic self-presentation online: A cross-cultural study. *Computers in Human Behavior*, *29*(1), 110–118. DOI: 10.1016/j.chb.2012.07.022

Safna, H. M. F. (2017). Negative impact of selfies on youth. *International Journal of Computer Science and Information Technology Research*, *5*(3), 68–73.

Salomon, I., & Brown, C. S. (2021). That selfie becomes you: Examining taking and posting selfies as forms of self-objectification. *Media Psychology*, *24*(6), 847–865. DOI: 10.1080/15213269.2020.1817091

Saltz, J. (2014). *Art at arm's length: A history of the selfie*. (https://www.vulture.com/2014/01/history-of-the-selfie.html)

Senft, T. M., & Baym, N. K. (2015). What does the selfie say? Investigating a global phenomenon. *International Journal of Communication, 9*, 1588–1606.

Shah, R., & Tewari, R. (2016). Demystifying 'selfie': A rampant social media activity. *Behaviour & Information Technology, 35*(10), 864–871. DOI: 10.1080/0144929X.2016.1201693

Shavelson, R. J., Hubner, J. J., & Stanton, G. C. (1976). Self-concept: Validation of construct interpretations. *Review of Educational Research, 46*(3), 407–441. DOI: 10.3102/00346543046003407

Shin, Y., Kim, M., Im, C., & Chong, S. C. (2017). Selfie and self: The effect of selfies on self-esteem and social sensitivity. *Personality and Individual Differences, 111*, 139–145. DOI: 10.1016/j.paid.2017.02.004

Siibak, A. (2009). Constructing the self through the photo selection-visual impression management on social networking websites. *Cyberpsychology (Brno), 3*(1), 1–10.

Sorokowska, A., Oleszkiewicz, A., Frackowiak, T., Pisanski, K., Chmiel, A., & Sorokowski, P. (2016). Selfies and personality: Who posts self-portrait photographs? *Personality and Individual Differences, 90*, 119–123. DOI: 10.1016/j.paid.2015.10.037

Sorokowski, P., Sorokowska, A., Oleszkiewicz, A., Frackowiak, T., Huk, A., & Pisanski, K. (2015). Selfie posting behaviors are associated with narcissism among men. *Personality and Individual Differences, 85*, 123–127. DOI: 10.1016/j.paid.2015.05.004

Strimbu, N., & O'Connell, M. (2019). The relationship between self-concept and online self-presentation in adults. *Cyberpsychology, Behavior, and Social Networking, 22*(12), 804–807. DOI: 10.1089/cyber.2019.0328

Strimbu, N., O'Connell, M., Nearchou, F., & Ó'sé, C. (2021). Adaption and psychometric evaluation of the Presentation of Online Self Scale in adults. *Computers in Human Behavior Reports, 3*, 1–6. DOI: 10.1016/j.chbr.2021.100073

Sung, Y., Lee, J. A., Kim, E., & Choi, S. M. (2016). Why we post selfies: Understanding motivations for posting pictures of oneself. *Personality and Individual Differences, 97*, 260–265. DOI: 10.1016/j.paid.2016.03.032

Taber, K. S. (2018). The use of Cronbach's Alpha when developing and reporting research instruments in science education. *Research in Science Education, 48*, 1273–1296. DOI: 10.1007/s11165-016-9602-2

Taskin, T. E., Ferdowshi, N., & Islam, S. (2024). Is selfie taking behavior beneficial for the mental wellbeing of young adults? *Dhaka University Journal of Biological Sciences, 33*(2), 77–86. DOI: 10.3329/dujbs.v33i2.75818

Terán, L., Yan, K., & Aubrey, J. S. (2020). "But first let me take a selfie": US adolescent girls' selfie activities, self-objectification, imaginary audience beliefs, and appearance concerns. *Journal of Children and Media, 14*(3), 343–360.

Tiggemann, M., Anderberg, I., & Brown, Z. (2020). Uploading your best self: Selfie editing and body dissatisfaction. *Body Image, 33*, 175–182. DOI: 10.1016/j.bodyim.2020.03.002

Tiidenberg, K. (2018). *Selfies: Why we love (and hate) them.* Emerald Publishing Limited.

UOY. (2023). *How looking at other people's selfies can make us feel bad about our own bodies.* (https://www.york.ac.uk/institute-of-mental-health-research/news/2023/selfies-image-angle-study/)

Valkenburg, P. M. (2017). Understanding self-effects in social media. *Human Communication Research, 43*(4), 477–490. DOI: 10.1111/hcre.12113

Vandenbosch, L., Fardouly, J., & Tiggemann, M. (2022). Social media and body image: Recent trends and future directions. *Current Opinion in Psychology, 45*, 1–6. DOI: 10.1016/j.copsyc.2021.12.002

Veldhuis, J., Alleva, J. M., Bij de Vaate, A. J., Keijer, M., & Konijn, E. A. (2020). Me, my selfie, and I: The relations between selfie behaviors, body image, self-objectification, and self-esteem in young women. *Psychology of Popular Media, 9*(1), 3–13. DOI: 10.1037/ppm0000206

Wade, N. J. (2014). Guest editorial: The first scientific 'selfie'? *Perception, 43*(11), 1141–1144. DOI: 10.1068/p4311ed

Wang, Y., Xie, X., Fardouly, J., Vartanian, L. R., & Lei, L. (2021). The longitudinal and reciprocal relationships between selfie-related behaviors and self-objectification and appearance concerns among adolescents. *New Media & Society, 23*(1), 56–77. DOI: 10.1016/j.chb.2023.107906

Wehrle, K., & Fasbender, U. (2019). Self-concept. In Zeigler-Hill, V., & Shackelford, T. K. (Eds.), *Encyclopedia of personality and individual differences* (pp. 1–5). Springer., DOI: 10.1007/978-3-319-28099-8_2001-1

Xiao, L., Chu, D., Wang, F., & Yang, Y. (2023). Editing the self in pictures: Selfie editing promotes self-objectification among Chinese. *Current Psychology (New Brunswick, N.J.)*, *42*, 10656–10668. DOI: 10.1007/s12144-021-02327-w

Yang, J., Fardouly, J., Wang, Y., & Shi, W. (2020). Selfie-viewing and facial dissatisfaction among emerging adults: A moderated mediation model of appearance comparisons and self-objectification. *International Journal of Environmental Research and Public Health, 17*(2), 672, 1-16. http://dx.doi.org/DOI: 10.3390/ijerph17020672

Zeng, W., Luo, Y. J., & Chen, H. (2024). Does thin-ideal internalization increase adolescent girls' problematic social media use? The role of selfie-related behaviors and friendship quality. *Youth & Society*, *56*(3), 447–474. DOI: 10.1177/0044118X231176849

ADDITIONAL READING

Attrill-Smith, A., Fullwood, C., Keep, M., & Kuss, D. (2019). *The Oxford handbook of cyberpsychology*. Oxford University Press.

Conrad-Morray, D. (2022). *Visual culture approaches to the selfie*. Routledge.

Fiske, S. T., & Macrae, C. N. (2012). *The SAGE handbook of social cognition*. Sage.

Lindgreen, S. (2017). *Digital media and society*. Sage.

Miller, V. (2020). *Understanding digital culture*. Sage.

Orton-Johnson, K. (2024). *Digital culture and society*. Sage.

Rosen, L. D., Cheever, N. A., & Carrier, L. M. (2015). *The Wiley handbook of psychology, technology, and society*. John Wiley & Sons.

Saugstad, P. (2018). *A history of modern psychology*. Cambridge University Press.

Waskul, D. D., & Vannini, P. (2016). *Popular culture as everyday life*. Routledge.

Wright, K. B., & Webb, L. M. (2011). *Computer-mediated communication in personal relationships*. Peter Lang.

KEY TERMS AND DEFINITIONS

Digital Self: Thoughts about one's self in the digital world.

Online Self-Presentation: How an individual represents himself / herself in the online world.

Self: One's thoughts about oneself.

Selfie: Is a digital content where the individual taking the photograph is at the center.

Selfitis Behavior: Selfie addiction

Social Appearance Anxiety: An individual's anxiety about how others evaluate him / her.

Social Media: Platforms that enable interaction and content generation.

Chapter 10
The Digitalization of Visual Culture in Modern Spirituality:
How Video Games Became a Gateway to Occultism

Andrej Kapcar
https://orcid.org/0000-0002-6435-2609
Masaryk University in Brno, Czech Republic

ABSTRACT

This chapter explores the convergence of digital media, visual culture, and modern occultism, focusing on how video games function as both symbolic archives and ritual spaces. By tracing the evolution of esoteric imagery from literature and film into interactive digital environments, the study examines how players engage with magical systems, narratives, and symbols. Through case studies and ethnographic insights from online communities, the chapter reveals how games not only depict occult themes but simulate magical logic, thus transforming play into experiential ritual practice. It argues that the aestheticization and democratization of esoteric knowledge through digital platforms, particularly within the ethos of Chaos Magick, has created a new form of participatory, visually immersive, and affectively charged spirituality.

1. INTRODUCTION

Spiritual practice and occult knowledge, once confined to secretive circles, have increasingly entered public discourse. The spirituality of today has gradually adapted

DOI: 10.4018/979-8-3373-6970-9.ch010

© 2026, IGI Global Scientific Publishing. Copying or distributing in print or electronic forms without written permission of IGI Global Scientific Publishing is prohibited. Use of this chapter to generative artificial intelligence (AI) technologies is expressly prohibited. The publisher reserves all rights to license its use for generative AI training and machine learning model development.

to the modern era, exploiting various means of modern technology. Through social media, films, television, video games, and internet culture, spiritual symbols and practices now reach millions of households worldwide. In this age of touchscreens and global sharing, what has once belonged to the margins of society, hidden from plain sight, has become interactive and aesthetically pleasing, sometimes even playable. The digitalization of occultism is no longer a fringe phenomenon, but rather a cultural undercurrent found in the popular internet memes, video games, and online subcultures. The various digital channels have become a place where the sacred and the entertainment merge - a place where the symbolic becomes systematized and the digital becomes ritualized.

This chapter explores how the visual languages of popular culture, particularly video games, have transformed traditional occultism into a digital environment. From occult symbols embedded in video game narratives to online forums exploring digital ritual methods, we are witnessing not only the diffusion of magical symbols into digital culture, but the active transformation of modern magical practice itself.

As such, it tries to answer questions, such as, but not limited to:

- What kind of changes can be seen within the occult practice when its symbols and rituals become part of generally accessible entertainment?
- How can rituals be performed within the digital environment, and how does it influence the perception of the practice by the practitioners themselves?
- How do the changes of this popularization of magical practice influence the community of practitioners, that was for a long time relying on its secrecy and exclusivity?
- What are the risks of this change towards a democratization of the esoteric practice to the practice itself?

The answers lie in the cultural and technological process of digitalization. As culture increasingly operates through digital interfaces, its transmission, interpretation, and reimagination follow new logics. The visual culture of the 21st century is born not only in the studio or the temple, but in lines of codes, graphical interfaces, or game engines. In this environment, symbols are no longer fixed. They are malleable, remixable, and shareable. The internet becomes an archive and a laboratory for esoteric experimentation, and visual culture becomes a medium through which spiritual ideas are both communicated and transformed.

The structure of this chapter follows the following logic. First, it examines the broader context of digitalization and how visual culture has evolved under the influence of the internet, digital spaces, and aesthetic appreciation. Next, it traces the appearance of occult themes in contemporary culture, with an emphasis on their playful, experimental, and often social nature. The third part focuses on video games as a case study, analyzing how they embody and transmit esoteric ideas. Finally, the last part turns to Chaos Magick as the conceptual esoteric approach, that combines elements from all the previously covered domains and builds it into a practice that both exemplifies and exploits the possibilities of the digital occult. Methodologically, it adopts a cultural and media studies lens, combining textual analysis of video games, participant observation in online communities, and theoretical insights from digital anthropology and religious studies. It aims to map how occult symbols and spiritual practices are reimagined, performed, and shared within the digital sphere.

Occultism, historically rooted in secrecy, relying on the exclusivity of knowledge, often locked behind initiations, has paradoxically flourished in the hyper-visual, hyper-connected spaces of modern digital life. Its resurgence among the younger generation of enthusiasts and practitioners alike, is inseparable from the forms of cultural consumption, participation enabled by the internet. Platforms like Instagram, Reddit, Discord, and YouTube serve as modern libraries of esoteric knowledge, where aesthetics and ideology intertwine. On the other hand, video games serve as visual and narrative channels, where game designers, often inspired by various esoteric traditions, construct whole cosmologies that allow players to live their fantasy of being a powerful magician. The appeal lies not only in the mystery or subversion associated with the occult, but in its adaptability - its openness to personalization and aesthetic reimagination.

Among the modern schools of magic, Chaos Magick is particularly open to digital evolution and thrives in this context. Emerging in the 1970s as a postmodern rejection of esoteric orthodoxy, Chaos Magick embraces belief as a tool, not a dogmatic truth (Otto, 2020, p. 761) . Its practitioners, often referred to as "chaotes" (Cusack, 2011, p. 133), borrow freely from traditions, symbols, pop culture, and personal gnosis. This radical openness makes it uniquely compatible with the digital age, where access to various esoteric traditions and visual archives is always only a few clicks away. The ethos of Chaos Magick aligns with the remix culture of the internet and the modular narratives of video games, making the magical practice flexible, interactive, experimental and aesthetically pleasing.

To understand this convergence, video games must be analyzed not only as entertainment, but as cultural and symbolic sources. Popular games, such as The Elder Scrolls, Dark Souls, Shin Megami Tensei, Persona, or Control don't just feature occult themes only as decoration, but rather offer complex systems of ritual, myth, and metaphysical structure that is deeply interwoven into the story. They invite players into alternate cosmologies, where engagement in the game progress through nonlinear thinking is rewarded with arcane knowledge, often shrouded in symbolic language. The aesthetics of the occult become embedded in gameplay mechanics, environmental storytelling, and even in user interfaces.

In the aforementioned Elder Scrolls series, players learn magical languages to cast spells, meant not only for combat, but also to alter the immediate environment, or social interactions within the game world. In games such as Bloodborne, or other belonging to the so called "soulslike"[1] genre, cosmic horror merges with Victorian setting, creating an atmosphere where knowledge itself is transformative, but at the same time dangerous. Persona and Shin Megami Tensei take it even one step further, by blending psychology, social dynamics, and esotericism in systems where summoning deities and demons reflects one's multifaceted personality. Control turns an entire government building into a liminal space of magical realism, where sigils, objects of power, and modern, bureaucratic occultism intersect.

In all the aforementioned examples, the game settings go further than depict the occult, but rather they simulate its logic. They encourage players to navigate symbolic systems, decode patterns, and apply the gained knowledge to influence their environment to their benefit. This binary system of cause and effect mirrors the fundamental structure of magical thinking, rooted in the teachings of Chaos Magick - an intention manifested into a symbolic action (aka casting a spell) can shape reality according to the will of the mage. Through digital interaction, players are not merely watching or reading about occultism but are taking an active approach and participating in it, at least within the fictional environment. On the other hand, as I will demonstrate in later parts of this chapter, the emotional, psychological and aesthetic appeal of these actions, environments or characters can resonate so intensively with the player/practitioner of magic, that individual elements of gameplay can be implemented into the ritual practice in the real world.

Video games thus become places where popular culture, digital media, and esoteric experimentation collide. It is here, where the sacred is made playable, cultural narratives are re-enchanted, and where occultism is reimagined through aesthetic immersion. For many, in an environment of alienation from institutional religions, theological hierarchy, and growing skepticism in prescribed dogmas, video games and online occult aesthetics offer novel ways of engaging with the mystical, in a way that is experimental, modular and shaped by the visual culture.

To explore digital occultism is to investigate how esoteric symbols and ideas are reshaped within a media environment driven by images, interactivity, and constant connectivity. It involves examining how belief systems and practices adapt to the aesthetics and logic of digital platforms. In this context, the resurgence of the occult is not a rejection of modernity or a turn toward escapism, but a reflection of how contemporary culture processes meaning, identity, and the unknown in an increasingly virtual and mediated world.

2. HISTORICAL CONTEXT: THE EVOLUTION OF OCCULTISM IN POPULAR CULTURE

Long before the occult found its place within the modern digital culture, it was firmly contained within the traditional forms of entertainment, be it literature, film industry or music. These older, established forms of culture could be perceived as the precursors, which prepared the terrain for the digital age and its reimagination of occult practices. The themes of arcane knowledge, alternative worlds, fantastic beings, and hidden, symbolic systems occupied the imagination of authors for decades, likely building upon the even older tradition of myths and fairy tales.

Theosophy and the Foundations of Modern Occult Symbolism

The literary roots of modern esotericism are deeply entangled with the rise of Theosophy, a spiritual movement founded by Helena Petrovna Blavatsky and Colonel Henry Steel Olcott in the late 19th century (Clerbois, 2002, p. 1). Theosophy introduced broader Western audiences to older European philosophies, such as Neoplatonism, but more importantly, to esoteric aspects of Eastern religions such as Hinduism and Buddhism. Theosophy brought into the popular scope of western esotericism concepts such as reincarnation, karma, astral planes, and the idea of a hidden spiritual authorities (known as Masters in Blavatsky's writings) guiding humanity[2]. It remained one of the essential influences on the development of Western esotericism in the 20th century (Hanegraaff, 2013, p. 131; Partridge, 2004, p. 90) and as such has left also a noticeable impact on the development of art and culture. Among those who drew inspiration from Theosophy, or were even members of the Theosophical society, could be mentioned the painters Wassily Kandinsky, Piet Mondrian or Hilma af Klint (Almqvist & Belfrage, 2016; Borkhardt, 2017; Wallace, 1968), writers Algernon Blackwood, George Russel or William Butler Yeats (Campbell, 1980, p. 165), or composers Cyril Scott and Gustav Holst (Algeo, 1987, p. 322). Its popularity was flourishing also among scientists, with Tomas Edison, Alfred Wallace, or William Crookes being all active members of the Theosophical society (Campbell, 1980, p. 165).

Esotericism in Literature, Art, and Music

H. P. Lovecraft adapted the esoteric themes into what would become cosmic horror-narratives filled with non-human intelligences, and forbidden knowledge that warps the human mind into insanity (Engle, 2014, p. 86). Even though Lovecraft was a skeptic, his fiction reflects Theosophical themes of multi-layered realities and alien spiritual forces, refracted through a more nihilistic lens, where his work would later became a solid inspiration for newer occult movements (Engle, 2014, p. 87).

Even in the modern days its legacy is still alive, as Mark Frost, the screenwriter and co-creator of the mystery television series Twin Peaks, states Theosophy as a direct influence behind the creation of this beloved TV series (Jackson, 1992).

Theosophy might be one of the biggest esoteric groups of the late 19th, early 20th century, but it was by far not the only one. Among other occult group that had a major influence on art were the Hermetic Order of the Golden Dawn and Ordo Templi Orientis, usually connected with the name of the influential English occultist and ceremonial magician, Aleister Crowley (Hanegraaf, 2006, p. 281). The expansive cosmology and mythmaking of these various occult circles had significant influential on early fantasy literature. Many authors were directly or indirectly inspired by the occult teachings, some being in close contact with members of the occult groups or being members themselves.

Fantasy writers such as Lord Dunsany, George MacDonald or even J. R. R. Tolkien were indirectly influenced by the occult elements, such as revival of myth, archetype, and sacred narrative. While Tolkien explicitly rejected occultism, the mythopoeic method he employed, creating vast, interlocking cosmologies with moral and metaphysical depth, bears similarities to esoteric cosmological storytelling. Even Bram Stoker's famous story Dracula was directly inspired by an earlier occult novel, titled A Strange Story, by Edward Bulwer-Lytton, 1862 (Partridge, 2018, p. 38).

Occultism in Early Audiovisual Media

In cinema, occultism took on a visual and expressive form as early as the 1920s in iconic movies such as German Expressionist horror movie Nosferatu (1922)[3], or the Swedish Danish documentary-style horror movie Häxan (1922)[4]. The former is based on the aforementioned story of Dracula, by Bram Stoker. It contains references to demonology (the demon Belial being the one who created the vampire) or even Enochian language (an occult writing system promoted by the 16th century occultists John Dee and Edward Kelley). Häxan on the other hand was based on the director's own study of the infamous book Malleus Maleficarum (Hammer of Witches), the 15th century German guide for the inquisition on dealings with people accused of witchcraft.

Later films such as Rosemary's Baby (1968), The Exorcist (1973) brought ritual, demonology, and occult symbols into mainstream visibility, often framed through themes of hidden power and transgression. Both of the movies caused a significant outcry among the population of the time, due to the controversial topics of Satanism within the storyline. Nonetheless, these narratives helped establish visual codes (magical symbols, grimoires and rituals-that remain part of the visual grammar of occult storytelling) into the modern visual entertainment industry to this day.

When it comes to esoteric inspirations, music is of no exemption as well. The already mentioned magician, Aleister Crowley became a key reference point for rock and countercultural musicians in the 1960s and 1970s. From Jimmy Page, from Led Zeppelin to David Bowie, Crowley's ideas about magic, willpower and personal liberation influenced musical identities and stage aesthetics. The presence of Crowley on the Beatles' Sgt. Pepper's Lonely Hearts Club Band album cover (1967) is an excellent example of how esoteric symbols became pop-cultural representations for rebellion and otherworldly insight.

These media laid the symbolic and narrative foundation that video games would later inherit and further enhance through interactivity. The visual motifs, narrative archetypes, and spiritual ambiguities of traditional media helped establish the occult as a serious, even if often sensationalized, cultural theme. Video games, drawing explicitly from these traditions, continued this trend and reimagining magical practice through immersive elements. Where films show the magic, games allow players to perform it.

Thus, while the digital occult might appear novel, it is deeply rooted in a longer cultural history. The symbolic depictions of the occult have gradually evolved from literature, movie and music industry into the interactive narratives and aesthetic representations in modern gaming.

The Rise of Chaos Magick

Emerging in England during the 1970s, Chaos Magick (often spelled with a "k" to exemplify its connection to esoteric traditions) represented a radical shift within Western occultism. Its founding is associated primarily with Peter J. Carroll and Ray Sherwin, this new school of magic quickly positioned itself into opposition to the rigid, dogmatic structures of ceremonial magic and hierarchical esoteric orders. Carroll and Sherwin proposed instead a more pragmatic, experimental, and deeply personal approach to magical practice, often also described as do-it-yourself (DIY) magic (Hine, 1995, p. 9). Chaos Magick is less concerned with dogmatic form and rigid belief than with experimental playfulness and personal practicality, as it is built upon the principle that belief is a tool for altering reality, not a dogma. As such, the effectiveness of a magical act lies in its subjective impact, freely modified through personal practice, rather than in adherence to prescribed traditions (Woodman, 2003, p. 16).

The concept of Chaos Magick was heavily influenced by the earlier works of the English artist and occultist Austin Osman Spare (Baker, 2011), whose emphasis on the power of intention, belief and sigilization laid the foundation for Chaos

Magick's core methodology. Spare's revolt against the dominant ceremonial magic of the time, mostly represented through Crowley, was expressed in his blending of artistic expression with magical intent (Spare, 1913). This blending of art and individual ritual style, often rejecting formal structure, became a defining feature of the movement. Carroll and Sherwin advanced these ideas by creating a system that could incorporate any symbolic framework, including those drawn from religion, mythology, philosophy, psychology, and increasingly, popular culture (Clarke, 2004, p. 105).

The motto "do what works" epitomizes the ethos of Chaos Magick (Duggan, 2014, p. 408). It applies a syncretic combination of techniques, in which practitioners, or *chaotes*, may invoke ancient deities from established world religions one day, and video game characters or comic book superheroes the next. The only criterion is subjective efficacy, whether the ritual generates a desired psychological or material outcome. This radical openness has made Chaos Magick a controversial yet attractive system, particularly to artists, and those disillusioned with the formalism and hierarchy of traditional schools of magic.

This acceptance of pop cultural content within the ritual practice is also not an afterthought, but a fundamental feature. In Chaos Magick, symbols derived from movies, music, games and even internet memes are not treated as superficial references, but as legitimate tools of transformation, provided they carry emotionally charged intention of the practitioner (Carroll, 1987, p. 31). Drawing from Spare's view that belief is the key ingredient in magical effectiveness, symbols from pop culture, when invested with emotional intensity, can hold as much power as traditional occult imagery.

Not surprisingly, Chaos Magick found fertile ground among creative communities. The artist and occultist, as well as the founding member of the English experimental music and art group Throbbing Gristle, Genesis Breyer P-Orridge was a central figure in promoting Chaos Magick's experimental and transgressive nature. P-Orridge's founding of Thee Temple ov Psychick Youth (TOPY) and its sister project Psychic TV in 1981 merged magic, performance art, and countercultural rebellion (P-Orridge, 2010). Alongside the Illuminates of Thanateros (IOT), a more structurally defined organization for Chaos Magick practitioners (Otto, 2020, p. 771), these collectives formed a cultural matrix through which Chaos Magick gradually spread into music, literature, and later, digital media.

This merging with contemporary pop culture has only intensified in the recent years. Musicians like Danny Carey of Tool, avant-garde artists like Alejandro Jodorowsky, and comic book writers like Grant Morrison have all drawn from Chaos Magick in both theory and practice. Morrison's series The Invisibles (1994–2000) was intended by the author as a "hypersigil"- a complex magical narrative, incorporating visual elements as well as drama and plot, intended to affect both the reader and the world through its symbolism (Morrison, 2003, p. 21). These and similar artistic projects are not only magical practices by the author, but due to their artistic appeal often serve as gateways for new practitioners, some of whom first encountered magical concepts through such media.

Video games have become a logical continuation of this magical trend. Their interactive nature, narrative complexity, and immersive symbolism, not to mention tens, even hundreds of hours players are willing to invest into them, make them ideal platforms for ritual and esoteric experimentation. Based on my research consisting of interviews and participant observation on internet forums such as Reddit or Discord, or within online video game communities, many Chaos Magick practitioners cite games such as Persona, Shin Megami Tensei, Planescape: Torment, and Dark Souls as major influences on their magical worldview. These titles explore themes such as personal transformation, belief as reality-shaping force, and the connection between visible and invisible worlds, ideas that resonate strongly with Chaos Magick's theoretical foundation.

In these contexts, digital environments are not merely backdrops for fantasy, but potential ritual spaces where intention, belief, and aesthetic converge. Game avatars may become hypersigils, game lore a system of gnosis, and fictional deities invoked with the same intensity as the traditional ones. This mixture of magic and media exemplifies one of Chaos Magick's defining traits - its capacity to evolve, mutate, and adapt through individual cultural resonance rather than institutional preservation.

Early Digital Occultism

The emergence of the internet in the 1990s marked in a new era for occult practice - particularly for Chaos Magick, whose decentralized and experimental practices made it uniquely suited to the digital environment. Early digital communities, such as Usenet boards and web forums such as mIRC, offered practitioners a novel space to share experiences, discuss theory, and collaborate on ritual design without the necessity of any hierarchy or initiation. Now mostly defunct platforms like Alt.Magick.Chaos FAQ, The Order of Chaos, Choronzon.org, or Chaostatic allowed users from around the world to engage in discourse that would otherwise be geographically or socially impossible.

As Chaos Magick evolved in these online environments, its core principle, i.e. belief as a tool, merged seamlessly with the emerging participatory internet culture. Online forums, imageboards, and eventually Reddit and Discord servers functioned not only as communal spaces but also as virtual temples, where rituals could be performed, shared, and modified in real time. The aesthetic minimalism and DIY attitude of early websites mirrored the ethos of Chaos Magick itself – to be flexible, user-defined, and results-driven.

As an example of internet culture merging with occult practices, that I found during my research, can be mentioned the evocation of "Random Number Jesus", a games-related servitor[5], invoked for lucid dreaming and reality shifting into chosen video game worlds (in this case the aim was to dream-travel into the world of the popular franchise Pokemon). Practitioners created sigils, performed online rituals, and documented their experiences, blending gameplay with magical experimentation. Offerings included incense or dedicated playtime, as a digital form of sacrifice. The ritual was considered successful as several practitioners reported a dream content aligned with the aimed fictional setting, exemplifying the subjective, often gamified logic of Chaos Magick in the digital age.

These communities helped reshape occultism for a new generation, turning isolated acts of magic into shared, narrative experiences. The rise of digital platforms not only democratized magical knowledge but laid the groundwork for an increasingly aestheticized, playful and virtually networked form of spirituality.

3. DIGITALIZATION AND VISUAL CULTURE IN OCCULTISM

Chaos Magick and the DIY Spirit of Digital Magic

The digital age has radically transformed how occult symbols are produced, shared, and used. At the heart of this change lies a significant cultural shift – the turn towards visuality in magic. This turn marks a shift from oral and text-based traditions toward visuality, and aestheticized practices of enchantment. Particularly in modern instances of Chaos Magick and its online communities, the act of working with sigils, often represented through pictorial memes, and symbolic interfaces reveals the modern fusion of magical ideas with visual culture.

Modern sigil magic, inspired by Austin Osman Spare, has become one of the most widespread and popular forms of magical expression in the digital era. Spare's description of sigils as "monograms of thought" (Spare, 1913, p. 26) that encode desire into a graphic form, to be subsequently destroyed in order to release their power, found a natural habitat in the digital realm (Weston & Bennett, 2013, p. 197). Chaos magicians adapted this technique not only for hand-drawn use, but for online creation, sharing, and even crowd-charging via platforms such as Tumblr, Instagram, or Reddit. Sigils have emerged from secrecy and entered their new, aesthetic and viral existence[6]. Practitioners create and distribute personal sigils as image files, sometimes layered with glitch effects or pixel art, visually encoding intention in a form that mirrors the modern language of the digital world (Partridge, 2005, p. 157).

A similar phenomenon is the rise of a so called meme magic, where internet memes function both as jokes and as magical sigils at the same time. In this case, intention is embedded not only in the image but in its spread. Inspired by the viral logic of the internet, meme magicians often intend to charge the magical image with supernatural power through repetition and circulation. While this was popularized through controversial alt-right forums during the 2010s, the practice has since broadened and diversified, finding popularity also in leftist occult subreddits, Discord servers, and meme pages that combine humor with magical intent. One of the practitioners on the webpage blog.magick.me describes memes as a commentary on the state of the world, that speaks to a large group of people, making it a form of a viral hypersigil (Makar, 2021). One of the most used examples of meme magic is the association with a popular internet meme Pepe the Frog, who later became the central figure of a joke religion called Kekism[7] (MomJeans, 2016a, 2016b).

The Chaos Star, a central emblem of Chaos Magick, shows how online visual culture thrives on remixing symbols. Originally from 1970s fantasy fiction novels (Moorcock, 1970), it has been reimagined through tabletop games and online forums. Today, it's used as both a magical icon and an internet status symbol, capturing the practice's emphasis on fluid identity and open symbolism.

Video games are another element that gradually emerged as a key platform for visual magical interactions. Many games do not simply reference magical practice, but rather they embed magical systems that replicate the symbolic and structural features of ritual practice. Players cast spells via runes, unlock sigils, and interact with cosmologies based on symbolic logic. In The Elder Scrolls V: Skyrim (B. G. Studios, 2011), for instance, players learn the "dragon tongue," a language of magical power whose runes are carved into the digital landscape and literally shout magic into the world. Thus, these runes act as both narrative tools and interactive sigils.

Some practitioners carry these visual elements from game worlds into their magical practice outside of the digital space. Several of my interlocutors reported using Skyrim's runic language in their rituals, or using so called sandbox game worlds, such as Minecraft, or The Sims as forms of sympathetic magic (building virtual settings that represent their real life aspirations). Minecraft (M. Studios, 2009), with its modular and creative world-building system, was particularly popular for constructing virtual memory palaces, and sacred spaces that mimic real-world ritual architecture.

This increasing orientation toward symbols and visuals reflects a broader shift in how modern spirituality operates. Contemporary magical practice, especially within Chaos Magick, tends to increase the importance of aesthetic engagement over theoretical coherence. Some practitioners explicitly claim that they are more often emotionally invested in modern visuals, characters, and narratives from games, comic books, or movies, in comparison to traditional esoteric doctrines. For many, these images serve not just as inspiration but as legitimate magical material. Characters like Cthulhu, the Chaos Gods from Warhammer 40k, or even fictional anti-heroes such as Deadpool or Kratos, from the God of War series, are used for invocation, evocation, or astral travel – often balancing somewhere between irony and serious, emotionally charged ritual practice, a dichotomy so typical for Chaos Magick.

This shift is deeply entangled with digital media. As the internet becomes the primary archive and platform for esoteric experimentation, magical knowledge becomes aestheticized, performative, and symbolic. Occult forums, Instagram sigil tags, TikTok spell demonstrations, and YouTube rituals function as ritual spaces and grimoire networks, built not on doctrinal fidelity but visual fluency. The magician becomes a curator of symbols, navigating an ever-growing palette of references, signs, and systems.

This visual turn also implies a new kind of literacy, that could be described as magical semiotics for the digital age. Symbols are no longer static but rather interactive. Mixed media are used for sigil creation, which are subsequently displayed and shared in hashtags. Rituals are no longer conducted exclusively in private but often as public art performances, sometimes even streamed live. In this landscape, the aesthetic power of the symbol is paramount, with its ability to provoke, seduce, shock, or inspire. This emphasis reflects the postmodern spirit of Chaos Magick itself, not as a return to tradition, but a progressive reconfiguration of meaning through imagery.

In this symbolic ecology, games and other digital media are not simply sources of inspiration, but rather a part of the magical process itself. When a practitioner invokes a game character for personal transformation, or constructs a ritual space in a sandbox game, they are blurring the boundary between fictional and spiritual realms, between code and intention. It is this fusion of visual, symbolic, and emotional elements that define the new magical logic of the digital age.

Role of Social Media & Online Communities

The role of social media platforms and online communities in shaping the contemporary landscape of magical practice is something that can't be overlooked. These digital spaces have not only facilitated the spread of magical ideas and aesthetics but have also redefined how practitioners connect, collaborate, and construct their spiritual identities. Reddit, Discord, YouTube and Instagram have become central nodes in a decentralized magical network, offering both a public stage and a private workshop for the modern occultist.

Reddit, with its subreddit structure and pseudonymous user culture, provides a semi-anonymous environment where users can engage in detailed, often heated discussions, share their views and rituals, and exchange magical experiences. Subreddits such as r/occult, r/occultlibrary or r/chaosmagick serve as both discussion boards and digital libraries of esoteric knowledge and spirituality, where users document the creation and application of magical practices. Threads analyzing the effectiveness of rituals, the symbolism in pop culture, or the construction of servitors exemplify how Reddit facilitates an ongoing, crowdsourced construction of magical knowledge.

Discord, by contrast, offers a more intimate and real-time platform. Servers dedicated to Chaos Magick, meme magic, or aesthetic occultism often include channels for spell-sharing, dream journals, and digital altar setups. The use of emoji reactions, bots, and customized visuals fosters a highly interactive magical environment, where identity and ritual become intertwined with platform-specific aesthetics. These communities often blur the lines between gaming culture and magical practice, using role-play, gamified rituals, and digital avatars as part of the spiritual experience.

Instagram and YouTube play a different role in this ecosystem by emphasizing the visual curation of magical identity and dominantly one sided presentation of a practitioner's views, opinions or aesthetical self-stylization. On Instagram, occult practitioners post sigils, tarot spreads, mood boards, and magical aesthetics using hashtags like #witchtok, #sigilcraft, or #chaosmagick. The image-oriented structure of the platform encourages a symbolic and performative approach to occultism, where the crafting of magical content becomes a form of both practice and presentation. On the other hand, YouTube provides a place for the recordings of full-fledged rituals, interviews, opinion sharing, with explanation and analysis of various forms of arcane knowledge. This aestheticization of the occult reflects broader trends in digital spirituality, where gradually the line between visual art, performance and magical intent is intentionally blurred.

Online communities have thus become not just tools for communication but infrastructures of belief. They enable distributed networks of magical experimentation, democratize access to esoteric knowledge, and allow practitioners to form social and intellectual ties with others who share similar spiritual orientations. The rise of digital occultism is inseparable from the social logics and technical affordances of these platforms, which together facilitate a new kind of collective, aesthetic, and collaborative magic.

Digital Rituals & Online Magic

The emergence of digital tools has not only reshaped communication and entertainment but has also fundamentally altered how magical rituals are conceived and performed. In contemporary occultism various forms of the practice, such as spell design, divination, or sigil creation have been increasingly adapted to the digital interface. What was once performed in solitude, with specific items, often difficult to obtain, is now enacted via smartphone screens, stylus pens, keyboards, and livestreams. These practices are not merely translations of analog methods into digital media, they represent a new ontology of ritual shaped by interactivity, connectivity, and simulation.

Digital spell work is often facilitated through apps and web-based tools designed for magical intent. Mobile applications for lunar tracking, tarot readings, astrology, and divination have become commonplace. Even an application for the creation of sigils exists. Platforms such as Labyrinthos, The Pattern, and Co–Star offer curated spiritual content in modern, slick, and user-friendly formats. These tools do not just reproduce occult systems, but rather algorithmically personalize them, blending data analytics with mystical symbolism. As a result, users engage with divinatory systems in ways that are at the same time unique, personal, but also programmed. By the expansion of generative AI systems, the potential for the simulated "human touch" increases even further.

Sigil creation, traditionally a physical process, has been wholly transformed in the digital space. Sigil generators, drawing apps, and online software allow practitioners to design complex magical symbols using styluses, filters, and layered graphics. These sigils are often stored on cloud platforms, posted to social media, or embedded in memes. Some practitioners report "charging" their sigils not only through traditional meditative focus and destruction, but by maximizing screen time, exposure, or even digital noise. The idea being that the symbol accumulates energy through views, reactions and shares. In this sense, online circulation and emotionally charged reaction, disregarding if positive or negative, becomes a form of magical activation.

Ritual performance has also adapted to the new digital possibilities. Practitioners conduct virtual rituals using group video calls, shared documents, and synchronized screens. It is not uncommon anymore for witch covens or other magical collectives to gather via Zoom or Skype to chant, invoke, or cast spells, often integrating digital music, virtual altars, or looping gifs as sensory tools. The digital ritual space is thus not static or symbolic alone, it is immersive, coordinated, and ephemeral. It leaves no physical trace, yet lingers as archived content, screenshots, or chat logs, contributing to a hybrid archive of magical experience.

Even more informal tools such as Instagram filters or TikTok boards are being co-opted for magical use. Practitioners build ritual routines around timing posts with planetary hours, layering spell intentions into captions or hashtags, and using filters as glamours or visual enchantments. These actions reflect a significant paradigm shift, one where the screen is no longer a barrier between practitioner and ritual, but the very surface upon which magic is projected.

In effect, digital rituals reconceptualize magic not as a departure from modernity, but as an engagement with its technologies. These practices embrace individuality, adaptability, reimagination and participatory culture - qualities native to the internet itself. The magician becomes a coder, a graphic designer, a performer, or even an influencer, while at the same time remaining a conjurer, crafting symbols that travel across networks, platforms, and timelines. Whether in a private sigil post or a live-streamed spell, digital magic reflects the ontological and aesthetic structures of the medium it inhabits. This merging of esoteric intention and digital interface represents a significant evolution in the nature of magical practice, one that no longer distinguishes between ritual and media, belief and interaction, magic and code.

4. VIDEO GAMES AS A MEDIUM FOR OCCULT EXPLORATION

The intersection of magic and video games represents an innovative mixture of digital interactivity and esoteric practice, one that transcends the passive consumption characteristic of traditional media. In contrast to movies or literature, where occult themes are experienced from the position of a passive observer, video games demand active participation, placing players into an alien world and transforming them into virtual practitioners of magic. These dynamics shift the epistemological framework of how occult knowledge is acquired and internalized. Within game worlds, players engage with systems that mirror real-world magical practices, from sigil crafting to ritual invocations, often without explicit awareness of their historical or philosophical roots. The ludic nature of these interactions, determined by the game logic, parallels the experimental ethos of modern Chaos Magick, where belief and practice are fluid, adaptable, and deeply personal. Magic in video games can be perceived in four major categories, whose combination create the most appropriate examples of complex, appealing narrative – the overarching mythologies, magical symbols, ritual techniques and emotional investment, usually represented by the feeling of dread, anxiety, of fear of the unknown.

Mythopoeia and Digital Cosmologies

Video games have become one of the most creative grounds for the reimagination of mythic and occult systems, forging what could be described as modern, digital mythologies. These are fictional cosmologies, often narratively complex and symbolically rich, that are inspired by real-world occult traditions but reworked into new forms. Through expansive worldbuilding, archetypal storytelling, and symbolic layering, many games construct internally consistent magical systems that mirror or reimagine esoteric ideologies like Hermeticism, Gnosticism, Kabbalah, not to mention religious influence from various world religions. The result is a mythopoetic terrain where players do not merely observe the myth, but rather take part on its creation, influencing the narrative along the way. Games like Cultist Simulator, developed by Weather Factory (2018) allow players to progress through a Gnostic-like[8] structure called "the Mansus," managing dream-states, emotions, and secret knowledge. The abstraction of magical resources like "Dread" and "Fascination" into mechanics shows how symbolic systems are gamified and ritualized.

The Elder Scrolls series, developed by Bethesda, particularly Morrowind (2002) and Skyrim (2011), exemplify this approach. Its cosmological narrative involves divine figures like Magnus, whose departure from the world left behind magic as an elemental residue, a concept echoing Gnostic notion of divine emanation. Similarly, the in-game book series titled "Thirty-Six Lessons of Vivec"[9] functions as an in-universe scripture blending esoteric symbolism, parable, and cryptic philosophy. These texts, written by the former Bethesda writer Michael Kirkbride, directly draw from Aleister Crowley's Book of the Law (Crowley, 2022) and other Hermetic traditions. They encourage players to decode symbolic layers and piece together metaphysical truths embedded in the lore. As the books are scattered throughout an already massive game world, it is painstakingly difficult to collect them all. The reward for those few who embark on this quest is collection of cryptic, semi-esoteric texts, mirroring the Gnostic quest for divine knowledge, described by some game critics as the greatest piece of lore in role playing game history (Byrd, 2022).

The Secret World by Funcom (2012) provides another example where mythic systems become playable. At the beginning of the game, players are able to join one of three secret societies and engage in quests that reference real-world ancient mythologies, occult groups, or conspiracy theories. The game's puzzle-based "investigation missions" are plentiful of occult references to Aleister Crowley, the Enochian language, or Tarot readings, merging historical esotericism with fictional worldbuilding. This convergence results in a "hyperstitional"[10] loop (CCRU, 1999, p. 39), where belief and fiction feed into one another.

FromSoftware's Dark Souls series (2011-2018) and Elden Ring (2022) present mythologies of cyclical death, forgotten gods, and fractured realities. These stories resemble ancient mystical ideas like the Kabbalistic "Breaking of the Vessels" (Dan, 2006, p. 58), a myth where divine creation shatters and must be repaired. In games like *Dark Souls* or *Elden Ring*, players piece together fragmented worlds and hidden truths in a similar spiritual journey.

Digital occultism finds adequate expression also in games that explore subjective realities. Control, developed by Remedy Entertainment (2019), blends conspiracy theory, (para)psychology, and occultism in a bureaucratic institution that catalogues and contains supernatural phenomena bound to a physical object. These "Objects of Power" require specific ritual acts to activate, resembling chaos-magical practices where function overrides dogma and belief, and perception shape reality (Carroll, 1987, p. 112).

Even games not explicitly focusing on the occult contribute to digital mythmaking. The long running Final Fantasy series, developed by Square Enix (1987-2024) fuses polytheism, elemental theory, and metaphysical conflict into new pantheons and magical systems. These games remix real-world mythologies through a syncretic lens, reinforcing the idea that myth evolves through reinterpretation and reimagination. As such, the hero can summon mythological beings from various religious traditions (even though heavily reimagined), such as Odin, Shiva, Ifrit or Leviathan to fight at his side. Thus, these digital mythologies don't just borrow from occult sources, rather they construct new symbolic ecosystems players are engaged with narratively and emotionally.

Visual Symbolism and Magical Interfaces

The visual language of video games plays a central role in how magic is represented and engaged with by players. Within the digital realm, magic is not only narrated or performed, but rather it is captured in glyphs, runes, diagrams, Tarot spreads, and even user interfaces that translate esoteric ideas into playable symbols. These visual elements are not merely ornamental, they constitute a semiotic system that players interact with, interpret, and sometimes even internalize. Various game designers actively choose to include spiritual and religious symbolism into world lore and mechanics (Rupcic, 2023, p. 247). In this sense, games become digital grimoires, turning sigils and spirits into dynamic interfaces that bind aesthetics to metaphysics.

In *Control*, the narrative is revolving around supernatural powers, pervading our everyday reality, kept at bay only through the afford of a clandestine government organization named The Federal Bureau of Control (FBC). Redacted documents found throughout the game world, geometrical seals, and the brutalist aesthetic all reinforce a vision of reality where power is activated through controlled symbolic systems. The tread of the supernatural is ever present, but visible only to those who know where to look, how to look, and how to decode the hidden knowledge.

The *Persona* and *Shin Megami Tensei* (SMT) series, both developed by Atlus company, offer even richer examples of visual esotericism. These games are steeped in occult iconography, including the use of Tarot cards, seals, mythological summoning circles, and symbolic character alignments. In *Persona*, the Velvet Room acts as a liminal space where archetypes are summoned and fused, reflecting Jungian psychoanalysis as well as ceremonial magic. The game's interface acts as a kind of ritual tool. It doesn't just guide the player through gameplay; it also mimics real-life magical systems. Players navigate choices based on symbolic logic, much like practitioners working with Tarot cards or astrological charts in traditional esotericism.

Visual magic extends into indie games as well. *The Witness* (2016) structures its puzzles around sacred geometry, compelling players to draw lines that reflect ley paths and energy circuits in nature. Similarly, *Monument Valley* (2014) uses impossible geometry, clearly inspired by the Dutch graphic artist Maurits Cornelis

Escher, to convey paradoxical states of being and perception. Many of these ideas reflect established mystical teachings, such as the annihilation of the self (fanaa) and journey of the soul in Sufi mysticism (Harmless, 2008, pp. 163–164) or Zen kōans, the paradoxical riddles challenging conventional logic in Zen Buddhism (Suzuki, 1991, p. 88).

Spell menus, skill trees, and crafting systems across many RPGs (role playing games) also function as magical diagrams. These systems often resemble alchemical charts or Kabbalistic trees, where the player's progression through nodes and elements mimics the path of initiation or spiritual refinement. In games like *Skyrim* and *The Witcher 3*, magic is divided into schools or disciplines, each with its own color-coded progression path, geometry, or elemental logic. These are not just mechanics; they are visual grammars of magic that reinforce symbolic coherence within the game's world.

Summoning mechanics, whether calling demons, spirits, or avatars, often involve intricate visual sequences that highlight magical transformation and agency. Games like *SMT*, *Final Fantasy*, and *Elden Ring* elevate these moments to cinematic spectacles, where glowing runes, sacred geometry, or astral light-play communicate the metaphysical stakes of the act. The summoning visual becomes both a narrative and experiential, awe-filled moment, affirming the player's role as a magical agent within a cosmological order.

Other games abstract magical interfaces entirely. In *Cultist Simulator*, cards represent archetypes, spirits, events and emotions. These must be combined in specific patterns to bring new, unexpected results, including experimentation with countless possibilities into the gameplay. This gamified ritual construction mirrors how modern magicians manipulate symbols to bypass conscious reasoning and affect subconscious processes, not that different from artistic techniques favored by occultists, such as the cut-up technique of Brion Gysin and favored by William Burroughs and Genesis P-Orridge (Asprem & Granholm, 2013, p. 127; Davis, 2015, p. 159).

These aesthetic strategies also tap into the magical logic of concealment and revelation. Symbols often function as gateways, revealing new dimensions of reality once decoded or activated. Hidden glyphs, encrypted messages, or symbolic riddles populate game spaces, drawing players into a gnostic mindset where knowledge must be earned through symbolic labor. Much like occult texts, these visual elements demand interpretation, pattern recognition, and a willingness to dedicate enough time to understand the underlaying meanings.

Through all these techniques, games cultivate what could be called "visual magical literacy." Players learn to navigate and manipulate symbolic systems that resonate with real-world magical practices. Even if players aren't consciously aware of the esoteric references, they learn to think through images, symbols, and actions. The result is a media form where symbolic immersion fosters a kind of secular mysticism, mediated through graphics, design, and interface logic.

Ritual Mechanics and Magical Systems

Game structures frequently function as vessels for ritual expression, embedding the logic of magical practice into mechanics, pacing, and progression. As Fanelli & Strobl (Fanelli & Strobl, 2023, p. 465) argue, games can serve as intentional ritual objects, tools for meaning-making and spiritual experimentation within fictional worlds. Video games operationalize rituals through repeatable patterns, crafting loops, and symbolic transformations that echo the structures of real-world esoteric systems. These ludic patterns allow players not only to witness, but to perform and internalize magic.

In *Tyranny*, developed by Paradox Interactive (2016) the magic system revolves around sigils, where the spell is constructed by a precise selection and combination of elemental cores, expressive forms, and accent modifiers. This system of constructing spells closely resembles the construction of sigils or ritual inscriptions in modern magical systems. There are various ways the magician manipulates symbolic elements to influence subconscious and metaphysical systems to his benefit (U.:D.:, 2012).

Games like *Noita,* developed by Nolla Games (2019) take this a step of spell creation even further. Each spell is constructed from component effects, with cascading consequences that simulate magical trial-and-error. As it is probably noticeable while discussing the nature of Chaos Magick, experimentation in contemporary magical practice is not only welcomed but directly suggested as a way of achieving the most desirable results (Carroll, 1987, p. 93; U.:D.:, 2012, p. 28). Here, ritual is not rigid, it is instead exploration, narrative, and deeply personal, reinforcing an experimental magical worldview. This playfulness of magical practice is embedded into the playstyle of Noite, where a new spell might clear the path from enemies for the player, but with the same chance might backfire and annihilate the avatar.

Temporal cycles, or time loops are also a powerful and popular magical element found in many games. In *The Legend of Zelda: Majora's Mask*, developed by Nintendo (2000) players are locked in a three-day time loop that must be repeated, refined, and ultimately mastered. Each cycle mirrors the logic of ceremonial timing, where rituals must be performed under specific astrological or temporal conditions for achieving the maximum efficacy, allowing progression in the game. Similarly, *Outer Wilds,* developed by Mobius Digital (2019) uses a 22-minute reset loop to simulate a cosmic rite of emergence and destruction of a whole planetary system, mirroring the system of birth, death and reincarnation, which can be escaped only by discovering the underlaying cause of (this) existence. These cycles transform repetition into revelation, encouraging players to achieve enlightenment through symbolic return, before being able to leave the cycle altogether, a belief directly inspired by Buddhism and Hinduism (Kremmerz, 2019, p. 36).

Crafting systems across many RPGs are additional elements that mimic traditional ritual preparation, or alchemy. In *The Witcher 3*, developed by CD Projekt (2013) the main character Geralt's combat preparations, brewing potions, inscribing sigils, aligning oils, are strongly inspired by folk magic practices. Each preparation must be done in a set order, reinforcing ritual logic through habitual play. These mechanics imbue the act of combat with additional supernatural consequences, turning a physical confrontation into spell play.

Ritual design is not limited to mechanics. It is also embedded in architecture and spatial logic. In *Journey,* developed by Thatgamecompany (2012) and *Hyper Light Drifter,* developed by Heart Machine (2016), sacred spaces marked by symmetry, light, and silence draw players into contemplative, almost meditative states. These environmental rituals echo not only real-world temple design and the use of sacred space in mystical experience, but also the state of mind one should adopt before seeking guidance in such spiritual places. Similarly, *Hellblade: Senua's Sacrifice,* developed by Ninja Theory (2017) uses binaural audio and visual sigils to transform perception, inducing semi-altered states similar to trancework or visionary rituals.

Finally, instead of design elements within the game lore or aesthetics, the act of playing itself can became a semi-spiritual experience on its own. A recent meta-ethnography outlined 28 dimensions of gameplay and motivation, several overlapping with the emotional experience of spiritual engagement and ritual behavior (McKechnie-Martin et al., 2024, p. 17). Speedrunning[11], often perceived among gamers as a performance of mastery, has also acquired almost ritual overtones. Runners perform frame-perfect inputs and exploit glitches in choreographed fashion, requiring absolute dedication to the goal through their runs. While for most of the players it's a fun new way to experience the game, sometimes perceived even as a sport, interesting are the descriptions of the emotions during the speedrun, reminiscent almost of a religious experience. The players report of no longer having an identity provided by the game, but rather they are transcending the gaming world in a new form, with a new goal. The sensitivity to various new stimuli (such as sound cues, or subtle movements) in the game increases, as they become vital information for successfully progressing through the game at the highest possible speed. The player no longer produces an experience based on their natural way of play style but rather exists in a new reality. Build upon the deep, and detailed knowledge of the game, the players are able to manipulate nuanced events and occurrences, that were invisible before, to change the game reality towards their goal (Bruett, 2017).

Next to the reality-changing element, of particular interest is also the radical devotion towards achieving the goal - running through the game at the shortest possible time. Speedrunners spend hundreds of hours repeating a level, or the whole game over and over again, with any minor mistake that is obstructing them from the "perfect run" is a reason to start the whole afford anew. This dedication and devotion to fulfilling a task while going through endless repetition is reminiscent of various esoteric practices, but mostly of alchemical experiments. There, in contrast to science, the goal is not objective observation, but rather a full personal involvement towards achieving the final goal of their experiment (Singer & Singer, 1995, p. 67). As such, the speedrunner becomes the element of transmutation, where time and the real-world temporarily seizes to hold any importance, the only importance is the transformation through understanding, that will allow the development of all the skills necessary for speedrunning the game.

Thus, when viewed through a magical lens, game systems simulate rites of passage, meditative cycles, and esoteric experimentation. The line between gameplay and ritual is not simply blurred, it is intentionally crossed. Games encode occult structures not only in aesthetics or narrative, but in ways players move, act, and repeat. These systems cultivate a procedural gnosis: a knowing-through-doing that mirrors the inner mechanics of ritual tradition

Occult Horror and the Transformation of the Self

A significant number of games that explore the occult do so through the lens of horror. These titles delve into spaces where knowledge is not only obscure but perilous, as insight itself becomes a form of dangerous transgression. Research into maldaimonic[12] play highlights how players across cultural settings use gaming to explore darker or transgressive spiritual expressions (Seaborn et al., 2024, p. 12). Usually drawing on Lovecraftian and Gnostic themes, such games construct their narrative architecture around the dangers of hidden truths and the breakdown of accepted reality. Magic in these games is not empowering in a conventional sense, as it rarely comes cheap. It is transformative, destabilizing, and often terrifying, a metaphor for the fact that power comes at a price.

Bloodborne, another game from the so called "soulslike" genre, developed by FromSoftware (2015) is perhaps the most exemplary case of this model. Its entire narrative structure revolves around the acquisition of so called "Insight," a mechanic used to summon other players and characters to your game world, but at the same time it increases the player's awareness of the cosmic horror surrounding them. As Insight rises, massive invisible entities become visible, architecture shifts, and the world reveals its hidden nature. This inspiration behind it reflects the Gnostic idea that true vision reveals the falsehood of the material world and the horror of the real. The game also aligns with Lovecraftian principles, specifically, the idea that the universe is vast, alien, and indifferent, and that magical knowledge leads to madness rather than mastery.

Other games are not just inspired by the writings of H.P. Lovecraft but directly bring his stories into interactive game worlds. In both *Call of Cthulhu: Dark Corners of the Earth*, developed by Headfirst Productions (2015) and *Call of Cthulhu*, developed by Cyanide (2018), this framework is even more explicitly tied to the mythos itself. The protagonists are investigators whose growing awareness of forbidden knowledge and accompanying events deteriorates their sanity up to the point of going insane, which equals a game over. This mechanic reflects a longstanding literary trope in esotericism, that spiritual truth is often unbearable to the uninitiated. As in many initiatory systems, access to deeper esoteric knowledge can come at a cost of mental stability, identity, or moral certainty and the practitioner should adequately prepare to receive it (Drury, 2011, p. 5).

The Medium, developed by Bloober Team (2021) explores the intersection of consciousness and the supernatural. In story, the protagonist navigates dual worlds simultaneously: the physical realm and a spirit plane strongly inspired by Zdzisław Beksiński's surreal and dystopian imagery. Magic here manifests itself through psychic sensitivity, and its revelations are tied to trauma, haunting, and unresolved emotional patterns. The player acts as a medium in the literal sense, channeling knowledge, suffering, and spectral resonance.

Similarly, *Alan Wake* and its sequel *Alan Wake* 2, developed by Remedy Entertainment (2010, 2023) uses metafictional magic to destabilize narrative itself. The protagonist is a writer trapped in his own story, where the act of writing alters reality. The text becomes a ritual space, and the language is an act of magic. This relationship between creation and occultism aligns with Chaos Magick's emphasis on narrative manipulation and belief as a tool of reality-bending (Burroughs, 1993, p. 48; Woodman, 2003, p. 35). Wake's descent into darkness is not merely psychological, it is very tangible and magical, structured as a poetic rite of transformation.

Across these examples, the experience of horror becomes a metaphor for initiation. The veil of ignorance is lifted, and the player must confront that which cannot be unseen through conventional means. Madness, often portrayed as a loss of rational agency, is reframed here as a liminal passage, an entry into unconventional logics, alternative landscapes, or symbolic realities. The transformation is both narrative and experiential, as is typical for the video game experience. The player not only witnesses the change but undergoes it personally, even if represented through a virtual avatar.

The already multiple times mentioned game *Control* builds horror through epistemological instability. It intensifies this with its haunted bureaucratic setting, where anomalous objects and spaces affect and destabilize the laws of physics. Similar to *Alan Wake* also here is magic framed as a disruption of ontological certainty[13]. As perception of reality is based on acquisition of information via receptors (Kišoňová,

2013, p. 17), a force that can rewrite the perception threatens the boundary between order and chaos.

This narrative design reflects the principle that true knowledge is hidden, protected, and only accessible through altered perception or ordeal. Many of these games excel at environmental storytelling. Information about the lore is divulged through fragmented notes and cryptic imagery, mirroring the way esoteric knowledge is traditionally hidden in plain sight, decoded only by the willing or the worthy. Such game itself becomes a kind of initiatory text, that is subsequently actively analyzed on discussion boards by hundreds of fans.

Importantly, these experiences challenge the notion of magic as control. Instead, they present magic as a pathway to chaos, or divinity. This reversal unsettles the player's expectations and aligns with magical systems that prioritize dissolution and transcendence. Whether it's the H. R. Giger inspired body horror of *Scorn*, developed by Ebb Software (2022), the Lovecraftian existential dread of the *Amnesia* series, developed by Frictional Games (2010-2016), or the existential and metaphysical horror of the long running *Silent Hill* series, developed by Konami (1999-2025), these narratives engage magic as a force that unravels as much as it reveals.

Some games use horror to explore the transformational dangers of knowledge and wisdom. In *Hellblade: Senua's Sacrifice*, psychological trauma based on the death of a loved one is portrayed through haunting sounds and visual hallucinations. At the same time, the narrative reflects the esoteric hero journey (Tiaynen-Qadir & Qadir, 2023, p. 51), where the games' main character is forced to encounter their shadow self in order to overcome their deeply rooted trauma. Within the narrative, the obstacle to overcome is not some world ending event, or an external enemy, but rather the psyche of the character herself. This fight against oneself through magical psycho-metaphysical means is a popular trope in many of the modern narrative-driven games. The disturbing anxiety inducing aesthetics of horror games the ideal for the depiction of the dichotomies of a psychological breakpoint, often building on the symbolism of hellish landscapes.

At the same time, these games mirror the symbolic structure of magical initiation, where the neophyte descends into the abyss to confront the (dangerous) mystery. If he succeeds, he emerges changed, if not, he is broken or even killed. Thus, the logic of occult horror thus parallels the alchemical process of dissolution and re-combination, where transformation is necessarily preceded by breakdown (Jung, 1980, p. 296; Kyunghee, 2016, p. 53).

As such, occult horror in games is not only aesthetic. It can be understood as an engagement with the limits of perception and the costs of transformation. It dramatizes the fundamental esoteric tension between revelation and ruin, order and chaos. By inviting the players to cross those thresholds themselves, such games offer an immersive, even though often disturbing, experience of the esoteric path of descent and ascension.

Case Studies: Magic in Motion

In addition to previously discussed titles, games like *The Mortuary Assistant*, developed by DarkStone Digital (2022) and *Goetia* series, developed by Sushee (2016-2022) focus mostly on the interconnection between aesthetic occultism and ritual simulation. *The Mortuary Assistant* combines semi-real exorcism practices and sigil work, while using fictionalized Goetic seals in ways that still evoke the dangers and consequences of demonological rituals (Woodman, 2003, p. 72). On the other hand, *Goetia*, builds its puzzles around authentic demons and demonic seals from the eponymous book it took inspiration from[14]. As such, it serves not only as entertainment article but also provides brief glimpse into the real-world occult practice.

The previously mentioned Atlus role playing games, the Persona series, and Shin Megami Tensei series deal extensively with various psychological and esoteric teachings, as well as various religious traditions. These can be split into three main categories – spiritual deities, tarot cards and archetypes from Jungian psychanalysis. While the narrative and cosmology within the game is certainly fascinating, what makes these games stand out of the crowd are in-game school lectures which the player can visit, that deal with academic explanation of said categories (in Persona 4 they are even into the "Specials" section of the game menu). Here, there is not much gameplay per se, rather the player sits for several minutes and watches a fictional professor explain in detail Jung's theory of archetypes, the relation between the Ego, Superego and Id, or what is the shadow within in relation to the personality. All of these lectures are voluntary and can be skipped, with no impact on the gameplay other than the player will miss on gaining new knowledge. The game thus manifests a secondary goal, next to entertainment, and that is education. It becomes a virtual classroom, where players are invited, but not forced to participate. Mirroring the acquisition of esoteric wisdom in the real world, also here the knowledge is available, but only to those who are willing to dedicate themselves to the hardships of learning.

The process of communication between the video game and the player in a met-anarrative sense is exemplified in the case of the famous cypher "FF:06:B5" from the game *Cyberpunk 2077*, developed by CD Projekt RED (2020). The mentioned text appears on a statue within the game world with no further explanation given. It took a combined player collaboration[15], spanning over 3 years of investigations, uncovering further steps and traces in understanding what the code means, with each step leading to a clue more cryptic then the previous one. After the cypher was finally cracked, it has divulged a mysterious existentialist text discussing the perception of reality, determinism, transhumanism or the freedom of will.

The phenomenon of communal magical engagement is also on the rise, exploiting game mechanics, rather than the narrative content. Players construct sacred spaces or conduct digital rituals in sandbox games like *Minecraft*, developed by Mojang Studios (2011), or *Sims*, developed by Maxis (2000-2025). This is in line with the rise of game-based spiritual practices, a sort of "ludic syncretism", where belief and worship, manifested through a devotional action is bound to open a magical channel of communication (as one of my interlocutors mentioned). As such, playing any game with the intention of a magical result (be it divination, powering up sigils, or creating servitors) is considered a ritual act by the practitioners, all according to the teachings of Chaos Magick.

VR and Immersive Spirituality

A unique, but rather peripheral category of games are VR (virtual reality) games, which provide an incomparable level of immersion and sensory stimulation to the players (Yao & Kim, 2019, p. 239). Even though the numbers of VR titles are negligible in comparison to the massive non-VR game production, several popular titles are not shy about their obvious occult inspiration. One of such games is *DreadEye VR*, developed by Digital Happiness (2017), the VR spin-off of the popular DreadOut franchise. The player takes the role of a Dukan, an Indonesian shaman, whose role in the game is to exorcize spirits. This is done by physically mixing ingredients in an in-game cauldron which summons various spirits from Indonesian folklore. The aesthetics and soundscape are just magnified by the technology of virtual reality, providing a haunting but definitely memorable experience.

The Wizards - Dark Times: Brotherhood, developed by Vertigo Games (2021), focuses more on a high fantasy narrative, providing an aesthetically different kind of experience. Through hand gestures players are able to produce different, visually mesmerizing spells, that help them in traversing the immersive game world. Several of my interlocutors have mentioned that this game is about the feeling, about the emotional investment, as it makes them feel like a character from other popular magical franchises such as Harry Potter, or Doctor Strange. The difference between controlling the game through peripheral technology such as a gamepad, or mouse and keyboard compared to hand gestures, all while being visually surrounded by the game world, was for many an almost transcendental experience.

An undoubtedly unique audiovisual experience is provided by the title *Ayahuasca: Kosmik Journey*, developed by Mac Guff (2020). I intentionally described it as an experience rather than a game, as it is how the author was intending this project to be. The players in this case can't influence the environment but only experience the spiritual and psychedelic journey. Within the virtual world, the player embarks on a visionary journey under the guidance of a virtual shaman in the Amazonian jungle, where he gradually descends into the underworld, only to be lifted into the heaven and subsequently dissolves into surreal geometrical particles. Even though the whole experience is only several minutes long, it is extremely intensive. Several of my interlocutors, who tested the program under my supervision, weren't able to finish it and had to leave the virtual world already after the first few minutes of gameplay.

Outside of the various gaming experiences, VR provides an additional potential for occult practices – being able to visit various sacred spaces without the necessity to leave the comfort of our home. The interesting ongoing project titled *VR Mystery School*, that runs on the platform VRChat, is a gathering hub for esoteric practitioners. The author of this space intended it as a safe space for practitioners on one hand, and a freely accessible library of arcane knowledge on the other. This virtual space hosts regular lectures on esoteric topics, virtual group meditations, divination practices, gallery of occult art, and even a hermetic temple inspired by the teachings of the famous occultist Franz Bardon (currently in construction). VR Mystery school exemplifies the potential that VR technology holds for the occult practice – being decentralized, immersive to the level of personal in-place participation, an accessible from anywhere (in respect to the technology)[16].

Unfortunately, due to VR systems being still very marginal, and only a fracture of players owning one, these programs usually reach only a very niche audience. Nonetheless, the potential that VR holds is still remarkable, and only time, and the intentions of game developers will show if it will be more deeply integrated into the gaming environment, and as such also to the practices of digital occultism, or if it will remain on the fringes of digital entertainment.

Subsequently, these and similar practices point to the emergence of a digital occulture[17], where play, belief, and performance merge. While risks of aesthetic reductionism persist, the examples above demonstrate that games can and often are more than vehicles of superficial symbolism and shallow entertainment. They act as mythopoetic, symbolic, and ritual spaces, even digital temples of ritual practice. As players explore, manipulate, and explore these systems, the occult becomes not just something that is observed, but rather something experiential and lived. And lastly, under the influence of Chaos Magick, games can become vessels of ritual knowledge and practice.

5. THE FEEDBACK LOOP: FROM DIGITAL TO REAL-WORLD OCCULT PRACTICES

As digital culture becomes increasingly fused with everyday life, the influence of video games and online spaces on real-world occult practices has moved from speculative theory to experimental practice. As I briefly demonstrated on the above-mentioned examples, video games that incorporate magical systems, and esoteric lore are often perceived by the audience as more than just entertainment. They can also act as educational tools, inspirational texts, and virtual laboratories for a new generation of self-taught occult practitioners. This section, based on my research of the gamer-magic practitioner online community, explores the feedback loop between digital and physical magical practices. How gamers adapt virtual magic into real-world rituals, how accessibility fosters a wave of DIY occultism, and what ethical questions arise from this digital diffusion of esoteric knowledge.

From Game Space to Sacred Space: Digital Practices Becoming Ritual Experience

Video games have long employed semi-ritualistic mechanics, often centered on repetition, chronology, symbolism, and transformation. For many players, these elements resonate with the structures of actual magical practice. One of my interlocutors stated that video games are an excellent way to tap into the same class of space as the astral, and as such can be a great way to supplement magic activity[18]. While exploring the connections between video games and magic in discussions with esoteric practitioners, I encountered numerous examples of players seeking out games that either explicitly explore occult, esoteric, or magical themes - or those that evoke the feeling of a magical experience. While these two categories can sometimes overlap, as in titles like *Cultist Simulator* or *The Secret World*, they are often distinct.

Games that directly reference occult symbols, secret societies, or esoteric characters usually serve not only as entertainment but also as simplified esoteric knowledge hubs. Their narratives and aesthetic immersion can spark interest in deeper magical study. Practitioners sometimes describe their experience with these games as similar to reading an occult novel, one that either introduces them to new ideas or reinforces their existing knowledge, often with a sense of delight in recognizing symbolic references. Importantly, these games place the player in the role of an active agent within the story, deepening emotional investment. Titles like *The Council*, developed by Big Bad Wolf Studio (2018), *The Broken Sword* series, developed by Revolution Software (1996–2024), and *The Gabriel Knight* series, developed by Sierra On-Line (1993–2014) exemplify this narrative strategy.

Each blends fiction with real-world esoteric references, covering topics such as the Templar Order, the Voynich Manuscript, Gnostic texts, Voodoo, Freemasonry, and Vatican conspiracy theories.

The second category, games that invoke the feeling of a magical experience, is broader and more diverse. These titles span across various genres and aesthetics, often depending on personal preferences. Examples include the existentially humorous discussion on the concept of free will - *The Stanley Parable*, developed by Galactic Cafe (2013), the Jungian, psychologically immersive *Disco Elysium*, developed by ZA/UM (2019), or the experimental spell-building game *Noita*, developed by Nolla Games (2019), where each pixel is physically simulated. Despite their differences, these games provide deeply emotional or psychologically engaging experiences that spill over into the player's real life. Whether by prompting philosophical reflection, eliciting emotional intensity, or creating a visceral adrenaline rush, they often result in personal transformation. Many of my interlocutors described these experiences as close to magical initiations - emerging changed after playing, as if they were no longer the same person.

A unique category includes games that merge both approaches, offering explicit esoteric content and an immersive magical atmosphere. The most commonly cited examples among practitioners were *Cultist Simulator* and *The Secret World*. These titles combine deep gameplay with rich esoteric symbolism, appealing aesthetics, and layered narratives. For some, *Cultist Simulator* is more than a game, it is rather a spiritual practice. Intentionally cryptic and lacking explicit guidance, it relies on cycles of trial, failure, and eventual understanding, mirroring the real-world acquisition of occult knowledge. Though the symbolism is fictional, the emotional impact and sense of awakening it produces is strikingly real.

The Secret World, developed by Funcom (2012), later rebranded as *Secret World Legends* (2017), is (or was) a massive multiplayer online RPG set in a contemporary world, a bold departure from the typical fantasy or sci-fi settings. Players must join one of three secret cabals - the Illuminati, the Templars, or the Dragon, and work together to prevent the end of the world. The game's world is saturated with occult and philosophical references, often embedded in hundreds of cryptic texts scattered across the map. Solving these mysteries requires players to think outside the box, sometimes consulting real-world sources. Such examples include decoding morse code, analyzing the biographies of historical figures, or combining various technical details of fragmented information the game provides.

If this sounds appealing, there is just one important obstruction - the original game is now almost entirely abandoned. The developers ceased updates years ago, and only the newer iteration, *Secret World Legends,* remains barely officially operational. Curious about its current state, I revisited the original version (thought generally vastly superior in comparison to Secret World Legends), now inaccessible through official channels and only available via unofficial downloads. To my surprise, the servers still function. Yet the once-bustling world is now eerily silent, populated only by non-playable characters. Social hubs that once hosted hundreds of players are now empty. Though occasional system messages suggested that a few other players were online, I found no signs of life - no responses to messages, no sight of other avatars.

This desolation, however, enhances the game's esoteric atmosphere. According to my interlocutors, the emptiness transforms the game into a virtual echo of traditional occult secrecy. The game is now effectively inaccessible to newcomers - functioning servers exist, but new players cannot obtain a game-key necessary for joining the game. For the few who remain, *The Secret World* has become a digital temple: a quiet, mysterious space of forgotten knowledge, accessible only to those already inside. Its emptiness is thus not a failure but a feature. The haunting solitude, the obscured lore, and the absence of guidance replicate the experiential qualities of esoteric practice: solitude, mystery, and personal initiation. That's precisely why the game resonates so strongly on Chaos Magick forums and online communities - it has become more than a game. It is a sacred archive.

DIY Occultism and the Digital Mage

The rise of self-taught magical practitioners in the internet era cannot be separated from the visual and ludic languages of games. The large choice of various digital platforms has fostered decentralized and heavily aestheticized forms of occult instruction. For many players the first encounter with magical symbolism and practices is through games, such as Tarot in *Persona*, elemental magic in *Final Fantasy*, or Gnostic mechanics in *Dark Souls*. The appeal of these stimuli often transforms into online research, discussion, and eventually experiments with magical practice outside of the game world. Not to mention the possibilities of digital rituals that I already covered previously.

The democratization of magical knowledge was intensively profiting from this accessibility. Where previous generations of occultists relied on rare texts or secretive orders, modern practitioners often begin with wikis, livestreamed rituals, or curated aesthetics, subsequently freely sharing their results or ideas online, without any necessity for initiation or hierarchy. Games often act as the first encounter into a deeper magical study. Due to the narrative and aesthetical appeal, esoteric knowledge contained within is more easily digested for many, in contrast to the often menacing volumes of primary literature. Of course, one doesn't exclude the other, but many practitioners refer that prior to their game experience they didn't even knew that this or another practice exists.

This DIY occultism often embraces the postmodern pragmatism of Chaos Magick. Belief is treated as a tool as systems are borrowed, adapted, or invented. Players use screenshots as focal images for visualization, adapt spell creation systems from games like *Tyranny* or *Noita*, and even apply in-game calendars to organize real-world spell work. This syncretic practice reflects not only Chaos Magick's ethos but the broader logic of internet culture - to remix, iterate and personalize.

While these practices may lack the formal initiation rites or lineage of traditional occult paths, they foster real engagement. The experiential learning offered by games, where progress is tied to practice and exploration, aligns naturally with esoteric ideas of initiation, where knowledge is earned through symbolic labor and transformation. The result is an emerging generation of occultists for whom the esoteric knowledge hidden in online forums and video games complements the one hidden in books and teachings.

Democratization or Trivialization? Ethical and Philosophical Reflections

The gamification and digitalization of occult knowledge raises several questions about the ethics of accessibility and representation also in the community of esoteric practitioners. On one hand, games have opened up magical traditions to a wider and more diverse audience than ever before. They provide a safe, creative, and often beautifully designed space for exploring belief, archetype, and transformation.

On the other, critics of this pop cultural magic warn of the dangers of reductionism and sensationalism, where sacred symbols become aesthetic tropes stripped of context. According to some, the usage of sacred symbols in games like *Persona*, *Assassin's Creed: Valhalla*, or *Honkai Impact 3rd*, where Thelemic, Norse, or Kabbalistic elements are stripped of historical or spiritual depth, risks flattening established traditions into aesthetic tropes. This mirrors the concerns voiced in broader sociological and religious research on the commodification and simplification of religious practices, where they are transformed into a simplified, consumer-friendly version. This processes are known as McDonaldization (Ritzer, 2014) or McReligion (Špehar, 2010).

There's also the issue of epistemic confusion, as players sometimes mistake fictionalized magical systems for authentic ones. Hyperstitional games like *The Secret World*, which mix real and invented esoterica, blur the line between existing mythology and fictional narrative. Probably the most well known example is the iconic fictitious grimoire Necronomicon[19], invented by H. P. Lovecraft and first appearing in his short story The Hound (Lovecraft, 1924). Lovecraft repeatedly mentioned its fictitious nature, that he made the book up, as well as its presumed author, the mad Arab Abdul Allhazred (Louck, 2024). Despite that, the book started a life of its own, with occultists such as Kenneth Grant claiming validity of its content as well as Lovecraft's cosmology (Levenda, 2013).

From a philosophical perspective, these developments echo long-standing debates in esotericism itself. The tension between tradition and innovation, or exclusivity and inclusivity, has always been part of the magical discourse. The internet, and games still perceived mostly as shallow mediums of entertainment in particular, have simply made this tension more visible. The most revolutionary shift brought by Chaos Magick has rephrased the question of validity and tradition, to a question of functionality. For chaos magicians it was no longer important whether the practice was drawn from an established teaching, but rather if it works for the practitioner. Does the newly designed ritual create some meaning, invoke power, or achieve some transformation?

For many practitioners, the answer is a firm yes. Even if a magical practice originated in a video game, its impact on the practitioner's psyche or spiritual life can be extraordinary. This feedback loop, where digital spaces inspire real rituals, and real rituals inform digital creativity, suggests not a collapse of boundaries, but rather an evolution and reconfiguration of the sacred.

6. CONCLUSION: TOWARD A NEW PARADIGM OF THE DIGITAL OCCULT

The cultural landscape of the 21st century is undergoing a profound re-enchantment. One mediated not by institutional religion or traditional esotericism, but by networks, aesthetics, and digital spaces. Through the lens of this chapter, we have seen how video games, visual culture, and digital platforms have not only become vessels for occult representation but active spaces of ritual experimentation and knowledge sharing. The occult is no longer confined to exclusivity and wisdom locked behind initiation, but rather it can be found on computer screens and manifests itself in the digital architectures of everyday life. We are witnessing a shift in how spirituality is accessed, performed, as well understood - in a shift from oral tradition to visual simulation.

However, this transformation does not mark the death of the occult tradition but rather signals its adaptation to modern environment. What began as a trickle of aesthetic references in early fantasy games and films has become a full current of symbolic engagement. The architecture of video game worlds mirrors magical systems, offering players not only the passive consumption of mythic content but also an active mythic experience. From sigil-crafting mechanics and metaphysical progressions to gnostic horror and ceremonial gameplay loops, video games today provide immersive environments that simulate and inspire magical thinking. Players engage with these systems not passively, but performatively and immersive - becoming practitioners of magic in digital temples, enacting rituals of intention, transformation, and gnosis.

The practice of Chaos Magick, in particular, has proven to be a conceptual bridge between traditional magical philosophies and the fluid logic of digital culture. Rooted in subjectivity, personal efficacy, and the creative repurpose of symbolic material, Chaos Magick thrives in the liminal zones where fiction merges with reality. In many ways, it anticipates and underwrites the logic of contemporary digital magic. Its emphasis on belief as a tool, rather than as doctrine, allows for a novel engagement with occult symbols drawn from video games, memes, or procedurally generated interfaces. In the Chaos Magick worldview, the line between invoking Odin, or any other traditional deity and invoking Sephiroth (the character from Final Fantasy VII) is a question of affective investment and ritual purpose. Not to mention that many of the traditional deities have been reimagined through popular culture as well. The main theorem being, "if the symbol resonates, it is valid", or simplified, "if it works, it is real", regardless of whether it originated in a primary esoteric text or in a video game environment.

Importantly, this openness is not limited to individual practice. As we have explored, digital platforms have facilitated the emergence of entire online communities where magical knowledge is created, adapted, and distributed in real time. From Discord channels where digital rituals are coordinated to subreddits where users dissect video game symbolism for esoteric relevance, the occult has entered an era of sharing, liking and subscribing. As knowledge is no longer gatekept but virtually amplified, the magician is no longer a solitary adept but a participant in a digital ecosystem of shared signs and symbols.

On the other hand, this democratization brings with it ethical and epistemological tension. As symbols are decontextualized and aesthetics prioritized over doctrine, there are voices complaining about the risk of trivialization, as reflected in the discussions about "McReligion," and the seriousness of commodified spirituality. The challenge lies in balancing accessibility and experimentations, with depth and responsibility. Can a sigil generator app be trusted to convey the power of intention, or can ritual performed via Zoom carry the same impact as one performed in sacred space? These are not questions with easy answers and often differ from the varied perspectives of the practitioners. For the magician of the digital age, the key issue becomes not merely in choosing symbols, but in navigating the complicated terrains of authenticity, impact, and cultural context.

What is clear, however, is that the digital realm offers not just a stage for magical performance, but a new set of tools and logics that are themselves inherently magical. The principles of recursion, nonlinearity, symbolic interaction, and hidden meaning can be found in both game design and esoteric thought. Through these shared attributes, the interface can become a ritual diagram, a code a spell, or the avatar a hypersigil. Even the bugs and glitches, so often exploited by speedrunners, resonate with the idea of magical liminality, as moments where the system reveals its faults, and reality can be shifted and adapted.

Looking ahead, the future of digital occultism is poised for even more radical transformation. With the rise of virtual reality (VR), augmented reality (AR), and generative artificial intelligence, new paradigms of magical experience are already emerging. In VR spaces, rituals can be embodied with unprecedented sensory immersion. Already now there are VR games available that let the player experience what it's like to be a shaman (*DreadEye VR*, by Digital Happiness, 2017), a wizard (The *Wizards - Dark Times: Brotherhood*, by Carbon Studio, 2020) or experience an out of body experience (*Ayahuasca: Kosmik Journey*, by Mac Guff, 2020). In addition, the VRChat room *VR Mystery school* is a gathering hub for magic practitioners in virtual reality, equipped with a library on esoteric knowledge, interactive divination tables, or even a hermetic temple. AI, too, holds immense potential, as well as risk. Intelligent systems trained on magical texts could generate custom rituals, divine correspondence, or dream interpretations, blurring the line between magician and machine. The question regarding the authenticity of rituals would be even more pressing. Could a ritual generated and processed by AI be considered real? Who would be the magician in such a case – the person instructing the machine, or the machine itself?

As scholars, such questions require us to re-evaluate the boundaries between the sacred and the simulated, or the authentic and the constructed. The study of religion should now engage also with new categories, not just temple and scripture, but also server and screenshot. The old divisions between high and low culture, sacred and profane, initiated and uninitiated, are being reconfigured by networks of aesthetics, affect, and algorithmic flow. Game studies, likewise, should take seriously the spiritual dimensions of play, not only as metaphor or theme, but also as practice. To understand the modern occult, we must look not only to archives and fieldwork, but also to code, game engine, and online communities.

For practitioners, the digital occult invites a new kind of practice - one rooted in creativity, innovation, and aesthetic fluency. It requires not less seriousness, but more subtlety. Symbols are powerful, whether drawn from the Key of Solomon or a RPG spell book. But their power is shaped by the intention of the user and the ritual context in which they are deployed. To practice magic today is to engage with a symbolic system that is increasingly public, visual, participatory and often playful. It is to navigate between fictional, virtual and spiritual realities, in an attempt to find points of resonance and transformation.

Finally, what this new trend reveals is not a loss of the esoteric, but rather its transformation. In digital spaces, the occult is not diluted but diversified. It is fractured into a multiple individual paths where each one carries the possibility of meaningful magical engagement. We have to realize that video games and digital media have not trivialized the occult, but rather have made it playable, interactive, and emotionally impactful. They have returned magic to their oldest function - as a tool for shaping inner and outer worlds and providing other ways of existence. In a world saturated with simulation, magic survives, but not in spite of the digital, but through embracing it, using it for its own evolution. The sacred is no longer necessarily hidden behind the veil of secrecy. The screen itself has become both veil and revelation. What the digital occult loses in tradition, it gains in something radical - a magic that's alive in between the loading screens, waiting not for initiation, but for players willing to press X to cast the spell.

REFERENCES

Algeo, J. (1987). Theosophy and the Zeitgeist. *The American Theosophist*, *75*(10), 322–332.

Almqvist, K., & Belfrage, L. (2016). *Hilma af Klint: Seeing is Believing* (Almqvist, K., & Belfrage, L., Eds.). Koenig Books.

Asprem, E., & Granholm, K. (2013). *Contemporary Esotericism*. Equinox Publishing Ltd.

Baker, P. (2011). *Austin Osman Spare: The Life and Legend of London's Lost Artist*. Strange Attractor Press.

Blavatsky, H. P. (1877a). *Isis Unveiled - A Master Key To The Mysteries Of Ancient And Modern Science And Theology: Vol I: Science*. Bernard Quaritsch.

Blavatsky, H. P. (1877b). *Isis Unveiled - A Master Key To The Mysteries Of Ancient And Modern Science And Theology: Vol II: Theology*. Bernard Quaritsch.

Borkhardt, S. (2017). 7. 'Russian Messiah': On the Spiritual in the Reception of Vasily Kandinsky's Art in Germany, c. 1910–1937. In Hardiman, L., & Kozicharow, N. (Eds.), *Modernism and the Spiritual in Russian Art: New Perspectives* (pp. 149–164). Open Book Publishers.

Bruett, J. (2017). *Video Game Speedrunning As a Unique Form of Play*. Games by Arbitration. https://www.jaredbruett.com/2017/07/28/essay-video-game-speedrunning-as-a-unique-form-of-play/

Burroughs, W. S. (1993). *The Adding Machine: Collected Essays*. Arcade Publishing.

Byrd, M. (2022). *Why Morrowind's 36 Lessons of Vivec Is the Greatest Piece of Lore in RPG History*. Den of Geek. https://www.denofgeek.com/games/morrowind-36-lessons-of-vivec-history-explained-retrospective-theories-lore/

Campbell, B. F. (1980). *Ancient Wisdom Revived: A History of the Theosophical Movement*. University of California Press.

Carroll, P. J. (1987). *Liber Null & Psychonaut*. Weiser Book.

CCRU. (1999). *Abstract Culture Digital Hyperstition* (D. Barker (ed.)). Saddle stitch.

Chambers, R. W. (1895). *The King in Yellow*. F. Tennyson Neely.

Clarke, P. (2004). *Encyclopedia of New Religious Movements*. Routledge.

Clerbois, S. (2002). In Search of the Forme-Pensée: The Influence of Theosophy on Belgian Artists, Between Symbolism and the Avant-Garde (1890–1910) [A la recherche d'une forme-pensée. L'influence de la théosophie sur les artistes en Belgique, entre symbolisme et avant-garde. *Nineteenth-Century Art Worldwide, 1*(2), 1–24.

Crowley, A. (2022). *The Book of the Law, or Liber AL vel Legis*. Unicursal.

Cusack, C. (2011). Discordian Magic. *International Journal for the Study of New Religions, 2*(1), 125–145.

Dan, J. (2006). *Kabbalah: A Very Short Introduction*. Oxford University Press.

Davis, E. (2015). *High Weirdness: Visionary Experience in the Senventies Counterculture*. Rice University.

Drury, N. (2011). *Stealing Fire from Heaven. The Rise of Modern Western Magic*. Oxford University Press.

Duggan, C. (2014). Chaos magick. *The Occult World*, 406–411.

Engle, J. (2014). Cults of Lovecraft : The Impact of H. P. Lovecraft ' s Fiction on Contemporary Occult Practices. *Mythlore: A Journal of J.R.R. Tolkien, C.S. Lewis. Charles Williams, and Mythopoeic Literature, 33*(1), 85–98.

Fanelli, M., & Strobl, M. M. (2023). Unlocking the spiritual potential of games: Reflections and future directions. In L. Marcato & F. Schniz (Eds.), *Fictional Practices of Spirituality I: Interactive Media* (pp. 465–475). transcript Verlag.

Hanegraaf, W. J. (2006). *Dictionary of Gnosis & Western Esotericism* (Hanegraaf, W. J., Ed.). Brill.

Hanegraaff, W. (2013). *Western Esotericism: A Guide for the Perplexed*. Bloomsbury Press.

Harmless, W. (2008). *Mystics*. Oxford University Press.

Hine, P. (1995). *Condensed Chaos: An Introduction to Chaos Magic*. New Falcon Publications.

Jackson, K. (1992). *Higher peaks in view: The man who wrote Twin Peaks has plans to get weirder. Mark Frost talked to Kevin Jackson about Sherlock and warlocks*. The Independent. https://www.independent.co.uk/arts-entertainment/higher-peaks-in-view-the-man-who-wrote-twin-peaks-has-plans-to-get-weirder-mark-frost-talked-to-kevin-jackson-about-sherlock-and-warlocks-1541807.html

Joshi, S. T. (1989). *Afterword", History of the Necronomicon*. Necronomicon Press.

Jung, C. G. (1980). Psychology and Alchemy. In Ladner, G. B. (Ed.), *The Collected Works of C. G. Jung* (Vol. 12). Princeton University Press.

Kišoňová, R. (2013). *Cognitive Aesthetics*. FFTU.

Kremmerz, G. (2019). *The Hermetic Science of Transformation* (Picchi, F., & Rumsby, J., Trans.). Inner Traditions.

Kyunghee, K. (2016). Alchemic transformation of human creation. *Journal of Languages and Culture*, *7*(4), 46–53.

Levenda, P. (2013). *The Dark Lord: H.P. Lovecraft, Kenneth Grant, and the Typhonian Tradition in Magic Kindle Edition*. Ibis Press.

Louck, D. K. (2024). *Quotes Regarding the Necronomicon from Lovecraft's Letters*. H.P. Lovecraft Archive. https://www.hplovecraft.com/creation/necron/letters.aspx

Lovecraft, H. P. (1924). The Hound. *Weird Tales*, *3*(2), 50–52.

Makar, H. (2021). *Understanding Sigils, Hypersigils... and Even Meme Magick*. Magick.Me. https://blog.magick.me/2021/07/22/how-use-sigils-hypersigils-meme-magick/

McKechnie-Martin, C. T., Cunningham, A., Baumeister, J., & Von Itzstein, G. S. (2024). A Meta-Ethnography of Player Motivation in Digital Games: The 28 Dimensions of Play. *Games and Culture*.

MomJeans, S. O. (2016a). *Advanced Meme Magic (The Holy Books Of Kekism)*. CreateSpace Independent Publishing Platform.

MomJeans, S. O. (2016b). *Intermediate Meme Magic (The Holy Books Of Kekism)*. CreateSpace Independent Publishing Platform.

Moorcock, M. (1970). *The Eternal Champion*. Dell Books.

Morrison, G. (2003). Pop Magic! In Metzger, R., & Morrison, G. (Eds.), *The Book of Lies: The Disinformation Guide to Magick and the Occult* (pp. 16–25). The Desinformation Company.

Otto, B.-C. (2020). The Illuminates of Thanateros and the institutionalisation of religious individualisation. In Fuchs, M. (Ed.), *Religious Individualisation* (pp. 759–796). De Gruyter.

P-Orridge, G. B. (2010). *Thee Psychick Bible*. Feral House.

Partridge, C. (2004). *The Re-Enchantment of the West: Alternative Spiritualities, Sacralization, Popular Culture, and Occulture* (Vol. 1). T&T Clark International.

Partridge, C. (2005). *The Re-Enchantment of the West: Alternative Spiritualities, Sacralization, Popular Culture, and Occulture* (Vol. II). T&T Clark International.

Partridge, C. (2015). *The Occult World* (Partridge, C., Ed.). Routledge.

Partridge, C. (2018). *High Culture: Drugs, Mysticism & the Pursuit of Transcendence in the Modern World.* Oxford U.

Ritzer, G. (2014). *The McDonaldization of Society* (8th editio). SAGE Publications, Inc.

Rupcic, T. (2023). Techno-Religion and Cyberspace Spirituality in Dystopian Video Games. *Religions, 14*(2).

Seaborn, K., Iseya, S., Hidaka, S., Kobuki, S., & Chandra, S. (2024). Play Across Boundaries: Exploring Cross-Cultural Maldaimonic Game Experiences. *Conference on Human Factors in Computing Systems - Proceedings.*

Shaw, V. (2017). *Lemegeton: The Complete Books I-V: Ars Goetia, Ars Theurgia Goetia, Ars Paulina, Ars Almadel, Ars Notoria.* Erebus Society.

Singer, A., & Singer, L. (1995). *Divine Magick: the world of the supernatural.* Boxtree.

Spare, A. O. (1913). *The Book of Pleasure: The Psychology of Ecstasy.* I-H-O Books.

Špehar, H. (2010). McReligion, Contribution to the McDonaldization Theory in the Politology of Religion. *Politikologija Religije, 4*(1), 118–130.

Studios, B. G. (2011). *The Elder Scrolls V: Skyrim* (Microsoft Windows, PlayStation 3, Xbox 360, PlayStation 4, Xbox One, Nintendo Switch, PlayStation 5, Xbox Series X/S). Bethesda Softworks.

Studios, M. (2009). *Minecraft (Microsoft Windows).* Mojang Studios.

Suzuki, D. T. (1991). *An Introduction To Zen Buddhism.* Grove Press.

Tiaynen-Qadir, T., & Qadir, A. (2023). *Symbols and Myth-making in Modernity. Deep Culture in Art and Action.* Anthem Press.

Wallace, I. H. (1968). *Piet Mondrian: The Evolution of His Neo-Plastic Aesthetic 1908-1920.* University of British Columbia.

Weston, D., & Bennett, A. (2013). *Pop Pagans: Paganism and Popular Music* (D. Weston & A. Bennett (eds.)). Routledge.

Woodman, J. (2003). *Modernity, Selfhood, and the Demonic: Anthropological Perspectives on "Chaos Magick" in the United Kingdom.* Goldsmiths Collage, University of London.

Yao, S., & Kim, G. (2019). The Effects of Immersion in a Virtual Reality Game: Presence and Physical Activity. *Lecture Notes in Computer Science (Including Subseries Lecture Notes in Artificial Intelligence and Lecture Notes in Bioinformatics), 11595 LNCS*(April), 234–242.

KEY TERMS AND DEFINITIONS

Chaos Magick: a modern magical practice that emphasizes results over adherence to rigid systems or dogma. Experimental in nature, it is often described as do-it-yourself (DIY) magic.

Esotericism: a diverse range of spiritual, religious, and philosophical currents that emphasize hidden or inner knowledge, often transmitted through initiations and practices restricted to a select group.

Magic: a beliefs and practices involving the manipulation of supernatural forces or beings.

Ritual: a ceremony, consisting of a series of actions performed according to a prescribed order

Spirituality: a broad concept encompassing a person's sense of connection to something larger than themselves, often involving a search for meaning and purpose in life.

Video Game: an interactive entertainment platform, where the player is influencing, usually through the pressing of a dedicated button on a peripheral controller, the visual elements on the display.

Virtual Reality: is a simulated experience that employs 3D display technology (usually in the form of glasses or a helmet) and movement tracking to provide the user with an immersive feel of a virtual world.

ENDNOTES

1 As soulslike is described the subgenre of role playing video games, with very high difficulty and environmental storytelling, usually set in a dark, grim, and gloomy game world. This video game genre is named after the video games Demon Souls and the Dark Souls series by FromSoftware.

2 Blavatsky describes her ideas in her to most famous books, Isis Unveiled and The Secret Doctrine (Blavatsky, 1877a, 1877b).

3 Directed by Friedrich Wilhelm Murnau.

4 Directed by Benjamin Christensen.

5 Often written as Random Number Gesus, RNGesus, or simply RNG, referencing the process of random number generation. The origin of RNGesus is unclear, even though it was circulating several gaming communities already in 2009. His popularity started to spread in 2014, where his definition was added to Urban Dictionary, a crowdsourced online dictionary for slang words and phrases. Since then, he has become a popular meme for gamers trying to influence their luck in video games.

6 At the time of writing this text, hashtags #sigil and #sigilmagic have combined over 320,000 posts on Instagram.

7 The main idea being an association between the meme figure of Pepe the Frog and a Egyptian frog-headed god of primordial darkness named Kek.

8 Gnosticism is a term used by scholars to identify groups known as *gnostics* (from Greek, knowers). These groups shared a mythology, that distinguished God from an imperfect creator-being (the Demuirge), identifies a divine essence within humans and understands *knowledge* (gnosis) of God and human's divine origins as the only way of salvation (Partridge, 2015, p. 25).

9 Vivec, or Lord Vivec the Warrior-Poet is one of the three immortal god-kings within the cosmological lore of Morrowind. He is worshipped as a symbol of mastery and duality. The Thirty-Six Lessons of Vivec are a series of 36 books the players can find within the game, presumably written by Vivec himself. Each volume is usually described as a Sermon, dealing with various issues from religious questions to moral lessons. They are intentionally written in a rather cryptic and symbolic way.

10 Hyperstition, a term coined by the English philosopher Nick Land, describing a cultural belief, especially in the work of fiction, that makes itself real, through bringing into reality the thing it describes (CCRU, 1999, p. 39).

11 The act of playing a video game, or a section of a video game as fast as possible, often exploiting technical issues or design flows to achieve the shortest time possible. The process of achieving a successful speedrun if the result of endless, almost devotional repetitions, trials and errors and experiments within the gameplay.

12 Maldaimonic game experiences are interactions, where the player engage in personally fulfilling gameplay through egocentric, malicious, destructive, and/or exploitative acts (Seaborn et al., 2024, p. 1).

13 It was recently confirmed by the production company, that the stories of both Alan Wake games actually take place within the larger universe of Control, and thus the games are directly connected.

14 Ars Goetia is one of the five books of The Lesser Key of Solomon, also known by its Latin title Lemegeton Clavicula Salomonis, an anonymous 17th century grimoire on sorcery and magic. Ars Goetia contains the seals and descriptions of the 72 demonic spirits, divided into multiple infernal hierarchies (Shaw, 2017).

15 The subreddit dedicated to the investigation of this mystery has over 47000 members, and hundreds of posts trying to deduce the meaning through various ways, from mathematics, binary code programming, to astrology and chakras.

16 While occult rituals conducted in virtual reality are still an extremely marginal case, several pioneers of digital occultism have already noticed the potential of this technology. As such, we can find examples of rituals that previously relied on imagination, such as the cleansing Lesser ritual of the pentagram (or LRP), being carried out in virtual reality with the help of artistic application, such as Tilt Brush – an application for VR painting.

17 A term coined by Genesis P-Orridge and later introduced into academia by Christoper Partridge, combining the words occult, and culture. Instead of the previously hidden and secretive occult, according to Partridge, occulture is common, public and noticeable, through various artistic, as well as pop-cultural phenomena (Partridge, 2004, p. 68).

18 An interesting example is from a gamer who reports, that when he plays games from the tactical shooter series *Tom Clancy's Rainbow Six,* during the process of reinforcing walls within the game world, he imagines he is reinforcing a belief he wants to have. At the same time, when he's eliminating an enemy, he is imagining eliminating an excuse that is preventing him to achieving said beliefs.

19 The inspiration behind the book is unclear. Some sources claim that he appeared to Lovecraft in a dream (Louck, 2024), or that he was inspired by Robert Chambers book The King in Yellow (Chambers, 1895). Lovecraft himself claimed that an old dusty grimoire is a common item in gothic literature (Joshi, 1989)

Chapter 11
Exploring Video Game Monetization:
Analysis of Strategies, Trends, and Ethical Implications

Tatiana Ferreira
Instituto Politécnico de Bragança, Portugal

Tiago Lopes
Instituto Politécnico de Bragança, Portugal

Tatiana Batista
Instituto Politécnico de Bragança, Portugal

João Vitorino
Instituto Politécnico de Bragança, Portugal

Pedro Malheiro
Instituto Politécnico de Bragança, Portugal

João Paulo Sousa
https://orcid.org/0000-0002-9005-084X
CeDRI, SusTEC, Instituto Politécnico de Bragança, Portugal

ABSTRACT

This study offers a comprehensive mapping of the scientific literature on video game monetization, addressing a significant gap in the systematic exploration of this multidimensional topic. Drawing on data from the Scopus database and analytical tools, the research highlights key themes, influential authors, and emerging trends shaping the field. The analysis reveals distinct waves of scholarly interest, correlating with industry innovations like freemium models and battle passes, and highlights the interdisciplinary nature of the field. Co-citation and bibliographic coupling analyses uncover robust intellectual and social networks, with prominent contributors advancing knowledge on monetization's ethical, psychological, and

DOI: 10.4018/979-8-3373-6970-9.ch011

© 2026, IGI Global Scientific Publishing. Copying or distributing in print or electronic forms without written permission of IGI Global Scientific Publishing is prohibited. Use of this chapter to generative artificial intelligence (AI) technologies is expressly prohibited. The publisher reserves all rights to license its use for generative AI training and machine learning model development.

economic dimensions. Furthermore, the study explores the implications of monetization practices on player retention, engagement, and satisfaction, underscoring the balance between profitability and ethical considerations.

INTRODUCTION

Video games have solidified their position as a global phenomenon, shaping cultural, social, and economic landscapes worldwide. With a staggering player base of 3.182 to 3.381 billion individuals between 2021 and 2023 (Newzoo, 2023), gaming has become the most profitable segment of the creative industries, outpacing traditional forms of entertainment like film and music. This transmedia expansion, where franchises extend into movies, TV shows, and merchandise, highlights the sector's financial impact and cultural influence.

The global video game market continues to experience robust growth. Asia-Pacific dominates as the leading region, accounting for 53% of the market, driven by economic and cultural factors, particularly in countries like China, India, Japan, and South Korea. Mobile gaming leads this expansion due to the popularity of free-to-play models, affordability, and accessibility of mobile devices. Projections indicate sustained growth until 2026, even as the post-pandemic stabilization phase begins. While North America comprises only 7% of the global player base, it generates significant revenue by focusing on developing games for international markets (Newzoo, 2023).

In this competitive landscape, monetization has become a cornerstone of game design and business strategies. Initially reliant on single-purchase premium models, the industry has diversified its approaches to include subscriptions, microtransactions, freemium models, in-game advertising, and hybrid models such as battle passes. These frameworks generate revenue and influence player retention, engagement, and satisfaction. Hamari et al. (Hamari et al., 2020) and Leahy (Leahy, 2022) note that while lucrative, specific practices, such as microtransactions and loot boxes, raise concerns regarding fairness, consumer manipulation, and potential gambling parallels. Balancing profitability with ethical considerations remains a pressing challenge for the industry.

This study also takes a critical stance in exploring the challenges and opportunities associated with monetization practices, including player perceptions, the impact of these strategies on user retention, and potential solutions to balance economic sustainability with consumer satisfaction (Drummond & Sauer, 2018; King & Delfabbro, 2018b). The analysis of the results will provide insights into video game monetization's state of the art and identify gaps and potential directions for future research.

The structure of this work is organized as follows: the next section presents a literature review about game monetization. The third section presents the methodology used for data collection and analysis; the fourth section discusses the results and identifies trends; finally, the last section critically reflects on the main findings, their implications, and recommendations for future investigations.

Following the above considerations, this study presents a structured mapping of scientific publications on game monetization. Given the multidimensional nature of the topic, the following research questions were formulated to guide the investigation:

1. What is the current state of knowledge on monetization strategies in the gaming industry?
2. How do publication and citation metrics differ across research domains related to game monetization, and what do these metrics reveal about the field's scholarly impact and research productivity?
3. What are the intellectual and social structures of game monetization research, as revealed through co-citation analysis, bibliographic coupling, and co-authorship networks?
4. What are the main trends and future developments in gain-game monetization models?
5. How do monetization strategies affect player retention, engagement, and satisfaction?

By mapping the scientific literature, this study aims to trace the evolution of research on game monetization, highlight influential works, and identify opportunities to balance profitability with ethical practices. The findings will provide critical insights into the interplay between business strategies and player experiences in this rapidly evolving field.

LITERATURE REVIEW

The world of video game monetization has significantly changed, evolving from a simple retail model to a complex ecosystem with various strategies. Early video games relied on direct sales, where consumers purchased a physical copy of the game and had complete access to its content (Egenfeldt-Nielsen et al., 2008). However, the digital distribution revolution and the rise of online gaming have paved the way for new monetization methods, including subscriptions, microtransactions, and advertising (Zackariasson & Wilson, 2010). This shift has enabled developers to generate ongoing revenue streams, fostering continuous content updates and community engagement (Wanick & Mataruna, 2021). Furthermore, the advent of free-to-play games has significantly altered the dynamics of the industry, attracting a broader audience while relying on in-game purchases for monetization (Flunger et al., 2017). The freemium model, in particular, has gained considerable traction, offering a basic version of the game for free while incentivizing players to spend money on premium features or content (Zackariasson & Wilson, 2012).

A thorough understanding of a game's economy requires the careful integration of marketing strategies, gameplay mechanics, and monetization principles (Asadi & Hemadi, 2018). Game designers must navigate the interplay between these elements to create engaging yet financially sustainable experiences. This challenge becomes even more pronounced when balancing artistic vision with commercial demands, particularly for independent developers who often operate with limited resources (Styhre & Wikhamn, 2019). Unlike large studios with established revenue streams, indie developers face the dual pressure of preserving creative integrity while ensuring their projects remain economically viable. Consequently, the fusion of design innovation and business strategy remains critical in modern game development.

Existing literature categorizes monetization approaches in several ways. According to Alha et al. (2018), these models include:

- **Premium** is the most traditional model, where players acquire the full game for a fixed price, often associated with premium experiences without additional costs.
- **Subscriptions**, such as Xbox Game Pass or PlayStation Plus, grant continuous access to a library of games through recurring payments, providing companies with a stable revenue stream (Hamari & Keronen, 2017).
- **Microtransactions** involve purchasing in-game items, which can be cosmetic or functional, representing one of the most lucrative yet controversial approaches (King & Delfabbro, 2018b).
- **Freemium** removes entry barriers, making the game accessible to any user while monetizing through optional purchases or advertising, encouraging prolonged engagement and purchases driven by convenience or exclusivity (Hamari et al., 2020).
- **In-game advertising** generates revenue by integrating ads, either passively (e.g., billboards within the game) or actively (e.g., mandatory video ads for progression), commonly used in large-scale mobile games (Lehdonvirta, 2009).

In addition to these primary strategies, other forms of monetization such as DLCs (Downloadable Content), Paywalls, Loot Boxes and Gacha Games have also risen in prominence (Zaucha & Agur, 2023).

Downloadable content (DLC) has become one of the most prevalent monetization strategy in the gaming industry, moving away from traditional pay-for-product models to more complex systems (Janoščík, 2023). The monetization of games through DLC and other in-game purchases has significant economic implications. It transforms games into platforms for continuous revenue generation rather than one-time purchases (Rutz et al., 2019). DLCs offer additional content post-launch, extending the life of the game and maintaining player interest. At the same time, Paywalls restrict access to certain features or levels, requiring payment for full gameplay experiences. This model is particularly evident in free-to-play games, where microtransactions are the primary revenue source (Majander, 2019; Petrovskaya & Zendle, 2022; Stokes, 2024).

Loot boxes, which have garnered considerable controversy, allow players to purchase random rewards, often drawing comparisons to gambling (Spicer et al., 2022). Loot boxes, as ubiquitous monetization mechanisms in digital games, have attracted the attention of various academic disciplines and the industry. Instead of a simple summary, this literature review highlights the different lenses through which loot boxes have been analyzed. Initially, the perspective of behavioral psychology dominated the discussion, focusing on how the random elements and intermittent rewards of loot boxes align with principles of operant conditioning, potentially leading to repetitive and, in some cases, problematic seeking behaviors exemplified in the works of (Caffarone, 2023; D'Amico, 2021; Kuklenko, 2024; Zendle & Cairns, 2018a).

Subsequently, the ethical and legal viewpoint gained prominence. Researchers and legislators began to question whether the mechanics of loot boxes sufficiently resemble gambling to warrant regulation, especially concerning the protection of minors and vulnerable individuals, as argued by (Drummond & Sauer, 2018; D. L. King & Delfabbro, 2018a). This debate raises fundamental questions about the responsibility of the gaming industry and the need for transparency and control.

In parallel, industry analysis offers a pragmatic view, examining loot boxes as a tool for revenue generation and player engagement (Li, 2022; Xiao, 2021). This perspective weighs the economic benefits for developers against the potential for alienating the player base and damaging the game's reputation. The tension between profit maximization and maintaining a healthy player community is a central theme in this analysis.

Far from being a mere monetization mechanism, loot boxes serve as a point of convergence for discussions about behavioral psychology, ethics in game design, regulation, and the business models of the digital entertainment industry. The continuous evolution of this topic demands an interdisciplinary approach to understand its implications and fully shape its future in gaming.

More recently, hybrid models, such as the Battle Pass have emerged, which combines subscriptions with microtransactions and incentivizes players to complete in-game objectives to unlock exclusive rewards (Petrovskaya & Zendle, 2020). This diversification has brought challenges, particularly concerning the balance between maximizing revenue and maintaining an ethically fair player experience. Exploring these taxonomies provides a deeper understanding of how different strategies influence player relationships with games and shape perceptions of value and fairness in the current industry landscape.

More recently, hybrid monetization models, such as the increasingly popular *Battle Pass* system, have emerged as a dominant strategy in the video game industry. These models effectively combine elements of traditional subscriptions with à la carte microtransactions, creating a dynamic revenue stream while simultaneously enhancing player engagement (Hadan et al., 2024). The Battle Pass, in particular, incentivizes players to complete specific in-game objectives, such as completing daily challenges or reaching certain progression milestones, in exchange for exclusive cosmetic items, character upgrades, or other premium rewards. This approach not only fosters long-term player retention but also capitalizes on psychological motivators such as the *fear of missing out* (FOMO) and the satisfaction derived from achievement-based unlocks (Hamari & Alha, 2019).

More recently, hybrid monetization models, such as the increasingly popular *Battle Pass* system, have emerged as a dominant strategy in the video game industry. These models effectively combine elements of traditional subscriptions with à la carte microtransactions, creating a dynamic revenue stream while simultaneously enhancing player engagement (Petrovskaya & Zendle, 2020). The Battle Pass, in particular, incentivizes players to complete specific in-game objectives, such as completing daily challenges or reaching certain progression milestones, in exchange for exclusive cosmetic items, character upgrades, or other premium rewards. This approach not only fosters long-term player retention but also capitalizes on psychological motivators such as the *fear of missing out* (FOMO) and the satisfaction derived from achievement-based unlocks (Hamari & Alha, 2019).

However, this diversification in monetization strategies has introduced significant challenges for developers and publishers, particularly concerning the ethical implications of such systems. One major issue is the delicate balance between maximizing revenue—often driven by aggressive monetization tactics—and maintaining a fair, non-exploitative player experience. Critics argue that some implementations of the Battle Pass model may border on *predatory design*, where players feel pressured to spend money to keep up with time-limited content or risk falling behind their peers (Fredriksson Friman & Zätterlund, 2023; Kuklenko, 2024b). Additionally, concerns have been raised regarding *pay-to-win* mechanics in certain hybrid models, where premium rewards provide competitive advantages, thus undermining game balance and fairness (Ross & Nieborg, 2021).

Exploring these taxonomies of monetization is crucial for understanding how different strategies shape player behavior, influence perceptions of value, and redefine notions of fairness in digital gaming ecosystems. For instance, while some players may perceive Battle Passes as a fair exchange of effort for rewards, others may view them as manipulative or overly commercialized. Furthermore, the rise of these hybrid models reflects broader industry trends toward *live-service gaming*, where continuous content updates and seasonal monetization cycles dominate (Stanković, 2024). By critically analyzing these frameworks, researchers can gain deeper insights into the evolving relationship between players and games and the socio-economic implications of modern monetization practices in the digital entertainment landscape.

The growing phenomenon of gacha games in mobile gaming has attracted significant attention and concern from researchers and regulators alike. These games, which often involve the collection of virtual items through a randomized "gacha" system, have been likened to gambling due to their ability to trigger addictive behaviors and significant financial investments from players (King et al., 2015). One key factor contributing to the addictive nature of gacha games is the element of chance and the thrill of potentially obtaining rare or highly coveted virtual items (Woods, 2024). This uncertainty, combined with the visual and auditory cues accompanying successful "pulls" in the gacha system, can activate the brain's reward pathways and foster a sense of excitement and anticipation. The free-to-play nature of many gacha games, coupled with the opportunities for in-game microtransactions, can lead to impulsive spending and the blurring of the line between gaming and gambling. The psychological and financial aspects of gacha games have been the subject of extensive research, as scholars strive to unravel the underlying mechanisms that drive player engagement and the potential risks associated with these monetization models (Gong et al., 2025; Ross & Nieborg, 2021; Shibuya et al., 2019). Researchers have found that players who engage in higher levels of spending in these games are more likely to exhibit symptoms of gaming disorder, underscoring the potential for these monetization strategies to have detrimental effects on player well-being (Costes & Bonnaire, 2022).

Despite the growing academic output on video game monetization, there are still significant gaps in studies that systematically map the key themes, leading authors, and emerging trends in this field. Previous research highlights the value of structured literature mapping to understand publication patterns, influential contributors, and the thematic evolution over (Davidovici-Nora, 2014; Zendle & Cairns, 2018b).

MATERIALS AND METHODS

Data Collection and Preparation

Peer-reviewed articles and reviews were selected from the Scopus database to ensure high-quality and relevant sources. The search included all publications up to the present and covered document types such as journal articles, conference papers, conference reviews, book chapters, and reviews. Books and retracted papers were excluded to maintain the integrity and relevance of the dataset, and the language was restricted to English. The search query was designed to capture literature relevant to video game business models and monetization strategies. The final query string used for data collection was as follows:

((business AND model) AND (video AND games)) OR (freemium AND free-to-play) AND (LIMIT-TO (LANGUAGE, "ENGLISH"))

This query targeted publications discussing the business models and monetization strategies of video games, with a focus on freemium and free-to-play models. As a result, 339 documents were retrieved. These records were exported in BibTeX format and imported into Biblioshiny, a graphical interface for the Bibliometrix package (R version 4.4.2), for further literature mapping and analysis. The metadata extracted included citation counts, bibliographic information, abstracts, keywords, and other relevant fields for an in-depth examination.

Methods

The analysis was conducted using the Bibliometrix R-package, which provides a comprehensive set of tools for analyzing bibliographic data (Aria & Cuccurullo, 2017). This software enabled the analysis of scientific production, citation networks, and thematic trends in the literature on video game monetization. Key visualizations, such as keyword co-occurrence networks, citation maps, and thematic evolution graphs, were generated to identify the most influential studies and emerging research areas.

These methods were selected to explore the research field's structural and thematic aspects. Citation networks helped identify the most influential works, while thematic evolution graphs allowed us to observe changes in research focus over time. Combining these methods provided a detailed understanding of video game monetization literature's intellectual structure and conceptual trends.

RESULTS

Table 1 presents key data collected from the Scopus database on 6 November 2024. A total of 339 publications from 1984 to 2024 were retrieved, including 131 journal articles and 167 conference papers. The analysis identified 725 authors and 82.3% of the documents were written by multiple authors.

Table 1. Primary search information

Description	Results
Total of Publications	339
Journal Articles	131
Conference Articles	167
Period	1984-2024
Query Date	6-11-2024
Number of Identified Authors	725
Documents with Multiple Authors	2.46
Single Author Documents	60
Sources (Journals, Books, etc)	260
Countries	54

The results obtained through Bibliometrix and the Scopus platform were organized into topics and subtopics, namely: Overview (annual scientific production and average citations per year), Sources (most relevant sources and production over time), Authors (most relevant authors, author production over time, most relevant affiliations, author countries, scientific production by country, and most cited countries), Documents (most cited documents, most frequent keywords, word cloud, and trend topics), Conceptual Structure (co-occurrence network and thematic map), and Social Structure (collaboration between countries).

Overview

Figure 1 presents the representation of two different metrics: annual scientific production (a) and the average number of citations (b), also on a yearly basis. From the visualization of the graph, it is evident that scientific production (a) began around 1984, grew steadily until 2000, and then became a less prominent subject, as indicated by the lack of publications during that period. However, starting in 2002, interest in the topic grew significantly, nearly doubling over the following five years. There was a notable dip in 2006, followed by an increase, leading to the second peak of growth in 2008.

From 2010 to 2016, production remained stable and consistent, fluctuating between 10 and 20 published works annually. In 2018, a new production peak was observed, followed by a decline and then a sharp rise again in 2022. From 2022 to the time of the study, a new drop-in publication output on this topic was noted. Overall, the graph indicates three distinct periods of peak interest and publication on this subject between 1984 and 2024: 1984 to 1999, 2002 to 2008, and 2017 to 2023.

Regarding the number of citations (b), the analysis of the graph line clearly shows that the most relevant and outstanding years of publication are those between 1998 and 2000, and 2005 to 2009. Articles published in 2006 stand out as the most cited to date.

Figure 1. (a) Annual Scientific Production and (b) Average Citations per Year

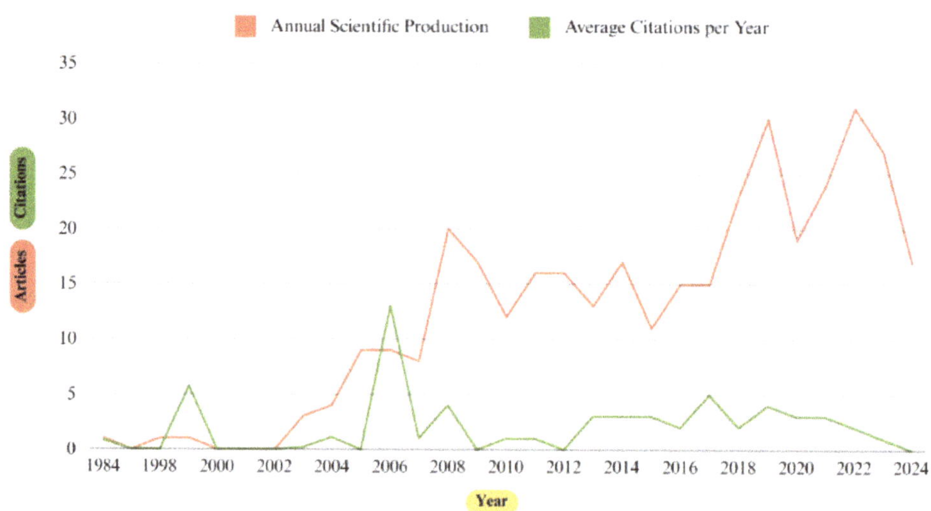

Sources

In Figure 2, the most relevant sources are represented, along with the number of publications over the years. It is noteworthy that these sources became more prominent after 2007. However, despite beginning in a later period, *Lecture Notes in Computer Science* stands out from the rest, having published a total of 16 articles to date. It is followed by the *ACM International Conference Proceeding Series* with a total of 10 articles, *Multimedia Tools and Applications* with 7, and the *18th Americas Conference on Information Systems 2012 (AMCIS 2012)* with 6. Meanwhile, the

Journal of Gambling Studies, Lecture Notes in Business Information Processing, Lecture Notes in Network and Systems, and *Proceedings of the European Conference on Games-Based Learning* each have a total of 5 articles.

Figure 2. Most Relevant Sources and Their Production Over Time

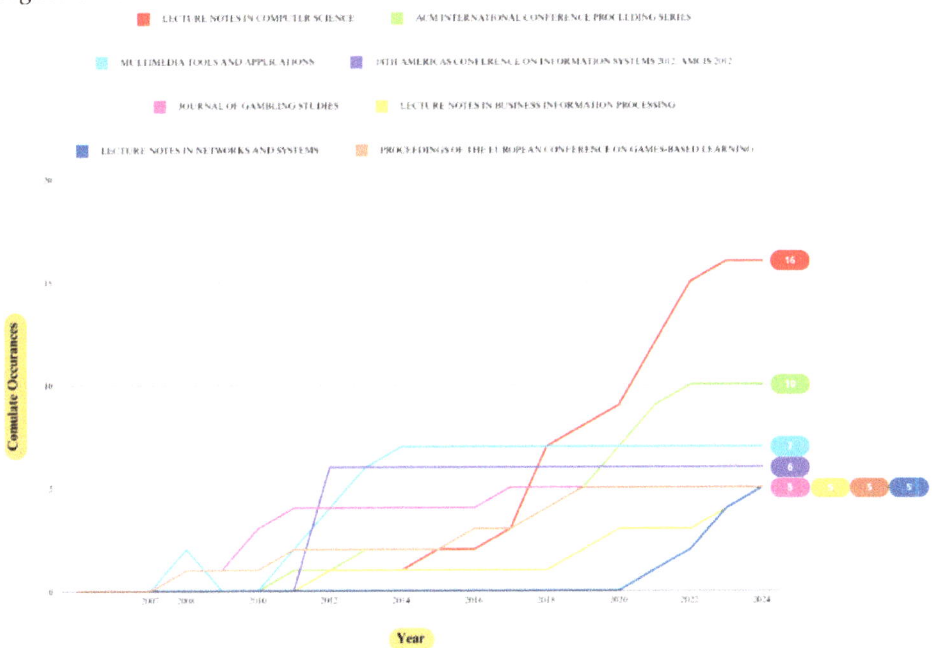

Authors

The analyzed documents are authored by 725 different researchers, with an average of 0.467 documents per author. Most of these authors, 595 (82.1%), produced co-authored documents, while 130 (17.9%) produced their work individually. A total of 60 (8.2%) documents were authored by a single individual.

Figure 3 highlights the 10 most relevant authors based on the number of documents produced and their year of publication. The leading author is Hamari, J., with 8 documents: 1 in 2015, 3 in 2017, 2 in 2019, and 2 in 2020. Other prolific authors include Drachen, A. (1 document each in 2014, 2015, and 2017); Koivisto, J. (2 in 2017 and 1 in 2020); King, D.L. (1 each in 2013, 2017, and 2020); Fitton, D. (1 in 2019, 1 in 2023, and 1 in 2024); Hanner, N. (1 in 2014, 2017, and 2020); Adachi, P.J.C. (2 in 2013); Alha, K. (1 in 2017 and 2019); and Baber, W.W. (1 in 2019 and 1 in 2022).

Figure 3. Most Relevant Authors and Their Production Over Time

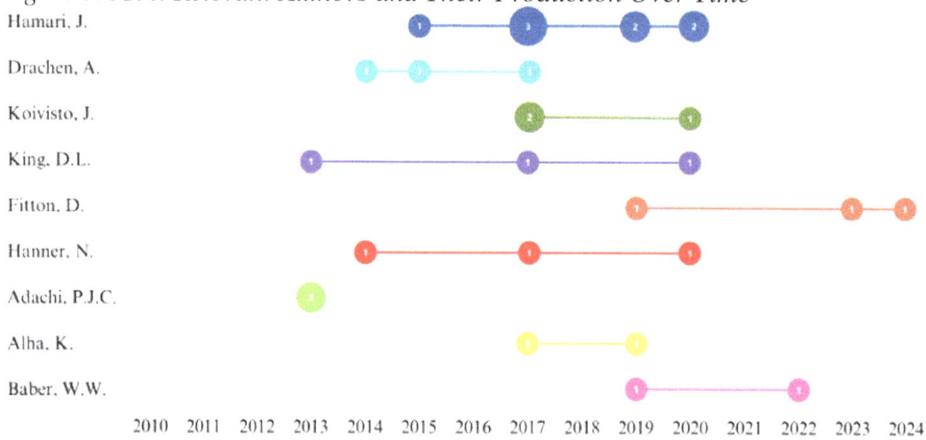

Among all articles collected using the query, Figure 4 (Figure 4) presents a graph of the most relevant affiliations by the number of associated articles. The University of Tampere leads with 12 affiliations, followed by Turun Yliopisto with 6. The University of Vienna ranks third with 5 affiliations. Other affiliations include groups with 4 (University of Adelaide, Technische University of Berlin, and Aalto University) and 3 (Nanyang Technological University, University of Texas at Dallas, Stanford University, and University of York).

Figure 4. Most Relevant Affiliations

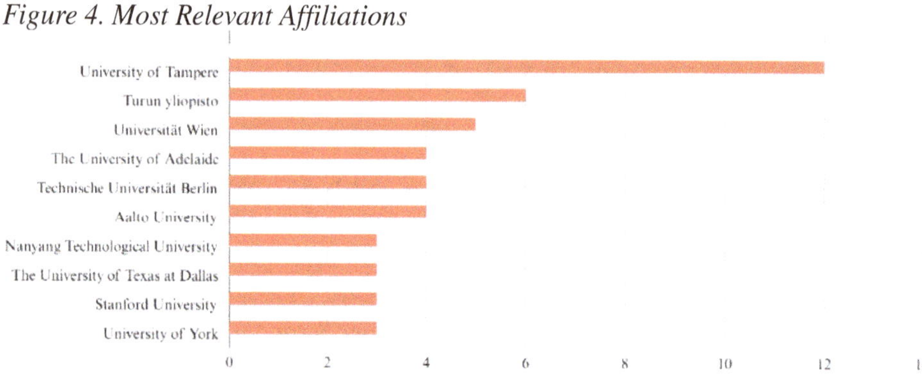

Figure 5 represents the number of documents authored by individuals from the same country versus those from different countries. For international collaborations, Finland and the UK top the list with 7 documents each, followed by the USA (6), China (4), Germany (3), South Korea (2), and 1 document each from Canada, Australia, Japan, Indonesia, Austria, Brazil, and Colombia. Countries like India, France, Italy, Spain, Portugal, Belgium, and Croatia had no cross-national publications.

For single-country authorships, the USA leads with 22 documents, followed by Canada (12), China (10), India (9), Finland and the UK (8 each), South Korea (6), Germany, France, Italy, and Spain (5 each), and others with fewer contributions.

Figure 5. Authors' Countries of Origin

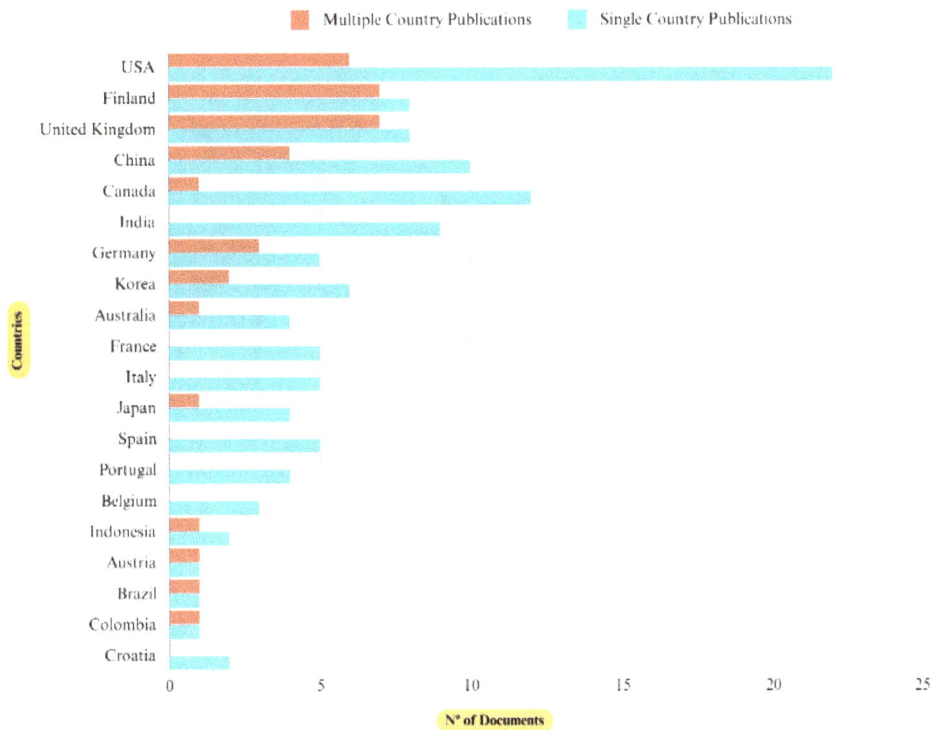

Figure 6 depicts a world map with varying shades of blue to indicate scientific output by country. Lighter shades signify lower production, while gray represents no output. Major contributors include the USA, Finland, the UK, and China. This map complements Figure 5, providing a deeper insight into document production by country.

Figure 6. Scientific Production by Country

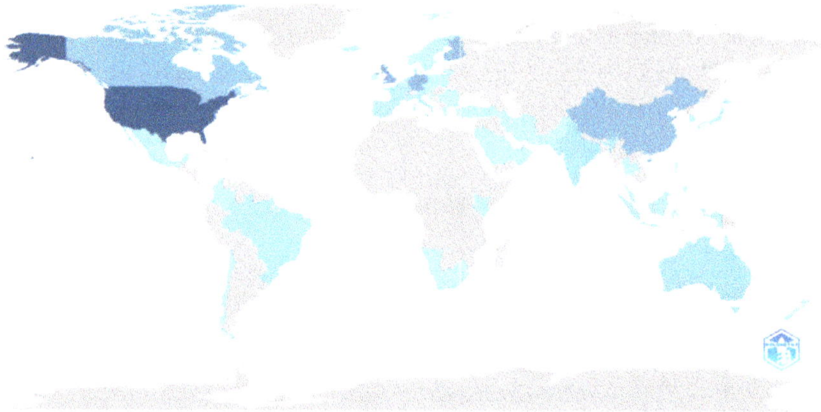

Similarly, regarding both the authors' nationalities and the scientific production by country, in the case of the most cited countries, the USA remains in first place with a total of 4,214 citations, as shown in the graph in Figure 7. This is followed by countries such as Georgia with 1,048 citations, Finland with 989, Canada with 418, the United Kingdom with 305, Hong Kong with 261, Germany with 225, Korea with 203, Saudi Arabia with 168, and finally, Australia with a total of 154 citations for their published scientific works.

Figure 7. Most Cited Countries

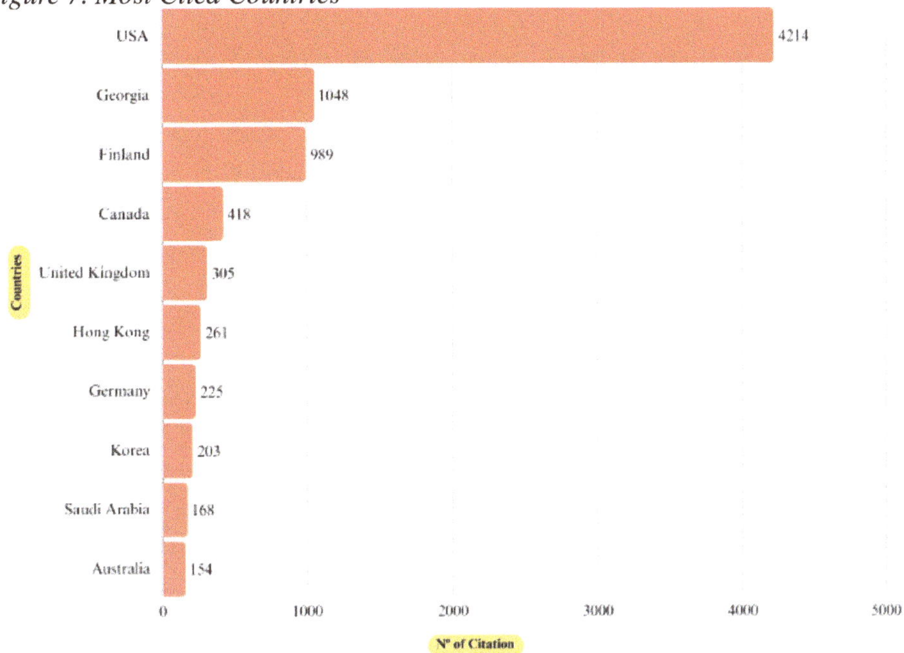

Documents

Table 2 shows the ten most cited documents within the subject in question, where the total number of citations represents the total number of times a given article has been cited from the beginning until the date of the research conducted.

One of the most cited and mentioned publications is by Ryan et al. (2006), with 2,229 citations. This publication applies Self-Determination Theory (SDT) to investigate motivation in digital gaming and its impact on well-being. The first three studies reveal that the perception of autonomy and competence during gameplay is associated with enjoyment, preferences, and well-being changes, influenced by the intuitiveness of the controls and immersion. The fourth study (LAM LT, 2014), with multiplayer players, confirms that autonomy, competence, and social relationships predict enjoyment and the intention to continue playing. The analysis compares SDT with Yee's motivational taxonomy, highlighting human motivation in virtual worlds.

In second place is the work by (Parker & Van Alstyne, 2005) (2005), with a total of 1,094 citations, where this paper explores how companies can profit by offering products for free through a formal model based on bilateral network externalities, integrating Katz and Shapiro's network effects, price discrimination, and product differentiation. The model demonstrates that even without competition, it is rational to invest in free products; both content providers and end consumers can be recipients of these products; the coupling of products between markets can simultaneously increase consumer well-being and business profits.

In third place in the table is Hertzog's (2008) work, which has a total of 1,048 citations and mentions, where his work reflects on whether intellectual, physical, and social activities produce cognitive enrichment effects throughout adult life, with an emphasis on old age, advocating for cognitive plasticity. The review of longitudinal studies and interventions shows that active lifestyles, including cognitive training and physical exercise, are associated with better maintenance of cognitive functions and a reduced risk of decline. Social and political implications are also explored, proposing interventions for promoting cognitive health and discussing the validity of commercial products aimed at cognitive aging.

In fourth place is the work of Lam (2014), which has a substantial drop in citations, with a total of 261 citations at the time of the research. This work presents a model to explain the relationship between online gaming addiction and depression. The systematic review included seven studies, three focusing on gaming addiction, especially MMORPGs, and four on problematic Internet use and sleep disorders. The results suggest that problematic Internet use is associated with sleep problems and that online gaming addiction may contribute to lower sleep quality, potentially influencing the mental health of young people.

Fifth in the citation ranking is the work by Postigo H. (2016), with a total of 204 citations, in his paper on the concept of "digital work architectures," using the case of game commentators and related research, highlighting the intersection between social practices and technological platforms that transform leisure activities into commercial work. This study analyzes how YouTube's functionalities shape user practices to benefit its business model.

The remaining papers have, in order, the following total citations: 187, 186, 184, 183, and 166.

Table 2. Most Global Cited Documents

Paper	Total Citations
RYAN RM, 2006, MOTIV EMOT (Ryan et al., 2006)	2229
PARKER GG, 2005, MANAGE SCI (Parker & Van Alstyne, 2005)	1094
HERTZOG, 2008, PSYCHOL SCI PUBL INTEREST SUPPL (Hertzog et al., 2008)	1048
LAM LT, 2014, CURR PSYCHIATRY REP (Lam, 2014)	261
POSTIGO H., 2016, NEW MEDIA AND SOCIETY (Postigo, 2016)	204

continued on following page

Table 2. Continued

Paper	Total Citations
ADACHI PJC, 2013, J YOUTH ADOLESC (Adachi & Willoughby, 2013)	187
KWON JH, 2011, COMMUNITY MENT HEALTH J (Kwon et al., 2011)	186
HAMARI J, 2015, INT J INF MANAGE (Hamari, 2015)	184
NAIR H., 2007, QUANT MARK ECON (Nair, 2007)	183
HAMARI J, 2017, COMPUT HUM BEHAV-a 10.10	166

To analyze the most cited words, it is necessary to do so with rigor and criteria, as some synonyms or terms encompass others. As can be seen in Figure 8, the term "video games" appears in different forms, without a hyphen in the 4th line of the graph and with a hyphen in the 9th line. Thus, when conducting a correct analysis, the term "video game" would account for a total of 54 occurrences by summing the variants. Another example is lines 6 with the term "business models", 8 with "freemium", and 10 with "free to play". In other words, the latter two terms are part of the first term, as they are monetization models, in this case, associated with games, which in turn are part of business models for a company. In total, they account for 71 occurrences, surpassing the term that, according to the graph, ranks first with 66 citations for "Human-Computer Interaction".

Figure 8. Most Frequent Words

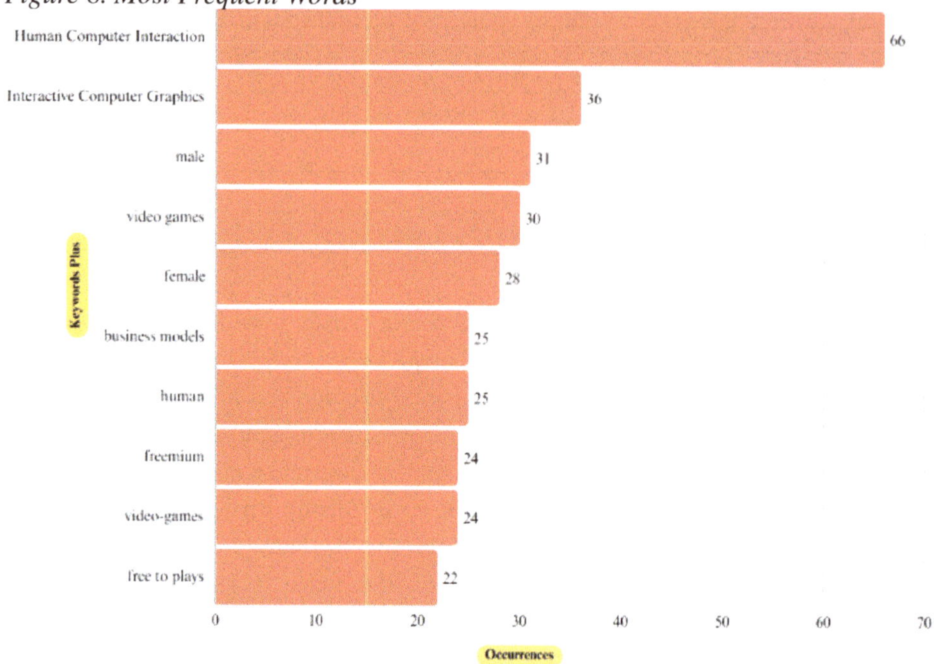

Figure 9 is a word cloud that visually complements the graph above (Figure 8), where we can get a better sense of the volume that the terms have in the published papers. In other words, the larger the font size, the greater the number of occurrences.

Figure 9. Word Cloud

By distinguishing between synonyms and topics, it becomes easier to perceive how words and topics have evolved over the years and when they were more prominent. Figure 10 is a graph that shows the topics that have been or are trending from 2004 to the present day. The analysis reveals that the term "artificial intelligence" emerged in 2020, one year before the rise in interest in "decision-making", topics that are directly related. It is also noteworthy that there were topics that maintained a high level of interest for a long period, such as "quality control" from 2008 to approximately 2024, or "marketing" from 2006 until mid-2021. Another highlighted topic is "human computer interaction", not only for its considerable time period but also due to the frequency of the term used.

Figure 10. Trend topics

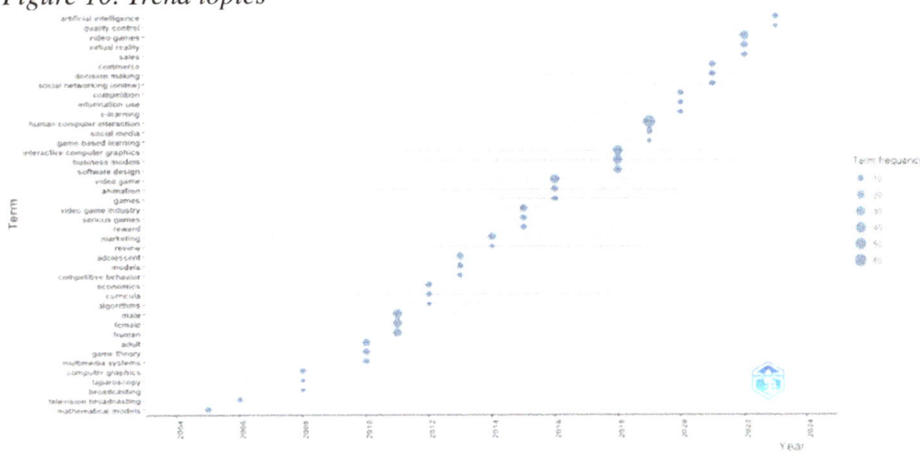

Conceptual Structure

Figure 11 provides a co-occurrence network based on keywords extracted from the titles, abstracts, and keywords of the cited papers. The network comprises "nodes", the individual words in the titles, and the lines between the "nodes" indicate the frequency with which the words co-occur in the same parameters. Although it is a graph with some complexity, it is easily visible that the terms "human computer interaction", are in red, and the terms "human", "humans", and "video games" are the ones with the most connections to other terms.

Figure 11. Co-occurrence Network

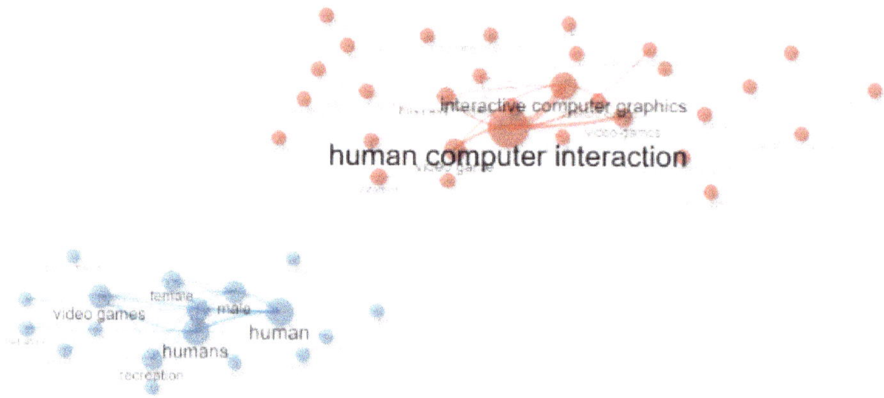

Figure 12 refers to the framework of the collected topics based on the following fields: Niche Topics, Emerging or Declining Topics, Driver Topics, and Basic Topics, as well as a content development density scale and a content relevance scale. In this graph, topics such as "humans" and "articles" already have substantial scientific development in the field and still maintain some relevance in scientific content production, categorizing them as Niche Topics. Topics such as "computer graphics", "multimedia systems", and "bandwidth" have some scientific content developed, but less than topics like "humans". On the relevance scale of the topic, these topics are categorized as Niche Topics. Topics like "internet", "education", and "economics" have little scientific content development, but they are highly relevant, thus categorized as Basic Topics. Topics like "human computer interaction", "interactive computer graphics", and "video games" are highly relevant in the scientific field and have some development, although less developed than topics like "multimedia systems". These topics are therefore categorized as Basic Topics.

Figure 12. Thematic Map

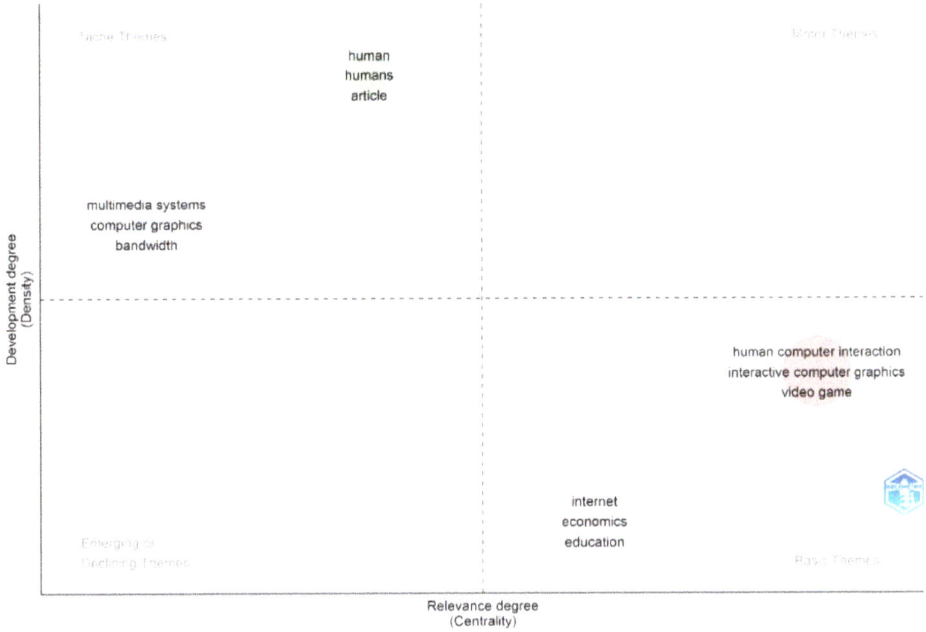

Social Structure

Figure 13 shows the countries that collaborated on the conducted studies. This graph reveals that the United Kingdom (UK) is one of the countries with the most international collaboration, with a total of 3 collaborations with Canada, 3 with Finland, and 3 with the United States of America (USA). The USA has the same number of international collaborations as the UK, collaborating 3 times with China, 3 with Germany, and, as previously mentioned, with the UK. Finland has 2 collaborations with Japan and 2 with Germany. Australia had 2 collaborations with the Netherlands. In addition to collaborating with Finland, Germany also collaborated with Denmark twice. Spain also had 2 collaborations with Brazil.

Figure 13. Country Collaboration

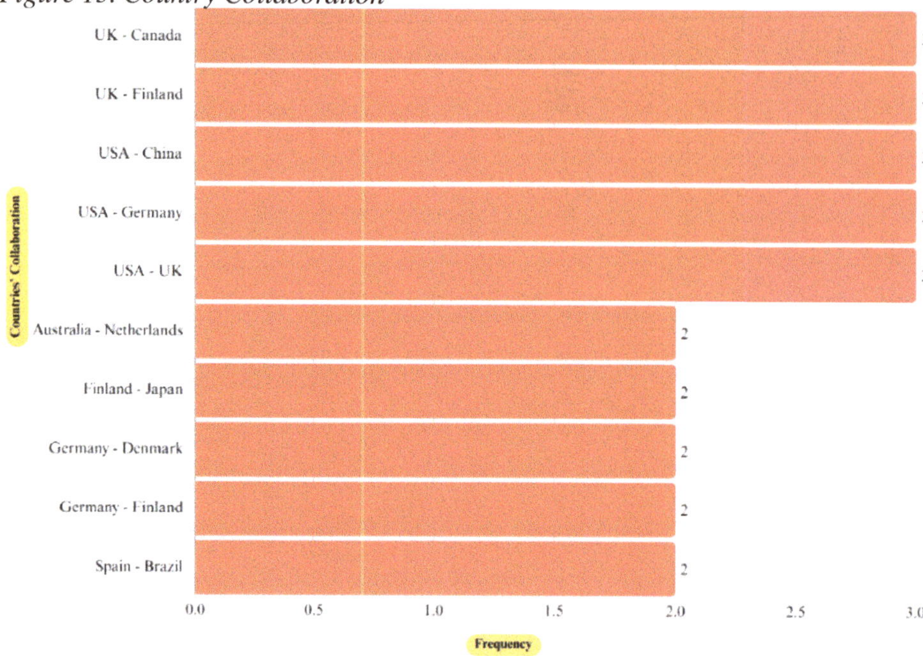

CONCLUSION

This study conducted a systematic mapping to chart the evolving landscape of research on game monetization, providing a structured overview of the field's development, intellectual framework, and emerging trends. Utilizing data from the Scopus database and employing advanced analytical tools like Biblioshiny for Bibliometrix in R, the study addressed key research questions related to publication patterns, intellectual networks, and the broader impact of monetization strategies on the gaming industry and player experiences.

Key Findings

State of Knowledge and Scholarly Contributions

The results demonstrate that research on game monetization has undergone three distinct waves of interest from 1984 to 2024, with heightened activity observed between 2002–2008 and 2017–2023. Peaks in scientific output are often aligned with pivotal industry developments, such as the rise of free-to-play (F2P) and freemium models. This directly answers the first question "What is the current state of knowledge on monetization strategies in the gaming industry?" regarding the current state of knowledge by outlining how the field has evolved and identifying its key academic contributions, such as Ryan's application of Self-Determination Theory, which significantly shaped the academic discourse.

Publication and Citation Metrics Across Domains

A total of 339 documents authored by 725 researchers were identified, reflecting a robust yet relatively niche scholarly interest. Journal articles and conference papers dominate the literature, with key publication sources including Lecture Notes in Computer Science and ACM International Conference Proceeding Series. The USA, Finland, and the UK emerged as leaders in both productivity and influence, evidenced by high citation counts and international collaborations. These findings address the second question "How do publication and citation metrics differ across research domains related to game monetization, and what do these metrics reveal about the field's scholarly impact and research productivity?" by revealing how publication and citation metrics vary across domains and illustrating their scholarly impact.

Intellectual and Social Structures

Through co-citation analysis, bibliographic coupling, and co-authorship networks, the study revealed that the field is highly collaborative, with 82.3% of documents authored by multiple researchers. This responds to the third question "What are the intellectual and social structures of game monetization research, as revealed through co-citation analysis, bibliographic coupling, and co-authorship networks?" by detailing the intellectual and social structures of game monetization research, highlighting key contributors like Hamari and Drachen and emphasizing the interdisciplinary nature of the field, which bridges psychology, economics, and computer science.

Emerging Trends and Future Directions

The thematic analysis identified trends that align with shifts in industry practices and player expectations. For example, the increasing prominence of "artificial intelligence" and "decision-making" reflects the growing reliance on data-driven models to optimize monetization while enhancing player satisfaction. This section answers the fourth question "What are the main trends and future developments in gain-game monetization models?" by outlining the main trends and predicting future developments in game monetization models.

Impact of Monetization on Player Experiences

A critical dimension of the research explored how monetization strategies affect player retention, engagement, and satisfaction. Studies highlighted in this analysis demonstrate that models like freemium and microtransactions can enhance or detract from player experiences depending on their design. This addresses the fifth question "How do monetization strategies affect player retention, engagement, and satisfaction?" by showing the nuanced effects of monetization strategies on players and emphasizing the importance of aligning these strategies with player motivations.

Implications and Recommendations

The findings offer several implications for researchers, industry practitioners, and policymakers. Measurement of scientific activity in this study provides academia with a foundation for future research to explore understudied areas, such as ethical frameworks for monetization or the role of artificial intelligence in personalizing player experiences. For the industry, the research highlights the importance of balancing profitability with ethical considerations, emphasizing strategies that prioritize long-term player satisfaction. Policymakers can draw on this analysis to develop guidelines that promote fair and transparent monetization practices, safeguarding consumer interests.

Limitations and Scope for Further Research

While this study offers a comprehensive analysis, it is important to acknowledge its limitations. The focus on English-language publications and the reliance on Scopus as the sole database may have excluded relevant works from other languages or sources. Future research could expand the dataset to include alternative databases and non-English publications, broadening the scope of analysis. Moreover, longitudinal studies could provide deeper insights into the causal relationships between monetization strategies and player behaviors.

Final Reflection

This study, through scientific impact assessment, underscores the significance of game monetization as a multidisciplinary field with far-reaching implications for the gaming industry and its stakeholders. By examining its intellectual foundations and research trends, the study provides a roadmap for future research and highlights the potential for innovative and ethical monetization models that benefit both players and developers. As the field continues to evolve, collaboration across disciplines and geographies will be crucial in addressing emerging challenges and opportunities in this dynamic area of research. Each section of this conclusion addresses one of the questions posed in the introduction, demonstrating how the study provides comprehensive answers and insights.

REFERENCES

Adachi, P. J. C., & Willoughby, T. (2013). More than just fun and games: The longitudinal relationships between strategic video games, self-reported problem solving skills, and academic grades. *Journal of Youth and Adolescence*, *42*(7), 1041–1052. DOI: 10.1007/s10964-013-9913-9 PMID: 23344653

Alha, K., Kinnunen, J., Koskinen, E., & Paavilainen, J. (2018). Free-to-Play Games: Paying Players' Perspective. *Proceedings of the 22nd International Academic Mindtrek Conference*, 49–58. https://doi.org/DOI: 10.1145/3275116.3275133

Aria, M., & Cuccurullo, C. (2017). Bibliometrix: An R-tool for comprehensive science mapping analysis. *Journal of Informetrics*, *11*(4), 959–975. DOI: 10.1016/j.joi.2017.08.007

Asadi, A., & Hemadi, R. (2018). Understanding Virtual Currencies in Video Games: A Review. *2018 2nd National and 1st International Digital Games Research Conference: Trends, Technologies, and Applications (DGRC)*, 109–117. https://doi.org/DOI: 10.1109/DGRC.2018.8712047

Caffarone, A. (2023). Virtual Gaming, Actual Damage: Video Game Design That Intentionally and Successfully Addicts Users Constitutes Civil Battery. *Duke Law & Technology Review*, *23*, 55.

Costes, J.-M., & Bonnaire, C. (2022). Spending Money in Free-to-Play Games: Sociodemographic Characteristics, Motives, Impulsivity and Internet Gaming Disorder Specificities. *International Journal of Environmental Research and Public Health*, *19*(23). *Artigo*, *23*. Advance online publication. DOI: 10.3390/ijerph192315709 PMID: 36497782

D'Amico, N. J. (2021). *MI* [Thesis, University of Tasmania]. https://doi.org/DOI: 10.25959/23249357.v1

Davidovici-Nora, M. (2014). *Paid and Free Digital Business Models Innovations in the Video Game Industry* (SSRN Scholarly Paper No. 2534022). Social Science Research Network. https://papers.ssrn.com/abstract=2534022

Drummond, A., & Sauer, J. D. (2018). Video game loot boxes are psychologically akin to gambling. *Nature Human Behaviour*, *2*(8), 530–532. DOI: 10.1038/s41562-018-0360-1 PMID: 31209310

Egenfeldt-Nielsen, S., Smith, J., & Tosca, S. (2008). *Understanding Video Games: The Essential Introduction*. https://doi.org/DOI: 10.4324/9780429431791

Flunger, R., Mladenow, A., & Strauss, C. (2017). The free-to-play business model. *Proceedings of the 19th International Conference on Information Integration and Web-based Applications & Services*, 373–379. https://doi.org/DOI: 10.1145/3151759.3151802

Fredriksson Friman, E., & Zätterlund, O. (2023). *The Dark Patterns of Battle Passes: Investigating player attitudes to a growing type of microtransaction*. https://urn.kb.se/resolve?urn=urn:nbn:se:umu:diva-211027

Gong, A.-D., Huang, Y.-T., Liu, K., & Sugiura, K. (2025). Getting hooked on mobile games: Strengthening purchase intentions towards mobile games using investment model and parasocial interactions. *Mobile Media & Communication*, *13*(1), 47–68. DOI: 10.1177/20501579241257907

Hadan, H., Sgandurra, S. A., Zhang-Kennedy, L., & Nacke, L. E. (2024). From Motivating to Manipulative: The Use of Deceptive Design in a Game's Free-to-Play Transition. *Proc. ACM Hum.-Comput. Interact.*, *8*(CHI PLAY), 309:1-309:31. https://doi.org/DOI: 10.1145/3677074

Hamari, J. (2015). Why do people buy virtual goods? Attitude toward virtual good purchases versus game enjoyment. *International Journal of Information Management*, *35*(3), 299–308. DOI: 10.1016/j.ijinfomgt.2015.01.007

Hamari, J., Hanner, N., & Koivisto, J. (2020). «Why pay premium in freemium services?» A study on perceived value, continued use and purchase intentions in free-to-play games. *International Journal of Information Management*, *51*, 102040. DOI: 10.1016/j.ijinfomgt.2019.102040

Hamari, J., & Keronen, L. (2017). Why do people play games? A meta-analysis. *International Journal of Information Management*, *37*(3), 125–141. DOI: 10.1016/j.ijinfomgt.2017.01.006

Hertzog, C., Kramer, A. F., Wilson, R. S., & Lindenberger, U. (2008). Enrichment Effects on Adult Cognitive Development: Can the Functional Capacity of Older Adults Be Preserved and Enhanced? *Psychological Science in the Public Interest*, *9*(1), 1–65. DOI: 10.1111/j.1539-6053.2009.01034.x PMID: 26162004

Janoščík, V. (2023). Behavioral capital: Gaming and monetization in post-marxist perspective. *Semiotica*, *2023*(254), 137–156. DOI: 10.1515/sem-2023-0124

King, D. L., & Delfabbro, P. H. (2018a). *Internet gaming disorder: Theory, assessment, treatment, and prevention* (pp. x, 276). Elsevier Academic Press.

King, D. L., & Delfabbro, P. H. (2018b). Predatory monetization schemes in video games (e.g. 'Loot boxes') and internet gaming disorder. *Addiction (Abingdon, England), 113*(11), 1967–1969. DOI: 10.1111/add.14286 PMID: 29952052

King, D. L., Gainsbury, S. M., Delfabbro, P. H., Hing, N., & Abarbanel, B. (2015). Distinguishing between gaming and gambling activities in addiction research. *Journal of Behavioral Addictions*, *4*(4), 215–220. DOI: 10.1556/2006.4.2015.045 PMID: 26690615

Kuklenko, P. (2024a). *The Role of Dark Design Patterns in Online Consumer Manipulation: A Critical Study with Emphasis on Video Game Monetisation* [fi=AMK-opinnäytetyö|sv=YH-examensarbete|en=Bachelor's thesis|]. https://www.theseus.fi/handle/10024/850304

Kuklenko, P. (2024b). *The Role of Dark Design Patterns in Online Consumer Manipulation: A Critical Study with Emphasis on Video Game Monetisation* [fi=AMK-opinnäytetyö|sv=YH-examensarbete|en=Bachelor's thesis|]. https://www.theseus.fi/handle/10024/850304

Kwon, J.-H., Chung, C.-S., & Lee, J. (2011). The effects of escape from self and interpersonal relationship on the pathological use of Internet games. *Community Mental Health Journal*, *47*(1), 113–121. DOI: 10.1007/s10597-009-9236-1 PMID: 19701792

Lam, L. T. (2014). Internet Gaming Addiction, Problematic Use of the Internet, and Sleep Problems: A Systematic Review. *Current Psychiatry Reports*, *16*(4), 444. DOI: 10.1007/s11920-014-0444-1 PMID: 24619594

Leahy, D. (2022). Rocking the Boat: Loot Boxes in Online Digital Games, the Regulatory Challenge, and the EU's Unfair Commercial Practices Directive. *Journal of Consumer Policy*, *45*(3), 561–592. DOI: 10.1007/s10603-022-09522-7

Lehdonvirta, V. (2009). Virtual item sales as a revenue model: Identifying attributes that drive purchase decisions. *Electronic Commerce Research*, *9*(1), 97–113. DOI: 10.1007/s10660-009-9028-2

Li, A. (2022). Deficiency of Loot Box Games in Chinese Video Game Market-. *RE:view, 1284–1288*. Advance online publication. DOI: 10.2991/aebmr.k.220307.212

Majander, V. (2019). *Revenue models for video games*. https://aaltodoc.aalto.fi/handle/123456789/39117

Nair, H. (2007). Intertemporal price discrimination with forward-looking consumers: Application to the US market for console video-games. *Quantitative Marketing and Economics*, *5*(3), 239–292. DOI: 10.1007/s11129-007-9026-4

Newzoo. (2023). Get Newzoo's newest free Global Games Market Report 2023. *Newzoo*. https://newzoo.com/resources/trend-reports/newzoo-global-games-market-report-2023-free-version

Parker, G. G., & Van Alstyne, M. W. (2005). Two-Sided Network Effects: A Theory of Information Product Design. *Management Science*, *51*(10), 1494–1504. DOI: 10.1287/mnsc.1050.0400

Petrovskaya, E., & Zendle, D. (2020). *The Battle Pass: A Mixed-Methods Investigation into a Growing Type of Video Game Monetisation*. https://doi.org/DOI: 10.31219/osf.io/vnmeq

Petrovskaya, E., & Zendle, D. (2022). Predatory Monetisation? A Categorisation of Unfair, Misleading and Aggressive Monetisation Techniques in Digital Games from the Player Perspective. *Journal of Business Ethics*, *181*(4), 1065–1081. DOI: 10.1007/s10551-021-04970-6

Postigo, H. (2016). The socio-technical architecture of digital labor: Converting play into YouTube money. *New Media & Society*, *18*(2), 332–349. DOI: 10.1177/1461444814541527

Ross, A., & Nieborg, D. (2021). Spinning is winning: Social casino apps and the platformization of gamble-play. *Journal of Consumer Culture*, *21*(1), 84–101. DOI: 10.1177/1469540521993931

Rutz, O., Aravindakshan, A., & Rubel, O. (2019). Measuring and forecasting mobile game app engagement. *International Journal of Research in Marketing*, *36*(2), 185–199. DOI: 10.1016/j.ijresmar.2019.01.002

Ryan, R. M., Rigby, C. S., & Przybylski, A. (2006). The Motivational Pull of Video Games: A Self-Determination Theory Approach. *Motivation and Emotion*, *30*(4), 344–360. DOI: 10.1007/s11031-006-9051-8

Shibuya, A., Teramoto, M., Shoun, A., & Akiyama, K. (2019). Long-Term Effects of In-Game Purchases and Event Game Mechanics on Young Mobile Social Game Players in Japan. *Simulation & Gaming*, *50*(1), 76–92. DOI: 10.1177/1046878118819677

Spicer, S. G., Nicklin, L. L., Uther, M., Lloyd, J., Lloyd, H., & Close, J. (2022). Loot boxes, problem gambling and problem video gaming: A systematic review and meta-synthesis. *New Media & Society*, *24*(4), 1001–1022. DOI: 10.1177/14614448211027175

Stanković, S. (2024). *Game Design for Free-to-Play Live Service*. Springer Nature Switzerland., DOI: 10.1007/978-3-031-56156-6

Stokes, J. (2024). Pocket Castles and Custom Skin: Championing Transparency in the Monetization of User-Generated Content in Video Games. *Cybaris: An Intellectual Property Law Review, 15*, 107.

Styhre, A., & Wikhamn, B. (2019). The ambiguities of money-making: Indie video game developers and the norm of creative integrity. *Qualitative Research in Organizations and Management: An International Journal, ahead-of-print*. https://doi .org/DOI: 10.1108/QROM-02-2019-1733

Wanick, V., & Mataruna, L. (2021). *The state of digital gaming and play post-COVID AUTHOR. 2*, 1.

Woods, O. (2024). The affective embeddings of gacha games: Aesthetic assemblages and the mediated expression of the self. *New Media & Society, 26*(2), 823–838. DOI: 10.1177/14614448211067756

Xiao, L. Y. (2021). *Regulating loot boxes as gambling? Towards a combined legal and self-regulatory consumer protection approach*. https://doi.org/DOI: 10.4337/ ielr.2021.01.02

Zackariasson, P., & Wilson, T. (2010). Paradigm shifts in the video game industry. *Competitiveness Review: An International Business Journal incorporating Journal of Global Competitiveness, 20*, 139–151. https://doi.org/DOI: 10.1108/10595421011029857

Zackariasson, P., & Wilson, T. (Eds.). (2012). *The Video Game Industry: Formation, Present State, and Future* (1st ed.). Routledge.

Zaucha, T., & Agur, C. (2023). Playbor, gamble-play, and the financialization of digital games. *New Media & Society, 14614448231190907*. Advance online publication. DOI: 10.1177/14614448231190907

Zendle, D., & Cairns, P. (2018a). Video game loot boxes are linked to problem gambling: Results of a large-scale survey. *PLoS One, 13*, e0206767. DOI: 10.1371/ journal.pone.0206767 PMID: 30462669

Zendle, D., & Cairns, P. (2018b). Video game loot boxes are linked to problem gambling: Results of a large-scale survey. *PLoS One, 13*(11), e0206767. DOI: 10.1371/ journal.pone.0206767 PMID: 30462669

Chapter 12
Impact of Smart Phones and Social Media Consumer Addiction Affecting Interpersonal Relationship

Ronit Kumar
https://orcid.org/0009-0005-6914-7099
Christ University, India

ABSTRACT

In this Chapter we will discuss the addiction of smartphones and Social Media Addiction. In this generation accessing the internet and getting connected online with people is very easy now people carry their smart devices with them everywhere and today people use mobile data more than calling someone because each and every individual with all age categories from a kid to senior citizen everyone is being Addicted. While the smartphone and social media platforms have played a crucial role in connecting people in a very easy manner. When people meet social gathering or in a parties they should interact with the people and have should socialise with the people but instead of that a notification from social media apps on smartphones pop's up and within a sec person get engaged with their phones or checking the notification. This is a major issue that is happening in today's time.

DOI: 10.4018/979-8-3373-6970-9.ch012

© 2026, IGI Global Scientific Publishing. Copying or distributing in print or electronic forms without written permission of IGI Global Scientific Publishing is prohibited. Use of this chapter to generative artificial intelligence (AI) technologies is expressly prohibited. The publisher reserves all rights to license its use for generative AI training and machine learning model development.

1. INTRODUCTION

Smartphones are loaded with quite innovative features. They can connect to the internet and allow versatile usage, be it social media or various types of applications like online shopping, computer games and so on. In this way, it is almost possible to say that smartphones have become an indispensable part of our lives, even more than an instrument of communication. People make all their job transactions with these smartphones, seek help from the most straightforward information they need, and, on the other hand, spend their entire free time communicating on social media without even noticing the loss of time. Instead of spending time with our families, on interpersonal relationships, and doing creative work, smartphone addiction has shortened our attention spans, causing us to miss many excitements of life. Smartphone addiction, which keeps increasing daily, causes certain problems in interpersonal relationships. This study, the first section of which is the introduction, focuses on the impact of smartphones and social media addiction on interpersonal relationships. In this direction, the study aims to evaluate smartphone and social media addiction in interpersonal relationships during the early adulthood period within the framework of different variables. The study is significant, with participants being young adults in the early adulthood period. It is believed that multiple variables, as well as various factors, will increase the constraints on the students who are in the training process and warn of the trap of smartphone and social media addiction. Furthermore, the study will shed light on the practices to be carried out to help students adapt to the educational atmosphere and social life.

1.1 Background and Significance

Many people are likely to remember a time when no one had an iPhone or when the closest they were to owning a phone was when they borrowed from their neighbor. It has been a decade since the first iPhone came out, and the changes it has brought about in human society are not debatable. Man's best friend and the self-proclaimed human extension, the smartphone and social media platforms, might well be portrayed as the inventions that have brought about a sense of community instead of actual human interaction. Smartphones and the social media platforms that people use via their phones have created man-to-man communication digitally; however, the number of hours that humans put into digital communication is slowly but surely taking time from their physical interaction. Smartphones and social media addiction combines the worst of all precedents of the vast knowledge of this generation: social anxiety combined with the mass merchandising that drives more and more people to adopt a virtual identity created via digital platforms and smartphones. Digital advancement is continuously taking humans' time from family, resulting in a social formation that is quite fragmented and simply impossible to make sense of altogether. However, the present society has also undertaken the belief that what we do not know does not hurt us, making it quite difficult to monitor and understand the complex relationships that emerge using our devices.

1.2 Purpose and Scope of the Study

The purpose of this study is to examine the impact of addiction to smartphones and associated social media on the quality of relationships between business travellers and their non-travelling partners. Several works in the field currently suggest a connection between the electronic usage of contemporary travellers abroad and affairs or relationship breakdowns at home. Furthermore, most business travel research neglects the influence of the partners remaining in their homes and argues that one logical group of professionals could be represented by the social community supporting them. This study examines these two research gaps and applies the addiction subset of excusable technology to the quality of variables. In some Situations They are prone to be very harmful a Staging 42.7% of road accidents were attributed to mobile phone use while driving (Zhou et al., 2016). Furthermore there is evidence use of smartphones in university may decrease academic performance (Rozgonjuk et al., 2018). Social media has taken on a central role in the lives of the majority of smartphone users and even influences the nature and composition of their face-to-face interactions. Its rapid growth has influenced the way people behave and interact with one another. Because of this, how people relate to their smartphones has been a trend scholars produced a growing amount of literature on as contemporary terms such as smartphone addiction and social media addiction summarize how much digital devices have entered the personal, social, and work lives of many individuals. The obsessive use of smartphones has been linked with issues ranging from anxiety and depression to community and friendship relationships. Furthermore, individuals use and engage with smartphones in different ways, for different purposes, and in different contexts, and their particular type of smartphone use can be addictive in itself if it undermines social, economic, or professional functioning.

2. OBJECTIVE

There is the more young, adult generation in today's time who has been addicted to Smartphones and social Media. It assesses the influence of smartphone and social media addiction on interpersonal relationships, with a special focus on friendships and romance. We aimed to find out if these addictions influence interpersonal interactions with best friends and romantic partners and deteriorate their intimacy and trust.

Moreover, we attempted to establish which addiction had a more negative impact: smartphone or social media addiction. The analysis included different behaviours in both addictions as well as the general use of other ICT devices. Women and men reported different general patterns of using smartphones and social media, but most of the impact of these devices on friendships and romantic relationships was uniform for both genders. Smartphone and social media addictions increase interactions with best friends and romantic partners, but they reduce relationship quality (especially in the case of romantic relationships) by lowering intimacy levels. Both girls and boys experienced the negative effects of addictions, but mostly in different ways—social media addiction had a greater impact on girls, while smartphone addiction had a stronger influence on boys. For addictions, the frequency of communication with best friends led to worse quality in these relationships.

2.1 Impact of Smartphones and Social Media Addiction on Relationships

The paper discusses whether smartphone addiction and other forms of social media addiction influence the quality of interpersonal relationships. These are friendships and romantic relationships, in which increased frequency of communication occurs on account of addictions, thus weakening the bonds with decreased intimacy and loss of trust. While it constantly connects, it replaces all meaningful and face-to-face communications that weaken emotional intimacy and fulfilment. The paradox it raises is that greater numbers of devices used for communication leave poorer quality between humans. This is because excessive exposure to technology tends to degrade the intensity of intimate relationships in youths.

2.2 Smartphone vs Social Media Addiction

This topic explores the influence of smartphone and social media addiction on interpersonal relationships, particularly friendships and romantic relationships. Smartphone addiction, often almost a synonym of gaming and general device use, is more common in young men, while social media addiction through constant comparison and validation-seeking affects females the most. Both addictions are proven to lower relationship quality differently: social media addiction causes dissatisfaction by forcing unrealistic comparisons, while smartphone addiction provokes distractions from personal relationships.

2.3 Gender Differences in Addiction and Relationship Impact

This study examines the trend of smartphone and social media addiction and its difference according to gender, showing insights into how both men and women are affected differently by these addictions. Women appeared to be more affected by social media addiction, but alongside these, other problems included comparators' anxiety and lower relationship satisfaction. Smartphone addiction was relatively higher in men; in fact, men have huge amounts for gaming or the consumption of media. Despite all these variations, the use of both smartphones and social media by either gender implies a decrease in intimacy and trust together with relationship quality due to their respective digital addictions.

3. UNDERSTANDING SMARTPHONE AND SOCIAL MEDIA ADDICTION

The smartphone is one of those indispensable tools that never stops changing society and moulding human behaviour and expectations this case, among the younger generation. Because accessibility to digital media can dramatically influence the user's life, it creates an increased chance of getting addicted. Nowadays, as technology advances, it is common to find people continuously operating digital media players and simulating complex interactions purely with their handheld devices. Most people have their smartphones without interruption during the day, and often, when there is a battery problem that prevents them from receiving a phone call, there is a sense of inconvenience accompanying that effect. Since too much dependence on such an apparatus can distort human contact, depress personality, and lead to a large number of injuries, resulting in a series of social problems, it is also often referred to as a "partial substitute" or called "electronic heroin." Moreover, since digital media players can exchange messages at a very low price or without charge, whether ordinary phone interconnection modes, text message communication, or regular information browsing are used, even with no moving fees, large-scale data transmission and receipt can be done within a short period. However, the generated fees can also be calculated based on the call fee. Also, the technological merits of these electronic products are enormous for young people who have limited living expenses. The vast majority of young people like to use mobile phones and are most likely to become addicted to the screens of digital media players. Their abilities are also quickly discovered and recognized by the vast majority of parents, who wish to purchase these advanced technology devices before obtaining the necessary economic resources. Due to the economic dependence of youth, who have developed a heavy reliance on digital products in today's popular digital era, adjustments in lifestyles are made to meet the demand for the use of electronic products. This means that the operation is not just chatting or communicating but generally buying, keeping, or consuming digital products which requires securing finances and after the mobile phone becomes a force unto itself, not just an ostentatious gadget, the computer becomes a force unto itself too.

4. LITERATURE REVIEW

This study explores the interconnection of social and psychological factors with varying levels of utilization of the widely used Asian social mobile application and among its users. It was found that high social identity and perception needs accompanied by low self-esteem and social competencies increase the likelihood of app addiction. Conversely, those who reported excessive use of social media apps, but no difficulties felt more satisfied with their lives and reported higher self-worth. Social and psychological factors do not influence casual users. The importance of analysing specific applications to understand the phenomenology of smartphone addiction as well as social factors that contribute to its development. The impact of social networking on mobile commerce (m-commerce), particularly how mobile applications affect people's views about online purchases and payments is noteworthy. Where social networking contributes to the interaction among consumers, thereby providing additional value for business. Hence, as most people tend to use social media through their smartphones, it is hard-pressed not to integrate m-commerce within these networks since it helps a lot in convenience (Hossain et al., 2020).

There are several factors including, but not limited to, the payment options offered as part of m-commerce, the value and fit of mobile shopping applications, the levels of trust and safety and how these elements influence consumers' perceptions of m-commerce. Mobile social networks contribute noticeably here as they motivate people to use mobile apps for shopping help to make this process quicker and easier and provide a greater sense of security as well. Higher levels of education, however, help to promote the use of cashless payment systems, mainly among frequent Internet users. The essay points out that improvements in technology will encourage more people to use the internet for business transactions as security risks will be addressed even more so than today.

The link between depressive states and excessive use of mobile phones, with particular attention paid to the role of friendship, as well as the quality of sleep. 450 medical students of Chinese descent provided assessments of these variables, and the results indicated that to a certain degree, sleep quality acts as a mediator in the relationship between depression and mobile phone addiction. Moreover, peer ties were found to reduce the impact of sleep quality on depression. These findings provide insight into the mechanisms that explain the association between depression and mobile phone addiction and highlight the role of interactions with peers and sleep in this connection. Also, limitations and further research concerns are addressed by Ziyi Feng et al. (2022).

In Turkey 1,274 high school students. Found more severe psychiatric disorders were associated with higher social media addiction and lower prosocial behaviours. It was observed in another research (Sümen & Evgin, 2021) that most of the pupils access social networks for one to three hours a day and even sleep with their handheld devices nearby which negatively impacts their sleep patterns. The findings underline the importance of health education because of the consequences of overusing social media on the mental health of adolescents and the vital role that adequate sleep plays for them. The investigation revolves around a notion called FOMO which embodies deficiency in the ability to connect because of the worry of missing something vital and is easily interfered with by social media. In this context, Fear of Missing Out is a young but widely used concept, as several means have been developed to measure Footprints in online social networking sites such as Facebook and Instagram. Every day more and more people use the Internet and are using a device such as a smartphone, and it is impossible to log off due to constant anticipation of something important or entertaining as well as the desire to check on other people's activities sold on social networks.

The On-FoMo inventory centres around the phenomenon where individuals tend to engage when they are aware that engagement in activity will alleviate the risks of Frustration Obsession What currency is you are spending time in? This currency Turn can be said to evolve with Urbanization and associated changes in lifestyle and incorporate all such electronic social networks such as Facebook and WhatsApp. FoMO translates into the Turkish language the On-FoMO Inventory and examines its reliability, validity, and applicability among Turkish speakers.

With this study, Translating the On-FoMO Inventory into Turkish and testing its reliability and validity on Turkish speakers was the main aim. The objective of the translation process was to make sure that the scale could be used in the hope of FoMO among the Turkish population with precision and relevance. Validity is ascertained by the scale in effect capturing the pull that it seeks to measure while reliability is how constant the scale is in measuring the construct.

The final goal was to examine the interrelationship among FOMO, mobile addiction, social networking, and life satisfaction. The researcher Fuad Bakioğlu et al. (2022) gave such a circumstance and focused on the focus of such dependence and how its parallel expansions fulfil the urge of not fearing of missing out, on the internet. Social network performers who are inclined toward more heavy smartphone use introduce factors that diminish life satisfaction and psychological well-being.

The focus of the investigation was on the aspects to explain how such a phenomenon as FoMO may incite people's deviant behaviour in the network process. All these endeavors, if successful, may help improve online security and promote healthy use of social media by preventing and mitigating FOMO.

Smartphones due to their multi-faceted functionality have become an essential part of higher education, aiding students in communication, learning activities, and accessing resources. However, an alarming trend of smartphone addiction has been noted among students of colleges and universities, which endangers academic performance and mental well-being. One of the factors that leads to such addictive behaviour is the neurotic personality trait that has been linked to higher levels of psychological distress and compulsive smartphone use over time (Lei et al., 2020).

Another study (Jeong et al., 2020) aimed at assessing the role of neuroticism and psychological well-being in smartphone addiction among medical students at University Sains Malaysia (USM). This is because medical students have to balance many aspects of their lives including learning therefore understanding what psychosocial factors would exacerbate smartphone addiction is of utmost importance(Oraison et al., 2020). Neuroticism involves poor emotional regulation and over-reactivity. Jeong et al. (2020) tried understand the correlates of the frequency of impairments in the activities of daily living among adult Koreans caused by excessive IGS (internet, games and smartphones) and other factors. Correlations were studied between the adverse effects of the excessive use of IGS and sociodemographic characteristics, social contacts, mainly with family members, mental characteristics, health conditions, and health-related quality of life. The work emphasises how unlimited access to certain digital platforms can affect people's functional capabilities and overall health. More importantly, the research intends to augment societal and public health theories by identifying such connections, understanding the dynamics of IGS addiction at a societal level and within the individual's health simply, therefore, justifying the need for effective treatments and support systems in place to manage the health deleterious.

It is established by an recent study (Zhang et al., 2023) that college students' involvement in social media has been increasing in recent years. Nevertheless, the influence of social media on students' well-being, particularly college students, is still a subject of contention. In as much as social media has been incorporated into Russian education, multiple types of research have shown contradictory trends when it comes to the overall impact of the said social media on students' well-being. Some writers, for instance, mention the adverse effects on mental health of the excessive usage of the Web – it escalates levels of anxiety and depression, while others focus on the bright side of such dependency – enhancement of social relations and cohesive communities. As such, these findings reveal the intricate role of social networking sites in the life of youth. What are the specific parameters that need to be sustained as to the link between one's social media use and wellness remains a major concern which also needs further analysis on the variations of the social media effect among different individuals. The provision of socializing will not be sufficient since it will be necessary to analyze these aspects to formulate measures that will foster appropriate interaction with social networks among students.

The psychological impact of the COVID-19 pandemic's swift international reach has triggered a fear of the virus. In their efforts to understand more about the symptoms that are innate to them, many individuals have sought the help of the internet through their mobile phones. There is a term for this behaviour, and it is called "cyberchondria." The focus of study by Faruk Caner Yam et al. (2023) is to determine the mediating and moderating effects of the severity of cyberchondria about COVID-19 fear and addiction to smartphones.

The mean age of the respondents was 28.61 years with the majority (64.4%) female. A total of 520 participants took part in the study and the age of the participants ranged from 17 to 65 years. Other surveys that the participants took include the Cyberchondria Severity Scale Short-Form, Smartphone Addiction Scale-Short Version, and the Fear of COVID-19 Scale. In the research design, for moderator variables, the study applied SPSS Process Macro and structural equation modelling.

The findings indicated that there was a positive relationship between the levels of cyberchondria symptoms, fear of COVID-19, and dependence on smartphones. More importantly, there was also a finding that showed the level of cyberchondria both mediated and moderated the relationship between COVID-19-related fear, and addiction to smartphones. This means that Cyberchondria severity may exaggerate the effects of smartphone addiction and the fear of the virus on individuals.

The study ends on the note that the extent of cyberchondria affects people's COVID-19 fears positively in the context of the pandemic. It emphasizes the need to address the challenges posed by prolonged use of mobile technology.

In an attempt to remedy an existing research deficit which on one hand depicts excessively the adverse effects of smartphone use, Yoon & Yun (2023) found out the usage patterns of teenagers. While previous studies have focused on the negative impacts, this research proposes that there are positive impacts, such as access to career information via smartphones and mobile learning. Three distinct smartphone usage profiles were developed from a survey of 2,341 high school students belonging to a larger longitudinal study: learning, recreational and little use profiles. To this end, students with lower levels of compliance and perseverance were assigned to the recreational group whereas students with higher levels of perseverance were assigned to the learning group. The leisure group had the lowest-rated achievement targets while the learning group had the highest-rated achievement targets. The academic performance of both the learning and low-use groups was enhanced significantly in comparison to that of the leisure group. These findings underscore the importance of understanding adolescent smartphone usage patterns and their implications for academic performance, self-control, and achievement orientation. Social Media Connection, or SMC, is the emerging trend of utilizing social media for work purposes outside regular working hours mostly practised in supply chain management. SMC has been found to have implications on the supply chain employees and the organisations, however, little is known about its implications on work attitudes, more specifically the intention to quit. This study by Guiyao Tang et al. (2020) seeks to understand how supply chain management (SMC) impacts the voluntary turnover of professionals in the supply chain, with a particular focus on the impact on employees and organizations. This in-depth comprehension of this relationship is particularly important because it will assist in dealing with the adverse effects of SMC which in turn might improve the performance of the organization and retention of employees. This study, in recognizing the gap in the existing literature focuses on the relationship between SMC and turnover intention and makes a call for organizations to recognize and address the challenges that may arise from using social networking sites for work engagement.

5. DISCUSSION

Interpersonal relationships are the social connections that exist between two or more individuals. They are based on personal or psychological factors rather than primarily sexual or biological ones. When communication in a relationship is face-to-face, the health of an interpersonal relationship can be assessed mostly by the expression of the eyes and facial muscles. If these elements are damaged, confidence, compassion, understanding, love, belonging, and other traits can be enhanced. All of these healthy relationship traits involve face-to-face interaction. The relationship depends on whether the two individuals have a fundamental, common interest in maintaining connection, engaging in conversations, and effective problem-solving. Trust, commitment, and positive outcomes will generate many long-term interpersonal relationships. At this stage, the common elements are understanding and trust. This is an informal interaction between people or parties who are related or concerned. It can also be separate or collective. Social development is positively correlated with general psychological adjustment, career performance, and social integration, and it increases well-being. Individual conversations play an important role in the construction and support of valued and admired partnerships. Interpersonal relationships include emotional or passionate policies; cooperation across geographical, community, political, economic, family, neighbourhood, and group lines; mutual support, expertise, and competence transfer mechanisms; and understanding combined with cultural exchange, irrespective of the personal or group status of a person or organization. Personal social networks and professions enable each area of life and are important to your physical and mental health.

5.1 Prevalence and Statistics

In recent years, the use of smartphones and social media applications has dramatically increased. Whereas a significant percentage of Indians own a smartphone, a large portion of 18-29-year-olds are using popular social media networks. Young adults are the most active users of the internet and these sites. One platform that remains one of the most widely used online platforms among Indians is Instagram. It also gets high traction rates with the younger generation, as a notable percentage of Indian adults use this Social Media. Among 18-24-year-olds, a large percentage of the users are on this platform. On the other hand, Facebook and site use is reduced in older generations. Only a smaller percentage of those aged 40 and older have a social media account.

Besides social media, in the last few years, people have started increasing their usage of dating sites. For the first time, a significant percentage of existing, committed relationships began on online dating sites or apps. Again, young adults accounted for the largest share of dating social media sites and app usage. As dating apps have become increasingly popular, they have also been implicated in high rates of social media and smartphone addiction. A significant percentage of the users admitted to spending excessive amounts of time on dating sites. Additionally, a notable percentage of the individuals used the apps to hook up; the majority of users are male. In some countries, individuals were spending higher amounts of time on dating apps than shopping online. Smartphones provide the ability to access dating apps, along with multiple social media networks, at any given time of day. The ease of use appears to contribute to the development of smartphone addiction for most smartphone owners.

Interpersonal Relationship: Importance and Dynamics

The Main Pillar of being a healthy and good person is very important. People are the most important during the tough times and good times. Interpersonal relationships, be they with parents, partners, children, friends, or people we meet in our day-to-day lives, enhance emotional and psychological well-being. Our social connections help us regulate stress, alleviate negative emotional states such as depression, heartaches, or loneliness, benefit both our physical and mental health, and provide social support. These relationships help us deal with our demanding work schedules, information saturation, and increasing financial pressures because, at the end of the day, we have someone to share these new experiences and our stories with. The dynamics of relationships are also changing, especially with the advent of social media apps. Platforms hold millions of subscribers. We communicate with each other, share personal information instantaneously, and see what the others are doing, how people are feeling, and where they are. We have become so absorbed that we check our smartphones when we wake up, send messages, and make calls in the middle of the night. As a result, these non-direct contacts that we maintain in our lives appear to be more important than face-to-face contacts. And the impact of this engagement promises to be enormous. Are we turning into a society where there are people everywhere but present nowhere? The importance of human relationships in having a healthy and fruitful life cannot be more eloquently said than this. Improved interpersonal relationships with parents, partners, children, friends, or acquaintances that we meet in daily life come with enhanced emotional and psychological well-being. Social bonding helps us tackle stress, erase the bad thoughts that come with depression, heartaches, and loneliness, benefit both our body and mind, and give us social support. Such relations help us deal with the difficulties in working hours, excess information, and increased pressures related to finance as, fundamentally speaking, by the end of the day, we do have someone to share these new experiences and our stories with. Yet another aspect of changing relations is evident; this time, it was brought about by social media applications. Platforms hold millions of subscribers. We communicate with each other, share personal information instantaneously, and see what the others are doing, how people are feeling, and where they are. We have become so absorbed that we check our smartphones when we wake up, send messages, and make calls in the middle of the night. As a result, these non-direct contacts that we maintain in our lives appear to be more important than face-to-face contacts. And the potential impact of this engagement promises to be significant. Are we morphing into a society surrounded by people who are present all the time but absent in their relationships?

An interpersonal relationship is an association or connection between individuals who are linked through communication, including social and emotional interactions. In an interpersonal relationship, two or more individuals are connected emotionally and socially in a business-to-business environment or a community; some connections are purpose-driven, while others are not. Interpersonal relationship refers to a one-on-one relationship here, and the 'interpersonal' has been used to mean a relationship between two or more people. And there are many kinds of interpersonal relationships, such as platonic friendship, romantic relationships, family relationships, etc.

5.2 Preposition Based on Existing Theory

Preposition 1: Understanding that they might miss out on something interesting.

Consequences: This hypothesis indicates that there is no empirical evidence to support the argument that this generation is at a greater risk of being addicted to the internet and/or mobile devices. That is, for several reasons i.e. engagement in a lot of social interactions, struggle to overcome inferiority complexes etc., high self-esteem individuals are in no way less vulnerable to smartphone use disorders.

Preposition 2: What is the Relation Between the Attention Restrictiveness Theory and Attachment Fear

Explanation: According to Keller, environmental pride can lead to excessive complacency attributed to an unjustified belief in the positive impact of environmental activism. The theory juxtaposes enjoyment in giving and the fear of losing the attention of others. Chih-Hsiu Shih et.al (2016) conducted a similar study confirming that competition for leisure resources has both positive and negative impacts on leisure activities.

Example: Young individuals who exhibit problematic internet use due to excessive fear of being left out often show signs of neglecting their usual academic and workplace responsibilities.

Consequences: This hypothesis posited that such causal attributions can result in a net decrease in emotional overreaches and in addictive behaviours specific to the individuals who have the most jeopardized self-concept. As noted earlier, their behaviour should not be considered analogous to preventing airtime abuse.

6. APPLICATION TO THE MODEL

In Educational Settings: This model could provide guidelines for smartphone usage policies in universities, to embrace ICT responsibly and for a good cause. For example, such programs may assist students in limiting their screen times or promoting the use of work-related applications.

In Mental Health Interventions: Given the causes of smartphone attachment disorder such as the fear of missing out (FoMO) and the syndrome of cyberchondria, the model helps to design the elements of therapy including cognitive behavioural therapy tasks directed at social anxiety, depression and dependence on the Smartphone.

Corporate Policy Formulation: This model offers the way forward for firms to formulate reasonable grading policies that encourage the use of social networks without infringing on the content of the policy and hence better employee well-being.

7. POTENTIAL IMPACT

Since smartphone use has led to a sense of addiction, it is undeniably one of the most detrimental factors influencing society today. Because it provided a range of perspectives from which the study could observe and comprehend cell phones, this segment that concentrated on the educational and professional setting was chosen for that reason. By doing this, the study has achieved its goal of creating a comprehensive understanding of the effects of SMC, FOMO, mobile purchasing, and cyberchondria. The theory-driven conceptual framework and the image that would serve as a model for future research as well as a source of possible topics that may be required for future investigations are the most suitable methodologies. This study had certain drawbacks.

7.1 Finding and Discussion

The study explored the effect of smartphones and social media consumer addiction on individuals' behavioural attitudes affecting interpersonal relationships and potential adverse effects in the long run. The present analysis reveals that smartphones and social media consumer addiction are significant issues in the modern age. If smartphones and social media addiction are left untreated over time, their effects can cause undesirable consequences. This problem arises because modern IT can alter perception, decision-making, values, locus of control, attention, impulse control, and inhibition, which, in turn, affect individuals' attitudes and behaviours, inevitably impacting communication and interpersonal relationships. The relationship between smartphone and social media addiction is significant, and social media consumer addiction influences interpersonal relationships. Social media consumer addiction affects the perception of individuals. Besides, it can affect individuals' attitudes, impulsiveness, and inhibitions. Smartphones and social media consumer addiction also have significant differences in terms of age, race, and background. Social media consumer addiction affects consumer intention and behaviour. Social media consumer addiction also triggers individuals' Internet addiction behaviours. Individuals' Internet addiction behaviours can become severe, leading to Internet addiction syndrome disorders that are considered to be a diagnostic problem. Individuals' Internet addiction syndrome disorders gradually evolve into severe Internet addiction behaviours that not only negatively affect individuals' physical and mental health but also disrupt individuals' interpersonal relationships. Social media consumer addiction affects individual values and locus of control. The more severe the addiction, the greater its impact. Due to the complexity of consumer behaviour, it is not easy to cut ties with social media. The promotion and support of technology have further developed. However, understanding and changing human behaviour has become even more difficult. There are various causes of social media addiction, such as emotional needs, self-enforcement theory, self-concept, social interaction theory, and social norms. Individuals who are addicted to smartphones and social media can be motivated by the need to perform tasks that they cannot accomplish offline. Individuals can exert more control through online interaction. They can fulfil their likes and desires and gain satisfaction via the use of social media. Individuals can set standard goals and be committed to achieving those standards. They feel accepted by peer groups. The more reposts and likes individuals receive from their followers, the greater the satisfaction, which results in a more positive self-concept, better image projection, increased followers' acceptance, and pursuit of higher standards from social media platform activities.

8. PREVALENCE OF SMART PHONE AND SOCIAL MEDIA USE

There is a growing body of literature on the individual level of smartphone and social media use. The majority of the study results suggest that the prevalence of smartphone and social media use is rapidly increasing. However, the extent varies across different age groups. It was found that 94% owned and used smartphones, and the average usage was more than 5.4 hours per day. An investigation of social media records demonstrated that 93.7% of adolescents had social media accounts. The figure increased to 97% for Turkish adolescents. Using time diaries kept in real time by participants for three consecutive days, patterns of daily smartphone-related behaviour of participants were studied and found that smartphone use is common among adults, with less than one quarter reporting that they never use the technology. As found in the study, smartphone use is no longer only concentrated in the adult population but also widespread among younger generations.

8.1 Impact of Consumer Addiction on Interpersonal Relationships

The term "loss of interest in significant interpersonal relationships" can be rephrased as 'affinities' in an informal sense, stressing more on an affluent lifestyle. In addition, the consumer places predominance on the substance or the behaviour of substance, which affects his or her personal life, consisting of family, interpersonal relationships, personal health, and personal goals. For some addicts, these enhance the excitement level, becoming a way of life that often leads to conflicts with significant goals in life. Consumerism today is not just limited to procuring goods; it has surpassed to the extent that one starts doing something idiosyncratically to excogitate and actualize those idiosyncrasies, believing that possessions will accord them their inherent value. This pursuit often violates human intimacy, familial relations, and aspirations to the extent that material well-being becomes more important than other people, particularly friends or family members.

8.2 Factors Influencing Consumer Addiction

The explosion of new technologies and the advancement of communication instruments have opened a virtual world composed of devices where the entire society has moved to live. The multifunctionality of innovative technology has brought different concepts to lifestyle. The attractiveness and pervasiveness of mobile phones and online social media have played a significant role in transforming social and consumer interaction. Today, the obsession with social media and mobile phones has resulted in consumer addiction, influencing the behaviour of consumers of all ages, which in turn impacts daily life relationships. Hence, the inquiry has been motivated to review the impact of smartphone and social media consumer addiction on interpersonal relationships in the context of consumer behaviour and its outcomes.

It is essential to understand the various factors that induce excessive social media and mobile phone behaviour. There are many factors such as social influence, fashion level, exposure level, phone brand, emotional attachment to the mobile phone, emotional state, and communication motives for excessive behaviour regarding mobile phones. Similarly, excessive social media use is due to various factors such as site attraction level and individuals' addiction level that arise from their motives for access and usage. Consequently, tying together the various factors for both mobile phone and social media addiction highlights the need to explore consumer attitudes and behaviours towards social media and smartphones.

9. SUGGESTED AREAS FOR FURTHER RESEARCH

Cultures and their Impact on FOMO and social media: Further studies may focus on exploring remoteness and fear of missing out in various countries to understand the differences between cultures and plan effective measures of prevention and treatment.

Research on the Use of Smartphones Based on Educational Purposes in Teenagers: The reliance on smartphones by students is expected to affect their educational performance over time and even the potential recovery from such damages after prolonged use.

The Aspect of Trust and Security in Mobile Commerce: Given the fact that trust has an important role in determining the level of m-commerce usage, other studies may endeavour to investigate how transparency of business processes, cybersecurity, and application features build the trust, especially in countries where m-commerce penetration is low.

Moderating Factors in Cyberchondria and Health Anxiety: As it is evident that cyberchondria contributes to increasing the fears about Covid 19, further studies must include the other moderating factors such as resilience and social support or even previous health anxiety to put forward a more thorough model of the anxieties surrounding health in the age of digital technologies.

Investigating the Positive Role of Smart Phones in Education: Research, instead of concentrating on the addiction to smartphones, could rather revolve around the positive aspects of the users such as their academic learning and success with the use of educational applications, access to information, and career advice. Impact of SMC on Other Industries: Given that the SMC is a concept that is on the rise apart from the supply CHA management, forward-looking studies seek to understand its application in other sectors such as health care, finance and education to comprehend the overall ramifications on the wellbeing and retention of the workers.

10. IMPLICATIONS FOR POLICY MAKERS

Given that this study's findings shed light on several policy and practice matters relating to the vital impact of growing consumer addiction to mobile phones and social media on face-to-face intimate relationship processes between people, created for the consumer society, including social structures, fellow consumers, industrial firms, and related industry actors among others, it has significant implications for society at large. As such, the study is key and useful for policy planners, lawmakers, business leaders, behavioral scholars, consumer activists, and citizens at large. Enhanced understanding of consumer addiction would help in the development of good public policies and specific strategies that would help neutralize and control consumer addiction, but also monitor multinational conglomerates, so that both positive societal outcomes and human values, along with consumer welfare and shareholder values, are jointly shared in the new environment. In particular, a consumer society, where business survives and thrives on the endless buying and spending activities of consumers, could greatly improve overall societal welfare, improve human relationships, diminish outsourcing woes, reduce demands on overstretched national health services, and particularly support the lives, careers, and future aspirations of the addicted younger generation. Findings here, shedding impressive light on consumers addicted to their mobile phones and social media, managed and manipulated by multinational technology firms disciplined and sometimes bullied by security agencies that have evolved for spying and snooping, which provide significant technological intelligence capability, are useful for the relevant professional networks, anti-business activists, behavioural researchers, consumer activists, policymakers, and business people, including business educators. The findings are important for politicians and contestants in national and local elections, as they help clarify and articulate to voters at large their unique positions on privacy, surveillance, and national cybersecurity interests. Undoubtedly, the vast majority of citizens are not bemused by the benefits that addiction to consumer society has to offer. Its day-to-day activities and functional purchases are essential and, in many cases, contribute to the being and function of society. But the alarming risk nowadays is that specific sectors of society are being swamped and consumed, sacrificing and suffering in their mortal fight with communication technologies, where smartphones are increasingly joining cigarettes and junk food as a key source of excess, addictive, and detrimental behaviour.

11. CONCLUSION

This present study aimed to examine the relationship between technology and social media with consumer addiction behaviour and its impact on interpersonal relationships among consumers. It is assumed that consumers are extensively aware of the consequences of the negative impact of engaging in consumer addiction behaviour but continue to engage with them despite its negative impact. In the result-of-review paper, negative consumer addiction behaviour in interpersonal relationships can be categorized into three parts; partnerships, family, and professional context. There are however noticeable limitations in this study. First, the current study only looked at psychological aspects affecting interpersonal relationships. There may be other determinants that have arisen during the growth of technology and social media from which researchers could draw to further explain addiction and negative consumer behaviour. The ethical perspective of consumer addiction behaviour especially in dealing with communication mental disorder, such phenomenon needs to be discussed together taking into account the views of multidisciplinary scholars. Secondly, the paper's research model is insufficient as it only includes a social interaction mechanism to predict addiction behaviour. Additional factors that can predict consumer addiction behaviour could be proposed to provide a collective explanation of consumer addiction. Hence the paper's motive is to invite future researchers to investigate other traits that contribute to consumer addiction behaviour. Third, the paper used a validated scale to measure consumer addiction behaviour. While the scale utilized is reliable and valid, the scale may not take into account other cultural and environmental factors that have been developed due to the rise of this phenomenon and come to notice in other countries. Lastly, future research could also focus on other specific media, such as Facebook, Shop Online and YouTube to further examine these new social trends which portray the highest usage growing pattern.

REFERENCES

Bakioğlu, F., Deniz, M., Griffiths, M. D., & Pakpour, A. H. (2022). Adaptation and validation of the Online-Fear of Missing Out Inventory into Turkish and the association with social media addiction, smartphone addiction, and life satisfaction. *BMC Psychology*, *10*(1), 154. DOI: 10.1186/s40359-022-00856-y PMID: 35717277

Feng, Z., Diao, Y., Ma, H., Liu, M., Long, M., Zhao, S., Wu, H., & Wang, Y. (2022). Mobile phone addiction and depression among Chinese medical students: The mediating role of sleep quality and the moderating role of peer relationships. *BMC Psychiatry*, *22*(1), 567. DOI: 10.1186/s12888-022-04183-9 PMID: 35999533

Hossain, S. F. A., Xi, Z., Nurunnabi, M., & Hussain, K. (2020). Ubiquitous Role of Social Networking in Driving M-Commerce: Evaluating the Use of Mobile Phones for Online Shopping and Payment in the Context of Trust. *SAGE Open*, *10*(3). Advance online publication. DOI: 10.1177/2158244020939536

Jeong, Y.-W., Han, Y.-R., Kim, S.-K., & Jeong, H.-S. (2020). The frequency of impairments in everyday activities due to the overuse of the internet, gaming, or smartphone, and its relationship to health-related quality of life in Korea. *BMC Public Health*, *20*(1), 954. DOI: 10.1186/s12889-020-08922-z PMID: 32552690

Lei, L. Y. C., Al-Aarifin Ismail, M., Mohammad, J. A. M., & Bahri Yusoff, M. S. (2020). The relationship of smartphone addiction with psychological distress and neuroticism among university medical students. *BMC Psychology*, *8*(1), 97. DOI: 10.1186/s40359-020-00466-6 PMID: 32917268

Oraison, H., Nash-dolby, O., Wilson, B., & Malhotra, R. (2020). Smartphone distraction-addiction: Examining the relationship between psychosocial variables and patterns of use. *Australian Journal of Psychology*, *72*(2), 188–198. DOI: 10.1111/ajpy.12281

Rozgonjuk, D., Saal, K., & Täht, K. (2018). Problematic Smartphone Use, Deep and Surface Approaches to Learning, and Social Media Use in Lectures. *International Journal of Environmental Research and Public Health*, *15*(1), 92. DOI: 10.3390/ijerph15010092 PMID: 29316697

Sümen, A., & Evgin, D. (2021). Social Media Addiction in High School Students: A Cross-Sectional Study Examining Its Relationship with Sleep Quality and Psychological Problems. *Child Indicators Research*, *14*(6), 2265–2283. DOI: 10.1007/s12187-021-09838-9 PMID: 34367373

Tang, G., Ren, S., Chadee, D., & Yuan, S. (2020). The dark side of social media connectivity: Influence on turnover intentions of supply chain professionals. *International Journal of Operations & Production Management*, *40*(5), 603–623. DOI: 10.1108/IJOPM-05-2019-0391

Yam, F. C., Korkmaz, O., & Griffiths, M. D. (2023). The association between fear of Covid-19 and smartphone addiction among individuals: The mediating and moderating role of cyberchondria severity. *Current Psychology (New Brunswick, N.J.)*, *42*(3), 2377–2390. DOI: 10.1007/s12144-021-02324-z PMID: 34690474

Yoon, M., & Yun, H. (2023). Relationships between adolescent smartphone usage patterns, achievement goals, and academic achievement. *Asia Pacific Education Review*, *24*(1), 13–23. DOI: 10.1007/s12564-021-09718-5

Zhang, C., Tang, L., & Liu, Z. (2023). How social media usage affects psychological and subjective well-being: Testing a moderated mediation model. *BMC Psychology*, *11*(1), 286. DOI: 10.1186/s40359-023-01311-2 PMID: 37737198

Zhou, R., Yu, M., & Wang, X. (2016). Why Do Drivers Use Mobile Phones While Driving? The Contribution of Compensatory Beliefs. *PLoS One*, *11*(8), e0160288. DOI: 10.1371/journal.pone.0160288 PMID: 27494524

Compilation of References

Abbass, H. (2021). Editorial: What is Artificial Intelligence? *IEEE Transactions on Artificial Intelligence*, *2*(2), 94–95.

Abdulkareem, A. K., Ishola, A. A., Bello, M. L., & Adejumo, A. (2024). The dark side of digitalization: Examining the impact of digital overload on job autonomy and job satisfaction. *Journal of Information. Communication and Ethics in Society*, *22*(3), 354–371.

Abel, J. P., Buff, C. L., & Burr, S. A. (2016). Social Media and the Fear of Missing Out: Scale Development and Assessment. *Journal of Business & Economics Research*, •••, 33–44.

Abel, J. P., Buff, C. L., & Burr, S. A. (2016). Social media and the fear of missing out: Scale development and assessment. *Journal of Business & Economics Research*, *14*, 33–43.

Abu-Bader, S., & Jones, T. V. (2021). Statistical mediation analysis using the sobel test and hayes SPSS process macro. *International Journal of Quantitative and Qualitative Research Methods*.

Adachi, P. J. C., & Willoughby, T. (2013). More than just fun and games: The longitudinal relationships between strategic video games, self-reported problem solving skills, and academic grades. *Journal of Youth and Adolescence*, *42*(7), 1041–1052. DOI: 10.1007/s10964-013-9913-9 PMID: 23344653

Adobe. (2025). Audio Enhancement Powered by Adobe Sensei. https://www.adobe.com/sensei.html

Adobe. (n.d.). Adobe Firefly. Retrieved May 4, 2025, from https://firefly.adobe.com/

Akanbi, P. A. (2011). Influence of extrinsic and intrinsic motivation on employees' performance. https://www.academia.edu/download/34792904/motivationworker.pdf

Akıncı, H., & Kahraman, Ü. G. (2024). Endüstri 4.0: Yönetim bilişim sistemleri bakış açısıyla değerlendirme. *MAKÜ Uygulamalı Bilimler Dergisi*, *8*(1), 76–99. DOI: 10.31200/makuubd.1442339

Akyazı, A. (2018). *Gazetecilikte Dijitalleşe ve Haber Üretimine Yansıması: Robot Gazeteciler, Dijital Medya ve Gazetecilik.* Eğitim Yayınevi.

Al-Badri, N. (2023). *Works.* https://www.nora-al-badri.de/works-index

Aldosari, B. (2020). Do filters and pose in selfies have an effect on cosmetic procedures? *Saudi Journal of Otorhinolaryngology Head and Neck Surgery*, *22*(1), 21–23. DOI: 10.4103/SJOH.SJOH_1_20

Algeo, J. (1987). Theosophy and the Zeitgeist. *The American Theosophist*, *75*(10), 322–332.

Alha, K., Kinnunen, J., Koskinen, E., & Paavilainen, J. (2018). Free-to-Play Games: Paying Players' Perspective. *Proceedings of the 22nd International Academic Mindtrek Conference*, 49–58. https://doi.org/DOI: 10.1145/3275116.3275133

Aliçavuşoğlu, Ç., & Boyraz, E. (2019). Kendimi Biliyorum, Kork(M)Uyorum! Yenilikleri Kaçırma Korkusu (Fomo) ve Sosyal Medya Dijital Üstbilişin Rolü. *International Journal of Social And Humanities Sciences Research (JSHSR)*, 682-697.

Aliefendioğlu, B. (2024). Artırılmış çağda yapay zekâ teknolojilerinin grafik tasarımı alanına etkisi. *International Journal of Media. Culture and Literature*, *10*(1), 69–96.

Aliyev, R. A. (2025). Artificial Intelligence as a Key Driver of Energy Security Transformation. *Post-Soviet Issues*, *12*(1), 30–48.

Alkharoubi, A. M. (2020) *Wayfinding for pedestrians in the crowded areas of Al-Hajj: How can wayfinding system designs increase the efficiency of wayfinding and navigation performances for pedestrian pilgrims during the Islamic pilgrimage (Al-Hajj)* [Doctoral dissertation, University of Minnesota]. https://search.proquest.com/openview/22bbf5a8b9a21dfcb66c8605586f8104/1?pq-origsite=gscholar&cbl=18750&diss=y

Almqvist, K., & Belfrage, L. (2016). *Hilma af Klint: Seeing is Believing* (Almqvist, K., & Belfrage, L., Eds.). Koenig Books.

Amatriain, X., & Basilico, J. (2012). Netflix Recommendations: Beyond the 5 stars. Netflix Tech Blog. https://netflixtechblog.com/netflix-recommendations-beyond-the-5-stars-part-1-55838468f429

Anderson, C. W., Bell, E., & Shirky, C. (2015), Post-Industrial Journalism: Adapting to the Present. Geopolitics, History, and International Relations, 7(2), 32–123. https://www.jstor.org/

Anderson, E., & Zettelmeyer, F. (Eds.). (2021). *Leading with AI and Analytics: Build your data IQ to drive business value*. McGraw Hill.

Andriasyan, S. (2025). How Artificial Intelligence Is Used in the Film Industry. https://smartclick.ai/articles/how-artificial-intelligence-is-used-in-the-film-industry

Anggarawati, S., Armelly, A., Salim, M., Odilawati, W., Saputra, F. E., & Atmaja, F. T. (2023). The mediating role of narcissistic behavior in the relationship between materialistic orientation and conspicuous online consumption behavior on social media. *Cogent Business & Management, 10*(3), 2285768. DOI: 10.1080/23311975.2023.2285768

Antonietti, C., Camerini, A. L., & Marciano, L. (2020). The impact of self-esteem, family and peer cohesion on social appearance anxiety in adolescence: Examination of the mediating role of coping. *International Journal of Adolescence and Youth, 25*(1), 1089–1102. DOI: 10.1080/02673843.2020.1858888

Arendt, H. (2006). *Between past and future: Eight exercises in political thought.* Penguin Books.

Aria, M., & Cuccurullo, C. (2017). Bibliometrix: An R-tool for comprehensive science mapping analysis. *Journal of Informetrics, 11*(4), 959–975. DOI: 10.1016/j.joi.2017.08.007

Asadi, A., & Hemadi, R. (2018). Understanding Virtual Currencies in Video Games: A Review. *2018 2nd National and 1st International Digital Games Research Conference: Trends, Technologies, and Applications (DGRC)*, 109–117. https://doi.org/ DOI: 10.1109/DGRC.2018.8712047

Asprem, E., & Granholm, K. (2013). *Contemporary Esotericism.* Equinox Publishing Ltd.

Ay, A. (2023). Gazetecilik 4.0: Yapay Zekâ Haberciliğinin Güncel Örneklerine Yönelik Bir İnceleme. *Süleyman Demirel Üniversitesi Vizyoner Dergisi, 14*(38), 412–435. 10.21076/ vizyoner.1141093

Bachman, L. F. (2004). *Statistical analyses for language assessment book.* Cambridge University Press.

Bagwell, L. S., & Bernheim, B. D. (1996). Veblen effects in a theory of conspicuous consumption. *The American Economic Review, 86*(3), 349–373.

Baker, P. (2011). *Austin Osman Spare: The Life and Legend of London's Lost Artist*. Strange Attractor Press.

Bakioğlu, F., Deniz, M., Griffiths, M. D., & Pakpour, A. H. (2022). Adaptation and validation of the Online-Fear of Missing Out Inventory into Turkish and the association with social media addiction, smartphone addiction, and life satisfaction. *BMC Psychology, 10*(1), 154. DOI: 10.1186/s40359-022-00856-y PMID: 35717277

Balakrishnan, J., & Griffiths, M. D. (2018). An exploratory study of "selfitis" and the development of the Selfitis Behavior Scale. *International Journal of Mental Health and Addiction, 16*(3), 722–736. DOI: 10.1007/s11469-017-9844-x

Barari, M. (2023). Unveiling the dark side of influencer marketing: How social media influencers (human vs virtual) diminish followers' well-being. *Marketing Intelligence & Planning, 41*(8), 1162–1177. DOI: 10.1108/MIP-05-2023-0191

Bartoli, C., Nosi, C., Mattiacci, A., & Sfodera, F. (2023). Consumer self-concept in the cyberspace: How digitization has shaped the way we self-disclose to others. *Journal of Strategic Marketing, 31*(6), 1133–1154. DOI: 10.1080/0965254X.2022.2056501

Batouei, A., Iranmanesh, M., Mustafa, H., Nikbin, D., & Ping, T. A. (2020). Components of airport experience and their roles in eliciting passengers' satisfaction and behavioural intentions. *Research in Transportation Business & Management, 37*, 100585. https://www.sciencedirect.com/science/article/abs/pii/S221053952030122X?via%3Dihub

Baudrillard, J. (1994). *Simulacra and simulation* (Glaser, S. F., Trans.). University of Michigan Press.

Belada, N. E. S. (2024). Deepfake disinformation. *Journal of Information Technology Law, 6*(1), 321–358. DOI: 10.55009/bilisimhukukudergisi.1387306

Black, J., & Fullerton, C. (2020). Digital deceit: Fake news, artificial intelligence, and censorship in educational research. *Open Journal of Social Sciences, 8*, 71–88. DOI: 10.4236/jss.2020.87007

Blackwell, D., Leaman, C., Tramposch, R., Osborne, C., & Liss, M. (2017). Extraversion, Neuroticism, Attachment Style and Fear Of Missing Out As Predictors of Social Media Use and Addiction. *Personality and Individual Differences*, •••, 66–72.

Blavatsky, H. P. (1877a). *Isis Unveiled - A Master Key To The Mysteries Of Ancient And Modern Science And Theology: Vol I: Science*. Bernard Quaritsch.

Blavatsky, H. P. (1877b). *Isis Unveiled - A Master Key To The Mysteries Of Ancient And Modern Science And Theology: Vol II: Theology*. Bernard Quaritsch.

Boden, M. A. (2016). *AI: Its nature and future*. Oxford University Press.

Borkhardt, S. (2017). 7. 'Russian Messiah': On the Spiritual in the Reception of Vasily Kandinsky's Art in Germany, c. 1910–1937. In Hardiman, L., & Kozicharow, N. (Eds.), *Modernism and the Spiritual in Russian Art: New Perspectives* (pp. 149–164). Open Book Publishers.

Boursier, V., Gioia, F., & Griffiths, M. D. (2020b). Do selfie-expectancies and social appearance anxiety predict adolescents' problematic social media use?. *Computers in Human Behavior, 110*, 1-8. 106395. https://doi.org/DOI: 10.1016/j.chb.2020.106395

Boursier, V., Gioia, F., & Griffiths, M. D. (2020a). Selfie-engagement on social media: Pathological narcissism, positive expectation, and body objectification–Which is more influential? *Addictive Behaviors Reports, 11*, 1–10. DOI: 10.1016/j.abrep.2020.100263

Boyd, D., & Crawford, K. (2012). Critical Questions for Big Data: Provocations for A Cultural, Technological, and Scholarly Phenomenon. *Information Communication and Society*, *15*(5), 662–679.

Bozüyük, T., Yağcı, C., & Gökçe, İ. (2005). Yapay zekâ teknolojilerinin endüstrideki uygulamaları. *Dicle Üniversitesi Mühendislik Fakültesi Mühendislik Dergisi*, *2*(2), 95–105.

Braidotti, R. (2013). *The posthuman*. Polity Press.

Breves, P. L., Liebers, N., Abt, M., & Kunze, A. (2019). The perceived fit between Instagram influencers and the endorsed brand: How influencer–brand fit affects source credibility and persuasive effectiveness. *Journal of Advertising Research*, *59*(4), 440–454.

Breytenbach, C. (2015, 02 10). *Tackling digital burnout in the workplace*. January 24, 2025 tarihinde http://www.destinyman. com/2015/02/10/tackling-digital-burnout-in-the-workplace/ adresinden alındı

Broussard, M. (2018). *Artificial Unintelligence: How Computers Misunderstand the World*. MIT Press.

Brown, T. (2012). From blueprint to genetic code: the merits of an evolutionary approach to design. *Rotman Magazine, Spring*.

Bruett, J. (2017). *Video Game Speedrunning As a Unique Form of Play*. Games by Arbitration. https://www.jaredbruett.com/2017/07/28/essay-video-game-speedrunning -as-a-unique-form-of-play/

Bukatman, S. (1997). *Blade Runner*. BFI Publishing.

Burns, R. P., & Burns, R. (2008). Business research methods and Sstatistics using SPSS. *Sage (Atlanta, Ga.).*

Burroughs, W. S. (1993). *The Adding Machine: Collected Essays.* Arcade Publishing.

Butler, J. (1990). *Gender trouble: Feminism and the subversion of identity.* Routledge.

Byrd, M. (2022). *Why Morrowind's 36 Lessons of Vivec Is the Greatest Piece of Lore in RPG History.* Den of Geek. https://www.denofgeek.com/games/morrowind-36-lessons-of-vivec-history-explained-retrospective-theories-lore/

Caffarone, A. (2023). Virtual Gaming, Actual Damage: Video Game Design That Intentionally and Successfully Addicts Users Constitutes Civil Battery. *Duke Law & Technology Review*, *23*, 55.

Campbell, B. F. (1980). *Ancient Wisdom Revived: A History of the Theosophical Movement.* University of California Press.

Campbell, C., & Farrell, J. R. (2020). More than meets the eye: The functional components underlying influencer marketing. *Business Horizons*, *63*(4), 469–479.

Caner, N., Efe, Y. S., & Başdaş, Ö. (2022). The contribution of social media addiction to adolescent LIFE: Social appearance anxiety. *Current Psychology (New Brunswick, N.J.)*, *41*(12), 8424–8433. DOI: 10.1007/s12144-022-03280-y

Canva. (2025). AI Video Editor – Create & Edit Videos with AI. https://www.canva.com/video-editor/ai/

Canva. (n.d.). Canva: Tasarım herkes için. Retrieved May 4, 2025, from https://www.canva.com/tr_tr/

Carlson, M. (2015). The Robotic Reporter: Automated Journalism and The Redefinition of Labor, Compositional Forms, and Journalistic Authority. *Digital Journalism (Abingdon, England)*, *3*(3), 416–431.

Carro, B. (2018). Pros and Cons of Robot Journalism, https://www.mediego.com/en/blog/pros-and-cons-of-robot-journalism/. Erişim Tarihi: 12.04.2025

Carroll, P. J. (1987). *Liber Null & Psychonaut.* Weiser Book.

Carter T. B. (1998), "Electronic Gatekeepers: Locking Out The Marketplace Of Ideas". Communication Law and Policy. 3:3., 389-408.

Carvalho, M., Yunus, A., & Lee, B. (2024) Tourism sector to bring in RM375bil over three years, Dewan Rakyat told. https://www.thestar.com.my/news/nation/2024/03/11/tourism-sector-to-bring-in-rm375bil-over-three-years-dewan-rakyat-told

Casale, S., Rugai, L., & Fioravanti, G. (2018). Exploring the Role of Positive Metacognitions in Explaining the Association Between the Fear of Missing Out and Social Media Addiction. *Addictive Behaviors*, •••, 83–87.

Castells, M. (2009). *Communication Power*. Oxford University Press.

Cave, S., & Dihal, K. (2020). *Imagining AI: How the World Sees Intelligent Machines*. Oxford University Press.

Çavuş, S. (2020). Gazetecilik ve Yapay Zekâ. H. Bakırtaş, & S. Çavuş içinde, Yapay Zekâ Disiplinleri Dönüştürüyor Değişime Hazır mıyız? (s. 242-255 S:250). Konya: Ekin

CCRU. (1999). *Abstract Culture Digital Hyperstition* (D. Barker (ed.)). Saddle stitch.

Çelik Durmuş, S., Gülnar, E., & Özveren, H. (2022). Determining digital burnout in nursing students: A descriptive research study. *Nurse Education Today*, (111), 1–7.

Chae, J. (2017). Virtual makeover: Selfie-taking and social media use increase selfie-editing frequency through social comparison. *Computers in Human Behavior*, *66*, 370–376. DOI: 10.1016/j.chb.2016.10.007

Chambers, R. W. (1895). *The King in Yellow*. F. Tennyson Neely.

Chaudhari, B. L., Patil, J. K., Kadiani, A., Chaudhury, S., & Saldanha, D. (2019). Correlation of motivations for selfie-posting behavior with personality traits. *Industrial Psychiatry Journal*, *28*(1), 123–129. DOI: 10.4103/ipj.ipj_30_19

Chávez Heras, D. (2024). *Cinema and machine vision: Artificial intelligence, aesthetics and spectatorship*. Edinburgh University Press.

Chen, H., & Magromo, K. (2024, May 4). Finance worker pays out $25 million after video call with deepfake 'chief financial officer'. *CNN*. https://edition.cnn.com/2024/02/04/asia/deepfake-cfo-scam-hong-kong-intl-hnk

Chen, Y., Rao, A., Jiang, X., Xiao, S., Ma, R., Wang, Z., Xiong, H., & Dai, B. (2024). CinePreGen: Camera Controllable Video Previsualization via Engine-powered Diffusion. arXiv preprint arXiv:2408.17424.

Chen, S., van Tilburg, W. A., & Leman, P. J. (2022). Self-objectification in women predicts approval motivation in online self-presentation. *British Journal of Social Psychology*, *61*(1), 366–388. DOI: 10.1111/bjso.12485

Chen, W., Xu, Z., Zheng, X., Yu, Q., & Luo, Y. (2020). Research on sentiment classification of online travel review text. *Applied Sciences (Basel, Switzerland)*, *10*(15), 52–75.

Chmielewska, E. (2001) *Implaced communication: wayfinding and informational environments.* https://escholarship.mcgill.ca/concern/theses/zk51vj42x

Choi, S.-Y., & Kim, J.-H. (2024). Validity and reliability of The Korean version of the Digital Burnout Scale. *Frontiers in Paublic Health*, 1-11.

Choi, G. Y., & Behm-Morawitz, E. (2018). Teach me about yourself (ie): Exploring selfie-takers' technology usage and digital literacy skills. *Psychology of Popular Media Culture*, *7*(3), 345–360. DOI: 10.1037/ppm0000130

Christensen, L., Johnson, B., & Turner, L. (2015). Araştırma Yöntemleri Desen ve Analiz. (A. Aypay, Çev.) Ankara: Anı Yayıncılık.

Christy, A., Sahrani, R., & Heng, P. H. (2020). Academic Burnout in Digital Era: Examining the Role of Problematic Smartphone Use, Core Self-Evaluations and Academic Achivement Burnout among Medical Students. *Advances in Social Science, Education and Humanities Research*, (439), 586–590.

Chua, T. H. H., & Chang, L. (2016). Follow me and like my beautiful selfies: Singapore teenage girls' engagement in self-presentation and peer comparison on social media. *Computers in Human Behavior*, *55*, 190–197. DOI: 10.1016/j.chb.2015.09.011

Claes, L., Hart, T. A., Smits, D., Van den Eynde, F., Mueller, A., & Mitchell, J. E. (2012). Validation of the social appearance anxiety scale in female eating disorder patients. *European Eating Disorders Review*, *20*(5), 406–409. DOI: 10.1002/erv.1147

Clanton Harpine, E. (2015). Is intrinsic motivation better than extrinsic motivation? Içinde E. Clanton Harpine (Ed.), *Group-Centered Prevention in Mental Health: Theory, Training, and Practice* (ss. 87-107). Springer International Publishing. https://doi.org/DOI: 10.1007/978-3-319-19102-7_6

Clarke, P. (2004). *Encyclopedia of New Religious Movements*. Routledge.

Clerbois, S. (2002). In Search of the Forme-Pensée: The Influence of Theosophy on Belgian Artists, Between Symbolism and the Avant-Garde (1890–1910) [A la recherche d'une forme-pensée. L'influence de la théosophie sur les artistes en Belgique, entre symbolisme et avant-garde. *Nineteenth-Century Art Worldwide, 1*(2), 1–24.

Cmsproductions (2025). https://www.cmsproductions.com/blog/ai-tools-for-film-producers

Çopuroğlu, F. (2021). Tüketicilerin Sosyal Medya Kullanımı, FoMO ve Hedonik Tüketim Arasındaki İlişki. *OPUS Uluslararası Toplum Araştırmaları Dergisi*, 4298-4326.

Corbetta, P. (2003). *Social Research Theory, Methods and Techniques*. Sage Publications.

Costa, B. M. (2018). Mas afinal, para que serve a Análise de Sentimento? *YouTube*. https//www.youtube.com/watch?v=JMQaFBYNLno

Costes, J.-M., & Bonnaire, C. (2022). Spending Money in Free-to-Play Games: Sociodemographic Characteristics, Motives, Impulsivity and Internet Gaming Disorder Specificities. *International Journal of Environmental Research and Public Health, 19*(23). *Artigo, 23*. Advance online publication. DOI: 10.3390/ijerph192315709 PMID: 36497782

Couldry, N., & Mejias, U. A. (2019). *The Costs of Connection: How Data Is Colonizing Human Life and Appropriating It for Capitalism*. Stanford University Press.

Coulthard, N., & Ogden, J. (2018). The impact of posting selfies and gaining feedback ('likes') on the psychological wellbeing of 16-25 year olds: An experimental study. *Cyberpsychology (Brno), 12*(2). Advance online publication. DOI: 10.5817/CP2018-2-4

Coursera. (2024). What Is AI Video Editing? https://www.coursera.org/articles/ai-video-editing

Creativani, K. (2023). Exploring the potential of visual communication design education: Transforming education paradigm. *Visual Heritage: Jurnal Kreasi Seni dan Budaya*, 5(2), 281–289. https://doi.org/DOI: 10.30998/vh.v5i2.8242

Crowley, A. (2022). *The Book of the Law, or Liber AL vel Legis*. Unicursal.

Cusack, C. (2011). Discordian Magic. *International Journal for the Study of New Religions*, *2*(1), 125–145.

D'Amico, N. J. (2021). *MI* [Thesis, University of Tasmania]. https://doi.org/DOI: 10.25959/23249357.v1

Dan, J. (2006). *Kabbalah: A Very Short Introduction*. Oxford University Press.

Daradkeh, M., & Atalla, S. (2023). From Data to Narrative: Automating and Engineering the Art of Data Storytelling. In *International Conference on Information Technology* (Vol. 23, pp. 550-555).

Daraj, L. R., AlGhareeb, M., Almutawa, Y. M., Trabelsi, K., & Jahrami, H. (2023). Systematic Review and Meta-Analysis of the Correlation Coefficients between Nomophobia and Anxiety, Smartphone Addiction, and Insomnia Symptoms. *Health Care*, *11*(14), 1–14.

Davidovici-Nora, M. (2014). *Paid and Free Digital Business Models Innovations in the Video Game Industry* (SSRN Scholarly Paper No. 2534022). Social Science Research Network. https://papers.ssrn.com/abstract=2534022

Davis, E. (2015). *High Weirdness: Visionary Experience in the Senventies Counterculture*. Rice University.

Dayo, F., Memon, A. A., & Dharejo, N. (2023). Scriptwriting in the Age of AI: Revolutionizing Storytelling withArtificial Intelligence. *Journal of Media & Communication*, *4*(1), 24–38.

De Jans, S., Van de Sompel, D., De Veirman, M., & Hudders, L. (2020). #Sponsored! How the recognition of sponsoring on Instagram posts affects adolescents' brand evaluations through source evaluations. *Computers in Human Behavior*, *109*, 106342.

De Jesus, S. C. (1994). *Environmental communication: design planning for way-finding. Design Issues, 10(3).* MIT Press., DOI: 10.2307/1511691

de Vaate, A. J. N. B., Veldhuis, J., Alleva, J. M., Konijn, E. A., & van Hugten, C. H. (2018). Show your best self (ie): An exploratory study on selfie-related motivations and behavior in emerging adulthood. *Telematics and Informatics*, *35*(5), 1392–1407.

de Vaate, A. J. N. B., Veldhuis, J., & Konijn, E. A. (2020). How online self-presentation affects well-being and body image: A systematic review. *Telematics and Informatics*, *47*, 101316. DOI: 10.1016/j.tele.2019.101316

De Veirman, M., Cauberghe, V., & Hudders, L. (2017). Marketing through Instagram influencers: The impact of number of followers and product divergence on brand attitude. *International Journal of Advertising*, *36*(5), 798–828.

Deguzman, K. (2023). What is Production Design in Film- How to Tell Stories Visually. https://www.studiobinder.com/blog/what-is-production-design-in-film

Delbaere, M., Michael, B., & Phillips, B. J. (2021). Social media influencers: A route to brand engagement for their followers. *Psychology and Marketing*, *38*(1), 101–112.

Deleuze, G. (1989). *Cinema 2: The time-image* (Tomlinson, H., & Galeta, R., Trans.). University of Minnesota Press.

Deleuze, G., & Guattari, F. (1987). *A thousand plateaus: Capitalism and schizophrenia* (Massumi, B., Trans.). University of Minnesota Press.

Desowitz, B. (2020). The Mandalorian: How ILM's Innovative StageCraft Tech Created a Star Wars Virtual Universe. https://www.indiewire.com/features/general/the-mandalorian-ilm-stagecraft-1202212389/

Diakopoulos, N. (2019). *Automating the News*. Harvard University Press.

D-ID. (2024). *Digital avatar*. https://www.d-id.com/resources/glossary/digital-avatar/

Diefenbach, S., & Christoforakos, L. (2017). The selfie paradox: Nobody seems to like them yet everyone has reasons to take them. An exploration of psychological functions of selfies in self-presentation. *Frontiers in Psychology*, *7*(8), •••. DOI: 10.3389/fpsyg.2017.00007

Dinh, T. C. T., & Lee, Y. (2021). "I want to be as trendy as influencers" – how "fear of missing out" leads to buying intention for products endorsed by social media influencers. *Journal of Research in Interactive Marketing*, *16*(3), 346–364. DOI: 10.1108/JRIM-04-2021-0127

Dinh, T. C. T., & Lee, Y. (2024). Social media influencers and followers' conspicuous consumption: The mediation of fear of missing out and materialism. *Heliyon*, *10*(16), e36387. DOI: 10.1016/j.heliyon.2024.e36387

Dinh, T. C. T., Wang, M., & Lee, Y. (2023). How Does the Fear of Missing Out Moderate the Effect of Social Media Influencers on Their Followers' Purchase Intention? *SAGE Open*, *13*(3), 21582440231197259. DOI: 10.1177/21582440231197259

Dipnot.tv. https://dipnot.tv/tr-TR/ilhan-sesen-son-yolculuguna-ugurlandi, Access Date: May 29, 2025 https://dipnot.tv/tr-TR, Access Date: May 29, 2025

DiTommaso, L. (2025). Conversations about Artificial Intelligence in Filmmaking. https://www.productiondesignerscollective.org/single-post/conversations-about-artificial-intelligence-in-filmmaking

Doğan, E. (2015). Türkiye'deki görsel iletişim tasarımı bölümleri üzerine genel bir durum analizi. *İletişim Çalışmaları Dergisi*, 1(1), 15–33.

Doğan, F., & Türkoğlu, İ. (2019). Derin öğrenme modelleri ve uygulama alanlarına ilişkin bir derleme. *Dicle Üniversitesi Mühendislik Fakültesi Mühendislik Dergisi*, *10*(2), 409–445. DOI: 10.24012/DUMF.411130

Donohue, G. A., Tichenor, P. J., & Olien, C. N. (1972). Gatekeeping: mass media systems and information control. In Kline, F. G., & Tichenor, P. J. (Eds.), *Current Perspectives in Mass Communication Research* (pp. 41–70). Sage.

Dossey, L. (2014). FOMO, Digital Dementia, and Our Dangerous Experiment. *Explore (New York, N.Y.)*, •••, 69–73.

Drummond, A., & Sauer, J. D. (2018). Video game loot boxes are psychologically akin to gambling. *Nature Human Behaviour*, *2*(8), 530–532. DOI: 10.1038/s41562-018-0360-1 PMID: 31209310

Drury, N. (2011). *Stealing Fire from Heaven. The Rise of Modern Western Magic*. Oxford University Press.

Duan, J., & Dholakia, R. R. (2017). Posting purchases on social media increases happiness: The mediating roles of purchases' impact on self and interpersonal relationships. *Journal of Consumer Marketing, 34*(5), 404–413. DOI: 10.1108/JCM-07-2016-1871

Duggan, C. (2014). Chaos magick. *The Occult World*, 406–411.

Durak, H., & Seferoğlu, S. S. (2016). Türkiye'de Sosyal Medya Okuryazarlığı Ve Sosyal Ağ Kullanım Örüntülerinin İncelenmesi. *Uluslararası Sosyal Araştırmalar Dergisi The Journal Of International Social Research*, 526-535.

Dykes, B. (2020). *Effective Data Storytelling: How to Drive Change with Data, Narrative and Visuals*. John Wiley & Sons.

Eckhardt, G. M., Belk, Russell W., & and Wilson, J. A. J. (2015). The rise of inconspicuous consumption. *Journal of Marketing Management, 31*(7-8), 807–826. DOI: 10.1080/0267257X.2014.989890

Egenfeldt-Nielsen, S., Smith, J., & Tosca, S. (2008). *Understanding Video Games: The Essential Introduction*. https://doi.org/DOI: 10.4324/9780429431791

El Khoueiry, C., Sacre, H., Haddad, C., Akel, M., Saade, S., Hallit, S., & Obeid, S. (2021). Selfie addiction: The impact of personality traits? A cross-sectional study among the Lebanese population. *Perspectives in Psychiatric Care, 57*(1), 167–178. DOI: 10.1111/ppc.12539

Eldaly, A. S., & Mashaly, S. M. (2022). The new dilemma of plastic surgery and social media: A systematic review. *European Journal of Plastic Surgery, 45*, 371–382. DOI: 10.1007/s00238-021-01891-5

Elgammal, A., Liu, B., Elhoseiny, M., & Mazzone, M. (2017). CAN: Creative adversarial networks—Generating "art" by learning about styles and deviating from style norms. In Goel, A., Jordanous, A., & Pease, A. (Eds.), *Proceedings of the 8th International Conference on Computational Creativity* (pp. 96–103). Georgia Institute of Technology. https://arxiv.org/abs/1706.07068

El-Masri, M., Altrabsheh, N., & Mansour, H. (2017). *Successes and challenges of Arabic sentiment analysis research: a literature review*. Qatar University.

Engle, J. (2014). Cults of Lovecraft : The Impact of H. P. Lovecraft ' s Fiction on Contemporary Occult Practices. *Mythlore: A Journal of J.R.R. Tolkien, C.S. Lewis. Charles Williams, and Mythopoeic Literature, 33*(1), 85–98.

Ergen, M. (2019). What is Artificial Intelligence? Technical Considerations and Future Perception. *The Anatolian Journal of Cardiology, 22*, 5–7.

Ermeydan, D., & Etlioğlu Erçetingöz, S. (2024). Avrupa Birliği Yapay Zekâ Tüzüğü uyarınca kişilik kapsamında yapay zekâ. *Bahçeşehir Üniversitesi Hukuk Fakültesi Dergisi, 19*(223), 1417–1454.

Erten, P. (2020). The Digital Burnout Scale Development Study. *İnönü University Journal of the Faculty of Education, 21*(2), 668-683.

eSafety. (2022). *Deepfake trends and challenges - Position statement.* https://www.esafety.gov.au/sites/default/files/2022-01/Deepfake-position-statement%20_v2.pdf

European Commission. (2019). *Ethics guidelines for trustworthy AI.* Publications Office of the European Union., DOI: 10.2759/346720

Faber, L. W. (2020). *The computer's voice: From Star Trek to Siri.* University of Minnesota Press.

Faber, L. W. (2023). *Robot suicide: Death, identity, and AI in science fiction.* Lexington Books.

Falmouth University. (2023). What is visual communication? Retrieved May 4, 2025, from https://www.falmouth.ac.uk/news/what-is-visual-communication

Fanelli, M., & Strobl, M. M. (2023). Unlocking the spiritual potential of games: Reflections and future directions. In L. Marcato & F. Schniz (Eds.), *Fictional Practices of Spirituality I: Interactive Media* (pp. 465–475). transcript Verlag.

Fastoso, F., González-Jiménez, H., & Cometto, T. (2021). Mirror, mirror on my phone: Drivers and consequences of selfie editing. *Journal of Business Research, 133*, 365–375. DOI: 10.1016/j.jbusres.2021.05.002

Feigenbaum, A., & Alamalhodaei, A. (2020). *The Data Storytelling Workbook.* Routledge.

Feng, Z., Diao, Y., Ma, H., Liu, M., Long, M., Zhao, S., Wu, H., & Wang, Y. (2022). Mobile phone addiction and depression among Chinese medical students: The mediating role of sleep quality and the moderating role of peer relationships. *BMC Psychiatry, 22*(1), 567. DOI: 10.1186/s12888-022-04183-9 PMID: 35999533

Figma. (n.d.). Your creativity, unblocked with Figma AI. Retrieved May 4, 2025, from https://www.figma.com/ai/

Flunger, R., Mladenow, A., & Strauss, C. (2017). The free-to-play business model. *Proceedings of the 19th International Conference on Information Integration and Web-based Applications & Services*, 373–379. https://doi.org/DOI: 10.1145/3151759.3151802

Folcu , O., Manta, O., & Militaru, I. (2024, January 15). Education, artificial intelligence, and the digital age. *Qeios.*

Fox, J., & Rooney, M. C. (2015). The Dark Triad and trait self-objectification as predictors of men's use and self-presentation behaviors on social networking sites. *Personality and Individual Differences*, *76*, 161–165. DOI: 10.1016/j.paid.2014.12.017

Fox, J., Vendemia, M. A., Smith, M. A., & Brehm, N. R. (2021). Effects of taking selfies on women's self-objectification, mood, self-esteem, and social aggression toward female peers. *Body Image*, *36*, 193–200. DOI: 10.1016/j.bodyim.2020.11.011

Fraenkel, J., & Wallen, N. (2008). *How to Design and Evaluate Research in Education*. McGraw-Hill Education.

Frawley, C. (2023). What Generative AI Could Look Like for Actors. https://www.backstage.com/magazine/article/ai-actors-explained-76361

Freberg, K., Graham, K., McGaughey, K., & Freberg, L. A. (2011). Who are the social media influencers? *Public Relations Review*, *37*(1), 90–92. DOI: 10.1016/j.pubrev.2010.11.001

Fredriksson Friman, E., & Zätterlund, O. (2023). *The Dark Patterns of Battle Passes: Investigating player attitudes to a growing type of microtransaction*. https://urn.kb.se/resolve?urn=urn:nbn:se:umu:diva-211027

Friedman, L. W., & Friedman, H. H. (2013). Using social media technologies to enhance online learning. *The Journal of Educators Online*, *10*(1). Advance online publication. DOI: 10.9743/JEO.2013.1.5

Fullwood, C., James, B. M., & Chen-Wilson, C. H. (2016). Self-concept clarity and online self-presentation in adolescents. *Cyberpsychology, Behavior, and Social Networking*, *19*(12), 716–720. DOI: 10.1089/cyber.2015.0623

Fullwood, C., Wesson, C., Chen-Wilson, J., Keep, M., Asbury, T., & Wilsdon, L. (2020). If the mask fits: Psychological correlates with online self-presentation experimentation in adults. *Cyberpsychology, Behavior, and Social Networking*, *23*(11), 737–742. DOI: 10.1089/cyber.2020.0154

Gartner. (2021). Definition of digitalization. Retrieved May 4, 2025, from https://www.gartner.com/en/information-technology/glossary/digitalization

Gawer, A. (2022). Digital platforms and ecosystems: Remarks on the dominant organizational forms of the digital age. *Innovation (North Sydney, N.S.W.), 24*(1), 110–124. DOI: 10.1080/14479338.2021.1965888

Georgetown University Library. (2023). Copyright and AI. https://guides.library.georgetown.edu/ai/copyright

Ghosh, A. (2023). Artificial Intelligence as an Innovation in the Film Industry. *Research Inspiration, 3*(3), 12–16.

Girmaji, R., Beri, B., Subramanian, R., & Gandhi, V. (2025). EditIQ: Automated Cinematic Editing of Static Wide-Angle Videos via Dialogue Interpretation and Saliency Cues. In *Proceedings of the 30th International Conference on Intelligent User Interfaces* (pp. 609-623).

Göldağ, B. (2022). An Investigation of the Relationship between University Students' Digital Burnout Levels and Perceived Stress Levels. *Journal of Learning and Teaching in Digital Age, 7*(1), 90–98.

Gong, A.-D., Huang, Y.-T., Liu, K., & Sugiura, K. (2025). Getting hooked on mobile games: Strengthening purchase intentions towards mobile games using investment model and parasocial interactions. *Mobile Media & Communication, 13*(1), 47–68. DOI: 10.1177/20501579241257907

Goodfellow, I., Pouget-Abadie, J., Mirza, M., Xu, B., Warde-Farley, D., Ozair, S., Courville, A., & Bengio, Y. (2014). Generative adversarial nets. *In Advances in Neural Information Processing Systems* (Vol. 27, pp. 2672–2680). https://www.researchgate.net/publication/263012109_Generative_Adversarial_Networks

Goodwin, R., & Sharp, O. (2020). *Zone Out* [Short film]. NYU AI Film Lab.

Gower, D., Kachaturoff, M., & Caboral-Stevens, M. (2023). Digital Experience Among Faculty and Students in One Midwest University. *Education Journal, 12*(3), 92–98.

Graefe, A. (2016). Guide to Automated Journalism. Tow Center for Digital Journalism Report. Erişim Tarihi (25.04.2025) http://towcenter.org/research/guide-to-automated-journalism/

Green, L. N. (2023) *The Variability of Typographic Wayfinding Systems.* Kent State University. https://search.proquest.com/openview/dbf12a2bbf207e3781714e2f39e9ff60/1?pq-origsite=gscholar&cbl=18750&diss=y

Griffiths, M. D., & Balakrishnan, J. (2018). The psychosocial impact of excessive selfie-taking in youth: A brief overview. *Education for Health, 36*(1), 3–6.

Griskevicius, V., Tybur, J. M., Sundie, J. M., Cialdini, R. B., Miller, G. F., & Kenrick, D. T. (2007). Blatant benevolence and conspicuous consumption: When romantic motives elicit strategic costly signals. *Journal of Personality and Social Psychology, 93*(1), 85–102. DOI: 10.1037/0022-3514.93.1.85

Günay, M. (2021). Design in visual communication. *Art and Design Review, 9*, 109–122. DOI: 10.4236/adr.2021.92010

Guo, H. (2022). Innovation and development of visual communication design in the new media era. *Frontiers in Business, Economics and Management, 3*(3), 49–51.

Gürdin, B. (2019). Sosyal Medyanın Hedonik Tüketimi ve FoMO"nun Gücü. *Üçüncü Sektör Sosyal Ekonomi Dergisi*, 1259-1278.

Hadan, H., Sgandurra, S. A., Zhang-Kennedy, L., & Nacke, L. E. (2024). From Motivating to Manipulative: The Use of Deceptive Design in a Game's Free-to-Play Transition. *Proc. ACM Hum.-Comput. Interact., 8*(CHI PLAY), 309:1-309:31. https://doi.org/DOI: 10.1145/3677074

Halpern, D., Valenzuela, S., & Katz, J. E. (2016). "Selfie-ists" or "Narci-selfiers"?: A cross-lagged panel analysis of selfie taking and narcissism. *Personality and Individual Differences, 97*, 98–101. DOI: 10.1016/j.paid.2016.03.019

Hamari, J. (2015). Why do people buy virtual goods? Attitude toward virtual good purchases versus game enjoyment. *International Journal of Information Management, 35*(3), 299–308. DOI: 10.1016/j.ijinfomgt.2015.01.007

Hamari, J., Hanner, N., & Koivisto, J. (2020). «Why pay premium in freemium services?» A study on perceived value, continued use and purchase intentions in free-to-play games. *International Journal of Information Management, 51*, 102040. DOI: 10.1016/j.ijinfomgt.2019.102040

Hamari, J., & Keronen, L. (2017). Why do people play games? A meta-analysis. *International Journal of Information Management, 37*(3), 125–141. DOI: 10.1016/j.ijinfomgt.2017.01.006

Hand, M. (2012). *Ubiquitous photography*. Polity Press.

Hanegraaff, W. (2013). *Western Esotericism: A Guide for the Perplexed*. Bloomsbury Press.

Hanegraaf, W. J. (2006). *Dictionary of Gnosis & Western Esotericism* (Hanegraaf, W. J., Ed.). Brill.

Harari, Y. N. (2011). Sapiens: História Breve da Humanidade - De Animais a Deuses. (7ª ed.). Elsinore.

Harari, N. Y. (2016). *Homo Deus Yarının Kısa Bir Tarihi. P. N. Taneli (Çev.).* Kolektif Kitap.

Harmless, W. (2008). *Mystics.* Oxford University Press.

Hart, T. A., Flora, D. B., Palyo, S. A., Fresco, D. M., Holle, C., & Heimberg, R. G. (2008). Development and examination of the social appearance anxiety scale. *Assessment, 15*(1), 48–59. DOI: 10.1177/1073191107306673

Hashem, R. E. S. M., Hassan, G. A. M., El-Sheikh, M. M., Hassan, H., & Azzam, L. A. B. I. (2022). Selfie phenomenon among a sample of Egyptian university students: Rate and psychiatric correlates. *Middle East Current Psychiatry, 29*(103), 1–12. DOI: 10.1186/s43045-022-00254-5

Hayes, A. F. (2022). *Introduction to mediation, moderation, and conditional process analysis: A regression-based approach* (3rd ed.). The Guilford Press.

Herman, D. (2020). Introducing Short-Term Brands: A New Branding Tool for a New Consumer Reality. *Journal of Brand Management*, •••, 330–340.

Hermida, A., & Young, M. L. (2019). *Data Journalism and the Regeneration of News.* Routledge.

Hertzog, C., Kramer, A. F., Wilson, R. S., & Lindenberger, U. (2008). Enrichment Effects on Adult Cognitive Development: Can the Functional Capacity of Older Adults Be Preserved and Enhanced? *Psychological Science in the Public Interest, 9*(1), 1–65. DOI: 10.1111/j.1539-6053.2009.01034.x PMID: 26162004

Hietajarvi, L., Salmela-Aro, K., Tuominen, H., Hakkarainen, K., & Lonka, K. (2019). Beyond screen time: Multidimensionality of socio-digital participation and relations to academic well-being in three educational phases. *Computers in Human Behavior*, (93), 13–24.

Hine, P. (1995). *Condensed Chaos: An Introduction to Chaos Magic.* New Falcon Publications.

Holdsworth, J., & Scappichio, M. (2024). *What is deep learning?* IBM. https://www.ibm.com/think/topics/deep-learning

Holroyd, M., & Olorunselu, F. (2022, March 16). Deepfake video shows Zelenskyy's false call for Ukraine to surrender. *Euronews.* https://www.euronews.com/my-europe/2022/03/16/deepfake-zelenskyy-surrender-video-is-the-first-intentionally-used-in-ukraine-war

Hong, S., Jahng, M. R., Lee, N., & Wise, K. R. (2020). Do you filter who you are?: Excessive self-presentation, social cues, and user evaluations of Instagram selfies. *Computers in Human Behavior, 104*, 1–6. DOI: 10.1016/j.chb.2019.106159

Hossain, S. F. A., Xi, Z., Nurunnabi, M., & Hussain, K. (2020). Ubiquitous Role of Social Networking in Driving M-Commerce: Evaluating the Use of Mobile Phones for Online Shopping and Payment in the Context of Trust. *SAGE Open, 10*(3). Advance online publication. DOI: 10.1177/2158244020939536

Hudders, L., De Jans, S., & De Veirman, M. (2021). The commercialization of social media stars: A literature review and conceptual framework on the strategic use of social media influencers. In De Jans, S., De Veirman, M., & Hudders, L. (Eds.), *Social media influencers in strategic communication* (pp. 24–67). Routledge.

Huitt, W. (2009). Self-concept and self-esteem. *Educational Psychology Interactive*. Valdosta, GA: Valdosta State University. (https://www.edpsycinteractive.org/topics/conation/self2.html). 25.02.2025.

Hunt, M., Marx, R., Lipson, C., & Young, J. (2018). No more FOMO: Limiting social media decreases loneliness and depression. *Journal of Social and Clinical Psychology*, •••, 751–768.

Hutto, C. J., & Gilbert, E. (2014). VADER: A Parsimonious Rule-based Model for Sentiment Analysis of Social Media Text. In *Proceedings of the Eighth International AAAI Conference on Weblogs and Social Media*. Association for the Advancement of Artificial Intelligence, 216-225.

IBM. (2024). What is artificial intelligence (AI)? Retrieved May 4, 2025, from https://www.ibm.com/think/topics/artificial-intelligence

Iftikhar, H., & Luximon, Y. (2022). The syntheses of static and mobile wayfinding information: An empirical study of wayfinding preferences and behaviour in complex environments. *Facilities, 40*(7/8), 452–474. DOI: 10.1108/F-06-2021-0052

Ilıcak, N. G., & Çinko, K. (2021). Yapay zekânın yarattığı masal: Prenses ile tilki. *Uluslararası Türkçe Edebiyat Kültür Eğitim Dergisi, 10*(2), 703–719.

Imran, H., Rehman, S., Khanum, S., & Shahzadi, M. (2024). Association of self-esteem, narcissistic tendencies, and selfie-posting behavior among young adults: Association between self-esteem, narcissism and selfies. *Pakistan Journal of Health Sciences, 5*(1), 26–31. DOI: 10.54393/pjhs.v5i01.1266

Ismail, A. F. (2024). Excessive editing of selfies on social media: The illusion of sustainability in mental health among female adolescents. *Journal of Ecohumanism, 3*(7), 3487–3494. DOI: 10.62754/joe.v3i7.4481

Jackson, K. (1992). *Higher peaks in view: The man who wrote Twin Peaks has plans to get weirder. Mark Frost talked to Kevin Jackson about Sherlock and warlocks.* The Independent. https://www.independent.co.uk/arts-entertainment/higher-peaks-in-view-the-man-who-wrote-twin-peaks-has-plans-to-get-weirder-mark-frost-talked-to-kevin-jackson-about-sherlock-and-warlocks-1541807.html

Jalees, D. (2020). Design thinking in the library space: Problem-solving signage like a graphic designer. *Art Libraries Journal, 45*(3), 114–121. DOI: 10.1017/alj.2020.17

Janoščík, V. (2023). Behavioral capital: Gaming and monetization in post-marxist perspective. *Semiotica, 2023*(254), 137–156. DOI: 10.1515/sem-2023-0124

Jeong, Y.-W., Han, Y.-R., Kim, S.-K., & Jeong, H.-S. (2020). The frequency of impairments in everyday activities due to the overuse of the internet, gaming, or smartphone, and its relationship to health-related quality of life in Korea. *BMC Public Health, 20*(1), 954. DOI: 10.1186/s12889-020-08922-z PMID: 32552690

Jin, S. V., & Ryu, E. (2018). "The paradox of Narcissus and Echo in the instagram pond" in light of the selfie culture from Freudian evolutionary psychology: Self-loving and confident but lonely. *Journal of Broadcasting & Electronic Media, 62*(4), 554–577. DOI: 10.1080/08838151.2018.1474881

Joshi, S. T. (1989). *Afterword", History of the Necronomicon*. Necronomicon Press.

Jung, C. G. (1980). Psychology and Alchemy. In Ladner, G. B. (Ed.), *The Collected Works of C. G. Jung* (Vol. 12). Princeton University Press.

Jun, X. Y. (2023). The construction of designers' visual design thinking in the visual communication design perspective. *World Journal of Educational Research (Los Angeles, Calif.), 10*(5), 88–93.

Jyoti, R. (2021). Unlock The True Power of Data Analytics with Artificial Intelligence. In Liebowitz, J. (Ed.), *Data Analytics and AI* (pp. 21–30). CRC Press.

Kant, I. (1998). *Critique of pure reason* (Guyer, P., & Wood, A. W., Trans.). Cambridge University Press.

Karaahmet Balcı, S. (2017). Değişen paradigmaların görsel iletişim tasarımı lisans ve lisansüstü eğitim programlarına yansımaları. *Turkish Studies International Periodical for the Languages. Literature and History of Turkish or Turkic, 12*(23), 151–172.

Karataşlıoğlu, R. E., & Özkanal, B. (2023). Digital Burnout in Distance Education Process: Examination of Secondary School Teachers' Opinions. *Journal of Advanced Education Studies, 5*(2), 319–341.

Karnouskos, S. (2020). Artificial intelligence in digital media: The era of deepfakes. *IEEE Transactions on Technology and Society*, *1*(3), 138–147. DOI: 10.1109/TTS.2020.3001312

Kavuran, T., & Çetinkaya, A. (2012). Görsel iletişim açısından film afişlerinin grafik çözümlemeleri (2000–2010 yılları arasında Antalya Altın Portakal Film Festivali'nde ödül alan sinema film afişlerinin değerlendirilmesi). *International Communication Symposium:* Kyrgyzstan Turkey Manas University Publications.

Kaynar, M. (2024). Yapay zekâ, yapay zekâ etiği ve insan doğasının geleceği (Yüksek lisans tezi, İstanbul Sabahattin Zaim Üniversitesi, Lisansüstü Eğitim Enstitüsü, Felsefe ve Din Bilimleri Anabilim Dalı, Felsefe ve Din Bilimleri Bilim Dalı). İstanbul, Türkiye.

Kellner, D. (1995). *Media culture: Cultural studies, identity and politics between the modern and the postmodern*. Routledge.

Kember, S., & Zylinska, J. (2012). *Life after new media: Mediation as a vital process*. MIT Press.

Kerlow, I. (2009). *The Art of 3D Computer Animation and Effects*. Wiley Publishing.

Ketenci, F., & Bilgili, C. (2006). *Görsel İletişim ve Grafik Tasarım: Yoncaların 10.000 Yıllık Gizemli Dansı*. Beta Yayınevi.

Kilavuz, İ. F. (2024). *Deepfaked democracy': The next-generation menace to global politics*. TRT World Research Centre. https://researchcentre.trtworld.com/wp-content/uploads/2024/09/Deepfaked-Democracy-to-publish-1.pdf

Kim, D. Y., Park, M., & Kim, H.-Y. (2023). An influencer like me: Examining the impact of the social status of Influencers. *Journal of Marketing Communications*, *29*(7), 654–675. DOI: 10.1080/13527266.2022.2066153

Kim, M. (2020). Instagram selfie-posting and young women's body dissatisfaction: Investigating the role of self-esteem and need for popularity. *Cyberpsychology (Brno)*, *14*(4), 1–15. DOI: 10.5817/CP2020-4-4

Kinder, M. (2024). Hollywood writers went on strike to protect their livelihoods from generative AI. Their remarkable victory matters for all workers. https://www.brookings.edu/articles/hollywood-writers-went-on-strike-to-protect-their-livelihoods-from-generative-ai-their-remarkable-victory-matters-for-all-workers/

King, D. L., & Delfabbro, P. H. (2018a). *Internet gaming disorder: Theory, assessment, treatment, and prevention* (pp. x, 276). Elsevier Academic Press.

King, D. L., & Delfabbro, P. H. (2018b). Predatory monetization schemes in video games (e.g. 'Loot boxes') and internet gaming disorder. *Addiction (Abingdon, England), 113*(11), 1967–1969. DOI: 10.1111/add.14286 PMID: 29952052

King, D. L., Gainsbury, S. M., Delfabbro, P. H., Hing, N., & Abarbanel, B. (2015). Distinguishing between gaming and gambling activities in addiction research. *Journal of Behavioral Addictions, 4*(4), 215–220. DOI: 10.1556/2006.4.2015.045 PMID: 26690615

Kišoňová, R. (2013). *Cognitive Aesthetics*. FFTU.

Knaflic, C. N. (2015). *Storytelling with data: A data visualization guide for business professionals*. John Wiley & Sons.

Kocaturk, T., Greuter, S., Hoang, T., & Wang, R. (2024) Enhancing human-building interaction and spatial experience in cultural spaces. *International Journal of Architectural Computing*. https://journals.sagepub.com/doi/epub/10.1177/14780771231225702

Koh, Y. J., Baldridge, J., Lee, H., & Yang, Y. (2020). Text-to-image generation grounded by fine-grained user attention. Google Research. https://arxiv.org/abs/2011.03775

Kozan, E. (2025). Emerging Opportunities and Threats for Filmmaking In The Age of Artificial Intelligence In Communications. 15th International Congresses on Social, Humanities, Administrative, and Educational Sciences in a Changing World Congress Proceedings Book, pp. 317-323. https://doi.org/DOI: 10.30546/19023.978-9952-8545-8-9.2025.601

Krämer, N. C., Feurstein, M., Kluck, J. P., Meier, Y., Rother, M., & Winter, S. (2017). Beware of selfies: The impact of photo type on impression formation based on social networking profiles. *Frontiers in Psychology, 8*(188), 1–14. DOI: 10.3389/fpsyg.2017.00188

Kremmerz, G. (2019). *The Hermetic Science of Transformation* (Picchi, F., & Rumsby, J., Trans.). Inner Traditions.

Krippendorff, K. (2004). *Content analysis: An introduction to its methodology* (2nd ed.). Sage Publications.

Kuklenko, P. (2024a). *The Role of Dark Design Patterns in Online Consumer Manipulation: A Critical Study with Emphasis on Video Game Monetisation* [fi=AMK-opinnäytetyö|sv=YH-examensarbete|en=Bachelor's thesis|]. https://www.theseus.fi/handle/10024/850304

Kuklenko, P. (2024b). *The Role of Dark Design Patterns in Online Consumer Manipulation: A Critical Study with Emphasis on Video Game Monetisation* [fi=AMK-opinnäytetyö|sv=YH-examensarbete|en=Bachelor's thesis|]. https://www.theseus.fi/handle/10024/850304

Kwon, J.-H., Chung, C.-S., & Lee, J. (2011). The effects of escape from self and interpersonal relationship on the pathological use of Internet games. *Community Mental Health Journal*, *47*(1), 113–121. DOI: 10.1007/s10597-009-9236-1 PMID: 19701792

Kyunghee, K. (2016). Alchemic transformation of human creation. *Journal of Languages and Culture*, *7*(4), 46–53.

Laili, E. F., Nadapdap, E., Respati, H., & Earlike, F. (2025). The influence of fear of missing out (FoMO) as a mediating variable between beauty influencers and brand image on purchase intention for Wardah products in Malang City. *East African Scholars Journal of Economics. Business and Management*, *8*(1), 30–36. DOI: 10.36349/easjebm.2025.v08i01.004

Lam, L. T. (2014). Internet Gaming Addiction, Problematic Use of the Internet, and Sleep Problems: A Systematic Review. *Current Psychiatry Reports*, *16*(4), 444. DOI: 10.1007/s11920-014-0444-1 PMID: 24619594

Largo.ai. (2025). https://home.largo.ai/

Latar, N. L. (2018). *Robot Journalism: Can Human Journalism Survive?* World Scientific.

Lau, G. S. J., & Idang, J. (2022). The relationship between selfie-editing, self-esteem, and social appearance anxiety among university students. *International Journal of Advanced Research in Future Ready Learning and Education*, *26*(1), 1–8. DOI: 10.37934/frle.26.1.18

Leahy, D. (2022). Rocking the Boat: Loot Boxes in Online Digital Games, the Regulatory Challenge, and the EU's Unfair Commercial Practices Directive. *Journal of Consumer Policy*, *45*(3), 561–592. DOI: 10.1007/s10603-022-09522-7

Lee, D., Wut, T. M., & Wan, C. (2023, July). The effect of fear-of-missing-out (FoMO) laden influencer marketing on travel destination promotion. In *Global Marketing Conference* (p. 118).

Lee, J. A., Bright, L. F., & Eastin, M. S. (2021). Fear of missing out and consumer happiness on Instagram: A serial mediation of social media influencer-related activities. *Cyberpsychology, Behavior, and Social Networking*, *24*(11), 762–766.

Lee, J. E., & Watkins, B. (2016). YouTube vloggers' influence on consumer luxury brand perceptions and intentions. *Journal of Business Research, 69*(12), 5753–5760.

Lee, M. K. O., Cheung, C. M. K., & Chen, Z. (2005). Acceptance of Internet-based learning medium: The role of extrinsic and intrinsic motivation. *Information & Management, 42*(8), 1095–1104. DOI: 10.1016/j.im.2003.10.007

Lees, D. (2024). Deepfakes in documentary film production: Images of deception in the representation of the real. *Studies in Documentary Film, 18*(2), 108–129. DOI: 10.1080/17503280.2023.2284680

Legere, C. (2020). *What's the difference between self-esteem and self-confidence?* (https://www.torontopsychologists.com/whats-the-difference-between-self-esteem-and-self-confidence). 25.04.2025.

Lehdonvirta, V. (2009). Virtual item sales as a revenue model: Identifying attributes that drive purchase decisions. *Electronic Commerce Research, 9*(1), 97–113. DOI: 10.1007/s10660-009-9028-2

Lei, L. Y. C., Al-Aarifin Ismail, M., Mohammad, J. A. M., & Bahri Yusoff, M. S. (2020). The relationship of smartphone addiction with psychological distress and neuroticism among university medical students. *BMC Psychology, 8*(1), 97. DOI: 10.1186/s40359-020-00466-6 PMID: 32917268

Lemay, D. J., Doleck, T., & Bazelais, P. (2019). Self-Determination, Loneliness, Fear of Missing Out, and Academic Performance. *Knowledge Management & ELearning*, 485-496.

Levenda, P. (2013). *The Dark Lord: H.P. Lovecraft, Kenneth Grant, and the Typhonian Tradition in Magic Kindle Edition*. Ibis Press.

Levinson, C. A., & Rodebaugh, T. L. (2011). Validation of the Social Appearance Anxiety Scale: Factor, convergent, and divergent validity. *Assessment, 18*(3), 350–356. DOI: 10.1177/1073191111404808

Levinson, C. A., Rodebaugh, T. L., White, E. K., Menatti, A. R., Weeks, J. W., Iacovino, J. M., & Warren, C. S. (2013). Social appearance anxiety, perfectionism, and fear of negative evaluation. Distinct or shared risk factors for social anxiety and eating disorders? *Appetite, 67*, 125–133. DOI: 10.1016/j.appet.2013.04.002

Levy, C. (2025). 'Not Just 50% Cheaper.' Netflix's Ted Sarandos Has His Own Take After James Cameron Revised His Thoughts On AI In Hollywood. https://www.cinemablend.com/movies/ted-sarandos-take-james-cameron-revised-thoughts-ai-in-hollywood

Li, A. (2022). Deficiency of Loot Box Games in Chinese Video Game Market-. *RE:view, 1284–1288.* Advance online publication. DOI: 10.2991/aebmr.k.220307.212

Li, H., Wang, Y., & Qu, H. (2024). *Where Are We So Far? – Understanding Data Storytelling Tools from the Perspective of Human-AI Collaboration.* The Hong Kong University of Science and Technology.

Lim, S. (2023). A qualitative study of the curriculum of visual communication design majors at University A: Based on NASAD, a design certification system in the U.S. *Archives of Design Research, 36*(2), 323–337.

Litmus Branding Pvt. Ltd. (n.d.). Ethical issues in AI-based design. Retrieved May 4, 2025, from https://www.litmusbranding.com/

Liu, X., Tai, Y.-W., & Tang, C.-K. (2024). ChatCam: Empowering Camera Control through Conversational AI. arXiv preprint arXiv:2409.17331.

Liu, Y., Zhu, J., & He, J. (2022). Can selfies trigger social anxiety? A study on the relationship between social media selfie behavior and social anxiety in Chinese youth group. *Frontiers in Psychology*, 13, 1-16. 1016538.

Liu, J., Li, C., Carcioppolo, N., & North, M. (2016). Do our Facebook friends make us feel worse? A study of social comparison and emotion. *Human Communication Research, 42*(4), 619–640. DOI: 10.1111/hcre.12090

Lo Duca, A. (2023). Towards a Framework for AI-Assisted Data Storytelling. In *Proceedings of the 19th International Conference on Web Information Systems and Technologies* (pp. 512-519).

Lobinger, K., & Brantner, C. (2015). In the eye of the beholder: Subjective views on the authenticity of selfies. *International Journal of Communication, 9*, 1848–1860.

Lobo, S. S., & Gowda, Y. (2016). The selfie phenomenon: Self-presentation and its implications. *International Journal of Computational Research and Development, 1*(1), 147–153.

Lodha, P., & De Sousa, A. (2019). Selfie taking: Is there a socio-cultural risk? *Indian Journal of Mental Health, 6*(4), 1–4.

Lonergan, A. R., Bussey, K., Mond, J., Brown, O., Griffiths, S., Murray, S. B., & Mitchison, D. (2019). Me, my selfie, and I: The relationship between editing and posting selfies and body dissatisfaction in men and women. *Body Image, 28*, 39–43. DOI: 10.1016/j.bodyim.2018.12.001

Lopez, J. (2023, May 17). Stability AI releases StableStudio, the open source future of DreamStudio. Stability AI. https://stability.ai/news/stablestudio-open-source-community-driven-future-dreamstudio-release

Lou, C., & Yuan, S. (2019). Influencer marketing. *Journal of Interactive Advertising*, *19*(1), 58–73. DOI: 10.1080/15252019.2018.1533501

Louck, D. K. (2024). *Quotes Regarding the Necronomicon from Lovecraft's Letters*. H.P. Lovecraft Archive. https://www.hplovecraft.com/creation/necron/letters.aspx

Lovecraft, H. P. (1924). The Hound. *Weird Tales*, *3*(2), 50–52.

Lubart, T. I. (2005). How can computers be partners in the creative process: Classification and commentary on the special issue. *International Journal of Human-Computer Studies*, *63*(4–5), 365–369.

Lumalabs.ai. (2025). https://lumalabs.ai/

Lu, Y., Zhao, T., Song, S., & Song, W. (2024). Can self-presentation on social media increase individuals' conspicuous consumption tendency? A mixed-method empirical study on Wechat in China. *Journal of Theoretical and Applied Electronic Commerce Research*, *19*(2), 2. Advance online publication. DOI: 10.3390/jtaer19020062

Majander, V. (2019). *Revenue models for video games*. https://aaltodoc.aalto.fi/handle/123456789/39117

Makar, H. (2021). *Understanding Sigils, Hypersigils... and Even Meme Magick*. Magick.Me. https://blog.magick.me/2021/07/22/how-use-sigils-hypersigils-meme-magick/

Manning, C. (2020). Artificial Intelligence Definitions. hai.stanford: https://hai.stanford.edu/sites/default/files/2020-09/AI-Definitions-HAI.pdf

Manovich, L. (2001). *The language of new media*. The MIT Press.

Manovich, L. (2002). *The Language of New Media. Londra*. The MIT Press.

Manovich, L. (2019). *AI Aesthetics*. Strelka Press.

Marconi, F. (2020). *Newsmakers: Artificial Intelligence and the Future of Journalism*. Columbia University Press.

Marshall, C. & Rossman, G. B. (2014). Designing Qualitative Research. New York: Sage.

Marshall, G. (1999). *Sosyoloji sözlüğü* (O. Akınhay & D. Kömürcü, Çev.). Bilim ve Sanat Yayınları.

Massive.ai. (2025). https://massive.io/

Mast, G., & Kawin, B. (2011). *A Short History of the Movies. 11Th Edition*. Pearson.

Matheson, E., & Sedgwick, D. (2021). Influencers and 21st Century Consumption. *Contexts*, *20*(2), 18–23. DOI: 10.1177/15365042211012066

McCarty, C. (2020). Resident assistant secondary trauma and burnout associated with student nonsuicidal self-injury. *Journal of American College Health*, *68*(7), 673–677.

McCormack, J., Gifford, T., & Hutchings, P. (2019). Autonomy, Authenticity, Authorship and Intention in Computer Generated Art. In *International Conference on Computational Intelligence in Music, Sound, Art and Design*, 35-50. Cham: Springer International Publishing.

McCosker, A., & Wilken, R. (2020). *Automating vision: The social impact of the new camera consciousness*. Routledge.

McKechnie-Martin, C. T., Cunningham, A., Baumeister, J., & Von Itzstein, G. S. (2024). A Meta-Ethnography of Player Motivation in Digital Games: The 28 Dimensions of Play. *Games and Culture*.

McLean, S. A., Paxton, S. J., Wertheim, E. H., & Masters, J. (2015). Photoshopping the selfie: Self photo editing and photo investment are associated with body dissatisfaction in adolescent girls. *International Journal of Eating Disorders*, *48*(8), 1132–1140. DOI: 10.1002/eat.22449

Merriam-webster. (n.d.). *Selfie*. (https://www.merriam-webster.com/dictionary/selfie). 23.02.2025.

Merrin, W. (2005). *Baudrillard and the media: A critical introduction*. Polity Press.

Meta, A. I. (2023). Voicebox: A Multilingual, Context-Aware Text-to-Speech System. https://ai.facebook.com/blog/voicebox-meta-generative-ai-model-speech

Metz, J. (2019). Fomo and Regret for Non-Doings. *Social Theory and Practice*, •••, 451–470.

Miller, E. (2024). Easy steps to make a talking avatar with AI from any photos. *Wondershare Virbo*. https://virbo.wondershare.com/talking-photo/make-ai-talking-avatar.html

Mills, J. S., Musto, S., Williams, L., & Tiggemann, M. (2018). "Selfie" harm: Effects on mood and body image in young women. *Body Image*, *27*, 86–92. DOI: 10.1016/j.bodyim.2018.08.007

Milmo, D., & Hawkins, A. (2024, May 18). How China is using AI news anchors to deliver its propaganda. *The Guardian*. https://www.theguardian.com/technology/article/2024/may/18/how-china-is-using-ai-news-anchors-to-deliver-its-propaganda

Mirzoeff, N. (2015). *How to see the world*. Pelican Books.

Misirlis, N., & Munawar, H. B. (2023). From deepfake to deep useful: Risks and opportunities through a systematic literature review (No. arXiv:2311.15809). *arXiv*. https://doi.org//arXiv.2311.15809DOI: 10.48550

MIT Open Learning. (2020). *Tackling the misinformation epidemic with "In Event of Moon Disaster"*. MIT News. Massachusetts Institute of Technology. https://news.mit.edu/2020/mit-tackles-misinformation-in-event-of-moon-disaster-0720

Modzelewski, P. (2020). FoMO (Fear of Missing Out) – An Educational and Behavioral Problem in Times of New Communication Forms. *Pedagogical Contexts*, 215-232.

Mohamed, E. (2025). Netflix's 'Deepfake Dubbing' Sparks Outrage. https://www.meer.com/en/92522-netflixs-deepfake-dubbing-sparks-outrage

MomJeans, S. O. (2016a). *Advanced Meme Magic (The Holy Books Of Kekism)*. CreateSpace Independent Publishing Platform.

MomJeans, S. O. (2016b). *Intermediate Meme Magic (The Holy Books Of Kekism)*. CreateSpace Independent Publishing Platform.

Moneva, J. C., Perolino, J. A., Jagobiao, M. C., & Ycong, S. T. (2020). Selfie and self-esteem. *International Journal of Social Science Research*, *8*(2), 131–142.

Moorcock, M. (1970). *The Eternal Champion*. Dell Books.

Morais, D. M., Oliveira, V., Junger, A. P., & Facó, J. F. (2020). O Conceito de Inteligência Artificial Usado no Mercado de Softwares, na Educação Tecnológica e na Literatura Científica. *Revista Educação Profissional e Tecnológica*, *4*(2), 98–109.

Moreno, S. (2018). Selfie-taking: A key semiotic practice within the 'show of the self'. *Punctum. International Journal of Semiotics*, *4*(2), 49–65. DOI: 10.18680/hss.2018.0019

Morozov, E. (2013). *To save everything, click here: The folly of technological solutionism*. PublicAffairs.

Morrison, G. (2003). Pop Magic! In Metzger, R., & Morrison, G. (Eds.), *The Book of Lies: The Disinformation Guide to Magick and the Occult* (pp. 16–25). The Desinformation Company.

Mulvey, L. (2006). *Death 24x a Second Stillness and the Moving Image*. Reaktion Books.

Mundel, J., Wan, Anan, & and Yang, J. (2024). Processes underlying social comparison with influencers and subsequent impulsive buying: The roles of social anxiety and social media addiction. *Journal of Marketing Communications*, *30*(7), 834–851. DOI: 10.1080/13527266.2023.2183426

Murphy, G., Ching, D., Twomey, J., & Linehan, C. (2023). Face/off: Changing the face of movies with deepfakes. *PLoS One*, *18*(7), e0287503. DOI: 10.1371/journal.pone.0287503 PMID: 37410765

Nair, H. (2007). Intertemporal price discrimination with forward-looking consumers: Application to the US market for console video-games. *Quantitative Marketing and Economics*, *5*(3), 239–292. DOI: 10.1007/s11129-007-9026-4

Nesi, J., Choukas-Bradley, S., Maheux, A. J., Roberts, S. R., Sanzari, C. M., Widman, L., & Prinstein, M. J. (2021). Selfie appearance investment and peer feedback concern: Multimethod investigation of adolescent selfie practices and adjustment. *Psychology of Popular Media*, *10*(4), 488–499. DOI: 10.1037/ppm0000342

Neville, S. (2021) *Immersive Participation: Futuring, Training Simulation, Dance and Virtual Reality*. [Doctoral dissertation, Coventry University]. https://pureportal.coventry.ac.uk/files/80837135/Neville2022PhD.pdf

Newzoo. (2023). Get Newzoo's newest free Global Games Market Report 2023. *Newzoo*. https://newzoo.com/resources/trend-reports/newzoo-global-games-market-report-2023-free-version

Nguyen, T., Ngamsiriudom, W., Pelton, L., & Dubinsky, A. J. (2015). Interrelationships among facets of self, motivation, and conspicuous and sustainable consumption behaviour. [IJBSAM]. *International Journal of Business Science and Applied Management*, *10*(2), 16–31.

Nilson, N. J. (2018). *Yapay Zekâ Geçmişi ve Geleceği*. Boğaziçi Üniversitesi Yayınevi.

Noble, S. U. (2018). *Algorithms of Oppression: How Search Engines Reinforce Racism*. NYU Press.

NYC DOT. (2024). WalkNYC. https://www.nyc.gov/html/dot/html/pedestrians/walknyc.shtml

Nyutu, E. N., Cobern, W. W., & Pleasants, B. A.-S. (2021). Correlational study of student perceptions of their undergraduate laboratory environment with respect to gender and major. [IJEMST]. *International Journal of Education in Mathematics, Science, and Technology*, *9*(1), 83–102. DOI: 10.46328/ijemst.1182

O'Rourke, N., Hatcher, L., & Stepanski, E. J. (2005). *A step-by-step approach to using SAS for univariate & multivariate statistics*. SAS Institute.

Oakes, O. (2019). "Deepfake" voice tech used for good in David Beckham malaria campaign. *Campaign*. https://www.campaignlive.co.uk/article/deepfake-voice-tech-used-good-david-beckham-malaria-campaign/1581378?utm_source=website&utm_medium=social

Oberst, U., Wegmann, E., Stodt, B., Brand, M., & Chamarro, A. (2017). Negative consequences from heavy social networking in adolescents: The mediating role of fear of missing out. *Journal of Adolescence*, •••, 51–60.

Okeke, A. O., Nwosu, C. J., Asogwa, J., & Dada, O. (2024). Utilization of deepfake technology in the film industry: Analysing AI-generated performances in the Hollywood film *The Irishman* and its impact on Artistic Integrity. *Scholarly Journal of Social Sciences Research*, *3*(6), 35–51. DOI: 10.5281/zenodo.13989607

Open, A. I. (2021). Organizational update. Retrieved January 14, 2021, from https://openai.com/blog/organizational-update/

Open, A. I. (2022). Whisper Speech Recognition System. https://openai.com/research/whisper

Open, A. I. (2023). DALL·E 2 [Computer software]. https://openai.com/dall-e-2

Open, A. I. ChatGPT. (2025, May 4). Görsel iletişim tasarımında kullanılan yapay zeka botları: Eğitim, profesyonel kullanım ve ücretsiz erişim özellikleri tablosu. OpenAI ChatGPT. https://chat.openai.com/

Oraison, H., Nash-dolby, O., Wilson, B., & Malhotra, R. (2020). Smartphone distraction-addiction: Examining the relationship between psychosocial variables and patterns of use. *Australian Journal of Psychology*, *72*(2), 188–198. DOI: 10.1111/ajpy.12281

Otto, B.-C. (2020). The Illuminates of Thanateros and the institutionalisation of religious individualisation. In Fuchs, M. (Ed.), *Religious Individualisation* (pp. 759–796). De Gruyter.

Oxford Learner's Dictionaries. (2025). Post-truth [adjective]. *Oxford Advanced Learner's Dictionary.* https://www.oxfordlearnersdictionaries.com/definition/english/post-truth?q=post+truth

Ozimek, P., Lainas, S., Bierhoff, H. W., & Rohmann, E. (2023). How photo editing in social media shapes self-perceived attractiveness and self-esteem via self-objectification and physical appearance comparisons. *BMC Psychology, 11*(99), 1–14. DOI: 10.1186/s40359-023-01143-0

Öztemel, E. (2020). Yapay zekâ ve insanlığın geleceği. In Şeker, M., Bulduklu, Y., Korkut, C., & Doğrul, M. (Eds.), *Bilişim Teknolojileri ve İletişim: Birey ve Toplum Güvenliği* (pp. 95–112). Türkiye Bilimler Akademisi Yayınları.

Pandey, E. (2024). The rise of fake influencers. *Axios*. https://www.axios.com/2024/09/07/fake-ai-influencers-lil-miquela

Pangarkar, A., & Rathee, S. (2023). The role of conspicuity: İmpact of social influencers on purchase decisions of luxury consumers. *International Journal of Advertising, 42*(7), 1150–1177. DOI: 10.1080/02650487.2022.2084265

Papapanou, T. K., Darviri, C., Kanaka-Gantenbein, C., Tigani, X., Michou, M., Vlachakis, D., Chrousos, G. P., & Bacopoulou, F. (2023). Strong correlations between social appearance anxiety, use of social media, and feelings of loneliness in adolescents and young adults. *International Journal of Environmental Research and Public Health, 20*(5), 4296. DOI: 10.3390/ijerph20054296

Parker, G. G., & Van Alstyne, M. W. (2005). Two-Sided Network Effects: A Theory of Information Product Design. *Management Science, 51*(10), 1494–1504. DOI: 10.1287/mnsc.1050.0400

Parsa, A. F. (2004). İmgenin gücü görsel kültürün yükselişi. In Işık, M. (Ed.), *Medyada Yeni Yaklaşımlar* (pp. 215–237). Eğitim Kitapevi Yayınları.

Partridge, C. (2004). *The Re-Enchantment of the West: Alternative Spiritualities, Sacralization, Popular Culture, and Occulture* (Vol. 1). T&T Clark International.

Partridge, C. (2015). *The Occult World* (Partridge, C., Ed.). Routledge.

Partridge, C. (2018). *High Culture: Drugs, Mysticism & the Pursuit ofTranscendence in the Modern World*. Oxford U.

Patton, M. Q. (2005). *Patton, M. Q. (2005). Qualitative Research*. John Wiley & Sons, Ltd.

Pavis, M. (2021). Rebalancing our regulatory response to deepfakes with performers' rights. *Convergence (London), 27*(4), 974–998. DOI: 10.1177/13548565211033418

Pavlik, J. V. (2023). Collaborating with ChatGPT: Considering the implications of generative artificial intelligence for journalism and media education. *Journal. Mass Commun. Educ.*, *78*, 84–93. DOI: 10.1177/10776958221149577

Pepple, S. (2014). Evaluating and Presenting Points of Interest in Wayfinding and Navigation Systems. *ResearchGate*. https://dl.acm.org/doi/pdf/10.1145/2541831.2541849?casa_token=41-kX6q9b00AAAAA:V10GPPClKSdp4lw_sB4EoNmA_smMS-VeOvVM3HcaiqF7CJv5peoXtlP1l4kOGJxg3jltWaStBeP0

Peretti, M. (2022). 10 Things You Should Know About AI in Journalism. gijn.org: https://gijn.org/stories/10-things-you-should-know-aboutai-in-journalism/

Peterka-Bonetta, J., Sindermann, C., Sha, P., Zhou, M., & Montag, C. (2019). The relationship between Internet Use Disorder, depression and burnout among Chinese and German college students. *Addictive Behaviors*, (89), 188–199.

Petrovskaya, E., & Zendle, D. (2020). *The Battle Pass: A Mixed-Methods Investigation into a Growing Type of Video Game Monetisation*. https://doi.org/DOI: 10.31219/osf.io/vnmeq

Petrovskaya, E., & Zendle, D. (2022). Predatory Monetisation? A Categorisation of Unfair, Misleading and Aggressive Monetisation Techniques in Digital Games from the Player Perspective. *Journal of Business Ethics*, *181*(4), 1065–1081. DOI: 10.1007/s10551-021-04970-6

Poeta, E., Ciravegna, G., Pastor, E., Cerquitelli, T., & Baralis, E. (2023). Concept-based Explainable Artificial Intelligence: A Survey. *Politecnico di Torino*.

P-Orridge, G. B. (2010). *Thee Psychick Bible*. Feral House.

Postigo, H. (2016). The socio-technical architecture of digital labor: Converting play into YouTube money. *New Media & Society*, *18*(2), 332–349. DOI: 10.1177/1461444814541527

Postman, N. (2004). *Teknopoli. (M. E. Yılmaz, Çev.)*. Gelenek Yayıncılık.

Pounders, K., Kowalczyk, C. M., & Stowers, K. (2016). Insight into the motivation of selfie postings: Impression management and self-esteem. *European Journal of Marketing*, *50*(9/10), 1879–1892. DOI: 10.1108/EJM-07-2015-0502

Preacher, K. J., & Hayes, A. F. (2004). Spss and sas procedures for estimating indirect effects in simple mediation models. *Behavior Research Methods, Instruments, & Computers*, *36*(4), 717–731.

Przybylski, A. K., Murayama, K., DeHaan, C. R., & Gladwell, V. (2013). Motivational, emotional, and behavioral correlates of fear of missing out. *Computers in Human Behavior, 29*(4), 1841–1848.

Przybylski, A., Murayama, K., DeHaan, C., & Valerie, G. (2013). Motivational, Motional and Behavioral Correlates of Fear of Missing Out. *Computers in Human Behavior*, •••, 1841–1848.

Pueyo, P., Dendarieta, J., Montijano, E., Murillo, A. C., & Schwager, M. (2024). Cinempc: A fully autonomous drone cinematography system incorporating zoom, focus, pose, and scene composition. *IEEE Transactions on Robotics, 40*, 1740–1757.

Puthiyakath, H. H., Anjali, R., Angel, S., & Goswami, M. P. (2024). Selfie syndrome: A study of selfitis and narcissism among young adults. *Journal of Creative Communications*, •••, 1–19. DOI: 10.1177/09732586231223603

Putranto, A., Utoyo, W. A., & Delliana, S. (2021). Robotic Journalısm Practıce, Journalis Twilight. The 3rd Open Society Conference (OSC 2021) (s. 218-228). Jakarta, Endonezya: Faculty of Law, Social and Political Sciences Universitas Terbuka.

Qattan, J., & Khasawneh, M. A. (2020). The psychological motivations of online conspicuous consumption: A qualitative study. [IJEBR]. *International Journal of E-Business Research, 16*(2), 1–16. DOI: 10.4018/IJEBR.2020040101

Qiu, Y. (2024). Social Comparison on Social Media Platforms: A media and communication Perspective. *SHS Web of Conferences, 185*, 03008. https://doi.org/DOI: 10.1051/shsconf/202418503008

Qiu, L., Lu, J., Yang, S., Qu, W., & Zhu, T. (2015). What does your selfie say about you? *Computers in Human Behavior, 52*, 443–449. DOI: 10.1016/j.chb.2015.06.032

Quan, H., Li, S., Zeng, C., Wei, H., & Hu, J. (2023). Big Data and AI-Driven Product Design: A Survey. *Applied Sciences (Basel, Switzerland).*

Quinn Emanuel Urquhart & Sullivan, LLP. (2023). Client Alert: Copyright Protection for Works Made With AI Tools. https://www.quinnemanuel.com/the-firm/publications/client-alert-copyright-protection-for-works-made-with-ai-tools

Radanliev, P. (2025). AI Ethics: Integrating Transparency, Fairness, and Privacy in AI Development. *Applied Artificial Intelligence, 39*(1). Advance online publication. DOI: 10.1080/08839514.2025.2463722

Rancière, J. (2009). *The emancipated spectator* (Elliott, G., Trans.). Verso Books.

Rashid, S., Warraich, U., Peerjan, G., & Salman, F. (2023). Impact of social media opinion leaders influencers on individual consumption decisions of visually conspicuous products. *Market forces, 18*, 139-162. https://doi.org/DOI: 10.51153/mf.v18i2.637

Ratner, B. (2009). The correlation coefficient: Its values range between+ 1/− 1, or do they? *Journal of Targeting. Measurement and Analysis for Marketing, 17*, 139–142. DOI: 10.1057/jt.2009.5

Recker, J. (2022). This deepfake exhibition shows how convincing the new technology can be. *Smithsonian Magazine*. https://www.smithsonianmag.com/smart-news/this-deepfake-exhibition-shows-how-convincing-the-new-technology-can-be-180979619/

Reer, F., Tang, W. Y., & Quandt, T. (2019). Psychosocial well-being and social media engagement: The mediating roles of social comparison orientation and fear of missing out. *New Media & Society, 21*(7), 1486–1505.

Reinecke, L., Hartmann, T., & Eden, A. (2014). The Guilty Couch Potato: The Role of Ego Depletion in Reducing Recovery Through Media Use. *Journal of Communication*, (64), 569–589.

Reinikainen, H., Munnukka, J., Maity, D., & Luoma-Aho, V. (2020). 'You really are a great big sister'–Parasocial relationships, credibility, and the moderating role of audience comments in influencer marketing. *Journal of Marketing Management, 36*(3–4), 279–298.

Ritzer, G. (2014). *The McDonaldization of Society* (8th editio). SAGE Publications, Inc.

Ross, A., & Nieborg, D. (2021). Spinning is winning: Social casino apps and the platformization of gamble-play. *Journal of Consumer Culture, 21*(1), 84–101. DOI: 10.1177/1469540521993931

Rothkopf, J. (2020, July 1). Deepfake technology enters the documentary world. *The New York Times*. https://www.nytimes.com/2020/07/01/movies/deepfakes-documentary-welcome-to-chechnya.html

Rousseau, A. (2021). Adolescents' selfie-activities and idealized online self-presentation: An application of the sociocultural model. *Body Image, 36*, 16–26. DOI: 10.1016/j.bodyim.2020.10.005

Rozgonjuk, D., Saal, K., & Täht, K. (2018). Problematic Smartphone Use, Deep and Surface Approaches to Learning, and Social Media Use in Lectures. *International Journal of Environmental Research and Public Health*, *15*(1), 92. DOI: 10.3390/ijerph15010092 PMID: 29316697

Rozgonjuk, D., Sindermann, C., Elhai, J. D., & Montag, C. (2020). Fear of missing out (FoMO) and social media's impact on daily life and productivity at work: Do WhatsApp, Facebook, Instagram, and Snapchat use disorders mediate that association? *Addictive Behaviors*, *110*, 106487.

Rui, J., & Stefanone, M. A. (2013). Strategic self-presentation online: A cross-cultural study. *Computers in Human Behavior*, *29*(1), 110–118. DOI: 10.1016/j.chb.2012.07.022

Runway. (n.d.). Studios. Retrieved May 4, 2025, from https://runwayml.com/studios

Rupcic, T. (2023). Techno-Religion and Cyberspace Spirituality in Dystopian Video Games. *Religions*, *14*(2).

Rüther, L., Jahn, J., & Marksteiner, T. (2023). #influenced! The impact of social media influencing on self-esteem and the role of social comparison and resilience. *Frontiers in Psychology*, *14*, 1–8. DOI: 10.3389/fpsyg.2023.1216195

Rutz, O., Aravindakshan, A., & Rubel, O. (2019). Measuring and forecasting mobile game app engagement. *International Journal of Research in Marketing*, *36*(2), 185–199. DOI: 10.1016/j.ijresmar.2019.01.002

Ryan, R. M., & Deci, E. L. (2000). Intrinsic and extrinsic motivations: Classic definitions and new directions. *Contemporary Educational Psychology*, *25*(1), 54–67. DOI: 10.1006/ceps.1999.1020

Ryan, R. M., Rigby, C. S., & Przybylski, A. (2006). The Motivational Pull of Video Games: A Self-Determination Theory Approach. *Motivation and Emotion*, *30*(4), 344–360. DOI: 10.1007/s11031-006-9051-8

Saad, N. (2019, November 8). Director says James Dean CGI film is still on despite backlash. *Los Angeles Times*. https://www.latimes.com/entertainment-arts/movies/story/2019-11-08/cgi-james-dean-director-backlash

Saboor, A., Ali, K., Mugheri, A., & Fatima, M. (2024). The Impact of Digital Transformation on Educational Leadership: Assessing Digital Burnout and Mental Health in Virtual Teaching. *Review of Applied Management and Social Sciences*, *7*(4), 391–408.

Safna, H. M. F. (2017). Negative impact of selfies on youth. *International Journal of Computer Science and Information Technology Research*, *5*(3), 68–73.

Sahota, N. (2024). The AI Takeover In Cinema: How Movie Studios Use Artificial Intelligence. https://www.forbes.com/sites/neilsahota/2024/03/08/the-ai-takeover-in-cinema-how-movie-studios-use-artificial-intelligence

Salomon, I., & Brown, C. S. (2021). That selfie becomes you: Examining taking and posting selfies as forms of self-objectification. *Media Psychology*, *24*(6), 847–865. DOI: 10.1080/15213269.2020.1817091

Saltz, J. (2014). *Art at arm's length: A history of the selfie*. (https://www.vulture.com/2014/01/history-of-the-selfie.html)

Salwen, M. B. (2005). Online News Trends. M. B. Salwen, B. Garrison, & P. D. Driscoll içinde, Online News and the Public, Lawrence Erlbaum Associates. stable/26805941

Santora, J. (2021, June 29). 12 types of influencers you can use to improve your marketing. *Influencer Marketing Hub*. https://influencermarketinghub.com/types-of-influencers/

Schwab, K. (2016). The fourth industrial revolution. World Economic Forum.

Seaborn, K., Iseya, S., Hidaka, S., Kobuki, S., & Chandra, S. (2024). Play Across Boundaries: Exploring Cross-Cultural Maldaimonic Game Experiences. *Conference on Human Factors in Computing Systems - Proceedings*.

Selby-Lara, A., & Howard, C. (2025). Robotic Rhythm: A Contemporary Look At AI-Driven Editing Tools. LMU Digital Commons. https://digitalcommons.lmu.edu/honors-thesis/572

Senft, T. M., & Baym, N. K. (2015). What does the selfie say? Investigating a global phenomenon. *International Journal of Communication*, *9*, 1588–1606.

Setiawan, R., Garliani, G., & Rahmawati, D. (2024). Analysis of the influence of fear of missing out (FoMO) and the role of influencers on tourism destination selection. *Jurnal Wacana Ekonomi*, *23*(2), 65–72.

Şeylan, S. (2023). Dijital ikiz teknolojilerinin sinemaya yansımaları ve etik sorunlar. *Motif Akademi Halkbilimi Dergisi*, *16*(43), 1450–1468.

Shabahang, R., Aruguete, M., & Shim, H. (2021). Online News Addiction: Future Anxiety, Fear of Missing Out on News, and Interpersonal Trust Contribute to Excessive Online News Consumption. *Online Journal of Communication and Media Technologies*, •••, 1–11.

Shah, R., & Tewari, R. (2016). Demystifying 'selfie': A rampant social media activity. *Behaviour & Information Technology, 35*(10), 864–871. DOI: 10.1080/0144929X.2016.1201693

Sharma, M. K., Anand, N., Ahuja, S., Thakur, P. C., Mondal, I., Singh, P., & Venkatesyan, S. (2020). Digital burnout: Covid-19 lockdown mediates excessive technology use stress. *World Social Psychiatry, 2*(2), 171–172.

Sharp, O., & Goodwin, R. (2016). *Sunspring* [Short film]. End Cue.

Shavelson, R. J., Hubner, J. J., & Stanton, G. C. (1976). Self-concept: Validation of construct interpretations. *Review of Educational Research, 46*(3), 407–441. DOI: 10.3102/00346543046003407

Shaw, L. (2024). Four Experts Explain How AI Will Change Hollywood. https://www.bloomberg.com/news/newsletters/2024-08-18/four-experts-explain-how-ai-will-change-hollywood

Shaw, V. (2017). *Lemegeton: The Complete Books I-V: Ars Goetia, Ars Theurgia Goetia, Ars Paulina, Ars Almadel, Ars Notoria*. Erebus Society.

Shen, X. (2020, March 12). Professor's online students prefer when he teaches classes as anime girl. *South China Morning Post*. https://www.scmp.com/abacus/news-bites/article/3074961/professors-online-students-prefer-when-he-teaches-classes-anime

Shibuya, A., Teramoto, M., Shoun, A., & Akiyama, K. (2019). Long-Term Effects of In-Game Purchases and Event Game Mechanics on Young Mobile Social Game Players in Japan. *Simulation & Gaming, 50*(1), 76–92. DOI: 10.1177/1046878118819677

Shin, Y., Kim, M., Im, C., & Chong, S. C. (2017). Selfie and self: The effect of selfies on self-esteem and social sensitivity. *Personality and Individual Differences, 111*, 139–145. DOI: 10.1016/j.paid.2017.02.004

Siepmann, C., Holthoff, L. C., & Kowalczuk, P. (2022). Conspicuous consumption of luxury experiences: An experimental investigation of status perceptions on social media. *Journal of Product and Brand Management, 31*(3), 454–468. DOI: 10.1108/JPBM-08-2020-3047

Siibak, A. (2009). Constructing the self through the photo selection-visual impression management on social networking websites. *Cyberpsychology (Brno), 3*(1), 1–10.

Silva Jasaui, D., Martí-Testón, A., Muñoz, A., Moriniello, F., Solanes, J. E., & Gracia, L. (2024). Virtual Production: Real-Time Rendering Pipelines for Indie Studios and the Potential in Different Scenarios. *Applied Sciences (Basel, Switzerland), 14*(6), 2530. DOI: 10.3390/app14062530

Singer, A., & Singer, L. (1995). *Divine Magick: the world of the supernatural.* Boxtree.

Şirin, T., Eratlı Şirin, Y., & Can, B. (2021). Beden Eğitimi Öğretmenlerinin Dijital Tükenmişlik Düzeylerinin İncelenmesi. *International Journal of Social. Humanities and Administrative Sciences, 7*(42), 1236–1245.

Sobchack, V. (1992). *The address of the eye: A phenomenology of film experience.* Princeton University Press.

Söğütlüler, T. (2024). The Future of the Moving Image: Virtual Production Technology. *Türkiye Film Araştırmaları Dergisi, 4*(2), 214–234. DOI: 10.59280/film.1530664

Sorokowska, A., Oleszkiewicz, A., Frackowiak, T., Pisanski, K., Chmiel, A., & Sorokowski, P. (2016). Selfies and personality: Who posts self-portrait photographs? *Personality and Individual Differences, 90,* 119–123. DOI: 10.1016/j.paid.2015.10.037

Sorokowski, P., Sorokowska, A., Oleszkiewicz, A., Frackowiak, T., Huk, A., & Pisanski, K. (2015). Selfie posting behaviors are associated with narcissism among men. *Personality and Individual Differences, 85,* 123–127. DOI: 10.1016/j.paid.2015.05.004

Soundraw. (2025). AI Music Generator for Creators. https://soundraw.io

Spangler, T. (2020). Warner Bros. Taps AI for Film Marketing Decision-Making. https://variety.com/2020/digital/news/warner-bros-cinelytic-ai-1203452420/

Spare, A. O. (1913). *The Book of Pleasure: The Psychology of Ecstasy.* I-H-O Books.

Špehar, H. (2010). McReligion, Contribution to the McDonaldization Theory in the Politology of Religion. *Politikologija Religije, 4*(1), 118–130.

Spicer, S. G., Nicklin, L. L., Uther, M., Lloyd, J., Lloyd, H., & Close, J. (2022). Loot boxes, problem gambling and problem video gaming: A systematic review and meta-synthesis. *New Media & Society, 24*(4), 1001–1022. DOI: 10.1177/14614448211027175

Stanković, S. (2024). *Game Design for Free-to-Play Live Service.* Springer Nature Switzerland., DOI: 10.1007/978-3-031-56156-6

Steg, L., & De Groot, J. I. (2019) *Environmental psychology: An introduction.* 2nd Ed. BPS Textbooks in Psychology. New Jersey: Wiley-Blackwell. https://www.hse.ru/data/2019/03/04/1196348199/%5BLinda_Steg_Judith_I._M._de_Groot%5D_Environmental_P(b-ok.cc).pdf

Stokes, J. (2024). Pocket Castles and Custom Skin: Championing Transparency in the Monetization of User-Generated Content in Video Games. *Cybaris: An Intellectual Property Law Review, 15*, 107.

Strimbu, N., & O'Connell, M. (2019). The relationship between self-concept and online self-presentation in adults. *Cyberpsychology, Behavior, and Social Networking, 22*(12), 804–807. DOI: 10.1089/cyber.2019.0328

Strimbu, N., O'Connell, M., Nearchou, F., & Ó'sé, C. (2021). Adaption and psychometric evaluation of the Presentation of Online Self Scale in adults. *Computers in Human Behavior Reports, 3*, 1–6. DOI: 10.1016/j.chbr.2021.100073

Studios, B. G. (2011). *The Elder Scrolls V: Skyrim* (Microsoft Windows, PlayStation 3, Xbox 360, PlayStation 4, Xbox One, Nintendo Switch, PlayStation 5, Xbox Series X/S). Bethesda Softworks.

Studios, M. (2009). *Minecraft (Microsoft Windows)*. Mojang Studios.

Styhre, A., & Wikhamn, B. (2019). The ambiguities of money-making: Indie video game developers and the norm of creative integrity. *Qualitative Research in Organizations and Management: An International Journal, ahead-of-print*. https://doi.org/DOI: 10.1108/QROM-02-2019-1733

Suls, J., Martin, R., & Wheeler, L. (2000). Three kinds of opinion comparison: The Triadic Model. *Personality and Social Psychology Review, 4*(3), 219–237. DOI: 10.1207/S15327957PSPR0403_2

Suls, J., Martin, R., & Wheeler, L. (2002). Social comparison: Why, with whom, and with what effect? *Current Directions in Psychological Science, 11*(5), 159–163. DOI: 10.1111/1467-8721.00191

Sümen, A., & Evgin, D. (2021). Social Media Addiction in High School Students: A Cross-Sectional Study Examining Its Relationship with Sleep Quality and Psychological Problems. *Child Indicators Research, 14*(6), 2265–2283. DOI: 10.1007/s12187-021-09838-9 PMID: 34367373

Sung, Y., Lee, J. A., Kim, E., & Choi, S. M. (2016). Why we post selfies: Understanding motivations for posting pictures of oneself. *Personality and Individual Differences, 97*, 260–265. DOI: 10.1016/j.paid.2016.03.032

Sun, Q., & Zhu, Y. (2022). Teaching analysis for visual communication design with the perspective of digital technology. *Hindawi Computational and Mathematical Methods in Medicine, 2022*, 1–10. DOI: 10.1155/2022/2411811 PMID: 35903440

Sun, Y., Wang, R., Cao, D., & Lee, R. (2021). Who are social media influencers for luxury fashion consumption of the Chinese Gen Z? Categorisation and empirical examination. *Journal of Fashion Marketing and Management*, *26*(4), 603–621. DOI: 10.1108/JFMM-07-2020-0132

Superscout.ai. (2025). https://superscout.ai/

Surjatmodjo, D., Unde, A. A., Cangara, H., & Sonni, A. F. (2024). Information pandemic: A critical review of disinformation spread on social media and its implications for state resilience. *Soc. Sci.*, *13*, 418. DOI: 10.3390/socsci13080418

Suzuki, D. T. (1991). *An Introduction To Zen Buddhism*. Grove Press.

Taber, K. S. (2018). The use of Cronbach's Alpha when developing and reporting research instruments in science education. *Research in Science Education*, *48*, 1273–1296. DOI: 10.1007/s11165-016-9602-2

Tableau. (2024). Artificial intelligence (AI) algorithms: a complete overview. Tableau: https://www.tableau.com/datainsights/ai/algorithms#:~:text=So%2C%20at%20the%20essential%20level,and%20their%20ability%20to%20learn

Tang, G., Ren, S., Chadee, D., & Yuan, S. (2020). The dark side of social media connectivity: Influence on turnover intentions of supply chain professionals. *International Journal of Operations & Production Management*, *40*(5), 603–623. DOI: 10.1108/IJOPM-05-2019-0391

Tang, Y., Li, H., Lan, M., Ma, X., & Qu, H. (2025). Understanding Screenwriters' Practices, Attitudes, and Future Expectations in Human-AI Co-Creation. In *CHI Conference on Human Factors in Computing Systems*. Yokohama, Japan. https://doi.org/DOI: 10.1145/3706598.3714120

Taskin, T. E., Ferdowshi, N., & Islam, S. (2024). Is selfie taking behavior beneficial for the mental wellbeing of young adults? *Dhaka University Journal of Biological Sciences*, *33*(2), 77–86. DOI: 10.3329/dujbs.v33i2.75818

Tatlerasia (2025). https://www.tatlerasia.com/lifestyle/entertainment/ai-in-movies

Teke, D., & Yılmaz, T. (2023). Sosyal Ortamlardaki Gelişmeleri Kaçırma Korkusu (Fomo) Ve İlişkili Faktörlerin Değerlendirilmesi: Lisans Öğrencileri Üzerine Bir Alan Araştırması. *Yönetim Bilimleri Dergisi/Journal Of. Administrative Sciences*, •••, 1–24.

Terán, L., Yan, K., & Aubrey, J. S. (2020). "But first let me take a selfie": US adolescent girls' selfie activities, self-objectification, imaginary audience beliefs, and appearance concerns. *Journal of Children and Media*, *14*(3), 343–360.

The Dali. (2025). *Dalí lives (via artificial intelligence).* https://thedali.org/exhibit/dali-lives/

The Guardian. (2023, October 2). Tom Hanks says AI version of him used in dental plan ad without his consent. *The Guardian.* https://www.theguardian.com/film/2023/oct/02/tom-hanks-dental-ad-ai-version-fake

The Guardian. (2025a). Collective licence to ensure UK authors get paid for works used to train AI, says trade body. https://www.theguardian.com/books/2025/apr/23/collective-licence-to-ensure-uk-authors-get-paid-for-works-used-to-train-ai

The Guardian. (2025b). EU accused of leaving devastating copyright loophole in AI act. https://www.theguardian.com/technology/2025/feb/19/eu-accused-of-leaving-devastating-copyright-loophole-in-ai-act

Thurman, N., & Lewis, S. C., ve Kunert, J. (2019). Algorithms, Automation, and News. *Digital Journalism (Abingdon, England)*, *7*(8), 980–992. DOI: 10.1080/21670811.2019.1685395

Tiaynen-Qadir, T., & Qadir, A. (2023). *Symbols and Myth-making in Modernity. Deep Culture in Art and Action.* Anthem Press.

Tiggemann, M., Anderberg, I., & Brown, Z. (2020). Uploading your best self: Selfie editing and body dissatisfaction. *Body Image*, *33*, 175–182. DOI: 10.1016/j.bodyim.2020.03.002

Tiidenberg, K. (2018). *Selfies: Why we love (and hate) them.* Emerald Publishing Limited.

Tokgöz, O. (2010). *Temel Gazetecilik.* İmge Kitabevi.

Trivedi, J., & Sama, R. (2020). The effect of influencer marketing on consumers' brand admiration and online purchase intentions: An emerging market perspective. *Journal of Internet Commerce*, *19*(1), 103–124.

Truong, Y., & McColl, R. (2011). Intrinsic motivations, self-esteem, and luxury goods consumption. *Journal of Retailing and Consumer Services*, *18*(6), 555–561. DOI: 10.1016/j.jretconser.2011.08.004

Tüfekçi, Z. (2014). Big Questions for Social Media Big Data: Representativeness, Validity and Other Methodological Pitfalls. *Proceedings of The Eighth International AAAI Conference On Weblogs And Social Media*, 505–514.

Türkoğlu, H. S., & Doğan, B. Ö. (2018). Sosyal Medya Üzerinden Okurun Değişimi ve Bilgi Güvenirliği. *Erciyes İletişim Dergisi*, *5*(4), 371–385.

Tutar, H., & Mutlu, H. T. (2024). Dijital Yorgunluk Ölçeği (DİYÖ): Geçerlilik ve Güvenirlik Çalışması. *İletişim Kuram ve Araştırma Dergisi*(67), 56-74.

U.S. Department of Education. (2023, May). Artificial intelligence and the future of teaching and learning: Insights and recommendations (M. A. Cardona, R. J. Rodríguez, & K. Ishmael, Eds.). Office of Educational Technology. https://eric.ed.gov/?q=source%3A%22Office+of+Educational+Technology%2C+US+Department+of+Education%22&id=ED631097

Uçar, T. F. (2004). *Görsel İletişim ve Grafik Tasarım*. İnkılap Kitapevi.

Unity. (2025). https://learn.unity.com/

UOY. (2023). *How looking at other people's selfies can make us feel bad about our own bodies.* (https://www.york.ac.uk/institute-of-mental-health-research/news/2023/selfies-image-angle-study/)

Vakhtin, D. (2023). AI for filmmaking: Script breakdowns in seconds. https://filmustage.com/blog/ai-for-filmmaking-script-breakdowns-in-seconds

Valkenburg, P. M. (2017). Understanding self-effects in social media. *Human Communication Research, 43*(4), 477–490. DOI: 10.1111/hcre.12113

Van Dalen, A. (2012). The algorithms behind the headlines: How machine-written news redefines the core skills of human journalists. *Journalism Practice, 6*(5-6), 648–658.

van Dijck, J. (2007). *Mediated memories in the digital age*. Stanford University Press.

Van Dijck, J. (2013). *The Culture Of Connectivity: A Critical History of Social Media*. Oxford University Press.

Vandenbosch, L., Fardouly, J., & Tiggemann, M. (2022). Social media and body image: Recent trends and future directions. *Current Opinion in Psychology, 45*, 1–6. DOI: 10.1016/j.copsyc.2021.12.002

Vault.ai. (2025). https://vault-ai.com/research-and-insights/

Veldhuis, J., Alleva, J. M., Bij de Vaate, A. J., Keijer, M., & Konijn, E. A. (2020). Me, my selfie, and I: The relations between selfie behaviors, body image, self-objectification, and self-esteem in young women. *Psychology of Popular Media, 9*(1), 3–13. DOI: 10.1037/ppm0000206

Vincent, J. (2020). Warner Bros. Signs AI Startup That Claims to Predict Film Success. https://www.theverge.com/2020/1/9/21058094/ai-film-decision-making-warner-bros-signs-cinelytic

Virilio, P. (1994). *The vision machine*. Indiana University Press.

Vogt, P., Gardner, D., & Haeffele, L. (2012). *When To Use What Research Design*. Guilford Press.

Vrontis, D., Makrides, A., Christofi, M., & Thrassou, A. (2021). Social media influencer marketing: A systematic review, integrative framework and future research agenda. *International Journal of Consumer Studies*, *45*(4), 617–644.

Wade, N. J. (2014). Guest editorial: The first scientific 'selfie'? *Perception*, *43*(11), 1141–1144. DOI: 10.1068/p4311ed

Wai, L. K., & Osman, S. (2019). The Influence of Self-esteem in the relationship of social media usage and conspicuous consumption. *International Journal of Academic Research in Business & Social Sciences*, *9*(2), 335–352. DOI: 10.6007/IJARBSS/v9-i2/5549

WalkMe. (n.d.). What is digitalization? Retrieved May 4, 2025, from https://www.walkme.com/glossary/digitalization/

Wallace, I. H. (1968). *Piet Mondrian: The Evolution of His Neo-Plastic Aesthetic 1908-1920*. University of British Columbia.

Wang, Y., Xie, X., Fardouly, J., Vartanian, L. R., & Lei, L. (2021). The longitudinal and reciprocal relationships between selfie-related behaviors and self-objectification and appearance concerns among adolescents. *New Media & Society*, *23*(1), 56–77. DOI: 10.1016/j.chb.2023.107906

Wanick, V., & Mataruna, L. (2021). *The state of digital gaming and play post-COVID AUTHOR*. *2*, 1.

Watercutter, A. (2023). The Hollywood Strikes Stopped AI From Taking Your Job. But for How Long? https://www.wired.com/story/hollywood-saved-your-job-from-ai-2023-will-it-last

Wegmann, E., Oberst, U., Stodt, B., & Brand, M. (2017). Online-Specific Fear of Missing Out and Internet-use Expectancies Contribute to Symptoms of Internet-Communication Disorder. *Addictive Behaviors Reports*, •••, 33–42.

Wehrle, K., & Fasbender, U. (2019). Self-concept. In Zeigler-Hill, V., & Shackelford, T. K. (Eds.), *Encyclopedia of personality and individual differences* (pp. 1–5). Springer., DOI: 10.1007/978-3-319-28099-8_2001-1

Weston, D., & Bennett, A. (2013). *Pop Pagans: Paganism and Popular Music* (D. Weston & A. Bennett (eds.)). Routledge.

Whissel, K. (2014). *Spectacular Digital Effects: CGI and Contemporary Cinema*. Duke University Press.

Whittaker, M., ... (2018). AI Now Report 2018. AI Now Institute. https://ainowinstitute.org/wp-content/uploads/2023/04/AI_Now_2018_Report.pdf

Wille, C. I. (2015). Shaping Dreams: Design Ideas and Design Fiction in Movie and Television Production Design. Artifact, Volume 3, Issue 4, 9.1-9.10. https://doi.org/DOI: 10.14434/artifact.v3i4.12812

Woodman, J. (2003). *Modernity, Selfhood, and the Demonic: Anthropological Perspectives on "Chaos Magick" in the United Kingdom*. Goldsmiths Collage, University of London.

Woods, O. (2024). The affective embeddings of gacha games: Aesthetic assemblages and the mediated expression of the self. *New Media & Society*, *26*(2), 823–838. DOI: 10.1177/14614448211067756

WorldOMeter. (2024) Malaysia Population (LIVE).https://www.worldometers.info/world-population/malaysia-population/#:~:text=The%20current%20population%20of%20Malaysia,latest%20United%20Nations%20data%201

Wortham, J. (2011, 4 9). *New York Times*. New York Times: https://www.nytimes.com/2011/04/10/business/10ping.html adresinden alındı

Xiao, L. Y. (2021). *Regulating loot boxes as gambling? Towards a combined legal and self-regulatory consumer protection approach*. https://doi.org/DOI: 10.4337/ielr.2021.01.02

Xiao, L., Chu, D., Wang, F., & Yang, Y. (2023). Editing the self in pictures: Selfie editing promotes self-objectification among Chinese. *Current Psychology (New Brunswick, N.J.)*, *42*, 10656–10668. DOI: 10.1007/s12144-021-02327-w

Yamazaki, A. (2024). Digital replicas and democracy: Issues raised by the Hollywood actors' strike. *Humanities & Social Sciences Communications*, *11*, 1661. Advance online publication. DOI: 10.1057/s41599-024-04204-w

Yam, F. C., Korkmaz, O., & Griffiths, M. D. (2023). The association between fear of Covid-19 and smartphone addiction among individuals: The mediating and moderating role of cyberchondria severity. *Current Psychology (New Brunswick, N.J.)*, *42*(3), 2377–2390. DOI: 10.1007/s12144-021-02324-z PMID: 34690474

Yang, J., Fardouly, J., Wang, Y., & Shi, W. (2020). Selfie-viewing and facial dissatisfaction among emerging adults: A moderated mediation model of appearance comparisons and self-objectification. *International Journal of Environmental Research and Public Health, 17*(2), 672, 1-16. http://dx.doi.org/DOI: 10.3390/ijerph17020672

Yang, M. (2021, July 16). Anthony Bourdain documentary sparks backlash for using AI to fake voice. *The Guardian.* https://www.theguardian.com/food/2021/jul/16/anthony-bourdain-documentary-ai-voiceover-roadrunner

Yao, S., & Kim, G. (2019). The Effects of Immersion in a Virtual Reality Game: Presence and Physical Activity. *Lecture Notes in Computer Science (Including Subseries Lecture Notes in Artificial Intelligence and Lecture Notes in Bioinformatics), 11595 LNCS*(April), 234–242.

Yener, S. (2018). Teknostresin İş Performansı Üzerindeki Etkisi; Tükenmişliğin Aracı Rolü. *Afyon Kocatepe Üniversitesi Sosyal Bilimler Dergisi, 20*(2), 85–101.

Yeniceler Kortak, İ. (2024). Gelişmeleri kaçırma korkusu ve haber tüketimi arasındaki ilişkinin incelenmesi. *Kastamonu İletişim Araştırmaları Dergisi (KİAD)*, 153-176.

Yeo, H.-J. P. (2014). An overview of research methods in visual communication design education. *International Journal of Design Creativity and Innovation, 2*(1), 51–62.

Yoon, M., & Yun, H. (2023). Relationships between adolescent smartphone usage patterns, achievement goals, and academic achievement. *Asia Pacific Education Review, 24*(1), 13–23. DOI: 10.1007/s12564-021-09718-5

Zackariasson, P., & Wilson, T. (2010). Paradigm shifts in the video game industry. *Competitiveness Review: An International Business Journal incorporating Journal of Global Competitiveness, 20*, 139–151. https://doi.org/DOI: 10.1108/10595421011029857

Zackariasson, P., & Wilson, T. (Eds.). (2012). *The Video Game Industry: Formation, Present State, and Future* (1st ed.). Routledge.

Zaucha, T., & Agur, C. (2023). Playbor, gamble-play, and the financialization of digital games. *New Media & Society, 14614448231190907*. Advance online publication. DOI: 10.1177/14614448231190907

Zendle, D., & Cairns, P. (2018a). Video game loot boxes are linked to problem gambling: Results of a large-scale survey. *PLoS One, 13*, e0206767. DOI: 10.1371/journal.pone.0206767 PMID: 30462669

Zengin, F. (2020). Akıllı Makine Çağı Sinemasına Giriş: Sinema Sanatında Yapay Zekâ Teknolojilerinin Kullanımı. İletişim Çalışmaları Dergisi, 6(2), 151-177.

Zeng, W., Luo, Y. J., & Chen, H. (2024). Does thin-ideal internalization increase adolescent girls' problematic social media use? The role of selfie-related behaviors and friendship quality. *Youth & Society*, *56*(3), 447–474. DOI: 10.1177/0044118X231176849

Zettl, H. (2016). *Sight, Sound, Motion: Applied Media Aesthetics* (8th ed.). Cengage Learning.

Zhang, C., Tang, L., & Liu, Z. (2023). How social media usage affects psychological and subjective well-being: Testing a moderated mediation model. *BMC Psychology*, *11*(1), 286. DOI: 10.1186/s40359-023-01311-2 PMID: 37737198

Zhang, Q., Lu, J., & Jin, Y. (2020).. . *Artificial Intelligence in Recommender Systems*, *7*(6), 1–19.

Zhang, Z., Jiménez, F. R., & Cicala, J. E. (2020). Fear of missing out scale: A self-concept perspective. *Psychology and Marketing*, *37*(11), 1619–1634. DOI: 10.1002/mar.21406

Zhang, Z., Jimenez, F., & Cicala, J. (2020). Fear Of Missing Out Scale: A Self-Concept Perspective. *Psychology and Marketing*, •••, 1619–1634.

Zhou, Q., & Ghazali, M. (2023). Research on the curriculum of visual communication design. *Journal of Humanities, Arts and Social Science*. https://doi.org/DOI: 10.26855/jhass.2023.07.031

Zhou, R., Yu, M., & Wang, X. (2016). Why Do Drivers Use Mobile Phones While Driving? The Contribution of Compensatory Beliefs. *PLoS One*, *11*(8), e0160288. DOI: 10.1371/journal.pone.0160288 PMID: 27494524

Zuboff, S. (2019). *The Age Of Surveillance Capitalism: The Fight for A Human Future at The New Frontier of Power*. Public Affairs.

Zuboff, S. (2019). *The age of surveillance capitalism: The fight for a human future at the new frontier of power*. PublicAffairs.

About the Contributors

Zuhal Akmeşe completed her first undergraduate studies in Social Studies Teaching at Afyon Kocatepe University Faculty of Education (2005). She then completed her second undergraduate degree with honors in the Department of Radio, Television, and Cinema at Ege University Faculty of Communication (2010). She completed her Master's degree in Radio, Television, and Cinema at the Institute of Social Sciences at Ege University with a thesis titled "Representation of Youth in Post-2000 Turkish Cinema" (2013), and her PhD at Istanbul University Institute of Social Sciences in the Department of Radio, Television, and Cinema with a thesis titled "Framing in Television and the Construction of Societal Perspective" (2017). In 2020, she earned the title of Associate Professor in the field of Communication Studies. Dr. Akmeşe's research interests include documentary cinema, new communication technologies, communication theories, social media, media literacy, visual communication design, production and direction in television and cinema, and the sociology of communication. She has authored several co-written studies in the field of communication and presented papers at international conferences and symposiums. She has also been involved as a consultant in film projects and has participated in numerous film and documentary film works as a director. Her documentary works have been shown at various national and international festivals, and her photographs have been exhibited in art galleries. Since 2013, Dr. Akmeşe has been conducting academic work at the Department of Radio, Television, and Cinema at Dicle University Faculty of Communication. In addition to her academic work, she has served as a member of the main jury at numerous national and international film festivals, as well as being part of the selection committees for many other events. She is a member of the editorial board of TRT Academy Journal, a board member of the Dicle University Cultural and Art Practice and Research Center, a member of the Dicle University Quality Board, and has held the position of Chair of the Department of Radio, Television, and Cinema at Dicle University Faculty of Communication. Dr. Akmeşe has authored several books in the fields of cinema and communication. She is also the founding president and current board chair of the Cinema Researchers' Culture and Arts Association, where she continues her work in cinema, arts, and communication. Within the association, she holds the roles of Festival President and Festival Director of the International Dicle Documentary and Short Film Festival. Additionally, she is the head editor of the SineAkademi cinema studies journal, which was initiated within the association.

Serhat Erdem, born in 1982 in Kırıkkale, completed his high school education at Samsun Ondokuz Mayıs High School. In 2004, he earned his bachelor's degree from Atatürk University, Faculty of Communication, Department of Radio, Television, and Cinema. In 2005, he began his academic career as a Research Assistant in the Department of Cinema and Television at Atatürk University's Faculty of Fine Arts. Erdem completed his master's degree in 2009 at Atatürk University, Institute of Social Sciences, Department of Journalism, with a thesis titled "An Analysis of the Transformations Caused by Matte Painting Applications in Cinema." In 2010, he began his doctoral studies at Istanbul University, Institute of Social Sciences, Department of Radio, Television, and Cinema. He received the title of Doctor in 2015 after successfully completing his dissertation titled "The Use of Visual Effects in the Reconstruction of Reality: Spatial Construction in the Spartacus Television Series." Between 2005 and 2022, Erdem served as an Assistant Professor in the Department of Cinema and Television at Atatürk University's Faculty of Fine Arts. In 2022, he earned the title of Associate Professor in the field of Visual Communication Design. Since February 2022, he has continued his academic work in the Department of Radio, Television, and Cinema at Atatürk University's Faculty of Communication.

***

Ali Arıcı is currently as an Associate Professor at Bilecik Şeyh Edebali University, Bozüyük Vocational School. He completed his undergraduate studies at Anadolu University, Faculty of Communication Sciences, Department of Journalism. He received his Master's degree from the Institute of Social Sciences, Department of Journalism, and his Ph.D. from the Institute of Social Sciences, Department of Public Relations and Advertising at Anadolu University. His research interests encompass new media, game advertising, virtual reality, advertising, public relations, and marketing communication.

Seril Çakmak Ekinci received her undergraduate degree from Anadolu University, Faculty of Communication Sciences, Department of Public Relations and Advertising in 2016. She completed her master's studies in 2021 in the Department of Advertising and Publicity at the Institute of Social Sciences, Marmara University.

She is currently a Ph.D. candidate in the Department of Public Relations and Advertising at the Graduate School of Social Sciences, Anadolu University. Seril Çakmak Ekinci currently holds the position of Research Assistant in the Department of Public Relations and Publicity at İnönü University, Faculty of Communication.

Sadık Çalışkan completed his undergraduate studies at Hacettepe University, Faculty of Letters, Department of English Language and Literature. He obtained his Master's degree from the Institute of Social Sciences, Department of Communication Sciences at İnönü University and earned his Ph.D. from the Institute of Social Sciences, Department of Public Relations and Publicity at Maltepe University. He is currently an Associate Professor at the Faculty of Communication, Department of Public Relations and Publicity at İnönü University. His primary research interests include culture and advertising, the history of advertising, storytelling in advertising, and brand management.

Nihan Dönmez completed her undergraduate degree in the Department of Cinema and Television at the Faculty of Communication Sciences, Anadolu University, in 2004. She earned her master's degree (2008) and PhD (2015) in the Department of Communication Sciences at the Institute of Social Sciences, Kocaeli University. Between 2008 and 2010, she worked as a Lecturer in the Public Relations and Publicity Program at Kandıra Vocational School. From 2011 to 2022, she continued her academic career as a Lecturer in the Department of Visual Communication Design at the Faculty of Communication, Kocaeli University. She is currently working at the same institution as an Assistant Professor. Her academic interests include television narrative, television programs and genres, television studies, and communication studies, and she has published scholarly work on these subjects.

Alper Erçetingöz is a Ph.D. Research Assistant at the Department of Radio, Television and Cinema, in Aydin Adnan Menderes University, Turkey. He received his master and Ph.D. degrees in Radio Television and Cinema in the Graduate School of Social Sciences from the Ege University. His research areas include film studies, cinema and philosophy, politic cinema.

Maria João Frade holds a Master's degree in Marketing Management from the Faculty of Economics of the University of Algarve, a postgraduate qualification in Communication, Culture and Arts from the Faculty of Human and Social Sciences of the University of Algarve, and a Bachelor's degree in Artistic Studies, also from the Faculty of Human and Social Sciences of the University of Algarve.

Andrej Kapcar is currently pursuing a PhD in Masaryk University in Brno at the Department for the Study of Religions. His academic background includes a BA in Archaeology, MAs in Economics, Archaeology and Comparative religions and a PhD in Archaeology. His research focuses on contemporary esotericism, occultism, and Chaos Magick in relation to the aesthetics of modern popular culture, predominantly video games. Among his other interests are philosophy, psychology, art (modern and classical alike) or cognitive studies. Outside of his academic endeavors, he also works as a graphic designer, specializing in occult inspired designs and art.

Özgür Kılınç completed his undergraduate studies at the Faculty of Communication, Department of Public Relations and Publicity at Ankara University. He received his Master's degree from the Institute of Social Sciences, Department of Communication Sciences at İnönü University, and earned his Ph.D. from the Institute of Social Sciences, Department of Public Relations and Advertising at Anadolu University. Currently, he is an Associate Professor at the Faculty of Communication, Department of Public Relations and Publicity at İnönü University. His main areas of interest include media relations, crisis communication, the history of public relations, and advertising.

Taner Kızılhan is an Assistant Professor in the Department of Visual Communication Design at the Faculty of Communication, Adnan Menderes University, Turkey. He received his Ph.D. and M.A. in Communication Design and Management from Anadolu University, where he previously worked as a research assistant. His doctoral research focused on digital citizenship, and his broader academic interests include digital media literacy, visual communication technologies, algorithmic design, and the socio-cultural implications of AI-driven media production. Kızılhan has authored several peer-reviewed articles in national and international journals and contributed chapters to academic books on smart cities, digital communication ethics, sexual expression in online environments, and data visualisation design. His work spans interdisciplinary topics such as deepfake aesthetics, post-truth visuality and new media theory. He has presented his research at numerous international conferences, and has participated in collaborative projects on smart cities and algorithmic governance. In 2019, he was a visiting Ph.D. researcher at McMaster University (Canada), where he conducted field research on public space decision-making in smart city infrastructures. In 2023, he was a visiting researcher at the University of Southern California (USA), focusing on data-driven civic practices. His current research explores the ethical and aesthetic boundaries of AI, visual misinformation, and the algorithmic shaping of public perception in the digital age.

Ronit Kumar is a dynamic and motivated student currently pursuing a Bachelor of Business Administration (BBA) at Christ University, a premier institution known for its academic excellence. With a keen interest in the ever-evolving domains of digital marketing and consumer behavior, Ronit aspires to carve a niche in the business world by blending creativity, strategic thinking, and analytical insights. At Christ University, Ronit has been actively engaging with coursework, projects, and extracurricular activities that provide a holistic understanding of business concepts. He is particularly focused on mastering skills like digital advertising, market research, content strategy, and data analytics, which are critical in today's competitive marketplace.

Anıl Uğur Oğuzcan completed his undergraduate studies with a scholarship in the Department of Public Relations and Advertising at Yaşar University. He received his master's degree from the Department of Public Relations and Publicity at Giresun University, and earned his PhD from the Department of Public Relations and Publicity at Marmara University with a dissertation titled "A Study on the Past, Present, and Future of Public Relations from the Perspective of Social Engineering." He worked as a research assistant at Giresun University Tirebolu Faculty of Communication and Marmara University Faculty of Communication. He is currently serving as a faculty member in the Department of Public Relations and Publicity at Tirebolu Faculty of Communication, Giresun University. He teaches courses on Public Relations Campaigns, Sustainability Communication, Corporate Social Responsibility Practices, Communication Technologies, and Research Planning in Public Relations. His academic work focuses on public relations theories, communication theories, corporate social responsibility and sustainability, social media, and social networks.

Deniz Oğuzcan graduated in 2018 with third place in her class from the Department of Radio, Television and Cinema at Istanbul University. She completed her M.A. in Radio, Television and Cinema at the same university in 2020, and earned her Ph.D. in the same field in 2024. She has participated in various short film projects as a director and screenwriter, alongside her academic research in the field of cinema. She is currently working as an Assistant Professor in the Department of Radio, Television and Cinema at the Faculty of Communication, Altınbaş University. Her academic work focuses on Digital Cinema, New Media, Sociology of Cinema, Philosophy of Cinema, and Artificial Intelligence and Cinema.

Stephen Poon is a social creative catalyst with a unique worldview, shaped by a rich multicultural background and extensive experience across Europe. Actively in research, his work spans in current issues and debates on SCHEI area (Sustainability,

Creativity, Human Factors, Entrepreneurship & Innovation), discourse across a wide range of disciplinarities in intra, cross, multi, inter and trans practices. His insights and versatile approach to social change and environmental stewardship bring valuable perspectives to the field of circularity and sustainability. He holds the lectureship for contextualising practice, integrated sustainability, design thinking, media marketplace and industry.

Célia M. Q. Ramos holds a PhD in Quantitative Methods Applied to Economics and Management from Faculty of Economics, University of Algarve, obtained her Master in Electrical and Computers Engineering from the Higher Technical Institute, Lisbon University, and is graduated in Computer Engineering from the University of Coimbra, Portugal. She is Coordinator Professor with Habilitation at School for Management, Hospitality and Tourism, also in the UALG, where she lectures mainly Information Systems. Current research interests includes, information systems, data analytics, electronic tourism, business intelligence, digital marketing, panel data models. Has published in the fields of information systems, marketing and tourism, She is reviewer of several scientific journals. At the level of applied research, she has participated in several funded projects. Researcher at the Centre for Tourism, Sustainability and Well-being (CinTurs). Email: cmramos@ualg.pt. ORCID ID: 0000-0002-3413-4897

Hülya Semiz Türkoğlu is a faculty member at the Department of Journalism at the Faculty of Communication at Istanbul University. She completed her undergraduate education at the Department of Journalism at the Faculty of Communication at Istanbul University between 2001-2005. She completed her master's degree at the same faculty between 2006-2008 and prepared her thesis titled "Journalist Sabiha Sertel's Views on the Period During the Second World War". She completed her doctorate between 2008-2014 and received her doctorate with her thesis titled "A Field Research on the Interactive Reader in Internet Journalism". Hülya Semiz Türkoğlu, who received the title of associate professor in 2022, currently serves as a faculty member at the Department of Journalism at the Faculty of Communication at Istanbul University. She has been serving as the Vice Head of the Department in the same department since 2022. In addition, she has been serving as a member of the University Board of Directors at the Women's Studies Application and Research Center within the Istanbul University Rectorate since 2019. Her research interests include Science, Technology and Society, Journalism, Communication Sciences, Disinformation, Artificial Intelligence, Privacy, Women, Children and Media. She teaches undergraduate courses "Information and Disinformation in Communication", "Agenda Setting and Public Opinion" and

"Communication Workshop"; and graduate courses "Women, Children and Media" and "Journalism and Social Media Management in the Digital Age".

João Paulo Sousa is graduated in Electrical and Computer Engineering from UTAD University. After three years, he gets a Master's degree in Engineering Technology. He received his Ph.D. degree in Computer Science at UTAD University. He published dozens of publications in international journals and conferences. He served as Chair of Videojogos2020 - 12th International Conference on Videogame Sciences and Arts and is on several scientific committees of international journals and conferences. His research activities concern video games, serious games, gamification, and artificial intelligence. In recent years he has been: director of the degree in Computer Science and Communications; director of the degree in Game Design and is the current director of the Master's Degree in Digital Game Design and Development at the Polytechnic Institute of Bragança (IPB), and director of the ESACT Computer Resources Center. He is currently an Adjunct Professor at the Polytechnic Institute of Bragança (IPB) and an internal member of the Digitization and Intelligent Robotics Research Centre (CeDRI) at the Polytechnic Institute of Bragança.

Süleyman Türkoğlu is a faculty member at the Department of Radio, Television and Cinema of the Faculty of Communication at Istanbul University. He completed his undergraduate education in the Department of Journalism at the Faculty of Communication at Istanbul University between 2000 and 2004. Then, he completed his graduate education at the same university between 2006 and 2008 and presented his thesis titled "Corporate Identity in Visual Communication Design and the Example of 'Istanbul University'". He completed his doctorate between 2008 and 2014 and received his doctorate with his thesis titled "A Field Research on Visual Design Presentation and News Websites in New Media". He has been working as a faculty member at the Department of Radio, Television and Cinema of the Faculty of Communication at Istanbul University since 2007. He worked as a Lecturer Dr. at the Press and Public Relations Directorate of the Presidency of Istanbul University between 2007 and 2019. He worked as an Assistant Professor at the Department of Radio, Television and Cinema of the Faculty of Communication at Istanbul University between 2014 and 2018. He has been working as an Assistant Professor in the same department since 2018. In addition to his academic studies, he has undertaken many administrative duties. Since 2022, he has been serving as the Vice President of the Department of Radio, Television and Cinema at the Faculty of Communication at Istanbul University. He also serves as a member of the Faculty Board of Directors. In 2024, he was appointed as the Vice Dean of the Faculty of Communication, and in 2025, he was appointed as the Vice Dean of the Faculty of

Open and Distance Education. His research areas include journalism, printing and publishing, media and communication systems, communication design, database systems, software, operating systems, and engineering and technology. Among the courses he has taught are "Media Workshop", "Digital Applications", "Page Design", "Data Journalism", "Graphic Design", "Printing and Communication Technologies" and "New Communication Environments" at the undergraduate level; and "Big Data Analytics and Management" at the graduate level. He has been continuing his academic career at Istanbul University, Faculty of Communication, Department of Radio, Television and Cinema since 2007.

Saadet Zeynep Varlı Gurer completed her undergraduate education in 1999 at Istanbul University, Faculty of Communication, Department of Public Relations and Publicity. She received her master's degree from Kocaeli University, Institute of Social Sciences, Department of Communication Sciences. In 2012, she completed her Ph.D. at Istanbul University, Institute of Social Sciences, Department of Public Relations and Publicity. Since 2014, she has been working as an Assistant Professor at Kocaeli University, Faculty of Communication, Department of Visual Communication Design. Gürer, who is the author of the book The Language of Clothing: The Role of Dress Codes in Political Communication, teaches courses such as Visual Media Analysis, Nonverbal Communication, and Semiotics, and conducts academic research in the field of visual media analysis. In 2021, she was awarded the title of Associate Professor in the field of Media Studies.

Nurcan Yılmaz completed her undergraduate studies in 2009 at Selçuk University, Faculty of Communication, Department of Public Relations and Publicity. She received her M.A. in 2014 and her Ph.D. in 2020 from the same department at the Graduate School of Social Sciences, Selçuk University. She is currently serving as an Associate Professor in the Department of Public Relations and Publicity at İnönü University, Faculty of Communication. Her scholarly work focuses on advertising, branding, social media, and corporate communication.

Index

A

C

D

F

G

H

I

M

O

P

S

U

V

W

www.ingramcontent.com/pod-product-compliance
Lightning Source LLC
LaVergne TN
LVHW062329300926
849161LV00007B/1631